Tools and Skills for .NET 10

Second Edition

Get the career you want with good practices and patterns to design, debug, and test your solutions

Mark J. Price

<packt>

Tools and Skills for .NET 10

Second Edition

Portfolio Director: Ashwin Nair
Relationship Lead: Nitin Nainani
Project Manager: Ruvika Rao
Content Engineer: Hayden Edwards
Technical Editor: Arjun Varma
Copy Editor: Hayden Edwards
Indexer: Manju Arasan
Proofreader: Hayden Edwards
Production Designer: Ajay Patule
Growth Lead: Priyadarshini Sharma

First published: July 2024
Second edition: January 2026

Production reference: 1171225

Published by Packt Publishing Ltd.
Grosvenor House
11 St Paul's Square
Birmingham
B3 1RB, UK.

ISBN 978-1-83588-250-4

`www.packtpub.com`

Contributors

About the author

Mark J. Price is a Microsoft Specialist: Programming in C# and Architecting Microsoft Azure Solutions, with over 20 years of experience. Since 1993, he has passed more than 80 Microsoft programming exams and specializes in preparing others to pass them. Between 2001 and 2003, Mark was employed to write official courseware for Microsoft in Redmond, USA. His team wrote the first training courses for C# while it was still an early alpha version. While with Microsoft, he taught "train-the-trainer" classes to get Microsoft Certified Trainers up-to-speed on C# and .NET. Mark has spent most of his career training a wide variety of students, from 16-year-old apprentices to 70-year-old retirees, with the majority being professional developers. Mark holds a BSc in Computer Science.

Thank you to all my readers. Your support means I get to write these books and celebrate your successes. Special thanks to the readers who give me actionable feedback via my GitHub repository and email, and interact with me and the book communities on Discord. You help make my books even better with every edition.

About the reviewer

Pavel P. Oleynik has a Ph.D. in Computer Science and is the author of more than 100 scientific papers in various languages. He organized and regularly conducted the International Theoretical and Practical Conference, Object Systems. He has been developing software since 1999 and has held the positions of team leader, technical leader, architect, and CTO in multibillion-dollar holdings. He is a recognized expert in areas such as heavy industry, coal industry, agricultural industry, banking, fintech, healthcare, retail, ERP/MES systems, SCM, ITSM, low-code/no-code systems, and foodtech.

Learn more on Discord

To join the Discord community for this book – where you can share feedback, ask questions to the author, and learn about new releases – follow this QR code:

`https://packt.link/TS2e`

Table of Contents

Chapter 12: Integration and Security Testing 461

Chapter 13: Benchmarking Performance, Load, and Stress Testing 487

Chapter 14: Functional and End-to-End Testing of Websites and Services 525

Chapter 15: Containerization Using Docker 555

Chapter 16: Cloud-Native Development Using Aspire 593

Preface

There are programming books that aim to be comprehensive references to individual subjects like security, dependency injection, unit testing, web testing, containerization, cloud deployment, design patterns, and soft skills including interview preparation.

This book is different. It is a step-by-step guide to learning all those tools and skills for professional .NET developers. It is concise and aims to be a brisk, fun read that is packed with practical hands-on walkthroughs of each topic. The breadth of the overarching narrative comes at the cost of some depth, but you will find many signposts to explore further if you wish.

In my experience, the hardest part of learning a new tool or skill is getting started. Once I have had the most important key concepts explained and been walked through some practical tasks, I then feel comfortable going deeper by exploring the official documentation on my own. You can feel confident experimenting on your own once you have seen how the basics work correctly.

This book is best for those who already know the fundamentals of the C# language and .NET libraries, have built some apps and services with .NET on their own, and now want to learn skills that are more relevant for working with a team in a professional organization.

I will cover the most important aspects of tools and skills for .NET professionals so that you can participate in conversations with colleagues about those tools and skills and get productive fast.

Who this book is for

This book is for .NET professionals seeking to enhance their expertise, as well as aspiring developers aiming to advance their careers in the field. This book caters to individuals eager to master essential .NET tools, refine their development practices, explore advanced techniques and cutting-edge tools, and prepare themselves for job opportunities and interviews in the competitive landscape of .NET development.

What this book covers

This preface briefly introduces each chapter. A longer description including why each topic is covered is in the first chapter.

Introduction

Chapter 1, Introducing Tools and Skills for .NET, is about setting up your development environment. You can use Visual Studio, VS Code, Rider, or any other code editor. I also review in more detail what the rest of this book covers and why. You will create some class libraries for an entity model and database that we will use in projects in later chapters. The chapter ends by covering how to use this book with future versions of .NET, for example, .NET 11, expected to be released in November 2026, and .NET 12, expected to be released in November 2027.

Tools

Important tools for professional .NET developers include your code editor, Git, debuggers, and memory analysis.

Chapter 2, Making the Most of the Tools in Your Code Editor, is about the less commonly used tools built into Visual Studio, VS Code, and Rider. You will learn how to customize your editor and how to create code snippets and refactoring features.

Chapter 3, Source Code Management Using Git, covers the most common tasks that you would perform with Git to manage your source code, especially when working in a team of .NET developers.

Chapter 4, Debugging and Memory Troubleshooting, is about using the debugging tools in your code editor and about using tools in your code editor to track the usage of memory to improve your apps and services.

Chapter 5, Logging, Tracing, and Metrics for Observability, is about how to instrument your code to enable observability during testing and production using telemetry.

Skills

Important skills for professional .NET developers include documentation, dynamic code, protecting data and code, implementing multitasking in your projects, and managing service dependencies.

Chapter 6, Documenting Your Code, APIs, and Services, discusses how to best document your code to help other developers maintain it in future using comments, and how to document your services and APIs to enable other developers to call them as designed.

Chapter 7, Observing and Modifying Code Execution Dynamically, introduces you to some common types that are included with .NET for performing code reflection and applying and reading attributes; working with expression trees; and creating source generators.

Chapter 8, Protecting Data and Apps Using Cryptography, is about protecting your data from being viewed by malicious users using encryption, and from being manipulated or corrupted using hashing and signing. You will also learn about authentication and authorization to protect applications from unauthorized users.

Chapter 9, Multitasking and Concurrency, covers how to allow multiple actions to occur at the same time to improve performance, scalability, and user productivity for the applications that you build.

Chapter 10, Dependency Injection, Containers, and Service Lifetime, is about reducing tight coupling between components, which enables you to better manage changes and software complexity, and is especially important to performing practical testing that we cover in the next part of the book.

Testing

Important testing tools and skills for professional .NET developers include all types of testing, from unit testing to web user interface testing.

Chapter 11, Unit Testing and Mocking, introduces testing practices that will improve your code quality. Unit testing is easy to get wrong and be useless, undermining the team's trust. Get it right, and you will save time and money, and smooth the development process.

Chapter 12, Integration and Security Testing, introduces two higher levels of testing, integration and security, that apply across all components of a solution.

Chapter 13, Benchmarking Performance, Load, and Stress Testing, introduces how to properly use the BenchmarkDotNet library to monitor your code to measure performance and efficiency. Then you will see how to perform load and stress testing on your projects to predict required resources and estimate the costs of deployment in production.

Chapter 14, Functional and End-to-End Testing of Websites and Services, introduces you to functional and end-to-end testing of service APIs and web user interfaces.

Containerization

Chapter 15, Containerization Using Docker, introduces you to the concept of containerization and specifically using Docker to virtualize hosts for services in complex solution architectures.

Chapter 16, Cloud-Native Development Using Aspire, introduces you to Aspire, an opinionated way to manage a simulated cloud-native development environment on your local computer.

Design and Career

Important design skills for professional .NET developers include common coding design patterns, algorithm implementations, and architectural patterns. Finally, you need to get the career you aspire to. To achieve this, you must impress with your job application documents and at an interview.

Chapter 17, Design Patterns and Principles, introduces you to the SOLID design patterns as well as other common design patterns like Singleton and Factory used by .NET.

Chapter 18, Software and Solution Architecture Foundations, covers software and solution architecture including Clean Architecture.

Chapter 19, Your Career, Teamwork, and Interviews, covers working in a team as a career professional, applying for jobs, and passing interviews for .NET software engineer and related job positions. This chapter includes 60 commonly asked questions in interviews. The first three questions have suggested answers in the print book. The full set of 60 questions and suggested answers are available online from the following link: `https://github.com/markjprice/tools-skills-net10/blob/main/docs/interview-qa/readme.md`.

Epilogue, describes your options for further study to master the tools and skills you need to become a well-rounded professional .NET developer.

Appendix A, Answers to the Test Your Knowledge Questions, has the answers to the test questions at the end of each chapter.

Appendix B, Setting Up Your Development Environment, has step-by-step instructions for setting up your development environment. This includes a code editor such as Visual Studio or VS Code, and a database named Northwind on a database server such as SQL Server in Docker, SQL Server locally, or Azure SQL Database in the cloud.

Appendix C, Looking For Help, is all about how to find quality information about programming on the web. You will learn about Microsoft Learn documentation, including its new MCP server for integration with AI systems, getting help while coding and using dotnet commands, getting help from fellow readers in the book's Discord channel, searching the .NET source code for implementation details, and finally making the most of modern AI tools like GitHub Copilot.

The *Appendix* chapters are available to download from a link in the README file in the GitHub repository: `https://github.com/markjprice/tools-skills-net10`.

You can also access a free PDF copy of the book (containing *Appendix A*, *B*, and *C*) through the following link: `https://packtpub.com/unlock`. Search for this book by name, ensure it's the correct edition, and have your invoice ready.

To get the most out of this book

You can develop .NET projects using Visual Studio, VS Code, or a third-party tool like Rider. VS Code, Rider, and the command-line tools work on most operating systems, including Windows, macOS, and many varieties of Linux. Visual Studio is Windows-only because Visual Studio for Mac has been retired, does not officially support .NET 8 or later, and it reached its end of life in August 2024.

Download the example code files

You can download or clone solutions for the step-by-step guided tasks and exercises from the GitHub repository at the following link: `https://github.com/markjprice/tools-skills-net10`.

If you don't know how, then I provide instructions on how to do this in *Chapter 1, Introducing Tools and Skills for .NET*.

We also have other code bundles from our rich catalog of books and videos available at `https://github.com/PacktPublishing`. Check them out!

Conventions used

There are a number of text conventions used throughout this book.

`CodeInText`: Indicates code words in text, database table names, folder names, filenames, file extensions, pathnames, dummy URLs, user input, and Twitter (X) handles. For example; "The `Controllers`, `Models`, and `Views` folders contain ASP.NET Core classes and the `.cshtml` files for execution on the server."

A block of code is set as follows:

```
// Storing items at index positions.
names[0] = "Kate";
names[1] = "Jack";
names[2] = "Rebecca";
names[3] = "Tom";
```

When we wish to draw your attention to a particular part of a code block, the relevant lines or items are highlighted:

```
// Storing items at index positions.
names[0] = "Kate";
names[1] = "Jack";
names[2] = "Rebecca";
names[3] = "Tom";
```

Any command-line input or output is written as follows:

```
dotnet new console
```

Bold: Indicates a new **term**, an important **word**, or words that you see on the screen, for example, in menus or dialog boxes. For example: "Clicking on the **Next** button moves you to the next screen."

> Warnings or important notes appear like this.

> Tips and tricks appear like this.

Get in touch

Feedback from our readers is always welcome.

General feedback: If you have questions about any aspect of this book or have any general feedback, please email us at `customercare@packt.com` and mention the book's title in the subject of your message.

Errata: Although we have taken every care to ensure the accuracy of our content, mistakes do happen. If you have found a mistake in this book, we would be grateful if you reported this to us. Please visit `http://www.packt.com/submit-errata`, click **Submit Errata**, and fill in the form.

Piracy: If you come across any illegal copies of our works in any form on the internet, we would be grateful if you would provide us with the location address or website name. Please contact us at `copyright@packt.com` with a link to the material.

If you are interested in becoming an author: If there is a topic that you have expertise in and you are interested in either writing or contributing to a book, please visit `http://authors.packt.com/`.

Share your thoughts

Once you've read *Tools and Skills for .NET 10, Second Edition,* we'd love to hear your thoughts! Scan the QR code below to go straight to the Amazon review page for this book and share your feedback.

`https://packt.link/r/183588251X`

Your review is important to us and the tech community and will help us make sure we're delivering excellent quality content.

Free Benefits with Your Book

This book comes with free benefits to support your learning. Activate them now for instant access (see the "*How to Unlock*" section for instructions).

Here's a quick overview of what you can instantly unlock with your purchase:

Free PDF copy with appendices

- Access a DRM-free PDF copy of this book to read anywhere, on any device.
- Unlock the book's appendices included with the free PDF.

Next-Gen Web-Based Reader

- **Multi-device progress sync:** Pick up where you left off, on any device.
- **Highlighting and notetaking:** Capture ideas and turn reading into lasting knowledge.
- **Bookmarking:** Save and revisit key sections whenever you need them.
- **Dark mode:** Reduce eye strain by switching to dark or sepia themes.

How to Unlock

Scan the QR code (or go to `packtpub.com/unlock`). Search for this book by name, confirm the edition, and then follow the steps on the page.

UNLOCK NOW

Note: Keep your invoice handy. Purchases made directly from Packt don't require one

1

Introducing Tools and Skills for .NET

In this first chapter, the goals are understanding the tools and skills that you will learn in this book, setting up your development environment to use Visual Studio 2026, Visual Studio Code, or JetBrains Rider, and then setting up a database and projects to use in the rest of the chapters. Throughout this book, I will use the names **Visual Studio**, **VS Code**, and **Rider** to refer to these three code editors respectively.

I use the term **modern .NET** to refer to .NET 10 and its predecessors like .NET 5, which derive from .NET Core. I use the term **legacy .NET** to refer to .NET Framework, Mono, Xamarin, and .NET Standard. Modern .NET is a unification of those legacy platforms and standards.

Every chapter in this book introduces some tools and some skills, but some chapters are more focused on a particular tool or a particular skill.

This chapter covers the following topics:

- Introducing this book and its contents
- Setting up your development environment
- Setting up a database and projects for this book
- Making good use of the GitHub repository for this book
- Where to go for help
- Using future versions of .NET with this book

> The GitHub repository for this book has solutions using full application projects for all code tasks: `https://github.com/markjprice/tools-skills-net10/`.
>
> After going to the GitHub repository, simply press the . (dot) key on your keyboard or change `.com` to `.dev` to change the repository into a live code editor based on VS Code using GitHub Codespaces. VS Code in a web browser is great to run alongside your chosen code editor as you work through the book's coding tasks. You can compare your code to the solution code and easily copy and paste parts if needed.

Free Benefits with Your Book

Your purchase includes a free PDF copy of this book (containing *Appendix A, B,* and *C*), along with other exclusive benefits. Check the *Free Benefits with Your Book* section in the Preface to unlock them instantly and maximize your learning experience.

Introducing this book and its contents

Before we dive into an overview of this book, let's set the context by understanding that this is one of four books about .NET 10 that I have written, covering almost everything a beginner to .NET needs to know.

Companion books to complete your learning journey

This book is the fourth of a quartet of books that completes your learning journey through .NET 10:

1. The first book, *C# 14 and .NET 10 – Modern Cross-Platform Development Fundamentals*, covers the fundamentals of the C# language, the .NET libraries, and using modern ASP.NET Core, Blazor, and Minimal API web services for web development. It is designed to be read linearly because skills and knowledge from earlier chapters build up and are needed to understand later chapters.
2. The second book, *Real-World Web Development with .NET 10*, covers mature and proven web development technologies like ASP.NET Core MVC and controller-based Web API web services, as well as OData, FastEndpoints, and Umbraco CMS for building real-world web projects on .NET 10. You will learn how to test your web services using xUnit and test the user interfaces of your websites using Playwright, and then how to containerize your projects ready for deployment.
3. The third book, *Apps and Services with .NET 10*, covers data using SQL Server, Dapper, and EF Core, as well as more specialized .NET libraries like internationalization and popular third-party packages including Serilog and Noda Time. You will learn how to build native **ahead-of-time** (**AOT**)-compiled services with ASP.NET Core Minimal API web services and how to improve performance, scalability, and reliability using caching, queues, and background services. You will also implement modern services using GraphQL, gRPC, and SignalR. Finally, you will learn how to build graphical user interfaces for websites, desktop, and mobile apps with .NET MAUI, Avalonia, and Blazor.
4. This fourth book (the one you're reading now), *Tools and Skills for .NET 10*, covers important tools and skills that a professional .NET developer should have. These include design patterns and solution architecture, debugging, memory analysis, all the important types of testing, whether it be unit, integration, performance, or web user interface testing, and then topics for testing cloud-native solutions on your local computer like containerization, Docker, and Aspire. Finally, we will look at how to prepare for an interview to get the .NET developer career that you want.

A summary of the .NET 10 quartet and their most important topics is shown in *Figure 1.1*:

C# language, including new C# features, debugging, unit testing, and object-oriented programming.

.NET libraries, including number types, text, regular expressions, collections, file I/O, and data with EF Core and SQLite.

Modern websites and web services with ASP.NET Core, Blazor, and Minimal API web services.

Mature websites using ASP.NET Core MVC and Umbraco CMS, including defining routes, controllers, models, and views.

Mature web services using Web API controllers, OData, and FastEndpoints, including authentication, authorization, and integration testing.

Caching, web testing, configuration, and containerizing for deployment.

Modern apps: .NET MAUI mobile apps, Avalonia desktop apps, and Blazor web apps.

Modern services: Minimal API web services, caching, queuing, GraphQL, gRPC, and SignalR.

Libraries: Popular third-party packages, integrating LLMs, and internationalization.

Data: SQL Server, ADO.NET SqlClient, Dapper, and EF Core.

Tools: IDEs, debugging, memory analysis, and AI assistants.

Libraries: Cryptography, multi-tasking and concurrency.

Tests: Unit, integration, performance, security, and web.

Develop: Docker and Aspire.

Design: Patterns, principles, software and solution architecture.

Career: Teamwork and interviews.

Figure 1.1: Companion books for learning .NET for beginner-to-intermediate readers

Audiences for this book

This book caters to two audiences:

- Readers who have completed my book for learning the fundamentals of the C# language, .NET libraries, and using ASP.NET Core for web development, *C# 14 and .NET 10 – Modern Cross-Platform Development Fundamentals*, and now want to take their learning further.
- Readers who already have basic skills and knowledge about C# and .NET and want to acquire practical skills and knowledge of common tools to become more professional with their .NET development, and in particular join a team of .NET developers.

Let's look at an analogy:

- First, an amateur cook might buy a book to learn fundamental skills, concepts, and terminology that any cook needs to make the most common dishes.
- Second, an amateur cook might also buy a recipe book to learn how to apply that knowledge and those skills to make complete meals. These meals might be traditional classics loved by most people, or daring dishes for a modern audience.
- Third, to become a professional cook, they would also need to understand the roles in a professional kitchen, learn more specialized tools and skills that are needed when cooking meals for many more people in a professional environment, and how to work in a team of cooks.

These three scenarios are why I wrote four books about .NET. (The second scenario covers two types of food, mature and modern.)

The preface briefly introduces each chapter, but many readers skip the preface. So, let's now review why each topic is covered in more depth.

Tools

There are many tools that a professional .NET developer should be familiar with. Some are built into most code editors like a debugger or source control integration, and some require separate applications and services like memory analysis and telemetry.

> Even beginner developers quickly become familiar with the basic tools included with a code editor like the main editing window, managing files in a project, how to set a breakpoint and start debugging, and then step through the code statement by statement, and how to run a project, so those topics will not be covered in this book. If you don't already have these skills, then I recommend that you read my book *C# 14 and .NET 10 – Modern Cross-Platform Development Fundamentals*.

Chapter 2, Making the Most of the Tools in Your Code Editor, is about the less commonly used tools built into Visual Studio, VS Code, and Rider. The major tools like a debugger or memory analysis tools are covered in separate later chapters. This chapter covers topics like refactoring features and how to customize your code editor using standards like `.editorconfig`.

Chapter 3, Source Code Management Using Git, covers the most common tasks that you would perform with Git to manage your source code, especially when working in a team of .NET developers. Git is a distributed source control system, so developers have a local copy of the entire repository. This enables offline work, fast branching, and merging. Git is the most popular source code control system for .NET projects, and there are tools and extensions available for seamless integration with all code editors and command-line tools. GitHub is a popular Microsoft platform for hosting Git repositories and collaborating on software projects.

Chapter 4, Debugging and Memory Troubleshooting, is about using the debugging tools in your code editor. You will learn how to use the built-in debugging features, how to decorate your own code with attributes to make it easier to see what's happening while debugging, and how to use tools in your code editor to track the usage of memory to improve your apps and services.

Chapter 5, Logging, Tracing, and Metrics for Observability, is about how to instrument your code to enable tracing, metrics, and logging during production, and how to implement telemetry using OpenTelemetry to monitor your code as it executes to enable observability.

Skills

As well as learning how to use the tools themselves, a professional .NET developer needs skills like documenting code, leveraging dynamic code, and implementing cryptographic techniques to protect code and data.

Chapter 6, Documenting Code, APIs, and Services, discusses how to best document your code to help other developers maintain it in the future using comments, and how to document your services and APIs to enable other developers to call them as designed. Forcing yourself to document your code has the side benefit that you will often spot places where you could improve the design and refactor your code and APIs.

Chapter 7, Observing and Modifying Code Execution Dynamically, introduces you to some common types that are included with .NET for performing code reflection, applying and reading attributes, working with expression trees, and most usefully, creating source generators.

Chapter 8, Protecting Data and Apps Using Cryptography, is about protecting your data from being viewed by malicious users using encryption, and from being manipulated or corrupted using hashing and signing. You will also learn about using authentication and authorization to protect applications from unauthorized users.

Chapter 9, Multitasking and Concurrency, covers how to allow multiple actions to occur at the same time to improve performance, scalability, and user productivity for the applications that you build.

Chapter 10, Dependency Injection, Containers and Service Lifetime, is about reducing tight coupling between components, which is especially critical to performing practical testing. This also enables you to better manage changes and software complexity.

Testing

One of the most important tools and skills for a .NET developer is testing to ensure quality. Testing spans the whole life cycle of development, from testing a small unit of behavior to end-to-end testing of the user experience and system integration. The earlier in the development process that you test, the lower the cost of fixing any mistakes that you discover.

Chapter 11, Unit Testing and Mocking, introduces testing practices that will improve your code quality. Unit testing is easy to get wrong and can become useless, undermining the team's trust. Get it right, and you will save time and money and smooth out the development process.

Chapter 12, Integration and Security Testing, introduces a higher level of testing across all components of a solution, and the types of testing needed to maintain the security of your projects.

Chapter 13, Benchmarking Performance, Load, and Stress Testing, introduces how to properly use the `BenchmarkDotNet` library to monitor your code to measure performance and efficiency. Then, you will see how to perform load and stress testing on your projects to predict required resources and estimate the costs of deployment in production using `Bombardier` and `NBomber`.

Chapter 14, Functional and End-to-End Testing of Websites and Services, introduces you to testing APIs and web user interfaces using Playwright for automation.

Chapter 15, Containerization Using Docker, introduces you to the concept of containerization and specifically using Docker to virtualize hosts for services in complex solution architectures.

Chapter 16, Cloud-Native Development Using Aspire, introduces you to Aspire, an opinionated way to manage a cloud-native development environment. It automates local deployments during development and includes integrations with tools you learned about earlier in the book like OpenTelemetry for observability, Docker containers for hosting microservices, and so on.

Design and career development

The final part of this book is about more theoretical concepts like design patterns, principles, and software and solution architecture, and ends with a chapter that wraps everything up with preparing for an interview to get the career that you want with a team of developers and other professionals.

Chapter 17, Design Patterns and Principles, introduces you to the SOLID design patterns as well as other common patterns and principles like **DRY** (**Don't Repeat Yourself**), **KISS** (**Keep It Simple, Stupid**), **YAGNI** (**You Ain't Gonna Need It**), and **PoLA** (**Principle of Least Astonishment**).

Chapter 18, Software and Solution Architecture Foundations, covers software and solution architecture, including using Mermaid to create architecture diagrams.

Chapter 19, Your Career, Teamwork, and Interviews, covers what you need to get the career you aspire to. To achieve this, you must impress with your resume and at an interview. This chapter covers commonly asked questions in interviews and suggested answers that fit with your experience to help you give realistic responses.

Setting up your development environment

Before you start programming, you'll need a code editor for C#. Microsoft has a family of code editors and **integrated development environments** (**IDEs**), which include:

- **Visual Studio**: Visual Studio 2026 for Windows. Visual Studio 2022 for Mac is no longer supported. You could also use Visual Studio in a virtual machine, or use Microsoft Dev Box as described at the following link: `https://azure.microsoft.com/en-us/products/dev-box`.
- **VS Code**: VS Code for Windows, Mac, Linux, the Web, or GitHub Codespaces.
- **Rider**: JetBrains Rider, which is available for Windows, Mac, or Linux. Since October 2024, it has a free version that you can read about at the following link: `https://blog.jetbrains.com/dotnet/2024/10/16/rider-reveal-livestream-big-news-for-dotnet-and-game-devs/`. Rider is popular with more experienced .NET developers.

Choosing the appropriate tool and application type for learning

What is the best tool and application type for learning how to use tools and skills with C# and .NET?

I want you to be free to choose any C# code editor or IDE to complete the coding tasks in this book, including Visual Studio, VS Code, Rider, or a code editor that I've never heard of.

In this book, I give general instructions that work with all tools, so you can use whichever tool you prefer.

Using Visual Studio for general development

Visual Studio can create most types of applications, including console apps, websites, web services, desktop, and mobile apps. Visual Studio only runs on Windows 10 version 1909 or later, or Windows Server 2016 or later, and only on 64-bit versions. Version 17.4 was the first version to support native ARM64.

> **Warning!** Visual Studio for Mac does not officially support .NET 8 or later and it reached its end-of-life in August 2024. If you have been using Visual Studio for Mac, then you should switch to VS Code for Mac or Rider for Mac, or use Visual Studio in a virtual machine on your local computer or in the cloud using a technology like Microsoft Dev Box. The retirement announcement can be read here: `https://devblogs.microsoft.com/visualstudio/visual-studio-for-mac-retirement-announcement/`.

Using VS Code for cross-platform development

The most modern and lightweight code editor to choose from, and the only one from Microsoft that is cross-platform, is VS Code. It can run on all common operating systems, including Windows, macOS, and many varieties of Linux, including **Red Hat Enterprise Linux** (**RHEL**) and Ubuntu. VS Code is a good choice for modern cross-platform development because it has an extensive and growing set of extensions to support many languages beyond C#.

Being cross-platform and lightweight, it can be installed on all platforms that your apps will be deployed to for quick bug fixes and so on. Choosing VS Code means a developer can use a cross-platform code editor to develop cross-platform apps.

VS Code is by far the most popular IDE, with over 75% of professional developers selecting it in the Stack Overflow 2025 survey, which you can read at the following link:

`https://survey.stackoverflow.co/2025/technology/#1-dev-id-es`.

Using GitHub Codespaces for development in the cloud

GitHub Codespaces is a fully configured development environment based on VS Code that can be spun up in an environment hosted in the cloud and accessed through any web browser. It supports Git repositories, extensions, and a built-in command-line interface so you can edit, run, and test from any device. Since it runs in the cloud and you interact with it via a web browser, there is nothing to download and install, and since it is based on VS Code, it works the same way VS Code does on your local computer.

> You can learn more about GitHub Codespaces at the following link: `https://github.com/features/codespaces`.

Reviews of GitHub Codespaces are available at the following links:

- `https://dev.to/github/github-codespaces-ga-any-good-reviewed-and-tested-3e62`
- `https://medium.com/@pooyan_razian/github-codespaces-a-different-way-to-code-da455777f9ab`

Using Rider for cross-platform development

Rider is a third-party code editor from JetBrains, the maker of IntelliJ IDEA, the leading Java and Kotlin IDE, and ReSharper, the popular Visual Studio plugin for .NET developers. Rider runs on multiple platforms: Windows, macOS, and Linux.

Developers who use it are often professionals who appreciate the extra features it has like live code inspections, context actions, and refactorings. Using Rider can be an indicator of a more advanced developer.

You should expect new versions of Rider to support the latest version of .NET a few weeks after Visual Studio. For example, .NET 8 was released on November 14, 2023, and Visual Studio with official support for .NET 8 was released on the same day. But Rider version 2023.3 with official support for .NET 8 was not released until December 7, 2023.

Although JetBrains is a fantastic company with great products, both Rider and the ReSharper extension for Visual Studio are software, and all software has bugs and quirky behavior. For example, they might show errors like "Cannot resolve symbol" in your Razor Pages, Razor views, and Blazor components. Yet, you can build and run those files because there is no actual problem.

> **Warning!** If you use Rider and you have installed the Unity Support or Heap Allocation Viewer plugins, then it will complain a lot about boxing. A common scenario when boxing happens is when value types like `int` and `DateTime` are passed as positional arguments to `string` formats. This is a problem for Unity projects because they use a different memory garbage collector than the normal .NET runtime. For non-Unity projects, like all the projects in this book, you can ignore these boxing warnings because they are not relevant. You can read more about this Unity-specific issue at the following link: `https://docs.unity3d.com/Manual/performance-reference-types.html`.

Will Microsoft merge Visual Studio and VS Code?

A reader, @automaton, posed a thought in the Discord channel for this book: "I wonder if the idea long term is to merge Code and VS."

My best guess is that .NET developers on Windows will continue to prefer Visual Studio (this is likely about 70% of my readers), and everyone else will split between VS Code and Rider, especially now that Rider is free for non-commercial use.

Microsoft has been clear about their commitment to improving both Visual Studio and VS Code but keeping them distinct in their roles. While VS Code continues to be enhanced with new features and cross-platform capabilities, Visual Studio remains focused on being a best-in-class IDE for development on Windows.

Visual Studio is deeply integrated with Windows-specific technologies and APIs. It leverages components such as the Windows Presentation Foundation (WPF), which is not natively supported on other operating systems. Rewriting or adapting these dependencies for other platforms would require significant effort and resources.

My belief is that Microsoft will never port Visual Studio to other platforms or merge the two products. Instead, they will continue to add features from one to the other. For example, Solution Explorer has been added to VS Code, and HTTP Editor has been added to Visual Studio.

What I used

To write and test the code for this book, I used the following hardware and software:

- Windows 11 on an HP Spectre (Intel) laptop and a Microsoft Surface Laptop 7 (ARM) with Visual Studio, VS Code, and Rider.
- macOS on an Apple Silicon Mac mini (M1) desktop with VS Code and Rider.

I hope that you have access to a variety of hardware and software too, because seeing the differences on various platforms deepens your understanding of development challenges, although any one of the preceding combinations is enough to learn how to build practical apps and websites.

Deploying cross-platform

Your choice of code editor and operating system for development does not limit where your code gets deployed.

.NET 10 supports the following platforms for deployment:

- **Windows**: Windows 10 version 1607 or later, Windows 11 version 22000 or later, Windows Server 2012 R2 SP1 or later, and Nano Server version 2019 or later
- **Linux**: Alpine Linux 3.22, Azure Linux 3.0, CentOS Stream 9 or 10, Debian 12 or 13, Fedora 42, openSUSE Leap 15.6, RHEL 9 or 10, SUSE Enterprise Linux 15.6, and Ubuntu 22.04, 24.04, or 25.04
- **Android**: API 21 or later is the minimum SDK target. Versions 12, 12.1, 13, 14, and 15
- **iOS** and **iPadOS**: 18. iOS 12.2 is used as the minimum SDK target
- **Mac**: macOS 14 or 15

> You can review the latest supported operating systems and versions at the following link: `https://github.com/dotnet/core/blob/main/release-notes/10.0/supported-os.md`.

Downloading and installing Visual Studio

Many professional .NET developers use Visual Studio in their day-to-day development work. Even if you choose to use VS Code to complete the coding tasks in this book, you might want to familiarize yourself with Visual Studio too.

If you do not have a Windows computer, then you can skip this section and continue to the next section, where you will download and install VS Code on macOS or Linux.

Since October 2014, Microsoft has made a professional-quality edition of Visual Studio available to students, open-source contributors, and individuals for free. It is called **Community Edition**. Any edition is suitable for this book. If you have not already installed it, let's do so now:

1. Download Visual Studio version 18.0 or later from the following link: `https://visualstudio.microsoft.com/downloads/`.

    > At the time of publishing in January 2026, the latest version of Visual Studio is version 18.0, and it is branded as Visual Studio 2026. If you choose to do so, you should be able to use Visual Studio 2022 to complete this book, although the user interface might move things around a bit.

2. Start the installer.
3. On the **Workloads** tab, select the following:
    - **ASP.NET and web development**
    - **.NET desktop development** (because this includes console apps).
    - **Desktop development with C++** with all default components (because this enables publishing console apps and web services that start faster and have smaller memory footprints).
4. On the **Individual components** tab, in the **Code tools** section, select the following:
    - **GitHub Copilot**
    - **Git for Windows**
5. Click **Install** and wait for the installer to acquire the selected software and install it.
6. When the installation is complete, click **Launch**.
7. The first time that you run Visual Studio, you will be prompted to sign in. If you have a Microsoft account, you can use that account. If you don't, then register for a new one at the following link: `https://signup.live.com/`.
8. The first time that you run Visual Studio, you will be prompted to configure your environment. For **Development Settings**, choose **Visual C#**. For the color theme, I chose **Light**, but you can choose whatever tickles your fancy.
9. If you want to customize your keyboard shortcuts, navigate to **Tools** | **Options...**, and then select the **Environment** | **Keyboard** option.

Visual Studio keyboard shortcuts

In this book, I will avoid showing keyboard shortcuts since they are often customized. Where they are consistent across code editors and commonly used, I will try to show them.

If you want to identify and customize your keyboard shortcuts, then you can, as shown at the following link: `https://learn.microsoft.com/en-us/visualstudio/ide/identifying-and-customizing-keyboard-shortcuts-in-visual-studio`.

Downloading and installing VS Code

VS Code has rapidly improved over the past couple of years and has pleasantly surprised Microsoft with its popularity. If you are brave and like to live on the bleeding edge, then there is the **Insiders** edition, which is a daily build of the next version.

Even if you plan to only use Visual Studio for development, I recommend that you download and install VS Code and try the coding tasks in this chapter using it, and then decide if you want to stick with just using Visual Studio for the rest of the book.

Let's now download and install VS Code, the .NET SDK, and the C# Dev Kit extension:

1. Download and install either the Stable Build or the Insiders edition of VS Code from the following link: `https://code.visualstudio.com/`.

   > If you need more help installing VS Code on any operating system, you can read the official setup guide at the following link: `https://code.visualstudio.com/docs/setup/setup-overview`.

2. Download and install the .NET SDK for version 10.0 from the following link: `https://www.microsoft.com/net/download`.

   > **Good practice:** The latest SDK version at the time of publishing is 10.0.101. Always install or update to the latest patched version.

3. To install the **C# Dev Kit** extension using the user interface, you must first launch the VS Code application.
4. In VS Code, click the **Extensions** icon or navigate to **View** | **Extensions**.
5. **C# Dev Kit** is one of the most popular extensions available, so you should see it at the top of the list, or you can enter `C# Dev Kit` in the search box.
6. Click **Install** and wait for supporting packages to download and install.

Good practice: Be sure to read the license agreement for the **C# Dev Kit.** It has a more restrictive license than the **C#** extension: `https://aka.ms/vs/csdevkit/license`.

Installing other extensions

In later chapters of this book, you will use more VS Code extensions. If you want to install them now, all the extensions that we will use are shown in *Table 1.1*:

Extension name and identifier	Description
C# Dev Kit `ms-dotnettools.csdevkit`	An official C# extension from Microsoft. Manage your code with a solution explorer and test your code with integrated unit test discovery and execution. It includes the **C#** and **IntelliCode for C# Dev Kit** extensions.
C# `ms-dotnettools.csharp`	This offers C# editing support, including syntax highlighting, IntelliSense, Go To Definition, Find All References, debugging support for .NET, and support for `csproj` projects on Windows, macOS, and Linux.
GitHub Copilot Chat `github.copilot-chat`	GitHub Copilot is an AI peer programming tool that helps you write code faster and smarter.
MSBuild project tools `tintoy.msbuild-project-tools`	This provides IntelliSense for MSBuild project files, including autocomplete for `<PackageReference>` elements.
SQL Server (mssql) for VS Code `ms-mssql.mssql`	This is for developing SQL Server, Azure SQL Database, and SQL Data Warehouse everywhere with a rich set of functionalities.
REST Client `humao.rest-client`	With this, you can send an HTTP request and view the response directly in VS Code.
ilspy-vscode `icsharpcode.ilspy-vscode`	With this, you can decompile **Microsoft Intermediate Language (MSIL)** aka .NET assemblies. It supports modern .NET, .NET Framework, .NET Core, and .NET Standard.

Table 1.1: VS Code extensions used in this book

Managing VS Code extensions at the command prompt

You can manage VS Code extensions at the command prompt or terminal, as shown in *Table 1.2*:

Command	**Description**
code --list-extensions	List installed extensions.
code --install-extension <extension-id>	Install the specified extension.
code --uninstall-extension <extension-id>	Uninstall the specified extension.

Table 1.2: Working with extensions at the command prompt

For example, to install the **C# Dev Kit** extension, enter the following at the command prompt:

```
code --install-extension ms-dotnettools.csdevkit
```

> I have created PowerShell scripts to install and uninstall the VS Code extensions in the preceding table. You can find them at the following link: https://github.com/markjprice/tools-skills-net10/tree/main/scripts/extension-scripts.

Understanding VS Code versions

Microsoft releases a new feature version of VS Code (almost) every month and bug-fix versions more frequently. For example:

- Version 1.106.0, October 2025 feature release
- Version 1.106.1, October 2025 bug fix release

The version of VS Code is less important than the version of the C# extension. While the C# extension is not required, it provides IntelliSense as you type, code navigation, and debugging features, so it's something that's very handy to install and keep updated to support the latest C# language features.

VS Code keyboard shortcuts

In this book, I will avoid showing keyboard shortcuts used for tasks like creating a new file since they are often different on different operating systems. The situations where I will show keyboard shortcuts are when you need to repeatedly press the key, for example, while debugging. These are also more likely to be consistent across operating systems.

If you want to customize your keyboard shortcuts for VS Code, then you can, as shown at the following link: https://code.visualstudio.com/docs/getstarted/keybindings.

I recommend that you download a PDF of keyboard shortcuts for your operating system from the following list:

- Windows: `https://code.visualstudio.com/shortcuts/keyboard-shortcuts-windows.pdf`
- macOS: `https://code.visualstudio.com/shortcuts/keyboard-shortcuts-macos.pdf`
- Linux: `https://code.visualstudio.com/shortcuts/keyboard-shortcuts-linux.pdf`

Downloading and installing Rider

According to the Stack Overflow Survey, about 20% of professional C# and .NET developers use Rider in their day-to-day development work. Rider is cross-platform, so you can install and run it on Windows, macOS, and varieties of Linux. You can use an evaluation license key for a free 30-day trial.

JetBrains also offers **Toolbox App** to manage your IDEs easily and it's free. It is especially useful for Linux users because Rider does not update through the apt (Advanced Package Tool) command like normal Linux programs. Plus, it gives you access to early access programs for software like JetBrains Fleet, a next-generation code editor.

If you have not already installed Rider and you want to use it, let's do so now:

1. Download the latest version of Rider from the following link: `https://www.jetbrains.com/rider/download/`.

   > If you're on Ubuntu 16.04 or later, you can install Rider from the command prompt or terminal, as shown in the following command: `sudo snap install rider --classic`

2. Run the installer.
3. Download the latest version of JetBrains Toolbox App from the following link: `https://www.jetbrains.com/toolbox-app/`.
4. Run the installer.
5. Navigate to `https://visualstudio.microsoft.com/downloads/#build-tools-for-visual-studio-2026` and install the **Build Tools for Visual Studio**. These are necessary to use the native ahead-of-time (AOT) compiler.

> If you have installed JetBrains ReSharper in Visual Studio, you will get similar tools as in Rider.

Other JetBrains tools

JetBrains offers a suite of tools designed to enhance productivity, code quality, and application performance for .NET developers. A brief overview of dotPeek, dotTrace, dotMemory, and dotCover, highlighting their capabilities and benefits, is included in the following list:

- **dotPeek**: This tool can decompile .NET assemblies back to readable C# code, making it easier to explore and understand external code that lacks a source. It allows browsing the contents of assemblies, helping developers explore the structure and dependencies without needing the source code. It provides advanced navigation and search capabilities within decompiled code, such as quick jumping to symbol definitions and usages. It's invaluable for understanding the inner workings of third-party libraries, frameworks, or any compiled .NET code without the original source. It can serve as a symbol server, making it possible to step into decompiled code during debugging sessions, aiding in the diagnosis of issues with external libraries. dotPeek is offered as a free tool, making advanced decompilation and assembly exploration accessible to all .NET developers.
- **dotTrace**: This tool provides detailed performance profiling for .NET applications, identifying performance bottlenecks by measuring execution times and call frequencies. It supports sampling, tracing, and timeline modes, each suited to different types of performance analysis. It offers a comprehensive set of views and filters to analyze the profiling data, including call trees, hot spots, and timeline views. It helps developers optimize application performance by pinpointing slow-running code and inefficient algorithms.
- **dotMemory**: This tool analyzes memory usage of .NET applications, identifying memory leaks and issues related to **Garbage Collector** (**GC**). It helps understand how memory is allocated and released, pinpointing excessive allocations that could lead to performance degradation. It allows the comparison of memory snapshots taken at different times, making it easier to identify memory leaks and the objects responsible. It facilitates memory optimization by providing insights into memory consumption patterns and detecting memory leaks.
- **dotCover**: This tool measures how much of the codebase is covered by tests, highlighting covered and uncovered code blocks. It works with various testing frameworks and supports all .NET applications, enhancing test effectiveness. It provides a continuous testing mode that automatically runs tests in the background as code changes, offering immediate feedback on test coverage and success. It helps improve code quality by ensuring higher coverage of tests, which can lead to fewer bugs and more stable applications. It facilitates an efficient testing process by identifying untested code, allowing developers to focus on areas lacking test coverage.

Together, these JetBrains tools form a comprehensive toolkit that can significantly enhance the productivity and efficiency of .NET development teams.

Setting up a database and projects for this book

We will set up a database and some initial projects for this book, but first, let's review some important features that make managing projects easier.

Central Package Management

By default, with .NET SDK CLI and most code editor-created projects, if you need to reference a NuGet package, you add the reference to the package name and version directly in the project file, as shown in the following markup:

```
<ItemGroup>
  <PackageReference Include="Microsoft.EntityFrameworkCore.SqlServer"
                    Version="10.0.0" />
  ...
</ItemGroup>
```

Central Package Management (CPM) is a feature that simplifies the management of NuGet package versions across multiple projects and solutions within a directory hierarchy. This is particularly useful for large solutions with many projects, where managing package versions individually can become cumbersome and error-prone.

Features and benefits of CPM

The key features and benefits of CPM include:

- **Centralized Control**: CPM allows you to define package versions in a single file, typically `Directory.Packages.props`, which is placed in the root directory of a directory hierarchy that contains all your solutions and projects. This file centralizes the version information for all NuGet packages used across the projects in your solutions.
- **Consistency**: Ensures consistent package versions across multiple projects. Having a single source of truth for package versions eliminates discrepancies that can occur when different projects specify different versions of the same package.
- **Simplified Updates**: Updating a package version in a large solution becomes straightforward. You update the version in the central file, and all projects referencing that package automatically use the updated version. This significantly reduces the maintenance overhead.
- **Reduced Redundancy**: Removes the need to specify package versions in individual project files (`.csproj`). This makes project files cleaner and easier to manage, as they no longer contain repetitive version information.

> **Good practice:** It is important to regularly update NuGet packages and their dependencies to address security vulnerabilities.

Defining project properties to reuse version numbers

Microsoft packages usually have the same number each month, like 10.0.2 in February, 10.0.3 in March. You can define properties at the top of your `Directory.Packages.props` file and then reference these properties throughout the file. This approach keeps package versions consistent and makes updates easier.

For example, in your Directory.Packages.props file. At the top of the file, within a <ProjectGroup> tag, define your custom property and then reference it for the package version, as shown in the following markup:

```
<Project>
  <PropertyGroup>
    <MicrosoftPackageVersion>10.0.2</MicrosoftPackageVersion>
  </PropertyGroup>

  <ItemGroup>
    <PackageVersion Include="Microsoft.EntityFrameworkCore"
                    Version="$(MicrosoftPackageVersion)" />
    <PackageVersion Include="Microsoft.Extensions.Logging"
                    Version="$(MicrosoftPackageVersion)" />
    <!-- Add more Microsoft packages as needed. -->
  </ItemGroup>

  <!-- Other packages with specific versions. -->
  <ItemGroup>
    <PackageVersion Include="Newtonsoft.Json" Version="13.0.4" />
  </ItemGroup>
</Project>
```

Note the following about the preceding configuration:

- **Define a property**: The line <MicrosoftPackageVersion>10.0.2</MicrosoftPackageVersion> defines the property. This value can be changed once at the top of the file, and all references will update automatically.
- **Reference the property**: Use the syntax $(PropertyName) to reference the defined property. All occurrences of $(MicrosoftPackageVersion) will resolve to the version number that you set.

When the monthly update rolls around, for example, from 10.0.2 to 10.0.3, you only have to update this number once.

You might want separate properties for related packages, such as:

```
<AspNetCorePackageVersion>10.0.3</AspNetCorePackageVersion>
<EFCorePackageVersion>10.0.3</EFCorePackageVersion>
```

This allows independent updates if packages diverge in their release cycles or versions later.

After making changes, at the terminal or command prompt, run the following command:

```
dotnet restore
```

This will verify the correctness of your references and quickly alert you if you've introduced errors. By adopting this pattern combined with CPM, you simplify version management, reduce redundancy, and make your projects easier to maintain over time.

Good practice: Choose clear and consistent property names, like `MicrosoftPackageVersion` or `AspNetCorePackageVersion`, to easily distinguish between different package ecosystems. Check your `Directory.Packages.props` file into source control. Regularly update and test after changing versions to ensure compatibility.

Configuring Central Package Management in a .NET solution

Let's set up CPM for a solution that we will use throughout the rest of the chapters in this book:

1. Create a new folder named `tools-skills-net10` that we will use for all the code in this book. For example, on Windows, create a folder: `C:\tools-skills-net10`.
2. In the `tools-skills-net10` folder, create a new file named `Directory.Packages.props`. You can do this at the command prompt or terminal using the following command:

```
dotnet new packagesprops
```

To save you time manually typing this large file, you can download it at the following link: `https://github.com/markjprice/tools-skills-net10/blob/main/code/Directory.Packages.props`.

3. In `Directory.Packages.props`, modify its contents, as shown in the following markup:

```
<Project>

  <PropertyGroup>
 <ManagePackageVersionsCentrally>true</ManagePackageVersionsCentrally>
    <Net10>10.0.1</Net10>
    <Aspire>13.0.2</Aspire>
    <OpenTelemetry>1.14.0</OpenTelemetry>
    <Testcontainers>4.9.0</Testcontainers>
    <MSExt>10.1.0</MSExt>
  </PropertyGroup>

  <ItemGroup Label="Chapter 1 Introducing Tools and Skills for .NET">
    <PackageVersion Include="Microsoft.EntityFrameworkCore.Design"
                    Version="$(Net10)" />
    <PackageVersion Include="Microsoft.EntityFrameworkCore.SqlServer"
                    Version="$(Net10)" />
```

```
    <!--For unit testing.-->
    <PackageVersion Include="coverlet.collector" Version="6.0.4" />
    <PackageVersion Include="Microsoft.NET.Test.Sdk" Version="18.0.1" />
    <PackageVersion Include="xunit" Version="2.9.3" />
    <PackageVersion Include="xunit.runner.visualstudio" Version="3.1.5"
/>
  </ItemGroup>

  <ItemGroup Label="Chapter 5 Logging, Tracing, and Metrics for
Observability">
    <!--For logging to console.-->
    <PackageVersion Include="Microsoft.Extensions.Logging.Console"
                    Version="$(Net10)" />

    <!--For generating OpenAPI documentation.-->
    <PackageVersion Include="Microsoft.AspNetCore.OpenApi"
Version="$(Net10)" />

    <!--For performance counters.-->
     <PackageVersion Include="System.Diagnostics.PerformanceCounter"
                       Version="$(Net10)" />

    <!--For OpenTelemetry.-->
    <PackageVersion Include="OpenTelemetry.Exporter.Console"
                    Version="$(OpenTelemetry)" />
    <PackageVersion Include="OpenTelemetry.Extensions.Hosting"
                    Version="$(OpenTelemetry)" />
    <PackageVersion Include="OpenTelemetry.Instrumentation.AspNetCore"
                    Version="$(OpenTelemetry)" />
    <PackageVersion Include="OpenTelemetry.Instrumentation.
EntityFrameworkCore"
                    Version="1.14.0-beta.2" />
    <PackageVersion Include="OpenTelemetry.Instrumentation.SqlClient"
                    Version="1.14.0-beta.1" />
  </ItemGroup>

  <ItemGroup Label="Chapter 7 Observing and Modifying Code Execution
Dynamically">
    <PackageVersion Include="Microsoft.CodeAnalysis.Analyzers"
                    Version="3.11.0" />
    <PackageVersion Include="Microsoft.CodeAnalysis.CSharp"
                    Version="5.0.0" />
  </ItemGroup>
```

```
  <ItemGroup Label="Chapter 9 Multitasking and Concurrency">
    <PackageVersion Include="Microsoft.Data.SqlClient" Version="6.1.3" />
  </ItemGroup>

  <ItemGroup Label="Chapter 10 Dependency Injection, Containers, and
Service Lifetime">
    <PackageVersion Include="Microsoft.Extensions.Hosting"
                    Version="$(Net10)" />
  </ItemGroup>

  <ItemGroup Label="Chapter 11 Unit Testing and Mocking">
    <PackageVersion Include="NSubstitute" Version="5.3.0" />
    <PackageVersion Include="Bogus" Version="35.6.5" />

    <!--FluentAssertions restricted its license with 8.0 and later.-->
    <!--Minimum 7.2.0 (inclusive) up to maximum 8.0.0 (exclusive).-->
    <PackageVersion Include="FluentAssertions" Version="[7.2.0,8.0.0)" />
  </ItemGroup>

  <ItemGroup Label="Chapter 13 Benchmarking Performance, Load, and Stress
Testing">
    <PackageVersion Include="BenchmarkDotNet" Version="0.15.8" />
    <PackageVersion Include="NBomber" Version="6.1.2" />
    <PackageVersion Include="NBomber.Http" Version="6.1.0" />
  </ItemGroup>

  <ItemGroup Label="Chapter 14 Functional and End-to-End Testing of
Websites and Services">
    <PackageVersion Include="Microsoft.Playwright" Version="1.57.0" />
    <PackageVersion Include="Microsoft.AspNetCore.Mvc.Testing"
                    Version="$(Net10" />
  </ItemGroup>

  <ItemGroup Label="Chapter 15 Containerization Using Docker">
    <PackageVersion Include="Spectre.Console" Version="0.54.0" />
    <PackageVersion Include="Testcontainers"
                    Version="$(Testcontainers)" />
    <PackageVersion Include="Testcontainers.MsSql"
                    Version="$(Testcontainers)" />
    <PackageVersion Include="Microsoft.AspNetCore.Diagnostics.
EntityFrameworkCore"
```

```
                    Version="$(Net10)" />
    <PackageVersion Include="Microsoft.AspNetCore.Identity.
EntityFrameworkCore"
                    Version="$(Net10)" />
    <PackageVersion Include="Microsoft.AspNetCore.Identity.UI"
                    Version="$(Net10)" />
    <PackageVersion Include="Microsoft.EntityFrameworkCore.Tools"
                    Version="$(Net10)" />
    <PackageVersion Include=
      "Microsoft.VisualStudio.Azure.Containers.Tools.Targets"
      Version="1.22.1" />
  </ItemGroup>

  <ItemGroup Label="Chapter 16 Cloud-Native Development Using Aspire">
    <PackageVersion Include="Aspire.Hosting.AppHost" Version="$(Aspire)"
/>
    <PackageVersion Include="Aspire.Hosting.Redis" Version="$(Aspire)" />
    <PackageVersion Include="Microsoft.Extensions.Http.Resilience"
                    Version="$(MSExt)" />
    <PackageVersion Include="Microsoft.Extensions.ServiceDiscovery"
                    Version="$(MSExt)" />
    <PackageVersion Include="Aspire.Hosting.Testing"
                    Version="$(Aspire)" />
    <PackageVersion Include="Aspire.StackExchange.Redis.OutputCaching"
                    Version="$(Aspire)" />
    <PackageVersion Include="OpenTelemetry.Exporter.
OpenTelemetryProtocol"
                    Version="$(OpenTelemetry)" />
    <PackageVersion Include="OpenTelemetry.Instrumentation.Http"
                    Version="$(OpenTelemetry)" />
    <PackageVersion Include="OpenTelemetry.Instrumentation.Runtime"
                    Version="$(OpenTelemetry)" />
    <PackageVersion Include="Aspire.Hosting.PostgreSQL"
                    Version="$(Aspire)" />
    <PackageVersion Include="Aspire.Hosting.SqlServer"
                    Version="$(Aspire)" />
    <PackageVersion Include="Aspire.Hosting.RabbitMQ"
                    Version="$(Aspire)" />
    <PackageVersion Include="Aspire.Hosting.Azure.CognitiveServices"
                    Version="$(Aspire)" />
  </ItemGroup>

</Project>
```

Warning! The `<ManagePackageVersionsCentrally>` element and its `true` value must all go on one line. Also, you cannot use floating wildcard version numbers like `10.0-*` as you can in an individual project. Wildcards are useful to automatically get the latest patch version, but with CPM, you must manually update the versions.

For any projects that we add underneath the folder containing this file, we can reference the packages without explicitly specifying the version, as shown in the following markup:

```
<ItemGroup>
  <PackageReference Include="Microsoft.EntityFrameworkCore.SqlServer" />
  <PackageReference Include="Microsoft.EntityFrameworkCore.Design" />
</ItemGroup>
```

CPM good practice

You should regularly review and update the package versions in the `Directory.Packages.props` file to ensure that you are using the latest stable releases with important bug fixes and performance improvements.

Good practice: I recommend that you set a monthly event in your calendar for the second Wednesday of each month. This will occur after the second Tuesday of each month, which is Patch Tuesday, the day when Microsoft releases bug fixes and patches for .NET and related packages. I do this myself and will try to keep the GitHub copy of this file updated every month (or so).

For example, throughout 2026, there are likely to be new versions each month, so you can go to the NuGet page for each of the packages. You can then update the versions in the `Directory.Packages.props` file, for example, as shown in the following markup:

```
<PackageVersion Include="Microsoft.EntityFrameworkCore.SqlServer"
                Version="10.0.3" />
```

Before updating package versions, check for any breaking changes in the release notes of the packages. Test your solution thoroughly after updating to ensure compatibility.

Educate your team and document the purpose and usage of the `Directory.Packages.props` file to ensure everyone understands how to manage package versions centrally.

You can override an individual package version by using the `VersionOverride` attribute on a `<PackageReference />` element in the specific project file. For example, to force the SQL Server for EF Core package to use version `10.0.0`, as shown in the following markup:

```
<PackageReference Include="Microsoft.EntityFrameworkCore.SqlServer"
                  VersionOverride="10.0.0" />
```

This can be useful if a newer version introduces a regression bug.

> You can learn more about CPM at the following link: `https://learn.microsoft.com/en-us/nuget/consume-packages/central-package-management`.

Package Source Mapping

If you use CPM and have more than one package source configured for your code editor, as shown in *Figure 1.2*, then you will see NuGet Warning `NU1507`, as shown in the following output:

```
There are 2 package sources defined in your configuration. When using central
package management, please map your package sources with package source mapping
(https://aka.ms/nuget-package-source-mapping) or specify a single package
source. The following sources are defined: https://api.nuget.org/v3/index.json
and  https://contoso.myget.org/F/development/.
```

Specifically in *Figure 1.2*, this warning occurs because we have both the default package source (`https://api.nuget.org/v3/index.json`) and a custom package source configured:

Figure 1.2: Visual Studio with two NuGet package sources configured

> NU1507 warning reference page can be found at the following link: `https://learn.microsoft.com/en-us/nuget/reference/errors-and-warnings/nu1507`.

Understanding Package Source Mapping

Package Source Mapping (PSM) can help safeguard your software supply chain if you use a mix of public and private package sources, as in the preceding example.

By default, when it needs to download a package, NuGet will search all configured package sources. When a package exists on multiple sources, it may not be deterministic which source the package will be downloaded from. With PSM, you can filter, per package, which source(s) NuGet will search.

PSM is supported by Visual Studio, .NET 6 and later, and NuGet 6 and later. Older tooling will ignore the PSM configuration.

Now let's see how to enable PSM.

Enabling Package Source Mapping

To enable PSM, you must have a `nuget.config` file.

> **Good practice:** Create a single `nuget.config` at the root of your source code directory hierarchy.

There are two parts: defining package sources, and mapping package sources to packages. All requested packages must map to one or more sources by matching a defined package pattern. In other words, once you have defined a `packageSourceMapping` element, you must explicitly define which sources every package, including transitive packages, will be restored from.

For example, if you want most packages to be sourced from the default `nuget.org` site, but there are some private packages that must be sourced from your organization's website, you would define the two package sources, and set the mapping (assuming all your private packages are named `Northwind.Something`), as shown in the following markup:

```
<?xml version="1.0" encoding="utf-8"?>
<configuration>
  <!-- `clear` ensures no additional sources are inherited from another config
file. -->
  <packageSources>
    <clear />
    <!-- `key` can be any identifier for your source. -->
    <add key="nuget.org" value="https://api.nuget.org/v3/index.json" />
    <add key="Northwind" value="https://northwind.com/packages" />
  </packageSources>

  <!-- All packages sourced from nuget.org except Northwind packages. -->
  <packageSourceMapping>
```

```
    <!-- key value for <packageSource> should match key values from
<packageSources> element -->
    <packageSource key="nuget.org">
      <package pattern="*" />
    </packageSource>
    <packageSource key="Northwind">
      <package pattern="Northwind.*" />
    </packageSource>
  </packageSourceMapping>
</configuration>
```

Let's create a `nuget.config` for all the solutions and projects in this book that will use `nuget.org` as the source for all packages:

1. In the `tools-skills-net10` folder, create a new file named `nuget.config`.
2. In `nuget.config`, modify its contents, as shown in the following markup:

```
<?xml version="1.0" encoding="utf-8"?>
<configuration>
  <!-- `clear` ensures no additional sources are inherited from another
config file. -->
  <packageSources>
    <clear />
    <!-- `key` can be any identifier for your source. -->
    <add key="nuget.org" value="https://api.nuget.org/v3/index.json" />
  </packageSources>

  <!-- All packages sourced from nuget.org. -->
  <packageSourceMapping>
    <!-- key value for <packageSource> should match key values from
<packageSources> element -->
    <packageSource key="nuget.org">
      <package pattern="*" />
    </packageSource>
  </packageSourceMapping>
</configuration>
```

3. Save changes.

> You can learn more about `nuget.config` at the following link: `https://learn.microsoft.com/en-us/nuget/reference/nuget-config-file`.
>
> You can learn more about PSM at the following link: `https://learn.microsoft.com/en-us/nuget/consume-packages/package-source-mapping`.

Treating warnings as errors

By default, compiler warnings may appear if there are potential problems with your code when you first build a project, but they do not prevent compilation and they are hidden if you rebuild. Warnings are given for a reason, so ignoring warnings encourages poor development practices.

Some developers would prefer to be forced to fix warnings, so .NET provides a project setting to do this, as shown highlighted in the following markup:

```
<Project Sdk="Microsoft.NET.Sdk">

  <PropertyGroup>
    <OutputType>Exe</OutputType>
    <TargetFramework>net10.0</TargetFramework>
    <ImplicitUsings>enable</ImplicitUsings>
    <Nullable>enable</Nullable>
    <TreatWarningsAsErrors>true</TreatWarningsAsErrors>
  </PropertyGroup>
```

I have enabled the option to treat warnings as errors in (almost) all the solutions in the GitHub repository.

If you find that you get too many errors after enabling this, you can disable specific warnings by using the `<WarningsNotAsErrors>` element with a comma-separated list of warning codes, as shown in the following markup:

```
<WarningsNotAsErrors>0219,CS8981</WarningsNotAsErrors>
```

You can learn more about controlling warnings as errors at the following link: `https://learn.microsoft.com/en-us/dotnet/csharp/language-reference/compiler-options/errors-warnings#warningsaserrors-and-warningsnotaserrors`.

Using a sample relational database

It would be useful to have a sample database that has a medium complexity and a decent number of sample records. Microsoft offers several sample databases, most of which are too complex for our needs, so instead, we will use a database that was first created in the early 1990s, known as **Northwind**.

Let's take a minute to look at a diagram of the Northwind database and its eight most important tables. You can refer to the diagram in *Figure 1.3* as we write code and queries throughout this book:

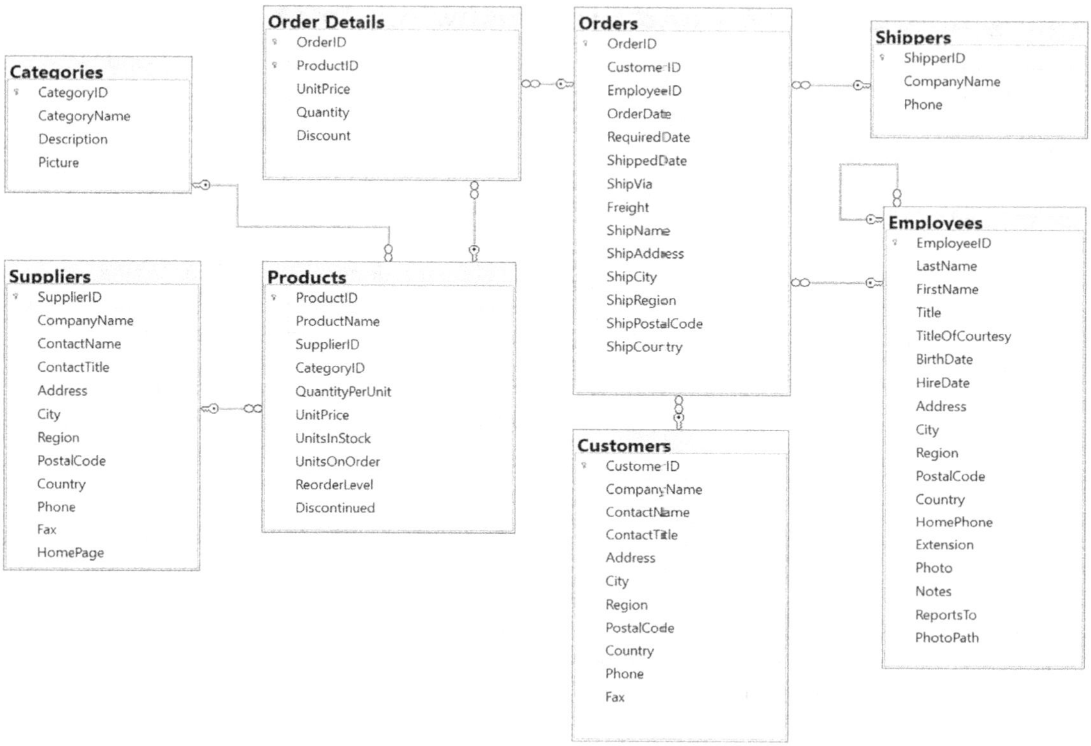

Figure 1.3: The Northwind database tables and relationships

Note that:

- Each category has a unique identifier, name, description, and picture. The picture is stored as a byte array in JPEG format.
- Each product has a unique identifier, name, unit price, number of units in stock, and other columns.
- Each product is associated with a category by storing the category's unique identifier.
- The relationship between `Categories` and `Products` is one-to-many, meaning each category can have zero, one, or more products.
- Each product is supplied by a supplier company indicated by storing the supplier's unique identifier.
- The quantity and unit price of a product is stored for each detail of an order.
- Each order is made by a customer, taken by an employee, and shipped by a shipping company.
- Each employee has a name, address, contact details, birth, and hire dates, a reference to their manager (except for the boss, whose `ReportsTo` field is `null`), and a photo stored as a byte array in JPEG format. The table has a one-to-many relationship to itself because one employee can manage many other employees.

Setting up SQL Server and the Northwind database

Microsoft offers various editions of its popular and capable SQL Server product for Windows, Linux, and Docker containers.

> If you have Windows, then you can use a free version that runs standalone, known as SQL Server Developer Edition. You can also use the free Express edition or the free SQL Server LocalDB edition that can be installed with Visual Studio. To install SQL Server locally on Windows, please see the detailed instructions in *Appendix B, Setting Up Your Development Environment*, which you can find here: `https://github.com/markjprice/tools-skills-net10/blob/main/docs/B31468_Appendix%20B.pdf`.
>
> If you prefer to install SQL Server locally on Linux, then you will find instructions at the following link: `https://learn.microsoft.com/en-us/sql/linux/sql-server-linux-setup`.

If you do not have a Windows computer or if you want to use a cross-platform database system, then please see the detailed instructions in *Appendix B, Setting Up Your Development Environment*.

You'll need to have set up SQL Server, run the SQL script to create the Northwind database and confirm that you can connect to the database and view the rows in its tables like `Products` and `Categories` before continuing with the project. The following two subsections provide detailed steps to help you do so using SQL Server in Docker. You can skip this if you already have this set up.

Northwind database SQL scripts

The script for SQL Server creates 13 tables as well as related views and stored procedures. The SQL scripts are found at the following link:

`https://github.com/markjprice/tools-skills-net10/tree/main/scripts/sql-scripts`.

I recommend that in your `tools-skills-net10` folder, you create a `sql-scripts` folder and copy all the SQL scripts to that local folder.

There are multiple SQL scripts to choose from, as described in the following list:

- `Northwind4SqlServerContainer.sql` script: To use SQL Server on a local computer in a container system like Docker. The script creates the Northwind database. It does not drop the database if it already exists because the Docker container should be empty anyway, as a fresh one can be spun up each time. Instructions to install Docker and set up a SQL Server image and container are in the next section of this book. This is my recommendation for using SQL Server in this book.

- `Northwind4SqlServerLocal.sql` script: To use SQL Server on a local Windows or Linux computer. The script checks if the Northwind database already exists and, if necessary, drops (deletes) it before creating it. Instructions to install SQL Server Developer Edition (free) on your local Windows computer can be found in the GitHub repository for this book at the following link: `https://github.com/markjprice/tools-skills-net10/blob/main/docs/sql-server/README.md`.
- `Northwind4SqlServerCloud.sql` script: To use SQL Server with an Azure SQL Database resource created in the Azure cloud. You will need an Azure account; these resources cost money as long as they exist! The script does not drop or create the Northwind database because you should manually create the Northwind database using the Azure portal user interface. The script only creates the database objects, including the table structure and data.

Before you can execute any of these SQL scripts, you need a SQL Server instance. My recommendation is to use Docker and a container, so that's what we will cover in the next section. If you prefer a local or cloud SQL Server, then you can skip this next section.

Installing Docker and an SQL Server container image

Docker provides a consistent environment across development, testing, and production, minimizing the "it works on my machine" issue. Docker containers are more lightweight than traditional virtual machines, making them faster to start up and less resource-intensive.

Docker containers can run on any system with Docker installed, making it easy to move databases between environments or across different machines. You can quickly spin up a SQL database container with a single command, making setup faster and more reproducible. Each database instance runs in its own container, ensuring that it is isolated from other applications and databases on the same machine.

You can install Docker on any operating system and use a container that has SQL Server installed. For personal, educational, and small business use, Docker Desktop is free to use. It includes the full set of Docker features, including container management and orchestration. The Docker CLI and Docker Engine are open source and free to use, allowing developers to build, run, and manage containers.

Docker also has paid tiers that offer additional features, such as enhanced security, collaboration tools, more granular access control, priority support, and higher rate limits on Docker Hub image pull.

The Docker image we will use has SQL Server 2025 hosted on Ubuntu 22.04. It is supported with Docker Engine 1.8 or later.

Let's install Docker and set up the SQL image and container now:

1. Install Docker Desktop from the following link: `https://docs.docker.com/engine/install/`.
2. Start Docker Desktop, which could take a few minutes on the initial start, as shown in *Figure 1.4*:

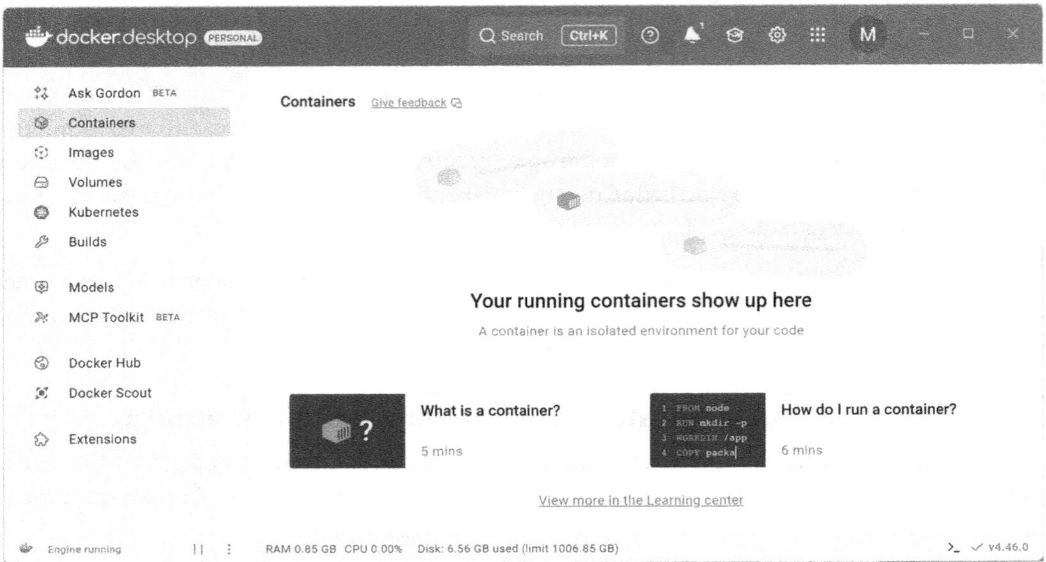

Figure 1.4: Docker Desktop on Windows

3. At the command prompt or terminal, pull down the latest container image for SQL Server 2025, as shown in the following command:

```
docker pull mcr.microsoft.com/mssql/server:2025-latest
```

> Unfortunately, the recent SQL Server images from Microsoft only support x64 architecture. If you want to use an image that runs without emulation on ARM CPUs, for example, if you have a Surface Laptop 7 or Mac, then you can use a minimal edition of SQL Server known as Azure SQL Edge that runs on either x64 or ARM64, with a minimum of 1 GB RAM on the host. But Azure SQL Edge is no longer supported by Microsoft, so use it at your own risk. I think that it's fine for learning purposes, but do not use unsupported software in production. To pull the Azure SQL Edge image, enter the following command: `docker pull mcr.microsoft.com/azure-sql-edge:latest`

4. Wait for the image as it downloads, and then note the results, as shown in the following output:

```
2025-latest: Pulling from mssql/server
a7f551132cc7: Pull complete
d39c64e0c073: Pull complete
04a0776f5c78: Pull complete
```

```
Digest:
sha256:e2e5bcfe395924ff49694542191d3aefe8636b3bd6c024f9ea01bf5a8856c56e
Status: Downloaded newer image for mcr.microsoft.com/mssql/server:2025-
latest
```

Running the SQL Server container image

You can create a container from the image and run it in a single `docker run` command with the following options:

- `--cap-add SYS_PTRACE`: This grants the container the `SYS_PTRACE` capability allows debugging tools (like `strace` or certain profilers) to attach to processes within the container. Microsoft recommends this for enabling debugging or diagnostic tools inside the container, but it's not strictly necessary for normal SQL Server operation.
- `-e 'ACCEPT_EULA=1'` or `-e "ACCEPT_EULA=1"`: This sets an environment variable to accept the SQL Server **End User License Agreement** (**EULA**). If you don't provide this, the container will exit immediately with a message saying you must accept the EULA.
- `-e 'MSSQL_SA_PASSWORD=s3cret-Ninja'` or `-e "MSSQL_SA_PASSWORD=s3cret-Ninja"`: This sets an environment variable to set the SQL Server `sa` (system administrator) account's password. The password must be at least eight characters long and contain characters from three of the following four sets: uppercase letters, lowercase letters, digits, and symbols. Otherwise, the container cannot set up the SQL Server engine and will fail. `s3cret-Ninja` satisfies those rules (lowercase, number, hyphen, uppercase), but feel free to use your own password if you wish.
- `-p 1433:1433`: This maps a port from the container to the host. `1433` is the default port for SQL Server. This allows applications on the host to connect to SQL Server inside the container as if it were running natively.
- `--name nw-container`: This gives the container a custom name. This is optional, but if you don't set a name, a random one will be assigned for you, like `frosty_mirzakhani`.
- `-d`: This runs the container in detached mode (in the background). Without it, Docker would run the container in the foreground, tying up your terminal or command prompt window.
- `mcr.microsoft.com/mssql/server:2025-latest`: This specifies the image to run. `mcr.microsoft.com` is Microsoft's official container registry. `mssql/server` is the SQL Server on Linux container image. `2025-latest` is the tag for the latest build of SQL Server 2025.

Now that you understand what you are about to do, we can run the image:

1. At the command prompt or terminal, run the container image for SQL Server with a strong password, and name the container `nw-container`, as shown in the following command:

```
docker run --cap-add SYS_PTRACE -e 'ACCEPT_EULA=1' -e 'MSSQL_SA_
PASSWORD=s3cret-Ninja' -p 1433:1433 --name nw-container -d mcr.microsoft.
com/mssql/server:2025-latest
```

Warning! The preceding command must be entered all on one line, or the container will not be started up correctly. In particular, the container might start up, but without a password set, and therefore, later, you won't be able to connect to it! All command lines used in this book can be found and copied from the following link: `https://github.com/markjprice/tools-skills-net10/blob/main/docs/command-lines.md`.

Also, different operating systems may require different quote characters, or none at all. To set the environment variables, you should be able to use either straight single-quotes or straight double-quotes. If the logs show that you did not accept the license agreement, then try the other type of quotes.

If running the container image at the command prompt fails for you, see the next section, titled *Running a container using the user interface*.

2. If your operating system's firewall blocks access, then allow access.
3. In Docker Desktop, in the **Containers** section, confirm that the image is running, as shown in *Figure 1.5*:

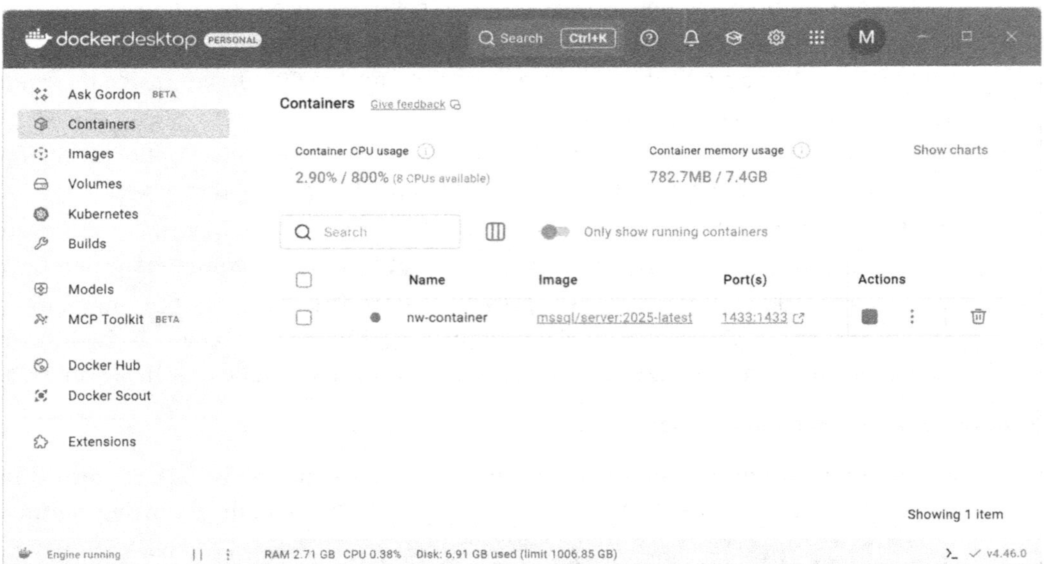

Figure 1.5: SQL Server container running in Docker Desktop on Windows

You might assume that the link in the **Port(s)** column is clickable and will navigate to a working website. But the container image only has SQL Server in it. SQL Server is listening on that port and can be connected to using a TCP address, not an HTTP address, so Docker is misleading you! There is no web server listening on port `1433`, so a web browser that makes a request to `http://localhost:1433` will get a **This page isn't working** error. This is expected behavior because a database server is not a web server. Many containers in Docker do host a web server, and in those scenarios, having a convenient clickable link is useful. But Docker has no idea which containers have web servers and which do not. All it knows is what ports are mapped from internal ports to external ports. It is up to the developer to know if those links are useful.

4. At the command prompt or terminal, ask Docker to list all containers, both running and stopped, as shown in the following command:

```
docker ps -a
```

5. Note the container `STATUS` is `Up 53 seconds` and listening externally on port `1433`, which is mapped to its internal port `1433`, as shown highlighted in the following output:

```
CONTAINER ID   IMAGE                                              COMMAND
CREATED          STATUS          PORTS                                        NAMES
183f02e84b2a   mcr.microsoft.com/ mssql/server:2025-latest   "/opt/mssql/
bin/perm..."   8 minutes ago   Up 53 seconds   1401/tcp, 0.0.0.0:1433-
>1433/tcp   nw-container
```

You can learn more about the `docker ps` command at `https://docs.docker.com/engine/reference/commandline/ps/`.

Running a container using the user interface

If you successfully ran the SQL Server container, then you can skip this section and continue with the next section, titled *Connecting to SQL Server in a Docker container*.

If entering a command at the prompt or terminal fails for you, try following these steps to use the user interface:

1. In Docker Desktop, navigate to the **Images** tab.
2. In the **mcr.microsoft.com/mssql/server** row, in the **Actions** column, click the **Run** button.
3. In the **Run a new container** dialog box, expand **Optional settings**, and complete the configuration, as shown in *Figure 1.6* and in the following items:
   - **Container name:** `nw-container`, or leave blank to use a random name.
   - **Ports:** Enter `1433` to map to **:1433/tcp**.
   - **Volumes:** Leave empty.

    - **Environment variables** (click + to add a second one):
        - Enter `ACCEPT_EULA` with the value `Y` (or `1`).
        - Enter `MSSQL_SA_PASSWORD` with the value `s3cret-Ninja`.
4. Click **Run**.

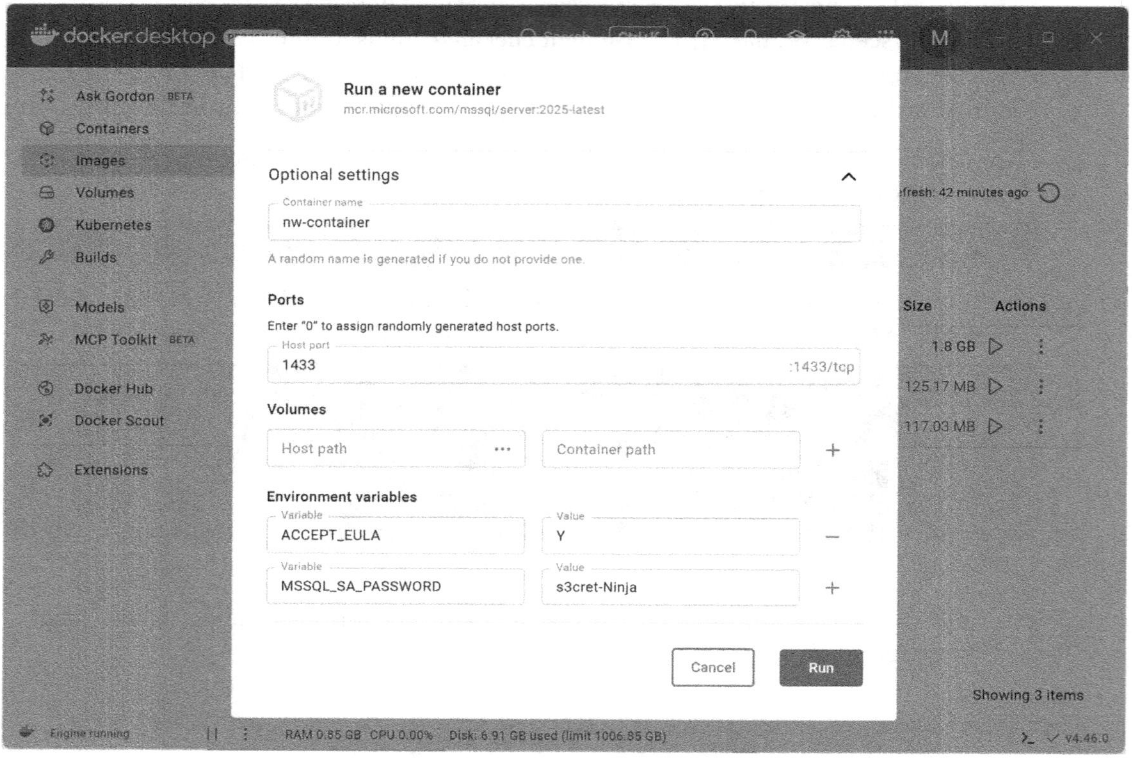

Figure 1.6: Running a container for SQL Server with the user interface

Connecting to SQL Server in a Docker container

Use your preferred database tool to connect to SQL Server in the Docker container. Some common database tools are shown in the following list:

- Windows only:
    - **SQL Server Management Studio (SSMS)**: The most popular and comprehensive tool for managing SQL Server databases. Free to download from Microsoft.
    - **SQL Server Data Tools (SSDT)**: Integrated into Visual Studio and free to use, SSDT provides database development tools for designing, deploying, and managing SQL Server databases.
- Cross-platform for Windows, macOS, Linux:
    - **VS Code's MS SQL extension**: Query execution, IntelliSense, database browsing, and connection to SQL Server databases.

Some notes about the database connection string for SQL Server in a container:

- **Data Source**, a.k.a. **Server Name:** `tcp:127.0.0.1,1433`
- **Authentication:** You must use **SQL Server Authentication**, a.k.a. **SQL Login**. That is, you must supply a username and password. The SQL Server image has the `sa` user already created, and you had to give it a strong password when you ran the container. We chose the password `s3cret-Ninja`.
- You must select the **Trust server certificate** checkbox.
- Optionally, you might want to save your password for future use.
- **Initial Catalog**, a.k.a. **database:** `master` or leave blank. (We will create the Northwind database using a SQL script, so we do not specify that as the database name yet.)

Warning! If you already have SQL Server installed locally, and its services are running, then it will be listening to port **1433**, and it will take priority over any Docker-hosted SQL Server services that are also trying to listen on port **1433**. You will need to stop the local SQL Server before being able to connect to any Docker-hosted SQL Server services. You can do this using Windows Services: in the **Services (Local)** list, right-click **SQL Server (MSSQLSERVER)** and choose **Stop**. (This can take a few minutes, so be patient.) You can also right-click and choose **Properties** and then set **Startup type** to **Manual**, as shown in *Figure 1.7* (it defaults to **Automatic**, so if you restart Windows, it will be running again). Or change the port number(s) for either the local or Docker-hosted SQL Server services so that they do not conflict.

Figure 1.7: SQL Server service properties

I have created a troubleshooting guide if you have trouble connecting to SQL Server: `https://github.com/markjprice/tools-skills-net10/blob/main/docs/errata/sql-container-issues.md`.

Connecting from Visual Studio

To connect to SQL Server using Visual Studio:

1. In Visual Studio, navigate to **View** | **Server Explorer**.
2. In the **Server Explorer** mini-toolbar, click the **Connect to Database...** button.
3. If prompted to **Change Data Source**, then choose **Microsoft SQL Server**.
4. Enter the connection details, as shown in *Figure 1.8*:

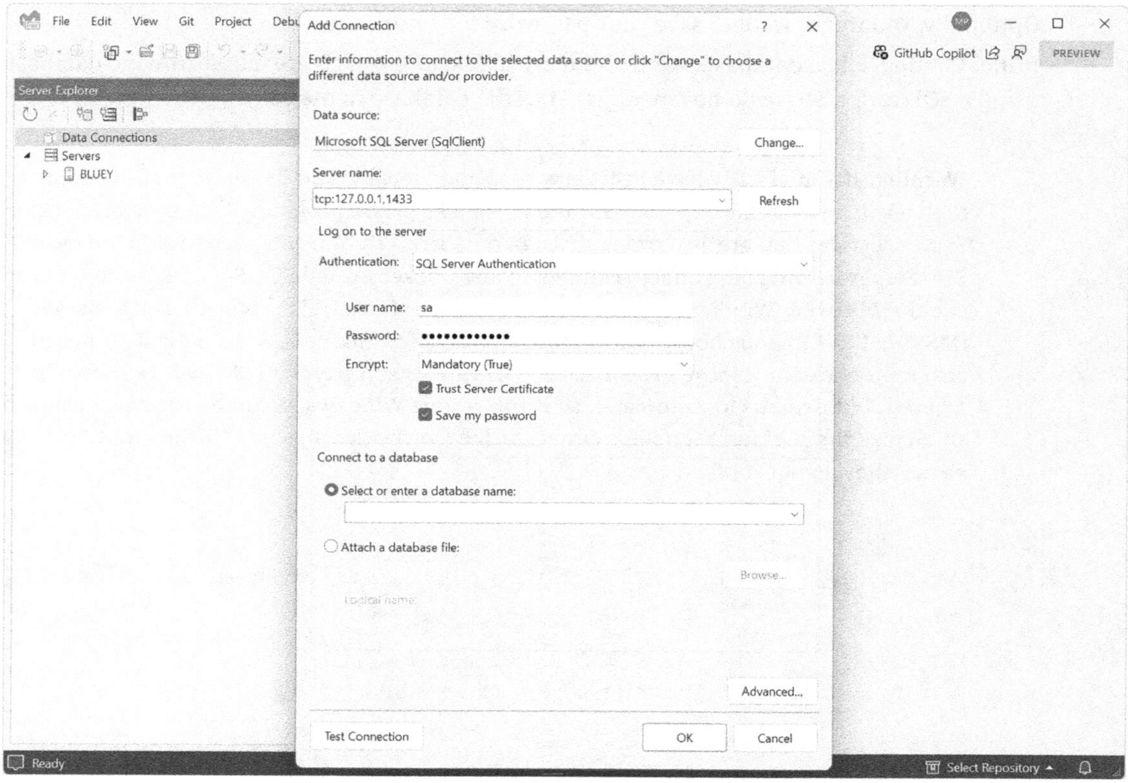

Figure 1.8: Connecting to your SQL Server in a container from Visual Studio

> **Warning!** If you get the error **Login failed for user 'sa'**, then the most likely causes are either that the password was not set correctly when you ran the Docker container, or you are connecting to a different SQL Server, for example, a local one instead of the one in the container.

Connecting from VS Code

To connect to SQL Server in a container using VS Code, follow these steps:

1. In VS Code, navigate to the **SQL Server** extension. Note that the `mssql` extension might take a few minutes to initialize the first time.

2. In the **SQL** extension, click **Add Connection...**.
3. In the **Connect to Database** pane, enter the connection details, as shown in *Figure 1.9*:
    - **Profile Name:** `SQL Server in Container`
    - **Connection Group: <Default>**
    - **Input type: Parameters**
    - **Server name:** `tcp:127.0.0.1,1433`
    - **Trust server certificate:** Selected
    - **Authentication type: SQL Login**
    - **User name:** `sa`
    - **Password:** `s3cret-Ninja`
    - **Save Password:** Cleared (or selected for convenience during learning)
    - **Database name:** `master` or leave blank (we will create the Northwind database using a SQL script, so we do not specify that as the database name yet)
    - **Encrypt: Mandatory**

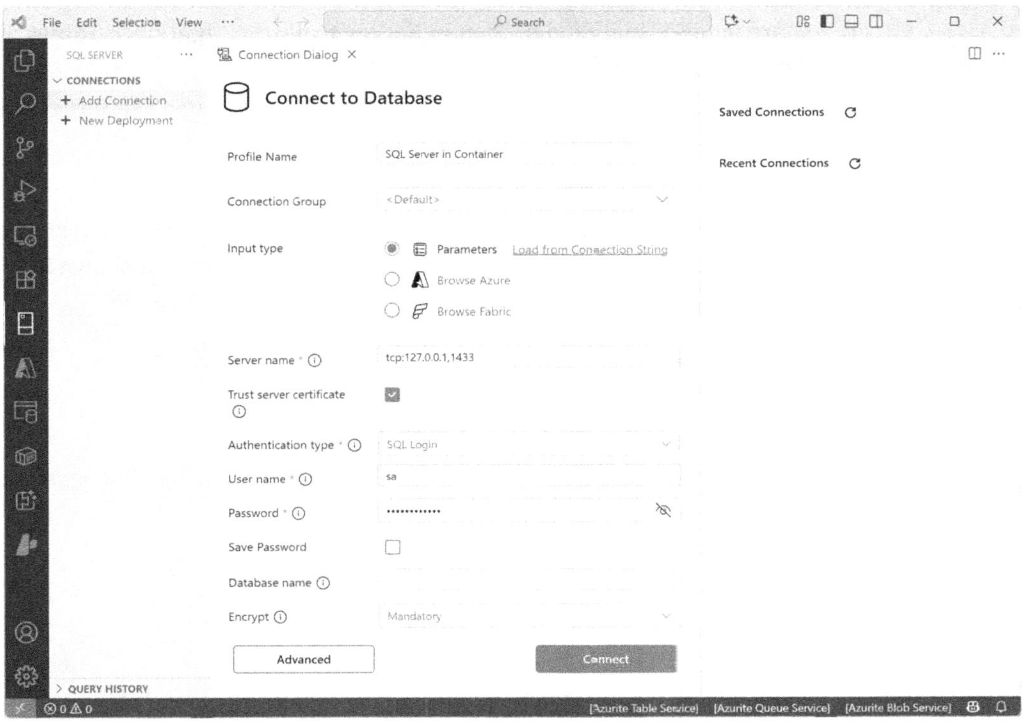

Figure 1.9: Connecting to your SQL Server in a container from VS Code

4. Click the **Connect** button and note the success notification message.

Creating the Northwind database using a SQL script

Now you can use your preferred code editor (or database tool) to execute the SQL script to create the Northwind database in SQL Server in a container:

1. Open the `Northwind4SqlServerContainer.sql` file. Note that this file does not know about the **Server Explorer** connection to the SQL Server database.
2. Connect the file to the SQL Server database. For example, in Visual Studio, right-click in the script file, navigate to **Connection** | **Connect...**, and then fill in the dialog box as before.
3. Execute the SQL script:
    - If you are using Visual Studio, right-click in the script file, select **Execute**, and then wait to see the **Command completed successfully** message.
    - If you are using VS Code, right-click in the script file, select **Execute Query**, select the **SQL Server in a Container** connection profile, and then wait to see the **Commands completed successfully** message.
4. Refresh the data connection:
    - If you are using Visual Studio, then in **Server Explorer**, right-click **Tables** and select **Refresh**.
    - If you are using VS Code, then right-click the **SQL Server in a Container** connection profile and choose **Refresh**.
5. Expand **Databases**, expand **Northwind**, and then expand **Tables**.
6. Note that 13 tables have been created, for example, `Categories`, `Customers`, and `Products`. Also note that dozens of views and stored procedures have also been created, as shown in *Figure 1.10*:

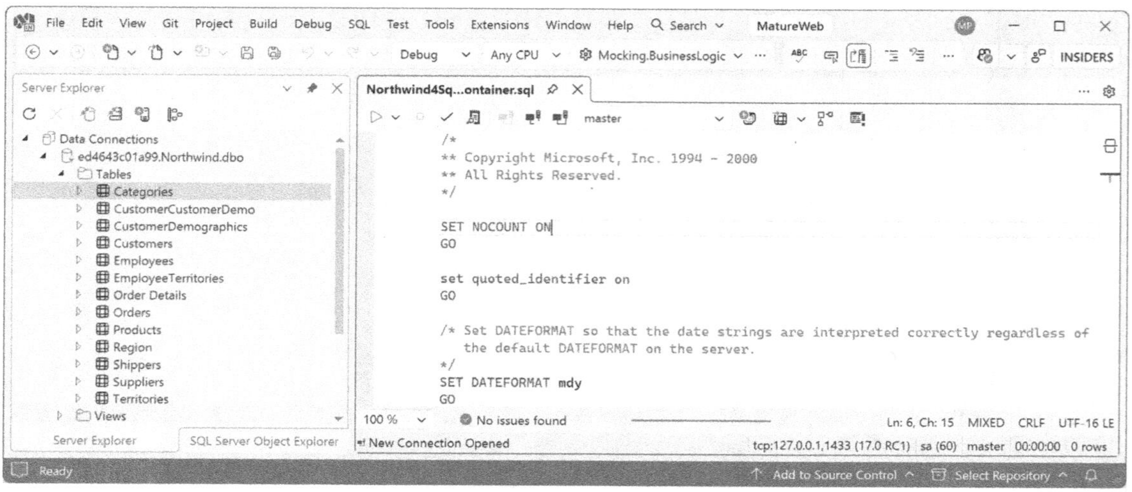

Figure 1.10: Northwind database created by SQL script in Visual Studio Server Explorer

You now have a running instance of SQL Server containing the Northwind database that you can connect to from your .NET projects.

You will want to keep the container while you work through all the chapters in this book. You can stop and start the container whenever you want, and the database will persist. Eventually, once you have finished this book, you might want to delete the container. This will also delete the database, so if you recreate the container, you will need to rerun the SQL script to recreate the Northwind database.

Removing Docker resources

When you have completed all the chapters in the book, or you plan to use a local SQL Server or Azure SQL Database in the cloud instead of a SQL Server container, and you want to remove all the Docker resources that it uses, then either use the Docker Desktop user interface or follow these steps at the command prompt or terminal:

1. At the command prompt or terminal, stop the `nw-container` container, as shown in the following command:

```
docker stop nw-container
```

2. At the command prompt or terminal, remove the `nw-container` container, as shown in the following command:

```
docker rm nw-container
```

> **Warning!** Removing the container will delete all data inside it.

3. At the command prompt or terminal, remove the image to release its disk space, as shown in the following command:

```
docker rmi mcr.microsoft.com/mssql/server:2025-latest
```

Setting up the EF Core CLI tool

The .NET CLI tool named `dotnet` can be extended with capabilities useful for working with EF Core. It can perform design-time tasks like creating and applying migrations from an older model to a newer model and generating code for a model from an existing database.

The `dotnet-ef` command-line tool is not automatically installed. You must install this package as either a **global** or **local tool**. If you have already installed an older version of the tool, then you should update it to the latest version:

1. At a command prompt or terminal, check if you have already installed `dotnet-ef` as a global tool, as shown in the following command:

```
dotnet tool list --global
```

2. Check in the list if an older version of the tool has been installed, like the one for .NET 9, as shown in the following output:

```
Package Id      Version      Commands
-------------------------------------
dotnet-ef       9.0.0        dotnet-ef
```

3. If an old version is installed, then update the tool, as shown in the following command:

```
dotnet tool update --global dotnet-ef
```

4. If it is not already installed, then install the latest version, as shown in the following command:

```
dotnet tool install --global dotnet-ef
```

If necessary, follow any OS-specific instructions to add the `dotnet tools` directory to your `PATH` environment variable, as described in the output of installing the `dotnet-ef` tool.

By default, the latest **general availability (GA)** release of .NET will be used to install the tool. To explicitly set a version, for example, to use a preview, add the `--version` switch. Or, to update to the latest .NET 11 preview or release candidate version (which will be available from February 2026 to October 2026), use the following command with a version wildcard:

```
dotnet tool update --global dotnet-ef --version 11.0-*
```

Once the .NET 11 GA release happens in November 2026, you can just use the command without the `--version` switch to upgrade.

You can also remove the tool, as shown in the following command:

```
dotnet tool uninstall --global dotnet-ef
```

Creating a class library for entity models using SQL Server

You will now create the entity models using the `dotnet-ef` tool:

1. Using your preferred code editor, create a new project, as defined in the following list:
   - Project template: **Class Library** / `classlib`
   - Project file and folder: `Northwind.EntityModels`
   - Solution file and folder: `Chapter01`

> **Good practice:** Make sure you create your solutions under the `tools-skills-net10` folder which contains the `Directory.Packages.props` and `nuget.config` files to benefit from central package management.

2. In the `Northwind.EntityModels` project, treat warnings as errors, and add package references (without version numbers) for the SQL Server database provider and EF Core design-time support, as shown highlighted in the following markup:

```
<Project Sdk="Microsoft.NET.Sdk">

  <PropertyGroup>
    <TargetFramework>net10.0</TargetFramework>
    <ImplicitUsings>enable</ImplicitUsings>
    <Nullable>enable</Nullable>
    <TreatWarningsAsErrors>true</TreatWarningsAsErrors>
  </PropertyGroup>

  <ItemGroup>
    <PackageReference Include="Microsoft.EntityFrameworkCore.SqlServer"
/>
    <PackageReference Include="Microsoft.EntityFrameworkCore.Design">
      <PrivateAssets>all</PrivateAssets>
      <IncludeAssets>runtime; build; native; contentfiles; analyzers;
buildtransitive</IncludeAssets>
    </PackageReference>
  </ItemGroup>

</Project>
```

If you are unfamiliar with how packages like `Microsoft.EntityFrameworkCore.Design` can manage their assets, then you can learn more at the following link: `https://learn.microsoft.com/en-us/nuget/consume-packages/package-references-in-project-files#controlling-dependency-assets`.

Good practice: By default, compiler warnings may appear if there are potential problems with your code when you first build a project, but they do not prevent compilation and they are hidden if you rebuild. Warnings are given for a reason, so ignoring warnings encourages poor development practices. I recommend that you force yourself to fix warnings by enabling the option to treat warnings as errors, as shown in the preceding code in Step 2.

3. Delete the `Class1.cs` file.
4. Build the `Northwind.EntityModels` project.

5. Open a command prompt or terminal for the `Northwind.EntityModels` folder.

> **Warning!** The next step assumes a database connection string for a local SQL Server authenticated with Windows Integrated Security. Modify it for SQL Server in a container with a user ID (`sa`) and password (`s3cret-Ninja`) if necessary.

6. At the command line, generate entity class models for all tables, as shown in the following commands:

```
dotnet ef dbcontext scaffold "Data Source=.;Initial
atalog=Northwind;Integrated Security=true;TrustServerCertificate=true;"
Microsoft.EntityFrameworkCore.SqlServer --namespace Northwind.
EntityModels --data-annotations
```

   Note the following:

   - The command to perform: `dbcontext scaffold`.
   - The connection string: `"Data Source=.;Initial Catalog=Northwind;Integrated Security=true;TrustServerCertificate=True;"`
   - Alternative connection string for SQL Server in a container: `"Data Source=127.0.0.1,1433;Initial Catalog=Northwind;User ID=sa;Password=s3cret-Ninja;TrustServerCertificate=true;"`
   - The database provider: `Microsoft.EntityFrameworkCore.SqlServer`
   - The namespace for the generated classes: `--namespace Northwind.EntityModels`
   - To use data annotations as well as the Fluent API: `--data-annotations`

Reviewing and modifying the generated code

Now we can review the code that was generated by the `dotnet-ef` tool:

1. Note that 28 classes were generated, from `AlphabeticalListOfProduct.cs` to `Territory.cs`.
2. In `NorthwindContext.cs`, note that the second constructor can have `options` passed as a parameter, which allows us to override the default database connection string in any projects, such as websites, that need to work with the Northwind database, as shown in the following code:

```
public NorthwindContext(
  DbContextOptions<NorthwindContext> options)
  : base(options)
{
}
```

3. In `NorthwindContext.cs`, both constructors give dozens of warnings, one for each of its `DbSet<T>` properties that represent tables and views. This is because they are marked as not nullable, and the compiler does not know that EF Core will automatically instantiate them all, so they will never actually be `null`. We can hide these warnings by disabling warning code `CS8618` just for those two constructors, as shown in the following code:

```
public partial class NorthwindContext : DbContext
{
#pragma warning disable CS8618
  public NorthwindContext()
#pragma warning restore CS8618
  {
  }

#pragma warning disable CS8618
  public NorthwindContext(DbContextOptions<NorthwindContext> options)
#pragma warning restore CS8618
      : base(options)
  {
  }
```

Good practice: We could simplify the code by disabling that warning code once at the top of the file and not restoring it anywhere in that file, but it is safer to re-enable warning codes in case you encounter more instances that you do need to handle differently.

You can learn more about this warning code at the following link: `https://learn.microsoft.com/en-us/dotnet/csharp/language-reference/compiler-messages/nullable-warnings#nonnullable-reference-not-initialized`.

4. At the top of the `NorthwindContext.cs` file, import the namespace for working with ADO.NET types, as shown in the following code:

```
using Microsoft.Data.SqlClient; // To use SqlConnectionStringBuilder.
```

5. Modify the `OnConfiguring` method to dynamically set the connection string and set any sensitive parameters using environment variables, as shown in the following code:

```
protected override void OnConfiguring(
  DbContextOptionsBuilder optionsBuilder)
{
  // If not already configured by a client project. For example,
  // a client project could use AddNorthwindContext to override
```

```
    // the database connection string.
    if (!optionsBuilder.IsConfigured)
    {
      SqlConnectionStringBuilder builder = new();
      builder.DataSource = "tcp:127.0.0.1,1433"; // SQL Server in
container.
      builder.InitialCatalog = "Northwind";
      builder.TrustServerCertificate = true;
      builder.MultipleActiveResultSets = true;

      // Because we want to fail faster. Default is 15 seconds.
      builder.ConnectTimeout = 3;

      // If using Windows Integrated authentication.
      // builder.IntegratedSecurity = true;

      // If using SQL Server authentication.
      builder.UserID = Environment.GetEnvironmentVariable("MY_SQL_USR");
      builder.Password = Environment.GetEnvironmentVariable("MY_SQL_PWD");

      optionsBuilder.UseSqlServer(builder.ConnectionString);
    }
  }
```

6. In `Customer.cs`, the `dotnet-ef` tool identified that the `CustomerId` column is the primary key and it is limited to a maximum of five characters, so it decorated the property with `[StringLength(5)]`. We also want the values to always be uppercase and always exactly five characters. So, add a regular expression to validate its primary key value to only allow five uppercase Western characters, as shown highlighted in the following code:

```
[Key]
[StringLength(5)]
[RegularExpression("[A-Z]{5}")]
public string CustomerId { get; set; } = null!;
```

Creating a class library for the data context using SQL Server

Next, you will move the context model that represents the database to a separate class library:

1. Add a new project, as defined in the following list:
    - Project template: **Class Library** / `classlib`
    - Project file and folder: `Northwind.DataContext`
    - Solution file and folder: `Chapter01`

2. In the `DataContext` project, add a project reference to the `EntityModels` project, and add a package reference to the EF Core data provider for SQL Server, as shown in the following markup:

```
<ItemGroup>
  <PackageReference Include="Microsoft.EntityFrameworkCore.SqlServer" />
</ItemGroup>

<ItemGroup>
  <ProjectReference Include=
    "..\Northwind.EntityModels\Northwind.EntityModels.csproj" />
</ItemGroup>
```

> After February 2026, you can try out previews of EF Core 11 by specifying `VersionOverride="11.0-*"`. The target framework for your project should continue to use `net10.0`. By using a wildcard, you will automatically download the latest monthly preview when you restore the packages for the project. Once the EF Core 11 GA version is released in November 2026, change the package version to `11.0.0` or later. After February 2027, you will be able to do similar with EF Core 12 (use a package version of `12.0-*`), but that will likely require a project targeting `net12.0`, so you will have to install a preview version of .NET 12 SDK as well.

3. In the `Northwind.DataContext` project, delete the `Class1.cs` file.
4. Build the `Northwind.DataContext` project.
5. Move the `NorthwindContext.cs` file from the `Northwind.EntityModels` project/folder to the `Northwind.DataContext` project/folder. You must *move* this file because if you copy it, there will be two database context classes with the same name and that will cause issues.

> In Visual Studio **Solution Explorer**, if you drag and drop a file between projects, it will be copied. If you hold down *Shift* while dragging and dropping, it will be moved. In VS Code **EXPLORER**, if you drag and drop a file between projects, it will be moved. If you hold down *Ctrl* while dragging and dropping, it will be copied.

6. In the `Northwind.DataContext` project, add a class named `NorthwindContextExtensions.cs`, and modify its contents to define an extension method that adds the Northwind database context to a collection of dependency services, as shown in the following code:

```
using Microsoft.Data.SqlClient; // SqlConnectionStringBuilder
using Microsoft.EntityFrameworkCore; // UseSqlServer
using Microsoft.Extensions.DependencyInjection; // IServiceCollection

namespace Northwind.EntityModels;

public static class NorthwindContextExtensions
```

```
{
  /// <summary>
  /// Adds NorthwindContext to the specified IServiceCollection. Uses the
SqlServer database provider.
  /// </summary>
  /// <param name="services">The service collection.</param>
  /// <param name="connectionString">Set to override the default.</param>
  /// <returns>An IServiceCollection that can be used to add more
services.</returns>
  public static IServiceCollection AddNorthwindContext(
    this IServiceCollection services,
    string? connectionString = null)
  {
    if (connectionString == null)
    {
      SqlConnectionStringBuilder builder = new();

      builder.DataSource = "tcp:127.0.0.1,1433"; // SQL Server in
container.
      builder.InitialCatalog = "Northwind";
      builder.TrustServerCertificate = true;
      builder.MultipleActiveResultSets = true;

      // Because we want to fail fast. Default is 15 seconds.
      builder.ConnectTimeout = 3;

      // If using Windows Integrated authentication.
      // builder.IntegratedSecurity = true;

      // If using SQL Server authentication.
      builder.UserID = Environment.GetEnvironmentVariable("MY_SQL_USR");
      builder.Password = Environment.GetEnvironmentVariable("MY_SQL_
PWD");

      connectionString = builder.ConnectionString;
    }

    services.AddDbContext<NorthwindContext>(options =>
    {
      options.UseSqlServer(connectionString);
```

```
        // Log to console when executing EF Core commands.
        options.LogTo(Console.WriteLine,
          new[] { Microsoft.EntityFrameworkCore
            .Diagnostics.RelationalEventId.CommandExecuting });
      },
      // Register with a transient lifetime to avoid concurrency
      // issues with Blazor Server projects.
      contextLifetime: ServiceLifetime.Transient,
      optionsLifetime: ServiceLifetime.Transient);

      return services;
    }
  }
```

7. Build the two class libraries and fix any compiler errors.

> **Good practice:** We have provided an optional argument for the `AddNorthwindContext` method so that we can override the SQL Server database connection string. This will allow us more flexibility, for example, to load these values from a configuration file.

Setting the user and password for SQL Server authentication

If you are using SQL Server authentication (i.e., you must supply a user and password), then complete the following steps:

1. In the `Northwind.DataContext` project, note the statements that set `UserId` and `Password`, as shown in the following code:

```
// SQL Server authentication.
builder.UserId = Environment.GetEnvironmentVariable("MY_SQL_USR");
builder.Password = Environment.GetEnvironmentVariable("MY_SQL_PWD");
```

2. Set the two environment variables at the command prompt or terminal, as shown in the following commands:

   - On Windows:

```
setx MY_SQL_USR <your_user_name>
setx MY_SQL_PWD <your_password>
```

   - On macOS and Linux:

```
export MY_SQL_USR=<your_user_name>
export MY_SQL_PWD=<your_password>
```

Unless you set a different password, <your_user_name> will be sa, and <your_password> will be s3cret-Ninja.

3. You **must** restart any command prompts, terminal windows, and applications like Visual Studio for this change to take effect.

Good practice: Although you could define the two environment variables in the `launchSettings.json` file of an ASP.NET Core project, you must then be extremely careful not to include that file in a GitHub repository! You can learn how to ignore files in Git at `https://docs.github.com/en/get-started/getting-started-with-git/ignoring-files`.

Registering dependency services

You can register dependency services with different lifetimes, as shown in the following list:

- **Transient:** These services are created each time they're requested. Transient services should be lightweight and stateless.
- **Scoped:** These services are created once per client request and are disposed of; then the response returns to the client.
- **Singleton:** These services are usually created the first time they are requested and then shared, although you can provide an instance at the time of registration, too.

In this book, you will use all three types of lifetime.

By default, a `DbContext` class is registered using the `Scope` lifetime, meaning that multiple threads can share the same instance. But `DbContext` does not support multiple threads. If more than one thread attempts to use the same `NorthwindContext` class instance at the same time, then you will see the following runtime exception thrown: `A second operation started on this context before a previous operation completed. This is usually caused by different threads using the same instance of a DbContext. However, instance members are not guaranteed to be thread-safe.`

This happens in Blazor projects with components set to run on the server side because, whenever interactions on the client side happen, a SignalR call is made back to the server, where a single instance of the database context is shared between multiple clients. This issue does not occur if a component is set to run on the client side.

Creating a test project to check the integration of the class libraries

xUnit is a popular unit testing framework for .NET applications. It was created by the original inventor of NUnit and is designed to be more modern, extensible, and aligned with .NET development practices.

Several benefits of using xUnit are shown in the following list:

- xUnit is open-source and has a strong community and active development team behind it. This makes it more likely that it will stay up to date with the latest .NET features and best practices. xUnit benefits from a large and active community, which means many tutorials, guides, and third-party extensions are available for it.
- xUnit uses a more simplified and extensible approach compared to older frameworks. It encourages the use of custom test patterns and less reliance on setup and teardown methods, leading to cleaner test code.
- Tests in xUnit are configured using .NET attributes, which makes the test code easy to read and understand. It uses `[Fact]` for standard test cases and `[Theory]` with `[InlineData]`, `[ClassData]`, or `[MemberData]` for parameterized tests, enabling data-driven testing. This makes it easier to cover many input scenarios with the same test method, enhancing test thoroughness while minimizing effort.
- xUnit includes an assertion library that allows for a wide variety of assertions out of the box, making it easier to test a wide range of conditions without having to write custom test code. It can also be extended with popular assertion libraries, like `FluentAssertions`, that allow you to articulate test expectations with human-readable reasons.
- By default, xUnit supports parallel test execution within the same test collection, which can significantly reduce the time it takes to run large test suites. This is particularly beneficial in continuous integration environments where speed is critical. However, if you run your tests in a memory-limited **Virtual Private Server (VPS)**, then that impacts how much data the server can handle at any given time and how many applications or processes it can run concurrently. In this scenario, you might want to disable parallel test execution. Memory-limited VPS instances are typically used as cheap testing environments.
- xUnit offers precise control over the test lifecycle with setup and teardown commands through the use of the constructor and destructor patterns and the `IDisposable` interface, as well as with the `[BeforeAfterTestAttribute]` for more granular control.

Since we will not be creating a client project in this chapter that uses the EF Core model, we should create a test project to make sure the database context and entity models integrate correctly:

1. Use your preferred code editor to add a new **xUnit Test Project [C#]** / `xunit` project named `Northwind.Tests` to the `Chapter01` solution.
2. In `Northwind.Tests.csproj`, modify the configuration to treat warnings as errors and add an item group with a project reference to the `Northwind.DataContext` project, as shown in the following markup:

```
<ItemGroup>
  <ProjectReference Include=
    "..\Northwind.DataContext\Northwind.DataContext.csproj" />
</ItemGroup>
```

Warning! The path to the project reference should not have a line break in your project file.

3. Build the `Northwind.Tests` project to build and restore project dependencies.
4. Rename the file `UnitTest1.cs` to `NorthwindEntityModelsTests.cs` (Visual Studio prompts you to rename the class when you rename the file).
5. In `NorthwindEntityModelsTests.cs`, if you are using VS Code, then manually rename the class to `NorthwindEntityModelsTests`.
6. In `NorthwindEntityModelsTests.cs`, modify the class to import the `Northwind.EntityModels` namespace and have some test methods for ensuring that the context class can connect, the provider is SQL Server, and the first product is named `Chai`, as shown in the following code:

```
using Northwind.EntityModels; // To use NorthwindContext and Product.

namespace Northwind.Tests;

public class NorthwindEntityModelsTests
{
  [Fact]
  public void DatabaseConnectTest()
  {
    using NorthwindContext db = new();
    Assert.True(db.Database.CanConnect());
  }

  [Fact]
  public void CategoryCountTest()
  {
    using NorthwindContext db = new();
    int expected = 8;
    int actual = db.Categories.Count();
    Assert.Equal(expected, actual);
  }

  [Fact]
  public void ProductId1IsChaiTest()
  {
    using NorthwindContext db = new();
```

```
            string expected = "Chai";
            Product? product = db?.Products?.Single(p => p.ProductId == 1);
            string actual = product?.ProductName ?? string.Empty;
            Assert.Equal(expected, actual);
        }
    }
```

Running tests

Now we are ready to run the tests and see the results using either Visual Studio or VS Code.

Using Visual Studio:

1. In **Visual Studio**, in **Solution Explorer**, right-click the `Northwind.Tests` project, and then select **Run Tests**.
2. In **Test Explorer**, note that the results indicate that three tests ran, and all passed, as shown in *Figure 1.11*:

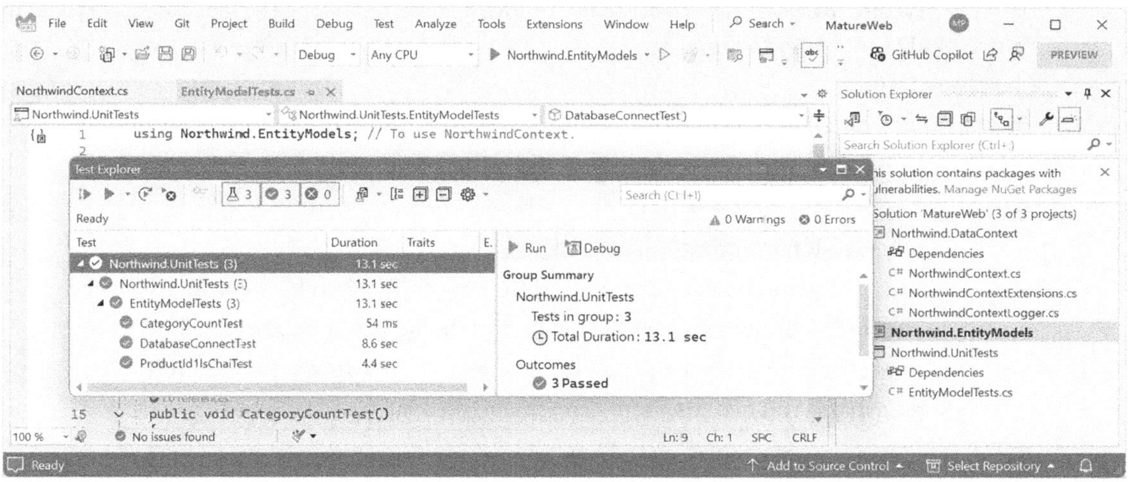

Figure 1.11: All the tests passed

Using VS Code:

1. In **VS Code**, in the `Northwind.Tests` project's **TERMINAL** window, run the tests, as shown in the following command:

```
dotnet test
```

> If you are using **C# Dev Kit**, then you can also build the test project and then run the tests from the **Testing** section in the **Primary Side Bar**.

2. In the output, note that the results indicate that three tests ran, and all passed.

Making good use of the GitHub repository for this book

Git is a commonly used source code management system. **GitHub** is a company, website, and desktop application that makes it easier to manage Git. Microsoft purchased GitHub in 2018, so it will continue to be closely integrated with Microsoft tools.

I created a GitHub repository for this book, and I use it for the following:

- To store the solution code for the book, which will be maintained after the print publication date
- To provide extra materials that extend the book, like errata fixes, small improvements, lists of useful links, and longer articles that cannot fit in the printed book
- To provide a place for readers to get in touch with me if they have issues with the book

Raising issues with the book

If you get stuck following any of the instructions in this book, or if you spot a mistake in the text or the code in the solutions, please raise an issue in the GitHub repository:

1. Use your favorite browser to navigate to the following link: `https://github.com/markjprice/tools-skills-net10/issues`.
2. Click **New Issue**.
3. Enter as much detail as possible that will help me to diagnose the issue. For example:
    - The specific section title, page number, and step number
    - Your code editor, for example, Visual Studio, VS Code, Rider, or something else, including the version number
    - As much of your code and configuration that you feel is relevant and necessary
    - A description of the expected behavior and the behavior experienced
    - If an exception is occurring, please include the full information about it
    - Screenshots (you can drag and drop image files into the issue box)

The following is less relevant but might be useful:

- Your operating system, for example, Windows 11 64-bit, or macOS Big Sur version 11.2.3
- Your hardware, for example, Intel, Apple Silicon, or ARM CPU

I want all my readers to be successful with my book, so if I can help you (and others) without too much trouble, then I will gladly do so.

Giving me feedback

If you'd like to give me more general feedback about the book, then you can email me at `markjprice@gmail.com`. My publisher, Packt, has set up Discord channels for readers to interact with authors and other readers. You are welcome to join us at the following link: `https://packt.link/TS1e`. The link will take you to the **Packt Web Dev Community** server and the **announcement** channel. From there, look for the appropriate book channel in the **Browse Channels** navigation bar.

I love to hear from my readers about what they like about my books, as well as suggestions for improvements and how they are working with C# and .NET, so don't be shy. Please get in touch!

Thank you in advance for your thoughtful and constructive feedback.

Downloading solution code from the GitHub repository

I use GitHub to store solutions to all the hands-on, step-by-step coding tasks throughout chapters and the practical exercises that are featured at the end of each chapter. You will find the repository at the following link: `https://github.com/markjprice/tools-skills-net10`.

If you just want to download all the solution files without using Git, click the green **Code** button and then select **Download ZIP**.

I recommend that you add the preceding link to your favorites or bookmarks.

> **Good practice:** It is best to clone or download the code solutions to a short folder path, like `C:\tools-skills-net10\` or `C:\net10-book\`, to avoid build-generated files exceeding the maximum path length. You should also avoid special characters like `#`. For example, do not use a folder name like `C:\C# projects\`. That folder name might work for a simple console app project but once you start adding features that automatically generate code, you are likely to have strange issues. Keep your folder names short and simple.

Where to go for help

This section is about how to find quality information about programming on the web. You will learn about Microsoft Learn documentation, including its new MCP server for integration with AI systems, getting help while coding and using `dotnet` commands, getting help from fellow readers in the book's Discord channel, searching the .NET source code for implementation details, and finally, making the most of modern AI tools like GitHub Copilot.

This is useful information that all readers should know and refer to throughout reading any of my .NET 10 books, especially if you are new to .NET.

This section has been made into a separate *Appendix C*, both to make it reusable in all four of my .NET 10 books, and to avoid wasting pages in the print book for those readers who have already read it from one of the other books.

An online Markdown version of *Appendix C* is available in the book's GitHub repository at the following link: `https://github.com/markjprice/markjprice/blob/main/articles/getting-help.md`. Since this is hosted in my personal GitHub account, I can keep it updated more frequently throughout the three-year support period of .NET 10.

As part of this book's free exclusive benefits, you can also access a PDF version of the book, which includes *Appendix C*. You can unlock it and the other benefits at the following link: `https://packtpub.com/unlock`, then search for this book by name. Ensure it's the correct edition. Have your purchase invoice ready before you start.

My books are specifically written in a tutorial style so that you can get started quickly and confidently before then switching to the official documentation for more details or specialized scenarios.

This technique is commonly used by developers to learn how to code. More than 50% use books or other physical media, and then more than 80% use other online resources, as shown in the Stack Overflow Survey 2023 at the following link: `https://survey.stackoverflow.co/2023/#section-learning-to-code-learning-how-to-code`.

Reading documentation on Microsoft Learn

The definitive resource for getting help with Microsoft developer tools and platforms is in the technical documentation on Microsoft Learn, and you can find it at the following link: `https://learn.microsoft.com/en-us/docs`.

Getting help for the dotnet tool

At the command prompt, you can ask the `dotnet` tool for help with its commands. The syntax is:

```
dotnet help <command>
```

This will cause your web browser to open a page in the documentation about the specified command. Common `dotnet` commands include `new`, `build`, and `run`.

> **Warning!** The `dotnet help new` command worked with .NET Core 3.1 to .NET 6, but it returns an error with .NET 7 or later: `Specified command 'new' is not a valid SDK command. Specify a valid SDK command. For more information, run dotnet help.` Hopefully, the .NET team will fix that bug soon!

Another type of help is command-line documentation. It follows this syntax:

```
dotnet <command> -?|-h|--help
```

For example, `dotnet new -?`, `dotnet new -h`, or `dotnet new --help` output documentation about the `new` command at the command prompt.

LLMs like ChatGPT

One of the biggest changes in coding and development in the past few years is the emergence of generative AI tools and LLMs that can help with coding tasks like completing a code statement, implementing an entire function, writing unit tests, and suggesting debugging fixes for existing code.

ChatGPT currently has several free models like 5.1 and 5.2, and the Plus individual subscription ($20 per month) or the Pro individual subscription ($200 per month). There are also Team and Enterprise subscriptions. You can compare options at the following link: `https://openai.com/chatgpt/pricing/`.

Let's say you need to understand more about .NET tools and skills. You might enter the following prompt: "What are the most important tools and skills for a professional .NET developer to learn?"

The response would be something like the following:

"Hey there! When it comes to being a professional .NET developer, there are several essential tools and skills you should consider mastering. Here's a detailed breakdown:

Tools:

- Visual Studio: This IDE is the go-to choice for .NET development. Make sure you're comfortable with its features and extensions.
- VS Code: While Visual Studio is powerful, VS Code is a lightweight, versatile code editor that's becoming increasingly popular among .NET developers.
- .NET Core/.NET 5 and beyond: Stay up to date with the latest versions of the .NET framework. .NET 5 and its successors offer cross-platform support and performance improvements.
- Git and GitHub: Version control is crucial. Git is a widely used distributed version control system, and GitHub provides a platform for collaborative development and code sharing.
- Azure DevOps: Familiarize yourself with Azure DevOps for managing projects and continuous integration and continuous deployment (CI/CD) pipelines.
- NuGet: Understanding package management with NuGet is essential for adding libraries and packages to your .NET projects.
- Docker: Containerization is becoming increasingly important for deploying .NET applications. Docker can help you create and manage containers effectively.

Skills:

- C#: As a .NET developer, C# is your primary language. Master object-oriented programming concepts, asynchronous programming, and LINQ.
- ASP.NET Core: For web development, ASP.NET Core is the framework of choice. Learn about MVC architecture, Razor Pages, and API development.
- Entity Framework Core: Understand how to work with databases using Entity Framework Core for efficient data access.
- Dependency injection: Grasp the principles of dependency injection and how it's used in .NET for managing object dependencies.
- Unit testing: Writing unit tests using tools like xUnit or NUnit is crucial for ensuring the reliability of your code.
- Web API design: If you're building APIs, learn about RESTful design principles, authentication, and versioning.
- Frontend technologies: Familiarize yourself with HTML, CSS, JavaScript, and frontend frameworks like React or Angular if you're involved in web development.
- Azure services: If you're working in the cloud, explore Azure services like Azure Functions, Azure SQL Database, and Azure App Service.
- Security: Understand security best practices, including authentication, authorization, and data protection.

- `Performance optimization: Learn about profiling, caching, and other techniques to optimize the performance of your applications.`
- `Agile methodologies: Agile practices like Scrum and Kanban are widely used in software development. Understanding them can improve team collaboration.`
- `Soft skills: Communication, problem solving, and teamwork are essential soft skills for any professional developer.`

`Now, I've covered quite a bit here, but remember that the tech landscape is always evolving. Staying curious and continuously learning is a vital skill in itself. If you have any specific questions or need more details on any of these topics, feel free to ask!"`

There are a few topics that ChatGPT mentions that my books do not cover. These are:

- **Azure DevOps** and **Azure Services**: For this book, I decided to remove requirements for Azure and other cloud services. I want all readers of my .NET books to be able to complete all the tasks on their local computer without paying for a cloud account. I want to avoid pushing readers toward any particular cloud provider, so from now on, my books will be cloud agnostic.
- **Front-end technologies**: HTML, CSS, and JavaScript, and the many, many client-side application frameworks like React and Angular.
- **Agile methodologies**: This and other methodologies really need a whole book to cover them in depth. If I can find a way to usefully introduce them in only a few pages, then the next edition might do that.

Getting better help from LLMs using prompt engineering

You might have heard the term **prompt engineering**. This is an important skill for any professional to have since modern tasks will commonly be completed more efficiently by collaborating with an AI.

> AI tools that integrate closely with your code editor like GitHub Copilot will be covered in *Chapter 2, Making the Most of Your Code Editor*.

To clarify or get a deeper understanding of a topic, or any piece of information, you can use the following prompt templates:

- Explain [insert specific topic] in simple terms.
- Explain to me like I'm a beginner in [field].
- Explain to me in a natural, human-like manner.
- Explain to me as if I'm 10 years old.
- Write a detailed [essay/text/paragraph] for me about [topic] by adding all the information necessary.

Use affirmative directives and avoid negative formulations like "don't."

For complex answers, or when it responds with a shallow answer, include the phrase "think step-by-step."

Assign a role to the large language models. For example, "You are an expert solution architect with decades of experience implementing .NET."

If you're unsure how to phrase a prompt, get the LLM to help you! For example:

"I want you to be my Prompt Engineer. Your goal is to assist me in creating the best prompt for my needs. The prompt will be used by you, ChatGPT. You will follow these steps: Your first response will be to ask me what the prompt should be about. I will provide my answer, but we will need to work together to improve it through continuous iterations by going through the next steps. Based on my input, you will generate three sections:

1. Revised prompt. Please provide your rewritten prompt. It should be clear, concise, and easily understood.
2. Suggestions. Please provide ideas on what details to include in the prompt to enhance it.
3. Questions. Please ask any relevant questions to gather additional information from me and improve the prompt.

We will continue this iterative process with me providing more information to you and you updating the prompt in the Revised prompt section until it's complete. Thank you!"

If you own a PC with an Nvidia GTX card, then you can download a free chat app to customize and converse with local LLMs. It can even process files like PDFs. If any of you try adding a PDF of any of my books so that you can ask questions about them, please let me know how you get on. You can find out more at the following link: `https://blogs.nvidia.com/blog/chat-with-rtx-available-now/`.

AI usage by developers

According to the Stack Overflow Survey (`https://survey.stackoverflow.co/2025/ai/#1-ai-tools-in-the-development-process/`), "84% of all respondents are using or are planning to use AI tools in their development process this year. Those learning to code are more likely than professional developers to be using or use AI tools."

Getting help on Discord and other chat forums

Asking questions in programming forums and Discord channels is an art as much as it is a science. To maximize your chances of receiving a helpful answer, there's a blend of clarity, specificity, and community awareness that you should aim for.

Here are some tips for asking questions:

- **Ask in a public channel, not in private: Please do not direct message an author with a question or a friend request.** Remember, every question asked and answered builds the collective knowledge and resourcefulness of the whole community. Asking in public also allows other readers to help you, not just the author. The community that Packt and I have built around my books is friendly and smart. Let us all help you.

- **Research before asking**: It's important to look for answers yourself before turning to the community. Use search engines, official documentation, and the search function within the forum or Discord server. This not only respects the community's time but also helps you learn more effectively. Another place to look first is the errata section of the book at the following link: `https://github.com/markjprice/tools-skills-net10/blob/main/docs/errata/README.md`.
- **Be specific and concise**: Clearly state what you're trying to achieve, what you've tried so far, and where you're stuck. A concise question is more likely to get a quick response.
- **Specify the book location**: If you are stuck on a particular part of the book, specify the page number and section title so that others can look up the context of your question.
- **Show your work**: Demonstrating that you've made an effort to solve the problem yourself not only provides context but also helps others understand your thought process and where you might have gone wrong.
- **Prepare your question**: Avoid too broad or too vague questions. Screenshots of errors or code snippets (with proper formatting) can be very helpful.

> **Good practice**: Oddly, I've been seeing more and more examples of readers taking photos of their screen and posting those. These are harder to read and limited in what they can show. It's better to copy and paste the text of your code or the error message so that others can copy and paste it themselves. Or at least take a high-resolution screenshot instead of a photo!

- **Format your code properly**: Most forums and Discord servers support code formatting using Markdown syntax. Use formatting to make your code more readable. For example, surround code keywords in single backticks like this: `` `public void` ``, and surround code blocks with three backticks with an optional language code, as shown in the following code:

````
```cs
using static System.Console;
WriteLine("This is C# formatted code.");
```
````

> **Good practice**: After the three backticks that start a code block in Markdown, specify a language code like `cs`, `csharp`, `js`, `javascript`, `json`, `html`, `css`, `cpp`, `xml`, `mermaid`, `python`, `java`, `ruby`, `go`, `sql`, `bash`, or `shell`.

> To learn how to format text in Discord channel messages, see the following link: `https://support.discord.com/hc/en-us/articles/210298617-Markdown-Text-101-Chat-Formatting-Bold-Italic-Underline`.

- **Be polite and patient:** Remember, you're asking for help from people who are giving their time voluntarily. A polite tone and patience while waiting for a response go a long way. Channel participants are often in a different timezone so may not see your question until the next day.
- **Be ready to actively participate:** After asking your question, stay engaged. You might receive follow-up questions for clarification. Responding promptly and clearly can significantly increase your chances of getting a helpful answer. When I ask a question, I set an alarm for three hours later to go back and see if anyone has responded. If there hasn't been a response yet, then I set another alarm for 24 hours later.

Incorporating these approaches when asking questions not only increases your likelihood of getting a useful response but also contributes positively to the community by showing respect for others' time and effort.

> **Good practice:** Never just say "Hello" as a message on any chat system. You can read why at the following link: `https://nohello.net/`. Similarly, don't ask to ask: `https://dontasktoask.com/`.

Using future versions of .NET with this book

Microsoft is expected to release .NET 11 at .NET Conf 2026 on Tuesday, November 10, 2026. Many readers will want to use this book with .NET 11 and future versions of .NET, so this section explains how.

Soon after the time of publishing in January 2026, .NET 11 is likely to already be available in preview, or you can wait for the final version in November 2026.

> **Warning!** Once you install a .NET 11 SDK, then it will be used by default for all .NET projects unless you override it using a `global.json` file. You can learn more about doing this at the following link: `https://learn.microsoft.com/en-us/dotnet/core/tools/global-json`.

You can easily continue to target the .NET 10 runtime while installing and using future C# compilers, as shown in *Figure 1.12* and illustrated in the following list:

1. **November 2025 onwards:** Install .NET SDK 10.0.100 or later and use it to build projects that target .NET 10 and use the C# 14 compiler by default. Every month, update to .NET 10 SDK patches on the development computer and update to .NET 10 runtime patches on any deployment computers.
2. **February to October 2026:** Optionally, install .NET SDK 11 previews each month to explore the new C# 15 language and .NET 11 library features. Note that you won't be able to use new library features while targeting .NET 10.
3. **November 2026 onwards:** Install .NET SDK 11.0.100 or later and use it to build projects that continue to target .NET 10 and use the C# 15 compiler for its new features. You will be using a fully supported SDK and fully supported runtime. You can also use new features in EF Core 11 because it will continue to target .NET 10.

4. **February to October 2027:** Optionally, install .NET 12 previews to explore new C# 16 language and .NET 12 library features. Start planning if any new library and ASP.NET Core features in .NET 11 and .NET 12 can be applied to your .NET 10 projects when you are ready to migrate.
5. **November 2027 onwards:** Install .NET 12.0.100 SDK or later and use it to build projects that target .NET 10 and use the C# 16 compiler.
6. You could migrate your .NET 10 projects to .NET 12 since .NET 12 is a **long-term support** (LTS) release. You have until November 2028 to complete the migration when .NET 10 reaches end-of-life.

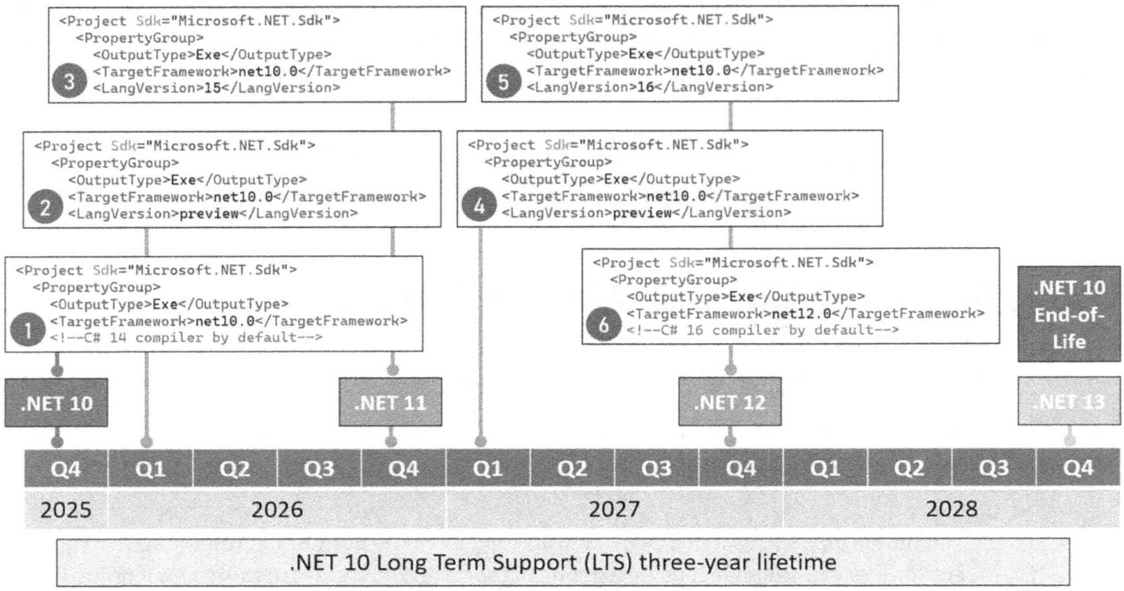

Figure 1.12: Targeting .NET 10 for long-term support while using the latest C# compilers

When deciding to install a .NET SDK, remember that the latest is used by default to build any .NET projects. Once you've installed a .NET 11 SDK preview, it will be used by default for all projects, unless you force the use of an older, fully supported SDK version like 10.0.100 or a later patch.

To gain the benefits of whatever new features are available in C# 15, while still targeting .NET 10 for long-term support, modify your project file, as shown highlighted in the following markup:

```
<Project Sdk="Microsoft.NET.Sdk">

  <PropertyGroup>
    <OutputType>Exe</OutputType>
    <TargetFramework>net10.0</TargetFramework>
    <LangVersion>15</LangVersion> <!--Requires .NET 11 SDK GA-->
    <ImplicitUsings>enable</ImplicitUsings>
    <Nullable>enable</Nullable>
  </PropertyGroup>
</Project>
```

Good practice: Use a **general availability** (GA) SDK release like .NET 11 to use new compiler features while still targeting older but longer supported versions of .NET like .NET 10.

Practicing and exploring

Test your knowledge and understanding by answering some questions, getting some hands-on practice, and exploring with deeper research the topics in this chapter.

Exercise 1.1 – Online-only material

Make sure that you are ready to use multiple code editors. *Chapter 1* of the *C# 14 and .NET 10 - Modern Cross-Platform Development Fundamentals* book has online sections showing how to get started with multiple projects using various code editors including Visual Studio, VS Code, or Rider.

You can read the sections at the following link:

`https://github.com/markjprice/cs14net10/blob/main/docs/code-editors/README.md`.

Exercise 1.2 – Practice exercises

If you do not yet have an OpenAI ChatGPT account, sign up for one and try asking it some questions: `https://chat.openai.com/`.

Exercise 1.3 – Test your knowledge

To get the best answer to some of these questions, you will need to do your own research. I want you to "think outside the book," so I have deliberately not provided all the answers in the book.

I want to encourage you to get into the good habit of looking for help elsewhere, following the principle of "teach a person to fish."

1. How are .NET developers who choose to use Rider perceived compared to developers who have only ever used Visual Studio?
2. What is a key phrase to use when prompt engineering ChatGPT?
3. When you ask a question in a forum or Discord channel, what should you keep in mind?
4. After its release in November 2026, you download and install .NET 11 SDK. How can you configure your projects to continue to target .NET 10 for long-term support and also enjoy the benefits of the C# 15 compiler?
5. What is the GitHub repository for this book used for?

Appendix A, Answers to the Test Your Knowledge Questions, is available to download from the following link: `https://github.com/markjprice/tools-skills-net10/blob/main/docs/B31468_Appendix%20A.pdf`.

Exercise 1.4 – Explore topics

Use the links on the following page to learn more about the topics covered in this chapter: `https://github.com/markjprice/tools-skills-net10/blob/main/docs/book-links.md#chapter-1---introducing-tools-and-skills-for-net`.

Summary

In this chapter:

- You were introduced to the tools and skills that you will learn about in this book
- You set up your development environment
- You learned where to get help and how to get the best help from AI tools like ChatGPT
- You set up a sample database named Northwind for SQL Server, and some .NET projects to define an EF Core model with tests for use in later chapters

In the next chapter, you will learn how to make the most of the tools in your code editor or IDE.

Learn more on Discord

To join the Discord community for this book – where you can share feedback, ask questions to the author, and learn about new releases – follow this QR code:

`https://packt.link/TS2e`

Join .NETPro – It's Free

Staying sharp in .NET takes more than reading release notes. It requires real-world tips, proven patterns, and scalable solutions. That's what .NETPro, Packt's new newsletter, is all about.

Scan the QR code or visit the link to subscribe:

`https://landing.packtpub.com/dotnetpronewsletter/`

2

Making the Most of the Tools in Your Code Editor

This chapter is about going beyond using the basic file management and editing tools in your code editor. We will look at the most common code editors or **integrated development environments (IDEs)**: Visual Studio and VS Code. For Rider, I have added links to online resources when relevant.

A modern code editor is far more than a place to type code. Used well, your code editor is a productivity engine packed with features designed to help you write better, cleaner software in less time. Whether you're refactoring a messy class, generating boilerplate code from snippets, or configuring the editor to fit your workflow, knowing how to make the most of these built-in tools can transform the way you develop.

In this chapter, we'll explore some of the most powerful capabilities of Visual Studio and other popular editors. You'll learn how to refactor code safely and efficiently, speed up development with reusable code snippets, fine-tune editor settings to match your personal workflow, leverage AI coding companions to boost productivity, navigate large projects and solutions like a pro, decompile .NET assemblies to understand third-party code, and create custom project and item templates to save time.

You only need to read the sections for the code editor that you use, although I recommend becoming familiar with them all while you are taking the opportunity to learn new things.

This chapter covers the following topics:

- Introducing common tools and features
- Tools in Visual Studio
- Tools in VS Code
- Decompiling .NET assemblies
- Custom project and item templates

Introducing common tools and features

Common tools and features in all code editors and IDEs include the following:

- Refactoring features
- Code snippets
- Editor configuration
- AI companions

Let's describe each of these tools and features in more detail so that you understand the concepts, and then, in later sections, you can see how specific code editors implement those features.

Refactoring features

Refactoring is the process of modifying the internal structure of existing project code without changing its external behavior. Most code editors and IDEs expose their refactoring features via their **Edit** menu and context (right-click) menus. But why would you want to spend effort rewriting code if there is no external effect?

The expected benefits are improved code readability and reduced complexity. In other words, you are investing in the future. Whoever must maintain the code should be able to do so with reduced effort and the likelihood of introducing bugs. You can think of this as preventively avoiding technical debt. Even a solo developer can benefit because future-you will appreciate the investment past-you made.

The most common types of refactoring include:

- **Rename Method/Variable**: Renaming makes code easier to understand by making it clearer what a method does or what a variable represents. This improves code readability so that it becomes almost self-documenting.
- **Extract Method**: When you first implement a method, you might end up with one that is hundreds of statements long. Some of that code could be extracted into its own method. By removing the statements from the main method and giving the new method a name that describes its purpose, the code becomes more readable and reusable.
- **Move Member**: This is about moving a member (like a method, property, or field) from one class to another, to put things where they logically belong.
- **Encapsulate Field**: This is about preventing direct access to a public field by making it private and then providing getter and setter methods, aka changing a field into a property. This allows more control over how and when the field is accessed and modified.
- **Extract Interface**: This refactoring is useful when you realize that you have classes that are used in different ways by different clients but share a common set of members. You can extract the subset of a class's members into its own interface.
- **Reorder Parameters in Method**: Methods can be called from many places within your code. If you decide to add, reorder, or remove parameters, then this refactoring can make sure all the calls to that method match correctly.

Refactoring is an essential skill in software development, and this skill becomes more important as codebases grow and evolve. By consistently refactoring, developers can make sure that the code remains clean, understandable, and maintainable over time.

Now let's see how you can reuse code that you frequently type.

Code snippets

Code snippets are small, reusable blocks of code statements that are used to perform a common task. The code snippets can be as simple as a single function or a few lines of code, and they can be written for any programming language. They are often defined using a cross-platform file format like XML or JSON with embedded code in any language.

Some of the benefits of using code snippets include the following:

- **Save Time**: Instead of writing code from a blank file, you can use a code snippet that performs the desired function. They are often used by presenters to demonstrate a specific programming concept when teaching coding or showing a new code feature.
- **Learning and Knowledge Sharing**: Snippets can be excellent learning tools. They often demonstrate how to implement a particular feature or use a specific technology. A third-party package could supply sample code snippets that show common starter code to use the package. For beginners, snippets can serve as practical examples of abstract concepts. For more experienced programmers, they can provide insights into best practices.
- **Consistency and Collaboration**: By using standardized code snippets, you can encourage your team to perform a task in the same way across different parts of a project or across different projects. This uniformity helps in maintaining code quality and reduces the likelihood of errors. Members of a team can share their snippets. This collaborative approach allows developers to benefit from the collective experience and expertise of the community. Once you have a library of snippets, you can easily reuse them in different projects. This not only saves time but also helps in maintaining a consistent coding style across your projects.
- **Documentation and Reference**: Code snippets can act as a form of documentation. If a snippet is well written and well commented, it can explain how certain functionalities work, making it easier for other developers to understand and use the code.

Code snippets are a practical tool, offering advantages like time efficiency, consistency, and learning. They facilitate quicker development processes and promote a collaborative coding culture within a team.

Now let's see how you can maintain consistent coding styles in a team of .NET developers working on the same project across various code editors.

Editor configuration

To configure code editors to define coding styles in a file, there is a standard file format named `.editorconfig`. This is paired with built-in support for processing the file format and enforcing its rules in most common code editors. These files are human-readable, easily editable directly or via a code editor user interface, and work well with version control systems like Git.

Your code editor will look for a file named `.editorconfig` in the directory of your project and in every parent directory. The search will stop if the `root` is reached or a file with `root=true` is found, as shown in the following configuration:

```
# Top-most .editorconfig file.
root = true
```

Comments in the `.editorconfig` file are prefixed with #.

Properties in the `.editorconfig` file are set with = on a single line.

Rules in the `.editorconfig` file can be divided into sections that are defined using `[ ]` and apply to files that match the file pattern. For example, you can set rules that only apply to C# files, as shown in the following configuration:

```
# This two-space indent rule only applies to C# code files.
[*.cs]
indent_style = space
indent_size = 2
```

The `.editorconfig` files are read top to bottom. Rules are applied in the order they are read, so later rules override earlier ones, while rules in files closer in the directory hierarchy take precedence.

Common properties in the `.editorconfig` file that can be set are shown in *Table 2.1*:

Property name	**Values**	**Property description**
root	true, false	If true, then stop the .editorconfig file search on the current file.
charset	latin1, utf-8, and others	Control the character set.
indent_style	tab, space	Use the specified character to indent. The values are case-insensitive.
tab_width	<integer>	Width of a single tab stop character.
indent_size	tab, <integer>	Indentation size in single-spaced characters.
end_of_line	lf, cr, or crlf	Control how line breaks are represented.
trim_trailing_whitespace	true, false	Remove all whitespace characters preceding newline characters in the file.
insert_final_newline	true, false	Ensure the file ends with a newline when saving.

Table 2.1: Common .editorconfig properties

> You can learn more about the `.editorconfig` file standard at the following link: `https://editorconfig.org/`.

The `.editorconfig` files are extensible, so most code editors add their own custom properties that they understand how to process. For example, Visual Studio will warn to remove unused namespace imports (`using` statements at the top of a code file) which is IDE rule number `0005`, but this can be disabled, as shown in the following configuration:

```
[*.cs]
dotnet_diagnostic.IDE0005.severity = none
```

To understand more about how `.editorconfig` files are processed by .NET projects to perform code analysis, you can review the following link: `https://learn.microsoft.com/en-us/dotnet/fundamentals/code-analysis/configuration-files`.

AI companions

Modern code editors include an **AI companion** or assistant. These can do some of the repetitive or specialized work for you, including:

- Improve code quality and security because the AI can highlight insecure coding patterns and API misuse.
- Answer general coding questions, or very specific questions about your codebase, because the AI has access to all the code in your project. When joining a new project, get the AI to walk you through the project and explain how it works. If the project uses a complex regular expression, then the AI can explain it to you.
- Suggest code completions as you enter code or comments. It turns natural language into code statements that match the project's context and existing coding style.
- Write Git pull request comments for you based on the code changes you've made. It can write unit tests for you based on the method parameters being tested.

Now that you understand the concepts behind the most common tools and features in most code editors, let's review each code editor in turn, looking at how they implement those and other features. We will start with Visual Studio since it is the most used by .NET developers.

Tools in Visual Studio

Visual Studio contains many useful built-in tools, including ones to implement the concepts just covered in this chapter.

By default, all links in this book for Visual Studio will go to the current version, i.e. to the 2026 version. To force a link to go to the older version, append `?view=vs-2022` to the end of the link.

Refactoring features

Visual Studio has dozens of refactoring features, aka refactorings, to modify code to make it easier to maintain, understand, and extend, but without changing its behavior. The most common refactorings are available by navigating to **Edit** | **Refactor**, and then selecting from the following menu items:

- **Rename** (*F2*): Safely rename a variable, type, or member in its definition and everywhere it is used
- **Encapsulate Field** (*Ctrl* + *R*, *E*): Convert a field into a property, and update all usages of that field to use the newly created property
- **Extract Interface** (*Ctrl* + *R*, *I*): Create an interface using existing members from a class, struct, or interface
- **Remove Parameter** (*Ctrl* + *R*, *V*): Remove a method's parameters
- **Reorder Parameter** (*Ctrl* + *R*, *O*): Change the order of a method's parameters

More specialized refactorings are context-dependent. You will need to position the editing cursor in some code that could be refactored and then activate **Quick Actions and Refactorings**.

Let's see some in action:

1. Use Visual Studio to add a new **Console App** / `console` project named `RefactoringDemos` to a `Chapter02` solution.
2. In the `RefactoringDemos` project, globally and statically import the `System.Console` class, as shown in the following markup:

```
<ItemGroup>
  <Using Include="System.Console" Static="true" />
</ItemGroup>
```

3. In the `RefactoringDemos` project, add a new class file named `Product.cs`.
4. In `Product.cs`, delete any existing statements, and then add statements to define a `Product` class with a field named `description`, as shown in the following code:

```
public class Product
{
  public string? description;
}
```

5. In `Program.cs`, delete any existing statements, and then add statements to instantiate a `Product` class and set its `description`, as shown in the following code:

```
Product product = new()
{
  description = "Seafood"
};

WriteLine(product.description);
```

6. In `Product.cs`, click in the statement that defines the `description` field, and then activate quick actions by clicking the **Quick Actions** icon, pressing *Alt* + *Enter*, or pressing *Ctrl* + . (dot). Then note the choices of refactorings, as shown in *Figure 2.1*:

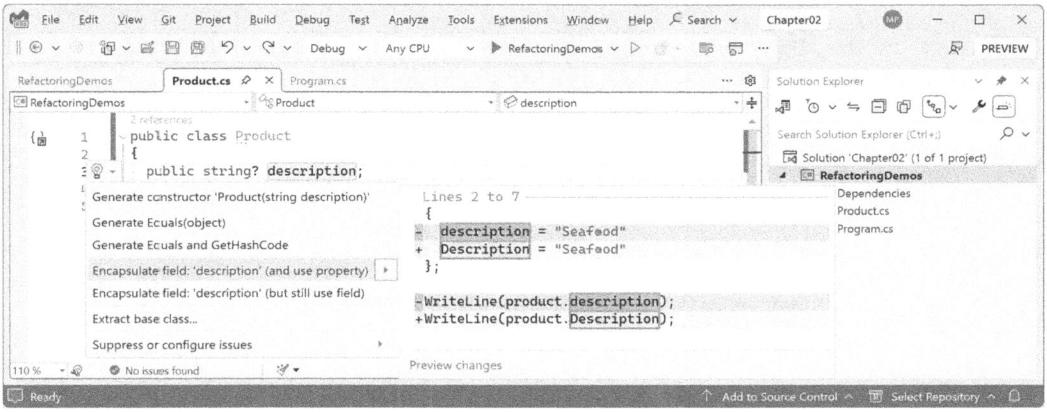

Figure 2.1: Refactorings for a field in a class

> The menu of choices is dependent on the exact position of the cursor when you activate the quick actions. For example, if the cursor is in the `public` keyword, you will see fewer options.

7. Select **Encapsulate field: 'description' (and use property)**, and note the field is made `private` and a public property is defined to get and set the field. In `Program.cs`, the member name has been changed to `Description` to match the public property.
8. In `Product.cs`, click in the statement that defines the `Product` class, and then click the **Quick Actions** icon, or press *Alt* + *Enter*, or press *Ctrl* + . (dot), and select **Generate constructor...**.
9. In the **Pick members** dialog box, clear **description** and leave **Description** selected, and then click **OK**.
10. Note a constructor has been added with a parameter to set the `Description` property, as shown in the following code:

```
public Product(string? description)
{
  Description = description;
}
```

11. In `Product.cs`, click in the statement that defines the `Product` class, and then click the **Quick Actions** icon, or press *Alt* + *Enter*, or press *Ctrl* + . (dot), select **Generate constructor 'Product()'**. Note a default constructor with no parameters is added.

12. In `Product.cs`, click in the statement that defines the `Product` class, and then click the **Quick Actions** icon, or press *Alt* + *Enter*, or press *Ctrl* + . (dot), select **Extract interface....** Note the options in the dialog box, as shown in *Figure 2.2*:

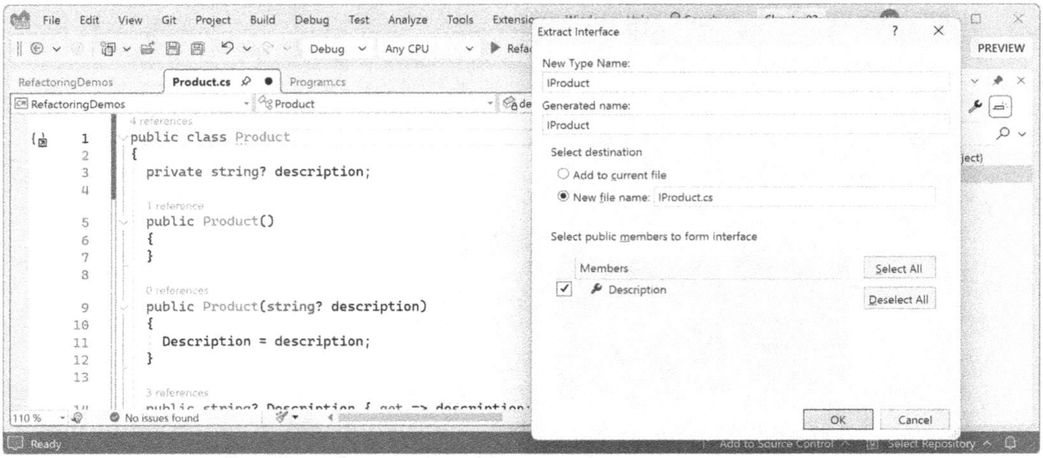

Figure 2.2: Extract Interface dialog box options

13. Click **OK**.
14. In `IProduct.cs`, note the interface that has been defined based on the members of the `Product` class, as shown in the following code:

```
public interface IProduct
{
  string? Description { get; set; }
}
```

15. In `Product.cs`, note the `Product` class implements the `IProduct` interface.

Now let's review some other useful refactorings like improving method parameters.

Add method parameter checks

It is good practice to add `if` statements that check the nullity of all the nullable, non-checked parameters in a method. There is a refactoring to help. Let's see:

1. In `Product.cs`, add a method, as shown in the following code:

```
public void Process(string name)
{
}
```

2. Click on the `name` parameter, activate quick actions, and note the option to add checks for `null`, empty, or whitespace, as shown in *Figure 2.3*:

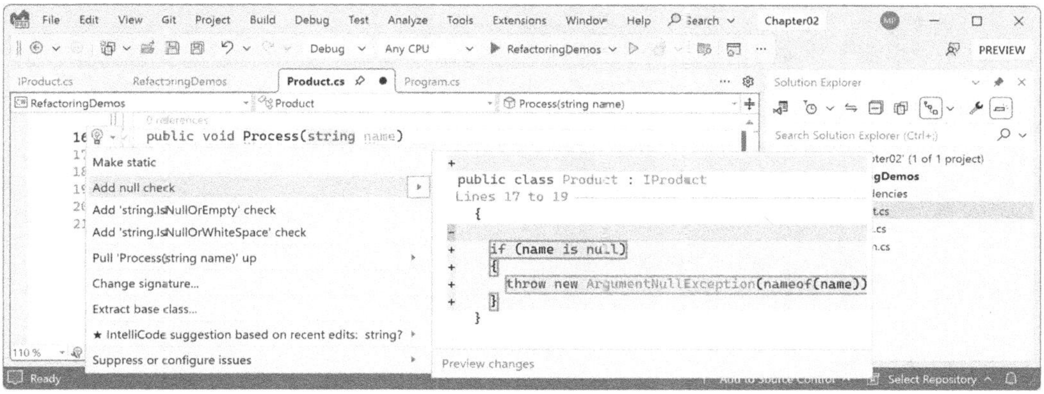

Figure 2.3: Adding method parameter checks

3. Select **Add 'string.IsNullOrWhiteSpace' check**, and note the new statements added, as shown in the following code:

```
if (string.IsNullOrWhiteSpace(name))
{
  throw new ArgumentException($"'{nameof(name)}' cannot be null or
whitespace.", nameof(name));
}
```

If you have multiple parameters, then you see an option to **Add null checks for all parameters**. I hope it will use guard clauses like `ArgumentException.ThrowIfNullOrWhiteSpace(name);` in future if it detects a project that targets a version of .NET that supports them.

Method parameter refactoring

Now let's look at method parameter refactoring:

1. In `Product.cs`, in the `Process` method, activate quick actions, and then select **Change signature...**.

2. In the **Change Signature** dialog box, note that you can add, remove, and reorder parameters, as shown in *Figure 2.4*:

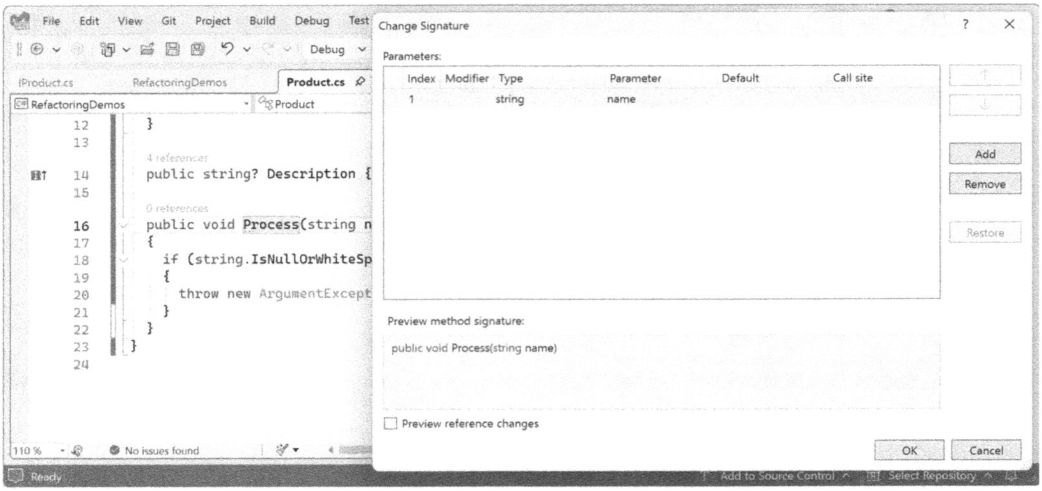

Figure 2.4: Changing the signature for a method's parameters

3. Optionally, try adding a new parameter to see the options available to you.
4. Click **Cancel**.

Convert foreach to for and vice versa

The `foreach` statement is a simple and convenient way to enumerate through an array or collection. But sometimes it is useful to know the index position of each item. For that reason, you might want to change a `foreach` into a `for` statement that uses an integer variable to enumerate. You can also switch back.

To use this refactoring, click in the `foreach` or `for` keyword, activate quick actions, and select **Convert to 'for'** or **Convert to 'foreach'**, as shown in *Figure 2.5*:

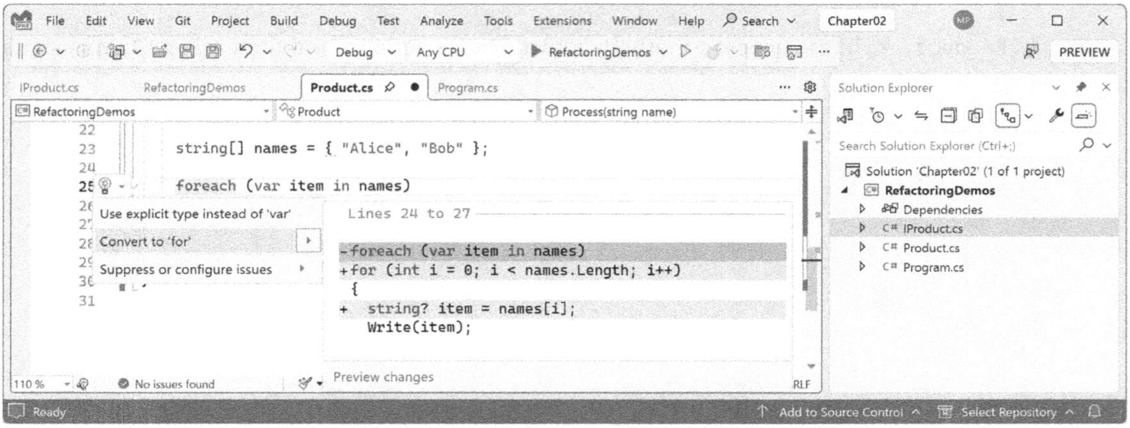

Figure 2.5: Converting a foreach statement to a for statement with an index

Simplify LINQ statements

A common mistake when writing LINQ statements to return one entity is to call `Where` to filter the sequence and then to separately call `Single`, `SingleOrDefault`, `First`, or `FirstOrDefault`.

What many developers do not realize is that those methods accept a delegate that can call a method or a lambda expression to perform the filtering. For example, take a look at the following code:

```
sequence.Where(item => item.ProductId == 27).Single();
```

This code can be simplified to the following:

```
sequence.Single(item => item.ProductId == 27);
```

To use this refactoring, click in the LINQ statement, activate quick actions, and select **Simplify LINQ expression**.

Align code elements

One of the most useful refactorings is a set that wraps, indents, and aligns long statements. The most common long statements in C# include:

- Methods with many defined parameters
- Statements with many method calls
- Binary statements with many operands

Each of these can be reformatted to make it easier to read (and are especially useful for book authors with limited horizontal space in print!).

For example, the following method has an example of the three most common scenarios that would benefit from aligning code elements:

```
public void Process(int number, string[] names, DateTime when, double height)
{
  if (names.Length > 10 && number < 0 && when.IsWeekend && height.IsNaN)
  {
    var query = names.Where(name.StartsWith("M")).OrderBy(name => name).
Select(name => name.Length);
    ...
  }
}
```

You can click in each code element, activate quick actions, and select **Wrap expression**, **Wrap every parameter**, **Wrap call chain**, **Wrap and align call chain**, and so on, to reformat, as shown in the following code:

```
public void Process(int number,
  string[] names,
  DateTime when,
```

```
    double height)
{
  if (names.Length > 10
    && number < 0
    && when.IsWeekend
    && height.IsNaN)
  {
    var query = names.Where(name.StartsWith("M"))
      .OrderBy(name => name)
      .Select(name => name.Length);
    ...
  }
}
```

You can read the full official documentation for refactoring features in Visual Studio at the following link: `https://learn.microsoft.com/en-us/visualstudio/ide/refactoring-in-visual-studio`.

Refactor to primary constructors

One of the new language features introduced with C# 12 with .NET 8 was primary constructors in `class` types. Primary constructors were already available for `record` types.

The C# team at Microsoft are trying to encourage .NET developers to embrace many of these new features. The first blog article in a series is about refactoring your code to use primary constructors, and you can read it at the following link: `https://devblogs.microsoft.com/dotnet/csharp-primary-constructors-refactoring/`.

Good practice: Personally, although primary constructors are great with `record` types, I am not a fan of using them in `class` types. Nor, it seems, are most other .NET developers, as you will see if you read the extremely negative comments section! But I do recommend that you read the article to see how to work with them, as well as some of the comments to see why developers don't like them. You can learn a language more deeply when developers with different opinions get excited!

Code snippets

In Visual Studio, you can review the currently available code snippets in a dialog box. Let's see:

1. Navigate to **Tools** | **Code Snippets Manager** or press *Ctrl* + *K*, *Ctrl* + *B*.
2. For **Language**, select **CSharp**, expand the **Visual C#** folder in the tree, and then select **class**, as shown in *Figure 2.6*:

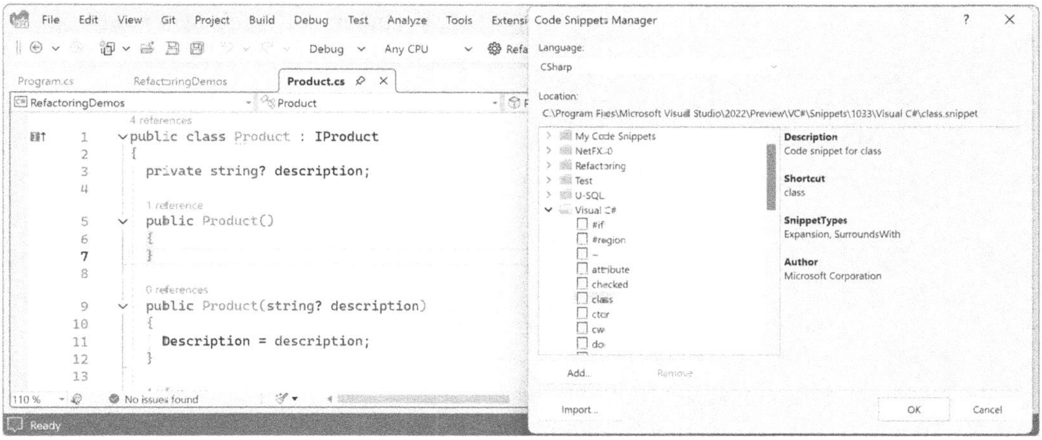

Figure 2.6: Reviewing C# code snippets in Code Snippets Manager

Note the following:

- A code snippet file has the extension `.snippet`.
- The built-in code snippets for C# are stored in the following folder: `C:\Program Files\Microsoft Visual Studio\18\Community\VC#\Snippets\1033\Visual C#`. (The culture number for US English is 1033.)

> If you have installed the Insiders edition instead of the Community edition, then the path will be: `C:\Program Files\Microsoft Visual Studio\18\Insiders\VC#\Snippets\1033\Visual C#`.

- You can add your own custom C# code snippet files to the following folder: `C:\Users\<yourname>\OneDrive\Documents\Visual Studio 18\Code Snippets\Visual C#\My Code Snippets`.
- Snippets have shortcuts, which can be entered in the code editor and then expanded by pressing *Tab*.
- Snippet types include **Expansion** and **SurroundsWith**. **Expansion** snippets are like `cw`, which expands to `Console.WriteLine`. **SurroundsWith** snippets are like `if`, in which you should select some existing statements before then inserting the snippet around those statements.
- You can click the **Add** and **Remove** buttons to add and remove folders that contain code snippet files.
- You can click the **Import...** button to import a code snippet file into the current folder.

3. In the **Location** box, select the full path to the **class** snippet file and copy it to the clipboard.
4. Navigate to **File** | **Open** | **File...** or press *Ctrl* + *O*, paste the path in the **File name** box, and then click **Open**.

5. Note the file format of a `.snippet` file is XML, as shown in the following markup:

```
<?xml version="1.0" encoding="utf-8" ?>
<CodeSnippets xmlns=
 "http://schemas.microsoft.com/VisualStudio/2005/CodeSnippet">
  <CodeSnippet Format="1.0.0">
    <Header>
      <Title>class</Title>
      <Shortcut>class</Shortcut>
      <Description>Code snippet for class</Description>
      <Author>Microsoft Corporation</Author>
      <SnippetTypes>
        <SnippetType>Expansion</SnippetType>
        <SnippetType>SurroundsWith</SnippetType>
      </SnippetTypes>
    </Header>
    <Snippet>
      <Declarations>
        <Literal>
          <ID>name</ID>
          <ToolTip>Class name</ToolTip>
          <Default>MyClass</Default>
        </Literal>
      </Declarations>
      <Code Language="csharp"><![CDATA[class $name$
  {
    $selected$$end$
  }]]>
      </Code>
    </Snippet>
  </CodeSnippet>
</CodeSnippets>
```

Note the following:

- The code that will be inserted is defined in an XML `CData` block. These start with `<![CDATA[` and end with `]]>`. Everything in between is the raw code.
- Variables within the code are identified with `$` at the start and end. For example, the special variable named `$selected$` identifies the current code selection when a **SurroundsWith** snippet is activated. The special variable named `$end$` is where the cursor will be after inserting the snippet. For example, after inserting the `cw` snippet, you would want the cursor to be in between the `()` parentheses of the `WriteLine()` method call.

- Custom variables are defined in the `<Declarations>` section, for example, `$name$`. These can be replaced with custom values after inserting the snippet. If there are multiple declarations of custom variables, then press *Tab* to navigate between them.

Code snippets schema

The XML that defines code snippets must conform to a predefined schema. Common allowed elements, attributes, and values are shown in *Table 2.2*:

Schema Item	Description	Required
`<CodeSnippets>` element	The root element in the XML file.	Yes
`<CodeSnippet>` element	Parent element for a `<Header>` and a `<Snippet>`.	Yes
`<Header>` element	Contains the general information like author and title that are shown in Code Snippets Manager. Child elements include `<Author>`, `<Description>`, `<HelpUrl>`, `<SnippetTypes>`, `<Keywords>`, and `<Shortcut>`. Only `<Title>` is required.	Yes
`<Snippet>` element	Contains the code that will be inserted.	Yes
`<Code>` element	Contains the actual code for the snippet. `$end$` and `$selected$` are special keywords. All other keywords surrounded by `$` must be defined in `<Literal>` or `<Object>` elements.	Yes
`Language` attribute	Sets the language for the code. Values can be `CSharp`, `VB`, `CPP` (C++), `XAML`, `XML`, `JavaScript`, `TypeScript`, `SQL`, or `HTML`.	Yes
`Kind` attribute	Use this to restrict where the snippet can be used. For example, `method body` will only show the snippet if you are in a method body, not in a type or empty file. Values can be `method body`, `method decl`, `type decl`, `file`, or `any`.	No
`Delimiter` attribute	Delimiter characters wrap replaceable parts of the code. By default, the delimiter for keywords is `$`. If you need to use a literal `$` in your code, for example, when using C# literal string values, then you can redefine the delimiter to something else like ~.	No
`<Declarations>` element	Defines literals and objects in the code snippet that can be edited after insertion. For example, in a `foreach` statement, the names of the variable and the collection.	No
`<Literal>` element	Literals are fixed values, like the maximum integer in a `for` statement.	No
`<Object>` element	Objects are names of objects used in the code snippet.	No
`<ID>` element	An identifier for a literal or object.	No
`<Default>` element	The default values for a literal or object.	No

Table 2.2: XML items defined in the code snippets schema

The code snippets schema is documented at the following link: `https://learn.microsoft.com/en-us/visualstudio/ide/code-snippets-schema-reference`.

Now let's see an example of creating and then distributing your code snippets.

Creating and importing code snippets

There are a few steps to creating a code snippet:

1. Create an XML file with the file extension `.snippet`
2. Fill in the appropriate elements, like the required `<Title>`
3. Add your code with optional replacement literals and objects

Let's see one in action:

1. Use Visual Studio to add a new **Console App** / `console` project named `CodeSnippetDemos` to a `Chapter02` solution.
2. In the `CodeSnippetDemos` project, add a new XML file named `CommonImports.snippet`.
3. In `CommonImports.snippet`, delete any existing statements, and then add statements to define a minimal template for a code snippet, as shown in the following markup:

```
<?xml version="1.0" encoding="utf-8"?>
<CodeSnippets xmlns=
 "http://schemas.microsoft.com/VisualStudio/2005/CodeSnippet">
  <CodeSnippet Format="1.0.0">
    <Header>
      <Title></Title>
    </Header>
    <Snippet>
      <Code Language="">
        <![CDATA[]]>
      </Code>
    </Snippet>
  </CodeSnippet>
</CodeSnippets>
```

Good practice: You can use the above as a template for future code snippets because it contains the minimum elements required.

4. In the `<Title>` element, add the following text: `Statically import common types globally`.
5. In the `<Language>` attribute, add the following text: `XML`.
6. Between the `[]` in the `<![CDATA[]]>` element, add code to import several commonly used types, as shown highlighted in the following markup:

```
<![CDATA[<ItemGroup>
  <Using Include="System.Console" Static="true" />
  <Using Include="System.Environment" Static="true" />
  <Using Include="System.IO.Path" Static="true" />
</ItemGroup>]]>
```

7. Save the file.
8. Navigate to **Tools** | **Code Snippets Manager**.
9. Click the **Import...** button, navigate to the `\tools-skills-net10\Chapter02\CodeSnippetDemos\` folder where you have saved the `CommonImports.snippet` file, select it, and then click **Open**.
10. In the **Import Code Snippet** dialog box, select **My Xml Snippets**, and then click **Finish**.
11. In **Code Snippets Manager**, click **OK**.
12. In the `CodeSnippetDemos.csproj` project file, place the insertion point on a blank line just before the `</Project>` element.
13. Insert a code snippet using one of the following options:
    - Navigate to **Edit** | **IntelliSense** | **Insert Snippet...**.
    - Right-click, and select **Snippet** | **Insert Snippet...**.
    - Press *Ctrl* + *K*, *X*.
14. Select **My Xml Snippets**, select **Statically import common types globally**, and note the code snippet is inserted.
15. In `Program.cs`, delete any existing statements and then add a statement to output the current directory using the statically imported types, as shown in the following code:

```
WriteLine(CurrentDirectory);
```

16. In the `CodeSnippetDemos` project, add a new XML file named `ConfigureConsole.snippet`.
17. In `ConfigureConsole.snippet`, delete any existing statements, and then add statements to define a code snippet for configuring the console, as shown in the following markup:

```
<?xml version="1.0" encoding="utf-8"?>
<CodeSnippets xmlns=
 "http://schemas.microsoft.com/VisualStudio/2005/CodeSnippet">
  <CodeSnippet Format="1.0.0">
    <Header>
      <Title>Configure console for culture</Title>
      <Description>Define a static method for Program to configure the
culture for the console.</Description>
```

```
      <Author>Mark J. Price</Author>
      <Shortcut>ccc</Shortcut>
    </Header>
    <Snippet>
      <Imports>
        <Import>
          <Namespace>System.Globalization</Namespace>
        </Import>
      </Imports>
      <Declarations>
        <Literal>
          <ID>defaultCulture</ID>
          <Default>en-US</Default>
          <ToolTip>The default culture when none is specified when
calling the method.</ToolTip>
        </Literal>
      </Declarations>
      <Code Language="CSharp" Delimiter="~">
        <![CDATA[partial class Program
{
  static void ConfigureConsole(string culture = "~defaultCulture~",
    bool useComputerCulture = false)
  {
    // To enable Unicode characters like Euro symbol in the console.
    OutputEncoding = System.Text.Encoding.UTF8;
    if (!useComputerCulture)
    {
      CultureInfo.CurrentCulture = CultureInfo.GetCultureInfo(culture);
    }
    WriteLine($"CurrentCulture: {CultureInfo.CurrentCulture.
DisplayName}");
  }
}]]>
      </Code>
    </Snippet>
  </CodeSnippet>
</CodeSnippets>
```

18. Save the file.
19. Navigate to **Tools** | **Code Snippets Manager**.
20. Click the **Import...** button, navigate to the `\tools-skills-net10\Chapter02\CodeSnippetDemos\` folder where you have saved the `ConfigureConsole.snippet` file, select it, and then click **Open**.
21. In the **Import Code Snippet** dialog box, select **My Code Snippets**, and then click **Finish**.
22. In **Code Snippets Manager**, for **Language**, select **CSharp**; in **Location**, expand **My Code Snippets** and select **Configure console for culture**, and note the information shown about the snippet, including its shortcut: **ccc**.
23. In **Code Snippets Manager**, click **OK**.
24. In the `CodeSnippetDemos` project, add a new class file named `Program.Functions.cs`.
25. In `Program.Functions.cs`, delete any existing code, type `ccc`, press *Tab* twice, and note the code snippet is inserted with the text `en-US` selected, ready for you to type over an alternative value.
26. Save the file.
27. In `Program.cs`, at the top of the file, call the method, as shown in the following code:

```
ConfigureConsole();
```

28. Run the project and note the result, as shown in the following output:

```
CurrentCulture: English (United States)
C:\tools-skills-net10\Chapter02\CodeSnippetDemos\bin\Debug\net10.0
```

Distributing code snippets

As you have seen, you could distribute code snippets as `.snippet` files and allow developers to manually import them using **Code Snippets Manager**.

If you want a more formal mechanism, then you can include your code snippet files in a Visual Studio extension so that developers can install the extension to obtain the snippets.

> You can read the full official documentation for code snippet features in Visual Studio at the following links: `https://learn.microsoft.com/en-us/visualstudio/ide/code-snippets` and `https://learn.microsoft.com/en-us/visualstudio/ide/visual-csharp-code-snippets`.

Editor configuration

One of the benefits of adding an `.editorconfig` file to your project is that it enforces coding standards not just for yourself but for everyone who works on that project because the settings take precedence over global Visual Studio text editor settings. Settings in the Visual Studio **Options** dialog box only take effect if there isn't an `.editorconfig` file with a setting that overrides them.

If you add an `.editorconfig` file to an existing project, then you will need to manually activate the settings to apply them to the existing code. You can do that by running **Code Cleanup** using the button in the status bar or by pressing *Ctrl + K, E*, as shown in *Figure 2.7*:

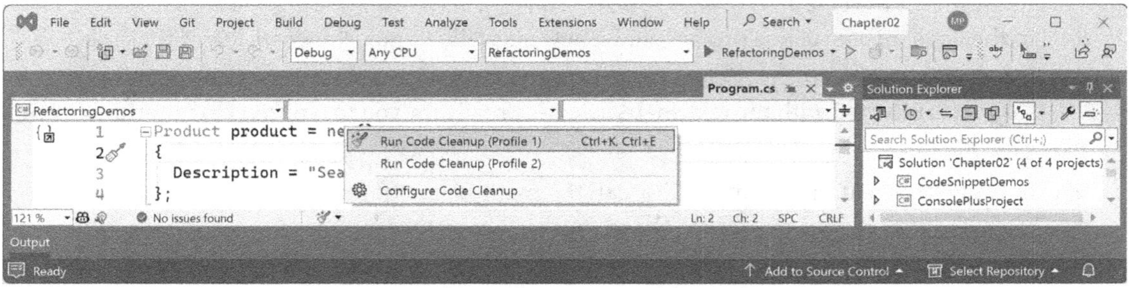

Figure 2.7: Code Cleanup options

To run **Code Cleanup** on an entire project or solution, in **Solution Explorer**, right-click a project or solution and then select **Analyze and Code Cleanup | Run Code Cleanup**.

> An alternative to Visual Studio's built-in Code Cleanup tool is the **CodeMaid** extension. Although I've never used it myself, some developers prefer it. You can learn more about it at the following link: `https://marketplace.visualstudio.com/items?itemName=SteveCadwallader.CodeMaid`.

Let's explore how to add an `.editorconfig` file to your project to encourage coding standards:

1. In the `RefactoringDemos` project, navigate to **Project** | **Add New Item...** or press *Ctrl + Shift + A*.
2. In the **Add New Item** dialog box, in the search box, enter `editor`, select **editorconfig File (.NET)**, and then click **Add**.

> **editorconfig File (.NET)** is prepopulated with default .NET code style, formatting, and naming conventions. **editorconfig File (default)** is only prepopulated with indent style and size.

3. Note that Visual Studio provides a graphical editor for the file with search capabilities, as shown in *Figure 2.8*:

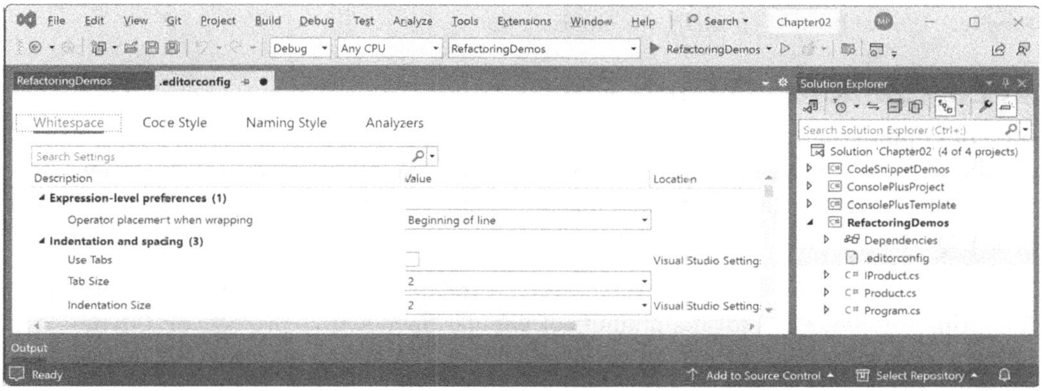

Figure 2.8: Visual Studio's graphical editor for an .editorconfig file

4. In the **Search Settings** box, enter `space` and note there are 24 space settings. (You are doing this to see the usage of the filter feature when editing settings, not because I want you to change any space-related settings.)
5. In **Solution Explorer**, right-click the `.editorconfig` file; select **Open With...**; in the dialog box, select **Common Language Editor Supporting TextMate Bundles**, and then click **OK**. This special editor provides IntelliSense for `.editorconfig` files.
6. Note the properties set, as partially shown in the following code:

```
[*.{cs,vb}]
#### Naming styles ####
# Naming rules
dotnet_naming_rule.interface_should_be_begins_with_i.severity =
suggestion
dotnet_naming_rule.interface_should_be_begins_with_i.symbols = interface
dotnet_naming_rule.interface_should_be_begins_with_i.style = begins_
with_i
...
dotnet_naming_style.pascal_case.capitalization = pascal_case
dotnet_style_operator_placement_when_wrapping = beginning_of_line
tab_width = 2
indent_size = 2
end_of_line = crlf
...
csharp_style_expression_bodied_constructors = false:silent
csharp_space_around_binary_operators = before_and_after
```

This section has shown how Visual Studio can apply and modify `.editorconfig` files. The actual properties that can be set were covered earlier in this chapter.

Now let's look at how AI companions can help you.

AI companions: GitHub Copilot

GitHub Copilot, the AI-powered coding companion, is now a recommended component in Visual Studio version 17.10 or later. If you only have Visual Studio version 17.9 or earlier, then you can find instructions to install GitHub Copilot at the following link: `https://devblogs.microsoft.com/visualstudio/how-to-install-github-copilot-in-visual-studio/`.

To use the new Copilot extension, you'll need a GitHub Copilot subscription. GitHub Copilot is free for verified students and for maintainers of popular open-source projects on GitHub. You can sign up for a 60-day free trial of GitHub Copilot and then pay $100 per year at the following link: `https://github.com/github-copilot/signup/`.

More advanced scenarios are supported by Copilot Enterprise, including building custom models based on your code repositories.

Making the most of GitHub Copilot

GitHub Copilot is now integrated tightly into Visual Studio version 17.10 or later. Features of the previously separate **GitHub Copilot** and **GitHub Copilot Chat** extensions are now combined into one button at the top right of the UI, as shown in *Figure 2.9*:

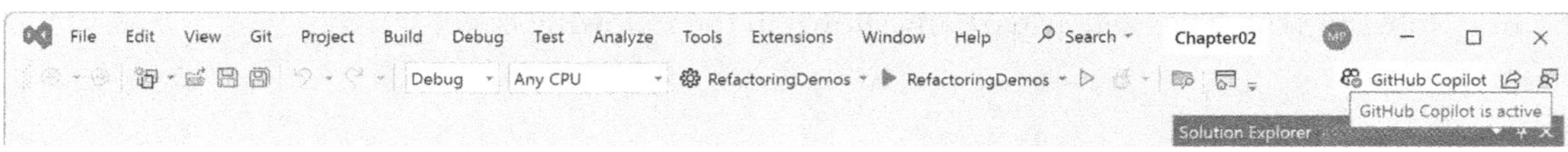

Figure 2.9: GitHub Copilot integrated in Visual Studio

GitHub Copilot provides an interactive experience via chat in a separate window and directly within your code editor. You can start a conversation or simply begin typing to receive context-aware code completions, suggestions, and even full code snippets. It's like having a pair programmer who assists with writing commit messages, debugging, generating unit tests, and more.

GitHub Copilot is a valuable resource for code-related information, offering documentation, definitions, references, error explanations, and best practices. Here are some tasks that Copilot can help you with:

- If you start writing code in the editor, then Copilot will suggest code as you type. Press *Tab* to accept a suggestion.
- Start an inline chat by right-clicking in a code file and then select **Ask Copilot** or press *Alt* + /. Inline chat will help you write your methods, classes, and unit tests by converting your prompts to code.
- To open a side panel for chat, click **GitHub Copilot** and then click **Open Chat Window**, as shown in *Figure 2.10*:

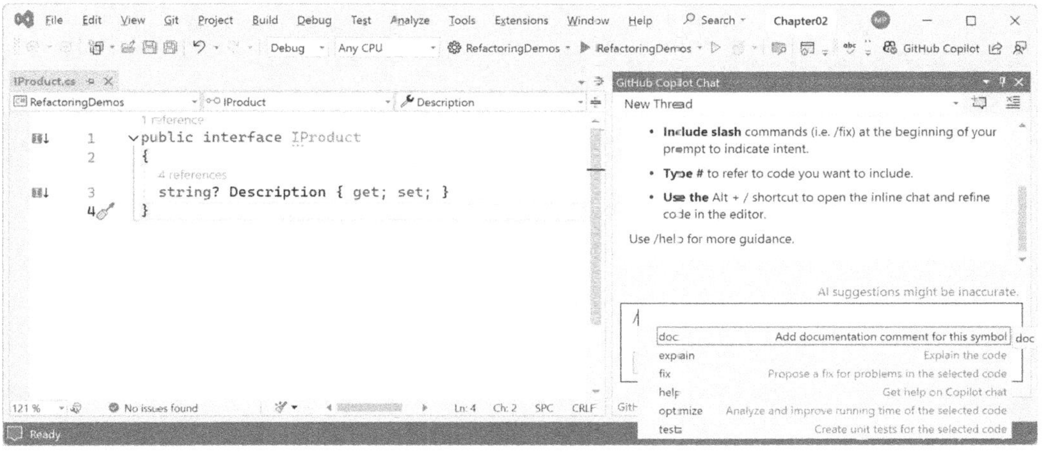

Figure 2.10: GitHub Copilot Chat window

Then, from the chat window:

- To state your intent, type /
- To refer to your files, type #
- To generate a unit test for a class, type `/test for #NorthwindContext.cs`
- To ask about the whole solution, type `#solution`

- To document a file, type `/doc #Program.Functions.cs` (you can select from a list of files as soon as you type the #), as shown in *Figure 2.11*:

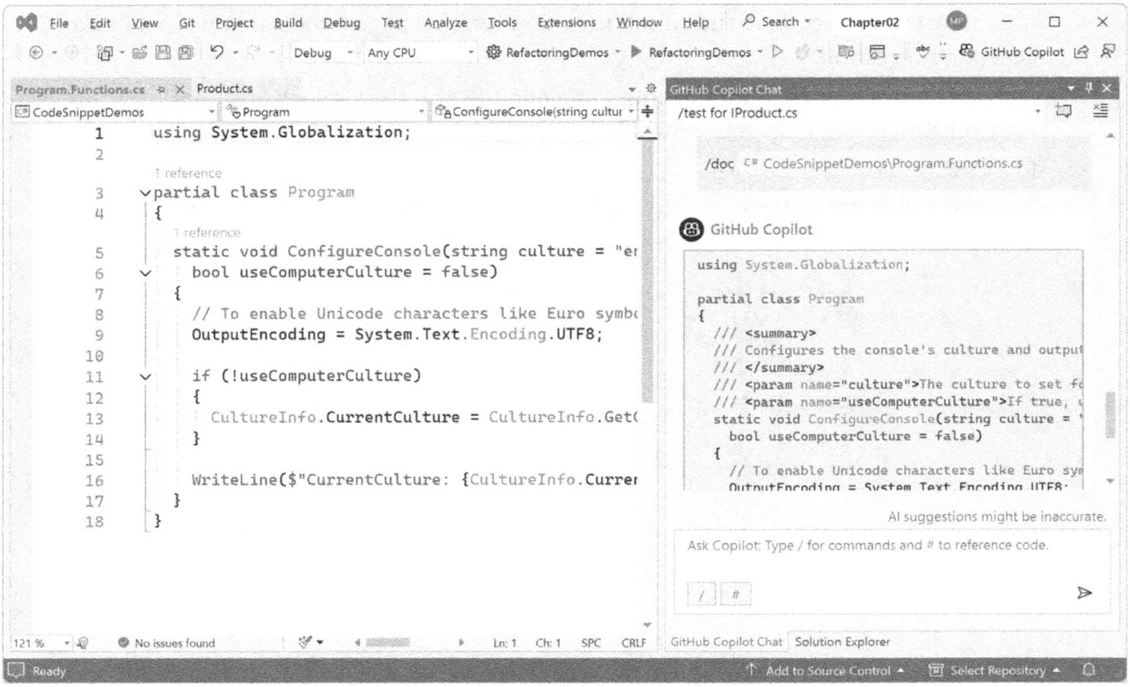

Figure 2.11: Documenting a class with GitHub Copilot

GitHub Copilot is also available in VS Code and Rider. You can read about GitHub Copilot in Rider at the following link: `https://github.blog/changelog/2024-03-07-github-copilot-chat-general-availability-in-jetbrains-ide/`.

Navigating Visual Studio

It might seem too basic, but it always used to surprise me when teaching in a classroom to see how many developers navigate their code editor user interface only by clicking with their mouse instead of using the keyboard, which is usually much faster.

Copying and pasting a statement

There is nothing more frustrating than waiting for a developer to carefully move their mouse to the start of a statement, then click, hold, and drag to select the statement, fumble it, and have to start again.

When moving or copying a statement, you can click anywhere in the statement without selecting any characters, then press *Ctrl* + *X* (to cut) or *Ctrl* + *C* (to copy) the whole statement. Then click anywhere in another statement and, as long as nothing is selected, you can then press *Ctrl* + *V* to paste to insert *above* that statement.

Switching between file tabs and tool windows

Most users are familiar with the Windows application switcher that is activated by pressing *Alt* + *Tab* (or *Alt* + *Shift* + *Tab* for reverse order), which allows quick switching between actively running applications.

IDE Navigator works like the Windows application switcher. Press *Alt* + *F7* (or *Ctrl* + *Tab*) to access the IDE Navigator or press *Alt* + *Shift* + *F7* (or *Ctrl* + *Shift* + *Tab*) to reverse the order in which you want to cycle through. Press multiple times to continue switching to the next active tool window or active file.

Note that while holding down the shortcut keys, you can also press the arrow keys to highlight either an active tool window or an active file. The full path of the active file is shown at the bottom of the window so that you can differentiate between files with the same name, like **Program.cs**, as shown in *Figure 2.12*:

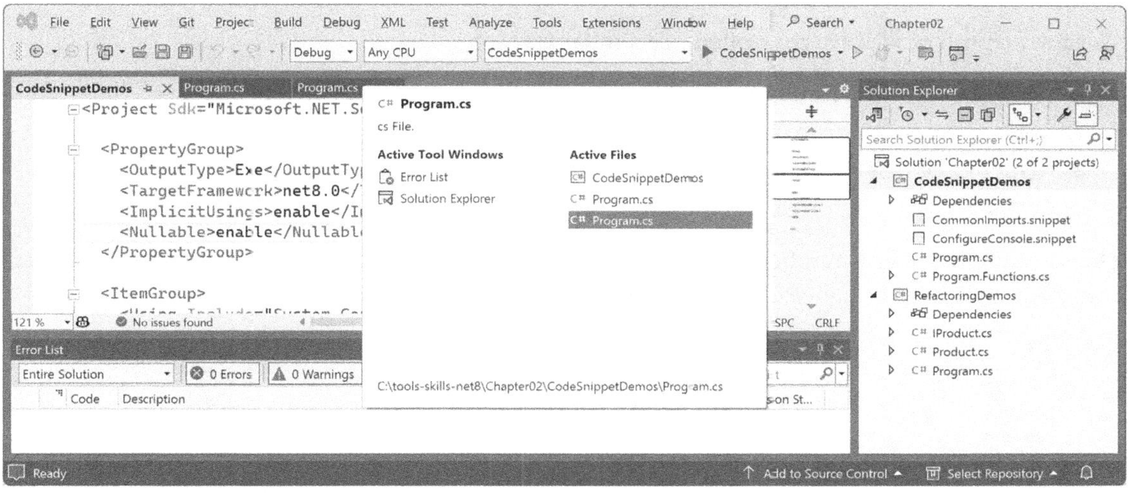

Figure 2.12: IDE Navigator to switch between active tool windows or active files

Common keyboard shortcuts for navigation are shown in *Table 2.3*:

Shortcut	**Description**
Ctrl + - (dash)	Activate open documents in the order they were most recently touched.
Ctrl + *Shift* + -	Activate open documents in the reverse order.
Alt + *F7* or *Ctrl* + *Tab*	Activate IDE Navigator and switch to the next active tool window or active file.
Alt + *Shift* + *F7* or *Ctrl* – *Shift* + *Tab*	Activate IDE Navigator and switch to the previous active tool window or active file.

Table 2.3: Common keyboard shortcuts for navigation

Features to improve the editing experience

Editing is one of the most important tasks for a developer, so features that help are important to know and understand how to properly use.

Line numbers and word wrap

Line numbers can be displayed in the left margin of the code window, but they are not shown by default.

Let's enable line numbers for C#:

1. Navigate to **Tools** | **Options** | **Text Editor** | **C#.**
2. Select the **Line Numbers** check box.
3. Click **OK.**

Word wrap preferences are controlled in a similar way:

1. Navigate to **Tools** | **Options** | **Text Editor** | **C#.**
2. Select the **Word wrap** check box.
3. Optionally, select the **Show visual glyphs for word wrap** check box.
4. Click **OK.**

The combination of line numbers and visual glyphs makes it especially easy to note when a statement is word-wrapped in the code editor, as shown in *Figure 2.13*:

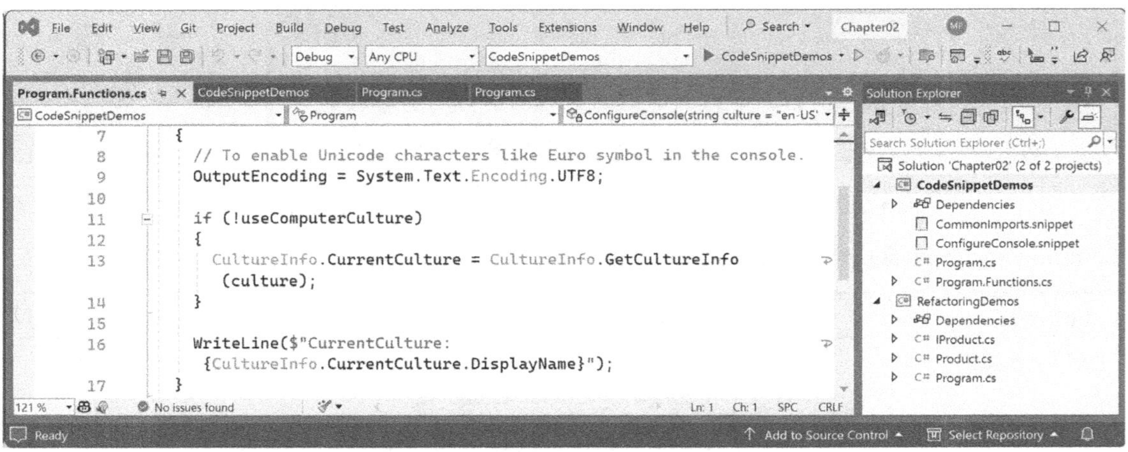

Figure 2.13: Word wrapping visual glyphs and line numbers

Keyboard shortcuts

Common keyboard shortcuts for editing are shown in *Table 2.4*:

Shortcut	Description
Alt + Up Arrow	Move the current statement or selected statements up one line.
Alt + Down Arrow	Move the current statement or selected statements down one line.
Ctrl + *K*, *C*	Comment the current statement or selected statements. The appropriate comment characters for the file type will be used automatically, for example, `<!-- -->` for an XML file and `//` for a C# file.
Ctrl + *K*, *U*	Uncomment the current statement or selected statements.

Table 2.4: Common keyboard shortcuts for editing

Let's try them out:

1. In the `CodeSnippetDemos.csproj` project file, click anywhere in one of the import statements, for example, `<Using Include="System.IO.Path" Static="true" />`.
2. Press *Alt* + Up Arrow and note the statement is moved up by one line.
3. Press *Alt* + Up Arrow again.
4. Press *Alt* + Down Arrow and note that the effect is moved down by one line.
5. Press *Alt* + Down Arrow again.
6. Press *Ctrl* + *K*, *C*, and note that XML comment characters are added around the statement to comment it out.
7. Press *Ctrl* + *K*, *U*, and note that the XML comment characters are removed to uncomment it.

Formatting code

You have always been able to set colors for different types of code. For example, blue for C# keywords and black for normal code. With Visual Studio version 17.10 or later, you can now also use bold and italic, which is especially nice for comments to make them distinct from code, and developers have been asking for this for decades.

Task list

Visual Studio has a handy task list where you can add and remove items manually, and it can automatically populate based on comments with tokens that you write. For example, there are three tokens that it recognizes by default, `TODO`, `HACK`, and `UNDONE`, as shown in the following code:

```
// TODO: Add caching.
// HACK: Fix this hack.
// UNDONE: Implement this method.
```

To view the task list, navigate to **View** | **Task List**, as shown in *Figure 2.14*:

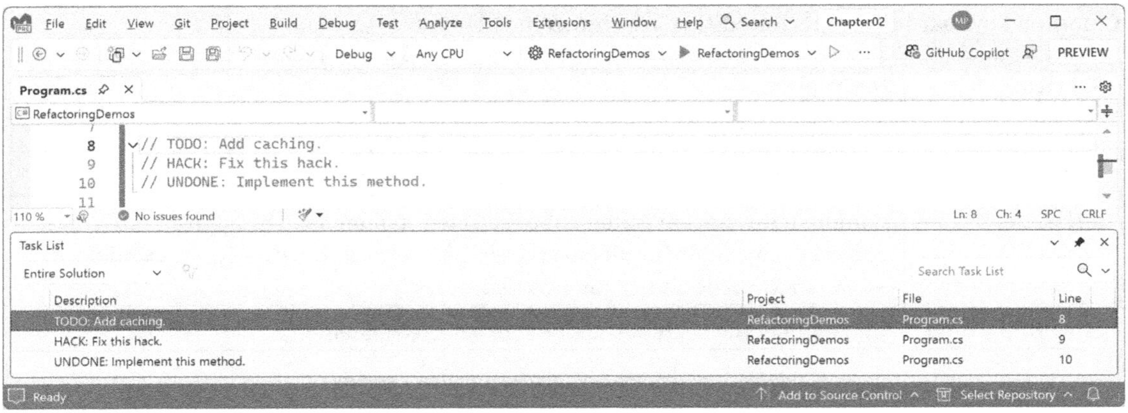

Figure 2.14: Visual Studio Task List showing comment tokens

Double-clicking a row in **Task List** will jump to the comment.

To define your own custom tokens, navigate to **Tools** | **Options** | **Environment** | **Task List.**

Extension Manager

Visual Studio version 17.10 or later includes a new extension manager, as shown in *Figure 2.15*:

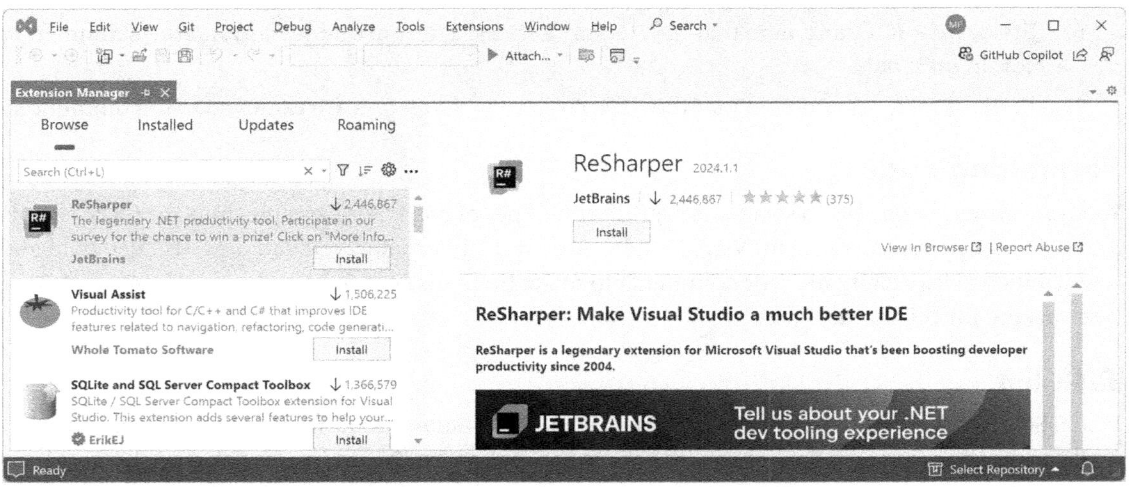

Figure 2.15: Visual Studio 17.10 or later improved Extension Manager

This design focuses on giving you more room for the content that matters when you're searching for extensions. The updated UI for your search results list now includes a large window displaying the detailed description of the selected extension.

If you want to filter your search results by category, click the filter icon in the toolbar to reveal the **category** and **subcategory** dropdown menus. These filters allow you to narrow your search, for instance, to find coding tools specifically or to display only C# templates.

Tools in VS Code

First, you should become familiar with VS Code's keyboard shortcuts. There are convenient single-page PDF files that you could print out on these keyboard shortcuts, one for each of the common operating systems, Windows, macOS, and Linux, and they are found at the following link: `https://code.visualstudio.com/docs/getstarted/keybindings#_keyboard-shortcuts-reference`.

Here are a couple of useful shortcuts you should definitely know. When you have multiple files (tabs) open simultaneously, you can use *Alt* + *Left Arrow* and *Alt* + *Right Arrow* to navigate between them. You can also use *Ctrl* + *Tab* and *Ctrl* + *Shift* + *Tab* (reverse order).

Refactoring features

Many of VS Code's refactoring features are activated by pressing *Ctrl* + *Shift* + *R*.

VS Code has a subset of refactoring commands, some of which are shown in the following list:

- **Rename symbol** (*F2*): Renaming is a common operation related to refactoring source code, and all instances of the symbol across all files will be renamed.
- **Extract method**: Select statements and pull them out into their own shared method.
- **Encapsulate field**: Turn a field into a property and update all usages of that field to use the newly created property.
- **Convert between auto property and full property**: Convert between an auto-implemented property to a full property.
- **Convert between if and switch statements**: Convert an `if` statement to a `switch` statement or to the C# 8 and later `switch` expression.
- **Wrap, indent, and align refactorings**: Wrap and align chains of method calls, or wrap, indent, and align parameters or arguments.

> You can read more about VS Code C# refactorings at the following link: `https://code.visualstudio.com/docs/csharp/refactoring`.

Code snippets

To insert a code snippet in VS Code, activate **Command Palette** and then select **Insert Snippet**, or enter the snippet's shortcut and press *Tab*.

Let's define some custom code snippets for VS Code:

1. Use VS Code to add a new **Console App** / `console` project named `SnippetDemos4Code` to the `Chapter02` solution. For example, in **Terminal**, in the `Chapter02` folder, enter the following commands:

```
dotnet new console -o SnippetDemos4Code
dotnet sln add SnippetDemos4Code
```

2. Navigate to **View** | **Command Palette** or press *Ctrl* + *Shift* + *P*.
3. Select **Snippets: Configure User Snippets** and then select **csharp (C#)**.
4. In the `csharp.json` file, read the comment.
5. In `csharp.json`, note the comment, and then add a JSON object to define a code snippet for configuring the console, using backslashes to escape double-quote characters, as shown in the following markup:

```
{
  // Place your snippets for csharp here. Each snippet is defined under a 
snippet name and has a prefix, body and
  // description. The prefix is what is used to trigger the snippet and 
the body will be expanded and inserted. Possible variables are:
  // $1, $2 for tab stops, $0 for the final cursor position, and 
${1:label}, ${2:another} for placeholders. Placeholders with the
  // same ids are connected.
  "Configure console for culture": {
    "prefix": "ccc",
    "body": [
      "using System.Globalization;",
      "using static System.Console;",
      ""
      "partial class Program",
      "{",
      " static void ConfigureConsole(string culture = \"${1:en-US}\",",
      " bool useComputerCulture = false)",
      " {",
      " // To enable Unicode characters like Euro symbol in the 
console.",
      " OutputEncoding = System.Text.Encoding.UTF8;",
      "",
      " if (!useComputerCulture)",
      " {",
      " CultureInfo.CurrentCulture = CultureInfo.
GetCultureInfo(culture);",
```

```
        "  }",
        "",
        "  WriteLine($\"CurrentCulture: {CultureInfo.CurrentCulture.
DisplayName}\");",
        "  }",
        "}",
      ],
      "description": "Define a static method for Program to configure the
culture for the console.",
      "isFileTemplate": true
  }
}
```

6. Save the file.
7. In the `SnippetDemos4Code` project, add a new class file named `Program.Functions.cs`.
8. In `Program.Functions.cs`, delete any existing code, type `ccc`, press *Tab*, and note the code snippet is inserted with the text `en-US` selected, ready for you to type over an alternative value.
9. Save the file.
10. In `Program.cs`, at the top of the file, call the method, as shown in the following code:

```
ConfigureConsole();
```

11. Run the project and note the result, as shown in the following output:

```
CurrentCulture: English (United States)
```

AI companions

AI companions can assist programmers in a range of practical ways generating boilerplate code, debugging errors, explaining unfamiliar syntax or libraries, reviewing code for best practices, and even suggesting more efficient algorithms. They can help refactor messy code, convert between languages, and write documentation or comments. Beyond pure coding, AI companions can serve as a sounding board for design decisions, simulate interview questions, and keep programmers up to date with evolving tools and frameworks—all in real time, without judgment or fatigue.

GitHub Copilot for VS Code

With GitHub Copilot for VS Code, you can get code suggestions as you type in the editor, or you can use natural language chat to ask about your code or start an editing session for implementing new features and fixing bugs.

You can access GitHub Copilot from the robot icon to the right of the **Search** box, and configure some of its settings from the robot icon on the right side of the status bar, as shown in Figure *2.16*:

Figure 2.16: Accessing GitHub Copilot in VS Code

You can choose the mode (**Ask**, **Edit**, **Agent**) and model from the GitHub Copilot Chat window, as shown in *Figure 2.17*:

Figure 2.17: Choosing a model for GitHub Copilot

Learn more about code completions at the following link:

`https://code.visualstudio.com/docs/copilot/ai-powered-suggestions`.

To set up GitHub Copilot in VS Code, you can read the instructions at the following link: `https://code.visualstudio.com/docs/copilot/setup`.

Gemini Code Assist for VS Code

Gemini Code Assist offers AI-powered assistance to help you build, deploy, and operate development projects.

Gemini Code Assist for individuals is available at no cost. Other editions are paid, like the Standard and Enterprise editions.

C# is one of dozens of verified coding languages trained on by the Gemini LLMs, as listed at the following link:

`https://developers.google.com/gemini-code-assist/docs/supported-languages#coding-languages`.

You can install Gemini Code Assist in common code editors including VS Code and Rider.

> To set up Gemini Code Assist, you can read the instructions at the following link: `https://developers.google.com/gemini-code-assist/docs/set-up-gemini`.

Decompiling .NET assemblies

One of the best ways to learn how to code for .NET is to see how professionals do it. Most code editors have an extension for decompiling .NET assemblies. Visual Studio and VS Code can use the **ILSpy** extension. Rider has a built-in **IL Viewer** tool.

> **Good practice:** You could decompile someone else's assemblies for non-learning purposes, like copying their code for use in your own production library or application, but remember that you are viewing their intellectual property, so please respect that.

Creating a console app to decompile

Let's create a console app that we can then decompile:

1. Use your preferred code editor to add a new **Console App** / `console` project named `DotNetEverywhere` to the `Chapter02` solution.
2. Modify the project file to statically import the `System.Console` class in all C# files.
3. In `Program.cs`, delete the existing statements, and then add a statement to output a message saying the console app can run everywhere and some information about the operating system, as shown in the following code:

```
WriteLine("I can run everywhere!");
WriteLine($"OS Version is {Environment.OSVersion}.");

if (OperatingSystem.IsMacOS())
{
  WriteLine("I am macOS.");
}
else if (OperatingSystem.IsWindowsVersionAtLeast(major: 10, build:
22000))
```

```
{
  WriteLine("I am Windows 11.");
}
else if (OperatingSystem.IsWindowsVersionAtLeast(major: 10))
{
  WriteLine("I am Windows 10.");
}
else
{
  WriteLine("I am some other mysterious OS.");
}

WriteLine("Press any key to stop me.");
ReadKey(intercept: true); // Do not output the key that was pressed.
```

4. Run the `DotNetEverywhere` project and note the results when run on Windows 11, as shown in the following output:

```
I can run everywhere!
OS Version is Microsoft Windows NT 10.0.22000.0.
I am Windows 11.
Press any key to stop me.
```

5. In `DotNetEverywhere.csproj`, add the **runtime identifiers (RIDs)** to target three operating systems inside the `<PropertyGroup>` element, as shown highlighted in the following markup:

```
<Project Sdk="Microsoft.NET.Sdk">

  <PropertyGroup>
    <OutputType>Exe</OutputType>
    <TargetFramework>net10.0</TargetFramework>
    <Nullable>enable</Nullable>
    <ImplicitUsings>enable</ImplicitUsings>
    <RuntimeIdentifiers>win-x64;osx-x64;linux-x64</RuntimeIdentifiers>
  </PropertyGroup>

</Project>
```

> **Warning!** There are two elements that you can use to specify runtime identifiers. Use `<RuntimeIdentifier>` if you only need to specify one. Use `<RuntimeIdentifiers>` if you need to specify multiple, as we did in the preceding example. If you use the wrong one, then the compiler will give an error, and it can be difficult to understand why with only one character difference!

6. At the command prompt or terminal, make sure that you are in the `DotNetEverywhere` folder.
7. Enter a command to build and publish the self-contained release version of the console application for Windows 10, as shown in the following command:

```
dotnet publish -c Release -r win-x64 --self-contained
```

8. Note the build engine restores any needed packages, compiles the project source code into an assembly DLL, and creates a `publish` folder, as shown in the following output:

```
MSBuild version 18.0.0+14c24b2d3 for .NET
  Determining projects to restore...
  All projects are up-to-date for restore.
  DotNetEverywhere -> C:\tools-skills-net10\Chapter02\DotNetEverywhere\
bin\Release\net10.0\win-x64\DotNetEverywhere.dll
  DotNetEverywhere -> C:\tools-skills-net10\Chapter02\DotNetEverywhere\
bin\Release\net10.0\win-x64\publish\
```

9. Enter the following commands to build and publish the release versions for macOS and Linux variants:

```
dotnet publish -c Release -r osx-x64 --self-contained
dotnet publish -c Release -r linux-x64 --self-contained
```

Decompiling using the ILSpy extension for Visual Studio

For learning purposes, you can decompile any .NET assembly with a tool like ILSpy:

1. In Visual Studio, navigate to **Extensions** | **Manage Extensions**.
2. In the search box, enter `ilspy`.
3. For the **ILSpy 2022** extension, click **Download**. (At the time of writing in November 2025, there is not a specific version of this extension for Visual Studio 2026, but the 2022 version should be compatible).
4. Click **Close**.
5. Close Visual Studio to allow the extension to be installed.
6. Restart Visual Studio and reopen the `Chapter02` solution.

7. In **Solution Explorer**, right-click the **DotNetEverywhere** project and select **Open output in ILSpy**.
8. In ILSpy, in the toolbar, make sure that **C#** is selected in the drop-down list of languages to decompile into.
9. In the **Assemblies** navigation tree on the left, expand **DotNetEverywhere (1.0.0.0, .NETCoreApp, v10.0)**.
10. In the **Assemblies** navigation tree on the left, expand **{ }** and then expand **Program.**
11. Select **<Main>$(string[]) : void** to show the statements in the compiler-generated `Program` class and its `<Main>$` method, as shown in *Figure 2.18*:

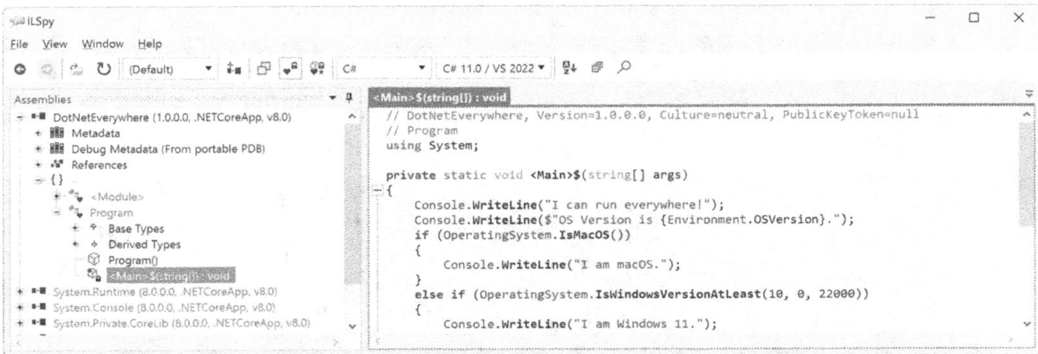

Figure 2.18: Revealing the <Main>$ method using ILSpy

12. Navigate to **File | Open....**
13. Navigate to the following folder:

```
tools-skills-net10/Chapter02/DotNetEverywhere/bin/Release/net10.0/
linux-x64
```

14. Select the `System.Linq.dll` assembly and click **Open**.
15. In the **Assemblies** tree, expand the **System.Linq (10.0.0.0, .NETCoreApp, v10.0)** assembly, expand the **System.Linq** namespace, expand the **Enumerable** class, and then click the **Count<TSource>(this IEnumerable<TSource>) : int** method.

16. In the `Count` method, note the good practice of checking the `source` parameter and throwing an `ArgumentNullException` if it is `null`, checking for interfaces that the source might implement with their own `Count` properties that would be more efficient to read, and finally, the last resort of enumerating through all the items in the source and incrementing a counter, which would be the least efficient implementation, as shown in *Figure 2.19*:

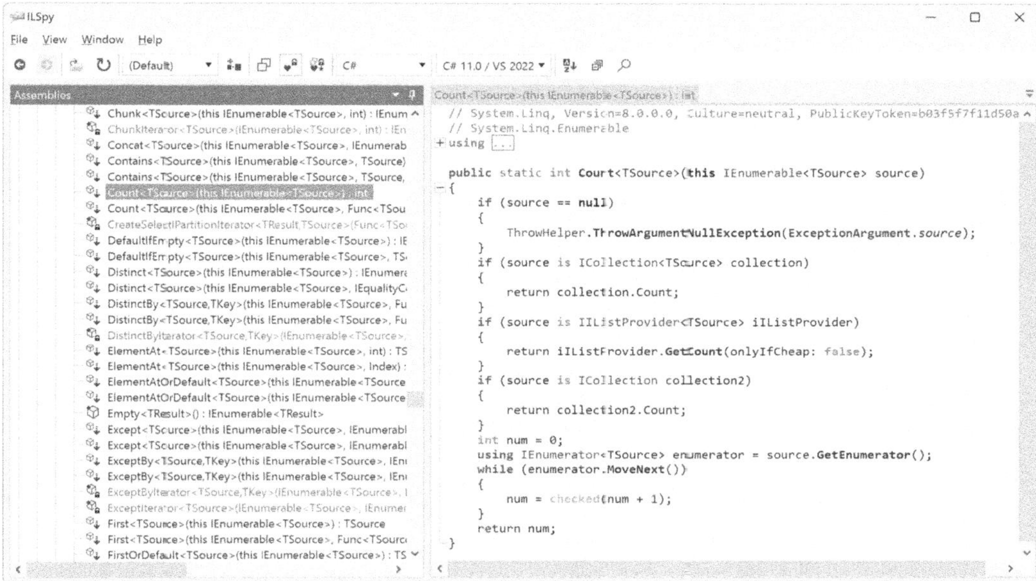

Figure 2.19: Decompiled Count method of the Enumerable class

Warning! Different decompiler tools are likely to produce slightly different code, for example, variable names, but the functionality will be the same.

17. Review the C# source code for the `Count` method, as shown in the following code, in preparation for reviewing the same code in **Intermediate Language (IL)**:

```
public static int Count<TSource>(this IEnumerable<TSource> source)
{
  if (source == null)
  {
    ThrowHelper.ThrowArgumentNullException(ExceptionArgument.source);
  }
  if (source is ICollection<TSource> collection)
  {
    return collection.Count;
  }
  if (source is IIListProvider<TSource> iIListProvider)
  {
    return iIListProvider.GetCount(onlyIfCheap: false);
  }
  if (source is ICollection collection2)
  {
    return collection2.Count;
  }
  int num = 0;
  using IEnumerator<TSource> enumerator = source.GetEnumerator();
  while (enumerator.MoveNext())
  {
    num = checked(num + 1);
  }
  return num;
}
```

Good practice: You will often see LinkedIn posts and blog articles warning you to always use the `Count` property of a sequence instead of calling the LINQ `Count()` extension method. As you can see above, this advice is unnecessary because the `Count()` method always checks if the sequence implements `ICollection<T>` or `ICollection` and then uses the `Count` property anyway. What it doesn't do is check if the sequence is an array and then use the `Length` property. If you have an array of any type, avoid `Count()` in favor of the `Length` property.

The final part of the `Count` method implementation shows how the `foreach` statement works internally. It calls the `GetEnumerator` method and then calls the `MoveNext` method in a `while` loop. To calculate the count, the loop increments an `int` value. It does all this in a `checked` statement so that an exception will be thrown in the case of an overflow. The `Count` method can therefore only count sequences with up to about 2 billion items. (For more items, you can use `LongCount` that goes up to about nine quintillion, two hundred twenty-three quadrillion, three hundred seventy-two trillion, and thirty-six billion.)

18. In the toolbar, click the **Select language to decompile** dropdown, select **IL**, and then review the IL source code of the `Count` method. To save two pages in this book, I have not shown the code here.

> **Good practice:** The IL code is not especially useful unless you get very advanced with C# and .NET development, when knowing how the C# compiler translates your source code into IL code can be important. The much more useful edit windows contain the equivalent C# source code written by Microsoft experts. You can learn a lot of good practices from seeing how professionals implement types. For example, the `Count` method shows how to check arguments for `null`.

19. Close ILSpy.

> You can learn how to use the ILSpy extension for VS Code at the following link: `https://github.com/markjprice/cs14net10/blob/main/docs/code-editors/vscode.md#decompiling-using-the-ilspy-extension-for-visual-studio-code`.

Viewing source links with Visual Studio

Instead of decompiling, Visual Studio has a feature that allows you to view the original source code using source links. This feature is not available in VS Code.

Let's see how it works:

1. In Visual Studio, enable **Source Link**:
    - Navigate to **Tools** | **Options**.
    - In the search box, enter `navigation to source`.
    - Select **Text Editor** | **C#** | **Advanced**.
    - Select the **Enable navigation to Source Link and Embedded sources** check box, and then click **OK**.
2. In Visual Studio, add a new **Console App** project to the `Chapter02` solution named `SourceLinks`.

3. In `Program.cs`, delete the existing statements. Add statements to declare a `string` variable and then output its value and the number of characters it has, as shown in the following code:

```
string name = "Timothée Chalamet";
int length = name.Count();
Console.WriteLine($"{name} has {length} characters.");
```

4. Right-click in the `Count()` method and select **Go To Implementation**.
5. Note the source code file is named `Count.cs` and it defines a partial `Enumerable` class with implementations of five count-related methods, as shown in *Figure 2.20*:

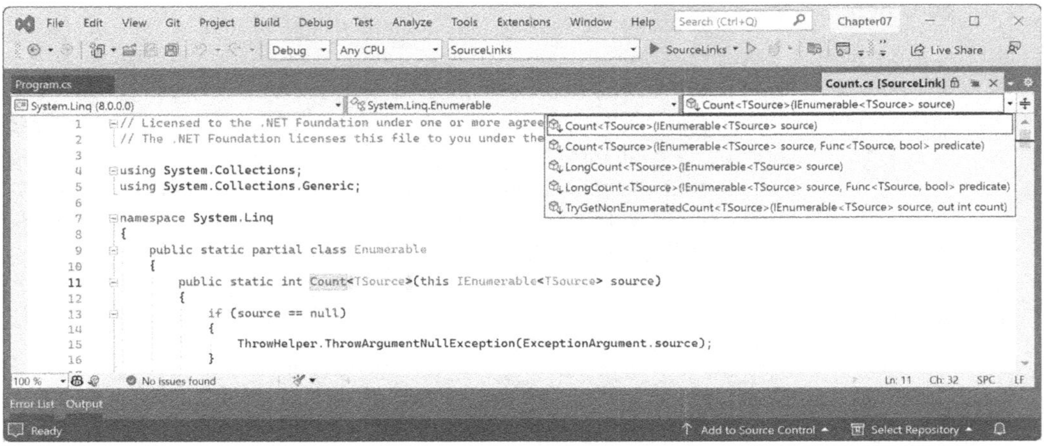

Figure 2.20: Viewing the original source file for LINQ's Count method implementation

You can learn more from viewing source links than decompiling because they show best practices for situations like how to divide up a class into partial classes for easier management. When we used the ILSpy compiler, all it could do was show all the hundreds of methods of the `Enumerable` class.

You can learn more about how Source Link works and how any NuGet package can support it at the following link: `https://learn.microsoft.com/en-us/dotnet/standard/library-guidance/sourcelink`.

6. If you prefer decompiling, then you can disable the **Source Link** feature now.

No, you cannot technically prevent decompilation

I sometimes get asked if there is a way to protect compiled code to prevent decompilation. The quick answer is no, and if you think about it, you'll see why this must be the case. You can make it harder using obfuscation tools like **Dotfuscator**, but ultimately, you cannot completely prevent it.

All compiled applications contain instructions for the platform, operating system, and the hardware on which they run. Those instructions must be functionally the same as the original source code, but are just harder for a human to read. Those instructions must be readable to execute your code; therefore, they must be readable to be decompiled. If you were to protect your code from decompilation using some custom technique, then you would also prevent your code from running!

Virtual machines simulate hardware and so can capture all interaction between your running application and the software and hardware that it thinks it is running on.

If you could protect your code, then you would also prevent attaching to it with a debugger and stepping through it. If the compiled application has a `pdb` file, then you can attach a debugger and step through the statements line by line. Even without the `pdb` file, you can still attach a debugger and get some idea of how the code works.

This is true for all programming languages. Not just .NET languages like C#, Visual Basic, and F#, but also C, C++, Delphi, and assembly language: all can be attached to for debugging or to be disassembled or decompiled. Some tools used by professionals for this are shown in *Table 2.5*:

Type	Product	Description
Virtual Machine	VMware	Professionals like malware analysts always run software inside a VM.
Debugger	SoftICE	Runs underneath the operating system, usually in a VM.
Debugger	WinDbg	Useful for understanding Windows internals because it knows more about Windows data structures than other debuggers.
Disassembler	IDA Pro	Used by professional malware analysts.
Decompiler	HexRays	Decompiles C apps. Plugin for IDA Pro.
Decompiler	DeDe	Decompiles Delphi apps.
Decompiler	dotPeek	.NET decompiler from JetBrains.

Table 2.5: Professional debugger, decompiler, and disassembler tools

Good practice: Debugging, disassembling, and decompiling someone else's software is likely against its license agreement and illegal in many jurisdictions. Instead of trying to protect your intellectual property with a technical solution, the law is sometimes your only recourse.

Lowering C# code

One of the best features of the **IL Viewer** plugin for Rider is its ability to convert high-level C# code to lower-level C# code rather than all the way to IL code. If you don't have Rider, then you can also use the `Sharplab.io` online tool, as you will see later.

But what is lowering?

Lowering refers to a technique used internally by the C# compiler to rewrite certain high-level language features, commonly known as "syntactic sugar," into lower-level language constructs.

You already know that compiling is the process of translating source code written in C# into IL code, which is then translated into native machine language for the specific CPU at runtime (unless you're using the AOT compiler!).

Probably the most common is `foreach` rewriting, as shown in the following code:

```
// A foreach loop is a high-level C# language feature.
foreach(Person person in people)
{
  Console.WriteLine(person);
}

// It is lowered to an interface and calls to its members.
List<Person>.Enumerator enumerator = people.GetEnumerator();
try
{
  while (enumerator.MoveNext())
    Console.WriteLine((object) enumerator.Current);
}
finally
{
  enumerator.Dispose();
}
```

There are many other examples of high-level language constructs that are lowered by the compiler, including:

- The `record` keyword, which is lowered to a `class` that implements the `IEquatable` interface.
- The `async` and `await` keywords, which are lowered to state machines. This allows asynchronous code execution without blocking the main thread.
- Lambdas and anonymous methods, which are lowered to delegate invocations or expression trees.
- Statements like `using` or `lock`, which are lowered to `try-finally` blocks to ensure proper resource cleanup.

Let's see some examples using Rider and the `SharpLab.io` website:

1. Start **Rider**. (If you do not have Rider, then just read the steps and review the screenshots until you get to step 7.)
2. In **Rider**, open the `Chapter02` solution, and then add a new **Console App** project named `LoweringCode`.
3. In **Rider**, in `Program.cs`, delete any existing statements and then add statements to define a list of two people and output them to the console using a `foreach` loop, as shown in the following code:

```
List<Person> people = [ new("Bob", 47), new("Alice", 23) ];

foreach(Person person in people)
{
  Console.WriteLine(person);
}

record Person(string FirstName, int Age);
```

> **Warning!** If you define a type in a file used as a top-level program, then it must be at the bottom of the file, as shown in the preceding code for the `Person` record.

4. In **Rider**, build the `LoweringCode` project.
5. In **IL Viewer**, select **Low-Level C#**, click on the end brace of the `foreach` loop, and note the IL Viewer automatically navigates to show the equivalent lowered C# code, as shown in *Figure 2.21*:

Figure 2.21: IL Viewer showing lowered C# code for a foreach loop

6. In `Program.cs`, click in the `record`, then in **IL Viewer**, scroll up a little, and note the equivalent lowered C# code is a class that implements `IEquatable<Person>`, as shown in *Figure 2.22*:

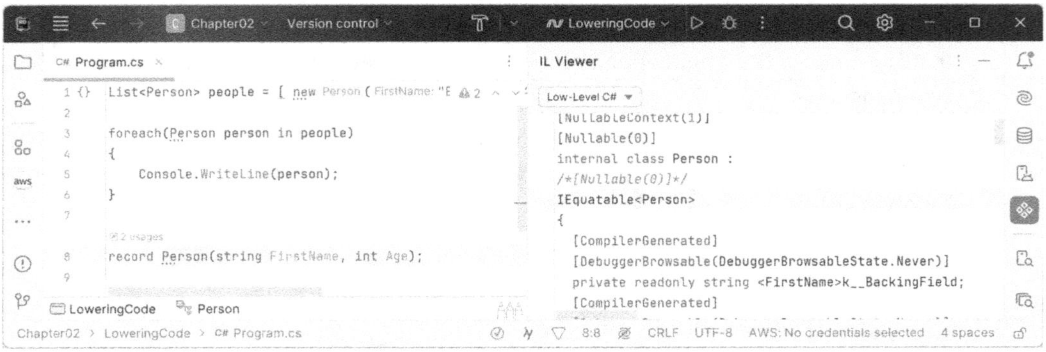

Figure 2.22: IL Viewer showing lowered C# code for a record class

7. Use your preferred browser to navigate to `https://sharplab.io/`.
8. In **SharpLab.io**, delete any existing statements and then add statements to define a list of two people and output them to the console using a `foreach` loop, as shown in the following code:

```
using System.Collections.Generic;

List<Person> people = [ new("Bob", 47), new("Alice", 23) ];

foreach(Person person in people)
{
  System.Console.WriteLine(person);
}

record Person(string FirstName, int Age);
```

9. In **SharpLab.io**, note the compiler-generated code for the `Program` class and its `<Main>$` method, as shown in *Figure 2.23* and the following code:

```
[CompilerGenerated]
internal class Program
{
  private static void <Main>$(string[] args)
  {
```

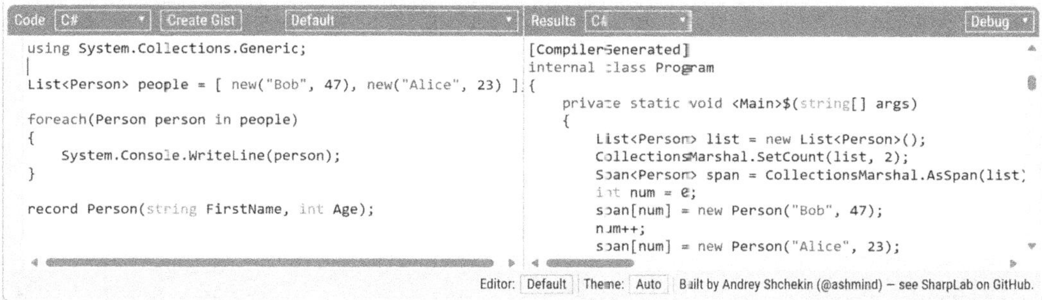

Figure 2.23: SharpLab.io website for decompiling and lowering .NET languages

10. Note how the collection expression is translated into a `Span` to efficiently populate the list of `Person` instances, as shown in the following code:

```
List<Person> list = new List<Person>();
CollectionsMarshal.SetCount(list, 2);
Span<Person> span = CollectionsMarshal.AsSpan(list);
int num = 0;
span[num] = new Person("Bob", 47);
num++;
span[num] = new Person("Alice", 23);
```

11. Note how the `foreach` statement is translated into calls to an enumerator, as shown in the following code:

```
List<Person>.Enumerator enumerator = list2.GetEnumerator();
try
{
  while (enumerator.MoveNext())
  {
    Person current = enumerator.Current;
    Console.WriteLine(current);
  }
}
finally
{
  ((IDisposable)enumerator).Dispose();
}
```

12. Note how the `record` is translated into a class that implements `IEquatable<Person>` with backing fields and properties, as shown in the following code:

```
internal class Person : IEquatable<Person>
{
  [CompilerGenerated]
  [DebuggerBrowsable(DebuggerBrowsableState.Never)]
  private readonly string <FirstName>k__BackingField;
...
  public string FirstName
  {
    [CompilerGenerated]
    get
    {
      return <FirstName>k__BackingField;
    }
    [CompilerGenerated]
    init
    {
      <FirstName>k__BackingField = value;
    }
  }
```

13. Note how the `ToString` method is implemented, as shown in the following code:

```
[CompilerGenerated]
public override string ToString()
{
  StringBuilder stringBuilder = new StringBuilder();
  stringBuilder.Append("Person");
  stringBuilder.Append(" { ");
  if (PrintMembers(stringBuilder))
  {
    stringBuilder.Append(' ');
  }
  stringBuilder.Append('}');
  return stringBuilder.ToString();
}

[CompilerGenerated]
protected virtual bool PrintMembers(StringBuilder builder)
{
  RuntimeHelpers.EnsureSufficientExecutionStack();
```

```
        builder.Append("FirstName = ");
        builder.Append((object)FirstName);
        builder.Append(", Age = ");
        builder.Append(Age.ToString());
        return true;
    }
```

There is a lot more code in the lowered equivalent of a `record`, for example, to implement equality comparisons, so take a few moments to review it all.

14. Run the **console app** project in **Rider**, or in `SharpLab.io`, in the **Result** dropdown, select **Run**, and note the result, as shown in the following output:

```
Person { FirstName = Bob, Age = 47 }
Person { FirstName = Alice, Age = 23 }
```

Now that you've seen how you can learn more details about how C# works underneath, so that you can both better understand it and improve performance, let's see how you can create custom templates for projects and project items.

Custom project and item templates

The .NET SDK comes with many project and item templates that can create a new project or item for you by calling the `dotnet new` command, for example, `console`, `classlib`, `web`, `mvc`, and `blazor`.

You can learn about the built-in project and item templates at the following link: `https://learn.microsoft.com/en-us/dotnet/core/tools/dotnet-new-sdk-templates`.

One of the most efficient ways to improve your code editor experience is to create custom .NET project templates. These are recognized by all the code editors. You can create templates for entire projects or individual project items. They are distributed as NuGet packages (`.nupkg` files) and installed through the `dotnet new install` SDK command.

All project and item templates use the same principles and have similar contents. Both project and item templates contain the following items:

- All the folders and files needed when the template is used, including source code files, embedded resources, sample data files, and so on.
- A `template.json` file, which provides the information needed to create a project or item from the template and to display the template in the appropriate user interface or help output.

You can quickly turn a normal .NET project into a project template simply by adding a `.template.config` folder that contains a `template.json` configuration file to the project.

The `template.json` file usually contains the following information, as shown in *Table 2.6*:

Member	Description	Required
`$schema`	The JSON schema for the `template.json` file, which should be `http://json.schemastore.org/template`.	Yes
`author`	The author of the template.	No
`classifications`	The tags for searching for the template. For example, `Common`, `Web`, `MAUI`, `Cloud`, `Test`, `ASP.NET`, `Blazor`, `Mobile`, `Console`, `.NET Aspire`, `Web API`, `Service`.	No
`identity`	A unique identifier for the template.	Yes
`name`	The visible full name for the template. For example, **Console App**.	Yes
`shortName`	The name used at the command prompt. For example, `console`.	Yes
`sourceName`	The name in the source tree to replace with the name the user specifies by using the `-n` or `--name` switch at the command prompt. By default, the current directory name will be used.	No
`preferNameDirectory`	A Boolean that indicates if a directory should be created if one is not specified.	No

Table 2.6: Minimal configuration in a template.json file

The full schema for the `template.json` file can be found at the following link: `https://json.schemastore.org/template`. Documentation for the file format can be found at the following link: `https://github.com/dotnet/templating/wiki`.

When distributed to the correct folder, your code editor or `dotnet` CLI can find and use the custom templates. Visual Studio automatically displays templates in the following places:

- Project templates are shown in the **Create a new project** page
- Item templates are shown in the **Add New Item** dialog box

Creating a project for a template

To create a project template, you need to start by creating a project that will act as the template. We can also install a project template for creating project templates.

Let's create a project template for a console app that includes extra files to define static methods to configure the culture used by the console app, and to import some extra types that are commonly used:

1. At the command prompt or terminal, enter the command to install the project template for creating project templates, as shown in the following command:

```
dotnet new install Microsoft.TemplateEngine.Authoring.Templates
```

2. Note the result, as shown in the following output:

```
The following template packages will be installed:
   Microsoft.TemplateEngine.Authoring.Templates
Success: Microsoft.TemplateEngine.Authoring.Templates::10.0.100 installed
the following templates:
Template Name                      Short Name     Language  Tags
--------------------------------  -------------  --------  -------------
-----
Template Package                   templatepack             Template
Authoring
template.json configuration file  template.json  JSON      Template
Authoring
```

3. Use Visual Studio to add a new **Template Package** / `templatepack` project named `ConsolePlusTemplate` to the `Chapter02` solution. Hint: you can select **Template Authoring** to filter by project types.
4. In the `ConsolePlusTemplate.csproj` project file, modify the configuration, as shown highlighted in the following markup:

```
<Project Sdk="Microsoft.NET.Sdk">

  <PropertyGroup>
    <!-- The package metadata. Fill in the properties marked as TODO
below -->
    <!-- Follow the instructions on https://learn.microsoft.com/en-us/
nuget/create-packages/package-authoring-best-practices -->
    <PackageId>Packt.ConsolePlus.Template</PackageId>
    <PackageVersion>10.0</PackageVersion>
    <Title>Console App (Packt)</Title>
    <Authors>Mark J. Price;Packt Publishing</Authors>
    <Description>A console app with extra imported types and a method to
configure the culture.</Description>
    <PackageTags>dotnet-new;templates;packt;console</PackageTags>
    <PackageProjectUrl>https://www.github.com/markjprice/tools-skills-
net10</PackageProjectUrl>
```

```
    <!-- Keep package type as 'Template' to show the package as a
template package on nuget.org and make your template available in dotnet
new search.-->
    <PackageType>Template</PackageType>
    <TargetFramework>net10.0</TargetFramework>
    <IncludeContentInPack>true</IncludeContentInPack>
    <IncludeBuildOutput>false</IncludeBuildOutput>
    <ContentTargetFolders>content</ContentTargetFolders>
    <NoWarn>$(NoWarn);NU5128</NoWarn>
    <NoDefaultExcludes>true</NoDefaultExcludes>
    <PackageReadmeFile>README.md</PackageReadmeFile>
  </PropertyGroup>

  <PropertyGroup>
    <LocalizeTemplates>false</LocalizeTemplates>
  </PropertyGroup>

  <ItemGroup>
    <PackageReference Include="Microsoft.TemplateEngine.Tasks"
Version="*" PrivateAssets="all" IsImplicitlyDefined="true"/>
  </ItemGroup>

  <ItemGroup>
    <Content Include="content\**\*" Exclude="content\**\
bin\**;content\**\obj\**" />
    <Compile Remove="**\*" />
  </ItemGroup>

  <ItemGroup>
    <None Include="README.md" Pack="true" PackagePath="" />
  </ItemGroup>

</Project>
```

Note the following:

- `<PackageType>` is set to `Template` to make the template package appear in `dotnet new search` results
- `<IncludeContentInPack>` is set to `true` to include the folders and files specified in the `<Content>` item group

5. In the `content` folder, delete the `SampleTemplate` folder.

6. Use Visual Studio to add a new **Console App** / `console` project named `ConsolePlusProject` to the `content` folder (ensure you change the **Location** to the `content` folder), as shown in *Figure 2.24*:

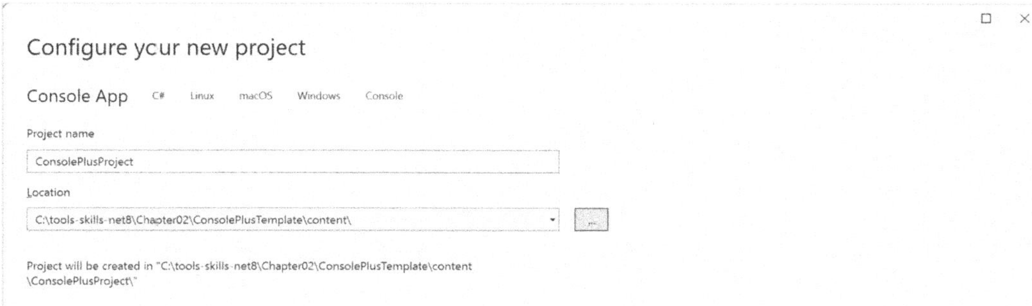

Figure 2.24: Configuring a console app project location

7. In the `ConsolePlusProject.csproj` project file, import some types, as shown in the following markup:

   If you completed the section that defined an XML code snippet, then you can add this `<ItemGroup>` using that.

```
<ItemGroup>
  <Using Include="System.Console" Static="true" />
  <Using Include="System.Environment" Static="true" />
  <Using Include="System.IO.Path" Static="true" />
</ItemGroup>
```

8. In the `ConsolePlusProject` project, add a new class file named `Program.Functions.cs`.
9. In `Program.Functions.cs`, delete any existing statements and add statements to define a partial class for `Program` with a method named `ConfigureConsole`, as shown in the following code:

   If you completed the section that defined a C# code snippet, then you can add this code using the `ccc` shortcut.

```
using System.Globalization;

partial class Program
{
  static void ConfigureConsole(
    string culture = "en-US",
    bool useComputerCulture = false)
```

```
  {
    // To enable Unicode characters like Euro symbol in the console.
    OutputEncoding = System.Text.Encoding.UTF8;

    if (!useComputerCulture)
    {
      CultureInfo.CurrentCulture = CultureInfo.GetCultureInfo(culture);
    }

    WriteLine($"CurrentCulture: {CultureInfo.CurrentCulture.
DisplayName}");
  }
}
```

10. In `Program.cs`, delete any existing statements and add a statement to call the `ConfigureConsole` method, as shown in the following code:

```
ConfigureConsole(); // en-US by default.

// Alternatives:
// ConfigureConsole("fr-FR"); // French in France.
// ConfigureConsole(useComputerCulture: true); // Your local culture.
// Add your code below here:
```

11. In the `ConsolePlusProject` project folder, add a new folder named `.template.config`.
12. In the `.template.config` folder, add a new JSON file named `template.json`.
13. In `template.json`, modify the contents to define the JSON schema for a template file, as shown in the following markup:

```
{
  "$schema": "http://json.schemastore.org/template",
}
```

14. On the blank line in the middle of the JSON file, press *Ctrl* + *Space* to pop up IntelliSense and note that the schema is recognized, with required elements shown in bold typeface, as shown in *Figure 2.25*:

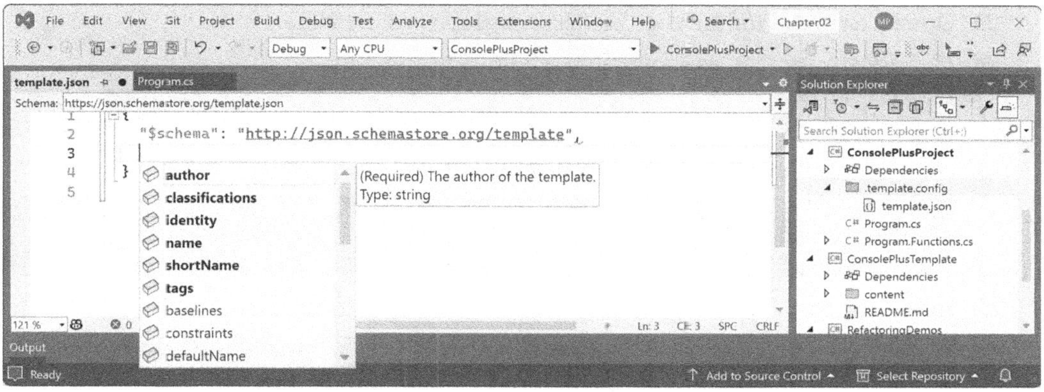

Figure 2.25: Specifying schema for editing a template.json file

15. Complete the rest of the file, as shown in the following markup:

```
{
  "$schema": "http://json.schemastore.org/template",
  "author": "Mark J. Price",
  "classifications": [ "Console", "Packt" ],
  "identity": "Packt.ConsolePlus.CSharp",
  "name": "Packt Console+ App",
  "shortName": "consoleplus",
  "tags": {
    "language": "C#",
    "type": "project"
  }
}
```

16. Save the file.
17. In the `ConsolePlusProject.csproj` project file, if Visual Studio has added configuration to include the file as content, then wrap it in XML comments, as shown highlighted in the following markup:

```
<!-- If Visual Studio adds an element like below, then
 you can delete it or comment it out. -->
<!--
<ItemGroup>
 <Content Include=".template.config\template.json" />
</ItemGroup>
-->
```

18. Open a terminal for the `ConsolePlusTemplate` project folder.
19. Package the project, as shown in the following command:

```
dotnet pack
```

20. Note the result, as shown in the following output:

```
Successfully created package 'C:\tools-skills-net10\Chapter02\
ConsolePlusTemplate\bin\Release\ConsolePlusTemplate.10.0.0.nupkg'.
```

21. Install the NuGet package, as shown in the following command:

```
dotnet new install .\bin\Release\ConsolePlusTemplate.10.0.0.nupkg
```

22. Note the result, as shown in the following output:

```
Success: ConsolePlusTemplate::10.0.0 installed the following templates:
Template Name       Short Name   Language  Tags
------------------  -----------  --------  -------------
Packt Console+ App  consoleplus  [C#]      Console/Packt
```

Testing the project template

Now let's test the template:

1. In Visual Studio, add a new project to the solution.
2. Optionally, search for your project template by entering `packt` in the search box, or it should be shown as a **New** project at the top of the list anyway, as shown in *Figure 2.26*:

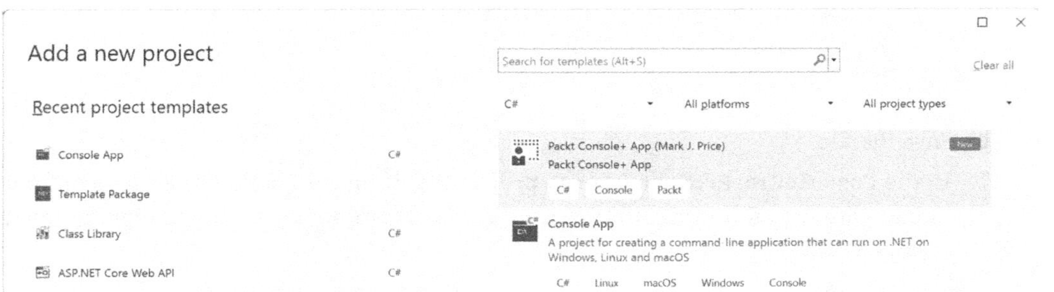

Figure 2.26: Searching for your project template

3. Click **Next**.
4. For the name of your project, enter `TemplateTest`, and then click **Create**.
5. Review the project file with its static and global type imports, the `Program.Functions.cs` file, and the code statements in the `Program.cs` file.

Practicing and exploring

Test your knowledge and understanding by answering some questions, getting some hands-on practice, and exploring the topics covered in this chapter with deeper research.

Exercise 2.1 – Online-only material

The print book mostly covers Visual Studio and VS Code. For similar coverage of tools in Rider, you can read an online-only section at the following link: `https://github.com/markjprice/tools-skills-net10/blob/main/docs/rider/ch02-tools.md`.

To read a summary of recent improvements to Visual Studio, you can read the following article: `https://devblogs.microsoft.com/visualstudio/visual-studios-full-year-in-review-2023/`.

To read a summary of recent improvements to GitHub Copilot, you can read the following article: `https://devblogs.microsoft.com/visualstudio/github-copilot-in-visual-studio-a-recap-of-2023/`.

Developers are quickly embracing AI tools in their developer workflows, as you can see from the Stack Overflow Survey 2023 and the following links:

- AI tool sentiment: `https://survey.stackoverflow.co/2023/#section-sentiment-and-usage-ai-tool-sentiment`
- Benefits of AI tools: `https://survey.stackoverflow.co/2023/#section-developer-tools-benefits-of-ai-tools`
- AI in the development workflow: `https://survey.stackoverflow.co/2023/#section-developer-tools-ai-in-the-development-workflow`

To read about the OpenAI and Stack Overflow partnership to improve models using Stack Overflow questions and answers, you can read the following article: `https://stackoverflow.co/company/press/archive/openai-partnership`.

Exercise 2.2 – Practice exercises

Create some code snippets for your own use.

Review articles about making the most of GitHub Copilot:

- Introducing the new Copilot experience in Visual Studio: `https://devblogs.microsoft.com/visualstudio/introducing-the-new-copilot-experience-in-visual-studio/`
- How to use GitHub Copilot Chat in Visual Studio: `https://devblogs.microsoft.com/visualstudio/how-to-use-github-copilot-chat-in-visual-studio/`
- Introducing Custom Agents for .NET Developers: C# Expert & WinForms Expert: `https://devblogs.microsoft.com/dotnet/introducing-custom-agents-for-dotnet-developers-csharp-expert-winforms-expert/`
- How to use Comments to Prompt GitHub Copilot for Visual Studio: `https://devblogs.microsoft.com/visualstudio/how-to-use-comments-to-prompt-github-copilot-visual-studio/`
- Code Faster and Better with GitHub Copilot's New Features: Slash Commands and Context Variables: `https://devblogs.microsoft.com/visualstudio/copilot-chat-slash-commands-and-context-variables/`

- Mastering Slash Commands with GitHub Copilot in Visual Studio: `https://devblogs.microsoft.com/visualstudio/mastering-slash-commands-with-github-copilot-in-visual-studio/`
- GitHub Copilot for Skeptics Who Still Think AI is Overrated: `https://www.youtube.com/watch?v=anI4Hr-ag80`

Exercise 2.3 – Test your knowledge

Answer the following questions. If you get stuck, try googling the answers, if necessary, while remembering that if you get totally stuck, the answers are in the Appendix:

1. Describe the steps to use the **Change Signature** refactoring feature in Visual Studio. Include in your answer how you would access this feature and what options are available to you during the process.
2. Explain how an `.editorconfig` file is used to standardize code formatting styles. Describe what an `.editorconfig` file is and provide an example of how to set the indentation style to spaces with a size of 4.
3. What is the difference between an **expansion** and a **surrounds with** code snippet? How do you use them? Give an example of each.
4. When defining a code snippet, what is the only required attribute of the `<Code>` element, and what are some common values for that attribute?
5. To create custom project templates for the .NET SDK, which project template do you need to install?

Appendix A, Answers to the Test Your Knowledge Questions, is available to download from the following link: `https://github.com/markjprice/tools-skills-net10/blob/main/docs/B31468_Appendix%20A.pdf`.

Exercise 2.4 – Explore topics

Use the links on the following page to learn more details about the topics covered in this chapter: `https://github.com/markjprice/tools-skills-net10/blob/main/docs/book-links.md#chapter-2---making-the-most-of-the-tools-in-your-code-editor`

Summary

In this chapter, you learned:

- About tools and features common to all code editors
- How to use tools in Visual Studio
- How to use tools in VS Code
- How to decompile .NET assemblies for learning purposes
- How to create a custom project template and use it to create a new project

In the next chapter, you will learn about Git, a popular source code control and management system.

3

Source Code Management Using Git

This chapter is about **source code management (SCM)** using Git. SCM is also known as **version control** as part of a **version control system (VCS)**. Version control involves tracking and managing changes to your codebase over time, ensuring that you can revisit earlier versions, experiment safely, and collaborate effectively with others. A VCS provides the tools to handle these tasks, and Git has become the industry standard thanks to its speed, flexibility, and wide adoption.

SCM isn't just for large teams working on complex projects. Even solo developers benefit from having a detailed history of changes, the ability to roll back mistakes, and the freedom to experiment without breaking working code. For teams, version control is indispensable. It enables multiple developers to work on the same project simultaneously, manage conflicting changes, and maintain a clean, reliable codebase.

There are many graphical user interfaces for working with Git, and most code editors include integrations with Git. Since I want this chapter to work for all my readers, it will explain concepts and show examples using the Git CLI because that is consistent and works across all platforms.

Once you have learned how to control Git at the command prompt and understand its concepts, you can switch to using any GUI tool that you prefer. At the end of this chapter, I link to online-only material that show common integrations, for example, for Visual Studio. Since the GUIs change frequently, I will be able to keep them updated online.

This chapter covers the following topics:

- Introducing source code management
- Introducing Git
- Working with Git
- Reviewing Git repositories
- Managing remote repositories
- Branching and merging

Introducing source code management

SCM is a set of practices and tools that developers use to track and manage changes to their source code throughout the lifecycle of software development. SCM is essential for collaboration among developer teams to ensure the ability to revert to previous versions if issues arise with code changes.

Features of source code management

SCM has the following features:

- **Version tracking**: SCM systems keep a record of every change made to the source code. This includes additions, deletions, and modifications to individual files. Each change is associated with a unique identifier and is known as a **commit**. A developer can easily view the history of changes made to the files in the codebase.
- **Collaboration**: A team of developers often work on the same project at the same time. SCM enables collaboration by allowing developers to work with their own local copies of the code and then later merge their changes back into the central codebase. Historically, the default branch was referred to as the **master branch** but, more recently, it is more commonly referred to as the **main branch** to avoid the association with slavery. This makes it easier for a team to work on the same project, regardless of geographical location.
- **Conflict resolution**: SCM systems maintain the integrity of the codebase by providing mechanisms to resolve conflicts caused by modifications to the same part of the code made by different developers.
- **Revert and rollback**: An invaluable feature of a good SCM system is the ability to revert to previous versions of the code. For example, if a new feature implementation introduces a critical bug, developers can quickly roll back to a previous revision.
- **Traceability**: SCM systems provide traceability by recording who made changes and comments to understand why. This can be used to link code changes to specific issues or requirements.
- **Backup and disaster recovery**: Although you should also implement proper backups of your filesystems, for small teams or solo developers, the code stored in an SCM system can serve as a backup. In case of data loss or system failure, the project's source code can be recovered from the SCM system.

Good practice: Understanding SCM is crucial because it plays a significant role in modern .NET development.

Types of SCM systems

There are two main types of SCM systems, **centralized version control systems** (CVCSs) and **distributed version control systems** (DVCSs), as described in the following list:

- **Centralized:** There is a single central repository that stores the entire history of the project and all its files. Developers check out files from this central repository to work on them. They check in their changes to the central repository frequently. The central repository is the one true copy of all source code files. Centralized control provides simplified management of branching and merging because there is less divergence of changes over time. But there is a single point of failure. If something goes wrong with the central repository, then everyone is immediately affected.
- **Distributed:** Every developer working on the project has their own complete local copy of the entire repository, including its complete history of changes. Developers work independently with their local repository copies. They can make commits, branches, and merges locally over an extended period without being limited by the actions of others in the team. Collaboration occurs through pulling and pushing changes to and from remote repositories. This is when branch merges (and potential conflicts) happen. Developers can work offline and independently and there is no single point of failure. But it is harder to learn and trickier to manage in large teams.

The choice between a centralized or distributed SCM depends on the nature of the project, team size, team experience, and your preferred process. In recent years, distributed systems have become more popular due to their advantages in terms of robustness and flexibility.

Common SCM systems

Commonly used SCM tools include:

- Mercurial (distributed): `https://www.mercurial-scm.org/`
- Git (distributed): `https://git-scm.com/`
- Subversion aka SVN (centralized): `https://subversion.apache.org/`

Git is most popular due to its powerful branching and merging capabilities, flexibility, and being a distributed system. We will learn more about it in the next section.

Introducing Git

Git is the most widely used **DVCS** that plays a key role in modern software development. It was created by Linus Torvalds in 2005. Git is known for its efficiency, speed, and robust capabilities.

But Git is also known for being complex. It has memes like: `git clone`, which leads to straightforward development, and `git fork`, which leads to a complex maze, implying that forking repositories can be confusing. Two comics from the ever-popular **xkcd** are shown in *Figure 3.1*:

Figure 3.1: xkcd comics about Git

> **Git** comic link: `https://xkcd.com/1597/`
>
> **Git Commit** comic link: `https://xkcd.com/1296/`

The point is that you do not need to learn much about Git to be way ahead of most other developers. They tend to memorize a few commands and use them without deep understanding.

Features of Git

Git has many key features, including the following:

- **Distributed version control:** Git is a distributed SCM, which means that each developer working on a project has a complete copy of the entire repository, including the entire history of changes. This allows developers to work offline and independently, making it ideal for collaborative and decentralized development.
- **Branching and merging:** Git has very powerful commands to control branching and merging. Developers can create branches to work on specific features or fixes without affecting the main codebase. Once their work is complete, they can merge their changes back into the main branch.
- **History and commits:** Git maintains a detailed history of all changes made to the codebase. Each change is recorded as a commit, which includes a unique identifier, author information, date, and a commit message explaining the changes. This history provides a clear audit trail and helps in understanding how the code has evolved over time. But as the xkcd comic implies, developers can become lazy and write worse and worse comments. This is why one of the most useful features of generative AI systems is integrating them with your code editor to perform tasks like writing commit messages for the developer by looking at the actual code change submitted. Of course, the most useful information is why the change was made, which still requires the developer to make an effort.

> Most AI integrations with Git are currently seen in graphical tools and development environments. Direct integration of AI with the Git CLI isn't widespread in terms of native support, but can be achieved through custom scripts or third-party tools. AI can be used to generate commit messages based on the changes made. Tools or scripts can analyze the diffs and automatically suggest a descriptive message for the commits. AI models can help manage branching strategies by analyzing development patterns and suggesting when to branch off, merge, or rebase, optimizing the development process. AI tools can predict the impact of merging branches based on historical data, potentially warning developers of likely conflicts or integration issues before they occur.

- **Fast and efficient:** Git is designed for speed and efficiency. It can handle large codebases with millions of files and commits without significant performance issues.
- **Open source and widely adopted:** Git is open source and has a vast user base. It is supported on multiple platforms, including Windows, macOS, and various Linux distributions, so it matches the cross-platform nature of modern .NET. GitHub, supported by the multi-trillion dollar Microsoft, provides hosting and collaboration features for Git repositories, and close integration with all modern code editors.

Git is a powerful and versatile tool, and while it can seem complex initially, learning it thoroughly can greatly improve a developer's workflow and collaboration capabilities. The biggest challenge with Git is arguably that it is up to each project team to define processes and procedures for managing the flow of changes to produce your apps and services.

Why is Git hard to learn?

Using Git, especially controlling it at the command prompt, is a challenge because basic commands like committing and pushing changes are straightforward, but recovering from scenarios like accidental commits or pushes is difficult without understanding the underlying complex conceptual graph model, as highlighted in the xkcd comic in *Figure 3.1*.

That is why the most common questions on Stack Overflow are topics like undoing your last commit, changing a commit message, and deleting a branch. In this chapter, I aim to help with learning Git by going beyond what most developers pick up by osmosis without overwhelming you with too much detail. To do so, I believe that it's important to see the Git CLI commands when you first learn Git, even if you plan to only use the GUI integration tools in real life, because they help you understand what is really happening underneath your code editor.

Roles in a team for Git

There are two official roles for team members that you should know about when using Git: authors and committers. Authors write the code. Committers publish changes to the repository. You will be both at different points in the process. Knowing the official role names is useful when reading official documentation that refers to them during those different process steps.

Downloading the latest Git

You might already have Git installed on your system. Regardless, to make sure you have the latest version, you can download it for your operating system from the following link: `https://git-scm.com/downloads`.

The most recent version of Git at the time of writing in December 2025 is 2.51.1. You can confirm the current version of Git that you have installed by entering the following command at the terminal or command prompt:

```
git --version
```

On Windows, the result is shown in the following output:

```
git version 2.51.1.windows.1
```

Git integration with Visual Studio

Git is such an important part of modern development that Visual Studio has a dedicated menu item for Git, as shown in *Figure 3.2*:

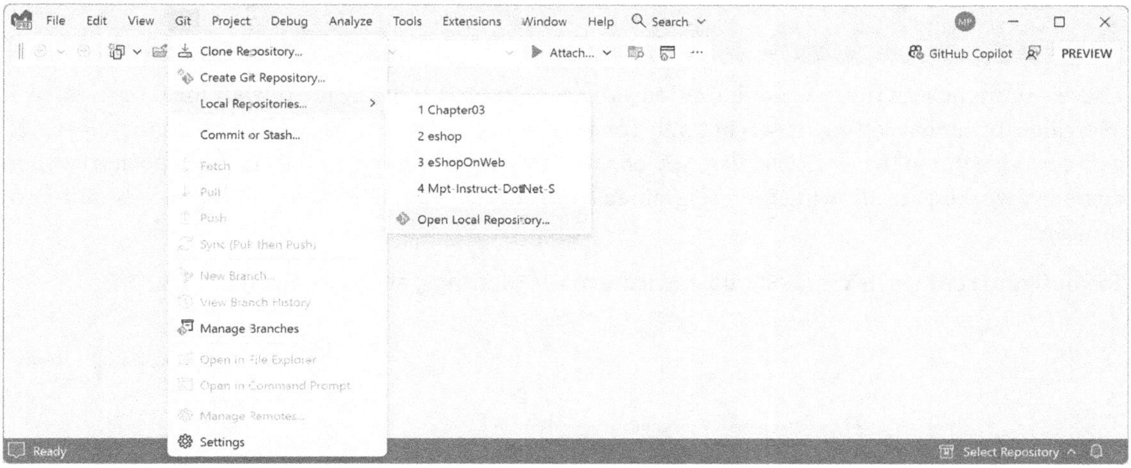

Figure 3.2: The Git menu in Visual Studio

You will see practical examples of using the Git integration with Visual Studio throughout this chapter.

Throughout this chapter, you can use either the Git CLI or Visual Studio to complete Git actions. I believe it is important to see the underlying Git commands so that you better understand what your code editor is doing for you. As well as being easier to use, Git integrations with your code editor also perform validations to make sure that you are executing commands correctly, which won't happen using the Git CLI.

Configuring your Git identity

After you install Git, you should set your name and email address. This is because every Git commit uses this information to track who made that change. At the terminal or command prompt, enter the following commands, but replace my name and email with your own:

```
git config --global user.name "Mark J Price"
git config --global user.email markjprice@gmail.com
```

You might prefer to set your name and email for individual repositories if you have different repositories for different organizations or personal projects. To do so, navigate to the repository directory, and then use the same commands but without the `--global` switch, as shown in the following commands:

```
git config user.name "Mark J Price"
git config user.email markp@corporation.com
```

These commands set the two configuration values in the `.git/config` file of your local repository. It overrides the global setting (if set) but only for actions taken within this specific repository. By using `git config` without the `--global` flag, you ensure that the settings apply only to the repository you're currently working in, allowing for fine-grained control over your Git identity settings across different projects.

To configure settings in Visual Studio, navigate to **Git** | **Settings**, as shown in *Figure 3.3*:

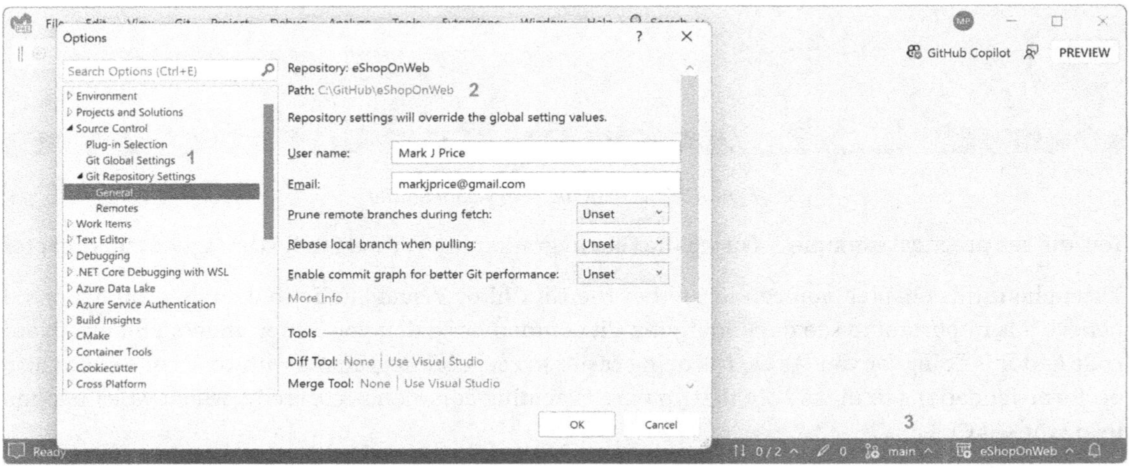

Figure 3.3: Configuring Git settings in Visual Studio

Note that you can configure the following via the **Options** dialog box, as shown in *Figure 3.3*:

1. Global Git settings
2. Repository-specific settings
3. Git status bar functionality

Configuring SSH signature enforcement

Enforcing SSH signatures in Git involves configuring your Git server to require that all Git operations (like pushing commits) are performed using SSH keys, and potentially setting up SSH signatures for verification. If you do not need this enforcement, then you can skip this section.

> **Good practice:** Enforcing SSH and using SSH signatures are advanced security measures that ensure that both the identity of the committer is verified and that the commit itself has not been tampered with since it was created.

The specific process varies based on the environment you're using, like GitHub or a self-hosted Git server, so let's just review the general steps:

1. **Setup SSH keys:** Make sure that you and every other Git user on your team has an SSH key pair generated and ready for use. To generate an SSH key pair, use each Git user's email as a label and the Ed25519 algorithm, which is modern and secure, as shown in the following command:

```
ssh-keygen -t ed25519 -C "your_email@example.com"
```

> `ssh-keygen` is available on Windows, as well as on Mac and Linux. This tool is part of the OpenSSH suite, which has become the standard for SSH operations across various operating systems.

> **Good practice:** The `-t ed25519` option specifies the use of the Ed25519 algorithm, which is recommended for its security and performance. Alternatively, RSA can be used with a recommended key size of at least 2,048 bits: `-t rsa -b 2048`.

2. **Add public keys to Git server:** Each Git user on your team must add their public SSH key to their account on the Git server. This is typically done through the Git server's user settings. For GitHub, navigate to **Settings** | **SSH and GPG keys** | **New SSH key**.
3. **Enforce SSH for repository access:** On the server, configure the repository settings to reject non-SSH connections for operations like `git push` or `git fetch`. This setting depends on the server. For GitHub, select SSH URLs for repository operations and disable them or not using HTTPS URLs.
4. **SSH signatures (commit signing with SSH keys):** Git version 2.34 introduced the ability to sign commits using SSH keys, providing a way to verify the authorship of commits like GPG signing but using SSH keys. Ensure your Git is updated and configure it to use your SSH key for signing commits, as shown in the following command:

```
git config --global user.signingkey <your-ssh-public-key-id>
git config --global commit.gpgformat ssh
```

You can now sign commits using the `-S` switch, as shown in the following command:

```
git commit -S -m "your commit message"
```

You can then verify the signatures, as shown in the following command:

```
git log --show-signature
```

To enforce SSH signatures server-side, you might need to use server-side hooks, such as pre-receive hooks in Git, to check for a valid SSH signature before accepting changes into the repository. This feature might not be supported directly out of the box on all platforms, and some configuration or script might be necessary to validate signatures.

Configuring your default branch

Let's check your default configuration and the files it is defined in, as shown in the following command:

```
git config --list --show-origin
```

Note the results, including the name and email you set in the previous section, and the default branch name of `master`, as shown highlighted in the following partial output:

```
file:C:/Program Files/Git/etc/gitconfig diff.astextplain.textconv=astextplain
...
file:C:/Program Files/Git/etc/gitconfig init.defaultbranch=master
...
file:C:/Users/markj/.gitconfig user.name=Mark J Price
file:C:/Users/markj/.gitconfig user.email=markjprice@gmail.com
```

Some configurations are set in a file where Git is installed and some configurations are set in a user file.

To change the default branch from `master` to something less culturally insensitive, like `main`, use the following command:

```
git config --global init.defaultBranch main
```

Git uses the last value for each unique key it sees so user configuration overrides application configuration.

Getting help for Git

To open a webpage with help for a Git command, use one of the following two commands:

```
git help <command>
git <command> --help
```

To get a command switch summary, use the following command:

```
git <command> -h
```

Now that you've set up Git locally and learned about some of the key concepts of Git, let's dive into some hands-on tasks to get started and work with a Git repository.

Working with Git

In this section you will learn how to start a Git repository, how to add files to it, how changes are tracked, how to commit files, how to undo commits, and how to stash and ignore files.

Starting with a Git repository

Ignoring the tool you use to do so, there are two ways to start with a Git repository:

- Cloning a remote Git repository to a local directory
- Initializing a repository in a local non-Git directory

To clone an existing repository into a directory, create and change to the target directory, and then use the `clone` Git command, as shown in the following command:

```
git clone https://github.com/markjprice/tools-skills-net10
```

To initialize a repository in a local non-Git directory, change to the directory, and then initialize a Git repository in that directory, as shown in the following command:

```
git init
```

The `init` Git command creates a new hidden subdirectory named `.git` that contains the needed Git repository files, as shown in the following output:

```
Initialized empty Git repository in C:/tools-skills-net10/Chapter03/RepoDemo/.
git/
```

In Visual Studio, you can either navigate to **Git** | **Create New Repository...** (if you do not currently have a repository active), or click the repository button in the status bar, then click the three dots button, and then click **Create Git Repository...**, as shown in *Figure 3.4*:

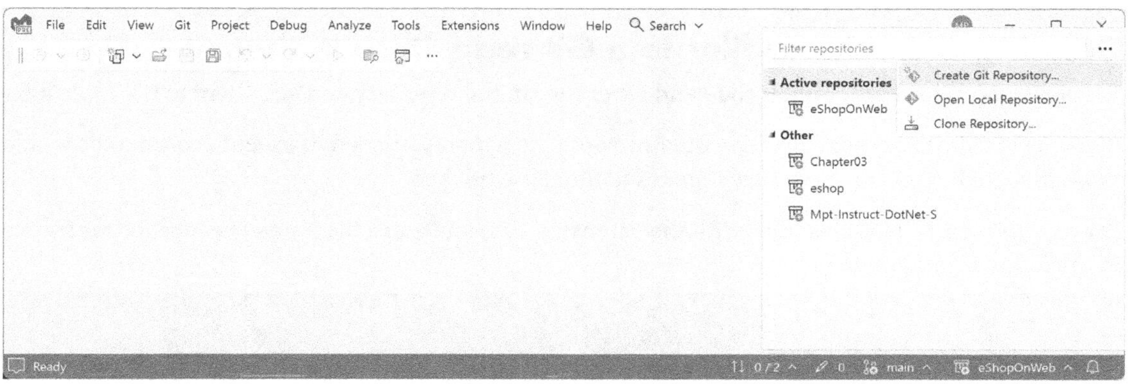

Figure 3.4: Menu to create a new Git repository in Visual Studio

Next, complete the **Create a Git repository** dialog box, as shown in *Figure 3.5*:

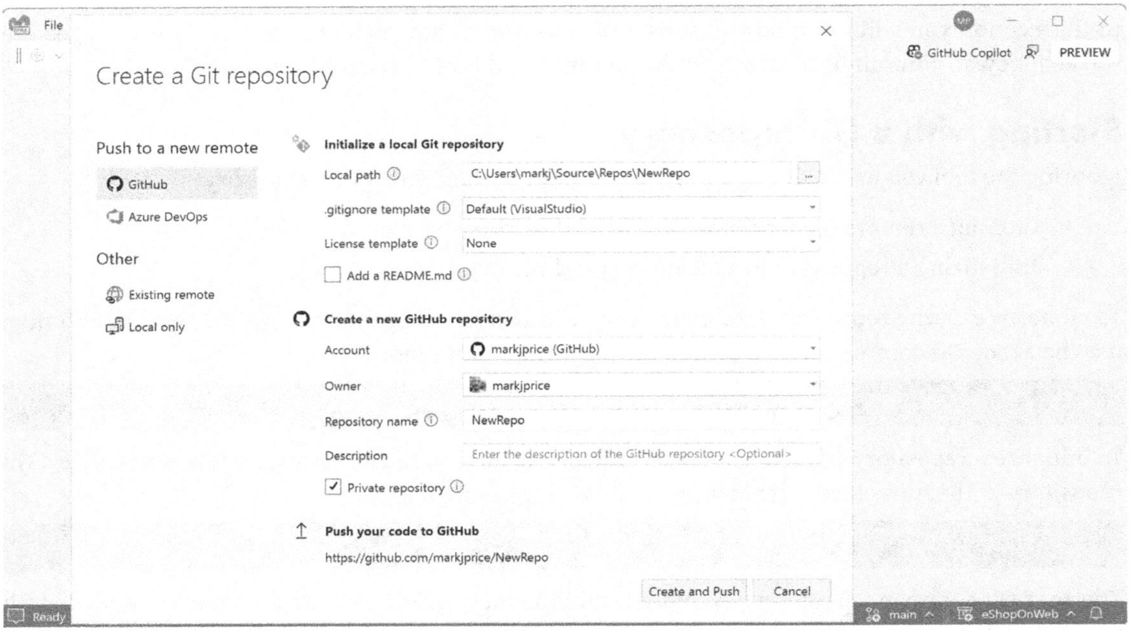

Figure 3.5: Creating a new Git repository in Visual Studio

Select **Local only** to hide the options for creating the repository remotely on GitHub as well as locally.

Creating and adding files to a Git repository in theory

The next step is to create source code and other files in the directory and add them to the repository.

If you have a directory that already contains some files, then you need to execute commands to add those files to the repository so that changes to them are tracked.

For example, add all C# files (files with the extension `.cs`) and add a file named `readme.md`, as shown in the following commands:

```
git add *.cs
git add readme.md
```

After adding files, you must commit them to the local repository, preferably with a message specified using the `-m` switch, as shown in the following command:

```
git commit -m 'Initial version'
```

Tracking changes in Git

A file in a directory used as a Git repository can be in one of four states, as described in *Table 3.1*:

State	Description
Untracked	A file in the directory for which Git is not tracking versions.
Staged	A file that has been added to the Git repository but not yet committed. For example, by using the `git add` command.
Unmodified	A file that is being tracked by Git because it has been added and committed.
Modified	A file that is being tracked by Git because it has been added and committed, and it has had changes made to it.

Table 3.1: File states in a Git repository

A diagram summarizing state flow is shown in *Figure 3.6*:

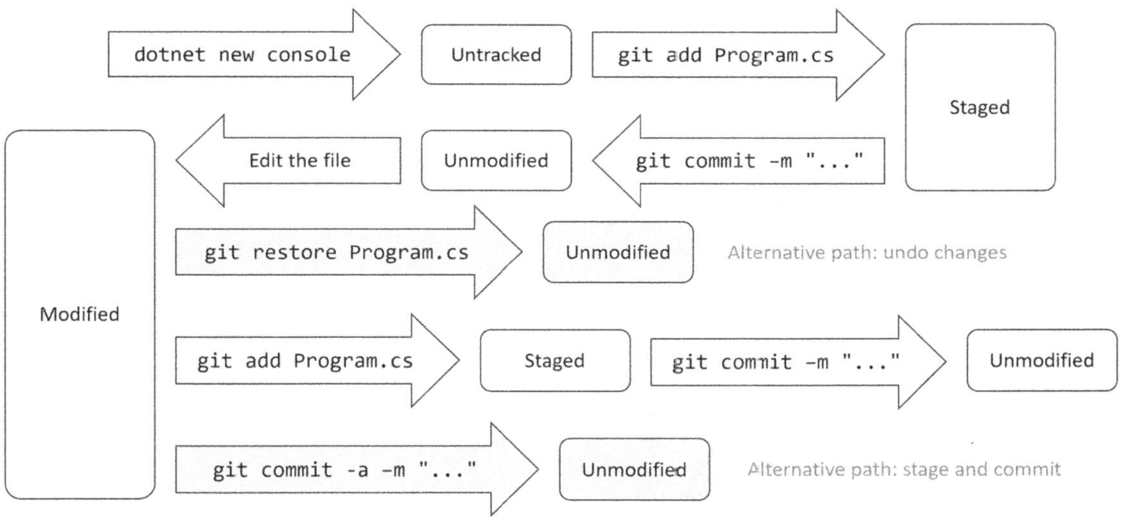

Figure 3.6: Flow of file states with Git

You can skip the staging area by adding the `-a` switch to the `commit` command. This will add (aka stage) all the modified files that are currently tracked before then committing them.

Let's see some of this flow in action.

Creating a Git repository in practice

To use the Git CLI:

1. Make a directory named `Chapter03` in the `tools-skills-net10` directory.
2. Using your preferred command prompt, change to the `Chapter03` directory.
3. Get the current Git status of the `Chapter03` directory, as shown in the following command:

```
git status
```

4. Note the result, as shown in the following output:

```
fatal: not a git repository (or any of the parent directories): .git
```

5. Initialize the `Chapter03` directory to become a Git repository:

```
git init
```

6. Note the result, as shown in the following output:

```
Initialized empty Git repository in C:/tools-skills-net10/Chapter03/.git/
```

To use Visual Studio:

1. Start **Visual Studio** (close it first if it is already running).
2. In the **Start** dialog, click **Continue without code.**
3. Navigate to **Git** | **Create Git Repository....**
4. In the **Create a Git repository** dialog box, click **Local only**, and then set options to initialize a local Git repository:
    - **Local path:** `C:\tools-skills-net10\Chapter03`
    - **.gitignore template: No .gitignore** (we will add one later)
    - **License template: None**
    - **Add a README.md:** Cleared
5. Click the **Create** button.

Creating a new project

Now we will create and add files for a new project.

To use the CLI tools:

1. Create a new console app in a subfolder named `RepoDemo`, as shown in the following command:

```
dotnet new console -o RepoDemo
```

2. Create a solution file named `Chapter03.sln` and add the `RepoDemo` project to it, as shown in the following commands:

```
dotnet new sln
dotnet sln add RepoDemo
```

3. Get the current Git status of the `Chapter03` directory, as shown in the following command:

```
git status
```

4. Note the result, as shown in the following output:

```
On branch main
No commits yet
Untracked files:
  (use "git add <file>..." to include in what will be committed)
        RepoDemo/
nothing added to commit but untracked files present (use "git add" to
track)
```

5. Stage the `RepoDemo` folder and all its files, as shown in the following command:

```
git add RepoDemo
```

6. Get the current Git status of the `Chapter03` directory, as shown in the following command:

```
git status
```

7. Note the result, as shown in the following output:

```
On branch main
No commits yet
Changes to be committed:
  (use "git rm --cached <file>..." to unstage)
        new file:   RepoDemo/Program.cs
        new file:   RepoDemo/RepoDemo.csproj
        new file:   RepoDemo/obj/RepoDemo.csproj.nuget.dgspec.json
        new file:   RepoDemo/obj/RepoDemo.csproj.nuget.g.props
        new file:   RepoDemo/obj/RepoDemo.csproj.nuget.g.targets
        new file:   RepoDemo/obj/project.assets.json
        new file:   RepoDemo/obj/project.nuget.cache
```

> **Good practice:** Whoops! We do not want to include the files in the `obj` directory because they are not source code. They are automatically generated by the Roslyn C# compiler.

8. Unstage all the files in the `RepoDemo` directory recursively (using the `-r` switch), as shown in the following command:

```
git rm --cached RepoDemo -r
```

9. Stage just the two important source code files in the `RepoDemo` folder, as shown in the following two commands:

```
git add RepoDemo/Program.cs
git add RepoDemo/RepoDemo.csproj
git add Chapter03.sln
```

10. Get the current Git status of the `Chapter03` directory, as shown in the following command:

```
git status
```

11. Note the result, as shown in the following output:

```
On branch main
No commits yet
Changes to be committed:
  (use "git rm --cached <file>..." to unstage)
        new file:   RepoDemo/Program.cs
        new file:   RepoDemo/RepoDemo.csproj
        new file:   Chapter03.sln
Untracked files:
  (use "git add <file>..." to include in what will be committed)
        RepoDemo/obj/
```

12. Get the current Git status of the `Chapter03` directory using the short switch, `-s`, which shows that status in a more concise format, as shown in the following command:

```
git status -s
```

13. Note the result, as shown in the following output:

```
A  RepoDemo/Program.cs
A  RepoDemo/RepoDemo.csproj
A  Chapter03.sln
?? RepoDemo/obj/
```

On the left are one or two characters: the left character indicates the status of the staging area, and the right character indicates the status of the working tree. ? means there is an untracked file in either the staging area or working tree, depending on if it is on the left or right. `A` means staged (added) and `M` means modified. In the preceding example output, no files are modified so you won't see an `M`.

To use Visual Studio:

1. In Visual Studio, navigate to **File** | **New** | **Project...**.
2. Select **Console App** and then click **Next**.
3. Complete the **Configure your new project** dialog box, as shown in *Figure 3.7*:

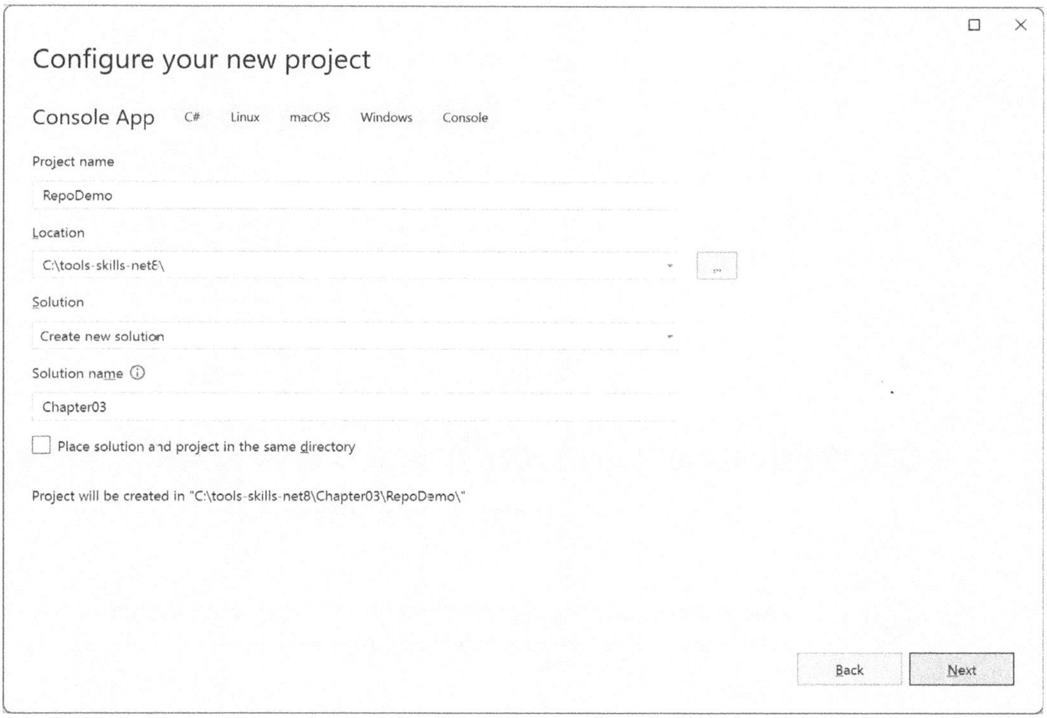

Figure 3.7: Creating a console app project and solution

4. Click **Next** and then click **Create**.

5. In the status bar, click the **Changes** button, and then in the **Git Changes** window, review the changes, as shown in *Figure 3.8*:

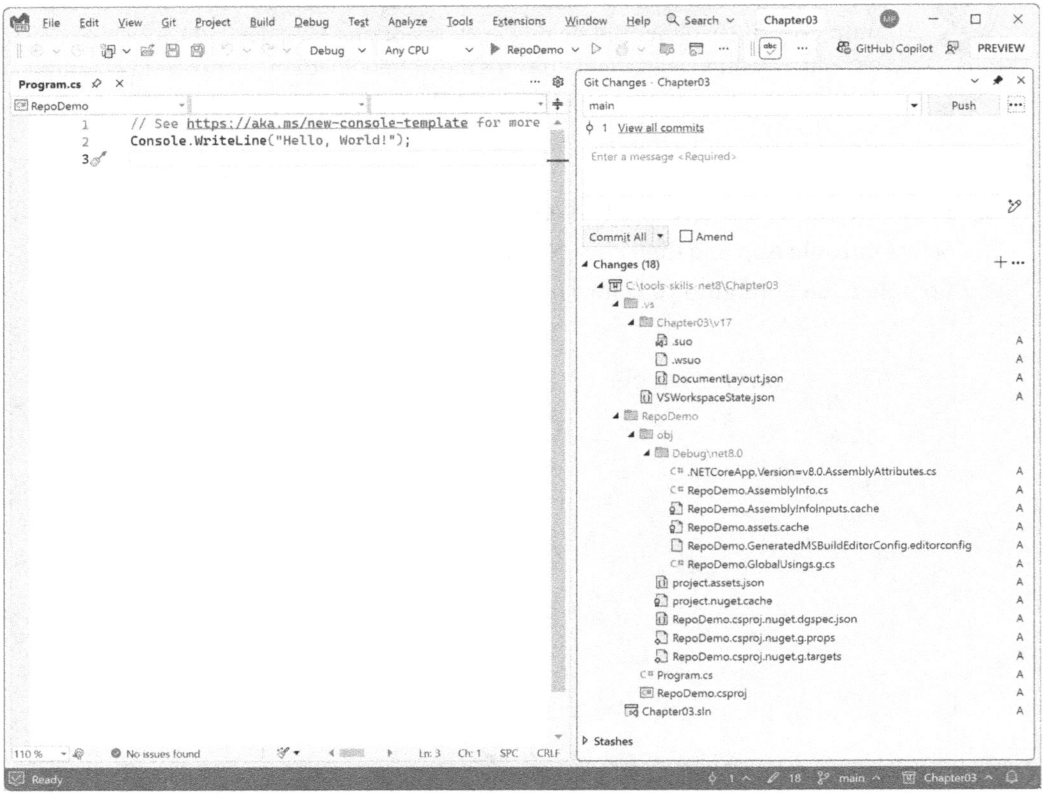

Figure 3.8: Git Changes in Visual Studio

Good practice: Accidentally adding more files than you meant to is why it is important to add a `.gitignore` file! We will do this later.

6. Hover your mouse over `Program.cs` and then click the + icon to stage it, and repeat for the `RepoDemo.csproj` and `Chapter03.sln` files so that you then have three staged files, as shown in *Figure 3.9*:

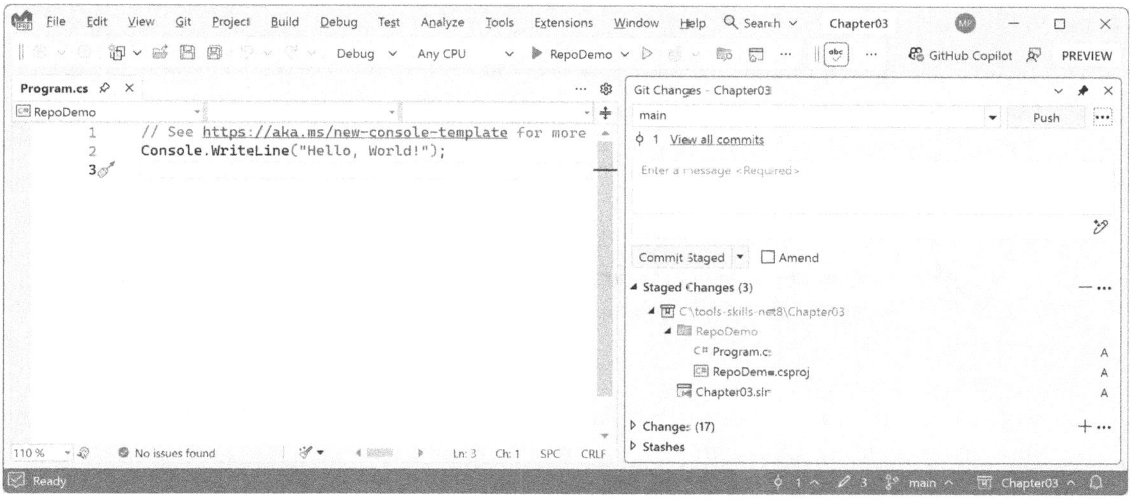

Figure 3.9: Staged files in Visual Studio

Staging the files is just part of the process. Next, we need to commit them.

Committing files

Now we will commit the changes to the staged files.

To use Git the CLI:

1. Commit the two files with a message, as shown in the following command:

```
git commit -m "Initial version"
```

2. Note the result, as shown in the following output:

```
[main (root-commit) 6549a99] Initial version
 3 files changed, 63 insertions(+)
 create mode 100644 RepoDemo/Program.cs
 create mode 100644 RepoDemo/RepoDemo.csproj
 create mode 100644 Chapter03.sln
```

When you commit changes to a repository, you're making a snapshot that you can revert to or compare to later.

To use Visual Studio:

1. At the top of the **Git Changes** window, enter a message, `Initial version`, and then click the **Commit Staged** button. (Note the pencil with sparkle button to add an AI-generated commit message, as shown in *Figure 3.10* with the red arrow pointing to the right. You will use this in a subsequent section.)

> The button is labeled **Commit Staged** because we selected a subset of the modified files to stage. If you do not stage any files, then the button is labeled **Commit All**.

2. Note the result is that a local commit was made successfully, as shown in *Figure 3.10* with the blue arrow pointing to the left:

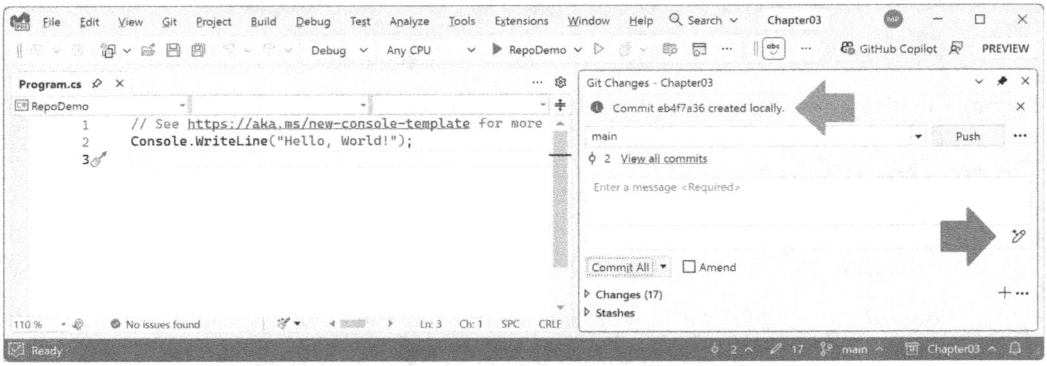

Figure 3.10: Committed information message in Visual Studio

3. Click **View all commits**, and in the **Git Repository - Chapter 3 (main)** window, note the most recent commit is at the top with its **Initial version** message, as shown in *Figure 3.11*:

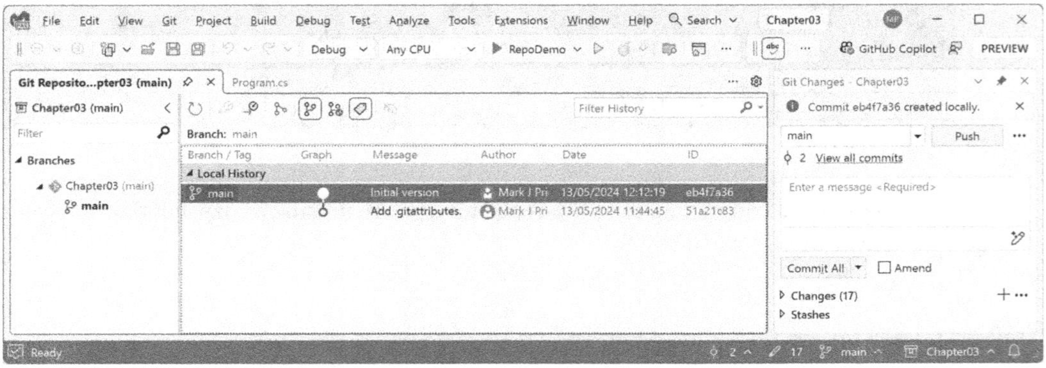

Figure 3.11: Git Repository window in Visual Studio

Undoing a commit

Undoing a Git commit can be done in several ways, depending on what exactly you want to achieve. A few common methods are shown in *Table 3.2*:

Git command	Description
`git reset --soft HEAD`	**Soft Reset:** Undoes the last commit but keeps your changes in the staging area. You can redo the commit message or make additional changes to the staged files.
`git reset HEAD`	**Mixed Reset:** Undoes the last commit and unstages the changes, but the changes are still in your working directory. You can edit these changes before recommitting.
`git reset --hard HEAD`	**Hard Reset:** This completely removes the last commit, along with any changes in the working directory. **Warning!** Potential loss of work.
`git revert <commit_hash>`	**Revert Commit:** Creates a new commit that undoes all changes made in the specified commit. This is the safest option, especially when working in a shared repository, as it doesn't rewrite the commit history.
`git commit --amend`	**Amend Commit:** Replaces the last commit with a new one, for example, to fix a typo in the commit message. This alters the commit history, so use it with caution in shared repositories.

Table 3.2: Git commands for undoing a commit

Choose the method based on your needs:

- If you're working alone and want to completely discard the last commit, use a hard reset
- If you want to keep the changes for further modification, use a soft or mixed reset
- If you're working in a shared environment and want to undo changes in a safe way that doesn't rewrite history, use `revert` or `amend`

To undo a commit in Visual Studio, in the **Git Repository** window, right-click a commit to see options, including to reset and delete changes, as shown in *Figure 3.12*:

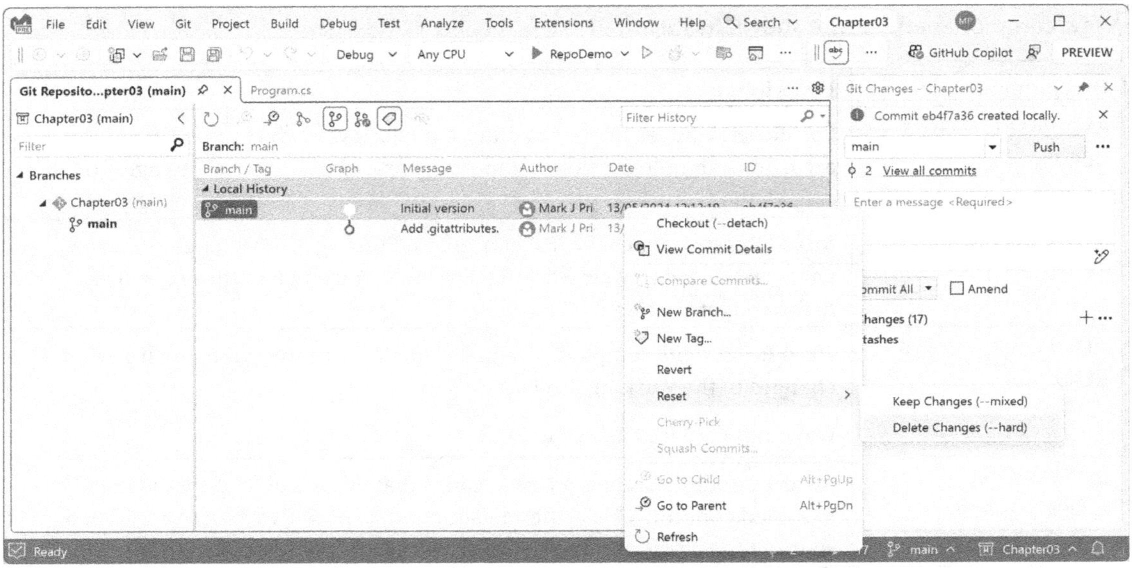

Figure 3.12: Menu for a Git commit including revert and reset options

Cleaning a commit

When you need to clean your working directory by removing files that should not be tracked by Git, like build residues or temporary files created by merge conflicts, use `git clean`.

`git clean` will permanently delete files that are not part of the index (staging area) nor included in any commit. This is useful for maintaining a clean working environment.

`git clean -d` can be used to remove untracked directories in addition to untracked files.

> **Warning!** `git clean` can be very destructive if used recklessly, as it permanently deletes files. Thus, it is often run with the `-n` option first to perform a dry run showing which files will be deleted, followed by the `-f` option to force the actual file deletion.

Always ensure you have backups or that your data is safely committed elsewhere before using these commands on important files.

Stashing

In Git, **stashing** is a handy feature that helps you temporarily save your modified and staged changes without committing them, allowing you to switch contexts and work on something else. It's particularly useful in scenarios where you are not ready to commit changes but need a clean working directory, for example, to switch branches or pull down updates.

When you run a stash command, Git takes both your staged and unstaged changes, saves them on a stack-like structure, aka the stash, and then reverts your working directory to match the HEAD commit. The changes are not lost; they're just set aside.

There are many reasons why you might want to stash, including the following common uses:

- **Context switching.** If you need to quickly switch to another branch to work on something else, you can stash your current changes, move to the other branch, and come back later and reapply the stashed changes.
- **Pulling updates.** If you have local changes that might conflict with upstream changes, you can stash your work, pull down the latest updates, and then reapply your stashed changes.
- **Experimenting.** If you want to experiment with something and aren't sure if you'll keep the changes, you can stash your current work, try out your ideas, and either restore the stashed work or discard it.

The basic commands for stashing are shown in *Table 3.3*:

Command	Description	Example
Stashing changes	You can use the `-m` switch to add a descriptive message to the stash entry for easier identification. If no changes are specified, `git stash` will stash all changes by default.	`git stash push -m "A descriptive message for the stash"`
Listing stashes	This command displays the list of stashed changes. Each entry is indexed and includes the message, if one was provided.	`git stash list`
Applying the last stash	This command re-applies the last stashed changes but does not remove the entry from the stash list.	`git stash apply`
Applying a stash	You can apply a specific stash by specifying its index.	`git stash apply stash@{0}`
Popping a stash	This applies the last stashed changes and then removes the entry from the stash list. Like apply, you can specify a stash index.	`git stash pop`
Dropping a stash	This command removes a specific stash entry from the list. If no index is specified, the last stash is dropped.	`git stash drop stash@{0}`
Clearing all stashes	This removes all stashed entries.	`git stash clear`

Table 3.3: Basic commands for stashing

You can stash specific files or changes by using `git stash push your_file.txt`, which only stashes changes related to the specified files.

Good practice: Frequent stashing can lead to a cluttered stash list. Regularly review and clean up old stashes to maintain clarity. Stashed changes are local to your repository; they are not transferred to the server when you push. If you rely heavily on stashes, ensure you have backups in case of machine failure.

Stashing will help you manage multiple work contexts in Git, keeping your working directory clean and your progress safe while you tackle different tasks.

In Visual Studio, in the **Git Changes** window, the **Commit All/Commit Staged** button has additional options for stashing, including:

- **Stash All** (`--include-untracked`)
- **Stash All and Keep Staged** (`--keep-index`)

Ignoring files

We never want to stage or commit files generated by the Roslyn C# compiler, for example, files in the `obj` or `bin` directories. We can create a file named `.gitignore` to control what files are excluded.

The rules for a `.gitignore` file are shown in the following list:

- Blank lines or lines starting with # are ignored.
- Use simplified regular expressions. For example, * matches zero or more characters, `[aeiou]` matches any character inside the brackets, and ? matches a single character.
- By default, the patterns will be applied recursively throughout the directory hierarchy. Start patterns with / to avoid recursion.
- End patterns with / to specify a directory. Use ** to match nested directories, for example, `a/**/z` would match `a/c/z` and `a/d/e/f/z`.
- Negate a pattern by starting it with `!`.

An example is shown in the following file:

```
# Ignore all files with .nuget. in its filename, like project.nuget.cache
# and RepoDemo.csproj.nuget.dgspec.json.
*.nuget.*
# Ignore all .pdf files in the doc directory and its descendants.
doc/**/*.pdf
# Ignore all files in directories named obj and bin.
obj/
bin/
```

> You can find a comprehensive set of sample `.gitignore` files at the following link: https://github.com/github/gitignore.

The .NET SDK CLI can create a suitable `.gitignore` file for you that works well for .NET projects. Visual Studio can also create one when you first create the Git repository, but we did not select that option.

Let's see how to add one if a Git repository already exists:

1. In the `Chapter03` directory, at the terminal or command prompt, create a `.gitignore` file using the .NET SDK CLI, as shown in the following command:

```
dotnet new gitignore
```

2. Open the file with your preferred text editor, and note its contents, as shown in the following partial file:

```
## Ignore Visual Studio temporary files, build results, and
## files generated by popular Visual Studio add-ons.
##
## Get latest from `dotnet new gitignore`
# dotenv files
.env
# User-specific files
*.rsuser
*.suo
*.user
*.userosscache
*.sln.docstates
# Build results
[Dd]ebug/
[Dd]ebugPublic/
[Rr]elease/
[Rr]eleases/
...
[Bb]in/
[Oo]bj/
[Ll]og/
[Ll]ogs/
...
```

3. Close the file.

4. Get the current Git status of the `Chapter03` directory, as shown in the following command:

```
git status
```

5. Note the result is that the files in the `obj` directory are now ignored and the new `.gitignore` file is recognized, as shown in the following output:

```
On branch main
Untracked files:
  (use "git add <file>..." to include in what will be committed)
        .gitignore
nothing added to commit but untracked files present (use "git add" to
track)
```

Good practice: A `.gitignore` file should be committed to the repository itself, so its rules apply to all members of your project team. You should also customize the `.gitignore` file to the specific needs of your project and not just use a generic template without reviewing it.

6. If you want to use the Git CLI, add and then commit the Git ignore file, as shown in the following commands:

```
git add .gitignore
git commit -m "Add Git ignore file."
```

7. In Visual Studio, note that all the compiler-generated files are now ignored, but we need to commit the new `.gitignore` file. This is a good opportunity to try the AI-generated commit message, so click the magic button (remember I told you earlier to note the pencil with sparkle button?) and review the suggested message, as shown in *Figure 3.13*:

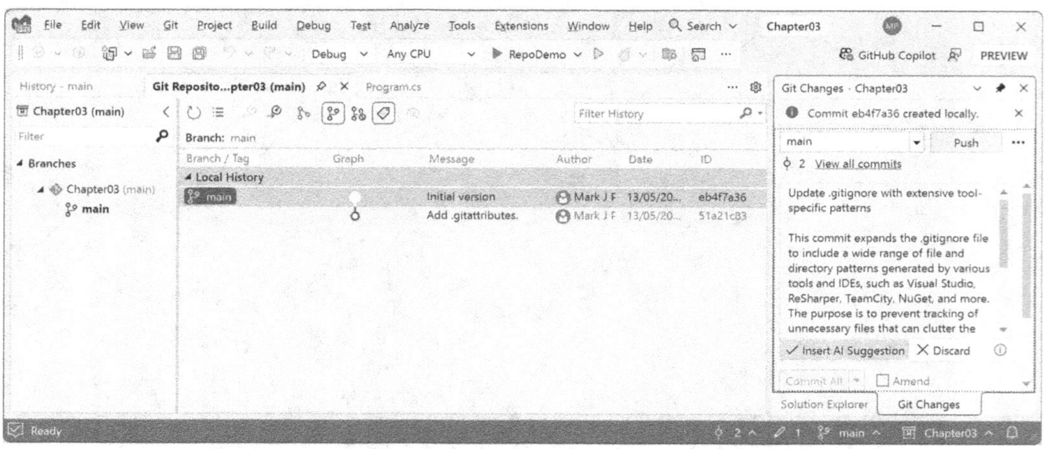

Figure 3.13: Committing a .gitignore file in Visual Studio

8. Click **Insert AI Suggestion**, or click **Discard** and then enter your own message.
9. Click the **Commit All** button.

Reviewing Git repositories

While working with Git repositories, you often want to review the changes you've made. For example, differences in files, commit history, and log output.

Viewing differences in files

You often want to know what you have changed but not yet staged and what you have staged but not yet committed. To find out, you can use the `git diff` command, which shows the code statements added and removed, also known as the **patch**.

Let's see an example:

1. To make it easier to work with the solution and project, open the `Chapter03` solution file in Visual Studio or Rider, or open the `Chapter03` folder in VS Code.
2. In the `RepoDemo` project, using your preferred code editor, in `Program.cs`, change the message from `Hello, World!` to `Hello, Git!`, as shown highlighted in the following code:

```
Console.WriteLine("Hello, Git!");
```

3. Save changes to the file.
4. At the terminal or command prompt, show the differences, as shown in the following command:

```
git diff
```

5. Note the results, as shown in the following output and in *Figure 3.14*:

```
diff --git a/RepoDemo/Program.cs b/RepoDemo/Program.cs
index 3751555..4ec9f4e 100644
--- a/RepoDemo/Program.cs
+++ b/RepoDemo/Program.cs
@@ -1,2 +1,2 @@
 // See https://aka.ms/new-console-template for more information
-Console.WriteLine("Hello, World!");
+Console.WriteLine("Hello, Git!");
```

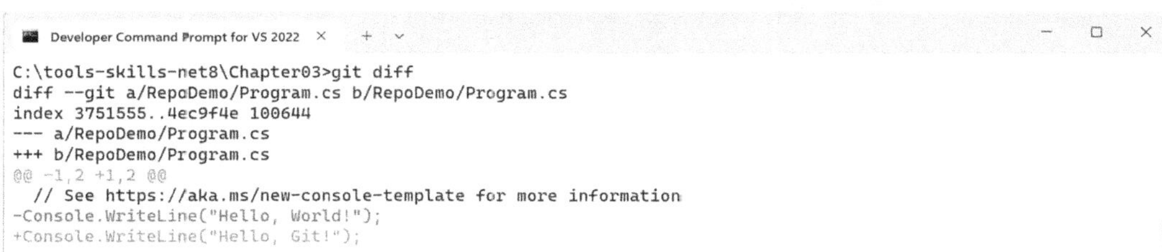

Figure 3.14: Showing differences at the command prompt

6. If you are using Visual Studio, then navigate to **View** | **Git Changes** and select **Program.cs**, as shown in *Figure 3.15*:

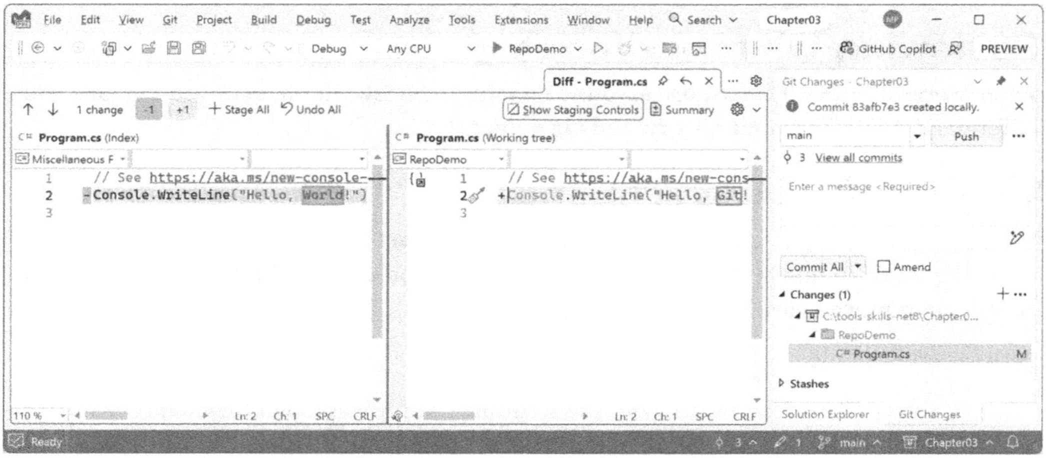

Figure 3.15: Showing differences in Visual Studio

7. If you are using VS Code, then navigate to **View** | **Source Control** and select **Program.cs**, as shown in *Figure 3.16*:

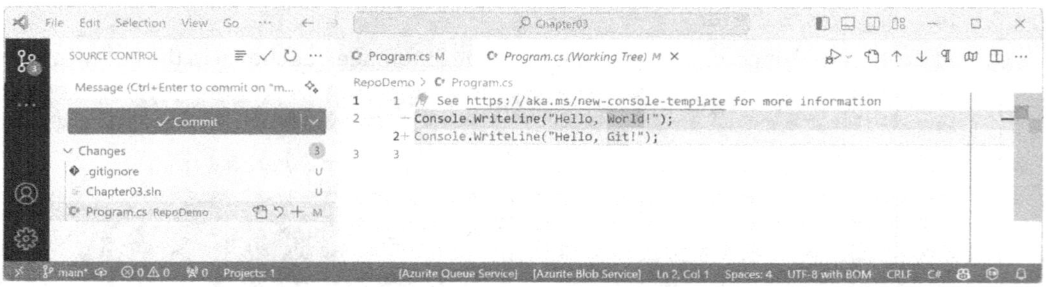

Figure 3.16: Showing differences in VS Code

> VS Code shows the two untracked files, `.gitignore` and `Chapter03.sln`, with a `U` character, and it shows the modified `Program.cs` file with an `M` character. When hovering over a file, the + button will stage the file and the undo arrow will discard changes.

8. Show what differences are currently staged, as shown in the following command:

```
git diff --staged
```

> The `--staged` and `--cached` switches mean the same thing so you can use either.

9. Note that nothing is currently staged. (In Visual Studio, the **Git Changes** window has a **Staged Changes** section that will be hidden when there are no staged changes.)
10. Stage the changes to `Program.cs`, as shown in the following command:

```
git add RepoDemo/Program.cs
```

Show what differences are currently staged, as shown in the following command:

```
git diff --staged
```

11. Note that you will see the first page of the results. When you see a colon (`:`), you can press *Page Down* to see the next page. You can press *Page Up* to go back a page. You can press *Q* to exit the pager at any time.
12. When you see `(END)`, then press *Q* to exit the pager.

> By default, Git uses a pager to show long results at the terminal or command prompt. You can disable this using the `--no-pager` switch immediately after the `git` command. For example, `git --no-pager diff --staged`.

13. Commit the changes with a message, as shown in the following command:

```
git commit -m "Changed output to say Hello Git."
```

14. Note the results for the `main` branch, as shown in the following output:

```
[main 6d2287d] Changed output to say Hello Git.
1 file changed, 1 insertion(+), 1 deletion(-)
```

15. If you were now to issue `diff` or `diff --staged` commands, then you would see nothing. If you issue a `git status` command, then you will see that your repository is up to date, as shown in the following output:

```
On branch main
nothing to commit, working tree clean
```

Viewing your commit history

Once you start committing, you will want to view the commit history. You do so using `git log`. It has many options, as shown in *Table 3.4*:

Switch	Description
`--patch` or `-p`	Show the details of the patches (additions, modifications, deletions). Limit the number with `-<number>`, for example, `-3` for the most recent three patches.
`--stat` and `--shortstat`	Show statistics about the commits.
`--name-status`	Show the list of changed files with added/modified/deleted information.
`--pretty`	Show in an alternate format, like `oneline`, `fuller`, and `format`, where you specify a custom format using special placeholders.
`--graph`	Display an ASCII graph of the branch and merge history.

Table 3.4: Common switches for the git log command

Let's see some examples:

1. Show the commit history, as shown in the following command:

```
git log
```

2. Note the results that show the two commits we have performed so far, in reverse-chronological order (most recent at the top), with each commit including its SHA-1 checksum, the author's name and email, the time stamp that the commit was written, and the commit message, as shown in the following output:

```
commit 6d2287d3ea630448f1bb112406b1834366652467 (HEAD -> main)
Author: Mark J Price <markjprice@gmail.com>
Date:   Tue Jan 30 11:17:45 2024 +0000
    Changed output to say Hello Git and add solution and Git ignore
files.
commit a4aa9557b71137a612cf7df430b3ad3c9faa3fde
Author: Mark J Price <markjprice@gmail.com>
Date:   Tue Jan 30 09:25:55 2024 +0000
    Initial version
```

A SHA-1 (Secure Hash Algorithm 1) checksum is a type of cryptographic hash function designed to create a unique, fixed-size (160-bit) hash value from input data of any size. This hash function is often used to verify data integrity. The SHA-1 hash is typically expressed as a 40-digit hexadecimal number. You will see a SHA algorithm in action in *Chapter 8, Protecting Data and Apps Using Cryptography*.

3. Show the commit history with the most recent three patches, as shown in the following command:

```
git log -p -3
```

4. Note the results show the details of the changes. Remember that you can page up and down, and you can quit the pager by pressing *Q*.
5. Show the commit history statistics, as shown in the following command:

```
git log --stat
```

6. Note the results that show the two commits we have performed so far, with statistics about the number of lines inserted or deleted (a modification would count as one insertion and one deletion, so two changes, for example, `RepoDemo/Program.cs | 2 +-`), as shown highlighted in the following output:

```
commit 6d2287d3ea630448f1bb112406b1834366652467 (HEAD -> main)
Author: Mark J Price <markjprice@gmail.com>
Date:   Tue Jan 30 11:17:45 2024 +0000
    Changed output to say Hello Git and add solution and Git ignore
files.
 .gitignore | 484 ++++++++++++++++++++++++++++++++++++++++++++++++++++
 Chapter03.sln | 25 +++
 RepoDemo/Program.cs | 2 +-
 3 files changed, 510 insertions(+), 1 deletion(-)
commit a4aa9557b71137a612cf7df430b3ad3c9faa3fde
Author: Mark J Price <markjprice@gmail.com>
Date:   Tue Jan 30 09:25:55 2024 +0000
    Initial version
 RepoDemo/Program.cs | 2 ++
 RepoDemo/RepoDemo.csproj | 10 ++++++++++
 2 files changed, 12 insertions(+)
```

7. Show the commit history statistics, as shown in the following command:

```
git log --pretty=oneline
```

8. Note the results that show the two commits we have performed so far, with only the messages, as shown in the following output:

```
6d2287d3ea630448f1bb112406b1834366652467 (HEAD -> main) Changed output to
say Hello Git and add solution and Git ignore files.
a4aa9557b71137a612cf7df430b3ad3c9faa3fde Initial version
```

> Other choices for `--pretty` include `short`, `medium`, `full`, and `fuller`. Try them all to see the differences. To take complete control, use `format:"<custom-format>"`. This is documented at the following link: `https://git-scm.com/docs/pretty-formats`.

9. Show the commit history with a custom format that shows the full commit hash (`%H`), the author's name (`%an`) in blue (`%Cblue`, `%Creset`), the author timestamp in ISO 8601 format (`%ai`), and then a new line (`%n`) with the commit message (`%s`), as shown in the following command:

```
git log --pretty=format:"Author of %H was %Cblue%an%Creset, at
%ai%nMessage: %s%n"
```

10. Note the results that show the two commits we have performed so far, with only the messages, as shown in the following output and *Figure 3.17*:

```
Author of 6d2287d3ea630448f1bb112406b1834366652467 was Mark J Price, at
2024-01-30 11:17:45 +0000
Message: Changed output to say Hello Git and add solution and Git ignore
files.
Author of a4aa9557b71137a612cf7df430b3ad3c9faa3fde was Mark J Price, at
2024-01-30 09:25:55 +0000
Message: Initial version
```

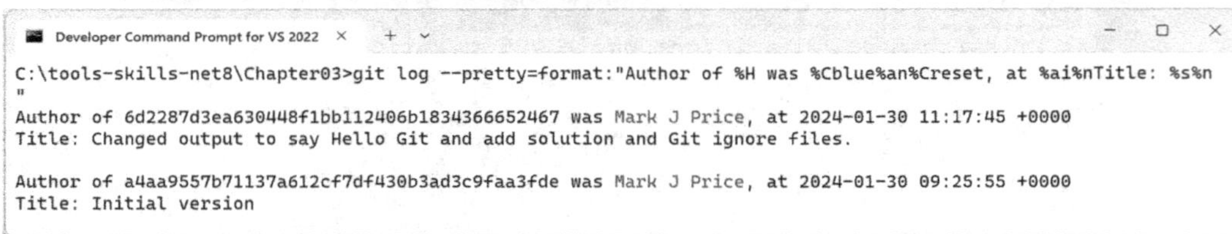

Figure 3.17: Pretty log output with customizations like blue color for author's name

11. Show the commit history with a custom format that shows the short commit hash (`%h`) and the commit message (`%s`), but with graphs for any branches, as shown in the following command:

```
git log --pretty=format:"%h %s" --graph
```

12. Note the results that show the two commits we have performed so far, with only the short commit hash and the commit message, as shown in the following output:

```
* 6d2287d Changed output to say Hello Git and add solution and Git ignore
files.
* a4aa955 Initial version
```

At the moment, it isn't very exciting because we do not have any branches (we will look at branching later in this chapter). A typical output might look like the following:

```
* 2d3acf9 Ignore errors from SIGCHLD on trap
*  5e3ee11 Merge branch 'master' of https://github.com/dustin/grit.git
|\
| * 420eac9 Add method for getting the current branch
* | 30e367c Timeout code and tests
* | 5a09431 Add timeout protection to grit
* | e1193f8 Support for heads with slashes in them
|/
* d6016bc Require time for xmlschema
*  11d191e Merge branch 'defunkt' into local
```

Filtering log output

You will quickly get too much log output to process sensibly unless you filter it. Two ways to filter by timestamp are the `--since` (or `--after`) and the `--until` (or `--before`) switches.

For example, to get the commits in the last two weeks, you would use either of the following two commands:

```
git log --since=2.weeks
git log --after=2.weeks
```

To get the commits starting in 2024, you could use the following commands:

```
git log --since=2024-01-01
git log --after=2024-01-01
```

To get the commits before 2024, you could use the following commands:

```
git log --until=2024-01-01
git log --before=2024-01-01
```

You also commonly want to filter by author, committer, or file path. For example:

```
git log --author "Mark J Price"
git log --committer "Mark J Price"
git log -- RepoDemo/RepoDemo.csproj
```

Good practice: The path or file to filter by must be the last option. It should be preceded by `--` to separate the path from other options.

To get the commits that contain the text string `ignore`, you could use the following command:

```
git log -S "ignore"
```

Managing remote repositories

Remote repositories are copies of your project files that are hosted over a network, including the internet. Working in a development team involves managing these remote repositories and pushing and pulling data to and from them when you need to share your work.

You will need an account on GitHub (or another Git host). If you do not have an account, then you can join and sign up at the following link:

`https://github.com/join`

> You can learn more about signing up for a GitHub account at the following link: `https://docs.github.com/en/get-started/quickstart/creating-an-account-on-github`.

You can list your configured remote repositories using `git remote -v`.

For example, if you have cloned the GitHub repository for this book, then in the folder you cloned it to, you could issue the `git remote -v` command, and you would see the following output:

```
origin  https://github.com/markjprice/tools-skills-net10.git (fetch)
origin  https://github.com/markjprice/tools-skills-net10.git (push)
```

In this case, the same URL is used to read (`fetch`) and write (`push`) to the remote repository.

To get more information, use the `show` command:

```
git remote show origin
```

You will see the following output:

```
* remote origin
  Fetch URL: https://github.com/markjprice/tools-skills-net10.git
  Push  URL: https://github.com/markjprice/tools-skills-net10.git
  HEAD branch: main
  Remote branch:
    main tracked
  Local branch configured for 'git pull':
    main merges with remote main
  Local ref configured for 'git push':
    main pushes to main (up to date)
```

Let's see how we can create a remote repository for our local demonstration project:

1. In the `Chapter03` directory, at the terminal or command prompt, list your configured remote repositories including the remote location, as shown in the following command:

```
git remote -v
```

2. Note that you won't have any yet, so the result is blank.
3. In your preferred web browser, navigate to `https://github.com` and sign in to your account.
4. On the GitHub home page, click the **New** button or navigate to `https://github.com/new`.
5. Enter a repository name of `repodemo`, note the other options (but you can leave them all at their defaults), and then click the **Create repository** button.
6. In the `Chapter03` directory, at the terminal or command prompt, add your remote repository with its URL (which will be unique to you!), as shown in the following command:

```
git remote add origin https://github.com/markjprice/repodemo.git
```

7. List your configured remote repositories, as shown in the following command:

```
git remote -v
```

8. Note that you now have a remote repository configured, as shown in the following output:

```
origin  https://github.com/markjprice/repodemo.git (fetch)
origin  https://github.com/markjprice/repodemo.git (push)
```

9. Push the `main` branch of your project up to the remote repositories, as shown in the following command:

```
git push origin main
```

> The syntax of the `push` command is `git push <remote> <branch>`. To read from the remote repository, use `git fetch <remote>`. For example, `git fetch origin`. To read from the remote repository and attempt to merge into your local code, use `git pull`.

10. You will be prompted to authenticate. You can use a web browser or mobile app. If you have configured two-factor authentication, then you will be prompted to enter a code into your GitHub app on your mobile device.
11. Note that files are pushed up to your remote repository, as shown in the following output:

```
info: please complete authentication in your browser...
Enumerating objects: 11, done.
Counting objects: 100% (11/11), done.
Delta compression using up to 8 threads
Compressing objects: 100% (10/10), done.
Writing objects: 100% (11/11), 4.76 KiB | 4.76 MiB/s, done.
```

```
Total 11 (delta 1), reused 0 (delta 0), pack-reused 0
remote: Resolving deltas: 100% (1/1), done.
To https://github.com/markjprice/repodemo.git
 * [new branch]      main -> main
```

12. Show the details of the remote repository, as shown in the following command:

```
git remote show origin
```

13. Note the result, as shown in the following output:

```
* remote origin
  Fetch URL: https://github.com/markjprice/repodemo.git
  Push  URL: https://github.com/markjprice/repodemo.git
  HEAD branch: main
  Remote branch:
    main tracked
  Local ref configured for 'git push':
    main pushes to main (up to date)
```

14. In your preferred web browser, navigate to `https://github.com/markjprice/repodemo` (your link will be different for your account name and repository name), and note the remote repository has been synchronized with your local directory, as shown in *Figure 3.18*:

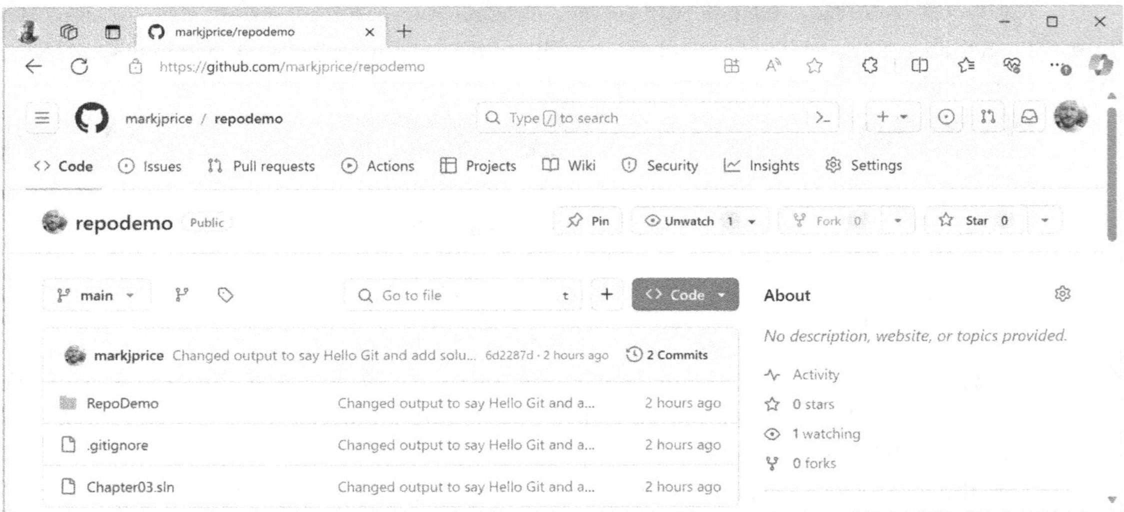

Figure 3.18: The RepoDemo repository hosted on GitHub

Next, we will look at branching and merging.

Branching and merging

Branching is a core concept in Git that significantly enhances the development workflow, making it more flexible and robust, especially in team environments. It's essential for managing large codebases and collaborating effectively on software projects.

A branch represents an independent line of development. You can think of it as a way to request a brand new working directory, staging area, and project history. New commits are recorded in the history of the branch, which results in a fork in the project's history.

Multiple branches allow different features or fixes to be developed in parallel. Changes made in a branch do not affect other branches, allowing you to work in an isolated sandbox.

Common uses of branches include:

- **Feature branching:** Each new feature is developed in its own branch and is merged back into the main branch upon completion.
- **Release branching:** When a version of the software is ready for release, it's branched off to allow for bug fixes and preparation for a release while development continues on the main branch.
- **Hotfix branching:** For urgent fixes, a branch is created from the stable version of the software. Once the fix is complete, it's merged into both the stable branch and the main development branch.

The way Git branches is lightweight so branching operations are very fast. This encourages workflows that branch and merge often, even multiple times in a day, which is quite different from rival version control systems. Mastery of branching and merging can change the way that you think about the development process.

Walking through a branching and merging example

In this example, you will perform the following steps:

1. Do some work in the `RepoDemo` project `main` branch to add a core calculator feature that can add two numbers.
2. Create a branch for a new feature in the `RepoDemo` project to configure the console culture.
3. Write the code for that new feature.
4. Switch back to the `main` branch because it needs a hotfix for a bug in the `Add` method.
5. Create a branch for the hotfix in the `RepoDemo` project.
6. Merge the hotfix to the `main` branch.
7. Switch back to the new feature and continue working on it.

Let's do it:

1. In the `RepoDemo` project, add a new file named `Calculator.cs`.
2. In `Calculator.cs`, define a `Calculator` class with an `Add` method (and a deliberate bug that will need a hotfix later!), as shown in the following code:

```
public static class Calculator
{
  public static int Add(int a, int b)
  {
    return a * b;
  }
}
```

3. In `Program.cs`, use the `Calculator` class to add 2 and 3 together and write the result to the console, as shown in the following code:

```
Console.WriteLine(Calculator.Add(2, 3));
```

4. In the `Chapter03` directory, at the terminal or command prompt, check the Git status, as shown in the following command:

```
git status
```

5. Note the result confirms that two changes need to be added to the staging area, as shown in the following output:

```
On branch main
Changes not staged for commit:
  (use "git add <file>..." to update what will be committed)
  (use "git restore <file>..." to discard changes in working directory)
        modified:   RepoDemo/Program.cs
Untracked files:
  (use "git add <file>..." to include in what will be committed)
        RepoDemo/Calculator.cs
```

6. In Visual Studio, in the **Git Changes** window, note one file is marked with **A** for added, and the other is marked with **M** for modified, as shown in *Figure 3.19*:

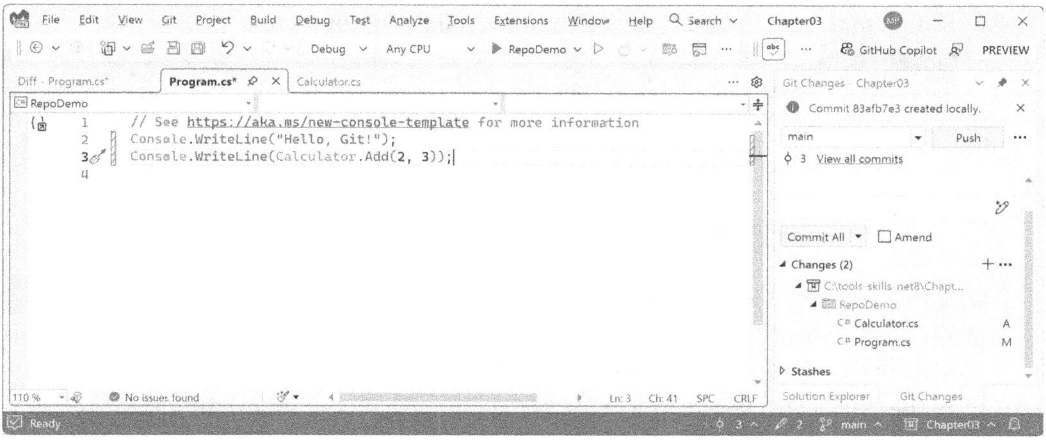

Figure 3.19: Added and modified files in Git Changes in Visual Studio

7. In the `Chapter03` directory, at the terminal or command prompt, add the untracked file to the staging area, as shown in the following command:

```
git add RepoDemo/Calculator.cs
```

> If you are using Visual Studio, then click the + button to move the `Calculator.cs` file to the **Staged Changes** section. You will also have to stage the modified file because Visual Studio does not have the ability to both stage and commit as the CLI does in the next step.

8. Stage the modified file and then commit the changes to both files with a comment message, as shown in the following command:

```
git commit -a -m "Add calculator functionality and call the Add method."
```

9. If you are using Visual Studio, enter the message and then click the **Commit Staged** button.
10. At the command prompt or terminal, note that a commit was made to the `main` branch, as shown in the following output:

```
[main dfc1ef8] Add calculator functionality and call the Add method.
 2 files changed, 8 insertions(+), 1 deletion(-)
 create mode 100644 RepoDemo/Calculator.cs
```

11. Confirm that there is nothing left to commit: `git status`.
12. Create a new feature branch named `configure-console`, as shown in the following command:

```
git branch configure-console
```

13. Switch to the new branch, as shown in the following command:

```
git switch configure-console
```

> You can combine creating and switching to a branch using `git switch -c <branch-name>`. The legacy command to switch branches is `git checkout <branch-name>` or `git checkout -b <branch-name>`.

14. If you are using Visual Studio, in the status bar, click the **main** branch icon, , click the **New Branch** button, enter a branch name of `configure-console` based on **main**, select the **Checkout branch** checkbox, and then click **Create**.
15. In the `RepoDemo.csproj` project file, statically and globally import the `Console` class, as shown in the following code:

```
<ItemGroup>
  <Using Include="System.Console" Static="true" />
</ItemGroup>
```

16. In the `RepoDemo` project folder, add a new file named `Program.Helpers.cs`.
17. In `Program.Helpers.cs`, define a partial `Program` class with a `ConfigureConsole` method, as shown in the following code:

> If you created a code snippet for this, then enter `ccc` and press *Tab* twice.

```
using System.Globalization;
partial class Program
{
  static void ConfigureConsole(string culture = "en-US",
 bool useComputerCulture = false)
  {
    // To enable Unicode characters like Euro symbol in the console.
    OutputEncoding = System.Text.Encoding.UTF8;
    if (!useComputerCulture)
    {
      CultureInfo.CurrentCulture = CultureInfo.GetCultureInfo(culture);
    }
    WriteLine($"CurrentCulture: {CultureInfo.CurrentCulture.
DisplayName}");
  }
}
```

18. In `Program.cs`, at the top of the file, configure the console, as shown in the following code:

```
ConfigureConsole();
```

19. In the `Chapter03` directory, at the terminal or command prompt, add the untracked file to the staging area, as shown in the following command:

```
git add RepoDemo/Program.Helpers.cs
```

If using Visual Studio, then click the **+ Stage All** button at the top of the **Changes** window to move all the added and changed files to the **Staged Changes** section.

20. Stage the modified file and then commit the changes to both files with a comment message, as shown in the following command:

```
git commit -a -m "Add new feature to configure the console culture."
```

If using Visual Studio, enter the message and then click the **Commit Staged** button. Or try the AI-generated message.

21. Note that a commit was made to the `configure-console` branch and three files were changed, as shown in the following output:

```
[configure-console f90cddb] Add new feature to configure the console
culture.
3 files changed, 23 insertions(+)
 create mode 100644 RepoDemo/Program.Helpers.cs
```

22. Confirm that there is nothing left to commit: `git status`.
23. Switch back to the main branch, as shown in the following command:

```
git switch main
```

To use Visual Studio, in the status bar, click the branches icon and select **main**.

24. Look at the files in the `RepoDemo` directory, and note that they are back to how they were before you created the `configure-console` branch.

To use Visual Studio, navigate to **Git** | **Manage Branches** and select **configure-console.**

25. Create and switch to a new branch named `calc-hotfix`, as shown in the following command:

```
git switch -c calc-hotfix
```

26. In `Calculator.cs`, fix the bug by changing the multiply operator to an addition operator, as shown in the following code:

```
return a + b;
```

27. Stage the modified file and then commit the changes to both files with a comment message, as shown in the following command:

```
git commit -a -m "Fix the Add method bug."
```

28. Note that a commit was made to the `configure-console` branch and three files were changed, as shown in the following output:

```
[calc-hotfix 9a9776a] Fix the Add method bug.
 1 file changed, 1 insertion(+), 1 deletion(-)
```

Good practice: You would now run your tests to confirm the hotfix works before continuing.

29. Switch back to the `main` branch, as shown in the following command:

```
git switch main
```

30. Merge the hotfix into the `main` branch, as shown in the following command:

```
git merge calc-hotfix
```

31. Note the result, as shown in the following output:

```
Updating dfc1ef8..9a9776a
Fast-forward
 RepoDemo/Calculator.cs | 2 +-
 1 file changed, 1 insertion(+), 1 deletion(-)
```

In Visual Studio, to merge a branch, right-click the branch, and then select **Merge '<branch_name>' into '<branch_name>'**, as shown in *Figure 3.20*:

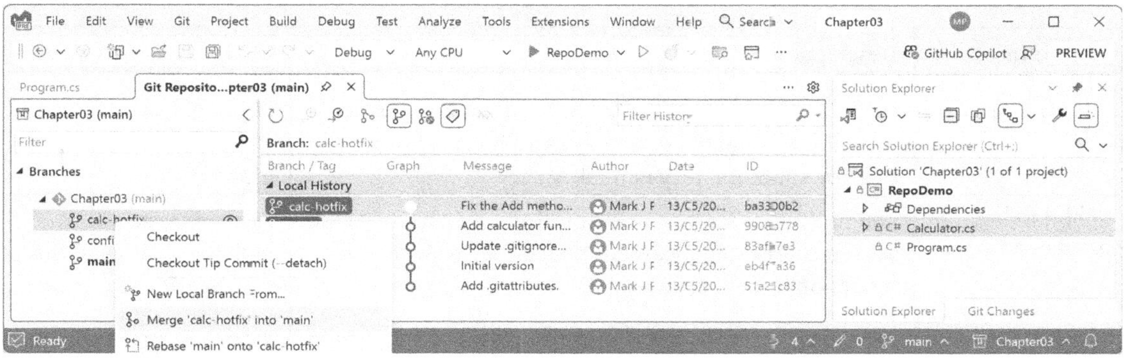

Figure 3.20: Merging a hotfix branch into main

Optionally, you can show the result at the command prompt or terminal, as shown in the following command:

```
git log --graph
```

Deleting and listing branches

Now that the hotfix has been applied to the `main` branch, we could delete the hotfix branch, as shown in the following command:

```
git branch -d calc-hotfix
```

But we will leave that branch for now.

We can switch back to the configure-console new feature branch and continue working on it, as shown in the following command:

```
git switch configure-console
```

You can list branches, as shown in the following command:

```
git branch
```

The results show the active branch with an asterisk, as shown in the following output:

```
  calc-hotfix
  configure-console
* main
```

Summary of common Git commands

The most common Git commands, including how to undo them, are described in *Table 3.5*:

Git command	Description	Undo
config	List (--list) or set configuration options.	n/a
init	Initialize the current directory as a Git repository. Creates a subdirectory named .git.	Delete the .git directory.
add <file-pattern>	Add file(s) that match the file or directory pattern to the Git repository staging area. Append the -r switch for recursion into directories.	rm --staged <file-pattern>. Append the -r switch for recursion into directories.
commit -m <message>	Commit currently staged files to the Git repository with a message. Timestamp and author will be automatically applied.	commit --amend, revert, or reset with various switches.
status	Show the status of the repository and its files. Append -s for short output.	n/a
log	Show to commit history. Append -p for patch details.	n/a
branch <branch-name>	Create and delete branches.	n/a
switch <branch-name>	Switch to (and optionally create with -c) a branch. The legacy command is checkout (and optionally create with -b).	n/a
merge <branch-name>	Merge a branch into the current branch.	n/a

Table 3.5: Common Git commands

Practicing and exploring

Test your knowledge and understanding by answering some questions, getting some hands-on practice, and exploring the topics covered in this chapter with deeper research.

Exercise 3.1 – Online-only material

Learn more about Git and Visual Studio at the following link: https://learn.microsoft.com/en-us/visualstudio/version-control/.

Free GitHub training is available at the following link: https://learn.microsoft.com/en-us/training/github/.

If you want to prove that you have GitHub skills, then GitHub certifications are available:

- **GitHub Foundations:** This exam covers collaboration, GitHub products, Git basics, and working within GitHub repositories.

- **GitHub Copilot**: This exam evaluates your skill in using the AI-driven code completion tool in various programming languages, certifying your capability to optimize software development workflows efficiently.
- **GitHub Actions**: Test your skills in streamlining workflows, automating tasks, and optimizing software pipelines, including CI/CD—all within customizable workflows.
- **GitHub Advanced Security**: Validate your expertise in vulnerability identification, workflow security, and robust security implementation—elevating software integrity standards.
- **GitHub Administration**: Highlight your expertise in repository management, workflow optimization, and efficient collaboration to support successful projects on GitHub.

Learn more at the following link: `https://resources.github.com/learn/certifications/`.

A great site for advanced beginners with Git is `https://think-like-a-git.net/`. As the site itself says, "You should know how to create a repository, add and commit files to it, and you should probably have some idea of why you might want to use a branch." The site only makes sense if you realize that it's aimed at existing Git users, not complete beginners. So, make sure you've read and understood most of what I've covered in this chapter before diving in.

Exercise 3.2 – Practice exercises

You can watch intermediate to advanced-level Git videos at the following link: `https://devblogs.microsoft.com/visualstudio/intermediate-and-advanced-git/`

Some online books about Git can be read at the following links:

- *Pro Git* (`https://git-scm.com/book/en/v2`): Written by Scott Chacon and Ben Straub, all content is licensed under the Creative Commons Attribution-NonCommercial-ShareAlike 3.0 license. The book is available in English, azərbaycan dili, български език, Deutsch, Español, Français, Ελληνικά, 日本語, 한국어, Nederlands, Русский, Slovenščina, Tagalog, Українська, and 简体中文.
- *Conversational Git* (`https://alanhohn.com/extras/conversational-git/`) Alan Hohn wrote this book because he "saw an ever-so-narrow niche for a book that introduced Git from the perspective of a person who uses it every day, but still remembers what it was like getting up to speed."

Exercise 3.3 – Test your knowledge

Answer the following questions. If you get stuck, try googling the answers, if necessary, while remembering that if you get totally stuck, the answers are in *Appendix A*:

1. What are five important features of a source code management system?
2. Why is Git hard to learn?
3. A file in a directory used as a Git repository can be in one of four states. What are those states?
4. When would you use the `git diff` command?
5. What are some common uses of Git branching?

Exercise 3.4 – Explore topics

Use the links on the following page to learn more details about the topics covered in this chapter: `https://github.com/markjprice/tools-skills-net10/blob/main/docs/book-links.md#chapter-3---source-code-management-using-git`.

Summary

In this chapter, you learned how to:

- Install and configure Git locally
- Create a local or clone a remote Git repository
- Track changes in Git
- Undo and clean a commit
- Work with the stash
- Review changes in Git repositories
- Manage branching and merging
- Continue your Git learning journey using videos and books

In the next chapter, you will learn about debugging your code and troubleshooting memory issues.

4

Debugging and Memory Troubleshooting

This chapter is about debugging tools and skills. You will also learn about tools for memory troubleshooting. For .NET developers, memory analysis is crucial to identify memory leaks, understand memory consumption, and optimize performance.

This chapter covers the following topics:

- Debugging strategies
- Interactive debugging with Visual Studio
- Understanding stack and heap memory
- Tools and skills for memory troubleshooting

Debugging strategies

Debugging can be the most challenging part of the development process. Professional .NET developers often spend more hours debugging than writing the original code, so keep that in mind when planning how much of your time you should invest in learning how to write code versus how much of your time you should invest in learning how to debug code.

Identifying and fixing bugs is the core purpose of debugging. Bugs in code can range from minor visual glitches that slightly affect the user interface to major issues that can cause data loss or security vulnerabilities. Debugging helps locate these problems so they can be corrected.

But fixing bugs is not the only use for debugging. For developers, especially those new to a project, stepping through the code during debugging provides a deeper understanding of the application's flow and logic. Debugging is an excellent learning tool.

Regular debugging sessions allow developers to not only fix errors but also refactor code, optimize processes, and ensure that the codebase remains maintainable and scalable. By understanding what went wrong and why a piece of code failed, developers can prevent similar issues in the future.

We will start this chapter by looking at a topic that is independent of any tool you might use: strategies for debugging a .NET project.

Introducing debugging strategies

Here are some strategies for effectively debugging a .NET project:

- **Understand the problem deeply**: Before diving into code, make sure you clearly understand the problem. This involves replicating the issue, reading error messages carefully, and understanding the context in which the bug occurs. Sometimes, the actual issue isn't where the error manifests but somewhere deeper in the code. Rushing to fix a bug can make the situation worse. Remember this maxim: First, do no harm!
- **Leverage the power of a debugger**: Use breakpoints, not just to pause execution but also to inspect the state of your application at various points. Conditional breakpoints are particularly useful for catching issues in specific scenarios. Don't overlook the **Immediate** window for evaluating expressions on the fly and the **Call Stack** to trace the sequence of method calls leading to the current state. You will learn about all these tools later in this chapter.
- **Write and run unit tests**: Unit testing can be a powerful debugging tool. By isolating pieces of your code and testing them individually, you can pinpoint the exact location of bugs. It's also a good practice to write tests for bug fixes to ensure that the issue doesn't reappear in the future. xUnit is a popular framework for .NET unit testing that you will learn about in *Chapter 11, Unit Testing and Mocking*.
- **Static code analysis**: Use static code analysis tools like the Roslyn compiler's code and style analyzers to detect potential bugs and code quality issues. The ReSharper extension for Visual Studio and the features built into Rider also help identify potential problem areas.
- **Memory and performance profiling tools**: Profiling tools can help you understand performance-related issues by highlighting memory leaks, inefficient database queries, or other resource bottlenecks. You will learn how to use some of these tools later in this chapter.
- **Logging and observability**: Implement robust logging in your application. Packages like Serilog can provide insights into what your application was doing leading up to an error. You will learn about the most popular modern extendable logging and observability framework, named OpenTelemetry, in *Chapter 5, Logging, Tracing, and Metrics for Observability*.

Debugging is as much an art as it is a science. It requires patience, a methodical approach, and sometimes a bit of creative thinking. The strategies above should give you a robust toolkit for tackling most debugging challenges in .NET.

Now let's look at the most important of those strategies in more detail: understanding the problem. The biggest mistake that developers make when debugging is rushing to implement a solution before they really understand the problem. This can lead to introducing more problems and, worse, not even fixing the original problem!

Understanding the problem

Understanding the problem thoroughly is a vital first step in debugging, and it's often more nuanced than it appears at first glance. Here's a deep dive into this strategy:

1. **Reproduce the issue consistently**: You must start by replicating the issue in a controlled environment like a development or staging environment where you can freely debug and test without affecting production. You must make sure that the bug can be reproduced consistently. Intermittent issues are harder to debug, so finding a repeatable way to reproduce the issue is vital. Then try to minimize the scenario to simplify what needs to be debugged. Initially, you might find a 7-step scenario that always produces the bug. If you can eliminate some of those steps, then you can focus on the few steps that actually contain the bug.
2. **Gather comprehensive information**: You should collect detailed error messages and logs. Sometimes, the stack trace or the exception details can point you directly to the issue. If the bug was reported by a user, gather as much information from them as possible, preferably in an automated way so that you are not reliant on their effort and attention to detail. The user who opened the bug report might not understand what the expected behavior should be so do not trust what they've written without confirming. What were they doing when the issue occurred? What specific steps led to the problem? Can you provide a quick and easy mechanism to take screenshots of the issue?

> You could configure services like Azure Application Insights or Sentry to know what a user was doing when an exception occurs, but I do not cover paid cloud services like these in this book.

3. **Document your findings**: Keep a record of what you find, even if it doesn't lead directly to a solution. This can be helpful if the issue resurfaces or if similar problems arise in the future.
4. **Analyze the context:** Look at recent changes in the codebase. Did the issue occur after a particular deployment or code change? The Git command `bisect` is useful in this scenario. Consider differences in environments, for example, between development, staging, and production. Sometimes bugs occur only under specific configurations or with certain data. For example, a database connection string in production might have a smaller timeout for executing commands, making them more likely to occur.

> You can learn about the Git `bisect` command at the following link: `https://git-scm.com/docs/git-bisect`.

5. **Seek historical knowledge**: Use a version control system like Git to understand the history of the affected code using the `git blame` command. Who wrote it and when? Were there any related issues in the past? Review any existing documentation or code comments that might provide insights into the intended behavior of the code.

6. **Understand the expected vs. actual behavior**: Clearly document what the expected behavior is and how it differs from what's currently happening. This not only aids in pinpointing the issue but also makes sure that you're solving the right issue.
7. **Hypothesize and test**: Formulate hypotheses about what might be causing the issue based on the gathered information. Then, design tests or experiments to confirm or refute these hypotheses. When an expected result is clear, you can write a unit test before using any debugging tools. This test should call the faulty methods and fail. Then you can debug the issue without running the app. Just fix the code and debug the test until it passes.
8. **Use interactive debugging tools effectively**: Familiarize yourself with the debugging tools in your code editor. Knowing how to use breakpoints effectively, stepping through your code, inspecting variables, and understanding the call stack can be invaluable.
9. **Collaborate and communicate**: Discuss the problem with teammates. Sometimes, just explaining the issue to someone else can help clarify your understanding of the problem. If you aren't working in a team, try rubber ducking (explain your issue to an inanimate object like a rubber duck). Even better these days is to have a conversation about the issue with an AI that has access to your codebase like GitHub Copilot Chat.
10. **Break down the problem**: If the issue is complex, break it down into smaller parts. Isolate components or functions and test them individually. This can help identify the specific area causing the problem.
11. **Verify the fix**: This is a vital step that is easy to overlook because when you spot the issue and fix it, you can be so excited and sure you've fixed it that you neglect to rerun your original reproduction scenario and confirm that the issue is truly and reliably fixed. Also note that fixes can cause regression bugs because they affect other parts of the system. If you have a suite of tests that run against other parts of the system, then run them before feeling confident that the bug is fixed without side effects.

Good practice: It is important to remember that software is not magic. There is always a logical reason behind every bug. Often, the solution is simple, and you kick yourself for overlooking something that becomes more obvious.

The goal of this phase is not just to find a quick fix but to truly understand why the issue is occurring. This thorough understanding not only leads to more effective and permanent solutions but also improves your knowledge of the system, making future debugging faster and more efficient.

How to start debugging

The best place to start is at the beginning. Although an issue might occur in the checkout of an e-commerce store, first, confirm that all the initialization happened as expected, for example, database connection strings, user account setup, and so on.

Imagine that you have some theories about what the issue is and think that it could be a database connection string, or something wrong with your entity model or the client code that calls it. It is tempting to save time by changing all those items at the same time. But if the issue is now fixed, which one fixed it? Only do one thing at a time, even though that takes more time. Make a single change, run tests, and then you'll know the minimum needed to safely fix the issue.

Even worse, imagine if the bug still exists after making those multiple changes. It could be that one of those changes on its own would have fixed the bug, but the other changes prevented it!

When to give up debugging

Sometimes it is better for the organization to give up on fixing a difficult bug in a superficial part of a system. This is especially true with user interface bugs. If the UI is still functional but some decorative part of it is glitchy, maybe it's best to move on to something more important. Or maybe there is some automated part of the system that can be done by a user manually so if the automation is buggy, the organization might be okay with it being disabled and removed instead of being unreliable.

Interactive debugging with Visual Studio

One of the most important debugging strategies is to use interactive debugging tools effectively. In this section, you will learn how to debug problems interactively at development time.

> The menu commands for debugging are on the **Debug** menu in Visual Studio or the **Run** menu in VS Code and Rider.

Creating code with objects to view

Let's explore debugging by creating a console app that references a class library, and we will then use the debugger tools in your code editor to step through and view objects live at runtime:

1. Use your preferred code editor to add a new **Class Library** / `classlib` project named `DebugLibrary` to a `Chapter04` solution.
2. Modify `DebugLibrary.csproj` to statically import `System.Console`, `System.Convert`, and `System.Text.Encoding` for all code files and treat warnings as errors, as shown highlighted in the following markup:

```
<Project Sdk="Microsoft.NET.Sdk">

  <PropertyGroup>
    <TargetFramework>net10.0</TargetFramework>
    <ImplicitUsings>enable</ImplicitUsings>
    <Nullable>enable</Nullable>
    <TreatWarningsAsErrors>true</TreatWarningsAsErrors>
  </PropertyGroup>
```

```
  <ItemGroup>
    <Using Include="System.Console" Static="true" />
    <Using Include="System.Convert" Static="true" />
    <Using Include="System.Text.Encoding" Static="true" />
  </ItemGroup>

</Project>
```

3. Rename `Class1.cs` to `WebConfig.cs`.
4. In `WebConfig.cs`, define a class with various properties that might be used in a web project, as shown in the following code:

```
namespace Packt.Shared;

public class WebConfig
{
  public string? DbConnectionString { get; set; }
  public string? Base64Encoded { get; set; }
  public string? JsonWebToken { get; set; }

  public WebConfig()
  {
    DbConnectionString = "Server="
      + "(localdb)\\mssqllocaldb;"
      + "Database=Northwind;"
      + "Trusted_Connection=true";

    byte[] data = UTF8.GetBytes("Debugging is cool!");
    Base64Encoded = ToBase64String(data);

    // Set a string for the JWT from the example at:
    // https://jwt.io/
    JsonWebToken =
      "eyJhbGciOiJIUzI1NiIsInR5cCI6IkpXVCJ9." +
      "eyJzdWIiOiIxMjM0NTY3ODkwIiwibmFtZSI6I" +
      "kpvaG4gRG9lIiwiaWF0IjoxNTE2MjM5MDIyfQ." +
      "SflKxwRJSMeKKF2QT4fwpMeJf36POk6yJV_adQssw5c";
  }

  public void OutputAll()
  {
```

```
    WriteLine($"DbConnectionString: {DbConnectionString}");
    WriteLine($"Base64Encoded: {Base64Encoded}");
    WriteLine($"JsonWebToken: {JsonWebToken}");
  }
}
```

5. Add a new class file named `Product.cs`.
6. In `Product.cs`, add statements to define a `Product` class, as shown in the following code:

```
namespace Northwind.EntityModels;

public class Product
{
  public int ProductId { get; set; }
  public string ProductName { get; set; } = null!;
  public int? SupplierId { get; set; }
  public int? CategoryId { get; set; }
  public string? QuantityPerUnit { get; set; }
  public decimal? UnitPrice { get; set; }
  public short? UnitsInStock { get; set; }
  public short? UnitsOnOrder { get; set; }
  public short? ReorderLevel { get; set; }
  public bool Discontinued { get; set; }
}
```

7. Use your preferred code editor to add a new **Console App** / `console` project named `DebugApp` to the `Chapter04` solution.
8. Modify `DebugApp.csproj` to statically import `System.Console` for all code files, treat warnings as errors, and reference the `DebugLibrary` project, as highlighted in the following markup:

```
<Project Sdk="Microsoft.NET.Sdk">

  <PropertyGroup>
    <OutputType>Exe</OutputType>
    <TargetFramework>net10.0</TargetFramework>
    <ImplicitUsings>enable</ImplicitUsings>
    <Nullable>enable</Nullable>
    <TreatWarningsAsErrors>true</TreatWarningsAsErrors>
  </PropertyGroup>

  <ItemGroup>
    <ProjectReference Include="..\DebugLibrary\DebugLibrary.csproj" />
  </ItemGroup>
```

```
  <ItemGroup>
    <Using Include="System.Console" Static="true" />
  </ItemGroup>

</Project>
```

9. In `Program.cs`, delete any existing statements and then write statements to instantiate a `WebConfig` object and output all of its properties, and then instantiate a `Product` instance, as shown in the following code:

```
using Packt.Shared; // To use WebConfig.
using Northwind.EntityModels; // To use Product.

WebConfig config = new();
config.OutputAll();

Product product = new()
{
  ProductId = 1,
  CategoryId = 1,
  ProductName = "Chai",
  UnitPrice = 1,
  UnitsInStock = 1,
  Discontinued = false
};

WriteLine("Press enter to exit.");
```

Setting a breakpoint and starting debugging

Breakpoints allow us to mark a line of code at which we want to pause to inspect the program state and find bugs. Here's where you should consider setting breakpoints when debugging, especially within the context of .NET development:

- **Areas of recent changes:** If a bug has appeared after recent modifications, setting breakpoints in these areas can help you quickly identify if and how the new changes are causing issues.
- **Known problem areas:** If certain parts of the codebase are known to be problematic or complex, it's wise to set breakpoints there when related functionality is behaving unexpectedly.
- **Start of faulty methods:** If you've identified a method where the problem manifests, set a breakpoint at the start of this method. This allows you to step through the entire method, watching how the input values are handled and how the outputs are generated.

- **Before and after important operations:** If your application interacts with databases, APIs, or other external services, set breakpoints just before and after these interactions. This can help you verify if the data being sent and received is correct.
- **User input points:** If the issue might be related to how user input is handled (like in a UI or a service endpoint), place breakpoints at the points where the user input is received and processed.
- **Exception handlers:** Setting breakpoints within exception handling blocks, for example, inside `catch` blocks, can be useful for examining the state when an exception is caught, helping to understand more about the error's context.
- **Unit tests:** If you're working with unit tests that fail due to a bug, set breakpoints within these tests. This is helpful to see why the expected outcomes are not being met. You will do this in the next section.
- **Entry and exit points of functions:** Especially in larger, more complex functions, setting breakpoints at the entry and the exit can help you understand what data is going into the function and what results it yields.
- **State changes:** If a bug is related to changes in the state of the application (like a variable that unexpectedly changes value), setting breakpoints at every point the variable is modified can help track down the source of the change.

Let's set a breakpoint and then start debugging using Visual Studio:

1. Click on the last statement, because we want all the code to execute to create the two objects so that we can view them in our debugging tools.
2. Navigate to **Debug** | **Toggle Breakpoint** or press *F9*. A red circle will appear in the margin bar on the left-hand side, and the statement will be highlighted in red to indicate that a breakpoint has been set. Breakpoints can be toggled off with the same action. You can also left-click in the margin to toggle a breakpoint on and off, or right-click a breakpoint to see more options, such as delete, disable, or edit conditions or actions for an existing breakpoint.
3. Navigate to **Debug** | **Start Debugging** or press *F5*. Visual Studio starts the console application and then pauses when it hits the breakpoint. This is known as *break mode*. Extra windows titled **Locals** (showing current values of local variables), **Watch 1** (showing any watch expressions you have defined), **Call Stack**, **Exception Settings**, and **Immediate Window** may appear, along with the **Debugging** toolbar. The line that will be executed next is highlighted in yellow, and a yellow arrow points at the line from the margin bar.
4. In the terminal or command prompt, note the output of the properties, and that two of the values are encoded, which is not very helpful for a human trying to debug code, as shown in the following output:

```
DbConnectionString: Server=(localdb)\
mssqllocaldb;Database=Northwind;Trusted_Connection=true
Base64Encoded: RGVidWdnaW5nIGlzIGNvb2wh
JsonWebToken: eyJhbGciOiJIUzI1NiIsInR5cCI6IkpXVCJ9.
eyJzdWIiOiIxMjM0NTY3ODkwIiwibmFtZSI6IkpvaG4gRG9lIiwiaWF0IjoxNTE2MjM5MDIyfQ.
SflKxwRJSMeKKF2QT4fwpMeJf36POk6yJV_adQssw5c
```

5. In the **Locals** window, expand the config variable and click the **View** button for **Text Visualizer** for the **Base64Encoded** property, as shown in *Figure 4.1*:

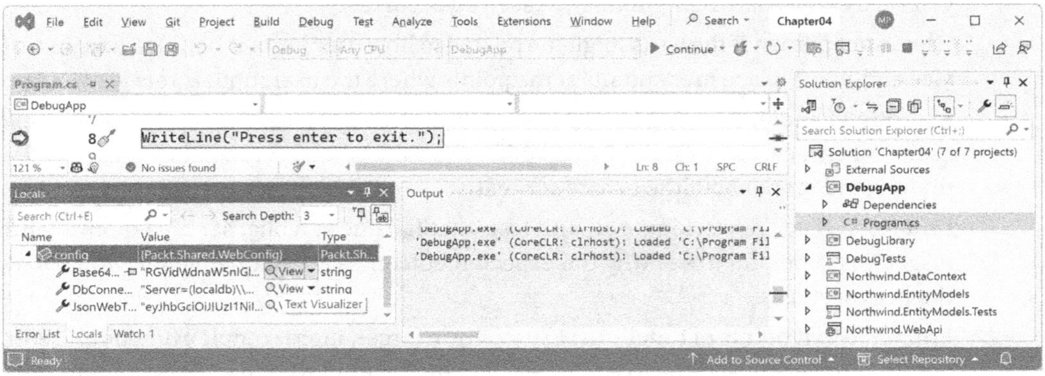

Figure 4.1: Locals window and View buttons for property values

6. In the **Text Visualizer** dialog box, for **String manipulation**, select **Base64 Decode**, and note that you can now read the original message, **Debugging is cool!**, as shown in *Figure 4.2*:

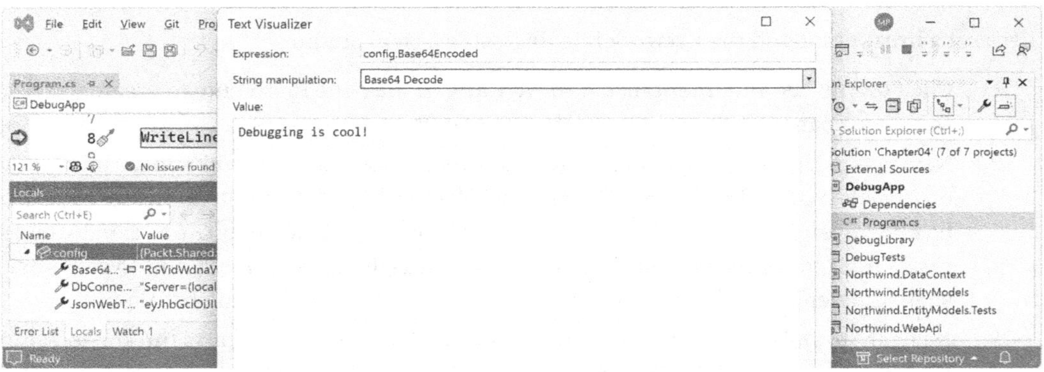

Figure 4.2: Decoding a Base64-encoded property in Text Visualizer

7. Close the **Text Visualizer** dialog box.
8. In the **Locals** window, click the **View** button for **Text Visualizer** for the **JsonWebToken** property.
9. In the **Text Visualizer** dialog box, for **String manipulation**, select **JWT Decode**, and note that you can now read the original JSON token, including information like the algorithm used and the user's name, as shown in *Figure 4.3*:

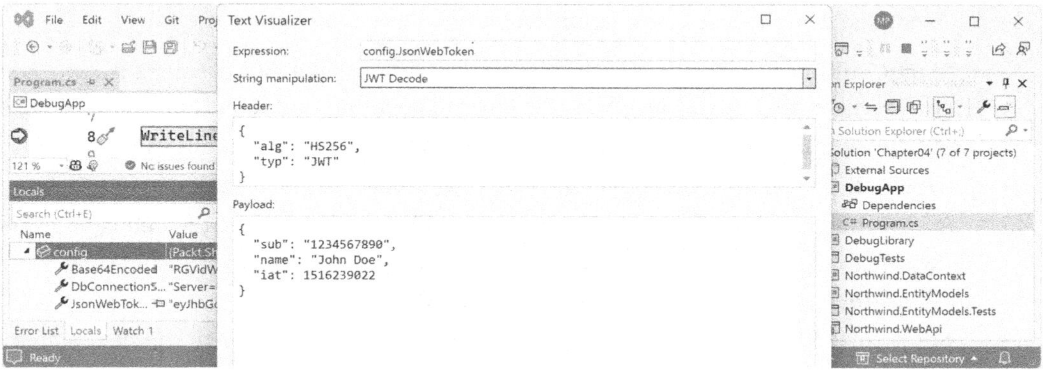

Figure 4.3: Decoding a JWT-encoded property in Text Visualizer

10. Close the **Text Visualizer** dialog box.

Navigating with the debugging toolbar

Visual Studio has two debug-related buttons in its **Standard** toolbar, one to start or continue debugging and another to hot reload changes to the running code, along with a separate **Debug** toolbar for the rest of the tools.

VS Code shows a floating toolbar with buttons to make it easy to access debugging features.

Both are shown in *Figure 4.4*:

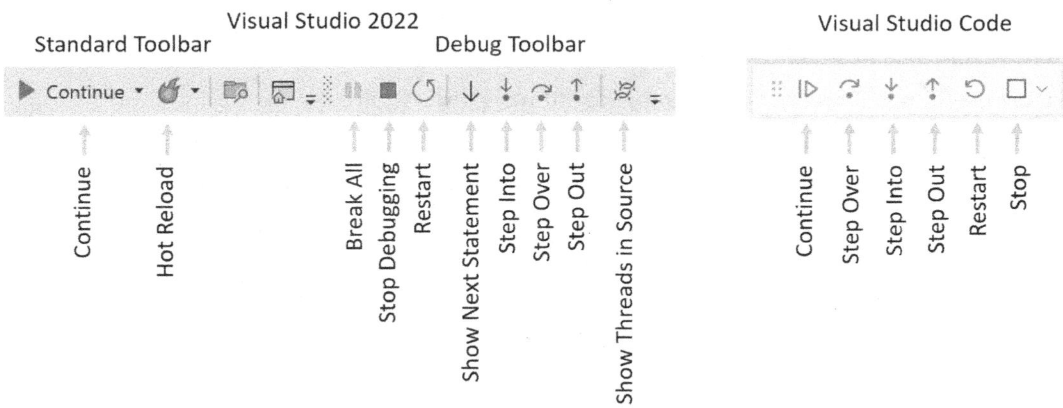

Figure 4.4: Debugging toolbars in Visual Studio and VS Code

The following list describes the most common buttons in the toolbars:

- **Start/Continue**/*F5*: This button is context-sensitive. It will either start a project running or continue running the project from the current position until it ends or hits a breakpoint.
- **Hot Reload**: This button will reload compiled code changes without needing to restart the app.
- **Break All**: This button will break into the next available line of code in a running app.
- **Stop Debugging/Stop**/*Shift* + *F5* (red square): This button will stop the debugging session.
- **Restart**/*Ctrl* or *Cmd* + *Shift* + *F5* (circular arrow): This button will stop and then immediately restart the program with the debugger attached again.
- **Show Next Statement**: This button will move the current cursor to the next statement that will execute.
- **Step Into**/*F11*, **Step Over**/*F10*, and **Step Out**/*Shift* + *F11* (blue arrows over dots): These buttons step through the code statements in various ways. The difference between Step Into and Step Over can be seen when you are about to execute a method call. If you click on Step Into, the debugger steps *into* the method so that you can step through every line in that method. If you click on Step Over, the whole method is executed in one go; it does not skip over the method without executing it. If you are already in a method, a click on Step Out will quickly execute the rest of the method until the point the method returns, when it will pause again.
- **Show Threads in Source**: This button allows you to examine and work with threads in the application that you're debugging.

Debugging windows

While debugging, both Visual Studio and VS Code show extra windows that allow you to monitor useful information, such as variables, while you step through your code.

The most useful windows are described in the following list:

- **VARIABLES**, including **Locals**, which shows the name, value, and type of any local variables automatically. Keep an eye on this window while you step through your code. See *Figure 4.5*.
- **WATCH** or **Watch 1**, which shows the value of variables and expressions that you manually enter.
- **CALL STACK**, which shows the stack of function calls.
- **BREAKPOINTS**, which shows all your breakpoints and allows finer control over them.

When in break mode, there is also a useful window at the bottom of the edit area:

- **DEBUG CONSOLE** or **Immediate Window** enables live interaction with your code. You can interrogate the program state, for example, by entering the name of a variable. For example, you can ask a question such as "What is 1+2?" by typing `1+2` and pressing *Enter*.

Controlling what appears in debug panes

Windows like **Locals** and **Watch 1** show the current values of variables and expressions as you step through your code with a debugger.

These windows already know how to show simple types like numbers and text strings. But for custom complex types, by default, it will show the return value of `ToString`. If your type has not overridden `ToString`, then that method will return the type name, like `Northwind.EntityModels.Product`.

You can take control of how your type displays in these debug panes by decorating your code with special attributes, as described in *Table 4.1*:

Attribute	Description
`DebuggerDisplay`	This string can contain braces, `{` and `}`. Text within a pair of braces is evaluated as a field, property, or method. For example, `{ProductName}` to output a field or property named `ProductName`. By default, string values will be surrounded by quotes. To indicate *no quotes*, suffix the name with `,nq`.
`DebuggerBrowsable`	Can be applied only as a single instance to properties and fields. You must choose a `DebuggerBrowsableState` enum value. `Never` means the member is not displayed. `Collapsed` is the default and means the member is displayed but not expanded. `RootHidden` means the member is not shown, but if it is an array or collection, then its child items are displayed.
`DebuggerStepThrough`	Tells the debugger to step through the code instead of stepping into the code.

Table 4.1: Attributes to control how your types display in debuggers

Warning! In the **Tools** | **Options** | **Debugging** dialog box, if the **Show raw structure of objects in variables windows** checkbox is selected, then the `DebuggerDisplay` attribute is ignored.

Let's try:

1. In the `DebugApp` project, navigate to **Debug** | **Start Debugging** or press *F5*.
2. Note the `product` variable displays its **Value** as `{Northwind.EntityModels.Product}`, as shown in *Figure 4.5*:

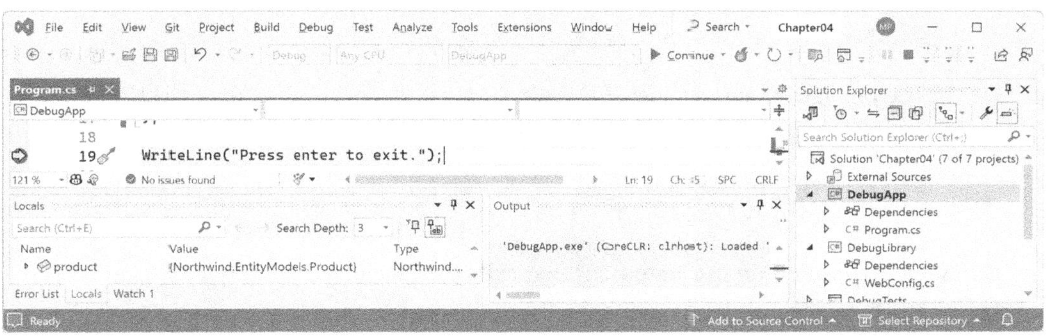

Figure 4.5: By default, a class displays its full type name in debug windows

3. Stop the debugger.
4. In the `Northwind.EntityModels` project, in `Product.cs`, decorate the class to control how it displays in the debugger to show its `ProductId` and `ProductName`, as shown highlighted in the following code:

```
[DebuggerDisplay("{ProductId}: {ProductName}")]
public class Product
```

5. In the `DebugApp` project, navigate to **Debug** | **Start Debugging** or press *F5*.
6. Note the `product` variable displays its **Value** as `1: "Chai"`, as shown in *Figure 4.6*:

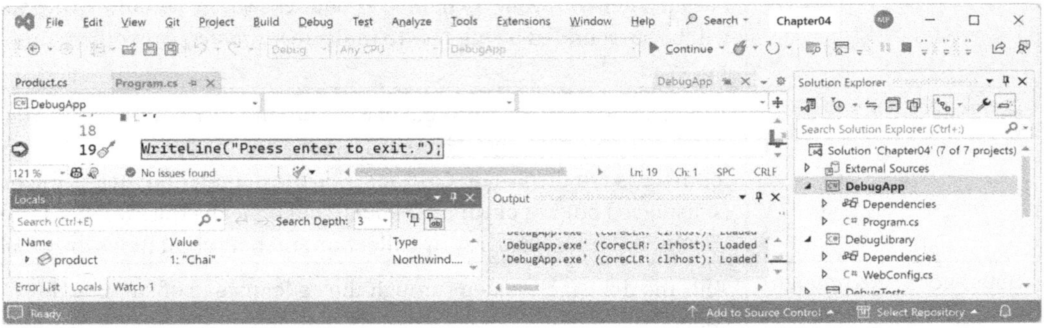

Figure 4.6: A class displaying its custom debug format

7. In the `Northwind.EntityModels` project, in `Product.cs`, add `,nq` after the field name to remove the quotes around the `ProductName`, as shown highlighted in the following code:

```
[DebuggerDisplay("{ProductId}: {ProductName,nq}")]
public class Product
```

8. In the `DebugApp` project, navigate to **Debug** | **Start Debugging** or press *F5*.
9. Note the output is now: `1: Chai`.
10. In the `DebugLibrary` project, in `WebConfig.cs`, decorate the database connection property to remove it from showing in debug windows, as shown highlighted in the following code:

```
[DebuggerBrowsable(DebuggerBrowsableState.Never)]
public string? DbConnectionString { get; set; }
```

11. In the `DebugLibrary` project, in `WebConfig.cs`, decorate the `OutputAll` method to prevent stepping into it, as shown highlighted in the following code:

```
[DebuggerStepThrough]
public void OutputAll()
```

12. Set a breakpoint on the statement that calls the `OutputAll` method.
13. In the `DebugApp` project, navigate to **Debug** | **Start Debugging** or press *F5*.

14. Click the **Step Into** button or press *F11* or navigate to **Debug** | **Step Into**, and note the dialog box that warns that you will automatically step over this method call (and how to override this option), as shown in *Figure 4.7*:

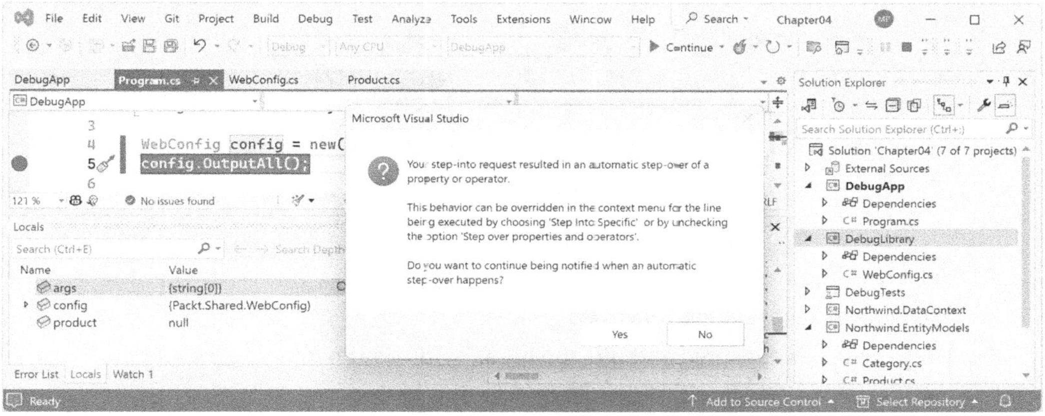

Figure 4.7: Preventing stepping into a method or property

15. In the **Locals** window, expand the `config` variable and note that the output does not show the `DbConnectionString` property.
16. Stop the debugger.

Debugging test projects

Let's see how you can debug a test project:

1. Use your preferred code editor to add a new **xUnit Test Project** / `xunit` project named `DebugTests` to the `Chapter04` solution.
2. In the `DebugTests.csproj` project file, add a project reference to the class library, as shown in the following markup:

```
<ItemGroup>
  <ProjectReference Include="..\DebugLibrary\DebugLibrary.csproj" />
</ItemGroup>
```

3. Build the `DebugTests` project.
4. In the `DebugTests` project, rename `UnitTest1.cs` to `DebugLibraryTests.cs`.
5. In `DebugLibraryTests.cs`, write statements in a test method to instantiate a `WebConfig` object and check that its properties are not `null`, as shown in the following code:

```
using Packt.Shared; // To use WebConfig.

namespace DebugTests;

public class DebugLibraryTests
```

```
{
  [Fact]
  public void WebConfigPropertiesInstantiated()
  {
    WebConfig config = new();
    Assert.NotNull(config.DbConnectionString);
    Assert.NotNull(config.Base64Encoded);
    Assert.NotNull(config.JsonWebToken);
  }
}
```

6. Set a breakpoint on the first assertion.
7. Navigate to **Test | Debug All Tests**.
8. Note the test is executed and hits the breakpoint, as shown in *Figure 4.8*:

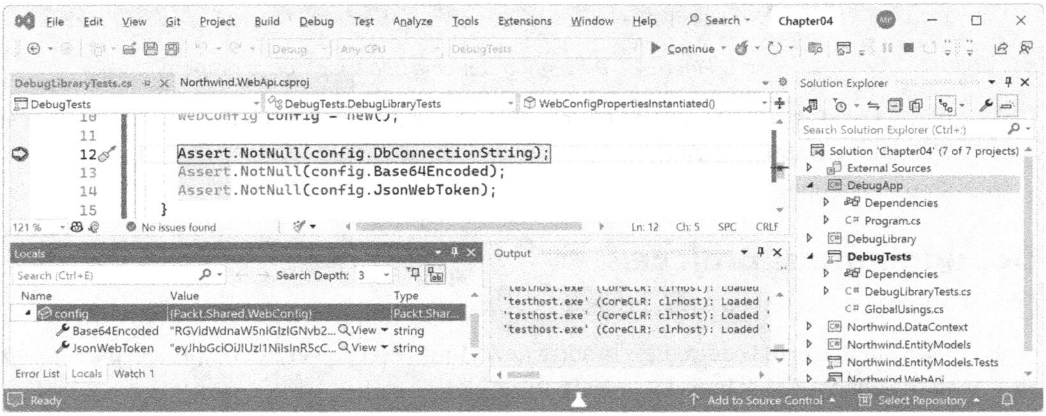

Figure 4.8: Hitting a breakpoint in a test project

9. Stop the debugger.

Asking GitHub Copilot Chat for debugging help

GitHub Copilot Chat is already a huge success for Microsoft. According to CEO Satya Nadella in a 2024 earnings conference call, GitHub Copilot is the world's most widely deployed AI developer tool. At the time of writing, there are over 1.3 million paid GitHub Copilot subscribers. Over half of the Fortune 500 use Azure OpenAI today, and Azure supports OpenAI's latest models, including GPT-4 Turbo, GPT-4 with Vision, and DALL-E 3.

> You can read more about Copilot's success at the following link: `https://visualstudiomagazine.com/articles/2024/02/05/copilot-numbers.aspx`.

GitHub Copilot Chat can help the debugging process by offering real-time guidance and suggestions. Since it has access to your codebase, it can understand the code context and generate code snippets, explanations, and debugging tips, especially when dealing with complex issues that are hard for a human to keep in their head at the same time.

Here are some ways that GitHub Copilot Chat can assist with debugging in a .NET project:

- **Generating hypotheses for bug causes.** When you encounter an unexpected `NullReferenceException`, you can describe the scenario to Copilot Chat, mentioning where the exception occurs. Copilot Chat can suggest potential causes for the exception, such as uninitialized objects or methods returning `null` unexpectedly.
- **Suggesting debugging techniques.** When your application experiences performance issues and you're unsure how to pinpoint the bottleneck, Copilot Chat can suggest specific .NET profiling tools or techniques. For instance, it might recommend using Visual Studio Diagnostic Tools or JetBrains dotTrace to profile your application and identify performance hotspots.
- **Writing test cases.** When you need to write unit tests to isolate a bug in a specific method, you can provide the method signature and a description of the expected behavior, and then Copilot Chat can generate unit test templates using xUnit. This includes setting up mock data, invoking the method with various inputs, and asserting the expected outcomes.
- **Fixing common coding mistakes.** When you're working with asynchronous code and encounter deadlocks or race conditions, Copilot Chat can identify common pitfalls in asynchronous programming, such as blocking on async code with `.Result` or `.Wait()`, and suggest best practices, like using `await` properly, to avoid these issues.
- **Refactoring suggestions for better code.** When your code works but is difficult to read or maintain due to poor structure or duplication, Copilot Chat can offer refactoring suggestions to improve code quality. This could involve breaking down large methods into smaller, more manageable ones, removing duplicate code, or applying design patterns to enhance code modularity and readability. Refactoring is covered in *Chapter 2, Making the Most of the Tools in Your Code Editor*.
- **Explaining error messages.** When you receive a compiler error or runtime exception message that is difficult to understand, you can copy the error message into Copilot Chat, and it can explain the error in simpler terms and offer common solutions. For example, if you encounter a `StackOverflowException`, Copilot Chat might suggest checking for infinite recursion or excessively large stack allocations.
- **Code snippets for debugging.** When you want to add logging to your application to capture more detailed information about an elusive bug, Copilot Chat can generate code snippets for integrating logging frameworks like Serilog into your .NET application, including configuring log levels and output sinks.

What might an interaction with Copilot Chat look like?

You: `"I'm getting a NullReferenceException when trying to access a property of my User object in a loop. What might be causing this?"`

Copilot: `A NullReferenceException occurs when you try to access a member on a null object reference. Here are a few things to check:`

- `Ensure that the User object is initialized before accessing its properties.`
- `If the User object is coming from a collection, verify that none of the elements in the collection are null.`
- `Add a null check before accessing the property. Here's a code snippet for safely accessing the User object's property:`

```
foreach (var user in users)
{
  if (user != null)
  {
    Console.WriteLine(user.PropertyName);
  }
}
```

GitHub Copilot Chat is a powerful tool when debugging, offering advice to solve many coding challenges. It can generate code snippets, explain concepts, and suggest best practices that reduce the time and effort required to debug and improve your .NET projects.

Before we look at memory troubleshooting tools, we should make sure you understand some of the basics of memory in .NET projects; we explore this next.

Understanding stack and heap memory

One of the most common issues with programming is managing memory. To troubleshoot memory issues, you need to start with a deep understanding of how memory is used in .NET projects.

There are two categories of memory: **stack** memory and **heap** memory. Stack memory is faster to work with but limited in size. It is fast because it is managed directly by the CPU, and it uses a last-in, first-out mechanism, so it is more likely to have data in its L1 or L2 cache. Heap memory is slower but much more plentiful.

On Windows, for ARM64, x86, and x64 machines, the default stack size is 1 MB. The .NET team decided to override the default so that .NET apps have 1.5 MB of stack memory, but this was a "completely accidental change", as you can read about in the following comment to a GitHub issue in the .NET repository:

`https://github.com/dotnet/runtime/issues/96347#issuecomment-1871528297`

It is 8 MB on a typical modern Linux-based operating system. For example, in a macOS or Linux Terminal, I can enter the command `ulimit -a` to discover that the stack size is limited to 8,192 KB and that other memory is "unlimited." This limited amount of stack memory is why it is so easy to fill it up and get a "stack overflow."

Mark Russinovich is a Microsoft expert and he wrote a deep dive article about memory and threads that is worth reading. For example, he writes, "for a thread's stack [...] the linker defaults to a reserve of 1MB and commit of one page (4K), but developers can override these values". You can read the article at the following link: `https://learn.microsoft.com/en-us/archive/blogs/markrussinovich/pushing-the-limits-of-windows-processes-and-threads`.

Warning! If the stack size limit might affect your projects, I recommend reading the following issue, especially the comments below from Microsoft employees who made the change from 1MB to 1.5MB. Migration from .NET Framework 4.7.2 to modern .NET results in `StackOverflowException` due to reduced stack size: `https://github.com/dotnet/runtime/issues/96347`.

Which of the two types of memory, stack or heap, is used by a type depends on how a .NET type is defined.

How reference and value types are stored in memory

There are three C# keywords that you can use to define .NET types: `class`, `record`, and `struct`. All can have the same members, such as fields and methods. One difference between them is how memory is allocated:

- When you define a type using `record` or `class`, you define a **reference type**. This means that the memory for the object itself is allocated on the heap, and only the memory address of the object (and a little overhead) is stored on the stack. Reference types always use a little stack memory. (If you're thinking that a reference sounds like a pointer, you'd be right, except that references are type-safe. We will look at pointers later in this chapter.)
- When you define a type using `record struct` or `struct`, you define a **value type**. This means that the memory for the object itself is allocated to the stack.

If a `struct` uses field types that are not of the `struct` type, then those fields will be stored on the heap, meaning the data for that object is stored in both the stack and the heap.

Good practice: All .NET BCL `struct` types avoid using field types that are not of the `struct` type. You should avoid doing this too. For example, do *not* do something like this:

```
public struct MyValueType
{
  // This is poor practice because string is a reference type.
  public string Name;
}
```

These are the most common `struct` types:

- Number `System` types: `byte`, `sbyte`, `short`, `ushort`, `int`, `uint`, `long`, `ulong`, `float`, `double`, and `decimal`
- Other `System` types: `char`, `DateTime`, `DateOnly`, `TimeOnly`, and `bool`
- `System.Drawing` types: `Color`, `Point`, `PointF`, `Size`, `SizeF`, `Rectangle`, and `RectangleF`

Almost all the other types are `class` types, including `string` (aka `System.String`) and `object` (aka `System.Object`).

> Apart from the difference in terms of where in memory the data for a type is stored, the other major differences are that you cannot inherit from a `struct`, and `struct` objects are compared for equality using values instead of memory addresses.

Imagine that you have a console app that calls some method that uses some reference and value type variables, as shown in the following code:

```
void SomeMethod()
{
  int number1 = 49;
  long number2 = 12;

  System.Drawing.Point location = new(x: 4, y: 5);

  Person kevin = new() { Name = "Kevin",
    Born = new(1988, 9, 23, 0, 0, 0, TimeSpace.Zero) };

  Person sally;
}
```

Let's review what memory is allocated on the stack and heap when this method is executed, as shown in *Figure 4.9* and as described in the following list:

- The `number1` variable is a value type (also known as `struct`), so it is allocated on the stack, and it uses 4 bytes of memory since it is a 32-bit integer. Its value, `49`, is stored directly in the variable.
- The `number2` variable is also a value type, so it is also allocated on the stack, and it uses 8 bytes since it is a 64-bit integer.
- The `location` variable is also a value type, so it is allocated on the stack, and it uses 8 bytes since it is made up of two 32-bit integers, `x` and `y`.
- The `kevin` variable is a reference type (also known as `class`), so 8 bytes for a 64-bit memory address (assuming a 64-bit operating system) are allocated on the stack, and enough bytes are allocated on the heap to store an instance of a `Person`.

- The `sally` variable is a reference type, so 8 bytes for a 64-bit memory address are allocated on the stack. It is currently unassigned (`null`), meaning no memory has yet been allocated for it on the heap. If we were to later assign `kevin` to `sally`, then the memory address of the `Person` on the heap would be copied into `sally`, as shown in the following code:

```
sally = kevin; // Both variables point at the same Person on heap.
```

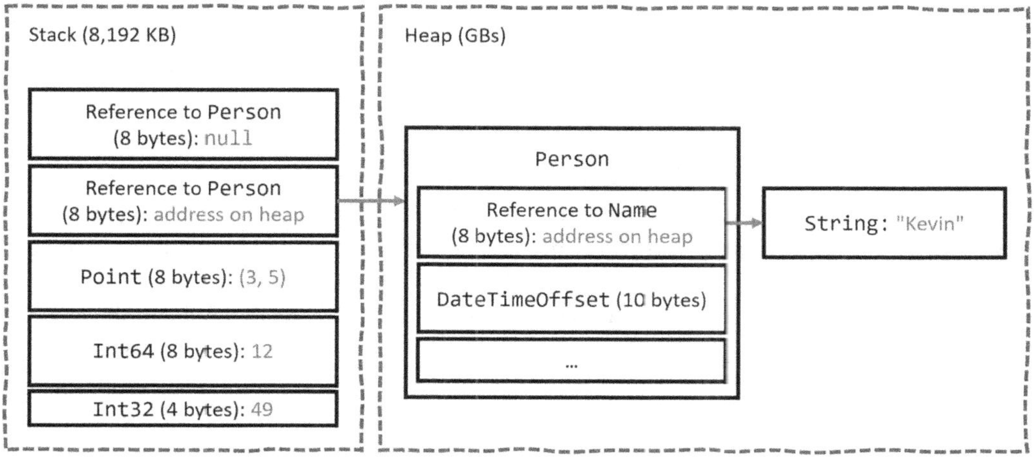

Figure 4.9: How value and reference types are allocated in the stack and heap

All the allocated memory for a reference type is stored on the heap except for its memory address on the stack. If a value type such as `DateTimeOffset` is used for a field of a reference type like `Person`, then the `DateTimeOffset` value is stored on the heap, as shown in *Figure 4.9*.

If a value type has a field that is a reference type, then that part of the value type is stored on the heap. `Point` is a value type that consists of two fields, both of which are themselves value types, so the entire object can be allocated on the stack. If the `Point` value type had a field that was a reference type, like `string`, then the `string` bytes would be stored on the heap.

When the method completes, all the stack memory is automatically released from the top of the stack. However, heap memory could still be allocated after a method returns. It is the responsibility of the .NET runtime's **garbage collector (GC)** to release this memory at a future date. Heap memory is not immediately released to improve performance. We will learn about the GC later in this section.

The console app might then call another method that needs some more stack memory to be allocated to it, and so on. Stack memory is literally a stack: memory is allocated at the top of the stack and removed from there when it is no longer needed.

C# developers do not have control over the allocation or release of memory on the stack. Technically, developers can force unreferenced memory on the heap to be collected, but they should leave that decision up to the garbage collector. Memory is automatically allocated when methods are called, and that memory is automatically released when the method returns. This is known as **verifiably safe code**.

Understanding unsafe code

C# developers can allocate and access raw memory using **unsafe code**, usually for performance benefits. The `stackalloc` keyword is used to allocate a block of memory on the stack. Memory allocated is released automatically when the method that allocated it returns.

> You can read about unsafe code and `stackalloc` at the following links: https://learn.microsoft.com/en-us/dotnet/csharp/language-reference/unsafe-code and https://learn.microsoft.com/en-us/dotnet/csharp/language-reference/operators/stackalloc.

Understanding pointers

Pointers are a low-level programming construct typically associated with unmanaged languages like C and C++. A pointer is a variable that stores the address of another variable. Pointers are powerful because they provide an efficient way to access and modify data. Pointers are used for implementing various data structures like linked lists, trees, and graphs. They enable the dynamic linking of elements without physically rearranging data in memory. Improper use of pointers, such as dereferencing uninitialized pointers (wild pointers) or pointers that have been freed (dangling pointers), can lead to undefined behavior, crashes, or security vulnerabilities like buffer overflow attacks.

.NET offers a managed environment designed to abstract away the complexities of direct memory management, providing automatic GC and type safety. Despite this, there are scenarios in .NET where pointers can be used, specifically in unsafe code blocks. This capability is primarily used for interoperability with unmanaged code, performance optimizations, or when accessing certain system resources directly.

To write unsafe code in C#, you must allow unsafe blocks at the project level and then use the `unsafe` keyword to mark a block of code or the declaration of a type or member. Unsafe code requires special permissions to run because it bypasses the safety of the .NET type system.

In unsafe code blocks, you can declare and use pointers similarly to how they are used in C or C++. For example, you can declare pointer types, allocate memory with the `stackalloc` keyword, and perform pointer arithmetic.

To declare a pointer in C#, suffix the data type with an asterisk, as shown in the following code:

```
int* pointer; // A pointer to an integer.
```

To dereference a pointer in C#, prefix the object with an asterisk, as shown in the following code:

```
int number = *pointer; // Dereferencing the pointer to get the data.
```

Let's see an example:

1. Use your preferred code editor to add a new **Console App** / `console` project named `PointersApp` to a `Chapter04` solution.

2. Modify `PointersApp.csproj` to statically import `System.Console` for all code files, treat warnings as errors, and allow unsafe code blocks, as shown highlighted in the following markup:

```
<Project Sdk="Microsoft.NET.Sdk">

  <PropertyGroup>
    <OutputType>Exe</OutputType>
    <TargetFramework>net10.0</TargetFramework>
    <ImplicitUsings>enable</ImplicitUsings>
    <Nullable>enable</Nullable>
    <TreatWarningsAsErrors>true</TreatWarningsAsErrors>
    <AllowUnsafeBlocks>true</AllowUnsafeBlocks>
  </PropertyGroup>

  <ItemGroup>
    <Using Include="System.Console" Static="true" />
  </ItemGroup>

</Project>
```

3. In `Program.cs`, delete any existing statements, and then write statements to sum an array of five numbers from 1 to 5 using pointers, as shown in the following code:

```
unsafe
{
  // Number of integers.
  const int size = 5;

  // Allocate a block of memory on the stack.
  // numbers is a pointer to the first element of the block.
  int* numbers = stackalloc int[size];

  // Initialize the array.
  for (int i = 0; i < size; i++)
  {
    *(numbers + i) = i + 1;
  }

  // Sum the array using pointer arithmetic.
  int sum = 0;
  for (int* ptr = numbers; ptr < numbers + size; ptr++)
  {
```

```
            sum += *ptr; // Dereference the pointer to get the value.
        }

        WriteLine($"The sum is: {sum}");
    }
```

Note the following about the preceding code:

- The unsafe block allows us to use pointers.
- The `int* numbers` statement declares a pointer to an integer.
- The `stackalloc` keyword allocates five (`size`) integers on the stack, and `numbers` points to the first integer. Memory allocated using `stackalloc` automatically gets freed when the current method scope ends, in this case, when the `Main` method ends when the console app stops.
- The loop for (`int* ptr = numbers; ptr < numbers + size; ptr++`) demonstrates pointer arithmetic, where `ptr` is incremented to point to the next integer in the allocated memory.
- The `*ptr` syntax is used to dereference the pointer to obtain and sum the integer values.

4. Start the project without the debugger and note the results, as shown in the following output:

```
The sum is: 15
```

You've now seen a simple example of using pointers in .NET. What else can they do?

Other uses of pointers

Other uses of pointers include platform invocation, aka **P/Invoke**, which allows calling unmanaged functions defined in DLLs (such as Win32 API functions). Pointers are often used to pass parameters by reference or to handle unmanaged structures and buffers.

For similar reasons, when interacting with COM objects using **COM Interop**, pointers may be used to handle references to COM interfaces or to pass data between managed and unmanaged code.

Component Object Model (COM) is a Microsoft technology that enables software components to interact and be used regardless of the languages in which they were developed. Despite being a relatively older technology, COM objects are still in use today in various forms and for multiple purposes, especially in Windows environments. COM is extensively used for automating tasks and integrating with Microsoft Office applications such as Word, Excel, Outlook, and PowerPoint. Many parts of the Windows OS user interface are extendable via COM objects. This includes context menu handlers, icon overlays, and toolbars in Windows Explorer, which are all implemented as COM components. **Windows Script Host** (**WSH**) and scripting languages like VBScript utilize COM for automating tasks in the Windows environment, interacting with the filesystem, and more.

In performance-critical sections of an application, pointers can be used to manipulate memory directly, potentially reducing overhead and increasing the speed of data processing or algorithms that require fine-grained control over memory.

Unsafe code can be more efficient for certain operations, such as manipulating large arrays or performing complex numeric computations, where bypassing array bounds checks can yield significant performance gains. Pointers can also be used to access memory-mapped files directly, allowing high-performance file I/O operations by mapping a file's contents to memory.

In scenarios requiring direct interaction with hardware or memory-mapped devices, unsafe code and pointers provide the necessary control and performance.

Warning! Unsafe code has the potential to introduce security risks and stability issues due to the possibility of memory corruption, buffer overruns, and similar problems typically associated with unmanaged code. Applications that rely on unsafe code may be less portable across different .NET runtimes and platforms due to direct memory access and platform-specific dependencies. Execution of unsafe code requires full trust security permissions, which may not be available in all environments, particularly in restricted or partially trusted environments like some web servers or client machines. The use of pointers and unsafe code in .NET is generally discouraged unless absolutely necessary due to the risks and complexities involved.

Understanding boxing

Boxing has nothing to do with being punched in the face, although for Unity game developers struggling to manage limited memory, it can sometimes feel like it.

Boxing in C# is when a value type is moved to heap memory and wrapped inside a `System.Object` instance. Unboxing is when that value is moved back onto the stack. Unboxing happens explicitly. Boxing happens implicitly, so it can happen without the developer realizing it. Boxing can take up to 20 times longer than without boxing.

For example, an `int` value can be boxed and then unboxed, as shown in the following code:

```
int n = 3;
object o = n; // Boxing happens implicitly.
n = (int)o; // Unboxing only happens explicitly.
```

A common scenario when boxing occurs without many developers realizing is passing value types to formatted strings, as shown in the following code:

```
string name = "Hilda";
DateTime hired = new(2024, 2, 21);
int days = 5;

// hired and days are value types that will be boxed.
Console.WriteLine("{0} hired on {1} for {2} days.", name, hired, days);
```

The `name` variable is not boxed because `string` is a reference type and is therefore already on the heap.

Boxing and unboxing operations have a negative impact on performance. Although it can be useful for a .NET developer to be aware of and to avoid boxing, for most .NET project types and for many scenarios, boxing is not worth worrying too much about because the overhead is dwarfed by other factors like making a network call or updating the user interface.

But for games developed for the Unity platform, its GC does not release boxed values as quickly or automatically; therefore, it is more critical to avoid boxing as much as possible. For this reason, JetBrains Rider with its Unity Support plugin will complain about boxing operations whenever they occur in your code. Unfortunately, it does not differentiate between Unity and other project types.

> You can learn more about boxing at the following link: `https://learn.microsoft.com/en-us/dotnet/csharp/programming-guide/types/boxing-and-unboxing`.

Understanding garbage collection

Stack memory is released when a method that allocates stack memory returns. This means it is simple to determine when it will be released.

Heap memory is released indeterminately. A special component of the .NET runtime known as the **garbage collector** (GC) decides when heap memory is released.

> In documentation, **GC** is used as a shorthand for both the concept of **garbage collection** and the specific component and class known as the **garbage collector.**

When your code creates an object, the .NET runtime allocates memory for it on the managed heap. As your application continues to create objects, the heap grows.

The GC periodically performs a collection to reclaim memory used by objects that are no longer accessible from the application. It starts by marking all live objects, which are objects accessible directly or indirectly from roots. Roots are static variables, local variables on the stack, and CPU registers holding references to objects.

Once live objects are identified, by default the collector compacts the generation 0 and 1 objects on the heap by moving these objects together, eliminating gaps created by reclaimed objects, which reduces heap fragmentation. For those who remember spinning hard drives, we used to run tools to defrag files, and this is similar.

Objects with finalizers (special methods that are like the opposite of constructors) are given a chance to execute the finalization code before the memory is reclaimed.

.NET uses a generational GC system, which organizes objects into generations (0, 1, and 2) based on their lifetime. New objects are placed in generation 0. If an object survives a GC, it's moved to the next higher generation. Higher generation objects are collected less frequently, optimizing GC performance since it's assumed that longer-lived objects will remain in memory longer, as shown in *Figure 4.10*:

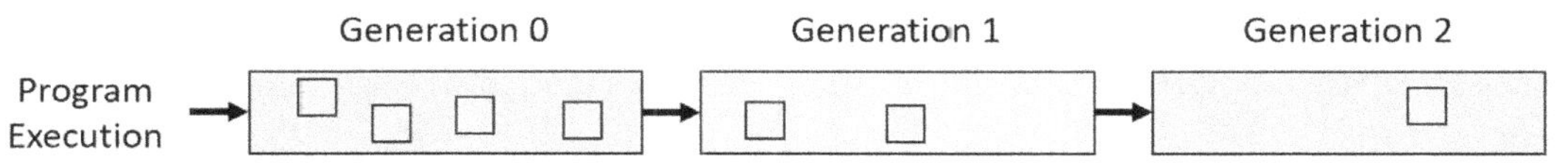

Figure 4.10: Garbage collection generations

GC generations are described in the following list:

1. **Program Execution:** Objects are allocated in Generation 0. GC occurs frequently in this generation. Newly allocated short-lived objects.
2. **Promotion:** Surviving objects in Generation 0 are promoted to Generation 1 after a GC. Objects in Generation 1 have survived at least one GC. GC is less frequent compared to Generation 0.
3. **Promotion:** Surviving objects in Generation 1 are promoted to Generation 2. Long-lived objects reside here. GC is rare in this generation.

You should also understand the **Large Object Heap (LOH)**. It's a special area of memory within the managed heap that the GC uses to store large objects separately from smaller ones. Understanding the LOH is important if you're dealing with performance tuning, memory optimization, or diagnosing memory-related issues:

- Small Object Heap (SOH): For most objects under 85,000 bytes.
- Large Object Heap (LOH): For objects 85,000 bytes or larger. LOH objects are always treated as Gen 2 objects.
- Pinned Object Heap (POH): Introduced in .NET 5 for long-lived, pinned objects.

The 85 KB threshold is hardcoded in the .NET runtime. If you allocate an object ≥ 85,000 bytes, it automatically goes onto the LOH instead of the SOH.

The LOH exists because large objects behave differently from small ones. Allocating and freeing large objects can fragment memory if handled the same way as small objects. Large objects are expensive to copy during garbage collection. Keeping them in a separate area allows the GC to optimize performance.

Good practice: Avoid unnecessary large allocations, especially in loops. Reuse large objects like buffers instead of reallocating them repeatedly. Enable LOH compaction if your app creates and discards many large objects, as shown in the following code:

```
GCSettings.LargeObjectHeapCompactionMode = GCLargeObjectHeapCompactionMode.
CompactOnce;

GC.Collect();
```

Controlling the GC

While the GC runs automatically, there are scenarios where you might want to influence its behavior manually using the `GC` class. For example, you might decide to force a GC in specific situations, such as after a large amount of memory has been freed, and you want to reclaim that memory immediately, as shown in the following code:

```
GC.Collect(); // Forces a GC of all generations: 0, 1, 2, and LOH.
```

If you have an object named `obj` that implements a finalizer but has already released its unmanaged resources, you can prevent the finalizer from running to improve performance, as shown in the following code:

```
GC.SuppressFinalize(obj);
```

You can inspect or influence the behavior of objects in different generations. For example, to check the generation of an object or to force a collection on a specific generation, as shown in the following code:

```
int objectGeneration = GC.GetGeneration(obj); // Gets the generation of obj.
GC.Collect(0); // Forces a collection of generation 0 only.
```

Managing resources with IDisposable

Unmanaged resources exist outside of the direct control of the .NET runtime, for example, database connections and files. These have both the external resources and some .NET memory allocated to represent them. If you forget to release unmanaged memory, the collector will never free it and there will be a resource leak.

If you correctly release unmanaged memory, when the GC releases the resource, it can then release the memory allocated too. But it must wait for a second garbage collection before safely removing this memory unless you implement the `IDisposable` interface and use the `GC` class to explicitly manage unmanaged resources effectively, as shown in the following code:

```
public class ResourceWrapper : IDisposable
{
  private bool disposed = false;

  // Implement IDisposable.
  public void Dispose()
  {
    Dispose(true);
    GC.SuppressFinalize(this); // Prevent finalizer from running.
  }

  protected virtual void Dispose(bool disposing)
  {
    if (!disposed)
```

```
    {
      if (disposing)
      {
        // Free managed resources.
      }
      // Free unmanaged resources.
      disposed = true;
    }
  }

  ~ResourceWrapper() // This is the finalizer.
  {
    Dispose(false);
  }
}
```

In this example, `Dispose` should be called to free the unmanaged resource. In the implementation, `GC.SuppressFinalize` is used to prevent the finalizer from running since resources are already released, optimizing GC. If the `Dispose` method is not called, then the finalizer will be used to release the unmanaged resource, but this will then require a second GC to release the allocated .NET memory.

Manual memory management with the `GC` class should be used sparingly, as improper use can negatively impact performance. Forcing GC can interfere with the optimized, automatic operation of the GC. It's typically used in scenarios with large, infrequent allocations of memory or when managing unmanaged resources.

Good practice: The .NET runtime's GC is highly optimized and best left to manage memory automatically in most cases.

Tools and skills for memory troubleshooting

Memory analysis is used to identify memory leaks, understand memory consumption, and optimize performance. The .NET ecosystem offers various tools and techniques for this purpose, tailored to the different needs and stages of application development.

Common memory tools and skills

Here's a list of some commonly used memory analysis tools and skills:

- **GC analysis:** Analyzing GC logs involves examining the GC's behavior to understand how memory is being managed, the frequency of collections, and the impact on application performance. You can enable GC logging using runtime configurations and then analyze the logs with tools like PerfView or GCStats.

- **Static code analysis:** This involves examining the code without executing it to find potential memory leaks and inefficiencies. .NET SDK includes built-in code analyzers that give warnings when APIs are misused in ways that could cause memory problems. Some third-party packages include their own code analyzers to do the same. Tools like ReSharper and CodeRush offer static code analysis features that can help identify code smells and potential memory issues early in the development cycle.
- **Profiling tools:** Profilers are the most direct way to analyze memory usage, allowing developers to measure the amount of memory objects consume and track memory allocation. Diagnostic tools are integrated directly within Visual Studio and include a memory profiler that offers insights into memory usage and potential leaks. JetBrains dotMemory is a comprehensive memory profiling tool that provides detailed analysis of memory usage, leakage detection, and memory traffic analysis.
- **Heap analysis:** Heap analysis will help you understand the allocation and lifetime of objects in the managed heap. It can identify memory leaks and the root cause of unwanted memory retention. WinDbg with the SOS debugging extension is a lower-level, powerful tool for analyzing complex memory issues, especially useful in production environments or for analyzing crash dumps. PerfView is an all-in-one performance tool that can collect and analyze memory usage data, among other metrics. It's particularly useful for its ability to analyze large volumes of data efficiently.
- **Memory tracing and leak detection:** This involves monitoring memory allocation and usage over time to detect leaks. This can be part of a testing phase or used in production with minimal overhead. For .NET projects, Visual Studio offers built-in tools for analyzing memory dumps and live monitoring of applications to detect memory anomalies.
- **Benchmarking analysis:** Combining memory profiling with performance benchmarking helps understand the memory footprint under different load conditions. BenchmarkDotNet is primarily a performance benchmarking tool, and it can be configured to collect memory diagnostics, providing a holistic view of how code changes affect both performance and memory usage.
- **Custom logging and monitoring:** Implementing custom logging around critical sections of code or for specific objects can help in tracking unexpected memory usage patterns. OpenTelemetry (OTel) or Serilog with custom metrics can be used to monitor and log memory usage, especially useful for applications running in production. You will learn about metrics and OTel in *Chapter 5, Logging, Tracing, and Metrics for Observability*.

The choice of tool and technique depends on the specific scenario, the development stage of the application, and the complexity of the memory issues being addressed.

Good practice: Early-stage development benefits more from static analysis and integrated IDE tools, while production environments might require robust profiling and heap analysis tools that have paid licenses.

For .NET developers, a combination of these tools and techniques ensures comprehensive memory analysis, helping to enhance application performance, reduce memory footprint, and improve overall stability.

Let's start with tools that are built into the most commonly used code editor, Visual Studio.

Visual Studio tools

Visual Studio tools are designed to provide insights into application performance and memory usage, helping identify and resolve issues that could impact efficiency. Visual Studio contains the following tools related to memory troubleshooting:

- **Performance profiler**: This combines various profiling tools, including CPU Usage, Memory Usage, and GPU Usage profilers, to give developers a comprehensive view of their application's performance. It collects detailed performance metrics, such as CPU time, memory allocations, and GPU usage, enabling developers to pinpoint performance bottlenecks. It allows the collection and analysis of performance data directly within the IDE, facilitating an efficient workflow for diagnosing and optimizing application performance.
- **Memory usage tool**: This tool enables developers to take snapshots of the .NET heap at various points in time, identifying memory allocations and potential leaks by comparing snapshots. It provides detailed information about object instances, their sizes, and their relationships, helping developers understand memory consumption patterns. It highlights potential memory leaks by showing objects that are being held in memory longer than expected, helping to identify the root cause of memory issues.
- **Live CPU profiling in the debugger**. This provides real-time CPU usage information while debugging, highlighting the most CPU-intensive lines of code and methods. It is available directly in the Debug toolbar; developers can quickly toggle CPU profiling on and off to diagnose performance issues while debugging. This allows developers to identify and address performance issues early in the development cycle, reducing the need for extensive profiling sessions later on.

> Visual Studio offers various editions, including the Community edition, which is free for individual developers, open-source projects, academic research, education, and small professional teams. There are differences in the availability of advanced diagnostic and performance profiling tools between the Community edition and the more premium editions. Performance Profiler (including CPU Usage, Memory Usage, GPU Usage profilers, etc.) and the Memory Usage tool are generally available in the Community edition. You can compare the Visual Studio editions at the following link: `https://visualstudio.microsoft.com/vs/compare/`.

Using Visual Studio Memory Usage

Using Visual Studio's Diagnostic Tools to measure memory usage is a great way to understand how your application allocates and uses memory over time. This can help you identify memory leaks, excessive allocations, and other inefficiencies that might affect your application's performance.

Let's create a console application that generates a list of objects in a loop, which is a common scenario where memory usage can be observed:

1. Use your preferred code editor to add a new **Console App** / `console` project named `MemoryApp` to a `Chapter04` solution.
2. Modify `MemoryApp.csproj` to statically import `System.Console` for all code files and treat warnings as errors.
3. In `Program.cs`, delete any existing statements, and then write statements to create a list of ten thousand people, which will have a measurable impact on memory usage, as shown in the following code:

```
List<Person> people = new();

for (int i = 0; i < 10_000; i++)
{
  people.Add(new Person { Name = $"Person {i}", Age = i });
}

WriteLine("Finished creating people.");

class Person
{
  public string? Name { get; set; }
  public int Age { get; set; }
}
```

4. Set two breakpoints: one on the statement that instantiates the people, and one on the statement that writes to the console.
5. Navigate to **Debug** | **Windows** | **Show Diagnostics Tools**, and then pin the pane.
6. In the **Diagnostics Tools** pane, click **Select Tools**, and make sure that **CPU Usage**, **.NET Counters**, and **Memory Usage** are selected, as shown in *Figure 4.11*:

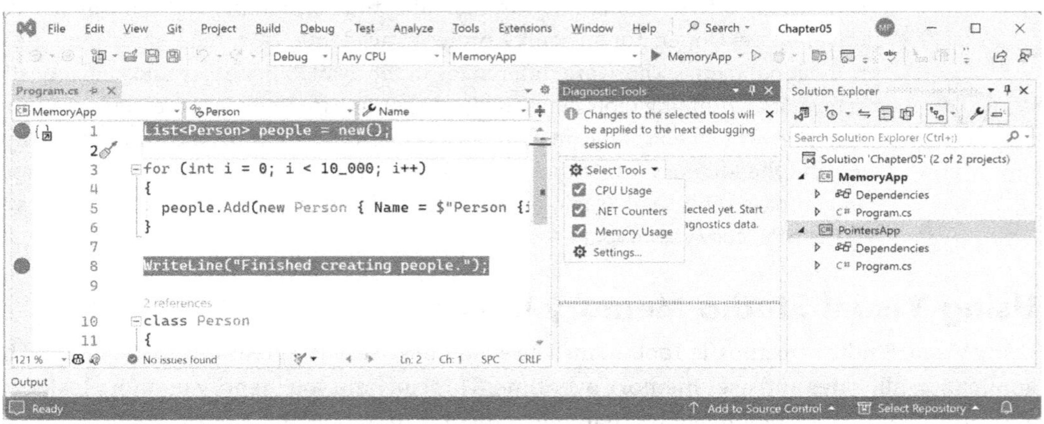

Figure 4.11: Enabling Diagnostic Tools

7. Navigate to **Debug** | **Start Debugging** or press *F5* or click the **MemoryApp** "play" button.
8. When the code stops at the first breakpoint, in the **Diagnostics Tools** pane, in the **Process Memory** section, on the **Summary** tab, click the **Take Snapshot** button Take Snapshot, as shown in *Figure 4.12*:

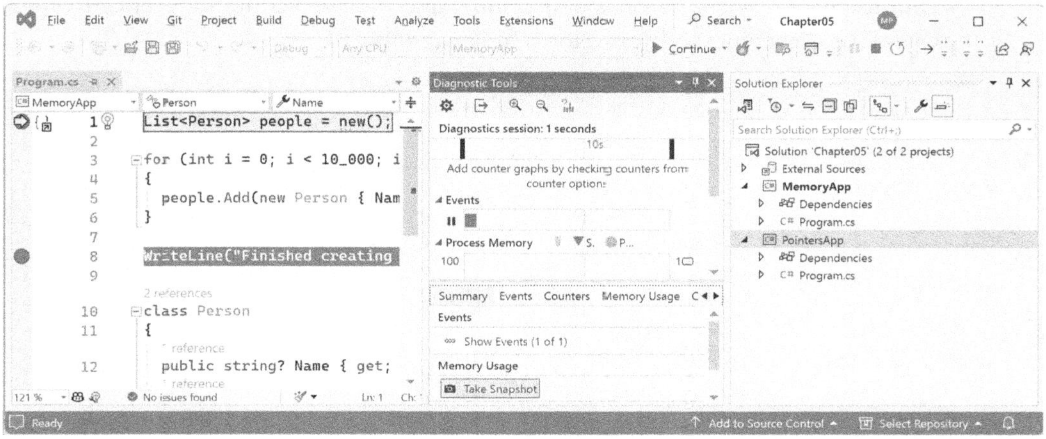

Figure 4.12: Taking a snapshot

9. Note the snapshot will be created as **Snapshot #1** and the **Memory Usage** tab becomes active, and a snapshot entry appears. This is your baseline snapshot before the list of people is allocated.
10. Navigate to **Debug** | **Continue** or press *F5*.
11. When the program stops at the second breakpoint, note the snapshot will be created as **Snapshot #2** and on the **Memory Usage** tab, in its mini toolbar, click the **Take Snapshot** button , and note that a second snapshot entry appears with up-pointing red arrows because memory usage has increased, as shown in *Figure 4.13*:

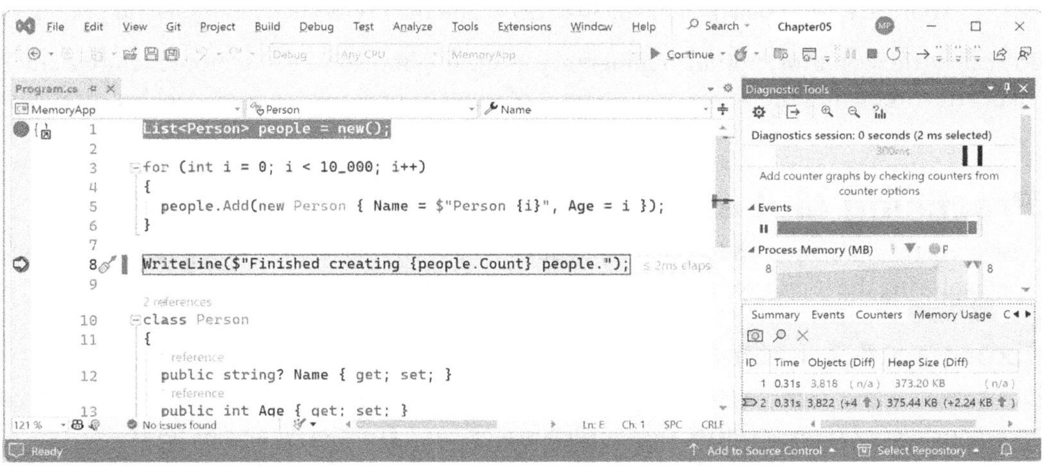

Figure 4.13: Multiple snapshots showing an increase in memory usage

12. Click on the second entry in the **Objects (Diff)** or **Heap Size (Diff)** columns to open the heap view for the selected snapshot, sorted by heap size.
13. At the top of the **Managed Memory** window, select the **Show dead objects** checkbox; in the **Filter types** box, enter `Person`; in the **Compare With Baseline** dropdown list, select **Snapshot #1**; in the list of **Types**, select **List<Person>**; and then select the **Referenced Types** tab and expand the object hierarchy, as shown in *Figure 4.14*:

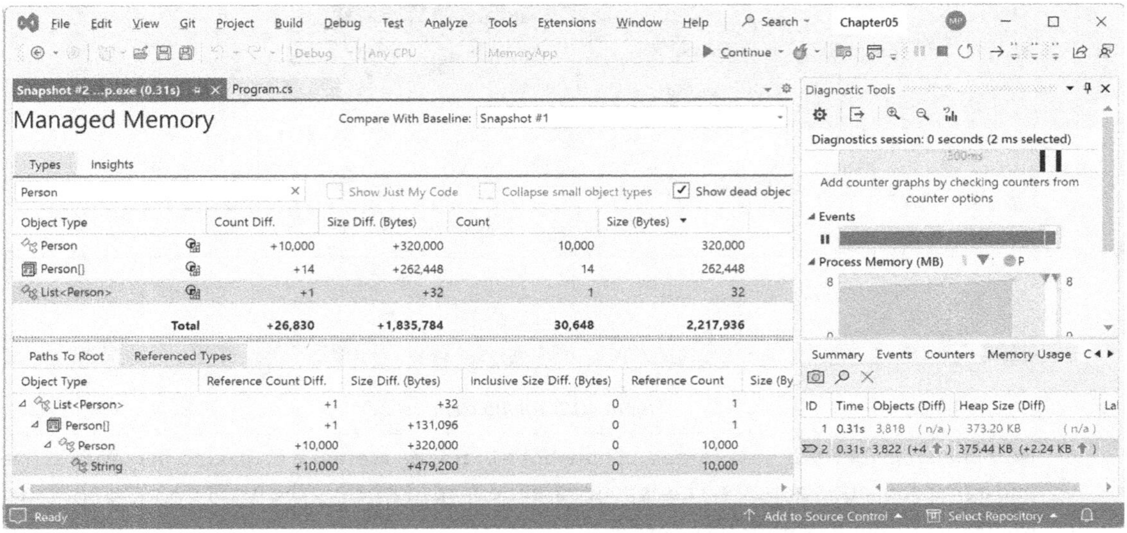

Figure 4.14: Comparing two snapshots

Note the following:

- `List<Person>` internally uses an array of `Person[]`
- There are ten thousand `Person` instances, and they reference ten thousand `string` values

In real-world scenarios, optimizing memory usage might involve using more memory-efficient data structures, reducing the scope and lifetime of objects, or implementing caching strategies where appropriate.

Practicing and exploring

Test your knowledge and understanding by answering some questions, getting some hands-on practice, and exploring the topics covered in this chapter with deeper research.

Exercise 4.1 – Online-only material

Read about some of the recent improvements with the Visual Studio debugger: `https://devblogs.microsoft.com/visualstudio/in-the-debuggers-spotlight-a-year-in-review/`.

Review the complete official documentation for profiling tools and skills with Visual Studio at the following link: `https://learn.microsoft.com/en-us/visualstudio/profiling/`.

A feature tour of Visual Studio profiling tools is available at the following link: `https://learn.microsoft.com/en-us/visualstudio/profiling/profiling-feature-tour`.

Exercise 4.2 – Practice exercises

In *Chapter 15, Containerization Using Docker*, you will learn about containerization. You can learn how to debug containers at the following link: `https://devblogs.microsoft.com/dotnet/debugging-dotnet-containers-with-visual-studio-code-docker-tools/`.

You can analyze memory usage by using the .NET Object Allocation tool, as described in the following link: `https://learn.microsoft.com/en-us/visualstudio/profiling/dotnet-alloc-tool`.

Exercise 4.3 – Test your knowledge

Answer the following questions. If you get stuck, try googling the answers, while remembering that if you get totally stuck, the answers are in *Appendix A*:

1. What are some important strategies for debugging?
2. What is the difference between the **Locals** and **Watch** windows when debugging?
3. How can you control what appears in debug panes like the **Locals** window?
4. By default, string values are surrounded by quotes when appearing in debug panes. How can you remove those quote characters?
5. What are some Visual Studio and JetBrains tools that are designed to provide insights into application performance and memory usage?

> *Appendix A, Answers to the Test Your Knowledge Questions*, is available to download from the following link: `https://github.com/markjprice/tools-skills-net10/blob/main/docs/B31468_Appendix%20A.pdf`.

Exercise 4.4 – Explore topics

Use the links on the following page to learn more about the topics covered in this chapter: `https://github.com/markjprice/tools-skills-net10/blob/main/docs/book-links.md#chapter-4---debugging-and-memory-troubleshooting`.

Summary

In this chapter, you learned:

- Strategies for debugging
- How to interactively debug code using Visual Studio
- How to define your types to control how they appear in debug windows
- How to debug test projects
- How memory, pointers, and resources are managed in .NET
- How to use Visual Studio to view memory usage

In the next chapter, you will learn about tracing, metrics, and logging for observability.

5

Logging, Tracing, and Metrics for Observability

This chapter is about logging, tracing, and monitoring with metrics, which are known as the pillars of observability.

Logging is the practice of recording events that happen within a system. Logs provide detailed information about system behavior, helping developers understand what went wrong and how to fix it. Logs can also track user actions, helping in understanding user behavior, which can help when debugging an issue, as well as serve as a historical record of what has happened in the system, which is important for security audits and compliance.

Tracing involves following the flow of a request through the various components of a system. It helps pinpoint where and why a problem occurred, making it easier to diagnose and fix issues.

Metrics are numerical data points that measure various aspects of system performance and behavior. By collecting metrics over time, you can identify trends and patterns that may indicate underlying issues or areas for optimization. Metrics also help in forecasting future resource needs and planning for scalability, ensuring that the system can handle growth.

This chapter covers the following topics:

- Logging and tracing in .NET
- Building a web service for logging
- Monitoring with metrics in .NET
- Introducing OpenTelemetry

Logging and tracing in .NET

Implementing effective logging and observability in a .NET project enables diagnosing issues, understanding system behavior, and ensuring application health. Here are the top strategies to optimize logging and observability in your .NET applications:

- **Use structured logging**: Unlike plain text logs, structured logs use a standard format (like JSON) to represent log messages, making them easier to query and analyze. This approach allows you to attach additional context to each log message, such as user IDs, session info, or environment details. For example, Serilog is highly configurable and integrates with various sinks (outputs). It enables logs to be written to files, databases, or cloud services.
- **Implement centralized logging**: You should store logs from all sources in a centralized logging system, like Serilog, that allows you to send logs to various destinations known as sinks. For example, to integrate Serilog with Elasticsearch (a distributed, RESTful search and analytics engine capable of storing and searching large amounts of data in real time), you can use the `Serilog.Sinks.Elasticsearch` package. This makes it easier to search across logs from different parts of your system and identify patterns or issues affecting multiple components.
- **Adopt a correlation ID for tracing requests**: Use a unique identifier for each request or transaction that flows through your system. This ID should be passed between microservices or components and included in all log messages related to that request. This allows you to trace the flow of requests and debugging issues in a distributed system. Good logging frameworks automatically include the correlation ID in every log entry.
- **Leverage observability tools**: Platforms like OpenTelemetry provide comprehensive observability solutions, integrating logs, metrics, and traces. Create dashboards that provide at-a-glance views of system health, **key performance indicators** (**KPIs**), and critical logs. Dashboards should be tailored to different audiences, from developers needing detailed troubleshooting data to executives interested in high-level KPIs.
- **Implement alerting and monitoring**: Configure alerts based on specific log events, error rates, or performance metrics exceeding predefined thresholds. Effective alerting means being notified before users are impacted, allowing for proactive issue resolution.
- **Educate your team**: Developers should know best practices for logging, including what to log, how to use logging levels effectively, and the importance of consistent log message formats. Be cautious not to log sensitive or **personally identifiable information** (**PII**). Foster a culture where observability is valued and understood by everyone involved in the software development lifecycle. This ensures that logging and monitoring are integrated into the development process from the start, rather than being an afterthought.

Implementing these strategies will significantly enhance your .NET project's logging and observability, leading to faster issue resolution, improved system reliability, and a better understanding of application behavior and performance.

Understanding ILogger in .NET

The `ILogger` interface is a fundamental part of the .NET logging framework, introduced as part of the `Microsoft.Extensions.Logging` namespace. It represents a generic, extensible logging interface that .NET developers can use across different types of applications. Understanding `ILogger` is crucial for implementing effective logging practices within .NET projects.

Here's what a .NET developer needs to know about `ILogger`:

- **Abstraction over logging providers:** `ILogger` provides an abstraction layer over various logging providers. This means developers can write logging code without being tied to a specific logging framework like Serilog. The actual logging implementation can be swapped without changing the application code, making it more flexible and maintainable.
- **Custom providers:** Developers can extend `ILogger`'s logging capabilities by implementing custom logging providers. This is useful for logging to custom storage systems, integrating with third-party logging services, or adding custom log processing logic.
- **Severity levels:** `ILogger` supports different logging levels or severities, allowing developers to categorize log messages by their importance. These levels are `Trace`, `Debug`, `Information`, `Warning`, `Error`, and `Critical`. This granularity helps in filtering logs based on the required verbosity and is crucial for identifying issues and understanding the application's behavior. Choose severity levels carefully to make sure that the log output is informative and not overwhelming.
- **Structured logging:** `ILogger` supports structured logging, enabling developers to log messages with placeholders and supplying the values separately. This approach keeps the log message template consistent, making it easier to query logs. Structured logging is more powerful than traditional string interpolation, as it allows for better searching and analysis in log management systems.
- **Scopes:** `ILogger` allows for the creation of logging scopes, providing a way to group a set of logical operations within a scope. This is particularly useful for associating logs with a specific operation, request, or transaction, making it easier to trace logs that are part of the same workflow or request lifecycle.
- **Integration with .NET dependency injection (DI):** `ILogger` integrates seamlessly with .NET's built-in DI framework. This integration allows `ILogger<T>` to be injected into classes, where `T` represents the class into which `ILogger` is injected.
- **Configurability in production:** Logging behavior can be configured in app settings, allowing developers and system administrators to control log levels and other settings for `ILogger` without changing the code, as shown in the following configuration:

```
{
  "Logging": {
    "LogLevel": {
      "Default": "Information",
      "Microsoft": "Warning",
      "Microsoft.AspNetCore": "Error",
```

```
        "System": "Warning"
      },
      "Console": {
        "IncludeScopes": true,
        "FormatterName": "simple",
        "FormatterOptions": {
          "TimestampFormat": "yyyy-MM-dd HH:mm:ss.fff",
          "UseUtcTimestamp": true
        }
      }
    }
  }
```

With the preceding configuration, the `ILogger` system will:

- Log messages at Information level or higher by default but use more restrictive levels for specific namespaces (`Warning` for `Microsoft` and `System`, and `Error` for `Microsoft.AspNetCore`).
- Write log messages to the console with included scopes, using a simple formatter. Scopes can be useful for adding contextual information to logs, like request identifiers or user context.
- Include timestamps in the `yyyy-MM-dd HH:mm:ss.fff` format, using UTC for the timestamps. The format here represents a full date and time with milliseconds.

> This configuration provides a balance between capturing enough information for troubleshooting (by logging information and higher levels) and avoiding excessive verbosity (by restricting `Microsoft` and `System` logs to warnings or errors). The formatted console output makes the logs easy to read and consistent in terms of timestamping.

- **Performance considerations**: While `ILogger` is designed to be efficient, developers should be mindful of logging in performance-critical paths. Excessive logging or logging at too fine-grained a level will negatively impact application performance.

Understanding and effectively utilizing `ILogger` is key to building robust, maintainable, and observable .NET applications. It not only aids in debugging and monitoring but also ensures that applications meet their logging and diagnostic requirements in a flexible and scalable manner.

How to log using ILogger

The `ILogger` abstractions and implementations are divided into separate packages, as described in *Table 5.1*:

Package	Description
`Microsoft.Extensions.Logging.Abstractions`	Provides abstractions of logging. Interfaces defined in this package are implemented by classes in other logging packages.
`Microsoft.Extensions.Logging`	Provides an abstract implementation used by the basic built-in implementations like console, event log, and debug logging.
`Microsoft.Extensions.Logging.Console`	Provides a `Console` logger provider implementation. It has dependencies on the above two packages so you do not need to reference them directly.
`Microsoft.Extensions.Logging.Debug`	Provides a `Debug` output logger provider implementation. It logs messages calling `System.Diagnostics.Debug.WriteLine()`.

Table 5.1: Logging packages and what they do

Let's see a basic logging example in a console app:

1. Use your preferred code editor to create a new **Console App** / `console` project named `LoggerApp` in a `Chapter05` solution.
2. In the `LoggerApp.csproj` project file, treat warnings as errors, and add a package reference for the console logger provider implementation, as shown in the following markup:

```
<ItemGroup>
  <PackageReference Include="Microsoft.Extensions.Logging.Console" />
</ItemGroup>
```

3. In `Program.cs`, delete any existing statements, create a logger factory with a console logger provider implementation, and then create a logger and output to the console, as shown in the following code:

```
// To use ILoggerFactory, LoggerFactory, ILogger.
using Microsoft.Extensions.Logging;

using ILoggerFactory factory = LoggerFactory.Create(builder =>
  {
    // This extension method is only available when you reference
    // the Microsoft.Extensions.Logging.Console package.
    builder.AddConsole();

    // Optionally, add other providers like:
    // AddDebug, AddEventLog, AddSerilog, AddLog4Net.
```

```
    // These methods are only available if you reference the
    // appropriate packages.
    // Optionally, add configuration like:
    // AddFilter, AddConfiguration.
  });

// The generic type parameter is used to categorize log messages.
ILogger logger = factory.CreateLogger<Program>();

string[] messageTemplates =
{
  "Logging is {Description}", // messageTemplates[0]
  "Product ID: {ProductId}, Product Name: {ProductName}"
};

logger.LogInformation(
  // The message parameter is poorly named. It is NOT a message.
  // It is a template format string that can contain placeholders.
  message: messageTemplates[0],
  args: "cool!");

logger.LogWarning(messageTemplates[1],
  // Passing a params array of objects for args parameter.
  1, "Chai");
```

Good practice: Although the parameter is named `message`, it is actually a *message template*. If you treat it like a message and pass different string values to it every time, then a string allocation is made on every method call. That wastes memory and reduces performance. To avoid these string allocations, define a limited number of message template strings and pass different values using the `args` parameter.

4. Start the `LoggerApp` project without debugging.
5. Note the result matches the message template, as shown in the following output and in *Figure 5.1*:

```
info: Program[0]
      Logging is cool!
warn: Program[0]
      Product ID: 1, Product Name: Chai
```

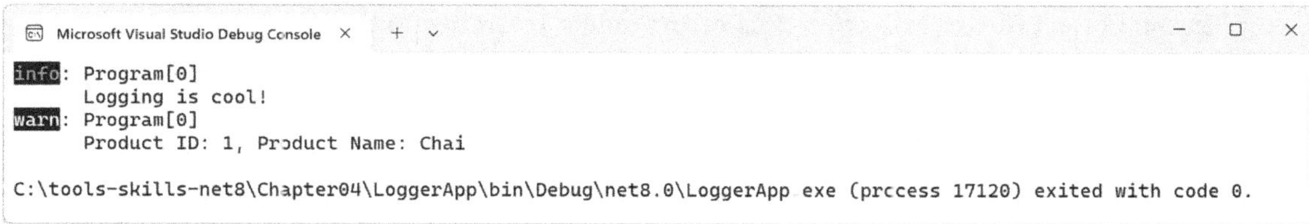

Figure 5.1: Logging information and warnings to the console

Good practice: When your application is using DI, then you should get the `ILoggerFactory` and `ILogger` objects from the DI container rather than creating them directly.

You can learn more about `ILogger` logging at the following link: `https://learn.microsoft.com/en-us/dotnet/core/extensions/logging`.

Building a web service for logging

Let's build a minimal web service project that we can then instrument with logging:

1. Use your preferred code editor to add a Web API project to the `Chapter05` solution, as defined in the following list:
    - Project template: **ASP.NET Core Web API** / `webapi`
    - Solution file and folder: `Chapter05`
    - Project file and folder: `Northwind.WebApi`
    - **Authentication type: None**
    - **Configure for HTTPS**: Selected
    - **Enable container support**: Cleared
    - **Enable OpenAPI support**: Selected
    - **Do not use top-level statements**: Cleared
    - **Use controllers**: Cleared
    - **Enlist in Aspire orchestration**: Cleared
2. Navigate to **File** | **Add** | **Existing Project...** and select the `Chapter01\Northwind.DataContext` project.

3. In the project file, treat warnings as errors, add a reference to the data context project that you created in *Chapter 1*, and remove the `version` attribute from any packages, as shown highlighted in the following markup:

```
<Project Sdk="Microsoft.NET.Sdk.Web">

  <PropertyGroup>
    <TargetFramework>net10.0</TargetFramework>
    <Nullable>enable</Nullable>
    <ImplicitUsings>enable</ImplicitUsings>
    <TreatWarningsAsErrors>true</TreatWarningsAsErrors>
  </PropertyGroup>

  <ItemGroup>
    <ProjectReference Include=
"..\..\Chapter01\Northwind.DataContext\Northwind.DataContext.csproj" />
  </ItemGroup>

  <ItemGroup>
    <PackageReference Include="Microsoft.AspNetCore.OpenApi" />
  </ItemGroup>

</Project>
```

4. Build the `Northwind.WebApi` project to restore packages and compile the referenced class library project.
5. In the `Properties` folder, in `launchSettings.json`, modify the `applicationUrl` of the profile named `https` to use port `5051` and `http` to use port `5052`, as shown highlighted in the following configuration:

```
"profiles": {
  ...
  "https": {
    "commandName": "Project",
    "dotnetRunMessages": true,
    "launchBrowser": false,
    "applicationUrl": "https://localhost:5051;http://localhost:5052",
    "environmentVariables": {
      "ASPNETCORE_ENVIRONMENT": "Development"
    }
```

6. In `Program.cs`, delete the statements about the weather service and replace them with statements to import the namespace to add the `NorthwindContext` to configured services, as shown highlighted in the following code:

```
using Northwind.EntityModels; // To use the AddNorthwindContext method.

var builder = WebApplication.CreateBuilder(args);

// Add services to the container.
// Learn more about configuring OpenAPI at https://aka.ms/aspnet/openapi
builder.Services.AddOpenApi();
builder.Services.AddNorthwindContext();

var app = builder.Build();

// Configure the HTTP request pipeline.
if (app.Environment.IsDevelopment())
{
  app.MapOpenApi();
}

app.UseHttpsRedirection();
app.Run();
```

Create extension methods for WebApplication

Let's create some extension methods for the `WebApplication` class to configure mappings for various HTTP `GET` requests that we want to handle:

1. In the `Northwind.WebApi` project folder, add a new folder named `Extensions`.
2. In the `Extensions` folder, add a new class file named `WebApplicationExtensions.cs`.
3. In `WebApplicationExtensions.cs`, import namespaces for controlling HTTP results, binding a parameter to a dependency service, and working with `Northwind` entity models. Then define an extension method for the `WebApplication` class to configure responses to all the HTTP `GET` requests documented in our API table, as shown in the following code:

```
using Microsoft.AspNetCore.Http.HttpResults; // To use Results.
using Microsoft.AspNetCore.Mvc; // To use [FromServices] and so on.
using Northwind.EntityModels; // To use NorthwindContext, Product.

namespace Northwind.WebApi.Extensions;

public static class WebApplicationExtensions
{
```

```
public static WebApplication MapGets(
  this WebApplication app, int pageSize = 10)
{
  app.MapGet("/", () => "Hello World!")
    .ExcludeFromDescription();

  app.MapGet("api/products", (
    [FromServices] NorthwindContext db,
    [FromQuery] int? page) =>
    db.Products?
      .Where(p => p.UnitsInStock > 0 && !p.Discontinued)
      .OrderBy(product => product.ProductId)
      .Skip(((page ?? 1) - 1) * pageSize)
      .Take(pageSize)
    )
    .WithName("GetProducts")
    .Produces<Product[]>(StatusCodes.Status200OK);

  app.MapGet("api/products/outofstock",
    ([FromServices] NorthwindContext db) => db.Products?
      .Where(p => p.UnitsInStock == 0 && !p.Discontinued)
    )
    .WithName("GetProductsOutOfStock")
    .Produces<Product[]>(StatusCodes.Status200OK);

  app.MapGet("api/products/discontinued",
    ([FromServices] NorthwindContext db) =>
      db.Products?.Where(product => product.Discontinued)
    )
    .WithName("GetProductsDiscontinued")
    .Produces<Product[]>(StatusCodes.Status200OK);

  app.MapGet("api/products/{id:int}",
    async Task<Results<Ok<Product>, NotFound>> (
      [FromServices] NorthwindContext db,
      [FromRoute] int id) =>
    {
      if (db.Products is null)
      {
        return TypedResults.NotFound();
      }
```

```
          else
          {
            return await db.Products.FindAsync(id) is Product product ?
              TypedResults.Ok(product) : TypedResults.NotFound();
          }
        })
        .WithName("GetProductById")
        .Produces<Product>(StatusCodes.Status200OK)
        .Produces(StatusCodes.Status404NotFound);

      app.MapGet("api/products/{name}", (
        [FromServices] NorthwindContext db,
        [FromRoute] string name) =>
          db.Products?.Where(p => p.ProductName.Contains(name)))
        .WithName("GetProductsByName")
        .Produces<Product[]>(StatusCodes.Status200OK);
      return app;
    }
  }
```

4. In `Program.cs`, import the namespace to use the extension methods you just defined, as shown in the following code:

```
using Northwind.WebApi.Extensions; // To use MapGets.
```

5. In `Program.cs`, before the call to `app.Run()`, call your custom extension method to map `GET` requests, noting that you can override the default page size of 10 entities when requesting all products, as shown highlighted in the following code:

```
app.MapGets(); // Default pageSize: 10.

app.Run();
```

Good practice: Instead of cluttering your `Program.cs` file with hundreds of lines of code, define extension methods for the common types that are configured in Minimal API web services, like `WebApplication` and `IServiceCollection`.

Testing the basic functionality of the web service

Now we can test the basic functionality of the web service:

1. Start the `Northwind.WebApi` project without debugging.
2. Navigate to `https://localhost:5051/api/products/outofstock`, and note the result, which should display the one product that is out of stock, as shown in the following output:

```
[
  {
    "productId": 31,
    "productName": "Gorgonzola Telino",
    ...
  }
]
```

3. Close the browser and shut down the web server.

We are now ready to try adding monitoring to these projects.

Monitoring with metrics in .NET

Metrics are fundamental concepts in monitoring applications and services in .NET. Metrics are closely related to alerts, as metrics provide the data that alerts use to determine when something requires attention, while

Alerts are notifications that something abnormal or noteworthy has happened within the system. By setting up alerts, you can catch issues before they become critical, thereby reducing downtime and improving system reliability.

Concepts for metrics and alerts

First, let's cover some basic concepts for monitoring with metrics and alerts, including what they are and what benefits they bring to .NET solutions.

Metrics

Metrics are quantitative measurements used to track and analyze the performance, health, and behavior of your application or system. Common .NET metrics include:

- **Performance:** CPU usage, memory consumption, request processing times, and so on.
- **Application:** Number of requests per second, error rates, response times, and so on.
- **Custom:** Any domain-specific measurements relevant to your application, such as the number of items processed, orders placed, or users logged in.

Metrics are collected over time and provide insights into the normal operation of your system. They help identify trends, diagnose issues, and optimize performance.

Common tools for recording and viewing metrics include:

- `System.Diagnostics`: A .NET built-in library for collecting performance counters.
- **Prometheus**: An open-source monitoring system often used with .NET applications via exporters.
- **Grafana:** A visualization tool that can be used with various data sources, including Prometheus.
- **Application Insights:** A comprehensive monitoring service that can collect and analyze metrics from .NET applications. This requires Azure, so we will not cover it in this book.

Alerts

Alerts are notifications triggered by specific conditions or thresholds defined on metrics. They inform you when something unusual or potentially harmful happens in your application or system. Alerts help you respond to issues promptly, minimizing downtime and impact on users.

Common scenarios for alerts include:

- **Threshold breaches:** For example, if CPU usage exceeds 80% for more than 5 minutes
- **Error rates:** If the rate of HTTP 500 responses exceeds a certain percentage
- **Custom conditions:** Any specific conditions based on your custom metrics

Common tools for alerts include:

- **Prometheus Alertmanager:** Works with Prometheus to define alert rules and send notifications.
- **Azure Monitor** with **Application Insights:** Provides powerful alerting capabilities for Azure-hosted .NET applications. Supports setting up alerts based on the metrics collected.

Scenarios for metrics and alerts

The working relationship between metrics and alerts is as follows:

1. Metrics are collected continuously from your application.
2. These metrics are monitored to understand the application's behavior and performance.
3. Alerts are set up based on specific conditions or thresholds applied to these metrics.
4. When the conditions are met, for example, a threshold is breached, then an alert is triggered, sending notifications via email, SMS, or other channels.

Suppose you have a .NET web application. You might set up the following metrics and alerts:

- **Metric:** Average response time of HTTP requests
- **Alert:** When the average response time exceeds 2 seconds over a 5-minute period
- **Metric:** Number of active users
- **Alert:** When the number of active users drops below a certain threshold, indicating potential availability issues
- **Metric:** Error rate of HTTP requests
- **Alert:** When the error rate exceeds 5%, indicating possible application issues

By continuously monitoring these metrics and setting up alerts, you can ensure your application runs smoothly and you can react promptly to any issues. Metrics provide the necessary data to understand and monitor your application, while alerts ensure you are promptly informed of any issues that require immediate attention.

Implementing metrics

In .NET, the `Meter`, `Counter<T>`, and `Histogram<T>` classes are part of the `System.Diagnostics.Metrics` namespace and are used to collect and record metrics for monitoring and diagnostic purposes.

> **Warning!** Avoid the `System.Diagnostics.PerformanceCounter` APIs because they are the legacy metric APIs. They're only supported on Windows and provide a managed wrapper for Windows OS Performance Counter technology. `System.Diagnostics.Metrics` APIs are the newest cross-platform APIs and are compatible with the OpenTelemetry project or with a .NET CLI tool for monitoring named .NET Counters, which you will see later in this section.

The `Meter` class represents a named group of instruments (such as counters and histograms) that are logically related. It acts as a factory for creating these instruments and provides a scope for them. Each `Meter` has a name and a version.

The `Counter<T>` class is a type of metric instrument that tracks the count of events or occurrences. It's typically used for metrics that accumulate over time, such as the number of requests received or the number of errors encountered. `Counter<T>` is an accumulating metric and should be used when you need to record a value that only increases.

You create a `Counter<T>` through a `Meter` instance and use its `Add` method to increment the count, as shown in the following code:

```
// Create a meter.
Meter meter = new("Northwind.WebApi.Metrics", "1.0");

// Create a counter.
Counter<int> counter = meter.CreateCounter<int>(
  "request_count", description: "Number of requests received.");

// Increment the counter.
counter.Add(1);
```

The `Histogram<T>` class is used to record the distribution of values, such as the duration of requests or the size of payloads. It helps in understanding the range and distribution of a set of measurements. You create a `Histogram<T>` through a `Meter` instance and use its `Record` method to log a value.

Good practice: In the preceding code, we created a new instance of the `Meter` class. In a project that uses DI, like ASP.NET Core, you should instead use the registered instance of `IMeterFactory`. You will learn all the reasons why in *Chapter 10, Dependency Injection, Containers, and Service Lifetime* and *Chapter 17, Design Patterns and Principles*. With .NET 8 or later, this will be registered by default in ASP.NET Core projects, or you can manually register the type in any `IServiceCollection` by calling `AddMetrics`.

Let's see a practical example of implementing a counter and histogram using a meter in our ASP.NET Core web service project.

Adding metrics to an ASP.NET Core project

We will create some endpoints in our web service to manage and update some metrics. We'll use a counter and histogram to track the number of requests and their durations:

1. In the `Northwind.WebApi.csproj` project file, add a package reference for working with performance counters, as shown in the following markup:

```
<PackageReference Include="System.Diagnostics.PerformanceCounter" />
```

2. In the `Northwind.WebApi` project, add a new folder named `Services`.
3. In the `Services` folder, add a new class file named `MetricsService.cs`.
4. In `MetricsService.cs`, import the namespace for metrics, and then define a class to configure and increment a counter for the number of requests received, as shown in the following code:

```
using System.Diagnostics.Metrics; // To use Meter, Counter, and
Histogram.

namespace Northwind.WebApi.Services;

public class MetricsService
{
  private readonly Meter _meter;
  private readonly Counter<int> _requestCounter;
  private readonly Histogram<double> _requestDuration;

  public int RequestCount { get; private set; }
  public List<double> RequestDurations { get; private set; } = [];

  public MetricsService(IMeterFactory meterFactory)
  {
    _meter = meterFactory.Create("Northwind.WebApi.Metrics", "1.0");

    _requestCounter = _meter.CreateCounter<int>(name: "request_count",
```

```
      description: "Number of requests received.");

    _requestDuration = _meter.CreateHistogram<double>(
      name: "request_duration", unit: "ms",
      description: "Request duration in milliseconds.");
  }

  public void IncrementRequestCount()
  {
    _requestCounter.Add(1);
    RequestCount++;
  }

  public void RecordRequestDuration(double duration)
  {
    _requestDuration.Record(duration);
    RequestDurations.Add(duration);
  }
}
```

5. In `Program.cs`, import the namespace for the metrics service, as shown in the following code:

```
using Northwind.WebApi.Services; // To use the MetricsService class.
```

6. In `Program.cs`, after the statement that registers the Northwind data context, add a statement to register the metrics service, as shown highlighted in the following code:

```
builder.Services.AddNorthwindContext();
builder.Services.AddSingleton<MetricsService>();
```

7. In the `Northwind.WebApi` project, add a new folder named `Middleware`.
8. In the `Middleware` folder, add a new class file named `MetricsMiddleware.cs`.
9. In `MetricsMiddleware.cs`, define a class to get the registered metrics service, record the duration of the current HTTP request, and increment a counter for the number of requests received, except for requests to the `/api/metrics` endpoint, as shown in the following code:

```
using System.Diagnostics; // To use Stopwatch.
using Northwind.WebApi.Services; // To use the MetricsService class.

namespace Northwind.WebApi.Middleware;

public class MetricsMiddleware
{
  private readonly RequestDelegate _next;
```

```
  private readonly MetricsService _metricsService;

  public MetricsMiddleware(RequestDelegate next, MetricsService
metricsService)
  {
    _next = next;
    _metricsService = metricsService;
  }

  public async Task InvokeAsync(HttpContext context)
  {
    Stopwatch timer = Stopwatch.StartNew();

    // Call the next middleware in the pipeline.
    await _next(context);
    timer.Stop();

    if (!context.Request.Path.StartsWithSegments("/api/metrics"))
    {
      _metricsService.IncrementRequestCount();
      _metricsService.RecordRequestDuration(timer.ElapsedMilliseconds);
    }
  }
}

public static class MetricsMiddlewareExtensions
{
  public static IApplicationBuilder UseMetricsMiddleware(
    this IApplicationBuilder builder)
  {
    return builder.UseMiddleware<MetricsMiddleware>();
  }
}
```

10. In `Program.cs`, import the namespace for the metrics middleware, as shown in the following code:

```
using Northwind.WebApi.Middleware; // To call UseMetricsMiddleware.
```

11. In `Program.cs`, after the statement that uses HTTPS redirection, add a statement to add the custom middleware to the request pipeline, as shown highlighted in the following code:

```
app.UseHttpsRedirection();
app.UseMetricsMiddleware();
```

12. In `WebApplicationExtensions.cs`, import the namespace for the metrics service and then add statements to define a new endpoint at `/metrics` that returns the request count and request durations stored in the metrics service, as shown highlighted in the following code:

```
public static WebApplication MapGets(
  this WebApplication app, int pageSize = 10)
{
  app.MapGet("api/metrics", (
  [FromServices] MetricsService metricsService) => new
  {
    metricsService.RequestCount, metricsService.RequestDurations
  });

  app.MapGet("/", () => "Hello World!")
    .ExcludeFromDescription();
```

13. Start the `Northwind.WebApi` project without debugging.
14. Navigate to `https://localhost:5051/api/metrics` and note there are no metrics, as shown in the following response body:

```
{
  "requestCount": 0,
  "requestDurations": []
}
```

15. Navigate to `https://localhost:5051/api/products` and note the first page of ten in-stock products is returned. (Product IDs: 1, 2, 3, 4, 6, 7, 8, 10, 11, and 12.)
16. Navigate to `https://localhost:5051/api/products?page=3`, and note the third page of ten in-stock products is returned. (Product IDs: 25, 26, 27, 30, 32, 33, 34, 35, 36, and 37.)
17. Navigate to `https://localhost:5051/api/products/discontinued` section, and note eight products are returned (5, 9, 17, 24, 28, 29, 42 and 53).
18. Navigate to `https://localhost:5051/api/metrics`, and note there are now metrics recorded, as shown in the following response body:

```
{
  "requestCount": 3,
  "requestDurations": [ 783, 21, 57 ]
}
```

19. Close the browser and shut down the web service.

Viewing metrics

You can install a global tool to view metrics, as follows:

1. Install the .NET Counters tool globally, as shown in the following command:

```
dotnet tool install -g dotnet-counters
```

2. Start the `Northwind.WebApi` project without debugging and leave it running.
3. Start **Task Manager**, search for `northwind`, right-click its entry and select **Go to details**, and then note the process ID or **PID**, which is **9552** on my system, as shown in *Figure 5.2*:

Figure 5.2: Finding the PID for the Northwind.WebApi service

> For MacOS, you can use **Activity Monitor.** For Linux, on GNOME use **System Monitor** and on KDE use **KSysGuard** or **System Activity.**

4. At the command prompt or terminal, start monitoring the web service by specifying its PID, as shown in the following command:

```
dotnet-counters monitor -p 9552 --counters Northwind.WebApi.Metrics
```

5. Make multiple calls to the web service, for example:
   - `https://localhost:5051/api/products`
   - `https://localhost:5051/api/products?page=2`
   - `https://localhost:5051/api/products/discontinued`
   - `https://localhost:5051/api/products/outofstock`
6. At the command prompt or terminal, note the results, as shown in the following output:

```
Press p to pause, r to resume, q to quit.
    Status: Running
Name
Current Value
[Northwind.WebApi.Metrics]
    request_count (Count)
3
    request_duration (ms)
        Percentile=50
49
```

```
            Percentile=95
    49
            Percentile=99
    49
```

7. Close the browser and shut down the web service.

Now let's see how we can combine all these techniques with OpenTelemetry.

Introducing OpenTelemetry

Telemetry is a combination of emitting logs and metrics from your code and then monitoring and analyzing the results. Unlike debugging, telemetry should not affect the operation and should have minimal impact on performance.

Logs are used to record a discreet operation and its success or failure. Metrics are used to record numbers, for example, completed requests, active requests, exceptions thrown, and so on.

OpenTelemetry (OTel) is an observability framework. It combines an API, an SDK, and tools that work together to generate and collect your solution's telemetry data such as metrics and logs. **Open Telemetry Protocol** (OTLP) is a vendor-neutral network protocol for transmitting telemetry data with OTel.

Since .NET provides its own logging API, you do not need to learn the OTel API. Instead, OTel integrates with `ILogger`. OTel requires the .NET 6 SDK or later.

The key benefits of using OTel with .NET projects are a common collection mechanism, common schemas and semantics for telemetry data, and an API for how third-party systems for analyzing data can integrate with OTel. These are called **exporters**. Common ones include Prometheus for metrics, Grafana for dashboards, and Jaeger for distributed tracing. Although you can manually configure these systems, in *Chapter 16, Cloud-Native Development Using Aspire*, you will see how you can easily integrate OTel with your projects and get dashboards built in.

Supported instrumentation packages

The OpenTelemetry Registry allows you to search for instrumentation libraries, collector components, utilities, and other useful projects in the OpenTelemetry ecosystem. Let's explore the registry:

1. Navigate to the OpenTelemetry Registry for .NET instrumentation packages at the following link: `https://opentelemetry.io/ecosystem/registry/?component=instrumentation&language=dotnet`.

2. Note that there are 902 total packages (at the time of writing) in the registry across all languages and package types. The list below the search filters only includes those that support .NET and are instrumentation packages, as shown in *Figure 5.3*:

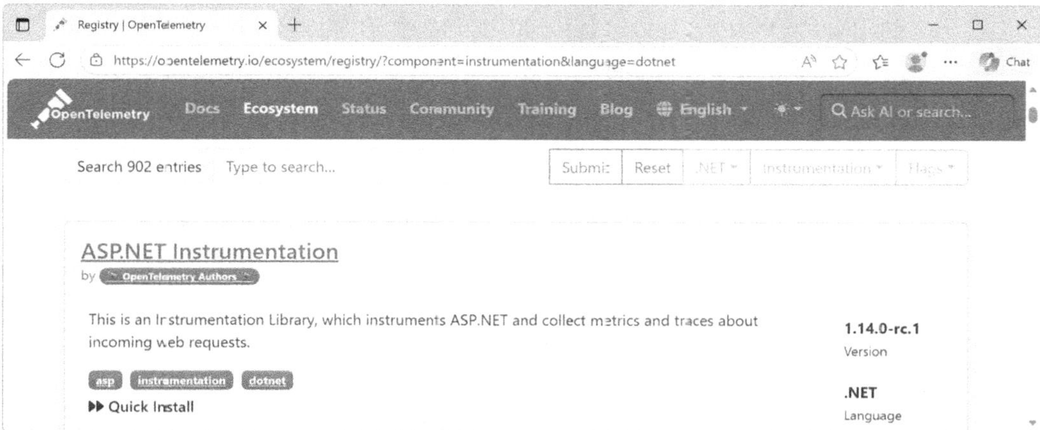

Figure 5.3: OpenTelemetry Registry instrumentation packages for .NET

3. In the **Type to search...** box, enter `sql`, click **Submit** or press *Enter*, and note the **SqlClient Instrumentation for OpenTelemetry** package is found.
4. In the **Type to search...** box, enter `entity`, click **Submit** or press *Enter*, and note the **EntityFrameworkCore Instrumentation for OpenTelemetry .NET** package is found.
5. In the **Type to search...** box, enter `aspnetcore`, click **Submit** or press *Enter*, and note the **ASP.NET Core Instrumentation for OpenTelemetry .NET** package is found.
6. In the **Type to search...** box, enter `grpc`, click **Submit** or press *Enter*, and note two packages are found, one just for client-side gRPC, and one for both the client and server side.
7. Try searching for packages and types that you commonly use in your .NET projects. For example, `HttpClient`, `Redis`, `Hangfire`, `Quartz`, `MassTransit`, `Azure`, `AWS`, and so on.

Instrumenting an ASP.NET Core project

The most common type of solution that you might want to add telemetry to is an ASP.NET Core project that stores data in SQL Server. We will use the projects that we created earlier to do this:

1. In the `Northwind.WebApi` project, add package references for OpenTelemetry integration with:
   - Export to the console
   - .NET hosting
   - Instrumentation for ASP.NET Core
   - Instrumentation for EF Core

- Instrumentation for SQL Server client, as shown in the following markup:

```
<PackageReference Include="OpenTelemetry.Exporter.Console" />
<PackageReference Include="OpenTelemetry.Extensions.Hosting" />
<PackageReference Include="OpenTelemetry.Instrumentation.AspNetCore" />
<PackageReference Include="OpenTelemetry.Instrumentation.
EntityFrameworkCore" />
<PackageReference Include="OpenTelemetry.Instrumentation.SqlClient" />
```

2. Build the `Northwind.WebApi` project to restore packages.
3. In the `Extensions` folder, add a new class named `WebApplicationBuilderExtensions.cs`.
4. In `WebApplicationBuilderExtensions.cs`, import namespaces for working with OpenTelemetry, and write statements to add and configure OpenTelemetry to the .NET logging infrastructure and to the registered DI services, as shown in the following code:

```
using OpenTelemetry.Logs; // To use AddConsoleExporter.
using OpenTelemetry.Metrics; // To use WithMetrics.
using OpenTelemetry.Resources; // To use ResourceBuilder.
using OpenTelemetry.Trace; // To use WithTracing.

namespace Northwind.WebApi.Extensions;

public static class WebApplicationBuilderExtensions
{
  private const string serviceName = "Northwind.WebApi";

  public static WebApplicationBuilder AddOTelForNorthwind(
    this WebApplicationBuilder builder)
  {
    builder.Logging.AddOpenTelemetry(options =>
    {
      options
        .SetResourceBuilder(ResourceBuilder
          .CreateDefault().AddService(serviceName))
        .AddConsoleExporter();
    });

    builder.Services.AddOpenTelemetry()
      .ConfigureResource(resource => resource.AddService(serviceName))
      .WithTracing(tracing => tracing
        .AddAspNetCoreInstrumentation()
        .AddEntityFrameworkCoreInstrumentation()
        .AddSqlClientInstrumentation()
```

```
        .AddConsoleExporter())
      .WithMetrics(metrics => metrics
        .AddAspNetCoreInstrumentation()
        .AddConsoleExporter());

    return builder;
  }
}
```

5. In `Program.cs`, before the statement that calls `builder.Build()`, call the extension method to configure OpenTelemetry for our Northwind web service, as shown in the following code:

```
builder.AddOTelForNorthwind();
```

This configuration will write trace logs about web requests, EF Core commands, and SQL client commands, and write metrics about ASP.NET Core including the Kestrel web server to the console.

Viewing the telemetry

Now we can start the project to view the telemetry:

1. Start the `Northwind.WebApi` project without debugging.
2. At the command prompt or terminal, note the additional logging associated with the setup of the HTTPS endpoint, as shown in the following output:

```
info: Microsoft.Hosting.Lifetime[14]
      Now listening on: https://localhost:5051
LogRecord.Timestamp:               2025-11-06T13:53:15.8008021Z
LogRecord.CategoryName:            Microsoft.Hosting.Lifetime
LogRecord.Severity:                Info
LogRecord.SeverityText:            Information
LogRecord.Body:                    Now listening on: {address}
LogRecord.Attributes (Key:Value):
    address: https://localhost:5051
    OriginalFormat (a.k.a Body): Now listening on: {address}
LogRecord.EventId:                 14
LogRecord.EventName:               ListeningOnAddress
Resource associated with LogRecord:
service.name: Northwind.WebApi
service.instance.id: 8074ba98-0800-4db8-805b-5fd76b3affd3
telemetry.sdk.name: opentelemetry
telemetry.sdk.language: dotnet
```

```
telemetry.sdk.version: 1.14.0
```

3. Note the additional logging associated with HTTP `GET` requests, for example, for the Swagger documentation home page, as shown in the following output:

```
Activity.TraceId:            d6efea25c5e02933af9c4f9cbfa42a8e
Activity.SpanId:             c20bd4cf4c41820d
Activity.TraceFlags:         Recorded
Activity.ActivitySourceName: Microsoft.AspNetCore
Activity.DisplayName:        GET
Activity.Kind:               Server
Activity.StartTime:          2025-11-06T13:53:16.8270755Z
Activity.Duration:           00:00:00.2663518
Activity.Tags:
    server.address: localhost
    server.port: 5051
    http.request.method: GET
    url.scheme: https
    url.path: /swagger/index.html
    network.protocol.version: 2
    user_agent.original: Mozilla/5.0 (Windows NT 10.0; Win64; x64)
AppleWebKit/537.36 (KHTML, like Gecko) Chrome/121.0.0.0 Safari/537.36
    http.response.status_code: 200
Resource associated with Activity:
    service.name: Northwind.WebApi
    service.instance.id: 8074ba98-0800-4db8-805b-5fd76b3affd3
    telemetry.sdk.name: opentelemetry
    telemetry.sdk.language: dotnet
    telemetry.sdk.version: 1.14.0
```

4. Note the additional logging associated with dozens of metrics for the Kestrel web server, for example, the number of active HTTP server requests (currently zero), as shown in the following output:

```
Metric Name: http.server.active_requests, Number of active HTTP server
requests., Unit: {request}, Meter: Microsoft.AspNetCore.Hosting
(2025-11-06T13:53:15.7220071Z, 2024-02-06T13:53:25.7214612Z] http.
request.method: GET url.scheme: https LongSumNonMonotonic
Value: 0
```

5. In the web browser, navigate to `https://localhost:5051/api/products/cha` to try out the endpoint that returns products by part of their name.

6. At the command prompt or terminal, use the search feature to look for `cha`, and note the HTTP GET request for products that contain `cha`, as shown in the following output:

```
Activity.TraceId:            dcf2799dd4b55a986bd1f899900d0fe2
Activity.SpanId:             7c799ce90ef0cc55
Activity.TraceFlags:         Recorded
Activity.ActivitySourceName: Microsoft.AspNetCore
Activity.DisplayName:        GET api/products/{name}
Activity.Kind:               Server
Activity.StartTime:          2025-11-06T14:13:15.8030496Z
Activity.Duration:           00:00:00.7640944
Activity.Tags:
    server.address: localhost
    server.port: 5051
    http.request.method: GET
    url.scheme: https
    url.path: /api/products/cha
    network.protocol.version: 2
    user_agent.original: Mozilla/5.0 (Windows NT 10.0; Win64; x64)
AppleWebKit/537.36 (KHTML, like Gecko) Chrome/121.0.0.0 Safari/537.36
    http.route: api/products/{name}
    http.response.status_code: 200
Resource associated with Activity:
    service.name: Northwind.WebApi
    service.instance.id: 53c0ed8b-a02c-4507-92ef-8bb118e614ac
    telemetry.sdk.name: opentelemetry
    telemetry.sdk.language: dotnet
    telemetry.sdk.version: 1.14.0
```

One of the most important pieces of data is the `Activity.TraceId`, which, in this HTTP `GET` request, is `dcf2799dd4b55a986bd1f899900d0fe2`. It represents the unique identifier for the entire trace, which is a set of operations that are related to the same request or workflow across services, threads, and processes. Related IDs are `SpanId`, which is ID for the current operation, and `ParentId`, which is the ID of the calling operation. `TraceId` stays the same for the entire distributed operation. `SpanId` changes for each activity within that trace. `ParentId` links to the caller's `SpanId` if the activity is nested.

7. At the command prompt or terminal, use the search feature to look for `SqlClient`, and note the `Activity.TraceId` is also `dcf2799dd4b55a986bd1f899900d0fe2`, indicating that it is the same trace through multiple tiers or layers of the solution (both the web service and data layer), as shown in the following output:

```
Activity.TraceId:            dcf2799dd4b55a986bd1f899900d0fe2
Activity.SpanId:             5afdcdd6e4d6a297
Activity.TraceFlags:         Recorded
Activity.ParentSpanId:       f344a4a64bc72502
Activity.ActivitySourceName: OpenTelemetry.Instrumentation.SqlClient
Activity.DisplayName:        Northwind
Activity.Kind:               Client
Activity.StartTime:          2025-11-06T14:13:16.4738201Z
Activity.Duration:           00:00:00.0219486
Activity.Tags:
    db.system: mssql
    db.name: Northwind
    peer.service: .
    db.statement_type: Text
Resource associated with Activity:
    service.name: Northwind.WebApi
    service.instance.id: 53c0ed8b-a02c-4507-92ef-8bb118e614ac
    telemetry.sdk.name: opentelemetry
    telemetry.sdk.language: dotnet
    telemetry.sdk.version: 1.14.0
```

8. At the command prompt or terminal, use the search feature to look for `Entity`, and note the `LogRecord.TraceId` is `dcf2799dd4b55a986bd1f899900d0fe2`, as shown in the following output:

```
info: Microsoft.EntityFrameworkCore.Database.Command[20101]
      Executed DbCommand (33ms) [Parameters=[@__name_0_rewritten='?'
(Size = 40)], CommandType='Text', CommandTimeout='30']
      SELECT [p].[ProductId], [p].[CategoryId], [p].[Discontinued], [p].
[ProductName], [p].[UnitPrice], [p].[UnitsInStock]
      FROM [Products] AS [p]
      WHERE [p].[ProductName] LIKE @__name_0_rewritten ESCAPE N'\'
LogRecord.Timestamp:                2025-11-06T14:13:16.5059590Z
LogRecord.TraceId:                  dcf2799dd4b55a986bd1f899900d0fe2
LogRecord.SpanId:                   5afdcdd6e4d6a297
LogRecord.TraceFlags:               Recorded
LogRecord.CategoryName:             Microsoft.EntityFrameworkCore.
Database.Command
LogRecord.Severity:                 Info
```

```
LogRecord.SeverityText:                 Information
LogRecord.Body:                         Executed DbCommand ({elapsed}
ms) [Parameters=[{parameters}], CommandType='{commandType}',
CommandTimeout='{commandTimeout}'][{newLine}{commandText}
LogRecord.Attributes (Key:Value):
    elapsed: 33
    parameters: @__name_0_rewritten='?' (Size = 40)
    commandType: Text
    commandTimeout: 30
    newLine:
    commandText: SELECT [p].[ProductId], [p].[CategoryId], [p].
[Discontinued], [p].[ProductName], [p].[UnitPrice], [p].[UnitsInStock]
FROM [Products] AS [p]
WHERE [p].[ProductName] LIKE @__name_0_rewritten ESCAPE N'\'
    OriginalFormat (a.k.a Body): Executed DbCommand ({elapsed}
ms) [Parameters=[{parameters}], CommandType='{commandType}',
CommandTimeout='{commandTimeout}'][{newLine}{commandText}
LogRecord.EventId:                      20101
LogRecord.EventName:                    Microsoft.EntityFrameworkCore.
Database.Command.CommandExecuted

Resource associated with LogRecord:
service.name: Northwind.WebApi
service.instance.id: 53c0ed8b-a02c-4507-92ef-8bb118e614ac
telemetry.sdk.name: opentelemetry
telemetry.sdk.language: dotnet
telemetry.sdk.version: 1.14.0
```

9. Stop the web server.

Viewing telemetry in the console is a terrible experience, but you can see the raw data that is captured and how `TraceId` values can be used to connect the many layers and technologies used in a complete .NET solution. We just need a friendly way to view and filter the raw data. To do so, you will need to export your data to a system like Jaeger, Zipkin, ElasticSearch or Prometheus.

You can learn about places that you can export OTel data to at the following link: `https://opentelemetry.io/docs/languages/net/exporters/`.

As you have seen, .NET 10 ships with first-class distributed tracing through `System.Diagnostics.Activity`. Tracing lets you follow a single request across process and service boundaries, which is invaluable when you need to understand latency, pinpoint a hot path, or reconstruct the sequence of events behind a failure.

- `TraceId` identifies the entire request across the system.
- `SpanId` identifies one operation within that request.
- `ParentId` ties spans together so you get a hierarchy rather than noise.
- .NET uses the W3C Trace Context standard, propagating IDs through the `traceparent` HTTP header.

To summarize, imagine a request from a client app to an API service that then calls a database and a payment service, as shown in *Figure 5.4*:

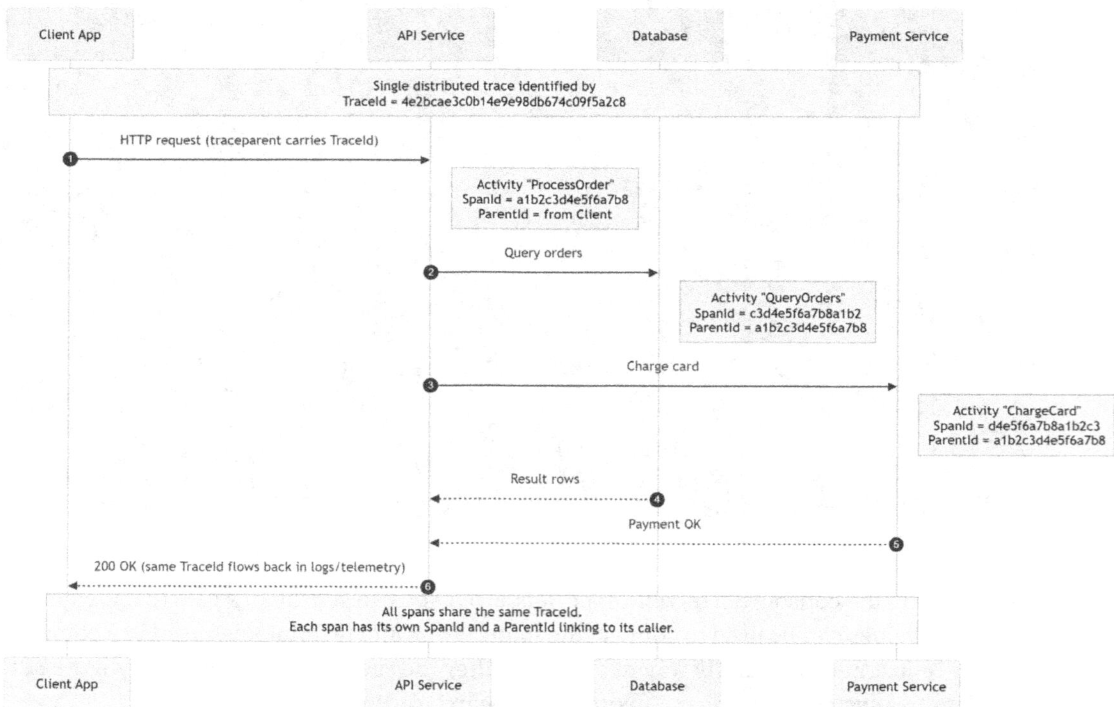

Figure 5.4: Tracing example diagram

Note the following about *Figure 5.4*:

- The `TraceId` is the umbrella ID for the entire request. Everything inside that umbrella is one story you can follow end to end.
- Each operation creates an `Activity` with a unique `SpanId`. That span reports timing, tags, and status for one step.

- `ParentId` links spans into a tree so tools can render a call graph instead of a pile of unrelated events.
- The W3C `traceparent` header keeps the `TraceId` and `SpanId` consistent as calls hop between services, as shown in the following header:

```
traceparent: 00-4e2bcae3c0b14e9e98db674c09f5a2c8-a1b2c3d4e5f6a7b8-01
```

- `TraceId` is 128 bits, `SpanId` is 64 bits, and the flags field tells you whether the trace is recorded.

But .NET developers can take advantage of an orchestration framework named Aspire, which you will learn about in *Chapter 16, Cloud-Native Development Using Aspire*.

Practicing and exploring

Test your knowledge and understanding by answering some questions, getting some hands-on practice, and exploring the topics covered in this chapter with deeper research.

Exercise 5.1 – Online-only material

Review the official OpenTelemetry documentation: `https://opentelemetry.io/docs/languages/net/`.

Exercise 5.2 – Practice exercises

You can explore some complete example solutions that implement OpenTelemetry in various types of .NET project at the following link: `https://github.com/open-telemetry/opentelemetry-dotnet/tree/main/examples`.

To learn how to use .NET and OTel with Prometheus, Grafana, and Jaeger, you can read the following article: `https://learn.microsoft.com/en-us/dotnet/core/diagnostics/observability-with-otel`.

Exercise 5.3 – Test your knowledge

Answer the following questions. If you get stuck, try googling the answers if necessary, while remembering that if you get totally stuck, the answers are in *Appendix A*:

1. What are some strategies to optimize logging and observability in your .NET applications?
2. What does a .NET developer need to know about `ILogger`?
3. Why is it important to understand that the `message` parameters of the `LogX` methods are message templates rather than individual messages?
4. What is the difference between logs, metrics, and alerts?
5. What is OpenTelemetry, and why does Microsoft recommend it for .NET development?

> *Appendix A, Answers to the Test Your Knowledge Questions,* is available to download from the following link: `https://github.com/markjprice/tools-skills-net10/blob/main/docs/B31468_Appendix%20A.pdf`.

Exercise 5.4 – Explore topics

Use the links on the following page to learn more details about the topics covered in this chapter: `https://github.com/markjprice/tools-skills-net10/blob/main/docs/book-links.md#chapter-5---logging-tracing-and-metrics-for-observability`.

Summary

In this chapter, you learned about:

- The `ILogger` interface and how it abstracts logging in .NET
- How to implement metrics for monitoring
- OpenTelemetry and how to instrument an ASP.NET Core project

In the next chapter, you will learn about documenting your code, public APIs, and services.

6

Documenting Your Code, APIs, and Services

This chapter is about documenting your code, public **APIs (Application Programming Interfaces)**, and services. Documentation improves code understandability, maintainability, team member onboarding, and the design of APIs and services, and is invaluable during debugging and support.

As well as documentation skills, we will look at some tools for helping you produce documentation efficiently. DocFX is a powerful tool provided by Microsoft that can generate API documentation, conceptual documentation, and more from your source code and Markdown files.

Mermaid is a markup language and toolset for generating diagrams and charts, for example, sequence diagrams and flow charts. Combined with the Markdown markup language, it is quick and easy to write good-looking documentation. Most code editors have built-in support for markup languages like Markdown and Mermaid, or extensions and plugins that you can install.

This chapter covers the following topics:

- Introducing documentation
- Documenting your source code
- Documenting public APIs in class libraries
- Documenting services
- Documenting visually with Mermaid diagrams

Introducing documentation

Documentation is one of those practices in software development that can be a pain while you're doing it, but its benefits will improve the quality, maintainability, and longevity of your software.

Benefits of documentation

Let's review why documentation is not just beneficial but essential, as shown in the following list:

- **Improved code understandability**: Well-documented code is far easier to understand. Poorly documented code can actually be worse than no documentation! When you're writing complex algorithms and under pressure from managers to deliver fast, it's easy to forget that what is obvious to you now will not be to someone else, or even your future self. Documentation can be used as a guide, or as a reminder, explaining why the code was written that way, and how it fits into the wider project. This is particularly crucial for complex code bases where the purpose of a block of code might not be immediately apparent.
- **Enhanced maintainability**: Software evolves over time with new features, bug fixes, and adaptations to new technologies. Documenting your code makes it easier for everyone, including yourself, to make changes in the future without breaking things. Good documentation outlines the expected behavior of the code, which means developers can make informed decisions about how to modify it.
- **Facilitates team member onboarding**: Bringing new team members up to speed is another area where documentation can save you time and effort. When you have documentation, new developers can familiarize themselves with the code base more quickly and independently and can find answers in the documentation rather than interrupting others. It also leads to faster adoption, fewer integration errors, and a smoother development process.
- **Eases knowledge transfer**: In any development team, there's always the risk of losing key personnel. If a developer who has been working on a critical piece of the system leaves and their knowledge hasn't been documented, it can leave a significant gap. Documentation ensures that knowledge is retained within the organization and not just stuck in the brains of individual developers. It should be a required step in the offboarding process.
- **Promotes best practices**: Documenting your code encourages you to write better code. When you're forced to explain your code, you're more likely to write it in a clear, logical manner from the start. You will sometimes discover bugs in your logic or conditions that your code does not account for because you've been forced to explain it. The process of documenting your code can also lead to refactoring your code to make it more efficient and understandable.
- **Improves the solution architecture and public APIs**: Documentation often includes external documents like API documentation, architecture diagrams, and usage guides. This comprehensive view of the system can help in identifying inconsistencies, redundant code, or areas where the design could be improved. When documentation is part of the development process, it encourages developers to think about the code from an outsider's perspective, which can lead to better-designed and more external-developer-friendly APIs.
- **Facilitates debugging and support**: Whether it's tracking down a bug or understanding why a system behaves in a certain way under specific conditions, documentation can provide crucial clues that lead to quicker resolution of issues. This is especially true in complex systems where the interactions between components might not be immediately obvious.

- **Enhanced cross-team understanding**: Documentation is not just written by developers, for developers. It can also be written by business analysts to explain business processes to the developers, or by technical team members for people outside the IT department.

The initial effort you put into documenting your code and APIs is an investment that pays dividends in the future, from making your code base more approachable and maintainable to ensuring knowledge transfer and facilitating debugging. It's a practice that not only benefits others but can also be a help to your future self.

Good practice: Offer a way for team members and external developers to provide feedback on the documentation. This can help identify areas for improvement or clarification. External developers are often willing to do the work to fix or extend documentation, if given the means.

When not to document

As important as knowing the benefits of documentation, and the specifics of what and how to document that are covered in the rest of this chapter, is knowing when *not* to document. Here are some scenarios where it might be justified to skip or minimize documentation:

- **Prototyping and experimentation**: When you're rapidly prototyping or experimenting with new ideas, extensive documentation can slow down the process. The nature of a prototype is often temporary, meant to test ideas or approaches rather than to serve as a final product. In these cases, it might be sufficient to use only inline comments to clarify complex logic or decisions that aren't immediately obvious from the code itself.
- **Self-documenting code**: If the codebase is written with clarity in mind, using meaningful variable and method names, consistent architectural patterns, and clear structure, the code can often be self-explanatory. This approach argues that the best kind of documentation is the code itself. However, this doesn't replace the need for high-level documentation that explains the architecture and flow of the application, but it can reduce the need for detailed inline comments.
- **Highly agile environments**: In very agile settings where changes are frequent and rapid, maintaining detailed documentation can be less feasible. Here, the documentation effort might focus more on critical areas like APIs exposed to external users or complex algorithms crucial for the system's functionality, rather than documenting every internal service or method.
- **Short-lived or temporary code**: Code that is intended to be used temporarily or that will be replaced in the near term (for example, workaround patches and temporary fixes) might not be documented extensively.
- **Internal tools for limited use**: Tools or scripts intended for internal use among a small team, particularly if all members are familiar with the project's context, might not need extensive documentation. Communication and direct knowledge transfer might be more efficient in these contexts.
- **Resource constraints**: In some scenarios, especially within start-ups or small teams, resources and time are limited, and the priority might be set on delivering functional software to meet business needs. Documentation might be deprioritized in favor of more critical tasks.

However, even in these scenarios, it's generally wise to at least document the intent and purpose of the software, key decisions that aren't obvious, and any external APIs that other developers or systems might interact with.

Now let's look at the specifics of how to document your source code.

Documenting your source code

Adding comments to your source code is an important part of software development. You will need to balance the need for documentation with the goal of keeping the codebase clean and maintainable. Every comment means extra work in the future when something changes because you must update the comments to match the code changes.

When should you document your source code?

Code can be over-commented, and it's not necessary to comment on everything. Let's review when developers should add comments to their code:

- **To explain "why" more than "what" or "how"**. The code itself should be clear enough to explain "what" it does and "how" it does it, through meaningful variable names, function names, and a clear structure aka self-documenting code. These days, "what" and "how" can also be easily explained using GitHub Copilot Chat. Therefore, comments should primarily be used to explain "why" decisions were made. This includes the reasoning behind choosing a specific algorithm, the purpose of a complex piece of logic, or why a workaround was necessary.
- **To clarify complex algorithms or logic**. When the code involves complex algorithms, mathematical calculations, or intricate logic that isn't immediately obvious, comments can be invaluable. They can guide the reader through your thought process, explain the steps of the algorithm, and clarify how the output is derived. This is especially important when the logic cannot be simplified or when the complexity is inherent to the problem being solved.
- **To highlight important behaviors or side effects**. If a piece of code has important side effects or behaviors that are not immediately obvious, either because the code itself is poorly written or the feature used is unfamiliar to the code reader, comments can be used to highlight them. This is crucial for functions or blocks of code where the implications of the operation are not apparent at first glance but are important for the correct functioning of the application.
- **When working around limitations or bugs**. This is one that developers often do not consider but it is more common than you might think. Sometimes you must implement workarounds for bugs in libraries, frameworks, or the language itself. In these cases, comments are essential to explain the context of the workaround, the nature of the bug, and, if available, provide a reference to the relevant bug report or documentation. This information is invaluable for future maintenance, especially once the bug is resolved and, therefore, the workaround can be safely removed.
- **To provide examples of usage**. In the case of libraries, frameworks, or complex functions, providing examples of usage within comments can be extremely helpful. This is particularly true for APIs or when the function is part of a public interface. Examples can show how to call a function, what parameters it expects, and the format of the expected output.

- **To mark to-dos and hacks.** Using comments to mark future tasks with tokens like `TODO` and `UNDONE`, or areas needing improvement with tokens like `HACK` can be useful for personal reminders or to inform team members of pending work. However, avoid an overabundance of `TODO`s since they can clutter the code and reduce readability. Ideally, these tasks should be tracked in a project management or issue tracker tool, but a code comment can provide immediate context within the code.

> **Good practice:** It's common to see dozens of `TODO` tokens in comments that are left undone for ages. A `TODO` comment isn't an excuse to never finish a feature or improvement. Complete your `TODO`s as soon as possible.

- **To document external dependencies.** When your code relies on external dependencies, such as APIs, libraries, or external data sources, comments can be used to document these dependencies. This includes version requirements, how the dependency is used, and potential alternatives. This information can be crucial during updates or when diagnosing issues related to these dependencies.

> **Good practice:** Document your code judiciously. Do not add comments everywhere that explain the obvious. Focus on explaining "why" and avoid "what" and "how."

Good practices for commenting your source code

Here are some good practices for commenting your source code:

- **Keep your comments up to date:** Outdated comments can be misleading and worse than no comments at all. Ensure that comments are updated alongside the code they describe.
- **Avoid redundant comments.** Do not state the obvious. Comments should provide additional value beyond what is clear from the code itself.
- **Use code as documentation:** Strive to make the code self-explanatory. Use clear naming conventions, refactor complex blocks into well-named functions, and keep the code structure intuitive. This is known as self-documenting code.
- **Leverage documentation comments:** Many languages support special formats for documentation comments that can be used to generate external documentation automatically. Use these for public APIs and interfaces. You will learn more about this in the next section of this chapter, *Documenting public APIs in class libraries*.

Comments should be used to convey the context, rationale, and additional information that cannot be clearly expressed through code alone. Keep in mind that the audience for source code comments are yourself and your team who have access to the complete source code for your projects.

Now let's turn to documenting public APIs in class libraries.

Documenting public APIs in class libraries

Documenting your source code potentially includes all code that you write, including `private` and `internal` types that are only used within your own projects. But you should pay special attention to code that forms a public API – any types that could be used outside your projects, perhaps even within your organization by other developers or teams, as well as outside your organization if you publicly publish NuGet packages.

Benefits of documenting your APIs

The importance of API documentation cannot be overstated, as it serves as the bridge between the capabilities of your software and its users, whether they are internal developers within the same organization, partners, or third-party developers. Here are some reasons why you should invest time and resources into documenting your APIs:

- **Enhances the developer experience**: Comprehensive, clear, and easy-to-navigate API documentation makes it easier for developers to find the information they need. Good documentation includes examples, error codes, and troubleshooting tips. Poor public API documentation is a major factor when developers abandon your API and choose a competing one.

  > For example, in the sixth edition of one of my books, in the section about GraphQL, I used the GraphQL.NET library (the `GraphQL.Server.Transports.AspNetCore` and related packages). However, I switched to the ChilliCream GraphQL platform because its API was better documented, and it had a much nicer API design.

- **Improves support and reduces costs**: Well-documented APIs can significantly reduce the number of support queries. When developers have access to detailed documentation, they can solve problems independently without needing to contact support. This not only improves that developer's satisfaction but also reduces the support workload on your team, leading to cost savings and allowing your team to focus on other areas of development.
- **Promotes best practices and consistency**: Creating documentation encourages you to think about your API from the consumer's perspective. This process can highlight inconsistencies, overly complex interfaces, or areas where the API might not adhere to best practices. By documenting your API, you're more likely to design a consistent, intuitive interface that follows industry standards, such as RESTful principles or GraphQL conventions.
- **Facilitates testing and integration**: API documentation often includes interactive elements, such as API explorers or sandboxes, which allow developers to test endpoints directly within the documentation. This interactive documentation can significantly speed up the integration process by allowing developers to experiment with the API in real time, understand the request and response formats, and debug issues on the fly.
- **Ensures longevity and scalability**: As your API evolves, maintaining up-to-date documentation ensures that changes are communicated effectively to users. This is crucial for ensuring backward compatibility, deprecating endpoints, or rolling out new features. Well-documented versioning strategies and change logs help users adapt to changes, ensuring the API's longevity and scalability.

- **Legal and security compliance**: For certain APIs, especially those dealing with sensitive data or operating in regulated industries, documentation can also serve a legal purpose. It can outline compliance with security standards, data protection regulations, and terms of use. Clear documentation of these aspects can mitigate legal risks and reassure users about the security and reliability of your API.
- **Marketability and community building**: API documentation can be a powerful marketing tool. It showcases your API's capabilities, demonstrates commitment to developer support, and can help build a community around your API. A vibrant developer community contributes to the API's success through feedback, bug reports, and even direct contributions in the case of open-source projects.

API documentation is much more than just a technical necessity; it's an integral part of the API's success, enhancing usability, fostering adoption, ensuring security, and assisting in the building of a developer community. Investing in high-quality API documentation is investing in the public success of your API.

So, now that you know why you should document your public APIs, how do you do it in practice?

XML comment documentation

.NET supports a standard way to document public APIs using **XML comments**. XML comments in .NET projects, denoted by `///`, are used for inline documentation and for creating automatically generated documentation for your codebase.

XML comments are used by Visual Studio's IntelliSense to provide inline documentation to developers as they write code. This feature improves developer productivity by providing quick access to function descriptions, parameter explanations, and return values directly in the coding environment as they enter code. This reduces the need to refer to external documentation, streamlining the development process and making it easier to understand and use APIs correctly.

As well as tooltips, one of the most significant benefits of XML comments is the ability to automatically generate documentation. Tools like DocFX or Sandcastle can parse these comments to produce detailed, structured documentation in various formats, such as HTML or PDF. This automated process ensures that the documentation is directly tied to the source code, reducing discrepancies and ensuring that the documentation is as up to date as the code itself.

Using XML comments encourages a standardized approach to documenting code within a project or across a team. The structure of XML comments—specifying summaries, parameters, return types, exceptions, and so on—promotes consistency in how information is documented, making it easier for anyone to understand and navigate the codebase.

In industries where documentation and compliance with certain standards are required, XML comments provide a way to ensure that all code is adequately documented according to these standards. This can be crucial for audits, regulatory compliance, and quality assurance processes.

XML comments can also be useful in unit testing and debugging. By documenting the expected behavior of a method, including edge cases and exceptions, developers can write more comprehensive tests. During debugging, these comments can provide quick insights into the intended behavior of the code, aiding in the diagnosis of issues.

Good practice: Given the relatively low effort required to maintain XML comments and the high value they bring, adopting this practice is a smart investment for any .NET project. A recent Copilot feature makes it even easier by using generative AI to automate the XML comment generation. You can learn more about this at the following link: https://devblogs.microsoft.com/visualstudio/introducing-automatic-documentation-comment-generation-in-visual-studio/.

How to document code using XML comments

.NET XML comments support a set of predefined tags that you can use to semantically structure your comments. These tags are recognized by documentation generation tools and IntelliSense, and they help organize the content clearly.

Some of the commonly used tags are shown in *Table 6.1*:

Tag	Description
<summary>	Provides a description of a type or a member.
<remarks>	Provides additional information about a type or member, complementing the summary.
<param name="name">	Describes one of the parameters for a method.
<paramref name="name" />	References a parameter in the summary or remarks.
<returns>	Describes the return value of a method.
<exception cref="member">	Specifies which exceptions can be thrown. This tag can be applied to definitions for methods, properties, events, and indexers. Use the cref attribute with a member reference to link directly to the exception class.
<example>	Gives an example of how to use a type or member. Commonly contains a <code> block.
<see cref="member" />, <seealso />	Creates a link to another type or member in the code that can be useful for providing related information or context.
<para>	Defines a paragraph (like <p> in HTML).
<c>, <code>	Applies code style to inline text and a block of text.
<list type="bullet">,	Applies bullet style. The type can be bullet, number, or table.
<item>	Defines an item in a list.
<b>, <i>, <u>	Applies bold, italic, and underline styles to text.
<inheritdoc [cref=""] [path=""]/>	Inherits XML comments from base classes, interfaces, and similar methods to avoid copying and pasting duplicate XML comments.

Table 6.1: Tags in XML comments

Good practice: The `inheritdoc` tag is especially important because it helps propagate comments, which reduces the chances of out-of-date documentation remaining in code.

Although you cannot apply complex styles, you can use the `<b>`, `<i>`, and `<u>` tags to apply bold, italic, and underline, respectively, and you can make code references stand out by using the `<c>` tag for inline code and the `<code>` tag for blocks of code. This can help distinguish code snippets or variable names from the rest of the text in documentation, as shown in the following markup and later in *Figure 6.3*:

```
/// <summary>
/// This method configures the console's culture.
/// For example, <c>ConfigureConsole()</c> sets culture to <i>en-US</i>.
/// The following code sets the console culture to <b>French in France</b>:
/// <code>
/// ConfigureConsole("fr-FR");
/// </code>
/// </summary>
```

Warning! Only bold `<b>` and italic `<i>` tags are supported in VS Code and Rider. Underline `<u>` only shows in Visual Studio.

For listing information, you can use the `<list type="<list_style>'>` tag to structure information in a bullet or number list format, which can help in organizing information clearly, such as enumerating steps, requirements, or considerations, as shown in the following markup:

```
/// <summary>
/// Consider the following points:
/// <list type="number">
///   <item><b>First</b> point.</item>
///   <item><u>Second</u> point.</item>
/// </list>
/// </summary>
```

Let's see it in action:

1. Use your preferred code editor to add a new **Class Library** / `classlib` project named `PacktLibrary` to a `Chapter06` solution.

2. Modify `PacktLibrary.csproj` to statically import `System.Console` and `System.Text.Encoding`, import the `System.Globalization` namespace for all code files, and treat warnings as errors, as shown highlighted in the following markup:

```
<Project Sdk="Microsoft.NET.Sdk">

  <PropertyGroup>
    <TargetFramework>net10.0</TargetFramework>
    <ImplicitUsings>enable</ImplicitUsings>
    <Nullable>enable</Nullable>
    <TreatWarningsAsErrors>true</TreatWarningsAsErrors>
  </PropertyGroup>

  <ItemGroup>
    <Using Include="System.Console" Static="true" />
    <Using Include="System.Text.Encoding" Static="true" />
    <Using Include="System.Globalization" />
  </ItemGroup>

</Project>
```

3. Rename `Class1.cs` to `Utility.cs`.
4. In `Utility.cs`, delete any existing statements and then define a class with two methods, as shown in the following code:

```
namespace PacktLibrary;

public class Utility
{
  public static string CurrentConsoleCulture()
  {
    return $"CurrentCulture: {CultureInfo.CurrentCulture.DisplayName}";
  }

  public static void ConfigureConsole(string culture = "en-US",
    bool useComputerCulture = false)
  {
    // To enable Unicode characters like Euro symbol in the console.
    OutputEncoding = UTF8;

    if (!useComputerCulture)
    {
      CultureInfo.CurrentCulture = CultureInfo.GetCultureInfo(culture);
    }
```

```
    WriteLine(CurrentConsoleCulture());
  }

  public static void WriteLineInColor(string text, ConsoleColor color)
  {
    ConsoleColor previousColor = ForegroundColor;
    ForegroundColor = color;
    WriteLine(text);
    ForegroundColor = previousColor;
  }
}
```

We could have implemented the `CurrentConsoleCulture` method as a property but, later in this section, I want to show how you can document the return value of a method.

5. Insert a blank line above the `ConfigureConsole` method.
6. Enter three slashes, `///`, or navigate to **Edit** | **IntelliSense** | **Insert Comment**, or right-click and select **IntelliSense** | **Insert Comment**.
7. Note that an XML comment is inserted with elements to document the two parameters named `culture` and `useComputerCulture`, as shown highlighted in the following code:

```
/// <summary>
///
/// </summary>
/// <param name="culture"></param>
/// <param name="useComputerCulture"></param>
public static void ConfigureConsole(string culture = "en-US",
  bool useComputerCulture = false)
```

8. Add text to set the following elements in the XML comment, as shown in the following code:

   - `<summary>`: Configure the console to support Unicode characters and set the culture to en-US (by default), or to a specified culture, or to the local computer culture.
   - `<param name="culture">`: Set to an ISO culture code like `fr-FR`, `en-GB`, or `es-AR`.
   - `<param name="useComputerCulture">`: Set to `true` to change the culture to the local computer's culture.

```
/// <summary>
/// Configure the console to support Unicode characters and set the
culture to en-US (by default), or to a specified culture, or to the local
computer culture.
```

```
/// </summary>
/// <param name="culture">Set to an ISO culture code like fr-FR, en-GB,
or es-AR.</param>
/// <param name="useComputerCulture">Set to true to change the culture to
the local computer's culture.</param>
public static void ConfigureConsole(string culture = "en-US",
  bool useComputerCulture = false)
```

Good practice: Remember that the text for the parameter descriptions will be shown in a tooltip so you should keep it short. It's best to give a brief description of the purpose of the parameter and, optionally, some example values.

9. Insert a blank line above the `CurrentConsoleCulture` method.
10. Enter three slashes, `///`, or navigate to **Edit** | **IntelliSense** | **Insert Comment**, or right-click and select **IntelliSense** | **Insert Comment**.
11. Add text to the XML comment to describe the summary and return value, as shown highlighted in the following code:

```
/// <summary>
/// Gets the current console culture in its native language.
/// </summary>
/// <returns>The current console culture as a string.</returns>
public static string CurrentConsoleCulture()
```

For now, we will not add XML comments to the third method.

Create a console app to use the documented library

Now let's create a console app to use the documented library:

1. Use your preferred code editor to add a new **Console App** / `console` project named `DocsApp` to the `Chapter06` solution.
2. Modify `DocsApp.csproj` to statically import `System.Console` for all code files, reference the `PacktLibrary` project, and treat warnings as errors, as shown highlighted in the following markup:

```
<Project Sdk="Microsoft.NET.Sdk">

  <PropertyGroup>
    <OutputType>Exe</OutputType>
    <TargetFramework>net10.0</TargetFramework>
    <ImplicitUsings>enable</ImplicitUsings>
    <Nullable>enable</Nullable>
```

```
    <TreatWarningsAsErrors>true</TreatWarningsAsErrors>
  </PropertyGroup>

  <ItemGroup>
    <ProjectReference Include="..\PacktLibrary\PacktLibrary.csproj" />
  </ItemGroup>

  <ItemGroup>
    <Using Include="System.Console" Static="true" />
  </ItemGroup>

</Project>
```

3. Build the `DocsApp` project to compile the referenced project and copy its assembly to the console app project's `bin` folder.
4. In `Program.cs`, delete any existing statements and then import the `PacktLibrary` namespace, as shown in the following code:

```
using PacktLibrary; // To use Utility.
```

5. On a new blank line, enter a statement to call the `ConfigureConsole` method, and note the IntelliSense that appears, as shown in *Figure 6.1*:

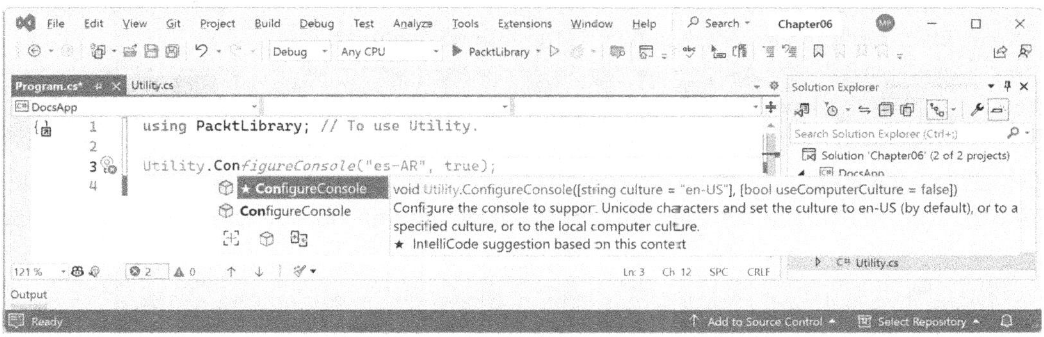

Figure 6.1: IntelliSense for a method documented using XML comments

In *Figure 6.1*, you can see that Visual Studio code completion tries to guess the arguments that you might want to pass to the method, like the string value `"es-AR"` and `true`. But that combination makes no sense because when `useComputerCulture` is `true`, the specified culture will be ignored. The AI in Visual Studio still needs some work. 😉

6. Complete the rest of the method name, type the open parenthesis, (, and note the IntelliSense that appears, as shown in *Figure 6.2*:

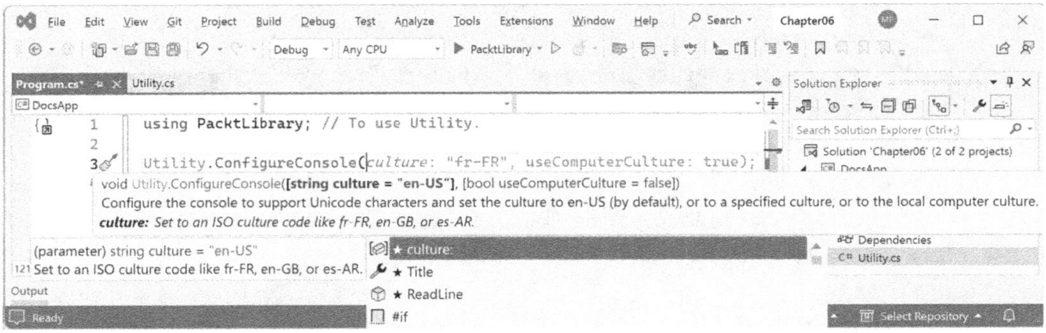

Figure 6.2: IntelliSense for the culture parameter

7. Complete the call to the `ConfigureConsole` method, and then add a statement to call the `WriteLineInColor` method to output the console's current culture in red, as shown in the following code:

```
Utility.ConfigureConsole();
Utility.WriteLineInColor(
  text: Utility.CurrentConsoleCulture(), color: ConsoleColor.Red);
```

8. Start the project and note the result is that the current console culture is US English, first in black and then in red, as shown in the following output:

```
CurrentCulture: English (United States)
CurrentCulture: English (United States)
```

While XML comments in .NET do not support direct styling within the comment blocks using something like CSS, the structure and presentation of the documentation can be enhanced using semantic tags.

Now let's see how we can generate documentation for this public API using DocFX.

Generating documentation using DocFX

DocFX builds a static HTML website from your source code (to document your public APIs) and Markdown files (so you can provide additional custom documentation pages). You can customize the layout and style of your website through templates.

When your XML comments are processed by documentation generators like DocFX, you have more control over the appearance of the final documentation. These tools allow you to apply stylesheets to the generated HTML documentation. This way, while the XML comments themselves are not styled, the output documentation can be styled extensively to match your branding or readability preferences.

Installing DocFX

DocFX is a `dotnet` CLI global tool. Let's install DocFX now:

1. At the command prompt or terminal, install DocFX, as shown in the following command:

```
dotnet tool install -g docfx
```

2. Optionally, if you have already installed DocFX, then update it to the latest version, as shown in the following command:

```
dotnet tool update -g docfx
```

3. Confirm that DocFX is installed, as shown in the following command:

```
dotnet tool list -g
```

4. Note the current version at the time of writing in November 2025 is `2.78.4`, as shown in the following output:

```
Package Id                          Version          Commands
------------------------------------------------------------------
docfx                               2.78.4           docfx
dotnet-ef                           10.0.0           dotnet-ef
microsoft.web.librarymanager.cli    2.1.175          libman
```

You can check the latest version of DocFX at the following link: `https://www.nuget.org/packages/docfx`.

Configuring a class library ready to be documented

Now we will configure the class library project to generate a documentation XML file from the source code that will then be used by DocFX:

1. In the `PacktLibrary.csproj` project file, add elements to generate documentation and control the path and filename that is created, as shown highlighted in the following markup:

```
<PropertyGroup>
  <TargetFramework>net10.0</TargetFramework>
  <ImplicitUsings>enable</ImplicitUsings>
  <Nullable>enable</Nullable>
  <TreatWarningsAsErrors>true</TreatWarningsAsErrors>
  <GenerateDocumentationFile>true</GenerateDocumentationFile>
  <DocumentationFile>
    bin\$(Configuration)\$(TargetFramework)\$(AssemblyName).xml
  </DocumentationFile>
</PropertyGroup>
```

`$(Configuration)` will be `Debug` or `Release` depending on how you build the project. `$(TargetFramework)` will be `net10.0` for this project. `$(AssemblyName)` will be `PacktLibrary` for this project. Alternatively, you could use `$(OutputPath)`, which would be the full path to where the assemblies are built in.

2. Build the `PacktLibrary` project. You will get compile errors.
3. Note the compile errors, as shown in the following output:

```
Error CS1591 Missing XML comment for publicly visible type or member
'Utility.WriteLineInColor()'
Error CS1591 Missing XML comment for publicly visible type or member
'Utility'
```

Good practice: Once you enable the generation of documentation, a code analyzer will warn you to add XML comments to all `public` types and their `public` members. Since we treat warnings as errors, we are forcing ourselves to do this work before we can build the project.

4. In the `PacktLibrary` project, in `Utility.cs`, insert a blank line above the `Utility` class.
5. Enter three slashes, `///`, or navigate to **Edit** | **IntelliSense** | **Insert Comment**, or right-click and select **IntelliSense** | **Insert Comment.**
6. Add formatted text with simple styles and a bulleted list to the XML comment, as shown in the following markup:

```
/// <summary>
/// This class contains utility methods like <c>ConfigureConsole</c>.
/// <para>
///   Sets console encoding to UTF-8 to support special characters like
Euro currency symbol,
///   and sets the current culture to one of the following:
///   <list type="bullet">
///     <item>A default culture of <b>US English</b> (<c>en-US</c>).</
item>
///     <item>A specified culture code like <i>French in France</i>
(<c>fr-FR</c>).</item>
///     <item>The <u>local</u> computer's culture.</item>
///   </list>
/// </para>
/// </summary>
```

7. Insert a blank line above the `WriteLineInColor` method.

8. Enter three slashes, `///`, or navigate to **Edit** | **IntelliSense** | **Insert Comment**, or right-click and select **IntelliSense** | **Insert Comment**.
9. Add text to the XML comment, as shown highlighted in the following code:

```
/// <summary>
/// Write a message to the console in the specified color.
/// </summary>
/// <param name="text">The text of the message.</param>
/// <param name="color">The color of the text.</param>
public static void WriteLineInColor(string text, ConsoleColor color)
```

10. Build the `PacktLibrary` project and note that the errors are gone.
11. In the `DocsApp` project, in `Program.cs`, hover your mouse cursor over `Utility` and note the tooltip, as shown in *Figure 6.3*:

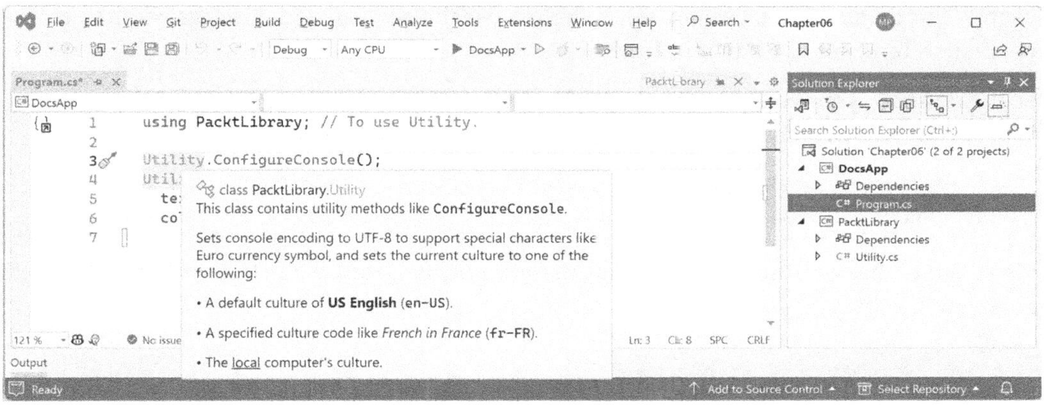

Figure 6.3: A custom formatted tooltip for the Utility class

12. In the `bin\Debug\net10.0` folder, open `PacktLibrary.xml`, and note that types are prefixed with a `T` like `T:PacktLibrary.Utility`, and members are prefixed with an `M` like `M:PacktLibrary.Utility.CurrentConsoleCulture`, as shown highlighted in the following partial markup:

```
<?xml version="1.0"?>
<doc>
  <assembly>
    <name>PacktLibrary</name>
  </assembly>
  <members>
    <member name="T:PacktLibrary.Utility">
      <summary>
        This class contains utility methods like <c>ConfigureConsole</c>.
        <para>
          ...
```

```
      </para>
    </summary>
  </member>
  <member name="M:PacktLibrary.Utility.CurrentConsoleCulture">
    <summary>
      Gets the current console culture in its native language.
    </summary>
    <returns>The current console culture as a string.</returns>
  </member>
  ...
</members>
</doc>
```

Other prefixes include `N` for a namespace, `F` for a field, `P` for a property, `E` for an event, and so on. It is useful to understand this because you can then use the `see` and `seealso` tags with the `cref` attribute to create references to these elements.

For example, you could create a reference from the `ConfigureConsole` method to the `CurrentConsoleCulture` method, as shown in the following markup:

```
/// <para>This method calls the <seealso cref="M:PacktLibrary.Utility.
CurrentConsoleCulture" /> method to output the current culture.</para>
```

Visual Studio has an auto-complete feature for doing this, so you don't necessarily need to know the complete syntax.

> You can learn more about creating links within API documentation at the following link: `https://learn.microsoft.com/en-us/dotnet/csharp/language-reference/xmldoc/recommended-tags#generate-links-and-references`.

Now we must create a DocFX documentation project that will use the XML files from the class library project.

Creating a DocFX project

Let's use DocFX to generate a web page and PDF to document the Packt class library and its `Utility` class:

1. At the command prompt or terminal, in the `PacktLibrary` project folder, initialize a DocFX project, as shown in the following command:

```
docfx init
```

2. Note the tool walks you through the process by asking you a sequence of questions. Answer them, as highlighted in the following output:

```
This utility will walk you through creating a docfx project.
It only covers the most common items, and tries to guess sensible
defaults.
Name (mysite): PacktLibrary
Generate .NET API documentation? [y/n] (y): y
.NET projects location (src): PacktLibrary
Markdown docs location (docs): docs
Enable site search? [y/n] (y): y
Enable PDF? [y/n] (y): y
About to write to C:\tools-skills-net10\Chapter06\PacktLibrary\docfx.
json:
{
  "metadata": [
    {
      "src": [
        {
          "src": "../PacktLibrary",
          "files": [
            "**/*.csproj"
          ]
        }
      ],
      "dest": "api"
    }
  ],
  "build": {
    "content": [
      {
        "files": [
          "**/*.{md,yml}"
        ],
        "exclude": [
          "_site/**"
        ]
      }
    ],
    "resource": [
      {
        "files": [
```

```
          "images/**"
        ]
      }
    ],
    "output": "_site",
    "template": [
      "default",
      "modern"
    ],
    "globalMetadata": {
      "_appName": "PacktLibrary",
      "_appTitle": "PacktLibrary",
      "_enableSearch": true,
      "pdf": true
    }
  }
}
Is this OK? [y/n] (y): y
Project created at C:\tools-skills-net10\Chapter06\PacktLibrary
Run docfx C:\tools-skills-net10\Chapter06\PacktLibrary\docfx.json --serve
to launch the site.
```

3. At the command prompt or terminal, in the `PacktLibrary` folder, host the DocFX project in a web server, as shown in the following command:

```
docfx docfx.json --serve
```

4. Note that HTML and PDF files are created in the project folder and subfolders like `api` and `docs`, and then a web server is started to immediately test the documentation website, as shown in the following output:

```
Using .NET Core SDK 10.0.100
Loading project C:/tools-skills-net10/Chapter06/PacktLibrary/
PacktLibrary.csproj
  Determining projects to restore...
  All projects are up-to-date for restore.
Processing PacktLibrary
Creating output...
Searching custom plugins in directory C:\Users\markj\.dotnet\tools\.
store\docfx\2.78.4\docfx\2.78.4\tools\net10.0\any\...
Post processor ExtractSearchIndex loaded.
No files are found with glob pattern images/**, excluding <none>, under
directory "C:\tools-skills-net10\Chapter06\PacktLibrary"
7 plug-in(s) loaded.
```

```
Building 3 file(s) in TocDocumentProcessor(BuildTocDocument)...
Building 2 file(s) in ManagedReferenceDocumentProcessor(BuildManagedRef-
erenceDocument=>SplitClassPageToMemberLevel=>ValidateManagedReference-
DocumentMetadata=>ApplyOverwriteDocumentForMref=>FillReferenceInforma-
tion)...
Building 3 file(s) in ConceptualDocumentProcessor(BuildConceptualDocu-
ment=>ValidateConceptualDocumentMetadata)...
Applying templates to 8 model(s)...
XRef map exported.
Extracting index data from 5 html files
 api\toc.pdf ---------------------------------------- 100%
docs\toc.pdf ---------------------------------------- 100%
     toc.pdf ---------------------------------------- 100%
Serving "C:\tools-skills-net10\Chapter06\PacktLibrary\_site" on http://
localhost:8080. Press Ctrl+C to shut down.
```

5. Start your preferred web browser and navigate to `http://localhost:8080`. On Windows, you can also press *Ctrl* and click on the link.
6. On the home page, in the top menu, click **Docs**. Note that the first page of the documentation is titled **Introduction** and it is a blank web page ready for you to write the content, and it has navigation links to a second documentation page titled **Getting Started**, as shown in *Figure 6.4*:

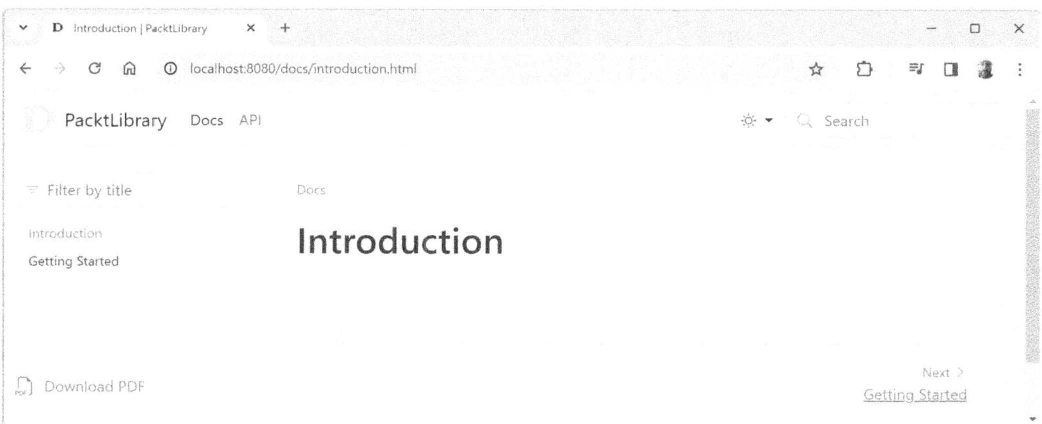

Figure 6.4: Introduction page of the documentation

7. On the **Introduction** page, in the top menu, click **API**, and note the custom formatted documentation for the `PacktLibrary` namespace and its `Utility` class, as shown in *Figure 6.5*:

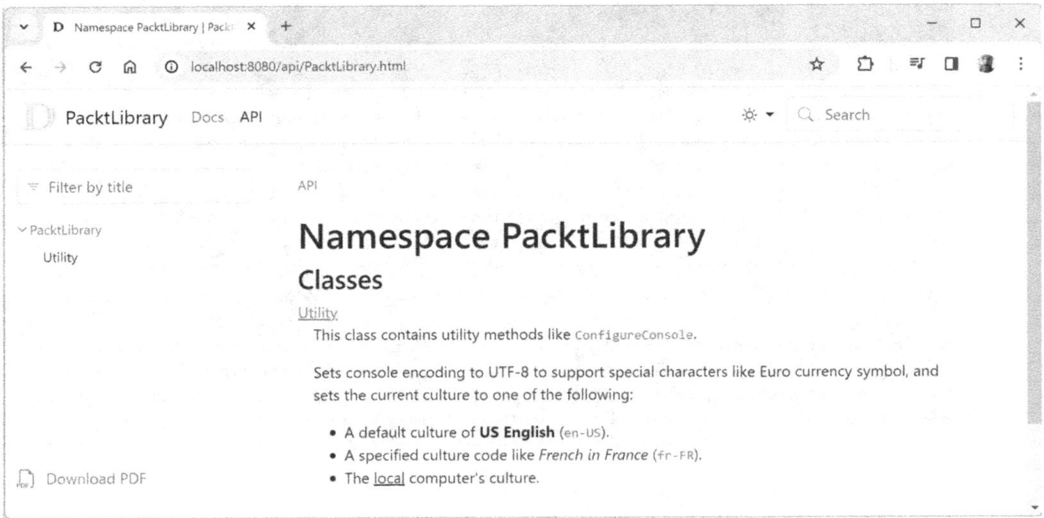

Figure 6.5: Custom formatted documentation for the PacktLibrary namespace

8. Click **Utility**, scroll down the page, and note the generated documentation for the `WriteLineInColor` method, as shown in *Figure 6.6*:

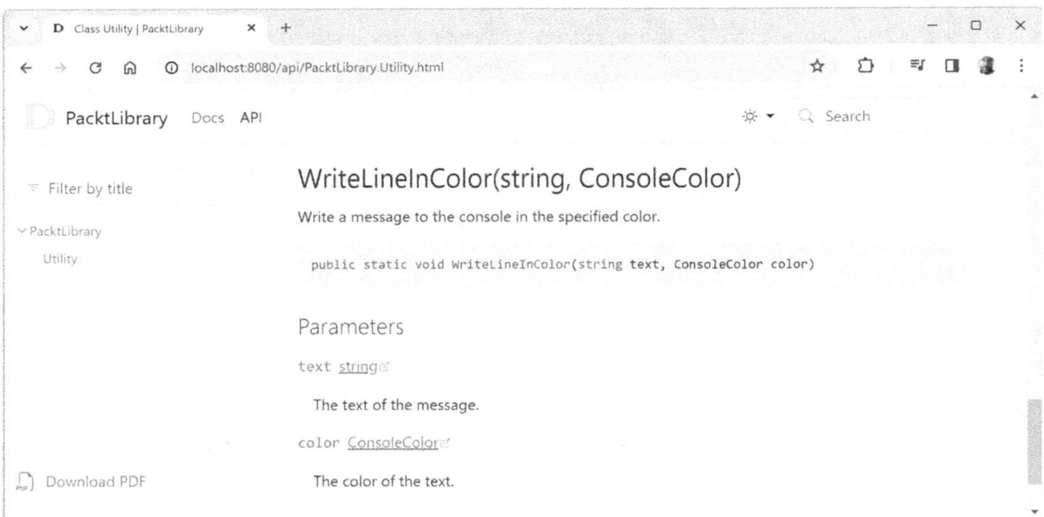

Figure 6.6: Generated documentation for the WriteLineInColor method

9. Click **Download PDF**, and note that a three-page PDF contains all the documentation for the class library.
10. Close the browser and shut down the web server by pressing *Ctrl* + *C* at the command prompt or terminal.

Now you know that you can change the XML comments to control the **API** section of the documentation website, but what about the **Docs** section? Let's find out.

Adding custom documentation content

To add new custom pages to your documentation site, you can add your own folder structure and Markdown files to the `docs` folder. Currently, the `docs` folder contains example empty pages for an **Introduction** page and a **Getting Started** page. The `docs` folder also contains a `toc.yml` file that is used to configure the table of contents, shown in the following code:

```
- name: Introduction
  href: introduction.md
- name: Getting Started
  href: getting-started.md
```

If you add more Markdown files, then you must update this `toc.yml` file to reflect the new files so that the static site is correct. For example, if you add a new Markdown file named `documenting-your-code.md`, then you would add an entry for it in the `toc.yml` file, as shown highlighted in the following code:

```
- name: Introduction
  href: introduction.md
- name: Getting Started
  href: getting-started.md
- name: Documenting Your Code
  href: documenting-your-code.md
```

On the DocFX site, there are community-built templates. You download and add these to a `templates` folder in your DocFX project. You must also update the `template` array in the `docfx.json` file to reference the new template.

> You can learn more about the DocFX template system at the following link: `https://dotnet.github.io/docfx/docs/template.html`.

Markdown markup language

Markdown is a lightweight markup language with plain text formatting syntax, designed so that it can be converted to HTML and many other formats using a tool by the same name. Created by John Gruber and Aaron Swartz in 2004, Markdown has become especially popular in the world of programming and technical documentation due to its simplicity and ease of use.

> Happy 21st birthday, Markdown!

Markdown aims to be as readable as possible in its raw form, making it intuitive for users to write structured documents without the overhead of heavier markup languages like HTML. Some of its syntax is shown in *Table 6.2*:

Syntax	Description
# Heading 1	Top-level heading
## Heading 2	Second-level heading
### Heading 3	Third-level heading, and so on
italic or _italic_	Italic text
bold or __bold__	Bold text
[Link Text](url)	Hyperlink
`![Image Alt Text](url)`	Image with alt text
> Blockquote	Blockquote text
- List item or * List item	Unordered list item
1. List item	Ordered list item
`Inline code`	Inline code block
``` or ```cs	Multi-line code block or with language label for syntax coloring
--- or ***	Horizontal rule

Table 6.2: Common Markdown syntax

Let's see some examples of the syntax in action.

Headings

Markdown allows you to create headings using the hash symbol, #. The number of hashes before the heading text determines the level of the heading, as shown in the following markup:

```
# Heading 1
## Heading 2
### Heading 3
#### Heading 4
```

This would render progressively smaller headings.

Formatting text

To emphasize text, you can make it bold or italic, as shown in the following markup:

```
*This text will be italic*
_This will also be italic_
**This text will be bold**
__This will also be bold__
**You _can_ combine them**
```

Creating lists

Both unordered and ordered lists are straightforward in Markdown, as shown in the following markup:

```
- Item 1
- Item 2
  - Item 2a
  - Item 2b
1. First item
2. Second item
```

Links and images

Adding links and images is done by enclosing the text in brackets and the URL in parentheses. For images, add an exclamation mark before the brackets, as shown in the following markup:

```
[OpenAI's Website](https://www.openai.com)
![Logo](https://example.com/logo.png)
```

Code blocks and syntax highlighting

For code blocks without syntax highlighting, you can use triple backticks, as shown in the following markup:

````
```
{
  "firstName": "John",
  "lastName": "Smith",
  "age": 25
}
```
````

For syntax highlighting, add the language identifier after the first set of backticks, as shown in the following markup:

````
```cs
void HelloWorld()
{
  Console.WriteLine("Hello, world!");
}
```
```python
def hello_world():
  print("Hello, world!")
```
````

Tables

Tables in Markdown can be created using a combination of vertical bars (|) and dashes (-). These symbols define the columns and separate the header from the body of the table. This approach makes it relatively straightforward to align columns and present data neatly.

To create a table in Markdown, you start by defining the headers, followed by a separator line that uses dashes to specify that the row above it is a header. Each column in the header and the separator line must be divided using the vertical bar (|). After the separator line, you can add each row of the table using the same format.

An example of a simple table in Markdown that organizes some information about different programming languages is shown in the following markup:

```
| Language | Creator          | Year |
|----------|------------------|------|
| C        | Dennis Ritchie   | 1972 |
| Python   | Guido van Rossum | 1991 |
| Java     | James Gosling    | 1995 |
```

This would render a table with three columns and a header row. The columns align neatly, and the data is easy to read. Markdown renderers typically style tables in a way that visually distinguishes the header row from the data rows, often by bolding the text in the header.

You can also align text within the columns of a Markdown table by including colons (:) in the separator line:

- To align text to the left, use a colon on the left side (:---)
- To align text to the right, use a colon on the right side (---:)
- To center text, use colons on both sides (:---:)

An example that demonstrates all three alignments is shown in the following markup:

```
| Left Aligned | Center Aligned | Right Aligned |
|:-------------|:--------------:|--------------:|
| text         | text           | text          |
| more text    | more text      | more text     |
```

Using these simple rules, you can create tables in Markdown that suit a wide range of needs, from displaying data compactly to organizing content in a visually appealing way.

Overall, Markdown's simplicity and ease of use make it an ideal choice for writing rich, well-structured technical documents. Mastering Markdown can significantly streamline your workflow.

You can view cheat sheets for Markdown at the following links: `https://www.markdownguide.org/cheat-sheet/` and `https://github.com/adam-p/markdown-here/wiki/Markdown-Cheatsheet`.

Documenting services

Documenting services, especially those exposed as web APIs, ensure that they are usable, maintainable, and accessible to developers. Several tools and formats have emerged as standards for documenting APIs and services, each with its own set of features and considerations.

Considerations for documenting services

The most important considerations for documenting services are shown in the following list:

- **Audience understanding**: Know your audience and their needs. Different stakeholders may require different levels of detail and technical depth. Microsoft has many tools like Power BI and other Power Platform products that are used by non-developers that can pull data from services so do not assume that the users of your service are all experienced developers.
- **Examples and tutorials**: Include practical examples and tutorials. Showing how to make common requests or implement typical use cases can greatly enhance understanding.
- **Versioning**: Services evolve over time so make sure your documentation reflects the correct version of the service and allow the user to switch to the documentation for older versions if they are still supported. Clearly indicate deprecated features or endpoints.
- **Accessibility**: Consider how users will access your documentation. Ease of navigation, search functionality, and responsive design are critical for their experience.
- **Security and authentication**: Document any authentication requirements clearly, including examples of how to authenticate requests.
- **Error handling**: Provide a dedicated documentation page with clear descriptions of possible errors, their meanings, and potential solutions or troubleshooting steps.

Tools for documenting services

Choosing the right tool and approach depends on your specific needs, the complexity of the service, and the preferences of your development team and API consumers. A combination of tools may be necessary to fully document larger or more complex services.

Popular standards and tools for documenting services include the following:

- **Swagger** aka **OpenAPI**: The **OpenAPI Specification (OAS)** is a widely used framework for API specification. It allows developers to describe the entire API including endpoints, request/response schemas, authentication methods, and so on in a JSON or YAML file. Although it can be verbose, its open ecosystem and tooling support make it a popular choice for documenting RESTful APIs.
- **Swashbuckle:** The OpenAPI ecosystem includes third-party tools that help generate the required files based on your .NET project. Swashbuckle is one of those tools and it includes an editor for writing and documenting your API specification, Swagger UI for generating dynamic API documentation that developers can interact with, and the ability to generate client libraries from an OpenAPI specification. Alternatives to Swashbuckle include **Scalar**, **NSwag** and **FastEndpoints**.

> **Warning!** Swashbuckle was used in .NET project templates since .NET 5, but it has been removed from the project templates since .NET 9, as you can read about at the following link: `https://github.com/dotnet/aspnetcore/issues/54599`. The Swashbuckle project is no longer actively maintained by its community owner. Microsoft plans to extend the capabilities introduced with `Microsoft.AspNetCore.OpenApi` to provide OpenAPI document generation. They have not yet decided if they will also implement dynamically producing a web-based UI to interactively test the API.

- **Postman**: Commonly known as a tool for API testing, this can also be used for documentation. You can document your API as you test it, but it is tied closely to the Postman ecosystem. Some organizations will not be comfortable using Postman for interaction with a public web service.
- **Read the Docs**: This is a documentation hosting platform that automatically updates your documentation from your version control system. It is often used for more comprehensive documentation needs beyond just API endpoints, covering the broader context, with examples and tutorials. It has good support for versioning services, which is critical for maintaining simultaneous documentation across different versions of your service.

Now let's look at how to use OpenAPI for documenting services.

Understanding the OpenAPI Specification (OAS)

OpenAPI aka Swagger is an open standard for describing, producing, consuming, and visualizing RESTful web services. It allows both humans and computers to discover and understand the capabilities of a service without requiring access to source code, additional documentation, or inspection of network traffic. In this section, we cover what a .NET developer should know about OpenAPI for documenting services.

You should understand the structure and syntax of the OpenAPI Specification. It's a language-agnostic definition format used to describe your API's endpoints, operations, input/output parameters, authentication methods, and other details. The specification can be written in YAML or JSON format. You can learn more at the following link: `https://spec.openapis.org/oas/latest.html`.

Familiarize yourself with the OpenAPI tooling ecosystem, which includes Scalar, NSwag, and FastEndpoints:

- **Scalar**: `https://scalar.com/`
- **NSwag**: `https://github.com/RicoSuter/NSwag`
- **FastEndpoints**: `https://github.com/FastEndpoints/FastEndpoints`

ASP.NET Core natively supports OpenAPI so it can automatically generate the OpenAPI documentation from your code. For .NET 5 to .NET 8, this was achieved using Swashbuckle packages. For .NET 9 and later, this is achieved using a Microsoft package.

You should learn the best practices for API design and documentation with OpenAPI. This includes defining clear and concise operation summaries and descriptions, using consistent naming conventions for paths, parameters, and schema, documenting all request and response models accurately, including status codes and error messages, versioning your API, and documenting changes clearly in the specification. You can learn more about Web API design at the following link: `https://swagger.io/solutions/api-design/`.

Ensure you understand how to describe security schemes in your OpenAPI document. OpenAPI supports various authentication mechanisms, including API keys, HTTP basic authentication, OAuth2, and OpenID Connect. Knowing how to properly document these schemes is important for securing your API and ensuring users know how to authenticate their requests. You can learn more at the following link: `https://learn.openapis.org/specification/security.html`.

Explore how to use OpenAPI specifications to generate client libraries and server stubs. This can speed up development, ensure consistency between your API's implementation and its documentation, and facilitate the development of client applications in various programming languages. You can learn more at the following link: `https://github.com/OpenAPITools/openapi-generator` and `https://swagger.io/tools/swagger-codegen/`.

For a .NET developer, mastering OpenAPI for services means not only understanding how to document APIs but also leveraging a suite of tools to design, test, secure, and generate code for APIs. It's about adopting a specification-first approach to API development, which can lead to more robust, understandable, and easily consumable web services.

Documenting a Minimal API web service using OpenAPI

The most widely used methods to document an ASP.NET Core Minimal API web service using OpenAPI are shown in *Table 6.3*:

Method	Description
`AddEndpointsApiExplorer`	Adds API exploration services, which are necessary for Swashbuckle to generate the OpenAPI specification from your Minimal API endpoints.
`AddSwaggerGen`	Configures Swashbuckle with a basic Swagger document named `v1` and sets up an API title and version.
`UseSwagger`	In the development environment, it enables Swagger UI and specifies the path to the generated OpenAPI specification.
`UseSwaggerUI`	Register the SwaggerUI middleware with optional setup action for DI-injected options.

Table 6.3: Methods to configure ASP.NET Core services for OpenAPI

As with documenting a public API for a class library, make sure to enable generation of documentation for the project, as shown in the following markup:

```
<GenerateDocumentationFile>true</GenerateDocumentationFile>
```

You need to configure OpenAPI to include any XML comments to enrich the generated OpenAPI documentation by modifying the `AddSwaggerGen` call in `Program.cs` to include the generated XML documentation file, as shown in the following code:

```
builder.Services.AddSwaggerGen(c =>
{
  c.SwaggerDoc("v1", new OpenApiInfo { Title = "Northwind API", Version = "v1"
});

  // Set the comments path for the Swagger JSON and UI.
  string xmlFile = $"{Assembly.GetExecutingAssembly().GetName().Name}.xml";
  string xmlPath = Path.Combine(AppContext.BaseDirectory, xmlFile);
  c.IncludeXmlComments(xmlPath);
});
```

Let's look at how to document an ASP.NET Core Minimal APIs web service using OpenAPI:

1. Use your preferred code editor to add a Web API project to the `Chapter06` solution, as defined in the following list:
    - Project template: **ASP.NET Core Web API** / `webapi`
    - Solution file and folder: `Chapter06`
    - Project file and folder: `Northwind.WebApi`
    - **Authentication type: None**
    - **Configure for HTTPS**: Selected
    - **Enable container support**: Cleared
    - **Enable OpenAPI support**: Selected
    - **Do not use top-level statements**: Cleared
    - **Use controllers**: Cleared
    - **Enlist in Aspire orchestration**: Cleared

    Warning! If you are using Rider, the option to create a Web API project using Minimal APIs is in the **Advanced Settings** section with a checkbox labeled **Use-MinimalAPIs.**

2. In the project file, treat warnings as errors, and then note the package reference for Microsoft's OpenAPI package, as shown highlighted in the following markup:

```
<Project Sdk="Microsoft.NET.Sdk.Web">

  <PropertyGroup>
    <TargetFramework>net10.0</TargetFramework>
```

```
    <Nullable>enable</Nullable>
    <ImplicitUsings>enable</ImplicitUsings>
    <TreatWarningsAsErrors>true</TreatWarningsAsErrors>
  </PropertyGroup>

  <ItemGroup>
    <PackageReference Include="Microsoft.AspNetCore.OpenApi" />
  </ItemGroup>

</Project>
```

3. Build the `Northwind.WebApi` project to restore packages.
4. In the `Properties` folder, in `launchSettings.json`, modify the `applicationUrl` of the profile named `https` to use port `50061` and `http` to use port `50062`, as shown highlighted in the following configuration:

```
"profiles": {
  ...
 "https": {
    "commandName": "Project",
    "dotnetRunMessages": true,
    "launchBrowser": true,
    "launchUrl": "swagger",
    "applicationUrl": "https://localhost:50061;http://localhost:50062",
    "environmentVariables": {
      "ASPNETCORE_ENVIRONMENT": "Development"
    }
```

Warning! I often use port numbers starting at `5000`, with the middle two digits as the chapter number, and ending with `1` for `https` and `2` for `http`. But ports `5060` and `5061`, both on TCP and UDP, are associated with the **Session Initiation Protocol** (**SIP**) by IANA.

5. In `Program.cs`, note the statements that configure OpenAPI, like `AddEndpointsApiExplorer` and `AddSwaggerGen`, as shown highlighted in the following code:

```
var builder = WebApplication.CreateBuilder(args);

// Add services to the container.
// Learn more about configuring Swagger/OpenAPI at https://aka.ms/
aspnetcore/swashbuckle
builder.Services.AddEndpointsApiExplorer();
builder.Services.AddSwaggerGen();
```

```
var app = builder.Build();

// Configure the HTTP request pipeline.
if (app.Environment.IsDevelopment())
{
  app.UseSwagger();
  app.UseSwaggerUI();
}

app.UseHttpsRedirection();

var summaries = new[]
{
  "Freezing", "Bracing", "Chilly", "Cool", "Mild", "Warm", "Balmy",
"Hot", "Sweltering", "Scorching"
};

app.MapGet("/weatherforecast", () =>
{
  var forecast = Enumerable.Range(1, 5).Select(index =>
      new WeatherForecast
      (
          DateOnly.FromDateTime(DateTime.Now.AddDays(index)),
          Random.Shared.Next(-20, 55),
          summaries[Random.Shared.Next(summaries.Length)]
      ))
      .ToArray();

  return forecast;
})
.WithName("GetWeatherForecast")
.WithOpenApi();

app.Run();

internal record WeatherForecast(DateOnly Date, int TemperatureC, string?
Summary)
{
  public int TemperatureF => 32 + (int)(TemperatureC / 0.5556);
}
```

6. Between the calls to `WithName` and `WithOpenApi`, add statements to further document the weather forecast endpoint, as shown highlighted in the following code:

```
.WithName("GetWeatherForecast")
.Produces (StatusCodes.Status200OK)
.WithTags("Weather")
.WithSummary("Retrieves the current weather for a specified city")
.WithDescription("Provides weather details including temperature and
summary for the city passed in the route parameter.")
.WithOpenApi();
```

7. Start the `Northwind.WebApi` project without debugging.
8. On the Swagger UI web page, click the GET request for the weather service and note the additional documentation for summary and description, as shown in *Figure 6.7*:

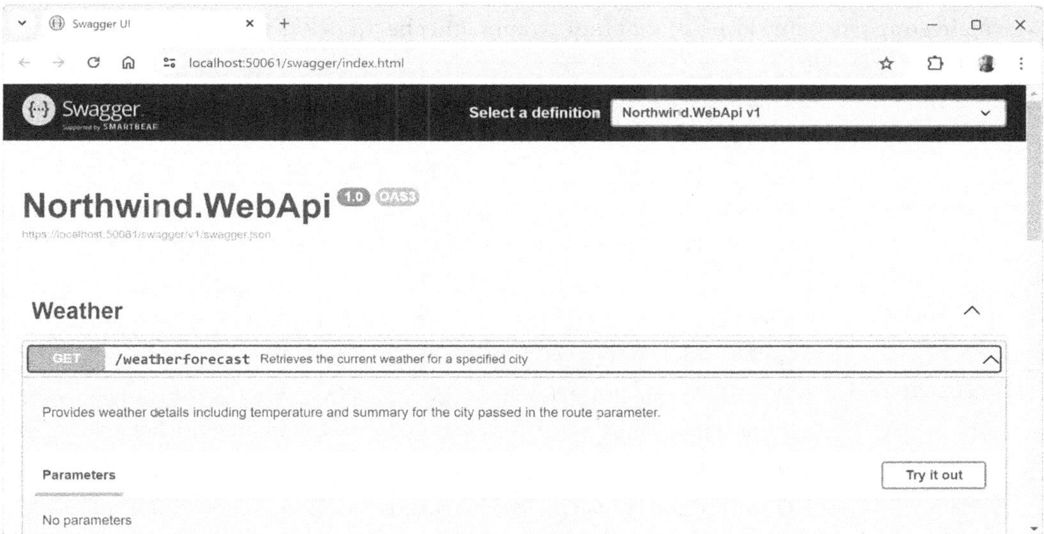

Figure 6.7: Swagger UI documentation

9. Close the browser and shut down the web server.

Next, let's see how we can create visual documentation using Mermaid diagrams.

Documenting visually with Mermaid diagrams

There's no better way to convey a concept than with a diagram, especially to non-techies like managers. Mastering the skill of diagramming will make you a more persuasive leader in meetings and accelerate your career because it will enhance your reputation with the people who sign the pay checks.

With the right tool, like Mermaid, you don't need graphic design skills to produce attractive, useful diagrams to bring the team together to all understand a solution architecture or code design decision. Mermaid is a good choice for .NET developers because Microsoft source code management hosts like GitHub have built-in support for rendering Mermaid diagrams.

In any Markdown file (`.md`), just define a Markdown code block and indicate the code is `mermaid`, as shown in the following code:

````
```mermaid

```
````

Mermaid's syntax is designed to be simple and intuitive, allowing developers to quickly create and incorporate various diagrams into their documentation, enhancing the understandability and readability of technical content.

Mermaid supports many types of diagram, graph, and chart, including those in *Table 6.4*:

Type	Description
`flowchart`, `graph`	Flowcharts and graphs allow you to visualize steps and decision points in a process or workflow, making complex processes easier to understand at a glance.
`sequenceDiagram`	These are used to show how objects interact in a given sequence, making them ideal for representing the flow of messages, events, or actions between different parts of a system.
`classDiagram`	These depict the structure of a system by showing its classes, attributes, operations, and the relationships among objects.
`stateDiagram`	These illustrate the states an entity can be in, as well as the transitions between these states. This type of diagram is useful in modeling the behavior of an application or system.
`erDiagram`	These are used in database design and modeling to show the relationships between data or entities in a database.
`gantt`	These are used in project management, offering a visual timeline for projects. They display tasks, their dependencies, and their duration over the project's lifecycle.
`journey`	These are used to show a user journey when interacting with a system.
`gitGraph`	These are used to visually display branches in a Git audit history.
`pie`	These are used to represent data distributions or proportions in a straightforward way.
`mindmap`	These are used to represent relationships between ideas when brainstorming.

Table 6.4: Common Mermaid diagram types

Rendering Mermaid diagrams

The main tools for rendering a Mermaid diagram include the following:

- **Mermaid Live**: This tool is a website that can interactively render Mermaid, found at the following link: `https://mermaid.live`, and is shown in *Figure 6.8*. It is great for quickly explaining a concept to a colleague, or during domain design decision meetings with mixed technical and non-technical participants. While in the room with the domain experts, you can interactively change the diagram, and everyone sees immediate results. Misunderstandings and issues can be spotted and fixed quickly without playing email ping-pong.

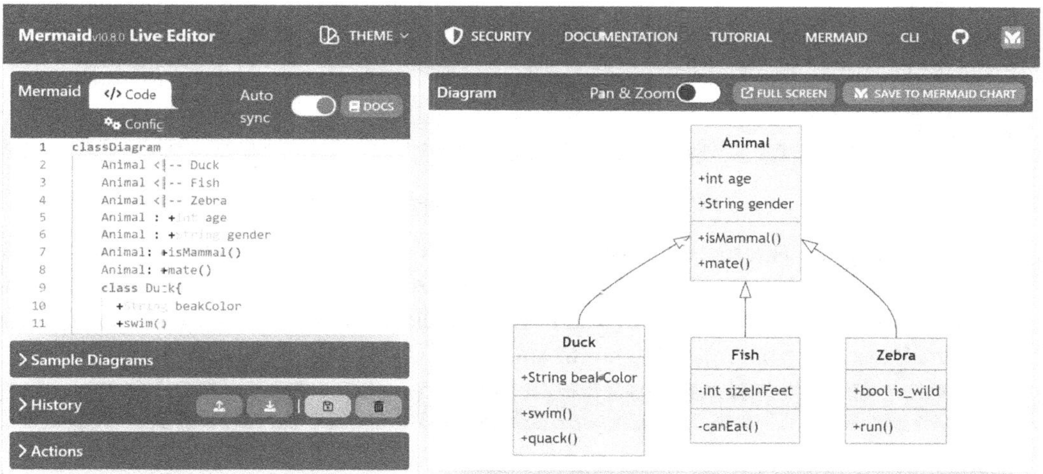

Figure 6.8: Mermaid Live website showing interactive diagramming

- **Markdown Preview Mermaid Support**: This tool is a VS Code extension with over a million downloads. It adds Mermaid diagram and flowchart support to VS Code's built-in Markdown preview, as shown in *Figure 6.9*, and to Markdown cells in notebooks. The extension's identifier is `bierner.markdown-mermaid`.

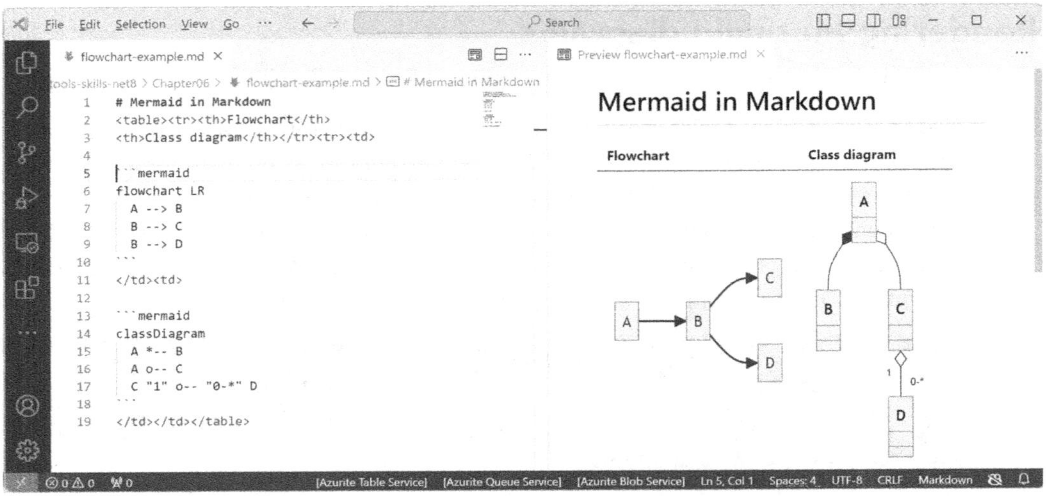

Figure 6.9: Markdown Preview Mermaid Support extension for VS Code

- **Mermaid CLI:** This tool converts Mermaid files into other graphical formats like PNG, SVG, and PDF. You can download the latest source code from the following link: `https://github.com/mermaid-js/mermaid-cli/`. If you have **Node Package Manager** (**npm**) then you can install the latest using the following command:

```
npm install -g @mermaid-js/mermaid-cli
```

> Instructions for downloading and installing Node.js and npm can be found at the following link: `https://docs.npmjs.com/downloading-and-installing-node-js-and-npm`. On Windows, you can download and install a **Node Version Manager (nvm)** from the following link: `https://github.com/coreybutler/nvm-windows`.

Now let's see some simple examples of the common diagram and chart types.

Flowcharts using Mermaid

Flowcharts are especially easy to understand even for non-technical users. For example, imagine you need to decide what type of electric vehicle (EV) you want to purchase. You could diagram the decisions, as shown in the following markup and in *Figure 6.10*:

```
flowchart
 A(Start) --> B{Budget?}
 B -->|Under $30k| C[Used EV]
 B -->|Between $30k-$50k| D[New Mid-Range EV]
 B -->|Over $50k| E[New Luxury EV]

 C --> F{Range Requirement?}
 D --> F
```

```
    E --> F

    F -->|Under 200 miles| G[City Car]
    F -->|200-300 miles| H[All-Purpose Vehicle]
    F -->|Over 300 miles| I[Long Range Vehicle]

    G --> J{Charging at Home?}
    H --> J
    I --> J

    J -->|Yes| K[Proceed with Purchase]
    J -->|No| L[Consider Charging Options]

    L --> M{Public Charging Available?}
    M -->|Yes| N[Proceed with Purchase]
    M -->|No| O[Reevaluate Requirements]
```

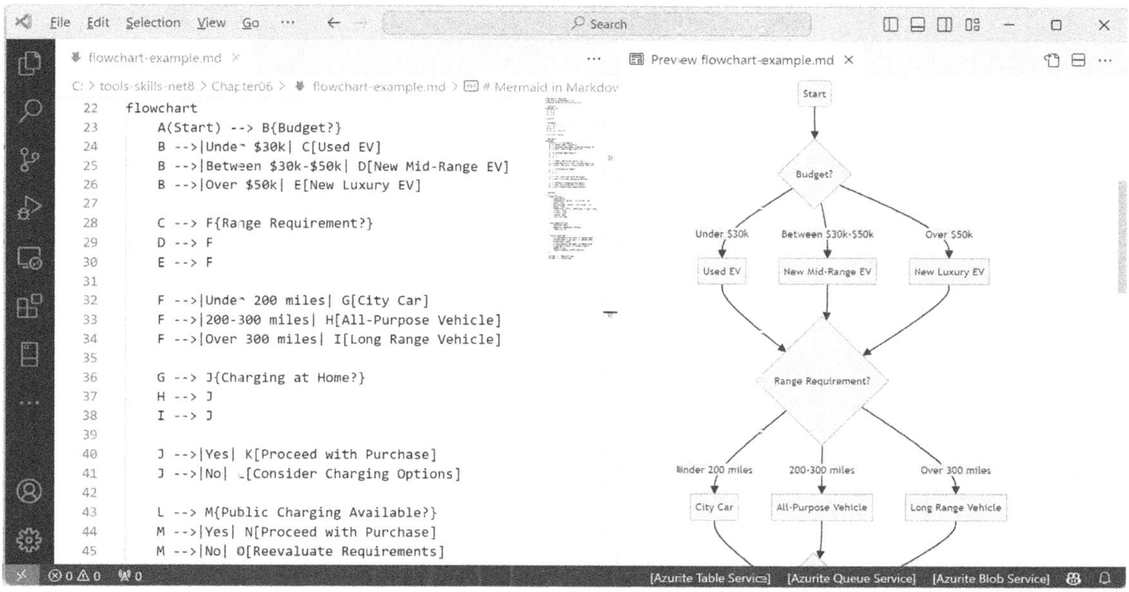

Figure 6.10: A flowchart to make decisions about buying an EV

Class diagrams using Mermaid

A common type of diagram used by developers is a class diagram. For example, you can show the inheritance relationship between the abstract `Stream` and concrete `FileStream` and `MemoryStream` classes, as shown in the following markup and in *Figure 6.11*:

```
classDiagram
  class Stream {
  <<abstract>>
```

```
+Read(byte[] buffer, int offset, int count) int
+Write(byte[] buffer, int offset, int count) void
+Seek(long offset, SeekOrigin origin) long
+Flush() void
+Close() void
-Length long
-Position long
}
class MemoryStream {
+MemoryStream()
+MemoryStream(byte[] buffer)
-Capacity int
}
class FileStream {
+FileStream(string path, FileMode mode)
+FileStream(string path, FileMode mode, FileAccess access)
+FileStream(string path, FileMode mode, FileAccess access, FileShare share)
-Name string
-SafeFileHandle SafeFileHandle
}
Stream <|-- MemoryStream
Stream <|-- FileStream
```

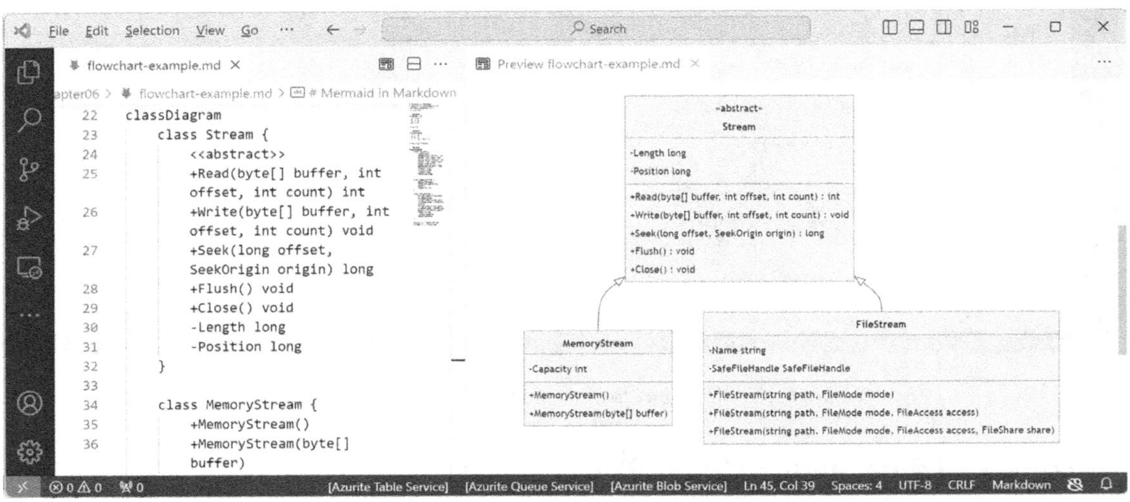

Figure 6.11: Class diagram of Stream class inheritance

Note the following about this diagram:

- The `Stream` class is an `abstract` class, showcasing some common methods (like `Read`, `Write`, `Seek`, and `Close`) and properties (`Length` and `Position`) that are relevant to stream operations.
- The `MemoryStream` and `FileStream` classes are shown as concrete implementations, including their constructors.
- Inheritance relationships show that both `MemoryStream` and `FileStream` derive from `Stream`.

You will learn more about the details of creating Mermaid diagrams in later chapters when we look at **Unified Modeling Language** (**UML**) and its common diagrams. For example, you will learn how to document sequences of actions within a system and use **Domain-Driven Design** (**DDD**) to diagram your domain in *Chapter 18, Software and Solution Architecture Foundations*.

Converting Mermaid to SVG

Finally, let's convert a Markdown file containing multiple Mermaid diagrams to SVG so it can be viewed in any web browser, not just in websites that support rendering Mermaid like GitHub and GitLab:

1. In the `Chapter06` folder, create a Markdown file containing multiple Mermaid diagrams. You can download an example at the following link: `https://github.com/markjprice/tools-skills-net10/blob/main/code/Chapter06/mermaid-examples.md`.
2. At the command prompt or terminal, in the `Chapter06` folder, convert a Markdown file containing Mermaid code blocks to SVG, as shown in the following command:

```
mmdc -i mermaid-examples.md -o output.md
```

> You must have installed Mermaid CLI as described earlier in this topic.

3. Note the results, as shown in the following output:

```
Found 4 mermaid charts in Markdown input
  ./output-1.svg
  ./output-2.svg
  ./output-4.svg
  ./output-3.svg
  output.md
```

4. Open the `output.md` file and note that it references SVG files instead of having Mermaid code blocks, as shown in the following code:

```
# Mermaid in Markdown
<table><tr><th>Flowchart</th>
<th>Class diagram</th></tr><tr><td>
![diagram](./output-1.svg)
</td><td>
![diagram](./output-2.svg)
</td></td></table>
![diagram](./output-3.svg)
![diagram](./output-4.svg)
```

You can download a cheat sheet for Mermaid at the following link: `https://jojozhuang.github.io/tutorial/mermaid-cheat-sheet/`.

Practicing and exploring

Test your knowledge and understanding by answering some questions, getting some hands-on practice, and exploring the topics covered in this chapter with deeper research.

Exercise 6.1 – Online-only material

Review more details of XML documentation at the following link: `https://learn.microsoft.com/en-us/dotnet/csharp/language-reference/xmldoc/`.

Review the recommended tags for use in XML documentation at the following link: `https://learn.microsoft.com/en-us/dotnet/csharp/language-reference/xmldoc/recommended-tags`.

Learn Markdown in detail: `https://www.markdownguide.org/`.

Learn Mermaid in detail: `https://mermaid.js.org/intro/getting-started.html`.

More Mermaid: `https://github.com/JakeSteam/Mermaid`.

When you read API reference documentation, you often want to review the actual source code. For .NET APIs that have Source Link enabled, have an accessible **program database** (PDB) file, and are hosted in a public GitHub repository, links to source code are included in the definition metadata. For example, the `String` class documentation page now has a new **Source** link, and its `IndexOf` method has a **Source** link to another of its source files, as shown in *Figure 6.12*:

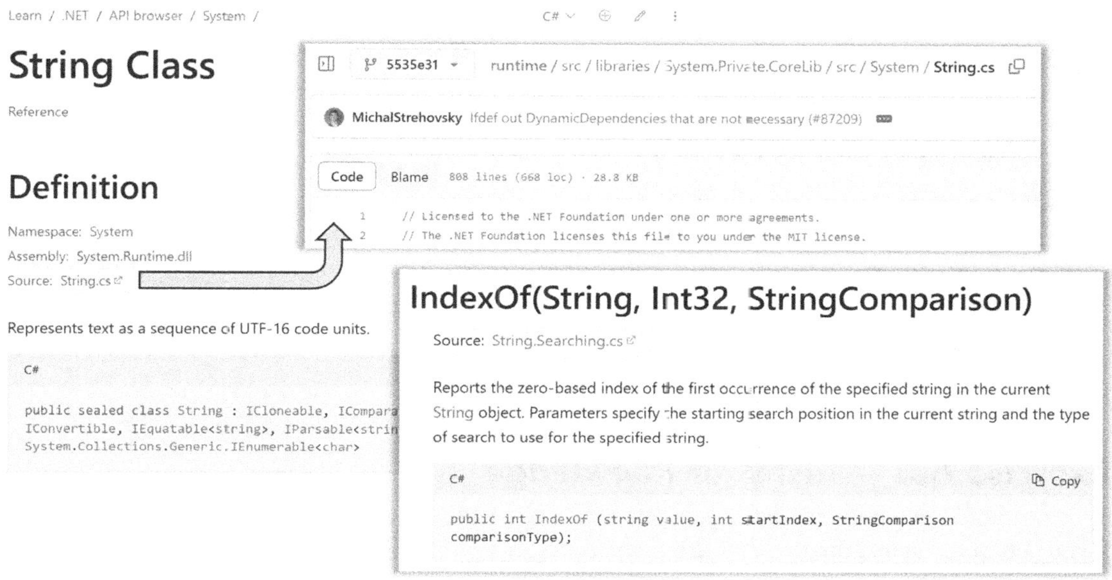

Figure 6.12: Examples of links to source code in the official documentation

You can read more about how the Microsoft team achieved this in the article **Introducing links to source code for .NET API Docs**, found at the following link: `https://devblogs.microsoft.com/dotnet/dotnet-docs-link-to-source-code/`.

Exercise 6.2 – Practice exercises

Review examples of XML documentation at the following link: `https://learn.microsoft.com/en-us/dotnet/csharp/language-reference/xmldoc/examples`.

Explore the sample diagrams at Mermaid Live, as shown in *Figure 6.13*: `https://mermaid.live/`.

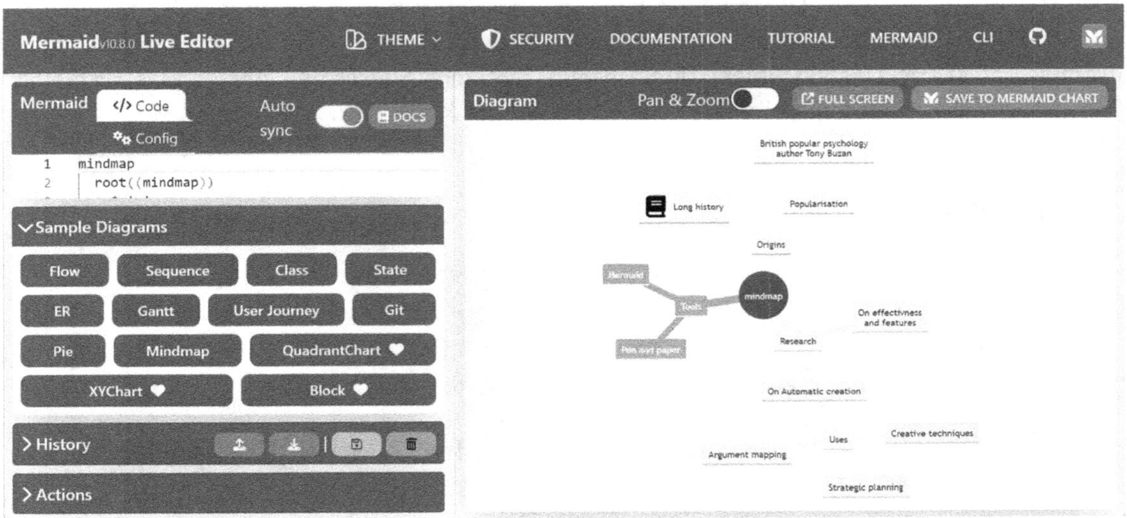

Figure 6.13: Mermaid Live sample diagrams

Exercise 6.3 – Test your knowledge

Answer the following questions. If you get stuck, try googling the answers, while remembering that if you get totally stuck, the answers are in *Appendix A*:

1. What are some good practices for adding comments to your source code?
2. How do you document a parameter for a method using XML comments?
3. Can you apply styles to the tooltip in XML comments?
4. What is DocFX?
5. How do you show inheritance in a Mermaid class diagram?

Appendix A, Answers to the Test Your Knowledge Questions, is available to download from the following link: `https://github.com/markjprice/tools-skills-net10/blob/main/docs/B31468_Appendix%20A.pdf`.

Exercise 6.4 – Explore topics

Use the links on the following page to learn more details about the topics covered in this chapter: `https://github.com/markjprice/tools-skills-net10/blob/main/docs/book-links.md#chapter-6---documenting-your-code-apis-and-services`.

Summary

In this chapter, you learned how to:

- Document your source code
- Document public APIs in class libraries
- Document services using OpenAPI
- Document visually with Mermaid diagrams

In the next chapter, you will learn about some common types that are included with .NET for performing code reflection and applying and reading attributes. You will also learn how to work with expression trees and how to create source generators.

Learn more on Discord

To join the Discord community for this book – where you can share feedback, ask questions to the author, and learn about new releases – follow this QR code:

`https://packt.link/TS2e`

7

Observing and Modifying Code Execution Dynamically

This chapter is about some common types that are included with .NET for performing code reflection and applying and reading attributes, working with expression trees, and creating source generators. These technologies enable a broad range of capabilities from code inspection and modification to runtime behavior alteration. This can significantly enhance the flexibility and efficiency of your applications.

Reflection is a powerful feature in .NET that allows programs to inspect and manipulate themselves. It can be used to access information about assemblies, modules, and types, and to dynamically create and invoke types and methods.

Expression trees represent code in a tree-like data structure, where each node is an expression, such as a method call or a binary operation. This feature can be used to inspect, modify, or execute code dynamically.

Introduced in .NET 5, source generators are a way to produce additional files during compilation. They run during compile time and can inspect the program to generate new source files that are compiled together with the rest of the code.

All of the topics in this chapter are usually considered advanced, so try not to worry about learning them deeply. For a topic like reflection, most readers only need to be able to briefly describe it and give examples of what it can do. After completing this chapter, you will be able to do that, and in an interview, say, "I'm not an expert at reflection/expression trees/source generators, but I've run code to see some of their capabilities. If you need me to implement more advanced scenarios, then I can learn that too."

This chapter covers the following topics:

- Working with reflection and attributes
- Working with expression trees
- Creating source generators

Working with reflection and attributes

Reflection is a programming feature that allows code to understand and manipulate itself. Key benefits of reflection include the following:

- **Dynamic type access:** Reflection enables you to access types in a dynamic manner at runtime. This is particularly useful for creating plug-in architectures where new functionality can be added without recompiling the application.
- **Late binding:** You can invoke methods and access properties on objects dynamically without knowing their types at compile time. This can be used to interact with APIs where the type information is not available beforehand. You will see this in action in a section titled *Dynamically loading assemblies and executing methods*.
- **Metadata inspection:** Reflection allows the examination of various types and their members, which is great for tools and libraries that need to handle types generically, for example, serialization frameworks and ORM tools.

Let's start by looking at metadata inspection.

Metadata in .NET assemblies

A .NET assembly is made up of up to four parts:

- **Assembly metadata and manifest:** Name, assembly, file version, referenced assemblies, and so on.
- **Type metadata:** Information about the types, their members, and so on.
- **Intermediate Language (IL) code:** Implementation of methods, properties, constructors, and so on. Source code like C# and F# is compiled into IL code by the Roslyn compiler and stored in the assembly.
- **Embedded resources** (optional): Images, strings, JavaScript, and so on.

The metadata is generated automatically from your code (for example, information about the types and members) or applied to your code using attributes.

Attributes can be applied at multiple levels: to assemblies, to types, and to their members, as shown in the following code:

```
// An assembly-level attribute.
[assembly: AssemblyTitle("Working with reflection and attributes")]

// A type-level attribute.
[Serializable]
public class Person
{
  // A member-level attribute.
  [Obsolete("Deprecated: use Run instead.")]
```

```
    public void Walk()
    {
...
```

Attribute-based programming is used a lot in app models like ASP.NET Core to enable features like routing, security, and caching.

Versioning of assemblies

Knowing the version number of a .NET assembly is quite valuable in various aspects of software development, maintenance, and deployment:

- .NET applications often depend on multiple libraries (assemblies) to function correctly. Each library can have different versions with varying functionalities and bug fixes. Tracking the version number helps developers know whether they are working with the most current iteration of an assembly.
- Different versions of assemblies might have different bugs or performance issues. Being able to identify which version of an assembly is being used can help you quickly diagnose problems and check against release notes to understand if a particular issue has been fixed in a later version.
- Knowing the assembly version helps to ensure that compatibility issues are addressed, which is particularly important when deploying applications across different environments or when upgrading existing systems.

.NET uses assembly version numbers as part of the binding and loading process. The **Common Language Runtime (CLR)** uses these numbers to resolve assembly references and load the correct assemblies at runtime. This is part of the assembly's identity and helps prevent "DLL Hell," where multiple versions of a component could interfere with each other.

Version numbers in .NET are a combination of three numbers, for example, `10.1.4`, with two optional additions, for example, `10.1.4.7628.345`.

If you follow the rules of semantic versioning, the three numbers denote the following:

- **Major:** Breaking changes
- **Minor:** Non-breaking changes, including new features, and often bug fixes
- **Patch:** Non-breaking bug fixes

Optionally, a version can include these:

- **Prerelease:** Unsupported preview releases
- **Build number:** Nightly builds

> An alternative within semantic versioning is having a year-based major number. For example, at the time of writing, Rider is version `2025.3.0.2`, meaning the third feature release in the year 2025, with its second patch.

Good practice: By default, your assemblies will start at a version number of `1.0.0.0` and stay that way unless you change them. You should update the version number every time you distribute a new version and follow the rules of semantic versioning, as described at the following link: `http://semver.org`.

Reading assembly metadata

Now that you know some of the kinds of metadata stored in a .NET assembly, like version information, let's see how you can dynamically read that metadata. To take control of some of the metadata stored in a .NET assembly, you use attributes.

Let's explore working with attributes:

1. Use your preferred code editor to add a new **Console App** / `console` project named `WorkingWithReflection` to the `Chapter07` solution.
2. In the project file, statically and globally import the `Console` class, as shown in the following markup:

```
<ItemGroup>
  <Using Include="System.Console" Static="true" />
</ItemGroup>
```

3. In `Program.cs`, delete any existing statements, and then:
   - Import the namespace for reflection.
   - Add statements to get the console app's assembly and output its name and location.
   - Get all assembly-level attributes and output their types, as shown in the following code:

```
using System.Reflection; // To use Assembly.

WriteLine("Assembly metadata:");
Assembly? assembly = Assembly.GetEntryAssembly();

if (assembly is null)
{
  WriteLine("Failed to get entry assembly.");
  return; // Exit the app.
}

WriteLine($" Full name: {assembly.FullName}");
WriteLine($" Location: {assembly.Location}");
WriteLine($" Entry point: {assembly.EntryPoint?.Name}");
```

```
IEnumerable<Attribute> attributes = assembly.GetCustomAttributes();

WriteLine($" Assembly-level attributes:");
foreach (Attribute a in attributes)
{
  WriteLine($" {a.GetType()}");
}
```

4. Run the code and view the result, as shown in the following output:

```
Assembly metadata:
  Full name: WorkingWithReflection, Version=1.0.0.0, Culture=neutral,
PublicKeyToken=null
  Location: C:\tools-skills-net10\Chapter07\WorkingWithReflection\bin\
Debug\net10.0\WorkingWithReflection.dll
  Entry point: <Main>$
  Assembly-level attributes:
    System.Runtime.CompilerServices.CompilationRelaxationsAttribute
    System.Runtime.CompilerServices.RuntimeCompatibilityAttribute
    System.Diagnostics.DebuggableAttribute
    System.Runtime.Versioning.TargetFrameworkAttribute
    System.Reflection.AssemblyCompanyAttribute
    System.Reflection.AssemblyConfigurationAttribute
    System.Reflection.AssemblyFileVersionAttribute
    System.Reflection.AssemblyInformationalVersionAttribute
    System.Reflection.AssemblyProductAttribute
    System.Reflection.AssemblyTitleAttribute
```

For security and trust reasons, the full name of an assembly must uniquely identify that specific assembly, so the full name of an assembly is a combination of the following:

- **Name**, for example, `WorkingWithReflection`
- **Version**, for example, `1.0.0.0`
- **Culture**, for example, `neutral`
- **Public key token**, although this can be `null`

Getting specific assembly attributes

Now that we know some of the attributes decorating the assembly, we can ask for them specifically.

1. At the bottom of `Program.cs`, add statements to get the `AssemblyInformationalVersionAttribute` and `AssemblyCompanyAttribute` classes and then output their values, as shown in the following code:

```
AssemblyInformationalVersionAttribute? version = assembly
  .GetCustomAttribute<AssemblyInformationalVersionAttribute>();

WriteLine($" Version: {version?.InformationalVersion}");

AssemblyCompanyAttribute? company = assembly
  .GetCustomAttribute<AssemblyCompanyAttribute>();

WriteLine($" Company: {company?.Company}");
```

2. Run the code and view the result, as shown in the following output:

```
  Version: 1.0.0
  Company: WorkingWithReflection
```

> Hmmm, unless you set the version, it defaults to `1.0.0`, and unless you set the company, it defaults to the name of the assembly. Let's explicitly set this information.

3. Edit the `WorkingWithReflection.csproj` project file to add elements for version and company, as shown highlighted in the following markup:

```
<Project Sdk="Microsoft.NET.Sdk">

  <PropertyGroup>
    <OutputType>Exe</OutputType>
    <TargetFramework>net10.0</TargetFramework>
    <ImplicitUsings>enable</ImplicitUsings>
    <Nullable>enable</Nullable>
    <Version>10.0.1</Version>
    <Company>Packt Publishing</Company>
  </PropertyGroup>
```

> The legacy .NET Framework way to set these values was to add attributes in the C# source code file, as shown in the following code:
>
> ```
> [assembly: AssemblyCompany("Packt Publishing")]
> [assembly: AssemblyInformationalVersion("10.0.1")]
> ```
>
> The Roslyn compiler used by .NET sets these attributes automatically, so we can't use the old way. Instead, they must be set in the project file.

4. Run the code and view the result, as shown in the following partial output:

```
Assembly metadata:
  Full name: WorkingWithReflection, Version=10.0.1.0, Culture=neutral,
PublicKeyToken=null
  ...
  Version: 10.0.1
  Company: Packt Publishing
```

Creating custom attributes

You can define your own attributes by inheriting from the `Attribute` class:

1. In the `WorkingWithReflection` project folder, add a class file named `CoderAttribute.cs`.
2. In `CoderAttribute.cs`, delete any existing statements and then define an attribute class that can decorate either classes or methods with two properties to store the name of a coder and the date they last modified some code, as shown in the following code:

```
namespace Packt.Shared;

[AttributeUsage(
  AttributeTargets.Class | AttributeTargets.Method,
  AllowMultiple = true)]
public class CoderAttribute(
  string coder, string lastModified) : Attribute
{
  public string Coder { get; set; } = coder;

  public DateTime LastModified { get; set; }
    = DateTime.Parse(lastModified);
}
```

3. In the `WorkingWithReflection` project folder, add a class file named `Animal.cs`.

4. In `Animal.cs`, delete any existing statements, then define a class with a method, and decorate the method with the `Coder` attribute with data about two coders, as shown in the following code:

```
namespace Packt.Shared;

public class Animal
{
  [Coder("Mark Price", "22 June 2024")]
  [Coder("Johnni Rasmussen", "13 July 2024")]
  public void Speak()
  {
    WriteLine("Woof...");
  }
}
```

5. In `Program.cs`, import namespaces for working with your custom attribute, as shown in the following code:

```
using Packt.Shared; // To use CoderAttribute.
```

6. In `Program.cs`, at the bottom of the file, add code to get the types in the current assembly, enumerate their members, read any `Coder` attributes on those members, and output the information, as shown in the following code:

```
WriteLine();
WriteLine("* Types:");
Type[] types = assembly.GetTypes();

foreach (Type type in types)
{
  WriteLine();
  WriteLine($"Type: {type.FullName}");

  MemberInfo[] members = type.GetMembers();

  foreach (MemberInfo member in members)
  {
    WriteLine($"{member.MemberType}: {member.Name} ({
      member.DeclaringType?.Name})");

    IOrderedEnumerable<CoderAttribute> coders =
      member.GetCustomAttributes<CoderAttribute>()
      .OrderByDescending(c => c.LastModified);

    foreach (CoderAttribute coder in coders)
```

```
      {
        WriteLine($"-> Modified by {coder.Coder} on {
          coder.LastModified.ToShortDateString()}");
      }
    }
  }
```

7. Run the code and view the result, as shown in the following partial output:

```
* Types:
Type: Program
Method: GetType (Object)
Method: ToString (Object)
Method: Equals (Object)
Method: GetHashCode (Object)
Constructor: .ctor (Program)
Type: Packt.Shared.Animal
Method: Speak (Animal)
-> Modified by Johnni Rasmussen on 13/07/2024
-> Modified by Mark Price on 22/06/2024
Method: GetType (Object)
Method: ToString (Object)
Method: Equals (Object)
Method: GetHashCode (Object)
Constructor: .ctor (Animal)
Type: Packt.Shared.CoderAttribute
Method: get_Coder (CoderAttribute)
Method: set_Coder (CoderAttribute)
Method: get_LastModified (CoderAttribute)
Method: set_LastModified (CoderAttribute)
Method: Equals (Attribute)
Method: GetHashCode (Attribute)
Method: get_TypeId (Attribute)
Method: Match (Attribute)
Method: IsDefaultAttribute (Attribute)
Method: GetType (Object)
Method: ToString (Object)
Constructor: .ctor (CoderAttribute)
Property: Coder (CoderAttribute)
Property: LastModified (CoderAttribute)
Property: TypeId (Attribute)
Type: Program+<>c
Method: GetType (Object)
```

```
Method: ToString (Object)
Method: Equals (Object)
Method: GetHashCode (Object)
Constructor: .ctor (<>c)
Field: <>9 (<>c)
Field: <>9__0_0 (<>c)
```

Most of the output should be self-evident to you, but what is the `Program+<>c` type and its strangely named fields?

Understanding compiler-generated types and members

The `Program+<>c` type is a compiler-generated **display class**. `<>` indicates compiler-generated and `c` indicates a display class. They are undocumented implementation details of the compiler and could change at any time. You can ignore them, so as an optional challenge, add statements to your console app to filter compiler-generated types by skipping types decorated with `CompilerGeneratedAttribute`.

Hint

Import the namespace for working with compiler-generated code, as shown in the following code:

```
using System.Runtime.CompilerServices; // To use CompilerGeneratedAttribute.
```

Making a type or member obsolete

Over time, you might decide to refactor your types and their members while maintaining backward compatibility. To encourage developers who use your types to use the newer implementations, you can decorate the old types and members with the `[Obsolete]` attribute.

Let's see an example:

1. In `Animal.cs`, add a new method named `SpeakBetter`, and mark the old `Speak` method as obsolete, as shown highlighted in the following code:

```
public void SpeakBetter()
{
  WriteLine("Wooooooooof...");
}

[Coder("Mark Price", "22 August 2024")]
[Coder("Johnni Rasmussen", "13 September 2024")]
[Obsolete($"use {nameof(SpeakBetter)} instead.")]
public void Speak()
{
  WriteLine("Woof...");
}
```

2. In `Program.cs`, modify the statements to detect obsolete methods, as shown highlighted in the following code:

```
foreach (MemberInfo member in members)
{
  ObsoleteAttribute? obsolete =
    member.GetCustomAttribute<ObsoleteAttribute>();

  WriteLine($"{member.MemberType}: {member.Name} ({
    member.DeclaringType?.Name}) {
   (obsolete is null ? "" : "Obsolete! " + obsolete.Message)}");
```

3. Run the code and view the result, as shown highlighted in the following output:

```
Type: Packt.Shared.Animal
Method: Speak (Animal) Obsolete! use SpeakBetter instead.
-> Modified by Johnni Rasmussen on 13/07/2024
-> Modified by Mark Price on 22/06/2024
Method: SpeakBetter (Animal)
Method: GetType (Object)
Method: ToString (Object)
Method: Equals (Object)
Method: GetHashCode (Object)
Constructor: .ctor (Animal)
```

You've seen practical examples of dynamic type access and metadata inspection. Let's see some other features of reflection: dynamic assembly loading and late binding.

Dynamically loading assemblies and executing methods

Normally, if a .NET project needs to execute in another .NET assembly, you reference the package or project, and then at compile time, the compiler knows the assemblies that will be loaded into the memory of the calling codebase during startup at runtime.

But sometimes you may not know the assemblies that you need to call until runtime. For example, a word processor does not need to have the functionality to perform a mail merge loaded in memory all the time. The mail merge feature could be implemented as a separate assembly that is only loaded into memory when it is activated by the user. This is sometimes referred to as late binding.

Another example would be an application that allows custom plugins, perhaps even created by other developers, such as extensions in Visual Studio and VS Code, and plugins in Rider.

You can dynamically load a set of assemblies into an `AssemblyLoadContext`, execute their methods, and then unload the `AssemblyLoadContext`, which unloads the assemblies too. An additional benefit of this technique is reduced memory usage.

In .NET 7 or later, the overhead of dynamically invoking a member of a type, like calling a method or setting or getting a property, has been made up to four times faster when it is done more than once on the same member.

Creating a class library to dynamically load

Let's see how to dynamically load an assembly, then instantiate a class and interact with its members:

1. Use your preferred code editor to add a new **Class Library** / `classlib` project named `DynamicLoadAndExecute.Library` to the `Chapter07` solution.
2. In the `DynamicLoadAndExecute.Library.csproj` project file, treat warnings as errors, statically and globally import the `Console` class, and globally import the namespace for working with reflection, as shown highlighted in the following markup:

```
<Project Sdk="Microsoft.NET.Sdk">

  <PropertyGroup>
    <TargetFramework>net10.0</TargetFramework>
    <ImplicitUsings>enable</ImplicitUsings>
    <Nullable>enable</Nullable>
    <TreatWarningsAsErrors>true</TreatWarningsAsErrors>
  </PropertyGroup>

  <ItemGroup>
    <Using Include="System.Reflection" />
    <Using Include="System.Console" Static="true" />
  </ItemGroup>

</Project>
```

3. Rename `Class1.cs` to `Dog.cs`.
4. In `Dog.cs`, define a `Dog` class with a `Speak` method that writes a simple message to the console based on a `string` parameter passed to the method, as shown in the following code:

```
namespace DynamicLoadAndExecute.Library;

public class Dog
{
  public void Speak(string? name)
  {
    WriteLine($"{name} says Woof!");
  }
}
```

Creating a console app to load the class library dynamically

Now we can create a console app that will dynamically load the class library and use its types:

1. Use your preferred code editor to add a new **Console App** / `console` project named `DynamicLoadAndExecute.Console` to the `Chapter07` solution.
2. In the `DynamicLoadAndExecute.Console.csproj` project file, treat warnings as errors, statically and globally import the `Console` class, and globally import the namespace for working with reflection, as shown highlighted in the following markup:

```
<Project Sdk="Microsoft.NET.Sdk">

  <PropertyGroup>
    <OutputType>Exe</OutputType>
    <TargetFramework>net10.0</TargetFramework>
    <ImplicitUsings>enable</ImplicitUsings>
    <Nullable>enable</Nullable>
    <TreatWarningsAsErrors>true</TreatWarningsAsErrors>
  </PropertyGroup>

  <ItemGroup>
    <Using Include="System.Reflection" />
    <Using Include="System.Console" Static="true" />
  </ItemGroup>

</Project>
```

3. Show all files for the two `DynamicLoadAndExecute` projects so that you can see their hidden folder hierarchies, as shown in *Figure 7.1*.
4. Build the `DynamicLoadAndExecute.Library` project to create the class library assembly in its `bin` folder hierarchy, as shown in *Figure 7.1*.
5. Build the `DynamicLoadAndExecute.Console` project to create its `bin` folder hierarchy.
6. Copy the three files from the `DynamicLoadAndExecute.Library` project's `bin\Debug\net10.0` folder to the equivalent folder in the `DynamicLoadAndExecute.Console` project, as shown in *Figure 7.1* and the following list:
    - `DynamicLoadAndExecute.Library.deps.json`
    - `DynamicLoadAndExecute.Library.dll`
    - `DynamicLoadAndExecute.Library.pdb`

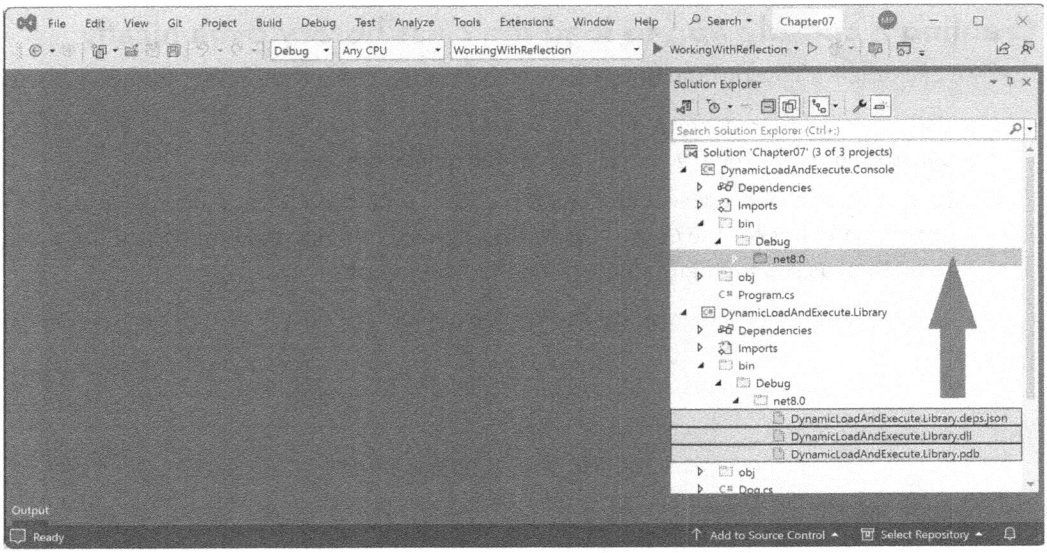

Figure 7.1: Copying the class library assembly into the console app project

An alternative to manually copying the assemblies would be to set the output directory for the `DynamicLoadAndExecute.Library` project to match the same directory as the `DynamicLoadAndExecute.Console` project, as shown in the following configuration:

```
<OutputPath>..\DynamicLoadAndExecute.Console\
bin\$(Configuration)\</OutputPath>
```

7. In the `DynamicLoadAndExecute.Console` project folder, add a new class file named `Program.Helpers.cs`, delete any existing statements, and then define a method for the `Program` class to output information about an assembly and its types, as shown in the following code:

```
// No explicit namespace!
partial class Program
{
  private static void OutputAssemblyInfo(Assembly a)
  {
    WriteLine($"FullName: {a.FullName}");
    WriteLine($"Location: {Path.GetDirectoryName(a.Location)}");
    WriteLine($"IsCollectible: {a.IsCollectible}");
    WriteLine("Defined types:");

    foreach (TypeInfo info in a.DefinedTypes)
    {
      if (!info.Name.EndsWith("Attribute"))
```

```
      {
        WriteLine($" Name: {info.Name}, Members: {
          info.GetMembers().Count()}");
      }
    }
    WriteLine();
  }
}
```

> **Warning!** You cannot collect (a.k.a. load) assemblies with active references, for example, the assemblies that your project references, nor can you collect the host assembly (the console app itself).

8. In `Program.cs`, delete the existing statements. Then, use the load context class to load the class library and output information about it, and then dynamically create an instance of the `Dog` class and call its `Speak` method, as shown in the following code:

```
using System.Runtime.Loader; // To use AssemblyLoadContext.

Assembly? thisAssembly = Assembly.GetEntryAssembly();
if (thisAssembly is null)
{
  WriteLine("Could not get the entry assembly.");
  return; // Exit the app.
}

OutputAssemblyInfo(thisAssembly);

WriteLine($"Creating load context for:\n  {
  Path.GetFileName(thisAssembly.Location)}\n");

AssemblyLoadContext loadContext = new(
  thisAssembly.Location, isCollectible: true);

string assemblyPath = Path.Combine(
  Path.GetDirectoryName(thisAssembly.Location) ?? "",
  "DynamicLoadAndExecute.Library.dll");

WriteLine($"Loading:\n  {Path.GetFileName(assemblyPath)}\n");

Assembly dogAssembly = loadContext.LoadFromAssemblyPath(assemblyPath);
```

```
OutputAssemblyInfo(dogAssembly);

Type? dogType = dogAssembly.GetType("DynamicLoadAndExecute.Library.Dog");

if (dogType is null)
{
  WriteLine("Could not get the Dog type.");
  return;
}

MethodInfo? method = dogType.GetMethod("Speak");

if (method != null)
{
  object? dog = Activator.CreateInstance(dogType);

  for (int i = 0; i < 10; i++)
  {
    method.Invoke(dog, new object[] { "Fido" });
  }
}
WriteLine();
WriteLine("Unloading context and assemblies.");
loadContext.Unload();
```

9. Start the `DynamicLoadAndExecute.Console` project and note the results, as shown in the following output:

```
FullName: DynamicLoadAndExecute.Console, Version=1.0.0.0,
Culture=neutral, PublicKeyToken=null
Location: C:\tools-skills-net10\Chapter07\DynamicLoadAndExecute.Console\
bin\Debug\net10.0
IsCollectible: False
Defined types:
  Name: DemoAssemblyLoadContext, Members: 29
  Name: Program, Members: 5
Creating load context for:
  DynamicLoadAndExecute.Console.dll
Loading:
  DynamicLoadAndExecute.Library.dll
```

```
FullName: DynamicLoadAndExecute.Library, Version=1.0.0.0,
Culture=neutral, PublicKeyToken=null
Location: C:\tools-skills-net10\Chapter07\DynamicLoadAndExecute.Console\
bin\Debug\net10.0
IsCollectible: True
Defined types:
  Name: Dog, Members: 6
Fido says Woof!
Fido says Woof!
Fido says Woof!
Fido says Woof!
Fido says Woof!
Fido says Woof!
Fido says Woof!
Fido says Woof!
Fido says Woof!
Fido says Woof!
Unloading context and assemblies.
```

Note that the entry assembly (the console app) is not **collectible**, meaning that it cannot be removed from memory, but the dynamically loaded class library is collectible.

You've now seen some of the basic features of reflection like reading metadata, dynamically loading an assembly, and calling methods on its types. There is a lot more that can be done with reflection, enough to fill an entire book! But reflection has some important limitations, as you will see next.

A warning about reflection and native AOT

One of the big themes of .NET in recent years is its growing support for native **ahead-of-time** (AOT) compilation.

Native AOT produces apps and services that are:

- **Self-contained**, meaning they can run on systems that do not have the .NET runtime installed.
- **AOT compiled to native code**, meaning a faster startup time and a potentially smaller memory footprint. This can have a positive impact when you have lots of instances (for example, when deploying massively scalable microservices) that are frequently stopped and restarted.

Native AOT compiles **intermediate code** (IL) to native code at the time of publishing, rather than at runtime using the **Just-In-Time** (JIT) compiler. But native AOT apps and services must target a specific runtime environment like Windows x64 or Linux ARM.

Native AOT has limitations, some of which are shown in the following list:

- No dynamic loading of assemblies
- No runtime code generation, for example, using `System.Reflection.Emit`
- It requires trimming, which has its own limitations
- The assembly must be self-contained, so they must embed any libraries they call, which increases their size

> **Warning!** If you use many of the features of reflection, then you cannot use and benefit from native AOT compilation.

Although your own apps and services might not use the features listed above, major parts of .NET do. For example, ASP.NET Core MVC (including Web API services that use controllers) and EF Core do runtime code generation to implement their functionality.

The .NET teams are hard at work making as much of .NET compatible with native AOT as possible, as soon as possible. But .NET 10 only includes support for ASP.NET Core if you use Minimal API web services, but it does not support controller-based Web API web services, and has no support for EF Core.

My guess is that it could take until .NET 10 before the teams can include native AOT compilation support for ASP.NET Core MVC and EF Core.

Native AOT does allow some reflection features, but the trimming performed during the native AOT compilation process cannot statically determine when a type has members that might be only accessed via reflection. These members would be removed by AOT, which would then cause a runtime exception.

> **Good practice:** Developers must annotate their types with `[DynamicallyAccessedMembers]` to indicate a member that is only dynamically accessed via reflection and should therefore be left untrimmed.

Doing more with reflection

This is just a taste of what can be achieved with reflection. Reflection can also do the following:

- Inspect assembly contents using MetadataLoadContext: `https://docs.microsoft.com/en-us/dotnet/standard/assembly/inspect-contents-using-metadataloadcontext`
- Dynamically generate new code and assemblies: `https://docs.microsoft.com/en-us/dotnet/api/system.reflection.emit.assemblybuilder`

You've seen how reflection enables runtime flexibility through features like late binding and dynamic assembly loading. But reflection focuses on working with existing types and members. Sometimes, you need a way to represent new code as data, modify it, and execute it dynamically. This is where expression trees come into play because they allow you to build a structured representation of code in memory. This is more efficient, easier to analyze, and central to technologies like LINQ, dynamic query generation, and runtime code transformations.

Working with expression trees

Expression trees represent code as a structure that you can examine or execute. Expression trees are immutable so you cannot change them, but you can create a copy with the changes you want.

If you compare expression trees to functions, then although functions have flexibility in the parameter values passed to the function, the structure of the function, what it does with those values and how, is fixed. Expression trees provide a structure that can dynamically change, so how a function is implemented can be dynamically changed at runtime.

Expression trees are also used to represent an expression in an abstract way, so instead of being expressed using C# code, the expression is expressed as a data structure in memory. This then allows that data structure to be expressed in other ways, using other languages.

When you write a LINQ expression for the EF Core database provider, it is represented by an expression tree that is then translated into an SQL statement. But even the simplest C# statement can be represented as an expression tree.

Let's look at a simple example, adding two numbers:

```
int three = 1 + 2;
```

To model the preceding statement, you need a local variable, an assignment, and a block that declares the variable and returns a value. To build that with `System.Linq.Expressions` you would use multiple expressions and then combine them into a block and lambda expression, as shown in the following code:

```
using System.Linq.Expressions;

// Variable declaration: int three;
ParameterExpression three = Expression.Variable(typeof(int), "three");

// Right-hand side: 1 + 2
BinaryExpression sum = Expression.Add(
  Expression.Constant(1), Expression.Constant(2));

// Assignment: three = 1 + 2
BinaryExpression assign = Expression.Assign(three, sum);

// Block:
BlockExpression block = Expression.Block(
  variables: new[] { three },
  expressions: new Expression[]
  {
    assign,
    three
```

```
    });

// Lambda that returns the block's final value (int)
var lambda = Expression.Lambda<Func<int>>(block);

// Sanity check
Console.WriteLine(lambda); // () => {var three; three = (1 + 2); three}
Console.WriteLine(lambda.Compile()()); // 3
```

Note the following about the preceding code:

- `ParameterExpression three` represents the local variable.
- `BinaryExpression sum` represents 1 + 2.
- `BinaryExpression assign` represents three = (1 + 2).
- `BlockExpression block` declares `three`, performs the assignment, and then yields `three` as the block's value.
- `LambdaExpression<Func<int>>` wraps the block so you can compile and execute it.

This statement would be represented as shown in the expression tree in *Figure 7.2*:

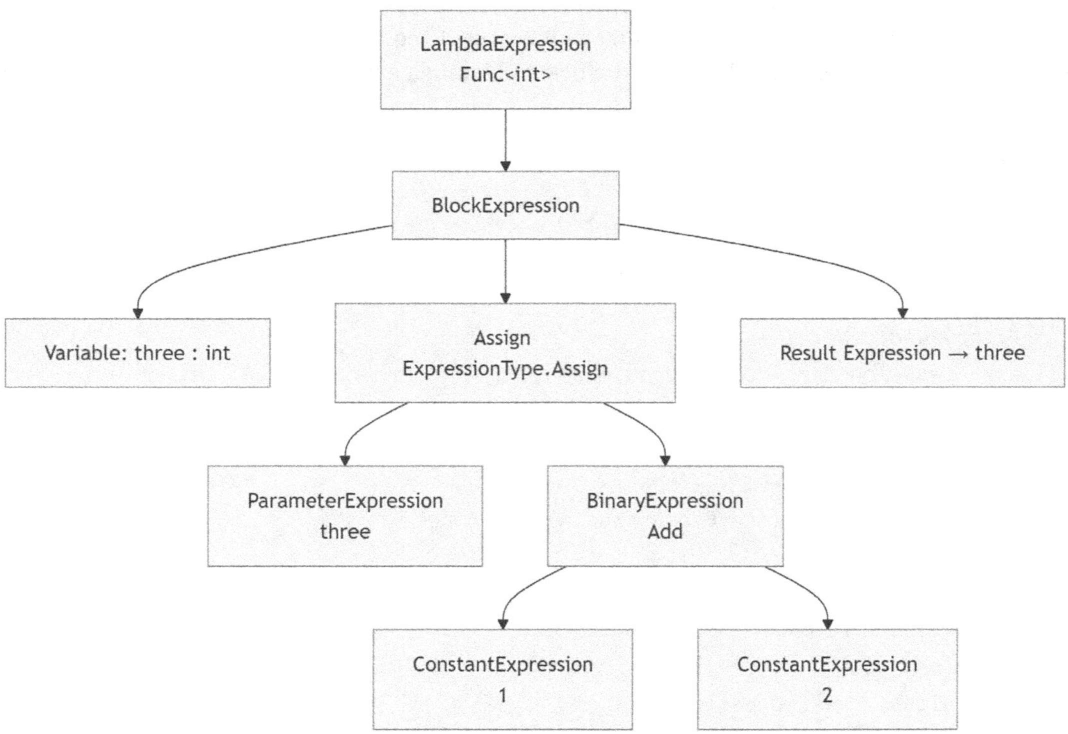

Figure 7.2: An expression tree of a simple statement adding two numbers

The preceding diagram shows us that even the simplest single statement like `int three = 1 + 2;` can be expressed as a tree structure. Compilers represent code statements as a tree structure for many reasons:

- **Hierarchical representation:** Code inherently has a hierarchical structure, with certain statements and expressions nested within others. A tree naturally represents this hierarchy: each node can have children that correspond to subcomponents of the code. For example, an `if` statement has branches for the conditions and any `else` block. This hierarchical arrangement allows the compiler to easily navigate and manipulate code structures during processing.
- **Ease of manipulation:** Trees allow easier manipulation of the code structure during various stages of the compilation process. Operations like transforming, optimizing, and generating code are more straightforward when the code is structured as a tree. For instance, if a compiler needs to optimize an expression, it can directly manipulate the subtree representing that expression without affecting the rest of the code structure.
- **Simplified parsing:** Parsing is the process of reading and understanding the source code. By representing code as a tree, the compiler simplifies the parsing process. Each node in the tree corresponds to a construct in the programming language (like loops, conditionals, and expressions), and the branches represent the relationships between these constructs. This makes it easier to apply grammar rules and syntactic validation.
- **Semantic analysis:** After parsing, the compiler performs semantic analysis, where it checks for semantic correctness like type checking, scope resolution, and usage of identifiers. The tree structure helps us navigate through different code elements systematically to perform these checks. Each node can be checked in isolation or in relation to its parent and children, ensuring the code adheres to the language's rules.
- **Code optimization:** The compiler can traverse the tree, looking for opportunities to simplify or enhance the code without changing its meaning. Common optimizations like constant folding (evaluating constant expressions at compile time), dead code elimination, and loop transformations are facilitated by the tree representation.
- **Target code generation:** The final stage of compilation involves generating target code, which can be machine code if you are using native AOT compilation, or IL byte code. The tree provides a systematic way to approach this generation, where each node can be translated into its equivalent in the target language. The tree helps to maintain the correct order and structure during this translation.
- **Debugging and error reporting:** When errors are detected in the source code, the tree structure helps to pinpoint the exact location of errors. Each node in the tree corresponds to a specific part of the source code, making it easier to generate meaningful error messages that can guide the programmer to the exact location and nature of the problem.

Overall, using a tree structure helps the compiler efficiently and effectively process source code through its various stages—parsing, analyzing, optimizing, and generating executable code.

Understanding components of expression trees

The `System.Linq.Expressions` namespace contains types for representing the components of an expression tree. For example, some common types are shown in *Table 7.1*:

Type	Description
`BinaryExpression`	An expression with a binary operator.
`BlockExpression`	A block containing a sequence of expressions where variables can be defined.
`CatchBlock`	A catch statement in a `try` block.
`ConditionalExpression`	An expression that has a conditional operator.
`ConstantExpression`	Represents a constant value like 1.
`Expression<Func<T>>`	A data structure that describes code, but it is not executable code. You can inspect it, transform it, or compile it to a delegate so it can be executed.
`LambdaExpression`	A lambda expression.
`MemberAssignment`	Assigning to a field or property.
`MemberExpression`	Accessing a field or property.
`MethodCallExpression`	A call to a method.
`NewExpression`	A call to a constructor.

Table 7.1: Common components when building expression trees

Only expression trees that represent lambda expressions can be executed.

Executing the simplest expression tree

Let's see how to construct, compile, and execute an expression tree representing the simplest single statement like `int three = 1 + 2;`:

1. Use your preferred code editor to add a new **Console App** / `console` project named `WorkingWithExpressionTrees` to the `Chapter07` solution.
2. In the `WorkingWithExpressionTrees.csproj` project file, statically and globally import the `Console` class, as shown in the following markup:

```
<ItemGroup>
  <Using Include="System.Console" Static="true" />
</ItemGroup>
```

3. In `Program.cs`, delete the existing statements, and then define an expression tree and execute it, as shown in the following code:

```
using System.Linq.Expressions; // To use Expression and so on.

ConstantExpression one = Expression.Constant(1, typeof(int));
ConstantExpression two = Expression.Constant(2, typeof(int));
BinaryExpression add = Expression.Add(one, two);

Expression<Func<int>> expressionTree = Expression.Lambda<Func<int>>(add);

Func<int> compiledTree = expressionTree.Compile();

WriteLine($"Result: {compiledTree()}");
```

4. Run the console app and note the result, as shown in the following output:

```
Result: 3
```

Now that you've seen the simplest example of an expression tree, you hopefully have a basic idea of what they are. Let's next look at one of the best features introduced to modern .NET: source generators.

Creating source generators

Source generators were introduced with C# 9 and .NET 5. They allow a programmer to get a compilation object that represents all the code being compiled, then dynamically generate additional code files, and compile those too.

A source generator is like a code analyzer that can add more code to the compilation process. In scenarios where you cannot use reflection to generate code, for example, if you also want to use native AOT compilation, then you can use source generators instead.

A great example is the `System.Text.Json` source generator. The classic method for serializing JSON uses reflection at runtime to dynamically analyze an object model, but this is slow. The better method uses source generators to create source code that is then compiled to give improved performance.

> You can read more about the `System.Text.Json` source generator at the following link: `https://devblogs.microsoft.com/dotnet/try-the-new-system-text-json-source-generator/`.

Implementing the simplest source generator

We will create a source generator that programmatically creates a code file that adds a method to the `Program` class, as shown in the following code:

```
// The source-generated code.
partial class Program
{
  static partial void Message(string message)
  {
    System.Console.WriteLine($"Generator says: '{message}'");
  }
}
```

This method can then be called in the `Program.cs` file of the project that uses this source generator.

Let's see how to do this:

1. Use your preferred code editor to add a new **Console App** / `console` project named `GeneratingCodeApp` to the `Chapter07` solution.
2. In the `GeneratingCodeApp.csproj` project file, statically and globally import the `Console` class, as shown in the following markup:

   ```
   <ItemGroup>
     <Using Include="System.Console" Static="true" />
   </ItemGroup>
   ```

3. In the `GeneratingCodeApp` project folder, add a new class file called `Program.Methods.cs`.
4. In `Program.Methods.cs`, define a partial `Program` class with a partial method with a `string` parameter, as shown in the following code:

   ```
   partial class Program
   {
     static partial void Message(string message);
   }
   ```

5. In `Program.cs`, delete the existing statements and then call the partial method, as shown in the following code:

   ```
   Message("Hello from some source generator code.");
   ```

Creating a class library to implement the source generator

Currently, source generators should target .NET Standard 2.0 as stated in the important note in the official documentation found at the following link: `https://learn.microsoft.com/en-us/dotnet/csharp/roslyn-sdk/source-generators-overview`. The default C# version used for class libraries that target .NET Standard 2.0 is C# 7.3, as shown at the following link: `https://docs.microsoft.com/en-us/dotnet/csharp/language-reference/configure-language-version#defaults`.

Let's create a class library for the source generator:

1. Use your preferred code editor to add a new **Class Library** / `classlib` project named `GeneratingCodeLib` that targets .NET Standard 2.0 to the `Chapter07` solution.
2. In the project file, set the C# language version to 12 or later (to support global `using` statements and raw string literals), statically and globally import the `Console` class, and add the NuGet packages `Microsoft.CodeAnalysis.Analyzers` and `Microsoft.CodeAnalysis.CSharp`, as shown highlighted in the following markup:

```
<Project Sdk="Microsoft.NET.Sdk">

  <PropertyGroup>
    <TargetFramework>netstandard2.0</TargetFramework>
    <LangVersion>12</LangVersion>
    <EnforceExtendedAnalyzerRules>true</EnforceExtendedAnalyzerRules>
  </PropertyGroup>

  <ItemGroup>
    <Using Include="System.Console" Static="true" />
  </ItemGroup>

  <ItemGroup>
    <PackageReference Include="Microsoft.CodeAnalysis.Analyzers">
      <PrivateAssets>all</PrivateAssets>
      <IncludeAssets>runtime; build; native; contentfiles; analyzers; 
buildtransitive</IncludeAssets>
    </PackageReference>
    <PackageReference Include="Microsoft.CodeAnalysis.CSharp" />
  </ItemGroup>

</Project>
```

> **Warning!** This project does not enable null warnings because the `<Nullable>enable</Nullable>` element is missing. If you choose to add it, then you will see some null warnings later.

3. Build the `GeneratingCodeLib` project.
4. Rename `Class1.cs` to `MessageSourceGenerator.cs`.

5. In the `GeneratingCodeLib` project, in `MessageSourceGenerator.cs`, define a class that implements `ISourceGenerator` and is decorated with the `[Generator]` attribute, as shown in the following code:

```
// To use [Generator], ISourceGenerator, and so on.
using Microsoft.CodeAnalysis;

namespace Packt.Shared;

[Generator]
public class MessageSourceGenerator : ISourceGenerator
{
  public void Execute(GeneratorExecutionContext execContext)
  {
    IMethodSymbol mainMethod = execContext.Compilation
      .GetEntryPoint(execContext.CancellationToken);
    string sourceCode = $$"""
 // The source-generated code.
 partial class {{mainMethod.ContainingType.Name}}
 {
 static partial void Message(string message)
 {
 System.Console.WriteLine($"Generator says: '{message}'");
 }
 }
 """;
    string typeName = mainMethod.ContainingType.Name;
    execContext.AddSource($"{typeName}.Methods.g.cs", sourceCode);
  }

  public void Initialize(GeneratorInitializationContext initContext)
  {
    // This source generator does not need any initialization.
  }
}
```

Good practice: It is a convention to include `.g.` or `.generated.` in the filename of source-generated files.

6. In the `GeneratingCodeApp.csproj` project file, add a reference to the class library project, as shown in the following markup:

```
<ItemGroup>
  <ProjectReference
    Include="..\GeneratingCodeLib\GeneratingCodeLib.csproj"
    OutputItemType="Analyzer"
    ReferenceOutputAssembly="false" />
</ItemGroup>
```

> **Good practice:** It is sometimes necessary to restart Visual Studio to see the results of working with source generators.

7. Build the `GeneratingCodeApp` project and note the auto-generated class file:

   - In Visual Studio, in **Solution Explorer**, expand the **Dependencies** | **Analyzers** | **GeneratingCodeLib** | **Packt.Shared.MessageSourceGenerator** nodes to find the `Program.Methods.g.cs` file, as shown in *Figure 7.3*:

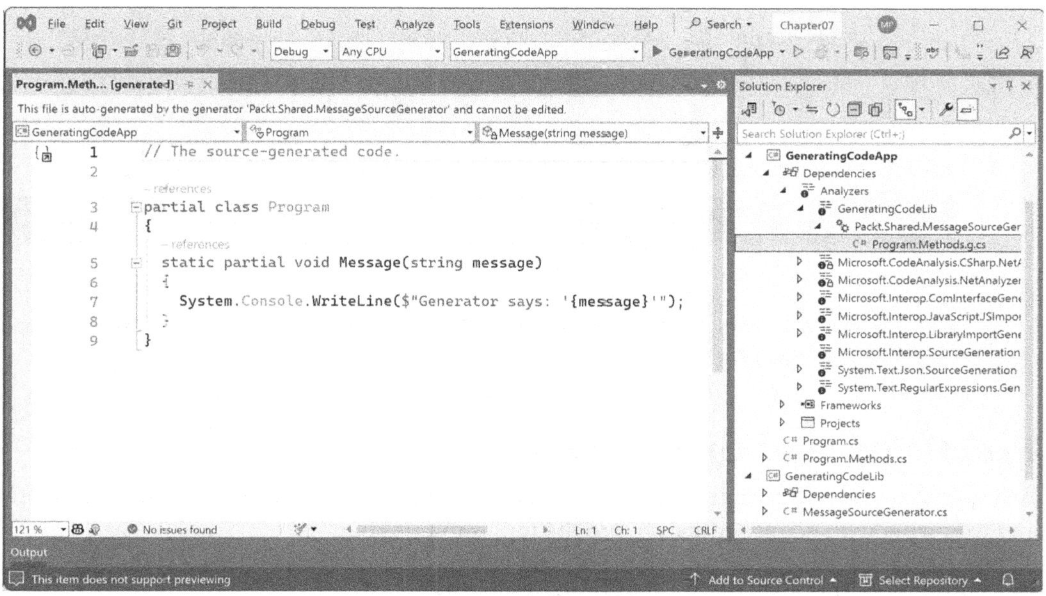

Figure 7.3: The source generated Program.Methods.g.cs file

Warning! VS Code does not automatically run analyzers. We must add an extra entry in the project file to enable the automatic generation of the source generator file, as shown in the following instructions:

1. In the `GeneratingCodeApp` project, in the project file, in the `<PropertyGroup>`, add an entry to enable the generation of the code file, as shown in the following markup: `<EmitCompilerGeneratedFiles>true</EmitCompilerGeneratedFiles>`.
2. In **Terminal**, build the `GeneratingCodeApp` project.
3. In the `obj/Debug/net10.0` folder, note the `generated` folder and its subfolder `GeneratingCodeLib/Packt.Shared.MessageSourceGenerator`, and the auto-generated file named `Program.Methods.g.cs`.

8. In the `Program.Methods.g.cs` file, note its contents, as shown in the following code:

```
// The source-generated code.
partial class Program
{
  static partial void Message(string message)
  {
    System.Console.WriteLine($"Generator says: '{message}'");
  }
}
```

9. Run the console app and note the message, as shown in the following output:

```
Generator says: 'Hello from some source generator code.'
```

You can control the path for automatically generated code files by adding a `<CompilerGeneratedFilesOutputPath>` element.

Practicing and exploring

Test your knowledge and understanding by answering some questions, getting some hands-on practice, and exploring with deeper research into the topics in this chapter.

Exercise 7.1 – Online-only material

To walk through another example of a source generator, you can complete an online-only section from my fundamentals book, found at the following link: `https://github.com/markjprice/cs14net10/blob/main/docs/ch07-source-generators.md`.

Exercise 7.2 – Practice exercises

Source generators are a massive topic. To learn more, use the following links:

- Source Generators design specification: https://github.com/dotnet/roslyn/blob/main/docs/features/source-generators.md.
- Source Generators samples: https://github.com/dotnet/roslyn-sdk/tree/main/samples/CSharp/SourceGenerators.
- Source Generators cookbook: https://github.com/dotnet/roslyn/blob/main/docs/features/source-generators.cookbook.md.
- Incremental Generators Cookbook: https://github.com/dotnet/roslyn/blob/main/docs/features/incremental-generators.cookbook.md.

Exercise 7.3 – Test your knowledge

Answer the following questions. If you get stuck, try googling the answers, if necessary, while remembering that if you get totally stuck, the answers are in *Appendix A*:

1. What are the four parts of a .NET assembly, and which are optional?
2. What can an attribute be applied to?
3. What are the names of the parts of a version number, and what do they mean if they follow the rules of semantic versioning?
4. How do you get a reference to the assembly for the currently executing console app?
5. How do you get all the attributes applied to an assembly?
6. How should you create a custom attribute?
7. What class do you inherit from to enable dynamic loading of assemblies?
8. What is an expression tree?
9. What is a source generator?
10. Which interface must a source generator class implement, and what methods are part of that interface?

Exercise 7.4 – Explore topics

Use the links on the following page to learn more about the topics covered in this chapter: https://github.com/markjprice/tools-skills-net10/blob/main/docs/book-links.md#chapter-7---observing-and-modifying-code-execution-dynamically.

Summary

In this chapter, you:

- Reflected on code and attributes
- Constructed, compiled, and executed a simple expression tree
- Built a source generator and used it in a console app project

In the next chapter, we will learn how to protect data using cryptography.

8

Protecting Data and Apps Using Cryptography

This chapter is about protecting your data from being viewed or manipulated by malicious users. You will learn how to protect your data using encryption, hashing, and signing. You will also learn how to properly generate random numbers for use with cryptographic operations, and how to implement basic authentication and authorization for users.

This chapter covers the following topics:

- Understanding the vocabulary of protection
- Encrypting and decrypting data
- Hashing data
- Signing data
- Generating random numbers for cryptography
- Authenticating and authorizing users

Warning! The code in this chapter covers security primitives for basic educational purposes only. You must not use any of the code in this chapter for production libraries and apps because the result will be that your data and projects are insecure. It is good practice to use libraries implemented by security professionals that are built using these security primitives and that have been hardened for real-world use following the latest best security practices. At the end of this chapter, you will find links to Microsoft best practices that you must follow if you intend to implement what you have learned in this chapter yourself.

Understanding the vocabulary of protection

Protecting data is important for many reasons, ranging from regulatory and compliance obligations to the direct and indirect impacts on users and organizations when data is poorly protected or exploited.

Most countries have specific laws and regulations that require businesses to protect the personal data of individuals. For example, the General Data Protection Regulation (GDPR) in the European Union, the California Consumer Privacy Act (CCPA) in the U.S., and similar regulations worldwide impose strict guidelines on data privacy and security. Non-compliance can result in significant penalties, legal fees, and damages.

Certain sectors, like healthcare and finance, have additional regulatory requirements (e.g., HIPAA in the U.S. for healthcare data protection, and PCI-DSS for payment data security). These regulations are designed to safeguard sensitive information specific to these sectors. Failing to comply with data protection laws can lead to hefty fines and legal costs.

When personal data is not properly safeguarded, it can lead to significant privacy breaches. This might expose individuals to unwanted publicity or intrusion into their private lives. Poor data security can lead to identity theft, where unauthorized individuals obtain and use personal data like Social Security numbers and credit card data to commit fraud or other crimes. When a company fails to protect user data, it often results in a loss of trust among its customers, potentially leading to churn and a damaged brand reputation.

For organizations that rely on proprietary data or intellectual property, inadequate data protection can lead to theft and unauthorized dissemination of their intellectual assets, which can compromise competitive advantages.

Techniques to protect your data

There are many techniques to protect your data. Here, we'll briefly introduce some of the most popular ones, and you will see more detailed explanations and practical implementations throughout this chapter:

- **Encrypting and decrypting:** This is a two-way process of converting your data from cleartext into ciphertext and back again. **Cleartext** is the original text that you want to protect. **Ciphertext** is the result of encrypting the cleartext.
- **Hashing:** This is a one-way process to generate a digest from any data. A digest of this paragraph might look like this: `DoBFtDhKeN0aaaLVdErtrZ3mpZSvpWDQ9TXDosTq0sQ=`. Hash is the verb; digest is the noun. No matter the size of the input, the digest is of fixed length, for example, a fixed-size byte array. Digests can be used to securely store passwords or to detect malicious changes or corruption of your data. Simple hashing algorithms should not be used for passwords. You should use PBKDF2, bcrypt, or scrypt for passwords because these algorithms guarantee that there cannot be two inputs that generate the same digest when used properly.
- **Signing:** This technique is used to ensure that data comes from a claimed source by validating a signature that has been applied to some data against someone's public key. For example, messages can be authenticated and validated by a receiver.

- **Authenticating**: This technique is used to identify someone by checking their credentials.
- **Authorizing**: This technique is used to ensure that someone has permission to perform an action or work with some data by checking the roles or groups they belong to.

> **Good practice:** If security is important to you (and it should be!), then hire an experienced security expert for guidance rather than relying on advice found online. It is very easy to make small mistakes and leave your applications and data vulnerable without realizing until it is too late!

Keys and key sizes

Protection algorithms often use a **key**. Keys are represented by byte arrays of varying sizes. Keys are used for various purposes, as shown in the following list:

- Encrypting and decrypting algorithms: AES, 3DES, RC2, Rijndael, and RSA
- Signing and verifying algorithms: RSA, ECDSA, and DSA
- Message authenticating and validating algorithms: HMAC
- Key agreement algorithms, a.k.a. safe encryption key exchange: Diffie-Hellman, Elliptical Curve Diffie-Hellman

> **Good practice:** Choose a bigger key size for stronger protection. This is an oversimplification because some RSA implementations support up to 16,384-bit keys that can take days to generate and would be overkill in most scenarios. A 2048-bit key should be sufficient until the year 2030, at which point you should upgrade to 3192-bit keys.

Keys for encryption and decryption can be **symmetric** (also known as **shared** or **secret** because the same key is used to encrypt and decrypt, and therefore must be kept safe) or **asymmetric** (a public-private key pair where the public key is used to encrypt, and only the private key can be used to decrypt).

> **Good practice:** Use symmetric key encryption algorithms in most cases because they are fast and can encrypt large amounts of data using a stream. Although asymmetric key encryption algorithms are slow and can only encrypt small byte arrays, use asymmetric keys for signature creation and validation because symmetric keys are inherently more of a risk since they must be shared, and if the key is stolen, then it can be used to decrypt the data.

In the real world, get the best of both worlds by using a symmetric key to encrypt your data and an asymmetric key to share the symmetric key. This is how **Transport Layer Security** (**TLS**) encryption on the internet works, which uses key agreement rather than RSA-encrypted session keys, as used by the legacy **Secure Sockets Layer** (**SSL**). Many people still use the acronym SSL when they mean TLS.

IVs and block sizes

When encrypting large amounts of data, there are likely to be repeating sequences. For example, in an English document, in any sequence of characters, `the` would appear frequently, and each time, it might get encrypted as `hQ2`. A good cracker would use this knowledge to make it easier to crack the encryption, as shown in the following output:

```
When the wind blew hard  umbrella broke.
5:s4&hQ2aj#D f9d1d£8fh"&s0)an DF8SFd#][1
```

We can avoid repeating sequences by dividing data into **blocks**. After encrypting a block, a byte array value is generated from that block, and this value is fed into the next block to adjust the algorithm. The next block is encrypted so the output is different even for the same input as the preceding block.

To encrypt the first block, we need a byte array to feed in. This is called the **initialization vector (IV)**.

An IV:

- Should be generated randomly along with every encrypted message
- Should be transmitted along with the encrypted message
- Is not itself a secret

Salts

A **salt** is a random byte array that is used as an additional input to a one-way hash function. If you do not use a salt when generating digests, then when many of your users register with `123456` as their password (from a 2023 survey, about 23 million users did this, making `123456` the most popular password globally), they will all have the same digest, and their accounts will be vulnerable to a rainbow table attack that uses precalculated digests.

> You can learn more about password statistics at the following links: `https://techjury.net/blog/password-statistics/` and `https://explodingtopics.com/blog/password-stats`.

When a user registers, the salt should be randomly generated and concatenated with their chosen password before being hashed. The generated digest (but not the original password) is stored with the salt in the database.

Then, when the user next logs in and enters their password, your code looks up their salt, concatenates it with the entered password, regenerates a digest, and then compares its value with the digest stored in the database. If they are the same, your code knows the user entered the correct password and lets them proceed into the app or website.

Even salting and hashing passwords is not enough for truly secure storage. You should do a lot more work, like peppering, key stretching, and regularly updating your hashing strategies. But that work is beyond the scope of this book. In this chapter, we will just look at a simple example of salting and hashing passwords.

Generating keys and IVs

Keys and IVs are byte arrays. Both parties that want to exchange encrypted data need the key and IV values, but byte arrays can be difficult to exchange reliably.

You can reliably generate a key or IV using a **password-based key derivation function** (**PBKDF2**). A good one is the `Rfc2898DeriveBytes` class, which takes a password, a salt, an iteration count, and a hash algorithm (the default is SHA-1, which is no longer recommended; you should use at least SHA-256 instead). It then generates keys and IVs by making calls to its `GetBytes` method. The iteration count is the number of times that the password is hashed during the process. The more iterations, the harder it will be to crack.

Although the `Rfc2898DeriveBytes` class can be used to generate the IV as well as the key, the IV should be randomly generated each time and transmitted with the encrypted message as plaintext because it does not need to be secret.

> **Good practice:** The salt size should be 8 bytes or larger, and the iteration count should be a value that takes about 100ms to generate a key and IV for the encryption algorithm on the target machine. This value will increase over time as CPUs improve. In the example code we write in the following section, we use 150,000, but that value will already be too low for some computers by the time you read this.

Encrypting and decrypting data

In .NET, there are multiple encryption algorithms you can choose from.

In legacy .NET Framework, some encryption algorithms are implemented by the **operating system** (**OS**) and their names are suffixed with `CryptoServiceProvider` or `Cng`. Some encryption algorithms are implemented in the .NET BCL and their names are suffixed with `Managed`.

In modern .NET, all encryption algorithms are implemented by the OS. If the OS encryption algorithms are certified by the **Federal Information Processing Standards** (**FIPS**), then .NET uses FIPS-certified encryption algorithms rather than implementing the encryption algorithm in the .NET base class library.

> Cryptographic operations are performed by OS implementations, so that when an OS has a security vulnerability fixed, .NET apps benefit immediately. But this means that those .NET apps can only use those features that the OS supports. You can read about which features are supported by which OS at the following link: `https://learn.microsoft.com/en-us/dotnet/standard/security/cross-platform-cryptography`.

Generally, you will always use an abstract class like `Aes` and its `Create` factory method to get an instance of an encryption algorithm, so you will not need to know if you are using `CryptoServiceProvider` or `Managed` anyway.

Some encryption algorithms use symmetric keys, and some use asymmetric keys. Symmetric encryption algorithms use `CryptoStream` to encrypt or decrypt large amounts of bytes efficiently. Asymmetric algorithms can only handle small amounts of bytes, stored in a byte array instead of a stream.

The main asymmetric encryption algorithm is RSA. Ron Rivest, Adi Shamir, and Leonard Adleman described the algorithm in 1977.

> A similar algorithm was designed in 1973 by Clifford Cocks, an English mathematician working for GCHQ, the British intelligence agency, but it was not declassified until 1997, so Rivest, Shamir, and Adleman got the credit and had their names immortalized in the RSA acronym.

The most common symmetric encryption algorithms derive from the abstract class named `SymmetricAlgorithm` and are shown in the following list:

- AES
- DESCryptoServiceProvider
- TripleDES
- RC2CryptoServiceProvider
- RijndaelManaged

If you need to write code to decrypt some data sent by an external system, then you will have to use whatever algorithm the external system used to encrypt the data. Likewise, if you need to send encrypted data to a system that can only decrypt using a specific algorithm, again, you do not have a choice of algorithm to use.

If your code will both encrypt and decrypt, then you can choose the algorithm that best suits your requirements for strength, performance, and so on.

> **Good practice:** Choose the **Advanced Encryption Standard (AES)**, which is based on the Rijndael algorithm, for symmetric encryption. Choose RSA for asymmetric encryption. Do not confuse RSA with DSA. The **Digital Signature Algorithm (DSA)** cannot encrypt data. It can only generate and verify signatures.

Encrypting symmetrically with AES

To make it easier to reuse your protection code in the multiple projects that you will build in this chapter, we will create a static class named `Protector` in its own class library and then reference it in a console app for our symmetric encryption.

Let's go!

1. Use your preferred code editor to create a new console app project, as defined in the following list:

    - Project template: **Console App** / `console`

- Solution file and folder: `Chapter08`
- Project file and folder: `EncryptionApp`

2. Add a new **Class Library** / `classlib` named `CryptographyLib` to the `Chapter08` solution.
3. In the `CryptographyLib` project, rename the `Class1.cs` file to `Protector.cs`.
4. In the `CryptographyLib` project, treat warnings as errors and globally and statically import the `System.Console` class.
5. In the `EncryptionApp` project, treat warnings as errors, globally and statically import the `System.Console` class, and add a project reference to the `CryptographyLib` library, as shown in the following markup:

```
<ItemGroup>
  <ProjectReference
    Include="..\CryptographyLib\CryptographyLib.csproj" />
</ItemGroup>
```

6. Build the `EncryptionApp` project and make sure there are no compile errors.
7. In `Protector.cs`, define a static class named `Protector` with fields for storing a salt byte array and a large number of iterations, along with methods to Encrypt and Decrypt, as shown in the following code:

```
using System.Diagnostics; // To use Stopwatch.
using System.Security.Cryptography; // To use Aes and so on.
using System.Text; // To use Encoding.

using static System.Convert; // To use ToBase64String and so on.

namespace Packt.Shared;

public static class Protector
{
  // Salt size must be at least 8 bytes, we will use 16 bytes.
  private static readonly byte[] salt =
    Encoding.Unicode.GetBytes("7BANANAS");

  // Default iterations for Rfc2898DeriveBytes is 1000.
  // Iterations should be high enough to take at least 100ms to
  // generate a Key and IV on the target machine. 150,000 iterations
  // takes 139ms on my 11th Gen Intel Core i7-1165G7 @ 2.80GHz.
  private static readonly int iterations = 150_000;

  public static string Encrypt(
    string plainText, string password)
```

```
{
  byte[] encryptedBytes;
  byte[] plainBytes = Encoding.Unicode.GetBytes(plainText);

  using (Aes aes = Aes.Create()) // abstract class factory method
  {
    // Record how long it takes to generate the Key and IV.
    Stopwatch timer = Stopwatch.StartNew();

    using (Rfc2898DeriveBytes pbkdf2 = new(
      password, salt, iterations, HashAlgorithmName.SHA256))
    {
      WriteLine($"PBKDF2 algorithm: {pbkdf2.HashAlgorithm
        }, Iteration count: {pbkdf2.IterationCount:N0}");

      aes.Key = pbkdf2.GetBytes(32); // Set a 256-bit key.
      aes.IV = pbkdf2.GetBytes(16); // Set a 128-bit IV.
    }

    timer.Stop();
    WriteLine($"{timer.ElapsedMilliseconds:N0
      } milliseconds to generate Key and IV.");

    int minimumMilliseconds = 100;

    if (timer.ElapsedMilliseconds < minimumMilliseconds)
    {
      ConsoleColor previousColor = ForegroundColor;
      ForegroundColor = ConsoleColor.Red;

      WriteLine(
        "WARNING: The elapsed time to generate the Key and IV " +
        "is less than {minimumMilliseconds} milliseconds which " +
        "is too short to provide a secure encryption key.");

      ForegroundColor = previousColor;
    }

    WriteLine($"Encryption algorithm: {nameof(Aes)}-{aes.KeySize
      }, {aes.Mode} mode with {aes.Padding} padding.");
```

```
      using (MemoryStream ms = new())
      {
        using (ICryptoTransform transformer = aes.CreateEncryptor())
        {
          using (CryptoStream cs = new(
            ms, transformer, CryptoStreamMode.Write))
          {
            cs.Write(plainBytes, 0, plainBytes.Length);
            if (!cs.HasFlushedFinalBlock)
            {
              cs.FlushFinalBlock();
            }
          }
        }
        encryptedBytes = ms.ToArray();
      }
    }
    return ToBase64String(encryptedBytes);
  }

  public static string Decrypt(
    string cipherText, string password)
  {
    byte[] plainBytes;
    byte[] cryptoBytes = FromBase64String(cipherText);

    using (Aes aes = Aes.Create())
    {
      using (Rfc2898DeriveBytes pbkdf2 = new(
        password, salt, iterations, HashAlgorithmName.SHA256))
      {
        aes.Key = pbkdf2.GetBytes(32);
        aes.IV = pbkdf2.GetBytes(16);
      }

      using (MemoryStream ms = new())
      {
        using (ICryptoTransform transformer = aes.CreateDecryptor())
        {
          using (CryptoStream cs = new(
            ms, transformer, CryptoStreamMode.Write))
```

```
          {
            cs.Write(cryptoBytes, 0, cryptoBytes.Length);
            if (!cs.HasFlushedFinalBlock)
            {
              cs.FlushFinalBlock();
            }
          }
        }
        plainBytes = ms.ToArray();
      }
    }
    return Encoding.Unicode.GetString(plainBytes);
  }
}
```

Note the following points about the preceding code:

- Although the salt and iteration count can be hardcoded (but preferably stored in the message itself), the password must be passed as a parameter at runtime when calling the `Encrypt` and `Decrypt` methods.
- The constructors for the `Rfc2898DeriveBytes` class require a `HashAlgorithmName` to be specified. We specify `SHA256`, which is better than the old default of `SHA1`.
- We use `Stopwatch` to record how long it takes to generate the key and IV so that we can make sure that it is at least 100ms. We output a warning if it is less than this minimum.
- We use a temporary `MemoryStream` type to store the results of encrypting and decrypting, and then call `ToArray` to turn the stream into a byte array.
- `CryptoStream` implements buffering, which is integral to how it handles data because cryptographic transformations often require a specific block size of data to operate correctly. It is therefore important to flush the final block if it has not already been flushed.
- We convert the encrypted byte arrays to and from a `Base64` encoding to make them easier to read for humans.

> **Good practice:** Never hardcode a password in your source code because, even after compilation, the password can be read in the assembly by using disassembler tools.

8. In the `EncryptionApp` project, in `Program.cs`, delete the existing statements, and then import the namespace for the `Protector` class and the namespace for the `CryptographicException` class, as shown in the following code:

```
using System.Security.Cryptography; // To use CryptographicException.
using Packt.Shared; // To use Protector.
```

> In a real project, you might statically import the `Packt.Shared.Protector` class so that you can call its methods like `Encrypt` without prefixing them with a class name like `Protector.Encrypt`. In this learning project, I want to make sure that you remember that those methods are ones you have written.

9. In `Program.cs`, add statements to prompt the user for a message and a password, and then encrypt and decrypt, as shown in the following code:

```
Write("Enter a message that you want to encrypt: ");
string? message = ReadLine();

Write("Enter a password: ");
string? password = ReadLine();

if ((password is null) || (message is null))
{
  WriteLine("Message or password cannot be null.");
  return; // Exit the app.
}

string cipherText = Protector.Encrypt(message, password);
WriteLine($"Encrypted text: {cipherText}");

Write("Enter the password: ");
string? password2Decrypt = ReadLine();

if (password2Decrypt is null)
{
  WriteLine("Password to decrypt cannot be null.");
  return;
}

try
{
  string clearText = Protector.Decrypt(cipherText, password2Decrypt);
  WriteLine($"Decrypted text: {clearText}");
}
catch (CryptographicException)
{
  WriteLine("You entered the wrong password!");
}
```

```
catch (Exception ex)
{
  WriteLine($"Non-cryptographic exception: {
    ex.GetType().Name}, {ex.Message}");
}
```

10. Run the code, try entering a message like `Hello Bob` and a password like `secret` to encrypt, enter the same password to decrypt, and view the result, as shown in the following output:

```
Enter a message that you want to encrypt: Hello Bob
Enter a password: secret
PBKDF2 algorithm: SHA256, Iteration count: 150,000
97 milliseconds to generate Key and IV.
WARNING: The elapsed time to generate the Key and IV may be too short to
provide a secure encryption key.
Encryption algorithm: AES-256, CBC mode with PKCS7 padding.
Encrypted text: eWt8sgL7aSt5DC9g74ONEPO7mjd55lXB/MmCZpUsFE0=
Enter the password: secret
Decrypted text: Hello Bob
```

If your output shows the number of milliseconds at less than 100, then adjust the number of iterations higher until the number of milliseconds is greater than 100. A different number of iterations will affect the encrypted text, so it will look different from the above output.

11. Run the console app and try entering a message and password to encrypt, but this time, enter the password incorrectly to decrypt, and view the result, as shown in the following output:

```
Enter a message that you want to encrypt: Hello Bob
Enter a password: secret
PBKDF2 algorithm: SHA256, Iteration count: 150,000
134 milliseconds to generate Key and IV.
Encryption algorithm: AES-256, CBC mode with PKCS7 padding.
Encrypted text: eWt8sgL7aSt5DC9g74ONEPO7mjd55lXB/MmCZpUsFE0=
Enter the password: 123456
You entered the wrong password!
```

Good practice: To support future encryption upgrades like switching to an improved algorithm or upgrading to a larger key size, record information about what choices you made. For example, for this project, record that we used AES-256, CBC mode with PKCS#7 padding, and PBKDF2 and its hash algorithm and iteration count. This good practice is known as **cryptographic agility**.

Hashing data

In .NET, there are multiple hash algorithms you can choose from. Some do not use any key, some use symmetric keys, and some use asymmetric keys.

There are two important factors to consider when choosing a hash algorithm:

- **Collision resistance**: How rare is it to find two inputs that share the same hash?
- **Preimage resistance**: For a hash, how difficult would it be to find another input that shares the same hash?

Some common non-keyed hashing algorithms are shown in *Table 8.1*:

Algorithm	Hash size	Description
MD5	16 bytes	This is commonly used because it is fast, but it is not collision resistant.
SHA-1	20 bytes	The use of SHA-1 on the internet has been deprecated since 2011.
SHA-256, SHA-384, SHA-512	32 bytes, 48 bytes, 64 bytes	These are the **Secure Hashing Algorithm 2nd generation** (**SHA-2**) algorithms with different hash sizes.
SHA3-256, SHA3-384, SHA3-512	32 bytes, 48 bytes, 64 bytes	These are the **Secure Hashing Algorithm 3rd generation** (**SHA-3**) algorithms with different hash sizes. They use stronger but slower algorithms. SHA-3 has been criticized for being slow on CPUs that do not have specific instructions meant for computing Keccak functions faster. For example, SHA2-512 is more than twice as fast as SHA3-512.

Table 8.1: Common non-keyed hashing algorithms

Good practice: Avoid MD5 and SHA-1 because they have known weaknesses. Choose a larger hash size to reduce the possibility of repeated hashes. The first publicly known MD5 collision happened in 2010. The first publicly known SHA-1 collision happened in 2017. You can read more at the following link: `https://arstechnica.co.uk/information-technology/2017/02/at-deaths-door-for-years-widely-used-sha1-function-is-now-dead/`.

Hashing with the commonly used SHA-256

Choosing between SHA-256, SHA-384, and SHA-512 for hashing depends on your specific security requirements, performance considerations, and system capabilities. SHA-256 is suitable for most applications where security is a priority. It's currently resistant to any known practical cryptographic attacks that could threaten its integrity or collision resistance. It is faster than SHA-384 and SHA-512 on 32-bit systems due to its smaller digest size and use of 32-bit words. It's often required for compliance with various security protocols and standards.

SHA-384 has a 384-bit hash and uses a larger block size compared to SHA-256. This makes it inherently more resistant to collision attacks, but it typically performs slower than SHA-256, although it can be faster on systems that optimize for 64-bit operations. It is used when there are specific regulatory or compliance requirements that dictate a hash length exceeding 256 bits, but where SHA-512 might be considered overkill or too slow.

SHA-512 provides a 512-bit hash, making it the most robust option in terms of raw security strength within the SHA-2 family. It's highly resistant to all known attack vectors, including collision and preimage attacks. It typically performs better than SHA-256 and SHA-384 on 64-bit systems due to its use of 64-bit words, which align well with the architecture of modern 64-bit CPUs. It is best suited for high-security environments where the integrity of very sensitive data is paramount.

If the highest level of security is a priority, SHA-512 is preferable. For most general applications, SHA-256 provides ample security, so that is what we will use in this chapter. As an optional challenge, add benchmarks and test all three hash algorithms on your machine to compare them.

.NET 8 introduced support for the SHA-3 family of hash algorithms, including SHAKE-128 and SHAKE-256. The SHAKE algorithms are different from traditional hash functions like SHA-128 or SHA-256 which are fixed-length hash functions. SHAKE-128 and SHAKE-256 are **Extendable Output Functions (XOFs)**, which means they can produce outputs of arbitrary length. This makes them highly flexible for various applications where different output sizes are needed. SHA-3 support is currently supported on Windows 11 build 25324 or later, and Linux with OpenSSL 1.1.1 or later.

Define a record and method to register users

We will now add a class to represent a user stored in memory, a file, or a database. We will use a dictionary to store multiple users in memory:

1. In the `CryptographyLib` class library project, add a new class file named `User.cs`, delete any existing statements, and then define a record with three properties for storing a user's name, a random salt value, and their salted and hashed password, as shown in the following code:

```
namespace Packt.Shared;

public record class User(string Name, string Salt,
  string SaltedHashedPassword);
```

2. In `Protector.cs`, add statements to declare a dictionary to store users and define two methods, one to register a new user and one to validate their password when they subsequently log in, as shown in the following code:

```
private static Dictionary<string, User> Users = new();

public static User Register(string username,
  string password)
{
  // Generate a random salt.
```

```
    RandomNumberGenerator rng = RandomNumberGenerator.Create();

    byte[] saltBytes = new byte[16];
    rng.GetBytes(saltBytes);

    string saltText = ToBase64String(saltBytes);

    // Generate the salted and hashed password.
    string saltedhashedPassword = SaltAndHashPassword(password, saltText);
    User user = new(username, saltText, saltedhashedPassword);
    Users.Add(user.Name, user);
    return user;
  }

  // Check a user's password that is stored in the Users dictionary.
  public static bool CheckPassword(string username, string password)
  {
    if (!Users.ContainsKey(username))
    {
      return false;
    }

    User u = Users[username];

    return CheckPassword(password,
      u.Salt, u.SaltedHashedPassword);
  }

  // Check a password using salt and hashed password.
  public static bool CheckPassword(string password,
    string salt, string hashedPassword)
  {
    // re-generate the salted and hashed password
    string saltedHashedPassword = SaltAndHashPassword(
      password, salt);

    return (saltedHashedPassword == hashedPassword);
  }

  private static string SaltAndHashPassword(string password, string salt)
  {
```

```
    using (SHA256 sha = SHA256.Create())
    {
      string saltedPassword = password + salt;

      return ToBase64String(sha.ComputeHash(
        Encoding.Unicode.GetBytes(saltedPassword)));
    }
  }
```

Implementing a hashing app

Now we will use the new hashing methods to work with users:

1. Use your preferred code editor to add a new console app named `HashingApp` to the `Chapter08` solution.
2. In the `HashingApp.csproj` project file, treat warnings as errors, add a project reference to `CryptographyLib`, and globally and statically import the `System.Console` class.
3. Build the `HashingApp` project.
4. In the `HashingApp` project, in `Program.cs`, delete the existing statements, and then add statements to register a user (Alice) and prompt to register a second user (Bob). Then, prompt to log in as one of those users and validate the password, as shown in the following code:

```
using Packt.Shared; // To use Protector.

WriteLine("Registering Alice with Pa$$w0rd:");
User alice = Protector.Register("Alice", "Pa$$w0rd");
WriteLine($" Name: {alice.Name}");
WriteLine($" Salt: {alice.Salt}");
WriteLine($" Password (salted and hashed): {
  alice.SaltedHashedPassword}");
WriteLine();

Write("Enter a new user to register: ");
string? username = ReadLine();
if (string.IsNullOrEmpty(username)) username = "Bob";

Write($"Enter a password for {username}: ");
string? password = ReadLine();
if (string.IsNullOrEmpty(password)) password = "Pa$$w0rd";

WriteLine("Registering a new user:");
User newUser = Protector.Register(username, password);
WriteLine($" Name: {newUser.Name}");
WriteLine($" Salt: {newUser.Salt}");
```

```
WriteLine($" Password (salted and hashed): {
  newUser.SaltedHashedPassword}");
WriteLine();

bool correctPassword = false;

while (!correctPassword)
{
  Write("Enter a username to log in: ");
  string? loginUsername = ReadLine();

  if (string.IsNullOrEmpty(loginUsername))
  {
    WriteLine("Login username cannot be empty.");
    Write("Press Ctrl+C to end or press ENTER to retry.");
    ReadLine();
    continue; // Return to the while statement.
  }

  Write("Enter a password to log in: ");
  string? loginPassword = ReadLine();

  if (string.IsNullOrEmpty(loginPassword))
  {
    WriteLine("Login password cannot be empty.");
    Write("Press Ctrl+C to end or press ENTER to retry.");
    ReadLine();
    continue;
  }

  correctPassword = Protector.CheckPassword(
    loginUsername, loginPassword);

  if (correctPassword)
  {
    WriteLine($"Correct! {loginUsername} has been logged in.");
  }
  else
  {
    WriteLine("Invalid username or password. Try again.");
  }
}
```

5. Run the code, register a new user (Bob) with the same password as Alice, and view the result, as shown in the following output:

```
Registering Alice with Pa$$w0rd:
  Name: Alice
  Salt: I1I1dzIjkd7EYDf/6jaf4w==
  Password (salted and hashed): pIoadjE4W/
XaRFkqS3br3UuAuPv/3LVQ8kzj6mvcz+s=
Enter a new user to register: Bob
Enter a password for Bob: Pa$$w0rd
Registering a new user:
  Name: Bob
  Salt: 1X7ym/UjxTiuEWBC/vIHpw==
  Password (salted and hashed):
DoBFtDhKeN0aaaLVdErtrZ3mpZSvpWDQ9TXDosTq0sQ=
Enter a username to log in: Alice
Enter a password to log in: secret
Invalid username or password. Try again.
Enter a username to log in: Bob
Enter a password to log in: secret
Invalid username or password. Try again.
Enter a username to log in: Bob
Enter a password to log in: Pa$$w0rd
Correct! Bob has been logged in.
```

Even if two users register with the same password, they have randomly generated salts so that their salted and hashed passwords are different.

Signing data

To prove that some data has come from someone we trust, it can be signed. You do not sign the data itself; instead, you sign a *hash* of the data, because all the signature algorithms first hash the data as an implementation step. They also allow you to shortcut this step and provide the data already hashed.

We will be using the SHA-256 algorithm for generating the hash, combined with the RSA algorithm for signing the hash.

We could use DSA for both hashing and signing. DSA is faster than RSA for generating a signature, but it is slower than RSA for validating a signature. Since a signature is generated once but validated many times, it is best to have faster validation than generation. That's why we will use RSA.

Good practice: DSA is rarely used today. The improved equivalent is **Elliptic Curve DSA (ECDSA)**. Although ECDSA is slower than RSA, it generates a shorter signature with the same level of security.

Signing with SHA-256 and RSA

Let's explore signing data and checking the signature with a public key:

1. In the `Protector` class, add statements to declare a field to store a public key as a `string` value, as shown in the following code:

```
public static string? PublicKey;
```

2. Add statements to declare a method to generate a signature, as shown in the following code:

```
public static string GenerateSignature(string data)
{
  byte[] dataBytes = Encoding.Unicode.GetBytes(data);
  SHA256 sha = SHA256.Create();

  byte[] hashedData = sha.ComputeHash(dataBytes);

  RSA rsa = RSA.Create();

  PublicKey = rsa.ToXmlString(false); // exclude private key

  return ToBase64String(rsa.SignHash(hashedData,
    HashAlgorithmName.SHA256, RSASignaturePadding.Pkcs1));
}
```

3. Add statements to declare a method to validate a signature, as shown in the following code:

```
public static bool ValidateSignature(
  string data, string signature)
{
  if (PublicKey is null) return false;

  byte[] dataBytes = Encoding.Unicode.GetBytes(data);
  SHA256 sha = SHA256.Create();

  byte[] hashedData = sha.ComputeHash(dataBytes);
  byte[] signatureBytes = FromBase64String(signature);

  RSA rsa = RSA.Create();
  rsa.FromXmlString(PublicKey);
  return rsa.VerifyHash(hashedData, signatureBytes,
    HashAlgorithmName.SHA256, RSASignaturePadding.Pkcs1);
}
```

Note the following from the preceding code:

- Only the public part of the public-private key pair needs to be made available to the code that is checking the signature so that we can pass `false` when we call the `ToXmlString` method. The private part is required to sign data and must be kept secret because anyone with the private part can sign data as if they are you!
- The hash algorithm used to generate the hash from the data by calling the `SignHash` method must match the hash algorithm set when calling the `VerifyHash` method. In the preceding code, we used `SHA256`.

Creating a signing app

Now we can test signing some data and checking the signature.

1. Use your preferred code editor to add a new console app named `SigningApp` to the `Chapter08` solution.
2. In the `SigningApp` project, treat warnings as errors, add a project reference to `CryptographyLib`, and globally and statically import the `System.Console` class.
3. Build the `SigningApp` project and make sure there are no compile errors.
4. In `Program.cs`, delete the existing statements and then import the `Packt.Shared` namespace. Add statements to prompt the user to enter some text, sign it, check its signature, then modify the data, and check the signature again to deliberately cause a mismatch, as shown in the following code:

```
using Packt.Shared; // To use Protector.

Write("Enter some text to sign: ");
string? data = ReadLine();
if (string.IsNullOrEmpty(data))
{
  WriteLine("You must enter some text.");
  return; // Exit the app.
}

string signature = Protector.GenerateSignature(data);
WriteLine($"Signature: {signature}");
WriteLine("Public key used to check signature:");
WriteLine(Protector.PublicKey);

if (Protector.ValidateSignature(data, signature)){
  WriteLine("Correct! Signature is valid. Data has not been
manipulated.");
}
else
```

```
{
  WriteLine("Invalid signature or the data has been manipulated.");
}

// Simulate manipulated data by replacing the first
// character with an X (or if already an X then Y).
char newFirstChar = 'X';

if (data[0] == newFirstChar)
{
  newFirstChar = 'Y';
}

string manipulatedData = $"{newFirstChar}{data.Substring(1)}";

if (Protector.ValidateSignature(manipulatedData, signature))
{
  WriteLine("Correct! Signature is valid. Data has not been manipulated.
");
}
else
{
  WriteLine($"Invalid signature or manipulated data: {manipulatedData}");
}
```

5. Run the code and enter some text, as shown in the following output (edited for length):

```
Enter some text to sign: The cat sat on the mat.
Signature: BXSTdM...4Wrg==
Public key used to check signature:
<RSAKeyValue><Modulus>nHtwl3...mw3w==</Modulus><Exponent>AQAB</
Exponent></RSAKeyValue>
Correct! Signature is valid. Data has not been manipulated.
Invalid signature or manipulated data: Xhe cat sat on the mat.
```

Generating random numbers for cryptography

Sometimes you need to generate random numbers for use with cryptography in encryption or signing. There are a couple of classes that can generate random numbers in .NET.

The `Random` class generates cryptographically weak **pseudo-random** numbers. However, this is not good enough for cryptography. If the random numbers are not truly random, then they are predictable, and then a cracker can break your protection.

For cryptographically strong pseudo-random numbers, you must use a `RandomNumberGenerator`-derived type, such as those created by calling the `RandomNumberGenerator.Create` factory method either with a named algorithm or using its default implementation.

We will now create a method to generate a truly random byte array that can be used in algorithms like encryption for key and IV values:

1. In the `Protector` class, add statements to define a method to get a random key or IV for use in encryption, as shown in the following code:

```
public static byte[] GetRandomKeyOrIV(int size)
{
  RandomNumberGenerator r = RandomNumberGenerator.Create();
  byte[] data = new byte[size];

  // The array is filled with cryptographically random bytes.
  r.GetBytes(data);
  return data;
}
```

   Now we can test the random bytes generated for a truly random encryption key or IV.

2. Use your preferred code editor to add a new console app named `RandomizingApp` to the `Chapter08` solution.
3. In the `RandomizingApp` project, treat warnings as errors, add a project reference to `CryptographyLib`, and globally and statically import the `System.Console` class.
4. Build the `RandomizingApp` project and make sure there are no compile errors.
5. In `Program.cs`, delete the existing statements and then import the `Packt.Shared` namespace. Add statements to prompt the user to enter a byte array size and then generate random byte values and write them to the console, as shown in the following code:

```
using Packt.Shared; // To use Protector.

Write("How big do you want the key (in bytes): ");

string? size = ReadLine();

if (string.IsNullOrEmpty(size))
{
  WriteLine("You must enter a size for the key.");
  return; // Exit the app.
}

byte[] key = Protector.GetRandomKeyOrIV(int.Parse(size));
```

```
WriteLine($"Key as byte array:");

for (int b = 0; b < key.Length; b++)
{
  Write($"{key[b]:x2} ");
  if (((b + 1) % 16) == 0) WriteLine();
}
WriteLine();
```

6. Run the code, enter a typical size for the key, such as 256, and view the randomly generated key, as shown in the following output:

```
How big do you want the key (in bytes): 256
Key as byte array:
f1 57 3f 44 80 e7 93 dc 8e 55 04 6c 76 6f 51 b9
e8 84 59 e5 8d eb 08 d5 e6 59 65 20 b1 56 fa 68
...
```

Authenticating and authorizing users

Authentication is the process of verifying the identity of a user by validating their credentials against some authority. Credentials include a username and password combination, or biometric data like a fingerprint or face scan. Once authenticated, the authority can make **claims** about the user, for example, what their email address is, and what groups or roles they belong to.

Authorization is the process of verifying membership of groups or roles before allowing access to resources such as application functions and data. Although authorization can be based on individual identity, it is good security practice to authorize based on group or role membership (which can be indicated via claims) even when there is only one user in the role or group. This is because that allows the user's membership to change in the future without reassigning the user's individual access rights.

For example, instead of assigning access rights for Buckingham Palace, Windsor Castle, and Sandringham House to *Charles Philip Arthur George* (a user), you would assign access rights to the *Monarch of the United Kingdom of Great Britain and Northern Ireland and other realms and territories* (a role) and then add *Charles* as the only member of that role. Then, at some point in the future, you do not need to change any access rights for the *Monarch* role; you just remove *Charles* and add the next person in the line of succession. And, of course, you would implement the line of succession as a queue.

Authentication and authorization mechanisms

There are multiple authentication and authorization mechanisms to choose from. They all implement a pair of interfaces in the `System.Security.Principal` namespace: `IIdentity` and `IPrincipal`.

Identifying a user

`IIdentity` represents a user, so it has a `Name` property and an `IsAuthenticated` property to indicate if they are anonymous or if they have been successfully authenticated from their credentials, as shown in the following code:

```
namespace System.Security.Principal;

public interface IIdentity
{
  string? AuthenticationType { get; }
  bool IsAuthenticated { get; }
  string? Name { get; }
}
```

A common class that implements this interface is `GenericIdentity`, which inherits from `ClaimsIdentity`, as shown in the following code:

```
namespace System.Security.Principal;

public class GenericIdentity : ClaimsIdentity
{
  public GenericIdentity(string name);
  public GenericIdentity(string name, string type);
  protected GenericIdentity(GenericIdentity identity);

  public override string AuthenticationType { get; }
  public override IEnumerable<Claim> Claims { get; }
  public override bool IsAuthenticated { get; }
  public override string Name { get; }
  public override ClaimsIdentity Clone();
}
```

The `Claim` objects have a `Type` property that indicates if the claim is for their name, their membership of a role or group, their date of birth, and so on, as shown in the following code:

```
namespace System.Security.Claims;

public class Claim
{
  // various constructors
  public string Type { get; }
  public ClaimsIdentity? Subject { get; }
  public IDictionary<string, string> Properties { get; }
```

```
  public string OriginalIssuer { get; }
  public string Issuer { get; }
  public string ValueType { get; }
  public string Value { get; }
  protected virtual byte[]? CustomSerializationData { get; }
  public virtual Claim Clone();
  public virtual Claim Clone(ClaimsIdentity? identity);
  public override string ToString();
  public virtual void WriteTo(BinaryWriter writer);
  protected virtual void WriteTo(BinaryWriter writer, byte[]? userData);
}

public static class ClaimTypes
{
  public const string Actor = "http://schemas.xmlsoap.org/ws/2009/09/identity/
claims/actor";
  public const string NameIdentifier = "http://schemas.xmlsoap.org/ws/2005/05/
identity/claims/nameidentifier";
  public const string Name = "http://schemas.xmlsoap.org/ws/2005/05/identity/
claims/name";
  public const string PostalCode = "http://schemas.xmlsoap.org/ws/2005/05/
identity/claims/postalcode";
  // Many other string constants.
  public const string MobilePhone = "http://schemas.xmlsoap.org/ws/2005/05/
identity/claims/mobilephone";
  public const string Role = "http://schemas.microsoft.com/ws/2008/06/identity/
claims/role";
  public const string Webpage = "http://schemas.xmlsoap.org/ws/2005/05/
identity/claims/webpage";
}
```

User membership

`IPrincipal` is used to associate an identity with the roles and groups that they are members of, so it can be used for authorization purposes, as shown in the following code:

```
namespace System.Security.Principal;

public interface IPrincipal
{
  IIdentity? Identity { get; }
  bool IsInRole(string role);
}
```

The current thread executing your code has a `CurrentPrincipal` property that can be set to any object that implements `IPrincipal`, and it will be checked when permission is needed to perform a secure action.

The most common class that implements this interface is `GenericPrincipal`, which inherits from `ClaimsPrincipal`, as shown in the following code:

```
namespace System.Security.Principal;

public class GenericPrincipal : ClaimsPrincipal
{
  public GenericPrincipal(IIdentity identity, string[]? roles);
  public override IIdentity Identity { get; }
  public override bool IsInRole([NotNullWhen(true)] string? role);
}
```

Implementing authentication and authorization

Let's explore authentication and authorization by implementing a custom authentication and authorization mechanism:

1. In the `CryptographyLib` project, in the `User.cs` record, add a property to store an array of roles, as highlighted in the following code:

   ```
   namespace Packt.Shared;

   public record class User(string Name, string Salt,
     string SaltedHashedPassword, string[]? Roles);
   ```

2. In `Protector.cs`, modify the `Register` method in the `Protector` class to allow an array of roles to be passed as an optional parameter, as shown highlighted in the following code:

   ```
   public static User Register(string username,
     string password, string[]? roles = null)
   ```

3. In the `Register` method, add a parameter to set the array of roles in the new `User` object, as shown highlighted in the following code:

   ```
   User user = new(username, saltText, saltedhashedPassword, roles);
   ```

4. At the top of the `Protector.cs` file, import the namespace for working with the user identity, as shown in the following code:

   ```
   // To use GenericIdentity, GenericPrincipal.
   using System.Security.Principal;
   ```

5. Add statements to the `Protector` class to define a `LogIn` method to log in a user, and if the username and password are valid, then create a generic identity and principal and assign them to the current thread, indicating that the type of authentication was a custom one named `PacktAuth`, as shown in the following code:

```
public static void LogIn(string username, string password)
{
  if (CheckPassword(username, password))
  {
    GenericIdentity gi = new(
      name: username, type: "PacktAuth");

    GenericPrincipal gp = new(
      identity: gi, roles: Users[username].Roles);

    // Set the principal on the current thread so that
    // it will be used for authorization by default.
    Thread.CurrentPrincipal = gp;
  }
}
```

Creating a secure app

Now we can create a console app that is secured:

1. Use your preferred code editor to add a new console app named `SecureApp` to the `Chapter08` solution.
2. In the `SecureApp` project, treat warnings as errors, add a project reference to `CryptographyLib`, and globally and statically import the `System.Console` class.
3. Build the `SecureApp` project and make sure there are no compile errors.
4. In the `SecureApp` project, in `Program.cs`, delete the existing statements, and then import required namespaces for working with authentication and authorization, as shown in the following code:

```
using Packt.Shared; // To use Protector.
using System.Security.Principal; // To use IPrincipal.
using System.Security.Claims; // To use ClaimsPrincipal, Claim.
```

5. In the `SecureApp` project, in `Program.cs`, add statements to register three users, named Alice, Bob, and Eve, in various roles, prompt the user to log in, and then output information about them, as shown in the following code:

```
WriteLine("Registering Alice, Bob, and Eve with passwords Pa$$w0rd.");
Protector.Register("Alice", "Pa$$w0rd", roles: new[] { "Admins" });
Protector.Register("Bob", "Pa$$w0rd",
```

```
  roles: new[] { "Sales", "TeamLeads" });

// Register Eve who is not a member of any roles.
Protector.Register("Eve", "Pa$$w0rd");
WriteLine();

// Prompt the user to enter a username and password to login
// as one of these three users.
Write("Enter your username: ");
string? username = ReadLine()!;

Write("Enter your password: ");
string? password = ReadLine()!;

Protector.LogIn(username, password);

if (Thread.CurrentPrincipal == null)
{
  WriteLine("Log in failed.");
  return; // Exit the app.
}

IPrincipal p = Thread.CurrentPrincipal;

WriteLine($"IsAuthenticated: {p.Identity?.IsAuthenticated}");
WriteLine(
  $"AuthenticationType: {p.Identity?.AuthenticationType}");
WriteLine($"Name: {p.Identity?.Name}");
WriteLine($"IsInRole(\"Admins\"): {p.IsInRole("Admins")}");
WriteLine($"IsInRole(\"Sales\"): {p.IsInRole("Sales")}");

if (p is ClaimsPrincipal principal)
{
  WriteLine($"{principal.Identity?.Name} has the following claims:");
  foreach (Claim claim in principal.Claims)
  {
    WriteLine($"{claim.Type}: {claim.Value}");
  }
}
```

6. Run the code, log in as `Alice` with `Pa$$w0rd`, and view the results, as shown in the following output:

```
Registering Alice, Bob, and Eve with passwords Pa$$w0rd.
Enter your username: Alice
Enter your password: Pa$$w0rd
IsAuthenticated: True
AuthenticationType: PacktAuth
Name: Alice
IsInRole("Admins"): True
IsInRole("Sales"): False
Alice has the following claims:
http://schemas.xmlsoap.org/ws/2005/05/identity/claims/name: Alice
http://schemas.microsoft.com/ws/2008/06/identity/claims/role: Admins
```

7. Run the code, log in as `Alice` with `secret`, and view the results, as shown in the following output:

```
Enter your username: Alice
Enter your password: secret
Log in failed.
```

8. Run the code, log in as `Bob` with `Pa$$w0rd`, and view the results, as shown in the following output:

```
Enter your username: Bob
Enter your password: Pa$$w0rd
IsAuthenticated: True
AuthenticationType: PacktAuth
Name: Bob
IsInRole("Admins"): False
IsInRole("Sales"): True
Bob has the following claims:
http://schemas.xmlsoap.org/ws/2005/05/identity/claims/name: Bob
http://schemas.microsoft.com/ws/2008/06/identity/claims/role: Sales
http://schemas.microsoft.com/ws/2008/06/identity/claims/role: TeamLeads
```

You've now seen how to register a user with a password and associate them with roles. Next, let's use those roles to authorize users to access application functionality.

Protecting application functionality

Now let's explore how we can use authorization to prevent some users from accessing some features of an application:

1. In the `SecureApp` project, at the top of `Program.cs`, add a statement to import the namespace for security exceptions, as shown in the following code:

```
using System.Security; // To use SecurityException.
```

2. At the bottom of `Program.cs`, add a method that is secured by checking for permission in the method, and throw appropriate exceptions if the user is anonymous or not a member of the `Admins` role, as shown in the following code:

```
static void SecureFeature()
{
  if (Thread.CurrentPrincipal is null)
  {
    throw new SecurityException(
      "A user must be logged in to access this feature.");
  }
  if (!Thread.CurrentPrincipal.IsInRole("Admins"))
  {
    throw new SecurityException(
      "User must be a member of Admins to access this feature.");
  }
  WriteLine("You have access to this secure feature.");
}
```

3. Above the `SecureFeature` method, add statements to call the `SecureFeature` method in a `try` statement, as shown in the following code:

```
try
{
  SecureFeature();
}
catch (Exception ex)
{
  WriteLine($"{ex.GetType()}: {ex.Message}");
}
```

4. Run the code, log in as `Alice` with `Pa$$w0rd`, and view the result, as shown in the following output:

```
You have access to this secure feature.
```

5. Run the code, log in as `Bob` with `Pa$$w0rd`, and view the result, as shown in the following output:

```
System.Security.SecurityException: User must be a member of Admins to
access this feature.
```

Real-world authentication and authorization

Although it is valuable to see some examples of how authentication and authorization can work, in the real world, you should not build your own security systems because it is too likely that you might introduce flaws.

Instead, you should look at commercial or open-source implementations. These usually implement standards like OAuth 2.0 and OpenID Connect. Microsoft's official position is that "Microsoft already has a team and a product in that area, Azure Active Directory, which allows 500,000 objects for free." You can read more at the following link: `https://devblogs.microsoft.com/aspnet/asp-net-core-6-and-authentication-servers/`.

A versatile OAuth 2.0 and OpenID Connect stack for .NET is available at the following link: `https://github.com/openiddict`.

Practicing and exploring

Test your knowledge and understanding by answering some questions, getting some hands-on practice, and exploring the topics covered in this chapter with deeper research.

Exercise 8.1 – Online-only material

Use the following link to review Microsoft recommendations and best practices for using encryption. The document is based on Microsoft's internal standards for their **Security Development Lifecycle** (**SDL**): `https://learn.microsoft.com/en-us/security/sdl/cryptographic-recommendations`.

Exercise 8.2 – Practice exercises

In the `Chapter08` solution, add a console app named `Exercise_EncryptData` that protects sensitive data like credit card numbers or passwords stored in an XML file, such as the following example:

```
<?xml version="1.0" encoding="utf-8" ?>
<customers>
  <customer>
    <name>Bob Smith</name>
    <creditcard>1234-5678-9012-3456</creditcard>
    <password>Pa$$w0rd</password>
  </customer>
  ...
</customers>
```

The customer's credit card number and password are currently stored in cleartext. The credit card number must be encrypted so that it can be decrypted and used later, and the password must be salted and hashed.

> **Good practice:** You should not store credit card numbers in your applications. This is just an example of a secret that you might want to protect. If you must store credit card numbers, then there is a lot more you must do to be **Payment Card Industry** (**PCI**)-compliant.

In the `Chapter08` solution, add a console application named `Exercise_DecryptData` that opens the XML file that you protected in the preceding code and decrypts the credit card number.

Exercise 8.3 – Test your knowledge

Answer the following questions. If you get stuck, try googling the answers if necessary, while remembering that if you get totally stuck, the answers are provided in *Appendix A*:

1. Of the encryption algorithms provided by .NET, which is the best choice for symmetric encryption?
2. Of the encryption algorithms provided by .NET, which is the best choice for asymmetric encryption?
3. What is a rainbow attack?
4. For encryption algorithms, is it better to have a larger or smaller block size?
5. What is a cryptographic hash?
6. What is a cryptographic signature?
7. What is the difference between symmetric and asymmetric encryption?
8. What does RSA stand for?
9. Why should passwords be salted before being stored?
10. SHA-1 is a hashing algorithm designed by the United States National Security Agency. Why should you never use it?

Exercise 8.4 – Explore topics

Use the links on the following page to learn more detail about the topics covered in this chapter: `https://github.com/markjprice/tools-skills-net10/blob/main/docs/book-links.md#chapter-08---protecting--data-using-cryptography`.

Summary

In this chapter, you learned how to:

- Encrypt and decrypt using symmetric encryption
- Generate a salted hash
- Sign data and check the signature on the data
- Generate truly random numbers
- Use authentication and authorization to protect the features of your applications

In the next chapter, you will learn how to allow multiple actions to occur at the same time to improve performance, scalability, and user productivity for the applications that you build.

9

Multitasking and Concurrency

This chapter is about letting multiple things happen at once, so your apps feel faster, scale better, and let users get more done. Modern software lives on multicore CPUs, talks to slow networks and disks, and runs in cloud environments where every blocked thread burns money. If you can express work concurrently and keep threads unblocked, you deliver smoother UIs, higher-throughput services, and happier customers.

This matters for your skills and your projects because:

- You will write asynchronous code that scales under load instead of code that works in development but stalls in production.
- You will keep apps responsive by moving expensive or I/O-bound work off the main thread without breaking cancellation or progress reporting.
- You will protect shared state with the right synchronization primitives, which means fewer heisenbugs, data races, and deadlocks.
- You will read code with confidence. Concurrency shows up everywhere in modern frameworks.

In this chapter, we will cover the following topics:

- Understanding processes, threads, and tasks
- Running tasks asynchronously
- Synchronizing access to shared resources
- Understanding `async` and `await`

Understanding processes, threads, and tasks

Let's start by defining some terms.

Processes

A **process** is a running instance of a program with its own private execution context. That context includes a virtual address space, one or more threads that execute the code, a unique process ID, open handles or file descriptors, security credentials, and other kernel-managed bookkeeping the OS uses to schedule and isolate it. In plain terms, a process is the container that the operating system gives your code so it can run safely alongside everything else. An example being each of the console apps that we have created in this book.

Processes matter because they provide isolation and safety. A buggy or compromised process is less likely to corrupt others because address spaces are separated. This is the OS's basic protection boundary. The OS tracks CPU time, memory, open files, and permissions per process, which is why tools can meter, limit, or kill a specific process.

Threads

While a process is the isolated environment that owns resources, a **thread** is the thing that runs inside it. Threads share the process's memory and handles, which is why they are cheaper to create but easier to trip over with race conditions.

A thread executes your code statement by statement. By default, each process only has one thread, and this can cause problems when we need to do more than one task at the same time. Threads are also responsible for keeping track of things like the currently authenticated user and any internationalization rules that should be followed for the current language and region.

Windows and most other modern operating systems use **preemptive multitasking**, which simulates the parallel execution of tasks. It divides the processor time among the threads, allocating a **time slice** to each thread one after another. The current thread is suspended when its time slice finishes. The processor then allows another thread to run for a time slice.

When Windows switches from one thread to another, it saves the context of the thread and reloads the previously saved context of the next thread in the thread queue. This takes both time and resources to complete.

As a developer, if you have a small number of complex pieces of work and you want complete control over them, then you could create and manage individual `Thread` instances. If you have one main thread and multiple small pieces of work that can be executed in the background, then you can use the `ThreadPool` class to add delegate instances that point to those pieces of work implemented as methods to a queue, and they will be automatically allocated to threads in the thread pool. In this chapter, we will use the `Task` type to manage threads at a higher abstraction level.

Threads may have to compete for and wait for access to shared resources, such as variables, files, and database objects. There are types for managing this that you will see in action later in this chapter.

Depending on the task, doubling the number of threads (workers) to perform a task does not halve the number of seconds that it will take to complete that task. In fact, it can increase the duration of the task due to resource contention, as shown in *Figure 9.1*:

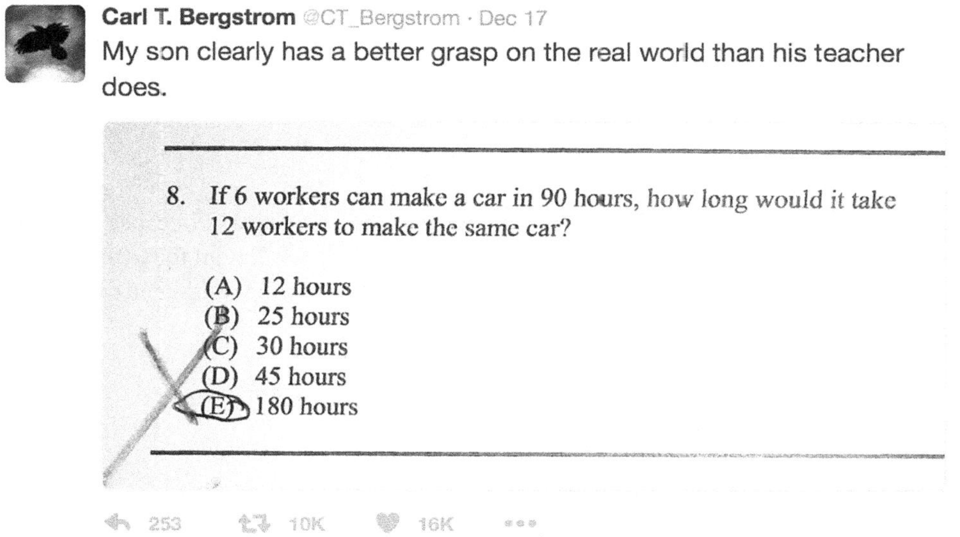

Figure 9.1: A tweet about tasks in the real world

Good practice: Never assume that more threads will improve performance! Run performance tests on a baseline code implementation without multiple threads, and then again on a code implementation with multiple threads. You should also perform performance tests in a staging environment that is as close as possible to the production environment.

Concurrency versus parallelism

The terms concurrency and parallelism are often used interchangeably but it is important to clarify the difference between them.

The core distinction between concurrency and parallelism is:

- **Concurrency** is about managing multiple tasks at once. In other words, interleaving multiple tasks, even on a single core.
- **Parallelism** is about executing multiple tasks at the same time. In other words, truly doing tasks simultaneously which requires multiple cores.

.NET enables concurrency through the `async` and `await` keywords, the `Task` and `Task<T>` classes, I/O-bound operations like file access or web requests, and `SynchronizationContext` and `TaskScheduler` classes.

Here's an example of concurrency:

```
public async Task RunAsync()
{
  var task1 = GetDataFromApiAsync();
  var task2 = ReadFileAsync();

  var results = await Task.WhenAll(task1, task2);
}
```

These tasks are concurrent. .NET doesn't necessarily run them in parallel because they could share the same thread via I/O completion ports. This pattern is extremely efficient for I/O-bound workloads because it doesn't block threads. Instead it lets the thread be reused while waiting on the I/O to complete.

Parallelism is different. In .NET, you achieve parallelism with:

- **Task Parallel Library (TPL)** APIs: `Parallel.For`, `Parallel.ForEach`
- `Thread`, `ThreadPool`, `Task.Run`
- PLINQ (Parallel LINQ)

Here's an example using `Parallel.ForEach`:

```
Parallel.ForEach(myCollection, item =>
{
  ProcessItem(item); // CPU-bound work.
});
```

This splits work across multiple threads and cores to execute simultaneously. This is useful when you're doing CPU-bound work like image processing, mathematical computation, and so on, or you just want to utilize multiple cores.

Common pitfalls of concurrency are race conditions and deadlocks (especially with `async void` and sync-over-async code).

Common pitfalls of parallelism are thread exhaustion, contention and locking issues, and wasted CPU on overhead, for example, spinning up threads for trivial work.

Table 9.1 summarizes some of the key differences:

Feature	Concurrency	Parallelism
Purpose	Managing many tasks	Speeding up work by doing it in parallel
Threads involved	1 or more (often just 1 for async)	Multiple threads / CPU cores
Use case	I/O-bound tasks	CPU-bound tasks
Common tools	`async`/`await`, `Task`, `ThreadPool`	`Parallel`, `Task.Run`, PLINQ
Example analogy	A waiter taking multiple orders	Multiple chefs cooking at once

Table 9.1: Key differences between concurrency and parallelism

So which should you use?

- If your code is mostly waiting (I/O-bound): use concurrency (`async`/`await`).
- If your code is mostly calculating (CPU-bound): use parallelism (`Parallel.For`, `Task.Run`).

And sometimes you might use both, as shown in the following code:

```
await Task.WhenAll(urls.Select(url =>
  Task.Run(() => DownloadAndProcess(url))
));
```

This uses concurrency (async coordination) and parallelism (spinning up tasks to run on different cores).

Running tasks asynchronously

To understand how multiple tasks can be run **simultaneously** (at the same time), we will create a console app that needs to execute three methods.

There will be three methods that need to be executed: the first takes 3 seconds, the second takes 2 seconds, and the third takes 1 second. To simulate that work, we can use the `Thread` class to tell the current thread to go to sleep for a specified number of milliseconds.

Running multiple actions synchronously

Before we make the tasks run simultaneously, we will run them **synchronously**, that is, one after the other:

1. Use your preferred code editor to add a console app project, as defined in the following list:
    - Project template: **Console App** / `console`
    - Solution file and folder: `Chapter09`
    - Project file and folder: `WorkingWithTasks`
    - **Do not use top-level statements**: Cleared.
    - **Enable native AOT publish**: Cleared.
2. In the `WorkingWithTasks` project, globally and statically import the `System.Console` class and treat warnings as errors.
3. In the `WorkingWithTasks` project, add a new class file named `Program.Helpers.cs`.
4. In `Program.Helpers.cs`, delete any existing statements, and then define a partial `Program` class with methods to output a section title and a task title, and to output information about the current thread, each in different colors to make them easier to identify in output, as shown in the following code:

```
partial class Program
{
  private static void SectionTitle(string title)
  {
```

```
    ConsoleColor previousColor = ForegroundColor;
    ForegroundColor = ConsoleColor.DarkYellow;
    WriteLine($"*** {title}");
    ForegroundColor = previousColor;
  }

  private static void TaskTitle(string title)
  {
    ConsoleColor previousColor = ForegroundColor;
    ForegroundColor = ConsoleColor.Green;
    WriteLine($"{title}");
    ForegroundColor = previousColor;
  }

  private static void OutputThreadInfo()
  {
    Thread t = Thread.CurrentThread;
    ConsoleColor previousColor = ForegroundColor;
    ForegroundColor = ConsoleColor.DarkCyan;
    WriteLine(
      "Thread Id: {0}, Priority: {1}, Background: {2}, Name: {3}",
      t.ManagedThreadId, t.Priority, t.IsBackground, t.Name ?? "null");
    ForegroundColor = previousColor;
  }
}
```

5. In the `WorkingWithTasks` project, add a new class file named `Program.Methods.cs`.
6. In `Program.Methods.cs`, delete any existing statements, and then add three methods that simulate work, as shown in the following code:

```
partial class Program
{
  private static void MethodA()
  {
    TaskTitle("Starting Method A...");
    OutputThreadInfo();
    Thread.Sleep(3000); // Simulate three seconds of work.
    TaskTitle("Finished Method A.");
  }

  private static void MethodB()
  {
```

```
    TaskTitle("Starting Method B...");
    OutputThreadInfo();
    Thread.Sleep(2000); // Simulate two seconds of work.
    TaskTitle("Finished Method B.");
  }

  private static void MethodC()
  {
    TaskTitle("Starting Method C...");
    OutputThreadInfo();
    Thread.Sleep(1000); // Simulate one second of work.
    TaskTitle("Finished Method C.");
  }
}
```

7. In `Program.cs`, delete the existing statements and then add statements to call the helper method to output information about the thread, define and start a stopwatch, call the three simulated work methods, and then output the milliseconds elapsed, as shown in the following code:

```
using System.Diagnostics; // To use Stopwatch.

OutputThreadInfo();

Stopwatch timer = Stopwatch.StartNew();

SectionTitle("Running methods synchronously on one thread.");
MethodA();
MethodB();
MethodC();
WriteLine($"{timer.ElapsedMilliseconds:#,##0}ms elapsed.");
```

8. Run the code, wait for all three methods to finish executing, and then review the result, noting that when there is only one unnamed foreground thread doing the work (with Thread Id: 1), and the total time required is just over 6 seconds, as shown in the following output:

```
Thread Id: 1, Priority: Normal, Background: False, Name: null
*** Running methods synchronously on one thread.
Starting Method A...
Thread Id: 1, Priority: Normal, Background: False, Name: null
Finished Method A.
Starting Method B...
Thread Id: 1, Priority: Normal, Background: False, Name: null
Finished Method B.
```

```
Starting Method C...
Thread Id: 1, Priority: Normal, Background: False, Name: null
Finished Method C.
6,028ms elapsed.
```

Introducing the Task class

The Thread class has been available since the first version of .NET in 2002 and can be used to create new threads and manage them, but it can be tricky to work with directly.

.NET Framework 4.0 introduced the Task class in 2010, which represents an asynchronous operation. A task is a high-level abstraction around the operating system thread that performs the operation, and the Task class enables easier creation and management of any underlying threads. Managing multiple threads wrapped in tasks will allow our code to execute at the same time, aka **asynchronously**.

Each Task has a Status property and a CreationOptions property. A Task has a ContinueWith method that can be customized with the TaskContinuationOptions enum, and it can be managed with the TaskFactory class.

Starting tasks

We will look at three ways to start the methods using Task instances. There are links in the GitHub repository to articles that discuss the pros and cons. Each has a slightly different syntax, but they all define a Task and start it:

- Instantiate a new task and then call its Start method.
- Call the Task.Factory.StartNew method.
- Call the Task.Run method.

Let's see each of them in action:

1. In Program.cs, comment out the previous statements that call methods A to C, and then add statements to create and start three tasks, one for each method, as shown highlighted in the following code:

```
Stopwatch timer = Stopwatch.StartNew();
/*
SectionTitle("Running methods synchronously on one thread.");
MethodA();
MethodB();
MethodC();
*/
SectionTitle("Running methods asynchronously on multiple threads.");
Task taskA = new(MethodA);
taskA.Start();
Task taskB = Task.Factory.StartNew(MethodB);
Task taskC = Task.Run(MethodC);
WriteLine($"{timer.ElapsedMilliseconds:#,##0}ms elapsed.");
```

> Instead of commenting out the previous statements, you could let them run, but then make sure to call the `timer.Restart()` method after outputting a new section title to reset the timings for each section.

2. Run the code, view the result, and note that the elapsed milliseconds appear almost immediately. This is because each of the three methods is now being executed by three new background worker threads allocated from the **thread pool (TP)** with different Thread Id values, as shown in the following output:

```
*** Running methods asynchronously on multiple threads.
Starting Method A...
Thread Id: 4, Priority: Normal, Background: True, Name: .NET TP Worker
Starting Method C...
Thread Id: 7, Priority: Normal, Background: True, Name: .NET TP Worker
Starting Method B...
Thread Id: 6, Priority: Normal, Background: True, Name: .NET TP Worker
6ms elapsed.
```

> In the preceding output I show the three methods in random order (A, C, B) because there is nothing to make the main thread wait for each method to finish before starting the next. But this output is just one example of many that you could see. Your output is unlikely to look the same as the book. It is even possible that the console app will end before one or even all the tasks have a chance to start and write to the console!

Waiting for tasks

Sometimes, you need to wait for a task to complete before continuing. To do this, you can use the `Wait` method on a `Task` instance, or the `WaitAll` or `WaitAny` static methods on an array of tasks, as described in *Table 9.2*:

Method	Description
`t.Wait()`	This waits for the task instance named `t` to complete execution.
`Task.WaitAny(Task[])`	This waits for any of the tasks in the array to complete execution.
`Task.WaitAll(Task[])`	This waits for all the tasks in the array to complete execution.

Table 9.2: Task class Wait methods

Let's see how we can use these wait methods to fix the problem with our console app:

1. In `Program.cs`, after creating the three tasks and before outputting the elapsed time, add statements to combine references to the three tasks into an array and pass them to the `WaitAll` method, as shown in the following code:

```
Task[] tasks = { taskA, taskB, taskC };
Task.WaitAll(tasks);
```

2. Run the code and view the result, and note the original thread will pause on the call to `WaitAll`, waiting for all three tasks to finish before outputting the elapsed time, which is a little over 3 seconds, as shown in the following output:

```
Starting Method A...
Starting Method B...
Thread Id: 4, Priority: Normal, Background: True, Name: .NET TP Worker
Thread Id: 6, Priority: Normal, Background: True, Name: .NET TP Worker
Starting Method C...
Thread Id: 7, Priority: Normal, Background: True, Name: .NET TP Worker
Finished Method C.
Finished Method B.
Finished Method A.
3,013ms elapsed.
```

The three new threads execute their code simultaneously, and they can potentially start in any order. `MethodC` should finish first because it takes only 1 second, then `MethodB`, which takes 2 seconds, and finally, `MethodA`, because it takes 3 seconds.

However, the actual CPU used has a big effect on the results. It is the CPU that allocates time slices to each process to allow them to execute their threads. You have no control over when the methods run.

Processing each task when it completes

In .NET 9, Microsoft introduced `Task.WhenEach`, a new API designed to simplify the handling of multiple asynchronous tasks by allowing developers to process each task as it completes, rather than waiting for all tasks to finish. This feature is particularly beneficial in scenarios involving I/O-bound operations, such as web requests or file I/O, where tasks may complete at different times.

`Task.WhenEach` returns an `IAsyncEnumerable<Task>`, enabling the use of `await foreach` to asynchronously iterate over tasks as they complete.

The benefits of `Task.WhenEach` include:

- Allows processing of each task's result as soon as it completes, improving responsiveness.
- Reduces boilerplate code required to track and manage the completion of multiple tasks.
- Particularly useful in high-throughput applications where tasks complete at varying times.
- Using `await foreach` with `Task.WhenEach` leads to more readable and maintainable code.

Let's review a code example:

```
using HttpClient httpClient = new();

List<string> urls = [
  "https://api.github.com",
  "https://jsonplaceholder.typicode.com/posts/1",
  "https://jsonplaceholder.typicode.com/posts/2"
];

List<Task<string>> tasks = new();

foreach (string url in urls)
{
  tasks.Add(httpClient.GetStringAsync(url));
}

await foreach (var completedTask in Task.WhenEach(tasks))
{
  try
  {
    string result = await completedTask;
    Console.WriteLine($"Response Length: {result.Length}");
  }
  catch (Exception ex)
  {
    Console.WriteLine($"Request failed: {ex.Message}");
  }
}
```

In this example, each HTTP request is processed as soon as it completes, without waiting for the other requests to finish. This approach enhances efficiency and responsiveness, especially when dealing with tasks that have varying completion times.

Before `Task.WhenEach`, developers often used `Task.WhenAny` in a loop to process tasks as they completed, as shown in the following code:

```
while (tasks.Any()) // Are there any tasks left to process?
{
  var completedTask = await Task.WhenAny(tasks);
  tasks.Remove(completedTask);
  var result = await completedTask;
  Console.WriteLine(result);
}
```

This method required manual tracking and removal of completed tasks, leading to more complex and error-prone code. `Task.WhenEach` provides a cleaner and more intuitive approach.

Continuing with another task

If all three tasks can be performed at the same time, then waiting for all tasks to finish will be all we need to do. However, often, a task is dependent on the output from another task. To handle this scenario, we need to define **continuation tasks.**

We will create some methods to simulate a call to a web service that returns a monetary amount, which then needs to be used to retrieve how many products cost more than that amount in a database. The result returned from the first method needs to be fed into the input of the second method. This time, instead of waiting for fixed amounts of time, we will use the `Random` class to wait for a random interval between 2 and 4 seconds for each method call to simulate the work:

1. In `Program.Methods.cs`, add two methods that simulate calling a web service and a database-stored procedure, as shown in the following code:

```
private static decimal CallWebService()
{
  TaskTitle("Starting call to web service...");
  OutputThreadInfo();
  Thread.Sleep(Random.Shared.Next(2000, 4000));
  TaskTitle("Finished call to web service.");
  return 89.99M;
}

private static string CallStoredProcedure(decimal amount)
{
  TaskTitle("Starting call to stored procedure...");
  OutputThreadInfo();
  Thread.Sleep((Random.Shared.Next(2000, 4000));
  TaskTitle("Finished call to stored procedure.");
  return $"12 products cost more than {amount:C}.";
}
```

2. In `Program.cs`, comment out the statements for the previous three tasks, and then add statements to start a task to call the web service and then pass its return value to a task that starts the database-stored procedure, as shown highlighted in the following code:

```
SectionTitle("Passing the result of one task as an input into another.");

Task<string> taskServiceThenSProc = Task.Factory
  .StartNew(CallWebService) // returns Task<decimal>
  .ContinueWith(previousTask => // returns Task<string>
```

```
    CallStoredProcedure(previousTask.Result));

WriteLine($"Result: {taskServiceThenSProc.Result}");

WriteLine($"{timer.ElapsedMilliseconds:#,##0}ms elapsed.");
```

3. Run the code and view the result, as shown in the following output:

```
Starting call to web service...
Thread Id: 4, Priority: Normal, Background: True, Name: .NET TP Worker
Finished call to web service.
Starting call to stored procedure...
Thread Id: 6, Priority: Normal, Background: True, Name: .NET TP Worker
Finished call to stored procedure.
Result: 12 products cost more than £89.99.
5,463ms elapsed.
```

The currency symbol is culture-specific so on my computer it uses a £. On your computer it will use your culture. You can control the culture by adding the following statement to the top of your `Program.cs` file:

```
using System.Globalization; // To use CultureInfo.
```

And then setting the culture using an ISO code like `en-US` for US English:

```
CultureInfo.CurrentCulture = CultureInfo.GetCultureInfo("en-US");
```

You might see two different threads running the web service and stored procedure calls, as in the previous output (for example, threads 4 and 6), or the same thread might be reused since it is no longer busy.

Nested and child tasks

As well as defining dependencies between tasks, you can define nested and child tasks. A **nested task** is a task that is created inside another task. A **child task** is a nested task that must finish before its parent task is allowed to finish.

Let's explore how these types of tasks work:

1. In `Program.Methods.cs`, add two methods, one of which starts a task to run the other, as shown in the following code:

```
private static void OuterMethod()
{
  TaskTitle("Outer method starting...");
  Task innerTask = Task.Factory.StartNew(InnerMethod);
  TaskTitle("Outer method finished.");
}
```

```
private static void InnerMethod()
{
  TaskTitle("Inner method starting...");
  Thread.Sleep(2000);
  TaskTitle("Inner method finished.");
}
```

2. In `Program.cs`, add statements to start a task to run the outer method and wait for it to finish before stopping, as shown in the following code:

```
SectionTitle("Nested and child tasks");
Task outerTask = Task.Factory.StartNew(OuterMethod);
outerTask.Wait();
WriteLine("Console app is stopping.");
```

3. Run the code and view the result, as shown in the following output:

```
Outer method starting...
Inner method starting...
Outer method finished.
Console app is stopping.
```

Although we wait for the outer task to finish, its inner task does not have to finish as well. In fact, the outer task might finish, and the console app could end before the inner task even starts, as shown in the following output:

```
Outer method starting...
Outer method finished.
Console app is stopping.
```

4. To link these nested tasks as parent and child, we must use a special option. In `Program.Methods.cs`, modify the existing code to add a `TaskCreationOption` value of `AttachedToParent`, as shown highlighted in the following code:

```
private static void OuterMethod()
{
  TaskTitle("Outer method starting...");

  Task innerTask = Task.Factory.StartNew(InnerMethod,
    TaskCreationOptions.AttachedToParent);

  TaskTitle("Outer method finished.");
}
```

5. Run the code, view the result, and note that the inner task must finish before the outer task can, as shown in the following output:

```
Outer method starting...
Inner method starting...
Outer method finished.
Inner method finished.
Console app is stopping.
```

6. Alternatively, the outer method could finish before the inner method starts, as shown in the following output:

```
Outer method starting...
Outer method finished.
Inner method starting...
Inner method finished.
Console app is stopping.
```

> The `OuterMethod` can finish its work before the `InnerMethod`, as shown by what it writes to the console, but its task must wait, as shown by the console not stopping until both the outer and inner tasks finish.

Wrapping tasks around other objects

Sometimes you might have a method that you want to be asynchronous, but the result to be returned is not itself a task. You can wrap the return value in a successfully completed task, return an exception, or indicate that the task was canceled by using one of the `Task` static methods, as shown in *Table 9.3*:

Method	Description
`FromResult<TResult>(TResult)`	Creates a `Task<TResult>` object whose `Result` property is the non-task result and whose `Status` property is `RanToCompletion`.
`FromException<TResult>(Exception)`	Creates a `Task<TResult>` that's completed with a specified exception.
`FromCanceled<TResult>(CancellationToken)`	Creates a `Task<TResult>` that's completed due to cancellation with a specified cancellation token.

Table 9.3: Methods to create a Task in various scenarios

These methods are useful when you need to:

- Implement an interface that has asynchronous methods, but your implementation is synchronous. This is common for websites and services.
- Mock asynchronous implementations during unit testing.

Imagine that you need to create a method to validate XML input and the method must conform to an interface that requires a `Task<T>` to be returned, as shown in the following code:

```
public interface IValidation
{
  Task<bool> IsValidXmlTagAsync(this string input);
}
```

Warning! The code in this section is for illustration only. You do not need to enter it in your project.

We could use these helpful `FromX` methods to return the results wrapped in a task, as shown in the following code:

```
using System.Text.RegularExpressions;

namespace Packt.Shared;

public static class StringExtensions : IValidation
{
  public static Task<bool> IsValidXmlTagAsync(this string input)
  {
    if (input == null)
    {
      return Task.FromException<bool>(
        new ArgumentNullException($"Missing {nameof(input)} parameter"));
    }

    if (input.Length == 0)
    {
      return Task.FromException<bool>(
        new ArgumentException($"{nameof(input)} parameter is empty."));
    }

    return Task.FromResult(Regex.IsMatch(input,
      @"^<([a-z]+)([^<]+)*(?:>(.*)<\/\1>|\s+\/>)$"));
  }
}
```

If the method you need to implement returns a `Task` (equivalent to `void` in a synchronous method), then you can return a predefined completed `Task` object, as shown in the following code:

```
public Task DeleteCustomerAsync()
{
  // ...
  return Task.CompletedTask;
}
```

When running tasks in parallel, the code will often need to access resources, and those resources are sometimes shared between tasks and threads. We, therefore, need to learn how to safely access those shared resources.

What is ValueTask and when should you use it?

If you're writing async methods in .NET, you'll mostly return `Task`, but `ValueTask` exists for some niche performance reasons.

Let's start by summarizing some important points about `Task`:

- `Task` represents an asynchronous operation.
- `Task` always involves heap allocation because it's a reference type.
- `Task` is used everywhere in .NET async APIs, for example, with `HttpClient`, EF Core, ASP.NET Core, and so on).
- `Task` is safe and simple. It supports `await`, chaining (`.ContinueWith()`), and so on.

Now let's review some important points about `ValueTask`:

- `ValueTask` was introduced in C# 7 and .NET Core 2.0.
- `ValueTask` is a value type aka `struct` that can avoid allocations if the result is already available.
- `ValueTask` can wrap a `Task` or an already computed result.
- `ValueTask` is useful in scenarios where you can return a result synchronously most of the time.

Here's a simplified common scenario of a method that returns a `Task`, as shown in the following code:

```
public async Task<int> GetDataAsync()
{
  await Task.Delay(1000); // Simulate async work
  return 42;
}
```

This always allocates a `Task<int>` object, even if the result is known quickly.

Alternatively, you might choose to use ValueTask when you might avoid the async overhead, as shown in the following code:

```
public ValueTask<int> GetDataFastAsync(bool cacheAvailable)
{
  if (cacheAvailable)
  {
    return new ValueTask<int>(42); // Return synchronously.
  }

  return new ValueTask<int>(GetFromDatabaseAsync()); // Wrap a Task.
}

private async Task<int> GetFromDatabaseAsync()
{
  await Task.Delay(1000);
  return 42;
}
```

If the data is already in cache, we avoid the overhead of async state machine and task allocation entirely.

Unlike `Task`, a `ValueTask` should be awaited exactly once. That's why it's not a drop-in replacement for `Task`. You must not do the following:

```
ValueTask<int> result = GetDataFastAsync();
result.GetAwaiter().GetResult(); // OK
result.GetAwaiter().GetResult(); // BAD: ValueTask should only be awaited once
```

APIs that return `ValueTask` can't be awaited multiple times or used easily in compositions, for example, with `Task.WhenAll()`, unless you first call `.AsTask()`, which defeats the performance purpose.

Use `ValueTask` when:

- The method is called a lot, like in a tight loop or in a performance-critical system. Some examples would include in ASP.NET Core middleware, serializers, and memory caches.
- The method often returns a result synchronously like from cache, memory pool, or quick I/O.
- You've benchmarked and proved `Task` allocation is a bottleneck.

Otherwise stick with `Task` because it's more readable, idiomatic, and less error-prone for most apps.

If you're building standard applications (desktop, web, API), don't worry about `ValueTask` yet. It's more relevant when you're writing reusable libraries, building high-throughput servers, and in control of how many allocations happen in your hot paths.

To summarize good practice recommendations:

- Use `Task` by default, unless profiling tells you otherwise. It's simple, widely supported, and fine for most use cases.

- Use `ValueTask` only if you're in a high-performance scenario and you can often return a result synchronously (without doing any actual asynchronous work).

> To learn more about `ValueType`, you should read the excellent article, Understanding the Whys, Whats, and Whens of ValueTask by Stephen Toub - MSFT: `https://devblogs.microsoft.com/dotnet/understanding-the-whys-whats-and-whens-of-valuetask/`.

Cancelling tasks

The cancellation pattern in .NET uses these two core pieces:

1. `CancellationTokenSource`: This is how you trigger the cancellation.
2. `CancellationToken`: This is what you pass into your async method. Your method must respect it.

The signature of a cancellable async method looks like the following code:

```
public async Task DoWorkAsync(CancellationToken cancellationToken)
```

Inside your method, you should:

- Periodically check `cancellationToken.IsCancellationRequested`.
- Or use `ThrowIfCancellationRequested()` to stop cleanly.
- Pass the token to cancellable methods like `Task.Delay()`, `HttpClient.SendAsync()`, and so on.

Let's try a simple example where a long-running operation is cancelled after 3 seconds:

1. Use your preferred code editor to add a new **Console App** / `console` project to the `Chapter09` solution named `CancellingTasks`.
2. Globally and statically import the `System.Console` class and treat warnings as errors.
3. In `Program.cs`, delete the existing statements. Add statements to create a cancellation token source that will auto-cancel after 3 seconds, and statements to call an async method and pass the cancellation token into it, and implement the async method to check for cancellations, as shown in the following code:

```
using var cts = new CancellationTokenSource();
cts.CancelAfter(3000); // Auto-cancel after 3 seconds.

try
{
  await DoWorkAsync(cts.Token);
}
catch (OperationCanceledException)
{
  WriteLine("Operation was cancelled.");
}
```

```
static async Task DoWorkAsync(CancellationToken token)
{
  WriteLine("Starting work...");

  for (int i = 0; i < 10; i++)
  {
    token.ThrowIfCancellationRequested();
    WriteLine($"Working... {i + 1}/10");
    // Pass cancellation token to deeper async methods.
    await Task.Delay(1000, token);
  }

  WriteLine("Work completed.");
}
```

4. Run the code and view the result, as shown in the following output:

```
Starting work...
Working... 1/10
Working... 2/10
Working... 3/10
Operation was cancelled.
```

To summarize, here are a few good practices for cancelling tasks:

- Pass a `CancellationToken` into your own async methods.
- Use `token.ThrowIfCancellationRequested()` or check `token.IsCancellationRequested`.
- Pass the token to any async API that supports it.
- Wrap `CancellationTokenSource` in `using` to avoid resource leaks.
- Only throw `OperationCanceledException` to indicate cancellation.

You now know how `Task` helps you express work, schedule it, await it, and cancel it. None of that, however, makes shared state safe by itself. The moment two tasks read or write the same data, you invite races, lost updates, and heisenbugs that only show up under load.

The next step is learning how to let tasks cooperate without stepping on each other: protecting shared data with `lock`/`Monitor`, coordinating access with `SemaphoreSlim` and `Mutex`, doing atomic updates with `Interlocked`, and choosing thread-safe structures like `ConcurrentDictionary`.

Although `Task` gives you concurrency and parallelism, while synchronization lets you keep your data correct while you use it.

Synchronizing access to shared resources

When you have multiple threads executing at the same time, there is a possibility that two or more of the threads may access the same variable or another resource at the same time, and as a result, may cause a problem. For this reason, you should carefully consider how to make your code **thread-safe**.

The simplest mechanism for implementing thread safety is to use an object variable as a flag or traffic light to indicate when a shared resource has an exclusive lock applied.

In William Golding's *Lord of the Flies*, Piggy and Ralph find a conch shell and use it to call a meeting. The boys impose a "rule of the conch" on themselves, deciding that no one can speak unless they're holding the conch.

I like to name the object variable I use for implementing thread-safe code the "conch." When a thread has the conch, no other thread should access the shared resource(s) represented by that conch. Note that I say *should*. Only code that respects the conch enables synchronized access. A conch is *not* a lock.

We will explore a couple of types that can be used to synchronize access to shared resources:

- `Monitor`: An object that can be used by multiple threads to check if they should access a shared resource within the same process.
- `Interlocked`: An object for manipulating simple numeric types at the CPU level.
- `Lock`: A new type introduced with .NET 9 for thread synchronization.

Accessing a resource from multiple threads

Let's create a console app to explore sharing resources between multiple threads:

1. Use your preferred code editor to add a new **Console App** / `console` project to the `Chapter09` solution named `SynchronizingResourceAccess`.
2. Globally and statically import the `System.Console` class and treat warnings as errors.
3. Add a new class file named `SharedObjects.cs`.
4. In `SharedObjects.cs`, delete any existing statements, and then define a static class with a field to store a message that is a shared resource, as shown in the following code:

```
public static class SharedObjects
{
  public static string? Message; // a shared resource
}
```

5. Add a new class file named `Program.Methods.cs`.
6. In `Program.Methods.cs`, delete any existing statements, and then define two methods that both loop five times, waiting for a random interval of up to two seconds and appending either `A` or `B` to the shared message resource, as shown in the following code:

```
partial class Program
{
  private static void MethodA()
```

```
  {
    for (int i = 0; i < 5; i++)
    {
      // Simulate two seconds of work on the current thread.
      Thread.Sleep(Random.Shared.Next(2000));

      // Concatenate the letter "A" to the shared message.
      SharedObjects.Message += "A";

      // Show some activity in the console output.
      Write(".");
    }
  }

  private static void MethodB()
  {
    for (int i = 0; i < 5; i++)
    {
      Thread.Sleep(Random.Shared.Next(2000));
      SharedObjects.Message += "B";
      Write(".");
    }
  }
}
```

7. In `Program.cs`, delete the existing statements. Add statements to import the namespace for diagnostic types like `Stopwatch`, and statements to execute both methods on separate threads using a pair of tasks, and wait for them to complete before outputting the elapsed milliseconds, as shown in the following code:

```
using System.Diagnostics; // To use Stopwatch.

WriteLine("Please wait for the tasks to complete.");
Stopwatch watch = Stopwatch.StartNew();
Task a = Task.Factory.StartNew(MethodA);
Task b = Task.Factory.StartNew(MethodB);

Task.WaitAll(new Task[] { a, b });
WriteLine();
WriteLine($"Results: {SharedObjects.Message}.");
WriteLine($"{watch.ElapsedMilliseconds:N0} elapsed milliseconds.");
```

8. Run the code and view the result, as shown in the following output:

```
Please wait for the tasks to complete.
..........
Results: BABABAABBA.
5,753 elapsed milliseconds.
```

This shows that both threads were modifying the message concurrently. In an actual application, this could be a problem. But we can prevent concurrent access by applying a mutually exclusive lock to a conch object, as well as adding code to the two methods to voluntarily check the conch before modifying the shared resource, which we will do in the following section.

Applying a mutually exclusive lock to a conch

Now, let's use a conch to ensure that only one thread accesses the shared resource at a time:

1. In `SharedObjects.cs`, declare and instantiate an `object` variable to act as a conch, as shown in the following code:

```
public static Lock Conch = new(); // A shared object to lock.
```

2. In `Program.Methods.cs`, in both `MethodA` and `MethodB`, add a `lock` statement for the conch around the `for` statements, as shown highlighted in the following code for `MethodB`:

```
lock (SharedObjects.Conch)
{
  for (int i = 0; i < 5; i++)
  {
    Thread.Sleep(Random.Shared.Next(2000));
    SharedObjects.Message += "B";
    Write(".");
  }
}
```

Good practice: Since checking the conch is voluntary, if you only use the `lock` statement in one of the two methods, the shared resource will continue to be accessed by both methods. Make sure that all methods that access a shared resource respect the conch by calling `lock` on it before trying to use any shared resources. Also note that you can't use `await` inside a `lock` block, and you shouldn't `await` after a call to `Monitor.Enter` either. The same thread that enters the monitor must exit it at the end of the block. `await` may suspend and resume on a different thread, so the compiler forbids it.

3. Run the code and view the result, as shown in the following output:

```
Please wait for the tasks to complete.
..........
Results: BBBBBAAAAA.
10,345 elapsed milliseconds.
```

Although the time elapsed was longer, only one method at a time could access the shared resource. Either `MethodA` or `MethodB` can start first. Once a method has finished its work on the shared resource, then the conch gets released, and the other method has the chance to do its work.

Understanding the lock statement

You might wonder what the `lock` statement does when it "locks" an object variable (hint: it does not lock the object!), as shown in the following code:

```
lock (SharedObjects.Conch)
{
  // Work with a shared resource.
}
```

In C# 12 (.NET 8) and earlier, the compiler changes the `lock` statement into a `try-finally` statement that uses the `Monitor` class to *enter* and *exit* the conch object (I like to think of it as *take* and *release* the conch object), as shown in the following code:

```
try
{
  Monitor.Enter(SharedObjects.Conch);
  // Work with a shared resource.
}
finally
{
  Monitor.Exit(SharedObjects.Conch);
}
```

When a thread calls `Monitor.Enter` on a reference type, it checks to see if some other thread has already taken the conch. If it has, the thread waits. If it has not, the thread takes the conch and gets on with its work on the shared resource. Once the thread has finished its work, it calls `Monitor.Exit`, releasing the conch.

If another thread was waiting, it could now take the conch and do its work. This requires all threads to respect the conch by calling `Monitor.Enter` and `Monitor.Exit` appropriately.

Good practice: You cannot use value types (`struct` types) as a conch. `Monitor.Enter` requires a reference type because it locks the memory address. Any internal data structures for that object are *not* locked.

In C# 13 with .NET 9 and later, you can use an instance of the `System.Threading.Lock` class instead of a `System.Object`, and continue to use similar coding techniques as shown in the following code:

```
private readonly Lock Conch = new();

public void Modify()
{
  // 1. Use the Lock statement.
  lock (Conch)
  {
    // Critical section associated with Conch.
  }

  // 2. Use the object's EnterScope method to return an object to Dispose.
  using (Conch.EnterScope())
  {
    // Critical section associated with Conch.
  }

  // 3. Call the Enter and Exit methods explicitly.
  Conch.Enter();
  try
  {
    // Critical section associated with Conch.
  }
  finally
  {
    Conch.Exit();
  }

  // 4. Use the Try pattern.
  if (Conch.TryEnter())
  {
    try
    {
      // Critical section associated with Conch.
    }
    finally
    {
      Conch.Exit();
    }
  }
}
```

You can learn more about the `Lock` object and how it works with the `lock` keyword at the following link: `https://learn.microsoft.com/en-us/dotnet/api/system.threading.lock`.

Avoiding deadlocks

Knowing how the `lock` statement is translated by the compiler to method calls on the `Monitor` class is also important because using the `lock` statement can cause a deadlock.

Deadlocks can occur when there are two or more shared resources (each with a conch to monitor which thread is currently doing work on each shared resource), and the following sequence of events happens:

- Thread X "locks" conch A and starts working on shared resource A.
- Thread Y "locks" conch B and starts working on shared resource B.
- While still working on resource A, thread X needs to also work with resource B, and so it attempts to "lock" conch B but is blocked because thread Y already has conch B.
- While still working on resource B, thread Y needs to also work with resource A, and so it attempts to "lock" conch A but is blocked because thread X already has conch A.

One way to prevent deadlocks is to specify a timeout when attempting to get a lock. To do this, you must manually use the `Monitor` class instead of using the `lock` statement. Let's see how:

1. In `Program.Methods.cs`, modify your code to replace the `lock` statements with code that tries to enter the conch with a timeout, outputs an error, and then exits the monitor, allowing other threads to enter the monitor, as shown highlighted in the following code for `MethodB`:

```
try
{
  if (SharedObjects.Conch.TryEnter(TimeSpan.FromSeconds(15)))
  {
    for (int i = 0; i < 5; i++)
    {
      Thread.Sleep(Random.Shared.Next(2000));
      SharedObjects.Message += "B";
      Write(".");
    }
  }
  else
  {
    WriteLine("Method B timed out when entering a monitor on conch.");
  }
}
finally
```

```
{
  SharedObjects.Conch.Exit();
}
```

2. Run the code and view the result. It should return the same results as before – although either A or B could grab the conch first – but is better code because it will prevent potential deadlocks.

Good practice: Only use the `lock` keyword if you can write your code such that it avoids potential deadlocks. If you cannot avoid potential deadlocks, then always use the `Monitor.TryEnter` method or the new `Lock` class instead of the `lock` keyword, in combination with a `try-finally` statement, so that you can supply a timeout and one of the threads will back out of a deadlock if it occurs. You can read more about good threading practices at the following link: `https://learn.microsoft.com/en-us/dotnet/standard/threading/managed-threading-best-practices`.

Synchronizing events

.NET events are not thread-safe, so you should avoid using them in multi-threaded scenarios.

After learning that .NET events are not thread-safe, some developers attempt to use exclusive locks when adding and removing event handlers or when raising an event, as shown in the following code:

```
// event delegate field
public event EventHandler? Shout;

// conch
private Lock eventConch = new();

// method
public void Poke()
{
  lock (eventConch) // bad idea
  {
    // If something is listening...
    if (Shout != null)
    {
      // ...then call the delegate to raise the event.
      Shout(this, EventArgs.Empty);
    }
  }
}
```

Good practice: Is it good or bad that some developers use locks in event handling? Well, it is complicated. It depends on complex factors so I cannot give a value judgement. You can read more about events and thread safety at the following link: `https://learn.microsoft.com/en-us/archive/blogs/cburrows/field-like-events-considered-harmful`. But it is complicated, as explained by Stephen Cleary in the following blog post: `https://blog.stephencleary.com/2009/06/threadsafe-events.html`.

Making CPU operations atomic

Atomic is from the Greek word **atomos**, which means *undividable*. It is important to understand which operations are atomic in multithreading because if they are not atomic, then they could be interrupted by another thread partway through their operation. Is the C# increment operator atomic, as shown in the following code?

```
int x = 3;
x++; // is this an atomic CPU operation?
```

It is not atomic! Incrementing an integer requires the following three CPU operations:

1. Load a value from an instance variable in memory into a register.
2. Increment the value.
3. Store the value in the instance variable in memory.

A thread could be interrupted after executing the first two steps. A second thread could then execute all three steps. When the first thread resumes execution, it will overwrite the value in the variable, and the effect of the increment or decrement performed by the second thread will be lost!

There is a type named `Interlocked` that can perform atomic actions like `Add`, `Increment`, `Decrement`, `Exchange`, `CompareExchange`, `And`, `Or`, and `Read` on the integer types in the following list:

- `System.Int32` (`int`), `System.UInt32` (`uint`)
- `System.Int64` (`long`), `System.UInt64` (`ulong`)

`Interlocked` does not work on numeric types like `byte`, `sbyte`, `short`, `ushort`, and `decimal`.

`Interlocked` can perform atomic operations like `Exchange` and `CompareExchange` that swap values in memory on the following types:

- `System.Single` (`float`), `System.Double` (`double`)
- `nint`, `nuint`
- `System.Object` (`object`)

Let's see it in action:

1. Declare another field in the `SharedObjects` class that will count how many operations have occurred, as shown in the following code:

   ```
   public static int Counter; // Another shared resource.
   ```

2. In `Program.Methods.cs`, in both methods A and B, inside the `for` statement and after modifying the `string` value, add a statement to safely increment the counter, as shown in the following code:

```
Interlocked.Increment(ref SharedObjects.Counter);
```

3. In `Program.cs`, before outputting the elapsed time, write the current value of the counter to the console, as shown in the following code:

```
WriteLine($"{SharedObjects.Counter} string modifications.");
```

4. Run the code and view the result, as shown highlighted in the following output:

```
Please wait for the tasks to complete.
..........
Results: BBBBBAAAAA.
10 string modifications.
13,531 elapsed milliseconds.
```

Observant readers will realize that the existing conch object protects all shared resources accessed within a block of code locked by the conch, and therefore, it is unnecessary to use `Interlocked` in this specific example. But if we had not already been protecting another shared resource like `Message`, then using `Interlocked` would be necessary.

Applying other types of synchronization

`Monitor` and `Interlocked` are mutually exclusive locks that are simple and effective, but sometimes, you need more advanced options to synchronize access to shared resources, as shown in *Table 9.4*:

Type	Description
`ReaderWriterLock`, `ReaderWriterLockSlim`	These allow multiple threads to be in **read mode**, one thread to be in **write mode** with exclusive ownership of the write lock, and one thread that has read access to be in **upgradeable read mode**, from which the thread can upgrade to write mode without having to relinquish its read access to the resource.
`Mutex`	Like `Monitor`, this provides exclusive access to a shared resource, except it is used for inter-process synchronization.
`Semaphore`, `SemaphoreSlim`	These limit the number of threads that can access a resource or pool of resources concurrently by defining slots. This is known as **resource throttling** rather than **resource locking**.
`AutoResetEvent`, `ManualResetEvent`	Event wait handles allow threads to synchronize activities by signaling each other and by waiting for each other's signals.

Table 9.4: Synchronization types

Now that we've explored the importance of synchronizing access to shared resources in multi-threaded applications, it's time to delve into how some new keywords introduced in C# 5 make writing asynchronous code easier.

Understanding async and await

C# 5 introduced two C# keywords when working with the `Task` type. They are especially useful for the following:

- Implementing multitasking for a **graphical user interface** (**GUI**)
- Improving the scalability of web applications and web services

Later in this chapter, you will see how the `async` and `await` keywords can implement multitasking for a GUI by building a WPF app that fetches data from the Northwind database asynchronously.

But for now, let's learn the theory of why these two C# keywords were introduced, and then later, you will see them used in practice.

Improving responsiveness for console apps

One of the limitations with console apps is that you can only use the `await` keyword inside methods that are marked as `async`, but C# 7 and earlier do not allow the `Main` method to be marked as `async`! A feature introduced in C# 7.1 provides support for `async` in `Main`. Let's explore that feature:

1. Use your preferred code editor to add a new **Console App** / `console` project to the `Chapter09` solution named `AsyncConsole`.
2. In `Program.cs`, delete the existing statements, statically import `Console`, and then add statements to create an `HttpClient` instance, make a request for Apple's home page, and output how many bytes it has, as shown in the following code:

```
using static System.Console;

HttpClient client = new();

HttpResponseMessage response =
  await client.GetAsync("http://www.apple.com/");

WriteLine("Apple's home page has {0:N0} bytes.",
  response.Content.Headers.ContentLength);
```

3. Build the project and note that it builds successfully. In .NET 5 and earlier, the project template created an explicit `Program` class with a non-async `Main` method, so you would have seen an error message, as shown in the following output:

```
Program.cs(14,9): error CS4033: The 'await' operator can only be used
within an async method. Consider marking this method with the 'async'
modifier and changing its return type to 'Task'. [/Users/markjprice/
tools-skills-net10/Chapter09/AsyncConsole/AsyncConsole.csproj]
```

4. You would have had to add the `async` keyword to the `Main` method and change its return type to `Task`. With .NET 6 and later, the console app project template uses the top-level program feature to automatically define the `Program` class with an asynchronous `<Main>$` method for you.
5. Run the code and view the result, which is likely to have a different number of bytes since Apple changes its home page frequently, as shown in the following output:

```
Apple's home page has 40,252 bytes.
```

Working with async streams

With .NET Core 3, Microsoft introduced the asynchronous processing of streams.

> You can complete a tutorial about async streams at the following link: https://learn.microsoft.com/en-us/dotnet/csharp/tutorials/generate-consume-asynchronous-stream.

Before C# 8 and .NET Core 3, the `await` keyword only worked with tasks that return scalar values. Async stream support in .NET Standard 2.1 allows an `async` method to return one value after another asynchronously.

Let's see a simulated example that returns three random integers as an async stream:

1. Use your preferred code editor to add a new **Console App** / `console` project to the `Chapter09` solution named `AsyncEnumerable`.
2. Globally and statically import the `System.Console` class and treat warnings as errors.
3. Add a new file named `Program.Methods.cs`.
4. In `Program.Methods.cs`, delete any existing statements and then define a method that uses the `yield` keyword to return a random sequence of three numbers asynchronously, as shown in the following code:

```
partial class Program
{
  private static async IAsyncEnumerable<int> GetNumbersAsync()
  {
    Random r = Random.Shared;

    // Simulate some work that takes 1.5 to 3 seconds.
    await Task.Delay(r.Next(1500, 3000));

    // Return a random number between 1 and 1000.
    yield return r.Next(1, 1001);

    await Task.Delay(r.Next(1500, 3000));
```

```
      yield return r.Next(1, 1001);

      await Task.Delay(r.Next(1500, 3000));
      yield return r.Next(1, 1001);
    }
  }
```

5. In `Program.cs`, delete the existing statements and then add statements to enumerate the sequence of numbers, as shown in the following code:

```
// Use async streams to iterate over a collection asynchronously.
await foreach (int number in GetNumbersAsync())
{
  WriteLine($"Number: {number}");
}
```

6. Run the code and view the result, as shown in the following output:

```
Number: 509
Number: 813
Number: 307
```

Improving responsiveness for GUI apps

So far in this book, we have only built console apps. Life for a programmer gets more complicated when building web applications, web services, and apps with GUIs such as Windows desktop and mobile apps.

One reason for this is that for a GUI app, there is a special thread: the **user interface** (UI) thread.

There are two rules for working in GUIs:

- Do not perform long-running tasks on the UI thread.
- Do not access UI elements on any thread except the UI thread.

To handle these rules, programmers used to have to write complex code to ensure that long-running tasks were executed by a non-UI thread, but once complete, the results of the task were safely passed to the UI thread to present to the user. It could quickly get messy!

With C# 5 and later, you have the use of `async` and `await`. They allow you to continue to write your code as if it is synchronous, which keeps your code clean and easy to understand, but underneath, the C# compiler creates a complex state machine and keeps track of running threads. It's kind of magical! The combination of these two keywords makes the asynchronous method run on a worker thread and, when it's complete, return the results on the UI thread.

Let's see an example. We will build a Windows desktop app using **Windows Presentation Foundation** (**WPF**) that gets employees from the Northwind database in a SQL Server database using low-level types like `SqlConnection`, `SqlCommand`, and `SqlDataReader`.

Warning! You will only be able to complete this task if you have Windows and the Northwind database stored in SQL Server. This is the only section in this book that is not cross-platform and modern (WPF is 17 years old!). You can use either Visual Studio or VS Code.

At this point, we are focusing on making a GUI app responsive. Since this book does not cover WPF elsewhere, I thought this task would be a good opportunity to at least see an example app built using WPF even if we do not look at it in detail. Let's go!

1. If you are using Visual Studio, add a new **WPF Application** [C#] project named `WpfResponsive` to the `Chapter09` solution. If you are using VS Code, use the following command: `dotnet new wpf`. If you are using JetBrains Rider, select **Desktop Application** and then select a **Type** of **WPF Application**.
2. Add a package reference for `Microsoft.Data.SqlClient` to the project.
3. In the project file, note the output type is a Windows EXE, the target framework is .NET for Windows (it will not run on other platforms, like macOS and Linux), and the project uses WPF, as shown in the following markup:

```
<Project Sdk="Microsoft.NET.Sdk">

  <PropertyGroup>
    <OutputType>WinExe</OutputType>
    <TargetFramework>net10.0-windows</TargetFramework>
    <Nullable>enable</Nullable>
    <UseWPF>true</UseWPF>
  </PropertyGroup>

  <ItemGroup>
    <PackageReference Include="Microsoft.Data.SqlClient"  />
  </ItemGroup>

</Project>
```

4. Build the `WpfResponsive` project to restore packages.
5. In `MainWindow.xaml`, in the `<Grid>` element, add elements to define two buttons, a text box and a list box, laid out vertically in a stack panel, as shown in the following markup:

```
<StackPanel>
  <Button Name="GetEmployeesSyncButton"
          Click="GetEmployeesSyncButton_Click">
    Get Employees Synchronously
  </Button>
```

```
  <Button Name="GetEmployeesAsyncButton"
          Click="GetEmployeesAsyncButton_Click">
    Get Employees Asynchronously
  </Button>

  <TextBox HorizontalAlignment="Stretch" Text="Type in here" />

  <ListBox Name="EmployeesListBox" Height="400" />
</StackPanel>
```

> Visual Studio has good support for building WPF apps and will provide IntelliSense as you edit code and XAML markup. VS Code does not.

6. In `MainWindow.xaml.cs`, import namespaces to work with ADO.NET and the stopwatch, as shown in the following code:

```
using Microsoft.Data.SqlClient; // To use SqlConnection and so on.
using System.Diagnostics; // To use Stopwatch.
```

7. In the `MainWindow` class, in the constructor, define two `string` fields for the database connection string and SQL statement, as shown in the following code:

```
private string connectionString;

private string sql = "WAITFOR DELAY '00:00:05';" +
  "SELECT EmployeeId, FirstName, LastName FROM Employees";
```

> The SQL command has two statements separated by a semicolon. The first waits for five seconds to simulate a long-running query.

8. In the `MainWindow` class, in the constructor, after the call to `InitializeComponent`, use an `SqlConnectionStringBuilder` to set the database connection string, as shown in the following code:

```
public MainWindow()
{
  InitializeComponent();

  // Change as needed to work with your Northwind database.
  SqlConnectionStringBuilder builder = new();
```

```
    builder.DataSource = "."; // SQL Server on local computer.
    builder.InitialCatalog = "Northwind";
    builder.Encrypt = false;
    builder.MultipleActiveResultSets = true;
    builder.ConnectTimeout = 5;

    // To use Windows Integrated authentication.
    builder.IntegratedSecurity = true;

    // To use SQL Server authentication.
    // builder.UserID = Environment.GetEnvironmentVariable("MY_SQL_USR");
    // builder.Password = Environment.GetEnvironmentVariable("MY_SQL_PWD");

    connectionString = builder.ConnectionString;
  }
```

9. Create event handlers for clicking on the two buttons. They must use the `string` constants to open a connection to the Northwind database and then populate the list box with the IDs and names of all employees, as shown in the following code:

```
private void GetEmployeesSyncButton_Click(object sender, RoutedEventArgs
e)
{
  Stopwatch timer = Stopwatch.StartNew();

  using (SqlConnection connection = new(connectionString))
  {
    try
    {
      connection.Open();

      SqlCommand command = new(sql, connection);
      SqlDataReader reader = command.ExecuteReader();

      while (reader.Read())
      {
        string employee = string.Format("{0}: {1} {2}",
          reader.GetInt32(0), reader.GetString(1),
          reader.GetString(2));

        EmployeesListBox.Items.Add(employee);
```

```
      }
      reader.Close();
      connection.Close();
    }
    catch (Exception ex)
    {
      MessageBox.Show(ex.Message);
    }
  }

  EmployeesListBox.Items.Add(
    $"Sync: {timer.ElapsedMilliseconds:N0}ms");
}

private async void GetEmployeesAsyncButton_Click(
  object sender, RoutedEventArgs e)
{
  Stopwatch timer = Stopwatch.StartNew();

  using (SqlConnection connection = new(connectionString))
  {
    try
    {
      await connection.OpenAsync();

      SqlCommand command = new(sql, connection);
      SqlDataReader reader = await command.ExecuteReaderAsync();

      while (await reader.ReadAsync())
      {
        string employee = string.Format("{0}: {1} {2}",
          await reader.GetFieldValueAsync<int>(0),
          await reader.GetFieldValueAsync<string>(1),
          await reader.GetFieldValueAsync<string>(2));

        EmployeesListBox.Items.Add(employee);
      }
      await reader.CloseAsync();
      await connection.CloseAsync();
    }
    catch (Exception ex)
```

```
        {
          MessageBox.Show(ex.Message);
        }
      }
      EmployeesListBox.Items.Add(
        $"Async: {timer.ElapsedMilliseconds:N0}ms");
    }
```

Note the following:

- Defining an `async void` method is generally bad practice because it is "fire and forget." You will not be notified when it is completed, and there is no way to cancel it because it does not return a `Task` or `Task<T>` that can be used to control it. As a result, the exception raised inside the event handler may be lost. That's why we use a `try-catch` inside the handler.
- The SQL statement uses the SQL Server `WAITFOR DELAY` command to simulate processing that takes five seconds. It then selects three columns from the `Employees` table.
- The `GetEmployeesSyncButton_Click` event handler uses synchronous methods to open a connection and fetch the employee rows.
- The `GetEmployeesAsyncButton_Click` event handler is marked as `async` and uses asynchronous methods with the `await` keyword to open a connection and fetch the employee rows.
- Both event handlers use a stopwatch to record the number of milliseconds the operation takes and add it to the list box.

Trying out the WPF app

Now we can run the WPF app:

1. Start the WPF app without debugging.
2. Click in the text box, enter some text, and note that the GUI is responsive.
3. Click the **Get Employees Synchronously** button.
4. Try to click in the text box, and note the GUI is not responsive.
5. Wait for at least five seconds until the list box is filled with employees.
6. Click in the text box, enter some text, and note the GUI is responsive again.
7. Click the **Get Employees Asynchronously** button.

8. Click in the text box, enter some text, and note that the GUI is still responsive while it performs the operation. Continue typing until the list box is filled with the employees, as shown in *Figure 9.2*:

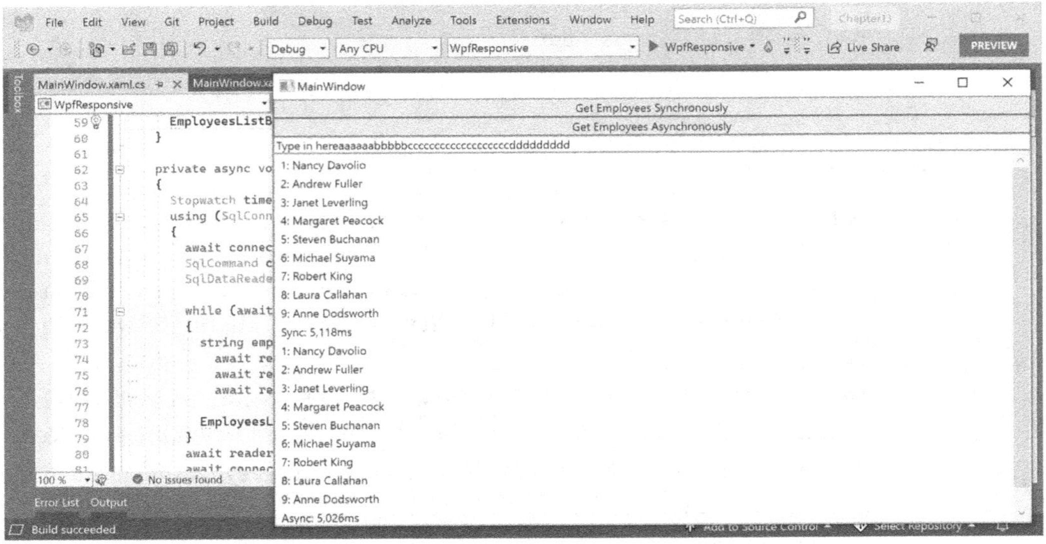

Figure 9.2: Loading employees into a WPF app synchronously and asynchronously

9. Note the difference in timings for the two operations. The UI is blocked when fetching data synchronously, while the UI remains responsive when fetching data asynchronously.
10. Close the WPF app.

Improving scalability for web applications and web services

The `async` and `await` keywords can also be applied on the server side when building websites, applications, and services. From the client application's point of view, nothing changes (or they might even notice a small increase in the time taken for a request to return). So, from a single client's point of view, the use of `async` and `await` to implement multitasking on the server side makes their experience worse!

On the server side, additional, cheaper worker threads are created to wait for long-running tasks to finish so that expensive I/O threads can handle other client requests instead of being blocked. This improves the overall scalability of a web application or service. More clients can be supported simultaneously.

Common types that support multitasking

There are many common types that have asynchronous methods that you can await, as shown in *Table 9.5*:

Type	Methods
`DbContext<T>`	`AddAsync`, `AddRangeAsync`, `FindAsync`, and `SaveChangesAsync`
`DbSet<T>`	`AddAsync`, `AddRangeAsync`, `ForEachAsync`, `SumAsync`, `ToListAsync` `ToDictionaryAsync`, `AverageAsync`, and `CountAsync`
`HttpClient`	`GetAsync`, `PostAsync`, `PutAsync`, `DeleteAsync`, and `SendAsync`
`StreamReader`	`ReadAsync`, `ReadLineAsync`, and `ReadToEndAsync`
`StreamWriter`	`WriteAsync`, `WriteLineAsync`, and `FlushAsync`

Table 9.5: Common types with asynchronous methods

Good practice: Any time you see a method that ends in the `Async` suffix, check to see whether it returns `Task` or `Task<T>`. If it does return `Task` or `Task<T>`, then you could use it instead of the synchronous non-`Async` suffixed method. Remember to call it using `await` and decorate your method with `async`.

Using await in catch and finally blocks

When `async` and `await` were first introduced in C# 5, it was only possible to use the `await` keyword in a `try` block, but not in a `catch` or `finally` block. In C# 6 and later, it is now possible to use `await` in `try`, `catch` and `finally` blocks.

Practicing and exploring

Test your knowledge and understanding by answering some questions, getting some hands-on practice, and exploring this chapter's topics with deeper research.

Exercise 9.1 – Read more online

Task Parallel Library (TPL): `https://learn.microsoft.com/en-us/dotnet/standard/parallel-programming/task-parallel-library-tpl`

Learn about `Parallel.ForAsync` and `ForEachAsync`:

`https://devblogs.microsoft.com/dotnet/performance-improvements-in-net-8/#parallel`.

Learn more about `async` and `await` in the article, How Async/Await Really Works in C#, by Stephen Toub - MSFT: `https://devblogs.microsoft.com/dotnet/how-async-await-really-works/`.

David Fowler, a Distinguished Engineer at Microsoft on the .NET team, has an excellent article about async good practices, found at the following link:

`https://github.com/davidfowl/AspNetCoreDiagnosticScenarios/blob/master/AsyncGuidance.md`.

Exercise 9.2 – Read more about parallel programming

Packt has a book that goes deeper into the topics in this chapter, *Parallel Programming and Concurrency with C# 10 and .NET 6: A modern approach to building faster, more responsive, and asynchronous .NET applications using C#*, by Alvin Ashcroft:

`https://www.packtpub.com/product/parallel-programming-and-concurrency-with-c-10-and-net-6/9781803243672`.

Exercise 9.3 – Test your knowledge

Answer the following questions:

1. What information can you find out about a process?
2. How accurate is the `Stopwatch` class?
3. By convention, what suffix should be applied to a method that returns `Task` or `Task<T>`?
4. To use the `await` keyword inside a method, what keyword must be applied to the method declaration?
5. How do you create a child task?
6. Why should you avoid the `lock` keyword?
7. When should you use the `Interlocked` class?
8. When should you use the `Mutex` class instead of the `Monitor` class?
9. What is the benefit of using `async` and `await` in a website or web service?
10. Can you cancel a task? If so, how?

Exercise 9.4 – Explore topics

Use the links on the following web page to learn more about the topics covered in this chapter:

`https://github.com/markjprice/tools-skills-net10/blob/main/docs/book-links.md#chapter-9---multitasking-and-concurrency`.

Summary

In this chapter, you learned:

- How to define and start a task.
- How to wait for one or more tasks to finish.
- How to control task completion order.
- How to synchronize access to shared resources.
- The magic behind `async` and `await`.

In the next chapter, you will learn about **dependency injection (DI)**, a cornerstone of modern software development because it promotes loosely coupled, testable, and maintainable code.

10

Dependency Injection, Containers, and Service Lifetime

This chapter is about **dependency injection (DI)**, a cornerstone of modern software development that promotes loosely coupled, testable, and maintainable code. DI decouples the creation of an object's dependencies from the object's behavior, allowing these dependencies to be provided externally.

DI containers automate the process of injecting dependencies, relieving developers from manually constructing and managing the lifecycle of dependencies. By configuring services within a container, applications can dynamically resolve and inject required dependencies at runtime, ensuring that each component receives the appropriate service instances. This not only simplifies the construction and wiring of dependencies but also enhances the modularity and flexibility of an application.

Understanding service lifetimes is essential for effective dependency management. Service lifetimes define the scope and duration for which a service instance is maintained by the DI container.

Whether you are building simple console applications or complex web services, mastering DI, containers, and service lifetimes will significantly enhance your development process and the quality of your software.

This chapter covers the following topics:

- Introducing dependency injection
- Implementing .NET Generic Host
- Special cases of DI with ASP.NET Core

Introducing dependency injection

Dependency injection (DI) is a design pattern used to implement **Inversion of Control (IoC)**, which resolves dependencies in a program. Traditionally, the flow of control is dictated by your code, as it makes calls to reusable libraries or frameworks to use their functionality. IoC inverts this control so that the framework controls it instead.

ASP.NET Core uses DI for IoC extensively. The framework controls the flow of request processing, and the developer's code is executed in response to specific events like HTTP `GET` or `POST` requests.

The main idea of DI is to decouple the creation of an object's dependencies from its own behavior, which allows for more modular, testable, and maintainable code. Instead of objects creating dependencies themselves using the `new` keyword, they are injected with their dependencies at runtime, often by an external framework or container.

For example, in *Figure 10.1*, on the left, you can see a statement that directly instantiates a calculator that implements an interface, and on the right, you can see a statement that requests the registered calculator from a service container:

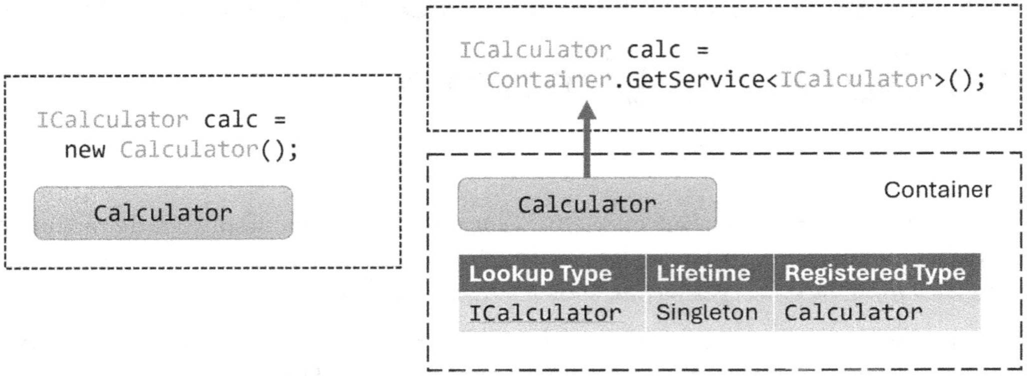

Figure 10.1: Comparing object creation directly with using a DI container

The service container is responsible for creating and managing the lifetime of services, aka dependency objects, allowing us to swap out the registered implementation class and even change its scope without changing the code.

Why use DI?

The most common reasons for using DI are shown in the following list:

- **Decoupling**: DI helps in decoupling components and their dependencies, making a system more modular. When software is divided into modules, changes can be made to individual parts without affecting the entire system. This makes it easier to update, fix bugs, or add new features. Modularity enforces a clear structure, making it easier for developers to understand and navigate the codebase. This reduces the learning curve for new developers joining the project.
- **Testability**: By injecting dependencies, it becomes easier to replace real dependencies with mocks or stubs during testing. You will see many examples of this in *Chapter 11, Unit Testing and Mocking*. Modules can be tested independently from the rest of the application. This makes it easier to identify and fix issues, as tests can be run on smaller, more manageable pieces of code. When an issue arises, debugging is simplified because the problem can often be isolated to a specific module rather than combing through the entire codebase.

- **Flexibility**: Changes in dependencies or their configurations have minimal impacts on the client code. Modularity allows for flexible architecture designs where modules can be easily added, removed, or replaced as needed. By encapsulating functionality within modules, it is easier to ensure that the internal workings of a module are hidden from other parts of an application, promoting better data integrity and reducing unintended side effects.
- **Maintainability**: With dependencies being centralized, updates and maintenance become more manageable. Different developers or teams can work on separate modules simultaneously without interfering with each other. This parallel development can significantly speed up the development process. Teams can progress independently on their modules, making it easier to manage large projects with multiple moving parts.

The mechanisms of DI in .NET

Imagine that we have an interface and an implementation, as shown in the following code:

```
public interface INotificationService
{
  void Notify(string message);
}

public class NotificationService : INotificationService
{
  public void Notify(string message)
  {
    // Send notification.
  }
}
```

There are primarily three ways to inject dependencies into other components that depend on them:

- **Constructor injection**: Dependencies are provided through a class constructor, as shown in the following code. This is the best practice, since it enables the easiest mocking of services during testing:

```
public class DataService
{
  private readonly INotificationService _service;

  // Constructor Injection
  public DataService(INotificationService service)
  {
    _service = service;
  }
```

```
    public void ProcessData(string data)
    {
        // Process data and send it using the notification service.
        _service.Notify(data);
    }
}
```

- **Property injection:** Dependencies are set on public properties of the class, as shown in the following code. Property injection is useful when the dependency is optional or when the dependency might change during the lifetime of an object. It provides more flexibility compared to constructor injection:

```
public class DataService
{
    // Property Injection
    public INotificationService Service { get; set; }

    public void ProcessData(string data)
    {
        // Process data and send it using the notification service.
        Service.Notify(data);
    }
}
```

- **Method injection:** Dependencies are provided through method parameters, as shown in the following code. This approach is suitable for dependencies that are only needed for a specific method. This keeps the rest of the class clean and focused on its core responsibilities:

```
public class DataService
{
    // ...other code.
    // Method Injection
    public void ProcessData(string data, INotificationService service)
    {
        // Process data and send it using the notification service.
        service.Notify(data);
    }
}
```

Examples in modern .NET

.NET includes built-in support for DI, making it straightforward to implement DI patterns in your applications. Let's look at an ASP.NET Core constructor injection example.

Constructor injection example

Suppose you have an `IEmailService` interface and an `EmailService` implementation. You want to inject this service into a consumer class, `UserRegistrationController`, that allows a user to register themselves with your website. The interface, class, and controller are shown in the following code:

```
public interface IEmailService
{
  void SendEmail(string to, string subject, string body);
}

public class EmailService : IEmailService
{
  public void SendEmail(string to, string subject, string body)
  {
    // Implementation to send an email.
  }
}

public class UserRegistrationController
{
  private readonly IEmailService _emailService;

  public UserRegistrationController(IEmailService emailService)
  {
    _emailService = emailService;
  }

  public void SendUserConfirmationEmail(string userId)
  {
    // Use _emailService to send an email to the user.
  }
}
```

In the ASP.NET Core project dependency services configuration section in `Program.cs`, you would register your dependencies as shown highlighted in the following code:

```
var builder = WebApplication.CreateBuilder(args);

// Add services to the container.
builder.Services.AddControllersWithViews();
builder.Services.AddSingleton<IEmailService, EmailService>();
// Other service registrations.

var app = builder.Build();
```

This setup tells the .NET DI container to inject an instance of `EmailService` whenever an `IEmailService` is required, using any method of injection including constructor injection.

Property injection examples

Blazor components allow the use of the `@inject` attribute, as shown in the following code:

```
@inject IWeatherService WeatherService
```

The `@inject` directive translates to a property with the `[Inject]` attribute, as shown in the following code:

```
[Inject]
public IWeatherService WeatherService { get; set; }
```

You can then use the property in the Blazor component, as shown in the following code:

```
weather = WeatherService.GetWeather();
```

The DI system recognizes this attribute and injects the corresponding service.

Property injection can also be achieved using third-party libraries or custom solutions. It's generally used in scenarios where constructor injection is not feasible or when optional dependencies are involved.

For example, in Autofac 7.0 or later, all required properties are automatically resolved, in a similar manner to constructor parameters, as shown in the following code:

```
public class NorthwindService
{
  // These properties will be automatically set by Autofac.
  public required ILogger Logger { protected get; init; }
  public required IConfigReader ConfigReader { protected get; init; }
  // More implementation.
}
```

All required properties of the component must be resolvable services; otherwise, an exception will be thrown when trying to resolve the component.

You would then need to use Autofac to register the services, as shown in the following code:

```
ContainerBuilder builder = new();
builder.RegisterType<NorthwindService>();
builder.RegisterType<ConsoleLogger>().As<ILogger>();
builder.RegisterType<ConfigReader>().As<IConfigReader>();
var container = builder.Build();
```

> Autofac is an alternative third-party DI/IoC container. You can learn more about it at the following link: `https://autofac.org/`.

Method injection example

Method injection is typically used when a specific method in a class requires a dependency but the rest of the class does not. It's not as commonly used as constructor injection but it can be useful in certain scenarios, especially with Minimal APIs, which do not use classes with constructors, as shown in the following code:

```
app.MapGet("/weather", (IWeatherService weatherService) =>
{
  return Results.Ok(new { Weather = weatherService.GetWeather() });
});
```

In the `MapGet` method, the `IWeatherService` parameter in the lambda expression indicates that this dependency should be provided by the DI container. Minimal APIs automatically resolve services like the `IWeatherService` from the DI container if the parameter is of a service type that has been registered in the container and injects it into the handler method.

Sometimes the parameter will be decorated with `[FromServices]`, as shown in the following code:

```
app.MapGet("/weather", ([FromServices] IWeatherService weatherService) =>
{
  return Results.Ok(new { Weather = weatherService.GetWeather() });
});
```

You may want to explicitly use `[FromServices]` in the following cases:

- **Ambiguity**: If there is ambiguity between where the parameter value comes from, for example, route parameters versus services.
- **Explicitness**: For code clarity and to signal that a parameter is explicitly being injected from services.
- **Non-service types**: If the parameter type isn't obviously a service, for example `HttpContext`, ASP.NET Core might not infer it correctly unless you specify `[FromServices]`.

In general, if the type is clearly a service and registered in the DI container, ASP.NET Core will resolve it without the `[FromServices]` attribute.

Registering dependency service lifetimes

Choosing the right service lifetime ensures that resources are used efficiently and that your application behaves correctly, with services being instantiated and disposed of at the appropriate times.

You can register dependency services with different lifetimes, as shown in the following list:

- **Transient**: These services are created each time they're requested. Transient services should be lightweight and stateless. Use them for lightweight, stateless services where a new instance is required for each operation, such as utility or helper services.
- **Scoped**: For ASP.NET Core projects, these services are created once per client request and are disposed of when the response returns to the client. For other types of projects, like console apps, you need to define a scope manually. You can also create custom additional scopes in ASP.NET Core projects if needed. Use them when you need a separate instance of a service for each request; they are useful for services that interact with per-request data, such as database contexts.
- **Singleton**: These services are usually created the first time they are requested and then shared, although you can provide an instance at the time of registration too. Use them when you need a single instance of a service for an entire application's lifetime, typically for shared resources or configurations.

In this chapter, you will use all three types of lifetimes, which are controlled by a service scope.

Registering multiple implementations of a dependency service

.NET 8 introduced the ability to set a key for a dependency service. This allows multiple services to be registered with different keys and then retrieved later using that key.

Let's see an example of a type of service, `IMemoryCache`, that might have multiple implementations registered with different keys to identify them, as shown in the following code:

```
builder.Services.AddKeyedSingleton<IMemoryCache, BigCache>("big");
builder.Services.AddKeyedSingleton<IMemoryCache, SmallCache>("small");

class BigCacheConsumer([FromKeyedServices("big")] IMemoryCache cache)
{
  public object? GetData() => cache.Get("data");
}

class SmallCacheConsumer(IKeyedServiceProvider keyedServiceProvider)
{
  public object? GetData() => keyedServiceProvider
    .GetRequiredKeyedService<IMemoryCache>("small").Get("data");
}
```

In the preceding code:

- The `AddKeyedSingleton` method is used to register services with a specific key in the DI container. In this case, it registers two implementations of the `IMemoryCache` interface: `BigCache` with the key `"big"`, and `SmallCache` with the key `"small"`.

- The `BigCacheConsumer` class takes an `IMemoryCache` parameter annotated with `[FromKeyedServices("big")]`. This means that when an instance of `BigCacheConsumer` is created, the DI container will inject the `IMemoryCache` implementation associated with the key `"big"`. This is my preferred mechanism to get a keyed service.
- Similarly, the `SmallCacheConsumer` class takes an `IKeyedServiceProvider` parameter. It retrieves the `IMemoryCache` implementation associated with the key `"small"` using the `GetRequiredKeyedService` method. This is an alternative mechanism to get a keyed service.

By associating services with specific keys, you can easily retrieve the correct implementation based on the key when injecting dependencies into your classes.

When are exceptions thrown?

When resolving dependencies in a DI container, several scenarios can lead to exceptions being thrown. Understanding these scenarios can help you diagnose and fix issues related to dependency resolution.

Here are some common scenarios:

- **Service not registered**: If a service is not registered with the DI container, attempting to resolve it will result in an exception – for example: `InvalidOperationException: Unable to resolve service for type 'IMyService' while attempting to activate 'MyComponent'`.
- **Circular dependency**: A circular dependency occurs when two or more components or projects depend on each other in a way that creates a loop. If there is a circular dependency, the DI container cannot resolve the services and will throw an exception – for example: `InvalidOperationException: A circular dependency was detected for the service of type 'ServiceA'`.
- **Missing constructor**: If a service requires a constructor with parameters that cannot be resolved by the DI container, it will throw an exception – for example: `InvalidOperationException: Unable to resolve service for type 'NonRegisteredDependency' while attempting to activate 'MyService'`.
- **Wrong lifetime configuration**: If services are registered with incompatible lifetimes, for example, a scoped service depending on a transient service in a singleton context, this can lead to exceptions or unexpected behavior. This may not throw an exception immediately but can lead to issues like `ObjectDisposedException` when the scoped service is disposed of while still referenced by the singleton.
- **Multiple implementations**: If multiple implementations of a service are registered without specifying which one to use, the DI container may throw an exception or resolve the wrong implementation – for example: `InvalidOperationException: Multiple constructors accepting all given argument types have been found in type 'MyService2'. There should only be one applicable constructor`.
- **Invalid service descriptor**: If a service is registered with an invalid descriptor, such as using a type that does not implement the interface, it can lead to exceptions – for example: `InvalidOperationException: Type 'MyService' does not implement interface 'IMyService'`.

Dependency resolution exceptions can arise from various misconfigurations. Understanding these scenarios helps developers better configure their DI containers and debug issues more effectively.

Best practices for DI

You should use best practices when implementing DI, as shown in the following list:

- **Prefer constructor injection**: This makes the dependencies of your class explicit and ensures that your class is always in a valid state.
- **Use interfaces for dependencies**: This makes it easier to swap out implementations without changing the consuming class.
- **Avoid the service locator pattern**: This is when your code explicitly gets a service inside its implementation. This is bad practice because it hides class dependencies, making the code harder to understand and maintain, and tests cannot mock the dependency or replace it when needed.
- **Keep scopes and lifetimes in mind**: Be aware of the scope and, therefore, lifetime of your dependencies to avoid memory leaks or unintended behavior.

DI in .NET simplifies managing dependencies, leading to cleaner, more maintainable code. By leveraging the built-in DI container in .NET, developers can focus more on business logic rather than the intricacies of object creation and management.

Now that we have reviewed managing dependency services, let's move up to a higher level and review the hosts that contain services, in particular, the .NET Generic Host.

Implementing .NET Generic Host

.NET Generic Host, introduced in .NET Core 2.1 in 2018, is a framework for hosting services and applications. It provides a standardized way to configure and run any application. It manages application lifetime, configuration, logging, DI, and so on. It can host a wide variety of applications, from web applications using ASP.NET Core to background services and workers.

Key features of the .NET Generic Host

The most important features of the .NET Generic Host are shown in the following list:

- **DI support**: The host sets up DI, making it easy to inject services throughout your application.
- **Logging**: The host comes with a pre-configured logging infrastructure that supports multiple logging providers.
- **Configuration**: It offers a unified API for application configuration, supporting various sources like JSON files, environment variables, and command-line arguments.
- **Lifecycle management**: The host provides interfaces to manage application start and stop events.

The introduction of the Generic Host has unified the way .NET applications are configured and run, providing a consistent approach across different types of applications. It abstracts the complexities of bootstrapping applications, managing configurations, and handling dependencies, allowing developers to focus more on application logic rather than boilerplate infrastructure code.

Building a .NET Generic Host

.NET Generic Host is responsible for app startup and lifetime management. Although it is mostly used in ASP.NET Core web projects and services of all kinds, the Generic Host can be used with any type of .NET project, including console apps.

The most important method related to setting up the host is `CreateDefaultBuilder`, which performs many actions like loading configuration and using it to set up components, including those shown in *Table 10.1*:

Action	Details
Loads host configuration.	Environment variables prefixed with `DOTNET_`. Command-line arguments.
Loads app configuration.	`appsettings.json`. `appsettings.{Environment}.json`. Secret Manager when the app runs in the `Development` environment. Environment variables. Command-line arguments.
Adds logging providers.	**Console**, **Debug**, **EventSource**, and **EventLog** (on Windows only).
Enables scope and dependency validation.	Only when the environment is the development environment.

Table 10.1: Configuration actions taken by CreateDefaultBuilder

Creating a .NET Generic Host involves using the `HostBuilder`, configuring services, and then starting the host. Let's see it in action:

1. Use your preferred code editor to add a new **Console App** / `console` project named `GenericHostApp` to a `Chapter10` solution.
2. In the `GenericHostApp.csproj` project file, treat warnings as errors, add a package reference to work with .NET Generic Host, and statically and globally import the `Console` class, as shown in the following markup:

```
<Project Sdk="Microsoft.NET.Sdk">

  <PropertyGroup>
    <OutputType>Exe</OutputType>
    <TargetFramework>net10.0</TargetFramework>
    <ImplicitUsings>enable</ImplicitUsings>
    <Nullable>enable</Nullable>
    <TreatWarningsAsErrors>true</TreatWarningsAsErrors>
  </PropertyGroup>
```

```
  <ItemGroup>
    <PackageReference Include="Microsoft.Extensions.Hosting" />
  </ItemGroup>

  <ItemGroup>
    <Using Include="System.Console" Static="true" />
  </ItemGroup>

</Project>
```

3. In the `GenericHostApp` project, add a new class file named `CounterService.cs`.
4. In `CounterService.cs`, define an interface and a class for a service that increments a counter, as shown in the following code:

```
namespace Packt.Shared;

public interface ICounterService
{
  int Counter { get; set; }
  void IncrementCounter();
}

public class CounterService : ICounterService
{
  public int Counter { get; set; } = 0;

  public void IncrementCounter()
  {
    ++Counter;
  }
}
```

`CounterService` is not a `static` class, nor are its members `static`. Any shared class instances will not be due to the `static` C# language feature.

5. In `Program.cs`, directly create and call an instance of the `CounterService` class, and then register, get, and call a registered instance of the `CounterService`, as shown in the following code:

```
// To use GetRequiredService, AddSingleton, AddScoped, AddTransient.
using Microsoft.Extensions.DependencyInjection;
using Microsoft.Extensions.Hosting; // To use IHostBuilder, Host.
```

```
using Packt.Shared; // To use ICounterService, CcunterService.

WriteLine("Creating a CounterService instance directly:");
ICounterService counterService = new CounterService();
counterService.IncrementCounter();
counterService.IncrementCounter();

WriteLine($"Counter: {counterService.Counter}");

WriteLine("Creating a CounterService instance indirectly using DI:");

// Create a host builder and pass the args passed to the console app.
IHostBuilder builder = Host.CreateDefaultBuilder(args);

builder.ConfigureServices(services =>
{
  services.AddSingleton<ICounterService, CounterService>();
});

IHost host = builder.Build();

ICounterService service1, service2;
service1 = host.Services.GetRequiredService<ICounterService>();
service2 = host.Services.GetRequiredService<ICounterService>();

WriteLine($"Are the instances the same? {service1 == service2}");
service1.IncrementCounter();
service2.IncrementCounter();
WriteLine($"service1.Counter: {service1.Counter}");
WriteLine($"service2.Counter: {service2.Counter}");

await host.RunAsync();
```

6. Start the `GenericHostApp` project without debugging, and note the result, which indicates that one instance of the service was created, as shown in the following output:

```
Creating a CounterService instance directly:
Counter: 2
Creating a CounterService instance indirectly using DI:
Are the instances the same? True
service1.Counter: 2
service2.Counter: 2
```

```
info: Microsoft.Hosting.Lifetime[0]
      Application started. Press Ctrl+C to shut down.
info: Microsoft.Hosting.Lifetime[0]
      Hosting environment: Production
info: Microsoft.Hosting.Lifetime[0]
      Content root path: C:\tools-skills-net10\Chapter10\GenericHostApp\
bin\Debug\net10.0
```

7. Press *Ctrl* + *C* to shut down the host.
8. In `Program.cs`, comment out the statement that registers the service as a singleton, and then add a statement that registers the service as transient, which will change the service's lifetime, as shown highlighted in the following code:

```
builder.ConfigureServices(services =>
{
  // services.AddSingleton<ICounterService, CounterService>();
  services.AddTransient<ICounterService, CounterService>();
});
```

9. Start the `GenericHostApp` project without debugging, and note the result, which indicates that two instances of the service were created, as shown in the following output:

```
Creating a CounterService instance indirectly using DI:
Are the instances the same? False
service1.Counter: 1
service2.Counter: 1
```

10. In `Program.cs`, comment out the statement that registers the service as transient, and then add a statement that registers the service as scoped, as shown highlighted in the following code:

```
builder.ConfigureServices(services =>
{
  // services.AddSingleton<ICounterService, CounterService>();
  // services.AddTransient<ICounterService, CounterService>();
  services.AddScoped<ICounterService, CounterService>();
});
```

11. In `Program.cs`, define a third service variable, wrap the statements that get the services and call them in a service scope. Then define an explicit scope that gets and calls the service, making sure to change the way you get the services, using the scoped service provider instead of the host services, as shown highlighted in the following code:

```
ICounterService service1, service2, service3;

// If we are getting a scoped service then we need at least one scope.
using (IServiceScope scope = host.Services.CreateScope())
```

```
{
  service1 = scope.ServiceProvider.GetRequiredService<ICounterService>();
  service2 = scope.ServiceProvider.GetRequiredService<ICounterService>();
  WriteLine($"Are the instances the same? {service1 == service2}");
  service1.IncrementCounter();
  service2.IncrementCounter();
  WriteLine($"service1.Counter: {service1.Counter}");
  WriteLine($"service2.Counter: {service2.Counter}");
}

using (IServiceScope scope = host.Services.CreateScope())
{
  service3 = scope.ServiceProvider.GetRequiredService<ICounterService>();
  WriteLine($"Are the instances the same? {service1 == service3}");
  WriteLine($"service1.Counter: {service1.Counter}");
  WriteLine($"service2.Counter: {service2.Counter}");
  WriteLine($"service3.Counter: {service3.Counter}");
}

await host.RunAsync();
```

You must make sure to get the services from the scoped service provider using `scope.ServiceProvider`, instead of from the host services using `host.Services`, because `host.Services` is in the default scope.

12. Start the `GenericHostApp` project without debugging, and note the result, which indicates that two instances of the service were created, as shown in the following output:

```
Creating a CounterService instance indirectly using DI:
Are the instances the same? True
service1.Counter: 2
service2.Counter: 2
Are the instances the same? False
service1.Counter: 2
service2.Counter: 2
service3.Counter: 0
```

In an ASP.NET Core project, a scope is automatically created for each HTTP request. Any services registered at the scope level and created during that request are, therefore, the same service instance. Any services registered at the transient level and created during that request are, therefore, different service instances. And, of course, singletons are always a shared instance.

Now that you've seen how to control the scope of services, let's see some other benefits of using a host.

Understanding host services and event handlers

A host service is a service that implements `IHostedService` and, therefore, implements `StartAsync` and `StopAsync` methods (event handlers) that will be called by the host once the service has been registered and whenever an instance starts and stops, as shown in the following code:

```
public class MyBackgroundService : IHostedService
{
  public Task StartAsync(CancellationToken cancellationToken)
  {
    // Code to start the background task.
    return Task.CompletedTask;
  }

  public Task StopAsync(CancellationToken cancellationToken)
  {
    // Code to stop the background task.
    return Task.CompletedTask;
  }
}
```

The `StartAsync` method is called when the `IHostedService` starts. It contains the logic to start the background task. The `StopAsync` method is called when the `IHostedService` stops. It contains the logic to gracefully shut down the background task. Both methods are asynchronous, allowing for the background task to be started and stopped asynchronously.

To use your `IHostedService` implementation, you need to register it in the DI container in your `Program.cs`, as shown in the following code:

```
var builder = WebApplication.CreateBuilder(args);

builder.Services.AddHostedService<MyBackgroundService>();

var app = builder.Build();

app.Run();
```

As well as registering your own services in the host container, some special ones get automatically registered, as shown in *Table 10.2*:

Service	**Description**
`IHostApplicationLifetime`	Provides three event handler methods to listen to: • `ApplicationStarted`: Triggered when an application has fully started. Useful for post-startup initialization. • `ApplicationStopping`: Triggered when an application performs a graceful shutdown. Useful for starting to release resources and stopping services. • `ApplicationStopped`: Triggered when an application has fully stopped. Useful for performing final cleanup tasks.
`IHostLifetime`	This interface is primarily implemented by infrastructure components rather than being used directly by application developers. Provides two event handler methods to listen to: `WaitForStartAsync`: Delays the start of an application until certain conditions are met. `StopAsync`: Handles the cleanup and shutdown process.
`IHostEnvironment`	Provides information about the current environment.
`ILogger`	Provides a service that implements logging. **Console**, **EventLog**, and so on are attached by default.

Table 10.2: Automatically registered services

Let's explore what these services can be used for:

1. In the `GenericHostApp` project, add a new class file named `WorkerService.cs`.
2. In `WorkerService.cs`, define a class that has methods for common events, as shown in the following code:

```
using Microsoft.Extensions.Hosting; // To use IHostedService.
using Microsoft.Extensions.Logging; // To use ILogger.

namespace Packt.Shared;

public sealed class WorkerService : IHostedService
{
  private readonly ILogger _logger;
  private readonly IHostEnvironment _environment;
  private readonly IHostApplicationLifetime _appLifetime;

  public WorkerService(
    ILogger<WorkerService> logger,
```

```
    IHostApplicationLifetime appLifetime,
    IHostEnvironment hostEnvironment)
  {
    _logger = logger;
    _logger.LogInformation("WorkerService constructor has been called.");

    appLifetime.ApplicationStarted.Register(OnStarted);
    appLifetime.ApplicationStopping.Register(OnStopping);
    appLifetime.ApplicationStopped.Register(OnStopped);

    _appLifetime = appLifetime;
    _environment = hostEnvironment;

    WriteLine($"_environment.EnvironmentName: {_environment.
EnvironmentName}");
    WriteLine($"_environment.ApplicationName: {_environment.
ApplicationName}");
    WriteLine($"_environment.ContentRootPath: {_environment.
ContentRootPath}");
  }

  public Task StartAsync(CancellationToken cancellationToken)
  {
    _logger.LogInformation("1. StartAsync has been called.");
    return Task.CompletedTask;
  }

  public Task StopAsync(CancellationToken cancellationToken)
  {
    _logger.LogInformation("4. StopAsync has been called.");
    return Task.CompletedTask;
  }

  private void OnStarted()
  {
    _logger.LogInformation("2. OnStarted has been called.");
  }

  private void OnStopping()
  {
    _logger.LogInformation("3. OnStopping has been called.");
```

```
  }

  private void OnStopped()
  {
    _logger.LogInformation("5. OnStopped has been called.");
  }

  private void GracefulShutdown()
  {
    _appLifetime.StopApplication();
  }
}
```

> **Good practice:** The quick and dirty way of shutting down an application is to call `Environment.Exit`. If your application uses hosting, then you can gracefully stop the host by calling `IHostApplicationLifetime.StopApplication` instead.

3. In `Program.cs`, register the worker service as a hosted service so that an instance will be created and started automatically when the host starts, as shown highlighted in the following code:

```
builder.ConfigureServices(services =>
{
  // services.AddSingleton<ICounterService, CounterService>();
  // services.AddTransient<ICounterService, CounterService>();
  services.AddScoped<ICounterService, CounterService>();

  // Register a hosted service that will start when the host starts.
  services.AddHostedService<WorkerService>();
});
```

4. In `Program.cs`, add a comment before the host starts, as shown highlighted in the following code:

```
// Start the host and any hosted services and wait for them to complete.
await host.RunAsync();
```

5. Start the `GenericHostApp` project without debugging, and note the results, including the environment information, as shown in the following output:

```
info: Packt.Shared.WorkerService[0]
      WorkerService constructor has been called.
_environment.EnvironmentName: Production
_environment.ApplicationName: GenericHostApp
```

```
_environment.ContentRootPath: C:\tools-skills-net10\Chapter10\
GenericHostApp\bin\Debug\net10.0
info: Packt.Shared.WorkerService[0]
      1. StartAsync has been called.
info: Packt.Shared.WorkerService[0]
      2. OnStarted has been called.
info: Microsoft.Hosting.Lifetime[0]
      Application started. Press Ctrl+C to shut down.
info: Microsoft.Hosting.Lifetime[0]
      Hosting environment: Production
info: Microsoft.Hosting.Lifetime[0]
      Content root path: C:\tools-skills-net10\Chapter10\GenericHostApp\
bin\Debug\net10.0
```

`Production` is the default environment if it is not explicitly set in a configuration, like an environment variable or at the command line. For example, you could start the project at the terminal or command prompt using the following command:

```
dotnet run --environment Development
```

6. Press *Ctrl* + *C* to gracefully shut down the host and note the result, as shown in the following output:

```
info: Packt.Shared.WorkerService[0]
      3. OnStopping has been called.
info: Microsoft.Hosting.Lifetime[0]
      Application is shutting down...
info: Packt.Shared.WorkerService[0]
      4. StopAsync has been called.
info: Packt.Shared.WorkerService[0]
      5. OnStopped has been called.
```

Service registration methods

There are multiple ways to register a service that supports different features, even at the same level of scope, for example, a singleton, as shown in *Table 10.3*.

In the feature columns for *Table 10.3*, **A** means automatic object disposal support, **M** means multiple implementations are supported, and **P** means you can pass arguments.

Method	A	M	P
`AddSingleton<IMyService, MyService>();` `AddSingleton<IMyService, Service2>();`	Yes	Yes	No

`AddSingleton<IMyService>(sp => new MyService());`
`AddSingleton<IMyService>(sp => new MyService(13));`
`AddSingleton<IMyService>(sp => new Service2(27));`
	Yes	Yes	Yes

`AddSingleton<MyService>();`	Yes	No	No

`AddSingleton<IMyService>(new MyService());`
`AddSingleton<IMyService>(new MyService(13));`
`AddSingleton<IMyService>(new Service2(27));`
	No	Yes	Yes

`AddSingleton(new MyService());` `AddSingleton(new MyService(13));`	No	Yes	Yes

Table 10.3: Service registration methods

To get multiple implementations that have been registered for the same interface, declare an `IEnumerable<T>` parameter, as shown in the following code:

```
public WorkerService(
  ILogger lastLoggerRegistered,
  IEnumerable<ILogger> allRegisteredLoggers)
```

`WorkerService` defines two constructor parameters. The single `ILogger` will be the last implementation to have been registered, and the `IEnumerable<ILogger>` will be all the registered `ILogger` implementations.

> If there is already an implementation of an interface registered, then calling `TryAddXxx` will fail.

Dependency graphs and service resolution

It is common to use DI in a chained fashion. Each requested dependency, like `WorkerService`, requests its own dependencies, like `ILogger`. The container finds the required dependencies in its graph of services and returns the fully resolved service.

The set of dependencies that must be resolved is referred to as a dependency tree, dependency graph, or object graph, as shown in *Figure 10.2*:

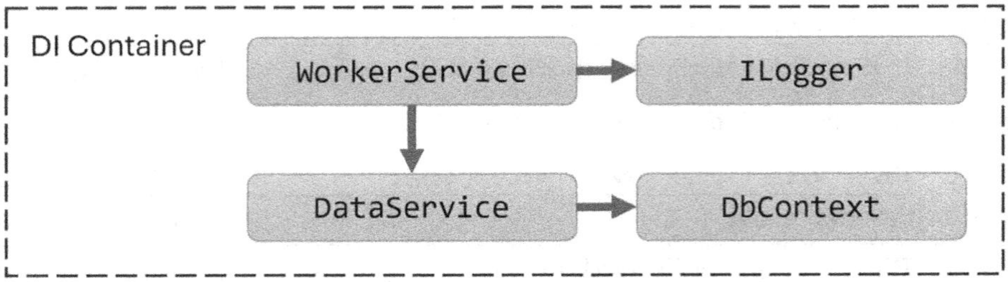

Figure 10.2: DI container and a dependency tree or graph

In *Figure 10.2*, the DI container manages the dependencies. `WorkerService` is a service that depends on other services. `ILogger` is a dependency required by the `WorkerService`. `DataService` is another dependency that might be needed by the `WorkerService` or other services. `DbContext` is a dependency required by the `DataService`.

The arrow from `WorkerService` to `ILogger` shows that `WorkerService` depends on `ILogger`. The DI container resolves the `WorkerService` and in the process resolves its dependencies, like `ILogger` and `DataService`, which in turn might have their own dependencies, like `DbContext`. This chained resolution ensures that all dependencies are fully resolved and injected where needed.

Disposing services

If a service implements `IDisposable`, then the container calls the `Dispose` method for the services that it creates automatically. You should never explicitly dispose of a service created by the container yourself because you do not know what the dependency tree or graph looks like, and just because you don't need a service anymore does not mean that it's not needed by other services. You also do not know what lifetime it has been registered with. If you dispose of it, other services are likely to fail.

However, if you use the technique of manually creating an instance of a service and passing that to the container, then you will have to dispose of it manually, as shown in the following code:

```
// The service is manually instantiated so must be manually disposed.
builder.Services.AddSingleton(new NorthwindService());
```

Special cases of DI with ASP.NET Core

The most common project type that uses DI extensively is an ASP.NET Core project. In this section, we will look at some of the special cases of DI when building web apps and services.

Registering services for features using extension methods

With a complex ASP.NET Core project, you are likely to need to register many related services for each feature of the website or web service in `Program.cs`, as shown in the following code:

```
builder.Services.AddScoped<IShoppingCart, InMemoryShoppingCart>();
builder.Services.AddScoped<ICustomerAccount, CustomerAccount>();
builder.Services.AddScoped<IUserRegistration, UserRegistration>();
```

It is good practice to define an extension method to group all these registrations, as shown in the following code:

```
public static class ServiceCollectionExtensions
{
  public static IServiceCollection AddNorthwindFeatures(
    this IServiceCollection services)
  {
    services.AddScoped<IShoppingCart, InMemoryShoppingCart>();
    services.AddScoped<ICustomerAccount, CustomerAccount>();
    services.AddScoped<IUserRegistration, UserRegistration>();
    return services;
  }
}
```

This will simplify the statements in `Program.cs`, as shown in the following code:

```
builder.Services.AddNorthwindFeatures();
```

The ASP.NET Core team does this themselves with methods like `AddControllers` and `AddRazorPages`.

When you cannot use constructor injection

If you are building ASP.NET Core MVC or controller-based Web API projects, then your controller classes can use constructor injection to get registered services, just like any other class. But there are other situations where you cannot use constructor injection to get registered services, as it forces a scoped service to behave like a singleton, which throws a runtime exception.

There are several situations in ASP.NET Core where using constructor injection may not be appropriate or possible. These scenarios typically arise when the service lifetimes are incompatible, or the context in which the service is needed does not support constructor injection. Here are some of those situations:

- **Background services**, such as those derived from `BackgroundService` or `IHostedService`, are typically singleton services. Injecting scoped services via the constructor is not appropriate due to their singleton nature. Injecting scoped services into background services via the constructor can cause them to be treated as singletons, leading to issues with resource management and state handling. The solution is to use method injection by resolving services within the `ExecuteAsync` method or create a scope using `host.Services.CreateScope()`.

- **Tag Helpers** are created per view instance, and injecting services via the constructor is not supported. Constructor injection is not feasible because Tag Helpers are not managed by the DI container in the same way controllers or other services are. The solution is to use property injection with the `[ViewContext]` attribute.
- **Filters** can be registered globally, per controller, or per action. Filters registered as singleton services cannot depend on scoped services directly via constructor injection. The solution is to use the `ServiceFilter` or `TypeFilter` attributes, or the DI container within the filter's methods.

Constructor injection is not always feasible, particularly when dealing with middleware, background services, Tag Helpers, and filters. In these cases, method injection, property injection, or resolving services within the method scope are preferred approaches to ensure that services are correctly instantiated and managed according to their intended lifetimes.

Let's look at one of these scenarios in more detail: dealing with middleware.

Using scoped services in middleware

Although singletons can be passed in the constructor to middleware, to use scoped and transient services in middleware, you should inject a service into the middleware's `Invoke` or `InvokeAsync` method, as shown in the following code:

```
public class NorthwindMiddleware
{
  private readonly RequestDelegate _next;
  private readonly ILogger _logger;
  private readonly ISingletonService _singleton;

  // Singleton services can use constructor injection.
  public MyMiddleware(RequestDelegate next,
    ILogger<MyMiddleware> logger,
    ISingletonService singleton)
  {
    _logger = logger;
    _singleton = singleton;
    _next = next;
  }

  public async Task InvokeAsync(HttpContext context,
    // Transient and scoped services must use method injection.
    ITransientService transient, IScopedService scoped)
  {
    _logger.LogInformation("Transient: " + transient.ProductId);
    _logger.LogInformation("Scoped: " + scoped.ProductId);
    _logger.LogInformation("Singleton: " + _singleton.ProduceId);
```

```
      await _next(context);
    }
  }
```

Resolving services at startup

To resolve a scoped service when an ASP.NET Core project starts, you must define a scope, as shown in the following code:

```
using Packt.Shared; // To use INorthwindService.

WebApplicationBuilder builder = WebApplication.CreateBuilder(args);

builder.Services.AddScoped<INorthwindService, NorthwindService>();
WebApplication app = builder.Build();

using (IServiceScope scope = app.Services.CreateScope())
{
  INorthwindService service = scope.ServiceProvider
    .GetRequiredService<INorthwindService>();

  // Use the service here.
}

app.MapGet("/", () => "Hello World!");

app.Run();
```

In the rest of the project, for example, in a controller class or Razor component, a service scope will be created automatically to handle each incoming HTTP request.

As well as constructor injection, you can get the services container from the current HTTP context, as shown in the following code:

```
IServiceProvider services = HttpContext.RequestServices;
```

DI and views

To inject a service into a Razor View or Razor Page, use the `@inject` directive, as shown in the following code:

```
@inject NorthwindService nw
```

DI, action methods, and Minimal APIs

If you are building controller-based MVC websites or Web API services, or Minimal API web services, then there are alternative techniques to constructor injection.

You can use action method injection using attributes like `[FromServices]` and `[FromKeyedServices]`.

First, register the services as normal, as shown in the following code:

```
builder.Services.AddSingleton<IOrderProcessor, OrderProcessor>();
builder.Services.AddKeyedSingleton<ICache, BigCache>("big");
```

Then, decorate action method parameters with attributes, as shown in the following code:

```
public IActionResult SubmitOrder([FromServices] IOrderProcessor processor)
{
  // Use processor.
}

public ActionResult<object> GetCatalog([FromKeyedServices("big")] ICache cache)
{
  return cache.Get("catalog");
}
```

Practicing and exploring

Test your knowledge and understanding by answering some questions, getting some hands-on practice, and exploring the topics covered in this chapter with deeper research.

Exercise 10.1 – Online-only material

You can read Martin Fowler's article, *Inversion of Control Containers and the Dependency Injection pattern*, from more than 20 years ago, at the following link: `https://www.martinfowler.com/articles/injection.html`.

You can read about ASP.NET Core Blazor DI at the following link: `https://learn.microsoft.com/en-us/aspnet/core/blazor/fundamentals/dependency-injection`.

Exercise 10.2 – Practice exercises

If you would prefer to use an alternative DI system to the built-in one, then **Autofac** is a good choice. You can learn a technique more deeply if you explore how other comparable systems do it. A simple tutorial for Autofac can be found at the following link: `https://autofac.readthedocs.io/en/latest/getting-started/index.html`.

Exercise 10.3 – Test your knowledge

Answer the following questions. If you get stuck, try googling the answers, if necessary, while remembering that if you get totally stuck, the answers are in *Appendix A*:

1. What is the main idea of DI?
2. What are the three main types of DI? Which type is not directly supported by .NET projects out of the box, except in special scenarios?
3. In .NET, you can register dependency services with different lifetimes. What are they?
4. What events can you listen to for a host service?
5. When do host services start?

> *Appendix A, Answers to the Test Your Knowledge Questions,* is available to download from the following link: `https://github.com/markjprice/tools-skills-net10/blob/main/docs/B31468_Appendix%20A.pdf`.

Exercise 10.4 – Explore topics

Use the links on the following page to learn more details about the topics covered in this chapter: `https://github.com/markjprice/tools-skills-net10/blob/main/docs/book-links.md#chapter-10---dependency-injection-containers-and-service-lifetime`.

Summary

In this chapter, you learned:

- The concepts around IoC and DI
- How dependency services are registered and resolved
- Dependency service lifetimes and when they should be used
- How to implement .NET Generic Host
- How ASP.NET Core uses DI

In the next chapter, you will be introduced to many types of testing, and then learn the details of unit testing and how to mock dependencies in your tests. It's a natural next step after this chapter.

Learn more on Discord

To join the Discord community for this book – where you can share feedback, ask questions to the author, and learn about new releases – follow this QR code:

`https://packt.link/TS2e`

Join .NETPro – It's Free

Staying sharp in .NET takes more than reading release notes. It requires real-world tips, proven patterns, and scalable solutions. That's what .NETPro, Packt's new newsletter, is all about.

Scan the QR code or visit the link to subscribe:

`https://landing.packtpub.com/dotnetpronewsletter/`

11

Unit Testing and Mocking

This chapter is about unit testing and mocking, but it will start with an introduction to all the types of testing that a .NET developer should know about. After that, we will move on to unit testing and mocking because these techniques target the smallest units of code – individual methods or functions. This granular focus makes them the natural foundation for any testing strategy. Unit tests verify that each part of the program works as intended in isolation, ensuring that small pieces of code function correctly on their own. Mocking complements this by allowing developers to simulate the behavior of complex dependencies, making unit tests more reliable and easier to write.

In later chapters, we will cover other types of testing, like integration, security, performance, functional, and end-to-end user interface testing, for websites and services. Covering all these topics will take multiple chapters. Integration testing will show us how different modules of our application interact and function together. Security testing will ensure that our code is resilient against malicious attacks and vulnerabilities. Performance testing will measure how well our application performs under various conditions, helping us identify bottlenecks and optimize efficiency. Functional testing will validate the end-to-end behavior of our application against user requirements, and end-to-end UI testing will focus on ensuring that our websites and services provide a seamless user experience from start to finish.

This chapter covers the following topics:

- Introducing all types of testing
- Pros and cons of test-driven development
- Unit testing using xUnit
- Mocking in tests
- Making fluent assertions in unit testing
- Generating fake data with Bogus

Introducing all types of testing

Testing is one of the most critical phases in the software development process. Good tests will ensure that your application is robust, reliable, and ready for production. But bad tests have a big cost. It is vital to spend the effort you put into writing tests effectively. What represents a good or bad test is one of the most important topics, and you will learn about it in detail in this and subsequent testing chapters.

Your testing strategy should cover various aspects of the application to catch bugs, avoid regressions, alleviate performance issues, and fix usability problems before they reach the end users. Let's review each of the major types of testing.

Unit testing

The purpose of a **unit test** is to verify individual units of behavior of your project in isolation to ensure that they work as expected. You should focus on business logic, algorithms, and individual functions or methods. Every method that is part of a public API should ideally have at least one corresponding unit test. Note I do not say *every* method!

Non-public methods typically do not require direct unit testing because:

- Testing through public interfaces naturally covers non-public methods
- Non-public methods have implementation details that are subject to change
- Focusing on behavior rather than implementation leads to more robust and maintainable tests.
- Simpler test suites are easier to manage
- Higher-level testing like integration and end-to-end testing can provide necessary coverage for complex interactions

By concentrating on public methods, you ensure that your tests remain meaningful, resilient to change, and focused on the class's intended behavior, promoting a more effective and maintainable testing strategy.

Now that you know what methods to test, it's worth emphasizing what makes a good unit test.

A good unit test should meet the following criteria:

- It verifies a single unit of behavior, for example, a method that implements some business logic.
- It executes as fast as possible. For example, it may use an in-memory data store instead of the production database to increase speed while testing business logic. A good test framework will allow you to set a timeout to stop a test from running for too long.
- It performs its work isolated from other tests (and optionally from its dependencies).

Common tools for unit testing .NET code include xUnit, NUnit, and MSTest. In this book, we will focus on xUnit but the others are similar enough that you will still benefit from this chapter even if you use alternative tools. We cover unit testing in detail later in this chapter.

Integration, end-to-end, and security testing

Higher-level types of testing include integration, end-to-end, and security testing.

An **integration test** can look like a unit test and use the same tools, like xUnit, but it does not meet one or more of the stricter criteria for a unit test. For example, they can test more than just a small piece of code, they often take longer to execute, and they are not isolated from other parts of the system.

The purpose of integration testing is to verify that different components, modules, or services of the project work together as intended. Integration tests should test database interactions, API integrations, and the interaction between different layers of the project. For example, they should test the interaction between the data access layer and the business logic layer.

An **end-to-end test** is a subtype of integration tests and it verifies a part of the system from the end user's point of view.

A **security test** is used to identify vulnerabilities in your apps and services and ensure that data is protected against unauthorized access. You should test authentication and authorization mechanisms, data encryption, as well as protection against common security threats, for example, SQL injection, cross-site scripting, and so on.

Common tools for integration testing include the same ones as for unit testing. The difference is what the tests do. Common tools for security testing include OWASP check lists and .NET security analyzers. We cover integration, end-to-end, and security testing in *Chapter 12, Integration and Security Testing*.

Performance, load, and stress testing

The purpose of performance, load, and stress testing is to ensure the application performs well under expected load conditions. You should test the response times of services, system throughput, and the ability to handle concurrent users or requests without degradation in performance.

Common tools include Apache JMeter, BenchmarkDotNet, and k6. We cover these types of testing in *Chapter 13, Benchmarking Performance, Load, and Stress Testing*.

Functional and usability testing

The purpose of **functional testing** is to ensure the application meets specified requirements and behaves correctly in all scenarios. You should test user scenarios, workflows, and end-to-end tasks. This includes testing form inputs and navigation flows.

The purpose of **usability testing** is to evaluate the application's user interface and overall user experience. You should test the ease of use, design consistency, navigation flow, and accessibility of your apps by getting user feedback, implementing A/B testing, and running usability testing sessions.

Common tools for functional testing include Playwright and Selenium for web apps and Appium for mobile applications. We cover functional and usability testing in *Chapter 14, Functional and End-to-End Testing of Websites and Services*.

Testing terminology

Let's review some of the common terms used in testing, as shown in *Table 11.1*:

Term	Definition
System under test (SUT), Method under test (MUT)	**SUT** is a type, like a class, being tested. You often create a test class with multiple test methods to group all the test methods for the SUT. **MUT** is a method within a SUT being tested.
Test double	An object that has the same public API as a dependency but with simplified and predictable behavior. The name is derived from the concept of a stunt double in film production. It has nothing to do with the `double` number type. It is an umbrella term for any non-production test-only dependencies.
Mock	A subtype of test double that is used to verify interactions between objects by setting up expectations and behaviors on the mock object and then asserting that these expectations were met during the test.
Regression	When the code stops working as intended after a code modification.
Coverage metric	Measures how much code a test project executes. This can be 0% to 100%. It's good practice to have a high level of coverage in the core business logic of your project but do not make this a requirement, especially in non-core parts. A good separation of business logic helps to make it clear what requires testing.
Test fixture	An object that the test needs to run, like a dependency. It could be an argument passed to the test, or some state in a file or database. The key point is that the value should be *fixed* so the test produces the same result each time it runs, hence the name *fixture*.

Table 11.1: Common testing terms

Attributes of all good tests

All good tests must have the following attributes:

1. **Verifies the most important parts of the codebase:** For unit tests, this is typically the domain model and business logic algorithms. For integration tests, it is typically controllers or orchestrators for a process that spans as many external systems as possible. But code coverage for tests does not need to be 100%. Tests should verify the end result of a process, not its implementation's technical details.
2. **Integrates automatically into the development process:** Set up your continuous integration and deployment system to run tests automatically.
3. **Avoids regressions:** As you add more features and your codebase becomes more complex, bugs can be introduced that break your code. Good tests will highlight these regressions so you can immediately fix them. They are an early warning system.

4. **Resistant to refactoring:** This means that if you refactor the implementation of a feature, its tests continue to pass. Tests that fail after refactoring lack resistance. They are false positives, aka false alarms.
5. **Balances costs and benefits:** Strikes a balance between the maintenance cost and the benefit gained from tests. Testing trivial code, like setting and getting properties on a model, is not worth the effort.

> **Good practice:** It is always better not to write a test than to write a bad test! Every statement adds to the maintenance costs of a project. If those statements do not provide value, that test is bad.

Test outcomes

When discussing test outcomes, we use the terms *positive* and *negative*, which refer to whether a test indicates the presence or absence of a defect or error. Like testing negative for a disease, a negative outcome is a good thing!

We also use the terms *true* and *false*, which refer to the correctness of the test result in relation to the actual condition of the code being tested. True is good and false is bad!

To summarize, by combining these terms, there are four possible test outcomes, as shown in *Table 11.2*:

	Positive	**Negative**
True	**True Positive (TP):** The test correctly identifies a defect. This means the code is faulty, and the test detects it. This is a good outcome. The test finds a defect that actually exists in the code.	**True Negative (TN):** The test correctly identifies that there is no defect. This means the code is correct, and the test confirms it. This is a good outcome. The test confirms that there are no defects in the code.
False	**False Positive (FP):** The test incorrectly identifies a defect. This means the code is correct, but the test mistakenly reports a defect. This is a bad outcome. The test reports a defect, but the code is actually correct.	**False Negative (FN):** The test fails to identify a defect. This means the code is faulty, but the test mistakenly reports that there are no defects. This is a bad outcome. The test fails to report a defect that exists in the code.

Table 11.2: Four possible test outcomes

Let's review some scenarios for a method to help you understand, as shown in *Table 11.3*:

	Scenario	**Test**	**Outcome**
TP	There's a bug in the method.	A unit test runs and fails, indicating an error.	The test correctly identifies the bug.
TN	The method is bug-free.	A unit test runs and passes, indicating no errors.	The test correctly confirms the method has no bugs.
FP	The method is bug-free.	A unit test runs and fails, indicating an error.	The test incorrectly reports a bug in the method.
FN	There's a bug in the method.	A unit test runs and passes, indicating no errors.	The test fails to identify the bug.

Table 11.3: Test outcome scenarios

Test doubles, mocks, and stubs

A **test double** is the umbrella term for any fake dependency in a test. They are used in tests in place of real dependencies that would be harder to set up consistently than a double.

There are multiple types of double. The most common are mocks and **stubs**:

- **Mocks** are doubles for outgoing interactions. For example, the test could call a mocked dependency that fakes sending an email during user registration. During the process, state could be changed in the external system, which could cause the test to fail when it shouldn't. Mocks are usually created using a mocking framework. When they are manually created, they are sometimes called **spies**.
- **Stubs** are doubles for incoming interactions. For example, the test could call a stubbed dependency that retrieves product information from a database. No state is changed in the external system. When the dependency does not yet exist, for example, if using TDD, then a stub is known as a **fake**. When a stub is a simple value and does not affect the outcome, then it is known as a **dummy**.

The separation of mocks and stubs is related to the **Command Query Separation (CQS)** principle. Every method should be either a command or a query. Mocks are for methods that could have side effects and do not return a value. Stubs are for methods that do not have side effects and return a value.

To improve your chances of success with testing, you and your team will need to commit to adopting a testing mindset.

Adopting a testing mindset

To get the best from testing, you will need to adopt a testing mindset. A comprehensive testing strategy will help in identifying and fixing bugs early in the development cycle. It will make sure that your projects meet the performance, security, and usability standards expected by users. As a .NET developer, investing time in learning about and implementing a broad range of testing methodologies will pay off in the form of more reliable, efficient, and user-friendly applications.

One of the strategies that you should consider is adopting **Test-Driven Development (TDD)**. This is where you write tests before writing the code itself. This approach can encourage better design and more maintainable code. But beware of the trade-offs. So, let's now look at the pros and cons of TDD.

Pros and cons of test-driven development

Test-Driven Development (TDD) is a software development approach that emphasizes writing tests before writing the actual code. This technique encourages developers to think through their design and requirements upfront, leading to better-designed, more reliable, and easier-to-maintain software from the very start.

Core principles of TDD

TDD is built around a simple cycle often described as "Red-Green-Refactor," as shown in the following list:

1. **Red**: Write a test for the next bit of functionality you want to add. The test assertions should fail because the functionality doesn't exist yet and the implementation throws a `NotImplementedException`. This step ensures that your tests are meaningful and that they truly verify the intended functionality.
2. **Green**: Write the minimum amount of code necessary to make the test pass. This encourages simplicity and focuses only on functionality that is needed.
3. **Refactor**: Clean up the new code, ensuring it fits well with the existing codebase, follows good practices, and remains readable and maintainable. Importantly, after refactoring, all tests should still pass, confirming that no existing functionality was broken by introducing a regression.

Pros of TDD

The benefits of TDD are shown in the following list:

1. **Higher code quality**: TDD can lead to a codebase that's better designed, more modular, and easier to maintain.
2. **Improved documentation**: The tests serve as documentation for your codebase, clearly explaining what each part of your application is supposed to do.
3. **Bug cost reduction**: By catching issues early in the development cycle, TDD can significantly reduce the cost of bugs and issues in your code.
4. **Facilitates change**: With a comprehensive suite of tests, developers can add new features or change existing ones without fear of inadvertently breaking other parts of the application.

Cons of TDD

The primary challenges and considerations of TDD are shown in the following list:

1. **Tricky for a team to adopt**: TDD requires a shift in mindset and approach, which can take time for teams to fully adopt and integrate into their workflows.
2. **Resistant management due to slower development at first**: Writing tests before code can initially slow down development as developers adjust to the TDD cycle. However, this is often offset by the reduced time spent debugging and fixing bugs later. But this can be tricky to explain to unconvinced management.
3. **Maintenance overhead of tests**: The test suite itself needs to be maintained and updated as the application evolves, which can add overhead. This is part of the investment in maintaining code quality over time.

Let's end the TDD section with a review of some good practices.

Good practices for TDD

Recommended good practices when implementing TDD include the following:

- Begin with simple tests and functionality before moving on to more complex scenarios. This helps in understanding the TDD process without getting overwhelmed. TDD makes more sense for unit testing than for integration testing. With unit testing, you can easily go through the red-green-refactor steps. With integration testing and larger features, this is more challenging.
- Focus on one test at a time to keep the development cycle tight and ensure that you are only working on implementing one piece of functionality at a time.
- Regularly refactor both your code and your tests for clarity, efficiency, and maintainability.
- Enhance the benefits of TDD by combining it with pair programming and code reviews. This helps to spread knowledge about your codebase and improve the quality of both code and tests.

You will learn more about pair programming and code reviews in *Chapter 19, Your Career, Teamwork, and Interviews*. But briefly, pair programming is a collaborative practice where two developers work together at one workstation, with one writing code (the "driver") while the other reviews each line of code as it's written (the "navigator"). Code reviews are a process where peers examine each other's code for mistakes, ensuring quality, improving codebase consistency, and fostering knowledge sharing within the team.

TDD is a software development methodology that, when properly applied, can lead to higher-quality software, a more thoughtful design process, and a codebase that is easier to maintain and extend. TDD requires an upfront investment in time and a shift in development culture, but the potential long-term benefits in terms of code quality and reduced debugging time are substantial.

Now let's dive into some practical examples of unit testing, specifically using a popular package named xUnit.

Unit testing using xUnit

You learned about the basics of unit testing in the introduction section. Now let's go a bit deeper. One of the most contentious aspects of unit testing is how isolated they must be. Let's look at this point in more detail.

How isolated should unit tests be?

There are two sides to this debate, as described in the following bullets:

- The traditional approach to writing unit tests is not to isolate them from their dependencies. In this approach, you are testing both the MUT and its dependencies. There could be a bug in one of the dependencies that would make the test fail. This can make it harder to track down the issue since you have more places to look. But you should have tests for just those dependencies too. However, each test should be isolated from other tests.
- The more modern approach to isolating unit tests involves separating the MUT from its dependencies by replacing them with test doubles. This removes any influence on the MUT's behavior and focuses the test on just the MUT.

Naming unit tests

Some advocate for a standardized naming scheme for unit test methods, for example, `[MethodName]_[Scenario]_[Result]`, where the three parts are as follows:

1. `MethodName` is literally the name of the MUT. For example, `CheckOut` for a shopping cart.
2. `Scenario` is a brief description of the action being tested. For example, the cart has an item in it that is out of stock.
3. `Result` is the expected result. For example, the checkout succeeds or fails.

However, adopting a mechanical naming scheme like this is less useful than you might think because as technical people, developers already focus too much on implementation details and this naming scheme just emphasizes that.

> **Good practice:** I do not recommend that you prefix all your unit test names with `[MethodName]_`.

Instead, simple phrases in plain language are best. They provide more flexibility than a strict naming scheme. You should use phrases that would be understood by an end user or a business domain expert. Cryptic names that need to be decoded impose a cognitive load on even developers. Keep it simple!

Here are three examples of test names that use simple phrases in plain language:

- `Checkout_fails_when_item_is_out_of_stock`
- `User_receives_confirmation_email_after_successful_registration`
- `Login_is_blocked_after_three_failed_attempts`

> `Checkout`, `User`, and `Login`, are not method names.

These names clearly describe the test's purpose in a way that is easily understood by both technical and non-technical stakeholders.

> **Good practice:** Name your test methods as if you are describing the scenario to a non-programmer who is familiar with the business functionality required. To improve readability, add underscores between words.

Unit testing using xUnit

xUnit.net, often simply referred to as **xUnit**, is a popular unit testing framework for the .NET ecosystem. xUnit has been specifically designed to address some of the limitations found in older testing frameworks like NUnit and MSTest.

Even internal Microsoft teams avoid MSTest in favor of xUnit. For example, the ASP.NET Core team uses xUnit, as shown at the following link: `https://github.com/dotnet/aspnetcore/tree/main/src/Testing/src/xunit`.

> If you are familiar with other testing frameworks, then you can review summary comparison tables at the following link: `https://xunit.net/docs/comparisons`.

Several benefits of using xUnit are shown in the following list:

1. xUnit is open-source and has a strong community and active development team behind it. This makes it more likely that it will stay up to date with the latest .NET features and best practices. xUnit benefits from a large and active community, which means many tutorials, guides, and third-party extensions are available for it.
2. xUnit uses a more simplified and extensible approach compared to older frameworks. It encourages the use of custom test patterns and less reliance on setup and teardown methods, leading to cleaner test code.

3. Tests in xUnit are configured using .NET attributes, which makes the test code easy to read and understand. It uses `[Fact]` for standard test cases and `[Theory]` with `[InlineData]`, `[ClassData]`, or `[MemberData]` for parameterized tests, enabling data-driven testing. This makes it easier to cover many input scenarios with the same test method, enhancing test thoroughness while minimizing effort.
4. xUnit includes an assertion library that allows for a wide variety of assertions out of the box, making it easier to test a wide range of conditions without having to write custom test code. It can also be extended with popular assertion libraries like `FluentAssertions` that allow you to articulate test expectations with human-readable reasons.
5. By default, xUnit supports parallel test execution within the same test collection, which can significantly reduce the time it takes to run large test suites. This is particularly beneficial in continuous integration environments where speed is critical. However, if you run your tests in a memory-limited **Virtual Private Server (VPS)**, then that impacts how much data the server can handle at any given time and how many applications or processes it can run concurrently. In this scenario, you might want to disable parallel test execution. Memory-limited VPS instances are typically used as cheap testing environments.
6. xUnit offers precise control over the test lifecycle with setup and teardown commands through the use of the constructor and destructor patterns and the `IDisposable` interface, as well as with the `[BeforeAfterTestAttribute]` for more granular control.

As noted, xUnit utilizes a range of .NET attributes to define and control the behavior of tests within your test suite. These attributes are crucial for organizing tests, specifying test behaviors, and managing test data. Let's review them next.

Common xUnit attributes

The most common xUnit attributes with examples of usage and descriptions are shown in *Table 11.4*:

Attribute example	Description
`[Fact]` `public void TestAdding2and2()`	`[Fact]` declares a test method that does not take any parameters and is run once by the test runner.

`[Theory]`
`[...]`
`public void TestAdding(`
` double expected,`
` double number1,`
` double number2)`
	`[Theory]` declares a test method that has one or more parameters that are run multiple times with different data. It must be used in conjunction with data-providing attributes like `[InlineData]`, `[ClassData]`, or `[MemberData]`.

`[InlineData(4, 2, 2)]` `[InlineData(5, 2, 3)]`	`[InlineData]` supplies fixed values for parameters in the defined order for a MUT decorated with `[Theory]`.

`[ClassData(typeof(AddingNumbersData))]`	`[ClassData]` supplies enumerated values for parameters in the defined order for a MUT decorated with `[Theory]`. The class can implement `IEnumerable<object[]>`. To provide strongly typed data, the class must derive from `TheoryData`.
`[MemberData(nameof(GetTestData))]`	`[MemberData]` supplies enumerated values for parameters in the defined order for a MUT decorated with `[Theory]`. The method must be `static` and return `IEnumerable<object[]>`.
`[Trait("Feature", "Shopping Cart")]`	Allows adding metadata to tests, categorizing them for filtering during test runs.

Table 11.4: Common xUnit attributes

`[Fact]` and `[Theory]` both allow you to change the display name of the test shown in results and set a timeout as an integer in milliseconds, as shown in the following code:

```
[Fact(Timeout = 3000)] // Test will timeout after 3 seconds.
```

If you want to temporarily skip running a `[Fact]` or `[Theory]` test, you can just set the `Skip` parameter to a text reason for skipping it, as shown in the following code:

```
[Fact(Skip = "Skipping this test for now.")]
```

Now let's write some code to explore xUnit features.

Creating a SUT

Let's start by creating a class library with a class (SUT) and method (MUT) that needs testing:

1. Use your preferred code editor to add a new **Class Library** / `classlib` project named `BusinessLogic` to the `Chapter11` solution.
2. In the `BusinessLogic.csproj` project file, treat warnings as errors and statically and globally import the `Console` class.
3. Rename `Class1.cs` to `Calculator.cs`.
4. In `Calculator.cs`, define a class with a method to add two real numbers together, with a deliberate bug, as shown in the following code:

```
namespace Packt.Shared;

// System under test (SUT)
public class Calculator
{
  // Method under test (MUT)
  public double Add(double number1, double number2)
  {
    return number1 * number2; // Deliberate bug!
  }
}
```

5. Build the `BusinessLogic` project.
6. Use your preferred code editor to add a new **xUnit Test Project [C#]** / `xunit` project named `BusinessLogicUnitTests` to the `Chapter11` solution. For example, at the command prompt or terminal in the `Chapter11` folder, enter the following commands:

```
dotnet new xunit -o BusinessLogicUnitTests
dotnet sln add BusinessLogicUnitTests
```

7. In the `BusinessLogicUnitTests` project, add a project reference to the `BusinessLogic` project, as shown in the following markup:

```
<ItemGroup>
  <ProjectReference Include="..\BusinessLogic\BusinessLogic.csproj" />
</ItemGroup>
```

> The path for a project reference can use either forward / or back \ slashes because the paths are processed by the .NET SDK and changed if necessary for the current operating system.

8. Build the `BusinessLogicUnitTests` project.

Writing simple unit tests

A well-written unit test must have three parts, commonly known as AAA or triple-A, as shown in the following list:

- **Arrange**: This part will declare and instantiate variables for inputs, the expected output, and the SUT, usually meaning instantiating a type that's being tested.
- **Act**: This part will execute the unit that you are testing. In our case, that means calling the MUT of the SUT that we want to test. If you have multiple statements in your Act section, then you are likely writing an integration test rather than a unit test. You should refactor the test into separate tests for each action.
- **Assert**: This part will make one or more assertions about the output of the act section. An assertion is a belief that, if not true, indicates a failed test. For example, when adding 2 and 2, we would expect the result to be 4. If you have multiple acts, each with their own assertions, then you're writing an integration test.

> **Good practice:** Although we only have one MUT, it is good practice to create multiple tests with different parameter values passed to the MUT to make sure a variety of scenarios are tested.

Now, we will write some unit tests for the `Calculator` class:

1. Rename the file `UnitTest1.cs` to `CalculatorUnitTests.cs` and then open it. If you are using VS Code, then you will need to manually rename the class in the source code to `CalculatorUnitTests`. (Visual Studio prompts you to rename the class when you rename the file, so you won't need to do this manually.)
2. In `CalculatorUnitTests.cs`, import the `Packt.Shared` namespace, and then modify the `CalculatorUnitTests` class to have two test methods, one for adding 2 and 2 and another for adding 2 and 3, as shown in the following code:

```
using Packt.Shared; // To use Calculator.

namespace BusinessLogicUnitTests;

public class CalculatorUnitTests
{
  [Fact]
  public void TestAdding2And2()
  {
    // Arrange: Set up the inputs, output, and the SUT.
    double number1 = 2;
    double number2 = 2;
    double expected = 4;
    Calculator sut = new();

    // Act: Execute the MUT.
    double actual = sut.Add(number1, number2);

    // Assert: Make assertions to compare expected to actual results.
    Assert.Equal(expected, actual);
  }

  [Fact]
  public void TestAdding2And3()
  {
    // Arrange: Set up the inputs, output, and the SUT.
    double number1 = 2;
    double number2 = 3;
    double expected = 5;
    Calculator sut = new();

    // Act: Execute the MUT.
```

```
        double actual = sut.Add(number1, number2);

        // Assert: Make assertions to compare expected to actual results.
        Assert.Equal(expected, actual);
    }
}
```

Visual Studio still uses an older project item template that uses a nested namespace. The preceding code shows the modern project item template used by `dotnet new` and JetBrains Rider that uses a file-scoped namespace.

> **Good practice:** Name the variable for the SUT as `sut` to make it clearly different from any dependencies. Consider using `#region` to define the three sections and make them collapsable. At a minimum, use blank lines between the three sections even if you do not add comments labeled Arrange, Act, and Assert. If you are consistent with the structure of your tests, then just a blank line should be enough to make them nicely readable.

3. Build the `BusinessLogicUnitTests` project.
4. Run the unit test and see the results:
    - If you are using Visual Studio, navigate to **Test | Run All Tests**, and then navigate to **Test | Test Explorer**. In **Test Explorer**, expand the test tree and note that the results indicate that two tests ran, one test failed, and one test passed. In the `BusinessLogic` project, in the `Calculator` class, note the information about the **1/2 passing** tests, as shown in *Figure 11.1*:

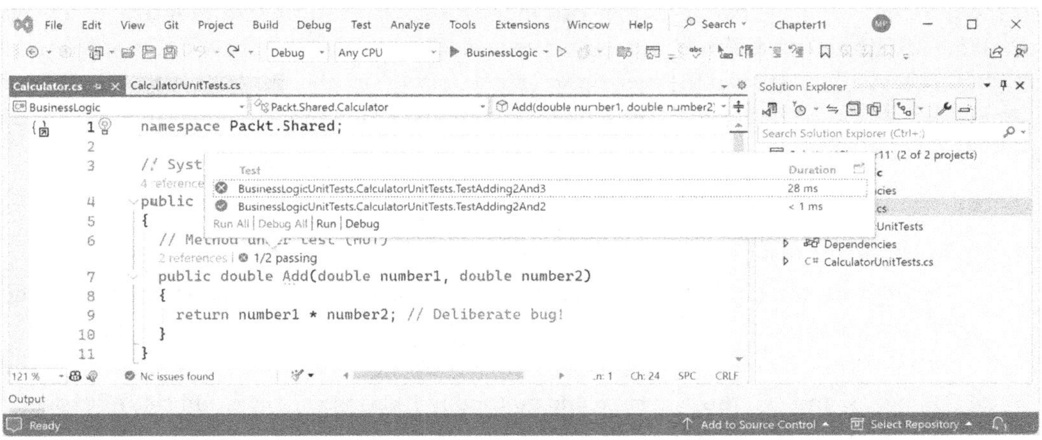

Figure 11.1: Number of passing and total tests for a MUT

- If you are using VS Code, navigate to **View | Testing**. Note the **TESTING** window has a mini toolbar with buttons to **Refresh Tests**, **Run Tests**, **Debug Tests**, and so on. Hover your mouse pointer over **CalculatorUnitTests** and then click the **Run Tests** button (black triangle icon) defined in that class. Click the **TEST RESULTS** tab and note that the results indicate that two tests ran, one test failed, and one test passed.
- If you are using the CLI, at the command prompt or terminal, in the `Chapter11` folder, run the unit test project, as shown in the following command: `dotnet test`. Note the result as shown in the following output:

```
Restore complete (0.5s)
  BusinessLogic succeeded (0.2s) → BusinessLogic\bin\Debug\net10.0\
BusinessLogic.dll
  BusinessLogicUnitTests succeeded (0.1s) → BusinessLogicUnitTests\bin\Debug\
net10.0\BusinessLogicUnitTests.dll
  BusinessLogicUnitTests failed with errors (0.0s)
    C:\tools-skills-net10\Chapter11\BusinessLogicUnitTests\CalculatorUnitTests.
cs(36): error VSTEST1: (BusinessLogicUnitTests.CalculatorUnitTests.
TestAdding2And3) BusinessLogicUnitTests.CalculatorUnitTests.TestAdding2And3()
Assert.Equal() Failure: Values differ  Expected: 5  Actual:   6 [C:\tools-
skills-net10\Chapter11\BusinessLogicUnitTests\BusinessLogicUnitTests.csproj]
Build failed with errors in 1.7s
```

At this point, we could fix the bug, but we want to leave it in so we can look at some more efficient ways to write tests by using parameters.

Test methods with parameters

At the moment, we have two tests that run independently, even though they are effectively testing the same MUT but with different parameter values. When there are only two sets of parameters, this might be acceptable, or even the best option since it is so simple. But once we have more sets of parameters, it would be better to write a single test method and pass those parameter values in using different techniques.

There are multiple ways to test methods with parameter values, including:

- Decorate the test method with `[InlineData]` and supply a `params` array of objects.
- Decorate the test method with `[ClassData]` and reference a class that represents an `IEnumerable` of arrays of objects.
- Decorate the test method with `[ClassData]`, reference a class that derives from `TheoryData<T1, T2, ...>`, and call the inherited `Add` method in its constructor to add sets of expected parameters and return values.
- Decorate the test method with `[MethodData]` and reference a method that returns an `IEnumerable` of arrays of objects.

Now let's see these four ways in detail.

Testing theory methods using InlineData

Let's explore some ways of doing this:

1. In the `BusinessLogicUnitTests` project, in `CalculatorUnitTests.cs`, add statements to define a test method with parameters, as shown in the following code:

```
[Theory]
[InlineData(4, 2, 2)]
[InlineData(5, 2, 3)]
public void TestAdding(double expected,
  double number1, double number2)
{
  // Arrange: Set up the SUT.
  Calculator sut = new();

  // Act: Execute the MUT.
  double actual = sut.Add(number1, number2);

  // Assert: Make assertions to compare expected to actual results.
  Assert.Equal(expected, actual);
}
```

> `[InlineData]` must be passed a `params` array of objects. This means any comma-separated literals or variables of any type can be passed and they will be converted to an array of objects: `System.Object[]`.

2. Build the `BusinessLogicUnitTests` project.

3. Run the unit test and see the results. For example, if you are using Visual Studio, then **Test Explorer** will show the `TestAdding` test method with two parameter sets passed, one that passes and one that fails, as shown in *Figure 11.2*:

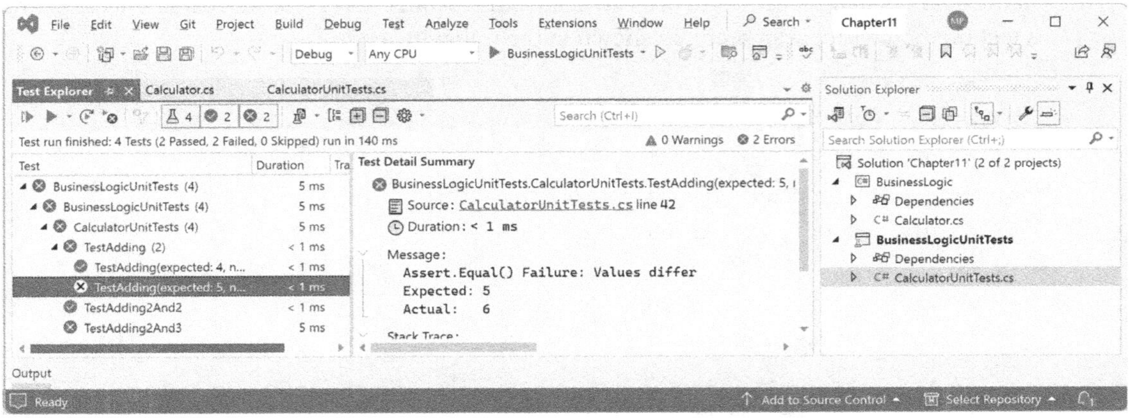

Figure 11.2: Test method with parameters showing one failed run

Testing theory methods using ClassData

Now let's use a class to supply the parameter values:

1. In the `BusinessLogicUnitTests` project, add a new class named `AddingNumbersData.cs`.
2. In `AddingNumbersData.cs`, define a class that implements `IEnumerable<object[]>`, meaning a class that returns a sequence of object arrays, and return two object arrays that represent the parameter sets that must be passed to the test method, as shown in the following code:

```
using System.Collections; // To use IEnumerable<T>.

namespace BusinessLogicUnitTests;

internal class AddingNumbersData : IEnumerable<object[]>
{
  public IEnumerator<object[]> GetEnumerator()
  {
    // Test adding 2 and 2 to give 4.
    yield return new object[] { 4, 2, 2 };

    // Test adding 2 and 3 to give 5.
    yield return new object[] { 5, 2, 3 };
  }

  // Non-generic implementation calls generic implementation.
  IEnumerator IEnumerable.GetEnumerator() => GetEnumerator();
}
```

Good practice: Instead of hardcoding the two (or more) sets of parameter values using `yield return`, it would be better to fetch the parameter sets from a file or database and then cache them because then the parameter values can be changed or added to without needing to hardcode them in source code and needing to recompile the test project every time they change.

3. In `CalculatorUnitTests.cs`, comment out the two `[InlineData]` attributes, and then add a `[ClassData]` attribute that references the class that we just created, as shown highlighted in the following code:

```
[Theory]
// [InlineData(4, 2, 2)]
// [InlineData(5, 2, 3)]
[ClassData(typeof(AddingNumbersData))]
public void TestAdding(double expected,
  double number1, double number2)
```

4. Build the `BusinessLogicUnitTests` project.
5. Run the unit test and see the results, which should be like earlier with `InlineData`.

Testing theory methods using strongly typed ClassData

Now let's use a strongly typed class to supply the parameter values:

1. In the `BusinessLogicUnitTests` project, add a new class named `AddingNumbersDataTyped.cs`.
2. In `AddingNumbersDataTyped.cs`, define a class that inherits from `TheoryData<T1, T2, T3>`, where `T1` is the expected value and `T2` and `T3` are the input values. Then call the inherited `Add` method to add two parameter sets that must be passed to the test method, as shown in the following code:

```
namespace BusinessLogicUnitTests;

internal class AddingNumbersDataTyped : TheoryData<double, double,
double>
{
  public AddingNumbersDataTyped()
  {
    // Test adding 2 and 2 to give 4.
    Add(4, 2, 2);

    // Test adding 2 and 3 to give 5.
    Add(5, 2, 3);
  }
}
```

The order of the types has to match the order of the parameters in the test method. Our test method has the expected value first and then the two inputs. You could order them with the expected value last instead, so `T1` and `T2` are the types of the two inputs, and `T3` is the type of the expected result.

3. In `CalculatorUnitTests.cs`, comment out the previous `[ClassData]` attribute and add a new one that references the class that we just created, as shown highlighted in the following code:

```
[Theory]
// [InlineData(4, 2, 2)]
// [InlineData(5, 2, 3)]
// [ClassData(typeof(AddingNumbersData))]
[ClassData(typeof(AddingNumbersDataTyped))]
public void TestAdding(double expected,
  double number1, double number2)
```

4. Build the `BusinessLogicUnitTests` project.
5. Run the unit test and see the results, which should be like earlier with `ClassData`.

Testing theory methods using MethodData

Now let's use a method to supply the parameter values:

1. In `CalculatorUnitTests.cs`, add a new `static` method that returns `IEnumerable<object[]>`, meaning it returns a sequence of object arrays, and return two object arrays that represent the parameter sets that must be passed to the test method, as shown highlighted in the following code:

```
public static IEnumerable<object[]> GetTestData()
{
  // Test adding 2 and 2 to give 4.
  yield return new object[] { 4, 2, 2 };

  // Test adding 2 and 3 to give 5.
  yield return new object[] { 5, 2, 3 };
}
```

The method must be static and return `IEnumerable<object[]>`. Instead of `yield return`, you could achieve this by returning a collection like `List<object[]>` or an array of objects. For example, you could use the C# 12 collection syntax, as shown in the following code: `return [ [4, 2, 2], [5, 2, 3] ];`

2. In `CalculatorUnitTests.cs`, comment out the `[ClassData]` attribute and then add a `[MemberData]` attribute that references the method that we just created, as shown highlighted in the following code:

```
[Theory]
// [InlineData(4, 2, 2)]
// [InlineData(5, 2, 3)]
// [ClassData(typeof(AddingNumbersData))]
[MemberData(memberName: nameof(GetTestData))]
public void TestAdding(double expected,
  double number1, double number2)
```

3. Build the `BusinessLogicUnitTests` project.
4. Run the unit test and see the results, which should be like earlier with `ClassData`.

Positive and negative test results

Using parameterized tests will significantly reduce the number of statements of code that you need to write, but they can make it harder to spot important differences between tests.

Some tests look for positive expected results, for example, a customer successfully checking out their shopping cart. Other tests look for negative expected results, for example, a customer failing to check out because there aren't enough units in stock. Even though they could all be tested in the same test methods with different parameters, you might choose to split positive and negative expected results into separate test methods.

Good practice: Keep positive and negative test results separated into different test methods with appropriate sets of parameters. If a particular scenario is complex and cannot be easily understood by seeing the raw parameter values, then create a separate `[Fact]` test method just for that scenario.

Now let's review some warning signs to look out for in unit tests and then how to run extra code to set up and tear down tests.

Red flags in unit tests

Here are some red flags (warning signs) to watch out for when writing your unit tests:

- If you are writing `if` or `switch` statements, then this is an anti-pattern because a unit test should not have branching. You are probably trying to test too many things within one test, and you should split the branches out into multiple separate tests.
- The Arrange section is usually the largest of the three, often with more statements than Act and Assert combined. If it gets too unmanageable, then create private methods to call within the test.

- The Act section should usually be a single statement. If the test requires you to make multiple method calls to test a unit of behavior, then it indicates a poor public API design. For example, imagine a public API that requires a call to a `ProcessOrder` method and then a `ReduceInventory` method when a product is bought on a commerce website. You might want to redesign the methods in the SUT. This is a good example of a benefit of TDD because it helps you refactor your public API and service designs before they become too rigid to change.
- The Assert section can have multiple assertions because a unit of behavior can have multiple outputs and they should all be evaluated using assertions. If you need to check multiple outputs, like a `bool`, an `int`, and a `string`, then consider redesigning the API to return a `record` type that combines those three values so that a single assertion can be made.

Seeing output during test execution

xUnit intentionally does not show output from `Console.WriteLine` during test execution because it runs tests in parallel by default, and console output could become jumbled. To write output in xUnit tests, you should use `ITestOutputHelper`, which is injected into your test class's constructor. This approach ensures that output is associated with the specific test that generated it.

A developer might want to write output during test execution for several reasons:

- **Debugging**: Output during test execution can help pinpoint where a test is failing. By printing the state of variables, the flow of execution, or other relevant details, a developer can better understand what is going wrong.
- **Intermediate results**: Printing intermediate results can help understand how data is being manipulated throughout the test, which can be crucial for debugging and verifying the correctness of the code under test.
- **Validation of assumptions**: Tests often involve certain assumptions about the state of the system or data. Output can be used to verify that these assumptions hold true during test execution.
- **Long-running tests**: For long-running tests, especially those involving performance testing, integration testing, or end-to-end testing, output can serve as a progress indicator, showing that the test is running and providing checkpoints. In environments where tests take considerable time to complete, having real-time feedback can help developers understand the current status and make decisions if intervention is needed.
- **Complex setup and teardown**: When tests involve complex setup and teardown processes, output can confirm that these processes are being executed correctly. This is especially important when dealing with external systems, databases, or configurations. Output can also help ensure that resources are being properly allocated and released, which is critical in avoiding resource leaks and ensuring test reliability.
- **Documentation and reporting**: Output can serve as a form of documentation, showing the steps taken during the test. This can be useful for audits, compliance, or just for maintaining a clear record of what the test does. Output can be captured and included in test reports, providing additional context that can be valuable for stakeholders who review the test results.

- **Understanding test behavior**: Sometimes output can help clarify what the test is doing and why. This can be particularly helpful for other developers who are reviewing the tests. For new developers or those unfamiliar with the codebase, output during test execution can serve as an educational tool, showing how the system behaves under different conditions and helping them understand the testing framework and methodologies used.

You will see an example of writing output during test execution in the next section.

Set up and tear down

Before a test can run, you sometimes need to execute some statements to set up some state or data to maintain a known start condition. And at the end of the test(s), you might need to clean things up.

This is a more common requirement of integration tests than unit tests because they tend to have more external dependencies, like files, services, and databases, but some unit tests will need it, so I introduce it in this chapter and cover it in more detail in *Chapter 12, Integration and Security Testing*.

If you need to execute statements for every test, you can put them in a constructor for the unit test class. If you need to clean up, implement `IDisposable` and put those statements in the `Dispose` method.

Let's see how with the calculator unit tests class:

1. In `CalculatorUnitTests.cs`, import the namespace for writing to test output, as shown in the following code:

   ```
   using Xunit.Abstractions; // To use ITestOutputHelper.
   ```

2. Add a constructor to set private fields for the SUT and xUnit's mechanism for writing test output, implement `IDisposable`, and output messages to show when the constructor, the `Dispose` method, and tests are executing, as shown highlighted in the following partial code:

   ```
   public class CalculatorUnitTests : IDisposable
   {
     private readonly Calculator _sut;
     private readonly ITestOutputHelper _output;

     public CalculatorUnitTests(ITestOutputHelper output)
     {
       _sut = new();
       _output = output;
       _output.WriteLine("Constructor runs before each test.");
     }

     [Fact]
     public void TestAdding2And2()
     {
       _output.WriteLine($"Running {nameof(TestAdding2And2)}.");
   ```

```
    ...
  }

  [Fact]
  public void TestAdding2And3()
  {
    _output.WriteLine($"Running {nameof(TestAdding2And3)}.");
    ...
  }

  [Theory]
  // [InlineData(4, 2, 2)]
  // [InlineData(5, 2, 3)]
  // [ClassData(typeof(AddingNumbersData))]
  [MemberData(memberName: nameof(GetTestData))]
  public void TestAdding(double expected,
    double number1, double number2)
  {
    _output.WriteLine($"Running {nameof(TestAdding)}.");
    _output.WriteLine($"  {nameof(number1)}: {number1}");
    _output.WriteLine($"  {nameof(number2)}: {number2}");
    _output.WriteLine($"  {nameof(expected)}: {expected}");
    ...
  }
  ...
  public void Dispose()
  {
    // Cleanup the _sut if necessary.
    _output.WriteLine("Dispose runs after each test.");
  }
}
```

3. In each test method, switch to use `_sut` instead of `sut` and comment out the statements to create an instance of `Calculator`.
4. Re-run the tests. If you are using the CLI, at the command prompt or terminal, enter the following command to see the extra test output:

```
dotnet test --logger "console;verbosity=detailed"
```

5. Note the tests' behavior remains the same, except that now additional output appears in **Test Detail Summary** in the **Standard Output** section of Visual Studio, as shown in *Figure 11.3*:

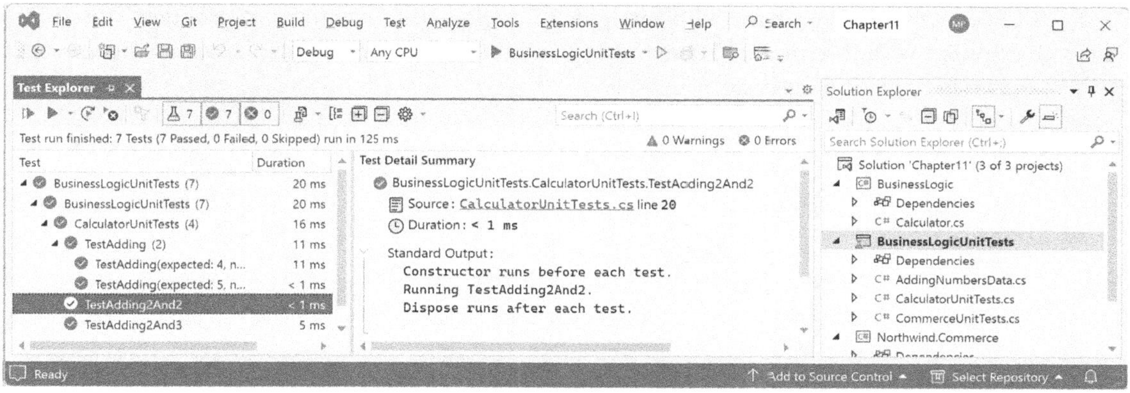

Figure 11.3: Standard output appearing in Test Detail Summary

> To see standard output written using `ITestOutputHelper` in `dotnet test`, use the command-line switch `--logger "console;verbosity=detailed"`.

Although it can be good practice to move shared code to a single location like the constructor, that does have some issues:

- When you read each test, you must read the constructor to see how the SUT and dependencies are being initialized that are being used in the test.
- The constructor initializes member variables for all tests, which makes the constructor fragile and violates the single responsibility pattern.

A better practice would be that each test must do the initialization for what it needs to run. This makes it easy to read each test as a single entity. Also, it becomes clearer when some tests are more complicated than others. It also makes tests isolated from each other. You may decide to never use common setup and teardown methods.

Controlling test fixtures

A common mistake is to assume that you should set test fixtures in the constructor. You can end up with test methods that do not have any statements for the arrange phase because it is all done in the constructor. This has the benefit of reducing the total number of statements of code, but this technique adds coupling between the tests and reduces readability.

Let's create a practical example and then improve it:

1. Use your preferred code editor to add a new **Class Library** / `classlib` project named `Northwind.Commerce` to the `Chapter11` solution.

2. In the `Northwind.Commerce.csproj` project file, treat warnings as errors.
3. Rename `Class1.cs` to `Store.cs`.
4. In `Store.cs`, define a class with methods to manage the inventory of products stored in a dictionary with the product ID as the key and the number of units in stock as the value, as shown in the following code:

```
namespace Northwind.Commerce;

public class Store
{
  // Key is ProductId, Value is Quantity.
  public Dictionary<int, int> Inventory { get; } = new();

  public void AddInventory(int productId, int quantity)
  {
    // Add the specified quantity of the specified product.
    if (Inventory.ContainsKey(productId))
      Inventory[productId] += quantity;
    else
      Inventory.Add(productId, quantity);
  }

  public bool RemoveInventory(int productId, int quantity)
  {
    if (Inventory[productId] >= quantity)
    {
      // Remove the specified quantity of the specified product.
      Inventory[productId] -= quantity;
      return true;
    }
    return false;
  }
}
```

5. Add a new class file named `Cart.cs`.
6. In `Cart.cs`, define a class to track product items that a customer has added to their shopping cart and will hopefully check out and purchase from our store later, as shown in the following code:

```
namespace Northwind.Commerce;

public class Cart
{
```

```
    private readonly Store _store;

    public Cart(Store store)
    {
      _store = store;
    }

    // Key is ProductId, Value is Quantity.
    public Dictionary<int, int> Items { get; } = new();

    public void AddItems(int productId, int quantity)
    {
      // Add the specified quantity of the specified product.
      if (Items.ContainsKey(productId))
        Items[productId] += quantity;
      else
        Items.Add(productId, quantity);
    }

    public void RemoveItems(int productId, int quantity)
    {
      // Remove the specified quantity of the specified product.
      Items[productId] -= quantity;
    }

    public bool Checkout()
    {
      // Process the cart and charge the customer.
      foreach (var item in Items)
      {
        if (!_store.RemoveInventory(item.Key, item.Value))
        {
          // Unable to remove the item from the inventory.
          return false;
        }
      }
      return true;
    }
  }
```

7. Build the `Northwind.Commerce` project.
8. In the `BusinessLogicUnitTests` project, add a project reference to the `Northwind.Commerce` class library, as shown highlighted in the following markup:

```
<ItemGroup>
  <ProjectReference Include="..\BusinessLogic\BusinessLogic.csproj" />
  <ProjectReference Include=
    "..\Northwind.Commerce\Northwind.Commerce.csproj" />
</ItemGroup>
```

9. In the `BusinessLogicUnitTests` project, add a new class file named `CommerceUnitTests.cs`.
10. In `CommerceUnitTests.cs`, define a class with tests that uses a factory method instead of a constructor to set up text fixtures like the store, as shown in the following code:

```
using Northwind.Commerce; // To use Store, Cart.

namespace BusinessLogicUnitTests;

public class CommerceUnitTests
{
  // Factory method to simplify setting up test fixtures.
  private Store CreateStore(int productId, int initialInventory)
  {
    Store store = new();
    store.AddInventory(productId, initialInventory);
    return store;
  }

  [Fact]
  public void Checkout_ShouldReduceInventoryLevel()
  {
    #region Arrange
    int productId = 1;
    int initialInventory = 10;
    Store store = CreateStore(productId, initialInventory);
    Cart sut = new(store);
    int quantityToBuy = 5;
    #endregion

    #region Act
    sut.AddItems(productId, quantityToBuy);
    bool success = sut.Checkout();
```

```
    #endregion

    #region Assert
    Assert.True(success);
    int updatedInventory = store.Inventory[productId];
    Assert.Equal(initialInventory - quantityToBuy, updatedInventory);
    #endregion
  }

  [Fact]
  public void Checkout_ShouldFailWhenLowInventory()
  {
    // Arrange
    int productId = 1;
    int initialInventory = 10;
    Store store = CreateStore(productId, initialInventory);
    Cart sut = new(store);
    int quantityToBuy = 15;

    // Act
    sut.AddItems(productId, quantityToBuy);
    bool success = sut.Checkout();

    // Assert
    Assert.False(success);
    int updatedInventory = store.Inventory[productId];
    Assert.Equal(initialInventory, updatedInventory);
  }
}
```

To allow you to explore ways of documenting your test methods, in the preceding code, we used simple comments for one test method and `#region` collapsable blocks for the other.

11. Run the tests and note they all pass.

Good practice: A modification of one test (or the constructor) should not affect other tests. Instead of declaring private fields to store shared state like the SUT and fixtures like `Store`, and setting them up in the constructor, define factory methods that simplify the Arrange code but still retain the context of what values are used to set up the dependencies.

Mocking in tests

Mocking in unit tests is a technique used to isolate the unit of code being tested by replacing its dependencies with controlled, pre-configured substitutes known as "mocks." This allows the developer to focus on testing the specific functionality of the unit without interference from its dependencies.

The key concepts of mocking include the following:

- **Isolation**: The primary purpose of mocking is to isolate the unit of code under test. This isolation ensures that the test is focused only on the behavior of the unit itself, rather than on the behavior of its dependencies. By using mocks, you create a controlled environment where you can precisely control the inputs and outputs of the dependencies.
- **Substitutes for real objects**: These include:
    - **Mocks**, which are stand-ins for the real objects that the unit under test interacts with. They mimic the behavior of real objects but are configured to return specific values or perform specific actions.
    - **Fakes**, which are simpler implementations of interfaces or classes used in the test environment. Unlike mocks, they provide working implementations but may not be as configurable or detailed.
    - **Stubs**, which provide predefined responses to specific calls, without implementing the entire behavior of the dependency. They are typically used for providing fixed inputs to the unit under test.
    - **Spies**, which are like mocks but also record information about how they were called, which can be useful for verifying interactions.
    - **Dummies**, which are objects passed around but never actually used. They are typically used to fill parameter lists.
- **Verification of interactions**: Mocks can be set up with expectations about how they should be used, such as which methods should be called, how many times they should be called, and with what arguments. After the test runs, the mock framework verifies whether these expectations were met. This helps ensure that the unit under test interacts with its dependencies as expected.

There are many benefits of mocking, such as:

- **Isolation and focus**: By isolating the unit under test from its dependencies, you can focus on testing its specific behavior without interference.
- **Control over your test environment**: Mocks allow you to simulate various scenarios by controlling the inputs and outputs of the dependencies.
- **Improved test reliability**: By removing the dependencies, you reduce the chance of flaky tests caused by external factors such as network issues or database states.
- **Faster tests**: Mocking often leads to faster tests since mocks usually run in-memory and do not involve time-consuming operations like database access or network communication.
- **Better coverage**: Mocks allow you to simulate edge cases and error conditions that might be difficult or impossible to reproduce with real dependencies.

A use case for mocking is mocking an interface to test a service method that depends on a repository layer without hitting the actual database. Another is creating a substitute for a logging service to verify that error logging occurs for a given input without actually writing to a log file.

Libraries for mocking

The choice of mocking framework often comes down to personal or team preference, the specific needs of the project, and the existing technological stack. **Moq**, **NSubstitute**, and **FakeItEasy** each offer a modern, developer-friendly approach to mocking, with active communities and ongoing development, making them excellent choices for most .NET projects today. When selecting a mocking framework, consider experimenting with a few to see which one best fits your development style and project requirements.

Moq

Moq is widely regarded as one of the easiest-to-use mocking libraries for .NET. It's particularly known for its straightforward syntax and ability to quickly set up mocks without needing to manage complex configurations or setup. Moq supports a wide range of features, including the ability to mock interfaces, abstract classes, and concrete classes, as well setting up returns, verifying method calls, and handling properties. It uses lambda expressions for setting up mocks in a strongly typed manner, which helps with refactoring and code readability.

> **Warning!** Moq developer kzu courted controversy by adding a component known as **SponsorLink** in version 4.20.0 on August 7, 2023. You can read the pull request at the following link: `https://github.com/devlooped/moq/pull/1363`. Moq "now ships with a closed-source obfuscated dependency that scrapes your Git email and phones it home" and was considered by many developers to be unacceptable, as you can read at the following link: `https://www.reddit.com/r/programming/comments/15m2q0o/moq_a_net_mocking_library_now_ships_with_a/`. Four days later, kzu removed SponsorLink from Moq version 4.20.69 but the damage had already been done. Many organizations have switched to alternatives like NSubstitute, as you can read at the following link: `https://www.reddit.com/r/dotnet/comments/173ddyk/now_that_the_controversy_from_moqs_dependencies/`.

NSubstitute

NSubstitute is designed with a focus on simplicity and ease of use, offering a concise API that can reduce the amount of mock-related code you need to write. It's a great choice for developers who prioritize readability and efficiency. Like Moq, NSubstitute allows for mocking interfaces and classes. It also supports argument matching and checking calls to specific methods and has a unique feature for automatically creating substitute instances for dependencies when constructing an object.

> You can discover more about NSubstitute at the following link: `https://github.com/nsubstitute/NSubstitute`.

FakeItEasy

FakeItEasy aims to be the most user-friendly mocking library for .NET, with a syntax that's designed to be easy to read and write. It's a good choice for teams looking for a balance between functionality and simplicity. It allows for easy creation of fake objects for interfaces and classes, with straightforward methods for configuring behavior, returns, and exceptions. FakeItEasy also supports advanced scenarios like calls to specific methods with certain arguments.

You can discover more about FakeItEasy at the following link: `https://fakeiteasy.github.io/`.

Using NSubstitute to create test doubles

NSubstitute is designed to make it easy to create test doubles like mocks, stubs, and so on for unit testing. This allows you to test components in isolation from their dependencies.

To create a mock, call the `Substitute.For<T>` method, where `T` is the interface or class that you need to mock, as shown in the following code:

```
ICalculator calc = Substitute.For<ICalculator>();
```

You can pass parameters if the class has a constructor, as shown in the following code:

```
var substitute = Substitute.For<ClassWithConstructor>(5, "Error");
```

The `substitute` object will not just have the members of the type it substitutes for, like `Add` for `ICalculator`. It will also have extension methods used to configure how the substitute should work, as shown in *Table 11.5*:

Extension method	Description
`Returns`	To set a return value for a method call on a substitute, call the method as normal, then follow it with a call to the `Returns()` extension method. For example: `calc.Add(2, 3).Returns(5)`. Instead of specifying a literal value to return, you can execute any lambda block, for example, to throw an exception.
`Received`	To check that a method has been called on a substitute, call the `Received()` extension method, followed by the call being checked. For example: `calc.Received().Add()`.

Table 11.5: NSubstitute extension methods

You can match arguments using `Args.Any<T>`. For example, when adding any integer to `5`, you could specify to return `7`, as shown in the following code:

```
calc.Add(Arg.Any<int>(), 5).Returns(7);
```

You can match specific arguments using `Args.Is<T>`. For example, when adding any integer greater than `3` to `5`, you could specify to return `9`, as shown in the following code:

```
calc.Add(Arg.Is<int>(x => x > 3), 5).Returns(9);
```

You can throw exceptions, as shown in the following code:

```
calc.Add(-1, -1).Returns(x => { throw new Exception(); });
```

Mocking with NSubstitute example

Let's explore mocking with NSubstitute:

1. In the `BusinessLogic` project, add a new interface file named `IEmailSender.cs`.
2. In `IEmailSender.cs`, define an interface for sending emails, as shown in the following code:

```
namespace Packt.Shared;

public interface IEmailSender
{
  bool SendEmail(string to, string subject, string body);
}
```

3. In the `BusinessLogic` project, add a new class file named `UserService.cs`.
4. In `UserService.cs`, define a class for creating a user that sends an email as part of its process, as shown in the following code:

```
namespace Packt.Shared;

public class UserService
{
  private readonly IEmailSender _emailSender;

  public UserService(IEmailSender emailSender)
  {
    _emailSender = emailSender;
  }

  public bool CreateUser(string email, string password)
  {
    // Create user.
    bool successfulUserCreation = true;

    // Send email to user.
    bool successfulEmailSend = _emailSender.SendEmail(
```

```
      to: email,
      subject: "Welcome!",
      body: "Your account is created.");

    return successfulEmailSend && successfulUserCreation;
  }
}
```

5. Build the `BusinessLogic` project.
6. In the `BusinessLogicUnitTests` project, add a package reference for `NSubstitute`, as shown in the following markup:

```
<PackageReference Include="NSubstitute"  />
```

7. Build the `BusinessLogicUnitTests` project to restore packages.
8. In the `BusinessLogicUnitTests` project, add a new class file named `EmailSenderUnitTests.cs`.
9. In `EmailSenderUnitTests.cs`, define a class with a test method that uses NSubstitute to create a mock of the `IEmailSender` interface, as shown in the following code:

```
using NSubstitute; // To use Substitute.
using Packt.Shared; // To use IEmailSender.
using Xunit.Abstractions; // To use ITestOutputHelper.

namespace BusinessLogicUnitTests;

public class EmailSenderUnitTests
{
  private readonly ITestOutputHelper _output;

  public EmailSenderUnitTests(ITestOutputHelper output)
  {
    _output = output;
  }

  [Fact]
  public void SendEmailTest()
  {
    #region Arrange
    IEmailSender emailSender = Substitute.For<IEmailSender>();

    emailSender.SendEmail(
      to: Arg.Any<string>(),
      subject: Arg.Any<string>(),
```

```
        body: Arg.Any<string>())
        .Returns(true);

      emailSender.When(x => x.SendEmail(
          to: Arg.Is<string>(s => s.EndsWith("example.com")),
          subject: Arg.Any<string>(),
          body: Arg.Any<string>()))
        .Do(x => _output.WriteLine("Email sent to example domain."));

      UserService sut = new(emailSender);
      #endregion

      #region Act
      bool result = sut.CreateUser("user@example.com", "password");
      #endregion

      #region Assert
      Assert.True(result);

      emailSender.Received(requiredNumberOfCalls: 1)
        .SendEmail(to: "user@example.com",
          subject: Arg.Any<string>(), body: Arg.Any<string>());
      #endregion
    }
  }
```

Note the following about the code for the test method:

- `Substitute.For<IEmailSender>()` creates a mock object for the `IEmailSender` interface.
- The `Returns` method is used to specify the return value when the `SendEmail` method is called with any arguments.
- The `When` and `Do` methods are used to specify an action that executes only when the email is sent to an address in the `example.com` domain, and if so, a message is written to the test output.
- The `Received` method checks that `SendEmail` was called exactly once with the expected arguments.

10. Run the test and note that it succeeds.

Making fluent assertions in unit testing

FluentAssertions is a set of extension methods that make writing and reading the code in unit tests and the error messages of failing tests more like a natural human language like English.

It works with most unit testing frameworks, including xUnit. When you add a package reference for a test framework, FluentAssertions will automatically find the package and use it to throw exceptions.

After importing the `FluentAssertions` namespace, call the `Should()` extension method on a variable and then one of the hundreds of other extension methods to make assertions in a human-readable way. You can chain multiple assertions using the `And()` extension method or have separate statements, each calling `Should()`.

Warning! Since version `8.0.0`, released on January 14, 2025, there has been a license change. Here's a statement from the project owner, `dennisdoomen`: "v7 will remain free indefinitely and will still receive critical fixes. v8 will only require a license when you use it in non-commercial projects." You can read more at the following links:

- `https://fluentassertions.com/releases/#800`
- `https://github.com/fluentassertions/fluentassertions/pull/2943`
- `https://github.com/fluentassertions/fluentassertions/pull/2943#issuecomment-2590187813`
- `https://github.com/fluentassertions/fluentassertions/pull/2943#issuecomment-2590286302`

Making assertions about strings

Let's start by making assertions about a single `string` value:

1. Use your preferred code editor to add a new **xUnit Test Project** / `xunit` named `FluentTests` to a `Chapter11` solution.
2. In the `FluentTests` project, add a package reference to `FluentAssertions`, as highlighted in the following markup:

```
<ItemGroup>
  <PackageReference Include="FluentAssertions" />
  <PackageReference Include="coverlet.collector" />
```

To avoid a commercial license, you should use a package version 7.2 or higher but less than 8.0. To do this, in `Directory.Packages.prop` I used the following entry:

```
<PackageVersion Include="FluentAssertions" Version="[7.2.0,8.0.0)"
/>
```

Alternatively, there is a v7-forked repo named AwesomeAssertions. You should be able to replace the package reference and everything will continue to work as before: `https://www.nuget.org/packages/AwesomeAssertions`.

3. Build the `FluentTests` project.
4. Rename `UnitTest1.cs` to `FluentExamples.cs`.

5. In `FluentExamples.cs`, import the namespace to make the `FluentAssertions` extension methods available and write a test method for a `string` value, as shown in the following code:

```
using FluentAssertions; // To use its extension methods.

namespace FluentTests;

public class FluentExamples
{
  [Fact]
  public void TestString()
  {
    string city = "London";
    string expectedCity = "London";

    city.Should().StartWith("Lo")
      .And.EndWith("on")
      .And.Contain("do")
      .And.HaveLength(6);

     city.Should().NotBeNull()
      .And.Be("London")
      .And.BeSameAs(expectedCity)
      .And.BeOfType<string>();

    city.Length.Should().Be(6);
  }
}
```

6. Run the test:
   - In Visual Studio, navigate to **Test** | **Run All Tests**.
   - In VS Code, in **Terminal**, enter `dotnet test`.
7. Note the test passes.
8. In the `TestString` method, for the `city` variable, delete the last `n` in `London`.
9. Run the test and note it fails, as shown in the following output:

```
Expected city "Londo" to end with "on".
```

10. Add the `n` back in `London`.
11. Run the test again to confirm the fix.

Making assertions about collections and arrays

Now let's continue by making assertions about collections and arrays:

1. In `FluentExamples.cs`, add a test method to explore collection assertions, as shown in the following code:

```
[Fact]
public void TestCollections()
{
  string[] names = { "Alice", "Bob", "Charlie" };

  names.Should().HaveCountLessThan(4,
    "because the maximum items should be 3 or fewer");

  names.Should().OnlyContain(name => name.Length <= 6);
}
```

2. Run the tests and note the collections test fails, as shown in the following output:

```
Expected names to contain only items matching (name.Length <= 6), but
{"Charlie"} do(es) not match.
```

3. Change `Charlie` to `Charly`.
4. Run the tests and note they succeed.

Making assertions about dates and times

Let's make assertions about date and time values:

1. In `FluentExamples.cs`, import the namespace for adding more extension methods for named months and other useful date/time-related functionality, as shown in the following code:

```
using FluentAssertions.Extensions; // To use February and so on.
```

2. Add a test method to explore date/time assertions, as shown in the following code:

```
[Fact]
public void TestDateTimes()
{
  DateTime when = new(
    hour: 9, minute: 30, second: 0,
    day: 25, month: 3, year: 2024);

  when.Should().Be(25.March(2024).At(9, 30));
  when.Should().BeOnOrAfter(23.March(2024));
  when.Should().NotBeSameDateAs(12.February(2024));
  when.Should().HaveYear(2024);
```

```
    DateTime due = new(
      hour: 11, minute: 0, second: 0,
      day: 25, month: 3, year: 2024);

    when.Should().BeAtLeast(2.Hours()).Before(due);
  }
```

3. Run the tests and note the date/time test fails, as shown in the following output:

```
Expected when <2024-03-25 09:30:00> to be at least 2h before <2024-03-25
11:00:00>, but it is behind by 1h and 30m.
```

4. For the `due` variable, change the hour from `11` to `13`.
5. Run the tests and note that the date/time test succeeds.

You can learn more details about FluentAssertions at the following link: https://fluentassertions.com/.

Generating fake data with Bogus

Bogus is a popular .NET library used to generate fake data for testing purposes. It is especially useful for creating realistic test data without the need to manually construct every piece of data.

Bogus provides a `Faker<T>` class that is highly versatile and configurable. It uses method chaining to define rules for generating values for properties of your class. The most common members of `Faker<T>` are shown in *Table 11.6*:

Member	Description
`RuleFor(property, generator)`	Defines a rule for a property using a lambda expression to specify how the value should be generated.
`Clone()`	Clones the `Faker<T>` instance so that you can make changes that do not affect the original. Useful if you want to temporarily change some of its rules.
`StrictMode(true)`	When set to `true`, ensures that all properties have rules defined and throws an exception if any are missing.
`Generate()`	Generates a single instance of the configured object.
`Generate(count)`	Generates `count` instances of the configured object in a `List<T>`.
`GenerateBetween(min, max)`	Generates a random number of instances between `min` and `max` of the configured object in a `List<T>`.
`GenerateLazy(count)`	Generates an `IEnumerable<T>` sequence of `count` objects using lazy evaluation.
`GenerateForever()`	Generates an infinite sequence of objects using immediate execution.

Table 11.6: Faker<T> common members

Bogus has a rich set of built-in value generators. Some common ones are shown in *Table 11.7*:

Member	Description
`IndexFaker`	Automatically incremented on every new object generated by the `Faker<T>` instance for its lifetime.

`Name.FirstName()`
`Name.LastName()`
`Name.FullName()`
	Generate names and related values.

`Internet.Email()`
`Internet.Url()`
`Internet.Ip()`
	Generate internet-related values, such as email addresses, URLs, and IP addresses.

`Address.StreetAddress()`
`Address.City()`
`Address.Country()`
	Generate address-related values.

`Phone.PhoneNumber()`	Generates phone numbers.

`Date.Between(start, end)`
`Date.Recent([days])`
`Date.Soon([days])`
`Date.Future(years, refDate)`
`Date.Past(years, refDate)`
	Generate dates and times. `Recent` and `Soon` are within a few days, or you can optionally specify a number of days. `Future` and `Past` are within a number of years after or before a reference date.

`Commerce.ProductName()`
`Commerce.Price()`
`Commerce.Categories(1).First()`
	Generate commerce-related values, such as product names, prices, and categories.

`Finance.CreditCardNumber()` `Finance.Currency().Code`	Generate finance-related values, such as credit card numbers and currency codes.
`Random.Int(18, 65)` `Random.Bool()`	Generate random values such as integers, Booleans, and strings.

`Image.DataUri(width, height)`
`Image.PicsumUrl(width, height)`
`Image.PlaceholderUrl(width, height)`
	Generate links to images using various websites.

`Company.CompanyName()`
`Company.Bs()`
`Company.CatchPhrase()`
	Generate company names and related values.

`Vehicle.Fuel()`
`Vehicle.Manufacturer()`
`Vehicle.Model()`
	Generate vehicle-related values, such as fuel type, manufacturer, and model names.

`Database.Column()` `Database.Engine()`	Generate database-related values, such as column names and database engines.

Table 11.7: Bogus built-in value generators

Imagine that you have a `User` class, as shown in the following code:

```
public class User
{
  public int Id { get; set; }
  public string FirstName { get; set; }
  public string LastName { get; set; }
  public string Email { get; set; }
  public DateTime DateOfBirth { get; set; }
  public string PhoneNumber { get; set; }
  public string StreetAddress { get; set; }
  public string City { get; set; }
  public string Country { get; set; }
  public decimal AccountBalance { get; set; }
}
```

You could define rules on a `Faker<User>` object to create a fake `User` instance in a test, as shown in the following code:

```
Faker<User> userFaker = new Faker<User>()
  .RuleFor(u => u.Id, f => f.IndexFaker + 1)
  .RuleFor(u => u.FirstName, f => f.Name.FirstName())
  .RuleFor(u => u.LastName, f => f.Name.LastName())
  .RuleFor(u => u.Email, f => f.Internet.Email())
  .RuleFor(u => u.DateOfBirth, f =>
    f.Date.Past(40, DateTime.Now.AddYears(-18)))
  .RuleFor(u => u.PhoneNumber, f => f.Phone.PhoneNumber())
  .RuleFor(u => u.StreetAddress, f => f.Address.StreetAddress())
  .RuleFor(u => u.City, f => f.Address.City())
  .RuleFor(u => u.Country, f => f.Address.Country())
  .RuleFor(u => u.AccountBalance, f => f.Finance.Amount());

User user = userFaker.Generate();
```

Now that you've seen the basics of how Bogus works, let's see a hands-on example project.

Faking data test project

Let's create a .NET test project that uses Bogus to generate fake data:

1. In the `BusinessLogic` project, add a new class file named `User.cs`.
2. In `User.cs`, define a class to represent a user, as shown in the following code:

```
namespace Packt.Shared;

public class User
{
  public int Id { get; set; }
  public string? FirstName { get; set; }
  public string? LastName { get; set; }
  public string? Email { get; set; }
  public DateTime DateOfBirth { get; set; }

  public override string ToString()
  {
    return $"{Id}, {FirstName} {LastName}, {Email}, {DateOfBirth:yyyy-MM-
dd}";
  }
}
```

3. In `UserService.cs`, add a method that accepts a `User` object and determines if the user is an adult, as highlighted in the following code:

```
namespace Packt.Shared;

public class UserService
{
  ...
  public bool IsAdult(User user)
  {
    return user.DateOfBirth <= DateTime.Now.AddYears(-18);
  }
}
```

4. Build the `BusinessLogic` project.
5. Use your preferred code editor to add a new **xUnit Test Project** / `xunit` named `BogusTests` to a `Chapter11` solution.

6. In the `BogusTests.csproj` project file, add package references to `NSubstitute` and `Bogus` and a project reference to the `BusinessLogic` project, as highlighted in the following markup:

```
<ItemGroup>
  <ProjectReference Include="..\BusinessLogic\BusinessLogic.csproj" />
</ItemGroup>

<ItemGroup>
  <PackageReference Include="NSubstitute" />
  <PackageReference Include="Bogus" />
  <PackageReference Include="coverlet.collector" />
```

7. Build the `BogusTests` project.

Writing a method with fake data

Now we can write a method that generates fake data to test the user service's `IsAdult` method:

1. Rename `UnitTest1.cs` to `BogusExamples.cs`.
2. In `BogusExamples.cs`, import the namespace working with `Bogus` and write two test methods that generate fake `User` objects to test if the `IsAdult` method works correctly to determine if the generated user is an adult, as shown in the following code:

```
using NSubstitute; // To use Substitute.
using Bogus; // To use Faker<T>.
using Packt.Shared; // To use User, UserService.
using Xunit.Abstractions; // To use ITestOutputHelper.

namespace BogusTests;

public class BogusExamples
{
  private readonly ITestOutputHelper _output;
  private readonly Faker<User> _userFaker;

  public BogusExamples(ITestOutputHelper output)
  {
    _output = output;

    _userFaker = new Faker<User>()
      // Configure an incrementing index for the Id property.
      .RuleFor(u => u.Id, f => f.IndexFaker + 1)
      // Configure the FirstName property to be a random first name.
      .RuleFor(u => u.FirstName, f => f.Name.FirstName())
```

```
    // Configure the LastName property to be a random last name.
    .RuleFor(u => u.LastName, f => f.Name.LastName())
    // Configure the Email property to be a random email address.
    .RuleFor(u => u.Email, f => f.Internet.Email())
    // Configure the DateOfBirth property to be a random date of birth
    // up to 30 years earlier than 18 years ago.
    .RuleFor(u => u.DateOfBirth, f => f.Date.Past(yearsToGoBack: 30,
      refDate: DateTime.Now.AddYears(-18)));
}

[Fact]
public void IsAdult_ShouldReturnTrue_WhenUserIs18OrOlder()
{
  // Arrange
  IEmailSender emailSender = Substitute.For<IEmailSender>();
  UserService userService = new(emailSender);
  User user = _userFaker.Generate();
  _output.WriteLine($"{user}");

  // Act
  bool result = userService.IsAdult(user);

  // Assert
  Assert.True(result);
}

[Fact]
public void IsAdult_ShouldReturnFalse_WhenUserIsUnder18()
{
  // Arrange
  IEmailSender emailSender = Substitute.For<IEmailSender>();
  UserService userService = new(emailSender);
  User user = _userFaker.Clone()
    // Override the DateOfBirth property to be a random date of birth
    // up to 10 years earlier than 8 years ago i.e. under 18.
    .RuleFor(u => u.DateOfBirth, f => f.Date.Past(yearsToGoBack: 10,
      refDate: DateTime.Now.AddYears(-8)))
    .Generate();
  _output.WriteLine($"{user}");
```

```
        // Act
        bool result = userService.IsAdult(user);

        // Assert
        Assert.False(result);
    }
}
```

3. Run the Bogus tests and note they both succeed, showing that the user service's `IsAdult` method correctly identifies adults and non-adults.

Practicing and exploring

Test your knowledge and understanding by answering some questions, getting some hands-on practice, and exploring the topics covered in this chapter with deeper research.

Exercise 11.1 – Online-only material

You can read the official documentation for xUnit at the following link: `https://xunit.net/`.

Learn more about the xUnit packages and when to use them at the following link: `https://xunit.net/docs/nuget-packages`.

If you use MS Test then you can read about its latest improvements in the article, *Introducing MSTest SDK – Improved Configuration & Flexibility*, found at the following link: `https://devblogs.microsoft.com/dotnet/introducing-mstest-sdk/`.

Exercise 11.2 – Practice exercises

Consider an `IProductService` interface that manages product information in an e-commerce system. This interface includes methods for getting product details, checking product availability, updating product information, handling notifications about product updates, and performing asynchronous operations related to products, as shown in the following code:

```
public interface IProductService
{
  Product GetProductById(int productId);
  Task<bool> IsProductAvailableAsync(int productId);
  Product UpdateProductPrice(int productId, decimal newPrice);
  string DefaultCurrency { get; set; }
  event EventHandler<ProductUpdatedEventArgs> ProductUpdated;
  IEnumerable<Product> GetProducts(string category = null);
}

public class Product
{
```

```
    public int Id { get; set; }
    public string Name { get; set; }
    public decimal Price { get; set; }
    public string Category { get; set; }
  }

  public class ProductUpdatedEventArgs : EventArgs
  {
    public int ProductId { get; set; }
    public decimal NewPrice { get; set; }
  }
```

Use xUnit and NSubstitute to write unit tests to:

1. Mock the `GetProducts` method to return different sets of products based on the category argument.
2. Mock the `DefaultCurrency` property to return a specific currency code when accessed, testing how the system reacts to different currencies.
3. Mock the `ProductUpdated` event to simulate a product update notification and verify that event subscribers react appropriately.
4. Mock `IsProductAvailableAsync` to return `true` or `false` asynchronously, allowing for testing of UI or service responses to stock availability.
5. Mock `GetProductById` and `UpdateProductPrice` to return specific `Product` instances, testing the system's handling of product details retrieval and updates.

Exercise 11.3 – Test your knowledge

Answer the following questions. If you get stuck, try googling the answers, if necessary, while remembering that if you get totally stuck, the answers are in *Appendix A*:

1. What criteria should a good unit test meet?
2. What is a MUT?
3. The Test-Driven Development (TDD) process is described as "Red-Green-Refactor." What do those three steps mean?
4. How are tests in xUnit configured?
5. For xUnit, what is a common parameter of the `[Fact]` and `[Theory]` attributes that is good practice to set and why?
6. To supply data for a `[Theory]` test, you can use the `[ClassData]` attribute and specify a class. What are the requirements for that class?
7. What is good practice for handling positive and negative test results?
8. What are the red flags that you should watch out for when writing or reviewing unit tests?
9. With xUnit, how can you see output during test execution?
10. Using NSubstitute, how do you configure the return value of a faked method?

Exercise 11.4 – Explore topics

Use the links on the following page to learn more details about the topics covered in this chapter: https://github.com/markjprice/tools-skills-net10/blob/main/docs/book-links.md#chapter-11---unit-testing-and-mocking.

Summary

In this chapter, you learned:

- About all the different types of testing, from unit to functional
- The pros and cons of TDD
- How to unit test using xUnit
- How to supply a test method with parameter values
- How to set up and tear down fixtures for a test
- How to use NSubstitue for mocking
- How to use Bogus to generate fake data

In the next chapter, you will learn about integration and security testing.

12

Integration and Security Testing

This chapter is about integration and security testing, both high-level types of testing. Unit tests are good at detecting errors in business logic, but you also need to verify that all the parts of your codebase work together with each other and external systems. This is where integration testing becomes important.

Some external systems should be used directly in integration tests, and some should be replaced with a test double. Integration tests commonly call out-of-process systems like databases, event buses, and message queues. This makes integration tests slower than unit tests, but integration tests cover more code, both in your codebase and external libraries. Integration tests are more likely to catch regressions.

> To learn about a real-world example regression in a .NET logging package, you can read a GitHub issue at the following link: `https://github.com/markjprice/cs11dotnet7/blob/main/docs/errata/errata.md#page-178---reviewing-project-packages`.

One tool available at the command line and in Visual Studio that makes it easier to perform integration tests on web services is dev tunnels. We will see how to use them to simplify testing services.

Security testing becomes more important every day. It is the trickiest type of testing because the best way to avoid security issues is to adopt security-by-design, which cannot be easily automated.

This chapter covers the following topics:

- Basics of integration testing
- Integration testing with data stores
- Testing services using dev tunnels
- Introducing security testing

Basics of integration testing

Integration testing is a phase of software testing where individual modules or components of an application are combined and tested as a group to ensure they work together correctly. This type of testing focuses on detecting issues that arise from the interaction between integrated units, such as data transfer errors, interface mismatches, and communication failures.

By validating the combined functionality of these interconnected components, integration testing helps ensure that the overall system operates seamlessly and meets specified requirements. It typically follows unit testing and precedes other types of high-level testing like security and performance testing in the software development lifecycle.

As mentioned in *Chapter 11, Unit Testing and Mocking*, integration testing uses similar tools to unit testing. For example, you can write integration tests using xUnit.

As a reminder, unit tests must be:

- A single unit of behavior.
- As fast-executing as possible.
- Isolated from other tests.

The simplest definition of an integration test is any coded test that does not meet the criteria for a unit test!

One other difference between the two types of testing is how many tests you typically write. One way of visually comparing integration testing to unit testing (and end-to-end testing) is the test pyramid, as shown in *Figure 12.1*:

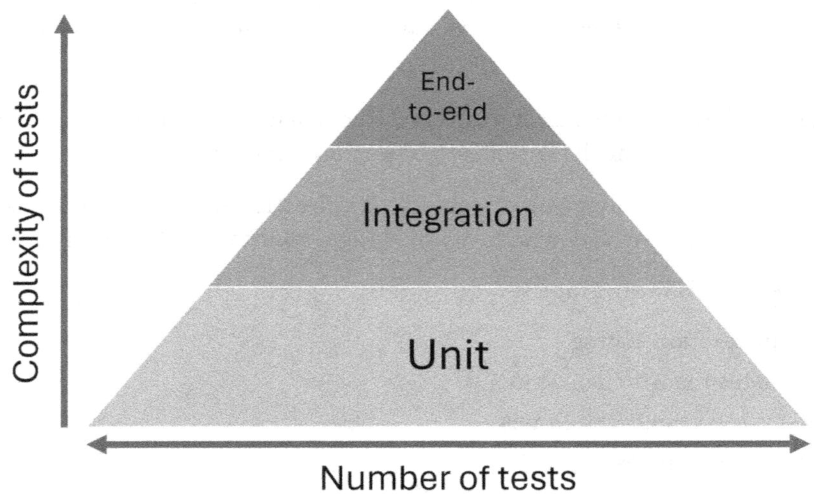

Figure 12.1: The test pyramid shows the weighting of test types

Lower-level tests like unit tests should have a higher number of tests than higher-level tests like end-to-end tests. Integration tests should have a number of tests in the middle.

Good practice: Define integration tests for the most common scenarios that occur in the real-world usage of your projects. Write enough integration tests to interact with every external system used. Edge cases are scenarios that result in errors and should mostly be covered by unit tests. Only define integration tests for edge cases that cannot be covered by unit tests.

Which external systems to test

External systems come in two types: ones under your control and ones outside your control. External systems under your control include data stores that only your project accesses. No other system updates the data. External systems outside your control include email systems and public services like weather or government systems.

As you can probably already guess, you should directly use external systems under your control, but mock external systems that you don't control.

What if the database is used by other systems? You might start with a database that's only used by your system, but over time other systems might want the convenience of direct access to it too. This breaks the design principles of microservices and leads to problems later, but it is very common in the real world. In this case, you will have to treat the database as out of your control and mock it.

Walkthrough of an example integration test

Let's review a complete example of an integration test for getting a product from a catalog by its identifier, as shown in the following code:

```
public class GetByIdTests
{
  private readonly CatalogContext _catalogContext;
  private readonly EfRepository<Order> _orderRepository;
  private OrderBuilder OrderBuilder { get; } = new OrderBuilder();
  private readonly ITestOutputHelper _output;

  public GetById(ITestOutputHelper output)
  {
    _output = output;

    DbContextOptionsBuilder<CatalogContext> dbOptions = new()
      .UseInMemoryDatabase(databaseName: "TestCatalog")
      .Options;

    _catalogContext = new CatalogContext(dbOptions);
    _orderRepository = new EfRepository<Order>(_catalogContext);
  }
```

```
    [Fact]
    public async Task GetsExistingOrder()
    {
      var existingOrder = OrderBuilder.WithDefaultValues();
      _catalogContext.Orders.Add(existingOrder);
      _catalogContext.SaveChanges();

      int orderId = existingOrder.Id;
      _output.WriteLine($"OrderId: {orderId}");

      var orderFromRepo = await _orderRepository.GetByIdAsync(orderId);
      Assert.Equal(OrderBuilder.TestBuyerId, orderFromRepo.BuyerId);

      // Note: Using InMemoryDatabase OrderItems is available. Will be null if
  using SQL DB.
      // Use the OrderWithItemsByIdSpec instead of just GetById to get the full
  aggregate
      var firstItem = orderFromRepo.OrderItems.FirstOrDefault();
      Assert.Equal(OrderBuilder.TestUnits, firstItem.Units);
    }
  }
```

The preceding code is an integration test class named `GetById` that tests the functionality of fetching an existing order from a repository. Note the following about the preceding code block:

- It uses an in-memory database for testing purposes.
- It has dependencies on `CatalogContext` (a custom `DbContext`) and `EfRepository<Order>` (a repository for the `Order` entity).
- The constructor initializes the in-memory database and the repository. It takes an `ITestOutputHelper` instance to output test information during execution.

Note the following about the test method `GetsExistingOrder` in the preceding code block:

- `GetsExistingOrder` uses an `OrderBuilder` class for constructing `Order` instances with default values.
- This `Order` instance is added to the `CatalogContext` and saved to the in-memory database.
- The order ID is extracted and logged using `_output`.
- The order is retrieved from the repository using the `GetByIdAsync` method.
- The test verifies that `BuyerId` of the retrieved order matches the expected value from `OrderBuilder`.
- It checks the first item in the `OrderItems` collection of the retrieved order to ensure it has the correct number of units.

This test ensures that the repository correctly retrieves an existing order from the in-memory database and verifies that the order's properties match the expected values.

Sharing fixtures in integration tests

There is a common scenario where you might want to initialize a fixture because it is genuinely shared between all tests: when using a database or EF Core model, especially when creating integration tests.

But in this case, use inheritance so that your unit test class still does not need a constructor, as shown in the following code:

```
public class NorthwindStoreTests : DatabaseIntegrationTests
{
  [Fact]
  public void Checkout_ShouldFailWhenLowInventory()
  {
    // Use the _db fixture here.
  }
  ...
}

public abstract class DatabaseIntegrationTests : IDisposable
{
  protected readonly NorthwindContext _db;

  protected DatabaseIntegrationTests(NorthwindContext db)
  {
    _db = db;
  }

  public void Dispose()
  {
    _db.Dispose();
  }
}
```

Improvements to integration testing of apps with top-level statements

In .NET 10, Microsoft has introduced a significant enhancement to streamline integration testing for ASP.NET Core applications utilizing top-level statements, a feature that became prevalent with C# 9.

Top-level statements simplify the entry point of C# applications by eliminating the need for an explicit `Main` method. For example, the `Program.cs` file might only contain the following code:

```
var builder = WebApplication.CreateBuilder(args);
var app = builder.Build();
app.MapGet("/", () => "Hello World!");
app.Run();
```

Under the hood, the compiler generates an internal `Program` class to encapsulate these statements. However, this internal designation poses a problem for integration testing. Testing frameworks often require access to the `Program` class to configure the test host or access services, which isn't possible if the class is `internal`.

Previously, developers had to manually add a `public partial class Program` declaration to expose the class for testing purposes:

```
public partial class Program { }
```

This workaround, while effective, was an extra step that could be easily overlooked, leading to confusion and potential errors.

To address this, .NET 10 introduces a source generator that automatically creates a `public partial class Program` when one isn't explicitly defined. This means that the compiler-generated `Program` class becomes accessible to test projects without any additional code from the developer.

Furthermore, an analyzer has been added to detect redundant explicit declarations of `public partial class Program`. If such a declaration is found, the analyzer will suggest its removal, keeping the codebase clean and adhering to best practices.

Integration testing with data stores

One of the most common systems that you will interact with integration tests are data stores, and they require special handling.

The schema for your data stores should be treated like code and be tracked in a source control system like Git. This allows you to keep all the schema changes over time in sync with changes to code that works on data in that structure.

The database schema includes table structure, index definitions, views, and stored procedures. For a SQL-based database, these are defined in SQL script files. You should also consider **reference data**, which is data that should be inserted into the database to prepopulate it. For example, you might need to add about 200 rows to a `CountryRegion` table used by your project for location lookups.

Developer instances of the database and migrations

Each developer in a team should have their own instance of the database to work with locally. This is so that tests run by different developers do not interfere with each other. Doing this also maximizes performance during test executions.

Over time, the database structure will change. New tables will be added. Columns will be added to tables. The best way to handle this is to use migrations. These are schema changes represented by the SQL statements that make the change. For example, `CREATE TABLE` and `ALTER TABLE`. **Object-Relational Mappers (ORMs)** like EF Core support migrations with classes with equivalent commands, as shown in the following code:

```
using Microsoft.EntityFrameworkCore.Migrations; // To use Migration.

namespace YourApp.Migrations;

public partial class AddPosts : Migration
{
  protected override void Up(MigrationBuilder migrationBuilder)
  {
    migrationBuilder.CreateTable(name: "Posts", columns: table => new
      {
        PostId = table.Column<int>(nullable: false)
          .Annotation("SqlServer:ValueGenerationStrategy",
            SqlServerValueGenerationStrategy.IdentityColumn),
        Title = table.Column<string>(nullable: true),
        Content = table.Column<string>(nullable: true),
        DateCreated = table.Column<DateTime>(nullable: false)
      },
      constraints: table =>
      {
        table.PrimaryKey("PK_Posts", x => x.PostId);
      });
  }

  protected override void Down(MigrationBuilder migrationBuilder)
  {
    migrationBuilder.DropTable(name: "Posts");
  }
}
```

Note the following about the preceding code:

- The `Up` method creates a new table called `Posts` with four columns: `PostId`, `Title`, `Content`, and `DateCreated`. The `PostId` column is configured as an identity column, which means its value will be automatically generated by the database when a new row is inserted. The `table.PrimaryKey` method is used to specify `PostId` as the primary key of the `Posts` table.

- The `Down` method reverses the changes made by the `Up` method. In this case, it simply drops the `Posts` table. This method ensures that you can revert your database schema to its previous state if needed.

> The actual SQL commands executed by these methods depend on the database provider you're using. EF Core translates the methods into the appropriate SQL commands for the configured database provider, like SQL Server, SQLite, or PostgreSQL.

A migration class can be auto-generated by the EF Core tools based on your model definitions and `DbContext` configuration. Whenever you make changes to your models that affect the database schema, you should create a new migration, as shown in the following command, where `<MigrationName>` would be something like `AddPosts`:

```
dotnet ef migrations add <MigrationName>
```

This technique allows you to version your database schema alongside your application code, making it easier to manage changes and deployments.

To run any outstanding migrations, which calls the `Up` methods in the migration classes, use the following command:

```
dotnet ef database update
```

To revert to a specified migration point, which calls the `Down` methods on the migration classes after that point, use the following command:

```
dotnet ef database update <MigrationName>
```

This will revert all migrations applied after the specified migration, so the database schema will match the state defined by the specified migration.

To revert all migrations so that the database returns to its original state, which calls all the `Down` methods of each migration in order, use the following command:

```
dotnet ef database update 0
```

Data lifecycle

Tests should not depend on the state of the database. Your tests should initialize the state of the database themselves to ensure consistency and remove data between test runs.

If you cannot do this, then your tests will need to execute sequentially so that the state of the database is known. If you execute tests in parallel, then you are more likely to get the state out of sync.

There are common ways to reset data between tests:

- Restore a database backup before each test. This can be slow depending on the size of the database.

- Create a database transaction and then roll it back at the end of the test. If the transaction is only used in the test, then production behavior is different.
- Scripting the cleanup of data after each test. This is fast but if a test fails without performing the cleanup, it will cause problems for other tests.
- Scripting the cleanup of data before each test. This is fast and less likely to leave the database in an unknown state if a test fails.

You should define a base class for integration tests that share a common database and the same initial state. Call a SQL script to clean up and initialize the database state, as shown in the following code:

```
using Microsoft.Data.SqlClient; // To use SqlConnection and so on.
using System.Data; // To use CommandType.

public abstract class DatabaseIntegrationTests
{
  private const string _connectionString;

  protected DatabaseIntegrationTests()
  {
    ResetDatabase();
  }

  public void ResetDatabase()
  {
    string sql = "DELETE FROM ...;" +
                 "DELETE FROM ...;" +
                 "INSERT INTO ...;";

    // Or load the SQL statements from a script file.
    using SqlConnection con = new(_connectionString);
    SqlCommand cmd = new(sql, con);
    cmd.CommandType = CommandType.Text;
    con.Open();
    cmd.ExecuteNonQuery();
  }
}
```

Good practice: Avoid in-memory database replacements. Although they are faster, modern databases are almost as fast, and only an integration test that uses the real database is a true integration test. Use the same data store system in tests as you will use in production.

You should define factory methods in a helper class to create entities, as shown in the following code:

```
public static class ObjectMother
{
  public static Category CreateCategory(
    int categoryId = 1,
    string categoryName = "Beverages",
    string description = "...")
  {
    using NorthwindContext db = new();

    Category category = new Category()
    {
      CategoryId = categoryId,
      CategoryName = categoryName,
      Description = description
    };

    db.Categories.Add(category);
    db.SaveChanges();
    return category;
  }
}
```

You should use the factory method in a test, as shown in the following code:

```
using static ObjectMother;

Category c1 = CreateCategory(); // Create Beverages.
Category c2 = CreateCategory(2, "Condiments", "..."); // Create Condiments.
```

Testing services using dev tunnels

Dev tunnels are a technology concept that's gained traction among web service developers. Dev tunnels create a secure, public URL that maps to a local server on your machine. This means you can share your local development environment with anyone in the world, without deploying the web service to a public server.

Imagine you're working on a web application on your laptop. Normally, the app would only be accessible to you, since it's running on your local server as `localhost`. If you wanted someone else to check it out, you'd have to deploy it to a public server, which can be a hassle, especially for quick feedback loops.

Dev tunnels work by establishing a secure connection between your local server and a service that creates a publicly accessible URL. This URL points directly back to your local server. When someone accesses this URL, the dev tunnel service routes that traffic to your machine, letting others interact with your local development project as if it were hosted online.

Dev tunnels provide several benefits, as shown in the following list:

- **Simplified collaboration**: Dev tunnels make it easy to share your work with clients, testers, or colleagues without the need to deploy it to a public staging environment. This is especially handy for quick reviews or collaborative debugging.
- **Real-world testing**: Dev tunnels allow for testing webhooks, third-party integrations, and mobile apps that require a public URL to function correctly, directly from your local environment.
- **Learning**: For learners and educators, dev tunnels provide a straightforward way to work on projects, experiment with new technologies, and share progress without the complexities of server management.

There is some dev tunnel terminology that you should be familiar with, as shown in *Table 12.1*:

Term	Description
Tunnel	Provides secure remote access to one host through a relay service. A dev tunnel has a unique DNS name, multiple ports, access controls, and other associated metadata.
Tunnel relay service	Facilitates secure connections between a dev tunnel host and clients via a cloud service, even when the host may be behind a firewall and unable to accept incoming connections directly.
Tunnel host	Accepts client connections to a dev tunnel via the dev tunnel relay service and forwards those connections to local ports.
Tunnel port	An IP port number (1-65535) that is allowed through a dev tunnel. A dev tunnel only allows connections on ports that have been added. One dev tunnel can support multiple ports, and different ports within a dev tunnel may use different protocols (HTTP, HTTPS, etc.) and may have different access controls.

Table 12.1: Dev tunnel terminology

While dev tunnels are secure, exposing your local environment to the public internet always comes with risks. It's important to use these tools judiciously, ensure that any sensitive data is protected, and possibly limit access using authentication or IP whitelisting.

The performance seen through a dev tunnel might not accurately reflect the performance of a fully deployed application, due to the overhead of tunneling and the specifics of your local development setup.

Installing the dev tunnel CLI

Before you can use dev tunnels, you must install the dev tunnel CLI.

- On Windows, use `winget`, as shown in the following command:

```
winget install Microsoft.devtunnel
```

- On MacOS, use Homebrew, as shown in the following command:

```
brew install --cask devtunnel
```

- On Linux, use `curl`, as shown in the following command:

```
curl -sL https://aka.ms/DevTunnelCliInstall | bash
```

> You will need to restart your command prompt or terminal before the `devtunnel` CLI will be available on your computer path.

Exploring a dev tunnel with the CLI and an echo service

An echo service is a simple server or endpoint that receives HTTP requests and sends back the same data in the response. It is often used for testing, debugging, and educational purposes because it allows developers to see exactly what data is being sent to the server and verify that it is correctly received and processed.

Let's explore how to use dev tunnels with an echo service to do a basic "sanity check" that it is working:

1. Before you can create a dev tunnel, you must log in with a Microsoft Entra ID, Microsoft personal account, or GitHub account, as shown in the following command:

```
devtunnel user login
```

2. Select your account and note the result, as shown in the following output:

```
Logged in as <your-email-account> using Microsoft.
```

> If you get an error, `Missing wamcompat_id_token in WAM case`, then try using device flow to log in instead, as shown in the following command: `devtunnel login -d`

3. Start hosting a simple service on port 8080 that just echoes any HTTP requests to it, as shown in the following command:

```
devtunnel echo http -p 8080
```

4. In another command prompt or terminal window, start hosting a dev tunnel for port `8080`, as shown in the following command:

```
devtunnel host -p 8080
```

5. Note the result, as shown in the following output:

```
Hosting port: 8080
Connect via browser: https://40bhwxgp.uks1.devtunnels.ms:8080,
https://40bhwxgp-8080.uks1.devtunnels.ms
Inspect network activity: https://40bhwxgp-8080-inspect.uks1.devtunnels.
ms
Ready to accept connections for tunnel: happy-hill-zw1k7n8
```

6. Start your preferred web browser and navigate to the URL specified in the output. For example, for me, it was the following link: `https://40bhwxgp.uks1.devtunnels.ms:8080`.
7. Log in using the same account as you used to host the dev tunnel because, by default, dev tunnels are only accessible to you.
8. Note the warning that confirms that you are about to connect to your dev tunnel, as shown in *Figure 12.2*:

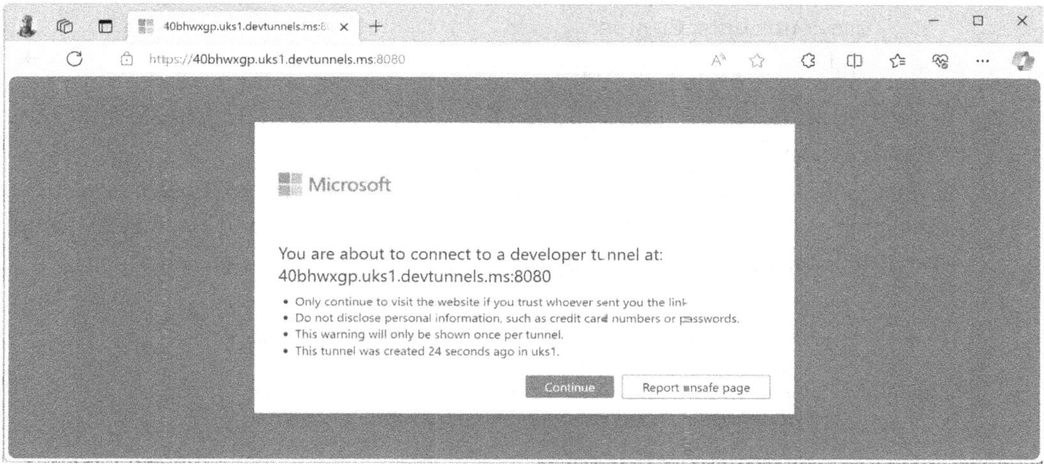

Figure 12.2: Connecting to a dev tunnel

9. Close the browser, because we don't actually need to connect to it at this point. We are just confirming that it's there.
10. At the command prompt or terminal, press *Ctrl* + *C* to shut down the dev tunnel host.
11. At the command prompt or terminal, press *Ctrl* + *C* to shut down the echo service.

Now let's see how to use a dev tunnel with an ASP.NET Core project.

Exploring a dev tunnel with an ASP.NET Core project

Now let's see a more practical example of how to use a dev tunnel with an ASP.NET Core project.

Let's explore:

1. Use your preferred code editor to add a Web API project to the `Chapter12` solution, as defined in the following list:

> **Warning!** To see all the options you might need to scroll down in the dialog box.

- Project template: **ASP.NET Core Web API** / `webapi`
- Solution file and folder: `Chapter12`

- Project file and folder: `Northwind.WebApi`
- **Authentication type: None**
- **Configure for HTTPS:** Selected
- **Enable container support:** Cleared
- **Enable OpenAPI support:** Selected
- **Do not use top-level statements:** Cleared
- **Use controllers:** Cleared
- **Enlist in Aspire orchestration:** Cleared

2. In the `Northwind.WebApi.csproj` project file, remove the `version` attribute from any packages because we are using CPM.
3. In the `Properties` folder, in `launchSettings.json`, modify the `applicationUrl` of the profile named `https` to use port `5121` and `http` to use port `5122`, and add an entry to navigate to the OpenAPI document, as shown highlighted in the following configuration:

```
"profiles": {
  ...
  "https": {
    "commandName": "Project",
    "dotnetRunMessages": true,
    "launchBrowser": false,
    "applicationUrl": "https://localhost:5121;http://localhost:5122",
    "environmentVariables": {
      "ASPNETCORE_ENVIRONMENT": "Development"
    }
```

4. In `Program.cs`, before the call to `app.Run()`, add statements to output the tunnel URL, as shown in the following code:

```
string? tunnelUrl = Environment.GetEnvironmentVariable("VS_TUNNEL_URL");

if (tunnelUrl is not null)
{
  Console.WriteLine($"Tunnel URL: {tunnelUrl}");
}
```

5. Start the `Northwind.WebApi` project without debugging.
6. Navigate to `https://localhost:5121/openapi/v1.json`.
7. Note the weather service shows the OpenAPI documentation page.
8. Navigate to `https://localhost:5121/weatherforecast` and note that it returns random weather.

9. At the command prompt or terminal, note that the web service is hosted on `localhost` and listening on ports `5121` and `5122`, as shown in the following output:

```
info: Microsoft.Hosting.Lifetime[14]
      Now listening on: https://localhost:5121
info: Microsoft.Hosting.Lifetime[14]
      Now listening on: http://localhost:5122
info: Microsoft.Hosting.Lifetime[0]
      Application started. Press Ctrl+C to shut down.
info: Microsoft.Hosting.Lifetime[0]
      Hosting environment: Development
info: Microsoft.Hosting.Lifetime[0]
      Content root path: C:\tools-skills-net10\Chapter12\Northwind.WebApi
```

10. Close the browser and shut down the web service.
11. In Visual Studio, in the standard toolbar, navigate to **https** | **Dev Tunnels (no active tunnel)** | **Create a Tunnel...**, as shown in *Figure 12.3*:

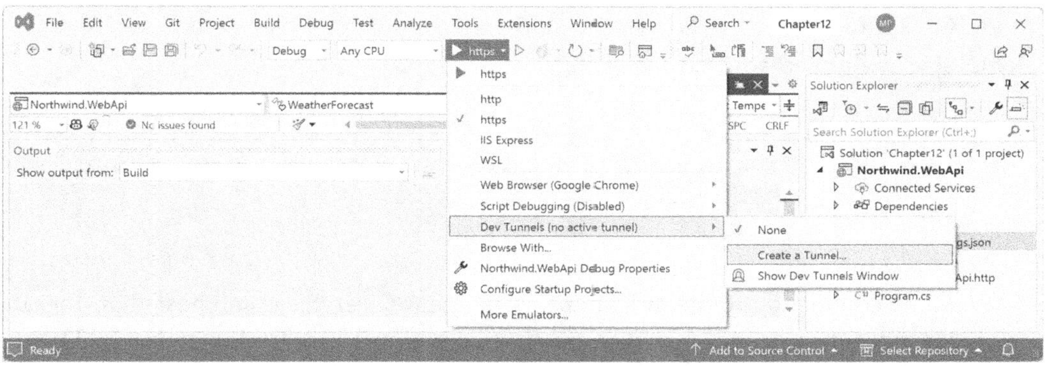

Figure 12.3: Creating a dev tunnel in Visual Studio

12. In the dialog box, fill in the following options, as shown in *Figure 12.4*:

   - **Account:** Select your Microsoft or GitHub account
   - **Name:** `Northwind Web API`
   - **Tunnel Type: Temporary**
   - **Access: Private**

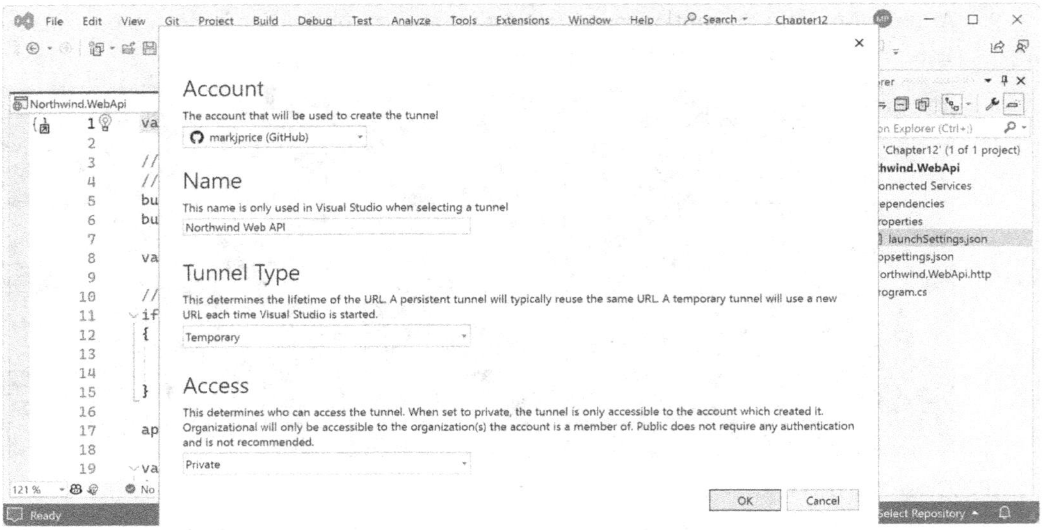

Figure 12.4: Creating a dev tunnel in Visual Studio

13. Click **OK**.
14. Start the project without debugging.

> If you are using a GitHub account, then you may need to authorize dev tunnels to verify your identity.

15. At the command prompt or terminal, note the web service is still hosted on `localhost` and listening on ports `5121` and `5122`. But now a dev tunnel is redirecting public HTTP requests via the public URL to your local web service so the environment variable containing the tunnel URL is available, as shown in the following output:

```
Tunnel URL: https://vk6q4272-5121.uks1.devtunnels.ms/
...
info: Microsoft.Hosting.Lifetime[14]
      Now listening on: https://localhost:5121
info: Microsoft.Hosting.Lifetime[14]
      Now listening on: http://localhost:5122
```

16. Copy the URL from the output and paste it into your browser address bar, then append `/weatherforecast`. For example, `https://vk6q4272-5121.uks1.devtunnels.ms/weatherforecast`, as shown in *Figure 12.5*:

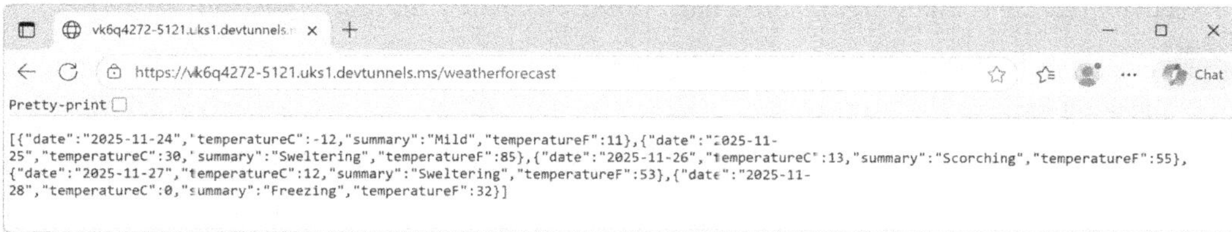

Figure 12.5: Random weather from a web service callable on the public internet

17. In Visual Studio, navigate to **View** | **Output**, select **Show output from: Dev Tunnels**, and note the results, as shown in the following output:

```
Getting dev tunnels for account 'Mark Price (markjprice@msn.com)':
Succeeded
Getting dev tunnels for account 'markjprice (GitHub)': Succeeded
Dev tunnel 'Northwind Web API' was created successfully
Successfully configured the following urls on dev tunnel 'Northwind Web
API':
        https://localhost:5121  ->  https://vk6q4272-5121.uks1.
devtunnels.ms/
```

> You can learn more about testing web services using dev tunnels at the following link: `https://learn.microsoft.com/en-us/aspnet/core/test/dev-tunnels`.

Whether you're a solo developer working on a side project or part of a team iterating rapidly on a complex application, dev tunnels offer a flexible, powerful way to bridge the gap between local development and public accessibility. Just remember to consider the implications of exposing your local environment and to use these tools wisely.

Introducing security testing

Security testing is a type of software testing that aims to uncover vulnerabilities, threats, and risks in a software application, ensuring that data and resources are protected from potential intruders. This process involves evaluating the application for security flaws that could be exploited by attackers, such as weaknesses in authentication, authorization, data encryption, and error handling. The goal is to identify and mitigate security issues to ensure the application can withstand malicious attacks and protect sensitive information, thereby maintaining the confidentiality, integrity, and availability of data.

For a .NET developer, security testing should not just be about ticking off a checklist. You need to embed a security-first mindset into the foundations of your development process. Given that .NET can create a wide range of applications—from web to mobile and desktop—understanding all aspects of security testing is challenging and I can't possibly cover it all in this section.

A professional .NET developer should know at least a minimum about security testing, as shown in the following list:

- **OWASP Top 10**: Start with the OWASP Top 10, which outlines the most critical web application security risks. For a .NET developer, being familiar with these risks is crucial because they represent the most common vulnerabilities that could be exploited in your applications. Understanding these risks helps in proactively designing and coding applications to be secure against known vulnerabilities.
- **Secure coding practices**: Security testing isn't just about finding bugs; it's about writing code that's secure by design. This involves adhering to secure coding practices that help prevent vulnerabilities in the first place. For .NET developers, this means understanding how to safely handle user input, implement proper authentication and authorization, manage sessions securely, and encrypt sensitive data.
- **.NET security features**: .NET provides a robust set of security features and libraries designed to help developers create secure applications. This includes mechanisms for authentication, authorization, secure communication (SSL/TLS), data protection APIs, and cryptographic services. A thorough understanding of these built-in features allows developers to leverage the framework's capabilities to enhance security. Many of the foundational elements were covered in *Chapter 8, Protecting Data and Apps Using Cryptography*.
- **Automated security testing tools**: Familiarize yourself with automated security testing tools that support .NET applications. Tools like OWASP ZAP offer automated scanning capabilities that can identify vulnerabilities in your code. Additionally, static code analysis tools that integrate with the .NET ecosystem can help analyze your source code for potential security issues before they become a problem. These tools are also known as **SAST** (**Static Application Security Testing**) and **DAST** (**Dynamic Application Security Testing**) and they can be integrated into the CI/CD pipeline, enabling continuous scanning and providing immediate feedback to developers.
- **Threat modeling**: Threat modeling is a proactive approach to identifying potential security threats to your application and determining the risks they pose. For .NET developers, engaging in threat modeling helps in understanding how an attacker might compromise your application and what controls or design changes can mitigate those risks. Microsoft offers guidance and tools for threat modeling that can be particularly useful in the .NET context.
- **Compliance requirements**: Depending on the domain your application operates in, there may be specific security compliance requirements you need to adhere to, such as GDPR for data protection, HIPAA for healthcare information, or PCI DSS for payment processing. Understanding these requirements and how they impact application development is crucial for .NET developers to ensure compliance and protect sensitive data.

Based on this list, we will look at OWASP and threat modeling in more detail.

Open Web Application Security Project

OWASP stands for the **Open Web Application Security Project**. It's a non-profit foundation that works to improve the security of software through its community-led open-source software projects – hundreds of chapters worldwide, tens of thousands of members – and by hosting educational events and training sessions.

OWASP is the collective wisdom of the best minds in application security worldwide. This means it provides insights, techniques, and solutions that have been vetted by experts. Its recommendations are not based on theoretical models but on real-world experiences and incidents, making its guidance incredibly practical and applicable.

OWASP's guidelines and tools often serve as benchmarks for security practices within the industry. For organizations, aligning with OWASP guidelines can help in establishing trust with clients and partners regarding the security posture of their services or products.

Increasingly, OWASP's guidelines are referenced in industry standards, regulations, and even legislation related to cybersecurity. This elevates the importance of being familiar with and adhering to OWASP recommendations, not just for best practices, but also for compliance purposes.

OWASP Top 10

The OWASP Top 10 is a critical awareness document for web application security, representing the most common and severe security risks affecting web applications today. At the time of writing in November 2025, the most recent version is 2021, but the next version has been "coming soon" for over a year and is already available as a release candidate, versioned as 2025 but this could change if the delays continue. The OWASP Top 10 reflects the evolving landscape of web application security, highlighting emerging risks alongside traditional vulnerabilities. While it gets updated periodically, for example, in 2017 and 2021, the core concerns tend to revolve around similar themes of input validation, authentication, access control, and data protection.

> **Warning!** If you use a search engine to find out more about this topic, make sure you search for "OWASP Top 10 2025," not just "OWASP Top 10," otherwise, you are likely to see lots of out-of-date results! And watch out for when they eventually release a new update. You can read more at the following link: `https://www.owasptopten.org/`.

For .NET developers, staying updated with the OWASP Top 10 is useful for securing applications against the most prevalent and dangerous web application security risks. A summary of the current top 10 web application security risks tailored for .NET developers, including examples and considerations for mitigating these risks in the .NET ecosystem, are shown in the following subsections.

A01:2025 – Broken Access Control

This is when you've allowed users to access other users' data or functionalities without proper authorization checks.

Use ASP.NET Core's built-in authorization mechanisms to enforce access controls. Always verify that the logged-in user has the appropriate permissions before performing sensitive operations or accessing sensitive data. Utilize ASP.NET Core Identity for authentication, which supports **multi-factor authentication** (**MFA**) and external authentication providers like OAuth.

Store passwords using a secure hashing algorithm such as bcrypt, scrypt, or Argon2. ASP.NET Core Identity uses secure password hashing by default. We learned about secure password hashing in *Chapter 8, Protecting Data and Apps Using Cryptography*.

Ensure users are only granted the minimum privileges necessary to perform their tasks, reducing the impact of a compromised account. Define roles and permissions clearly and use the built-in `[Authorize]` attribute in ASP.NET Core to protect resources and services.

A02:2025 – Security Misconfiguration

This includes improperly configured permissions, default settings, verbose error messages, and so on. For example, exposing sensitive information through misconfigured error handling in .NET applications.

Ensure all configurations are secure across all layers of the application. Regularly audit and update configurations. Use custom error pages in ASP.NET Core to avoid revealing sensitive information.

A03:2025 – Software Supply Chain Failures

Previously known as "Using Components with Known Vulnerabilities," software supply chain failures are breakdowns or other compromises in the process of building, distributing, or updating software. They are often caused by vulnerabilities or malicious changes in third-party code, tools, or other dependencies that the system relies on.

This emphasizes the risks of using software that is known to be vulnerable. For example, avoid using outdated or unsupported versions of .NET or third-party libraries, especially those with known vulnerabilities.

Regularly update .NET, third-party libraries, and dependencies. Use tools like NuGet Package Manager for managing updates and consider employing software composition analysis tools. Use tools to scan your project for known vulnerabilities in dependencies. Tools like OWASP Dependency Check can be integrated into your build process.

A04:2025 – Cryptographic Failures

Previously known as "Sensitive Data Exposure," this focuses on the failure to properly protect data in transit and at rest. For example, storing passwords in plaintext or using weak encryption methods for sensitive data.

Utilize the Data Protection API in ASP.NET Core to encrypt sensitive data stored in your application or database. This API provides a simple way to encrypt and decrypt data securely.

Ensure HTTPS is used for all data in transit and employ strong cryptographic practices for data at rest. In ASP.NET Core, you can enforce HTTPS by configuring the middleware to redirect all HTTP requests to HTTPS.

Implement **HTTP Strict Transport Security** (**HSTS**) to prevent man-in-the-middle attacks by forcing browsers to use secure connections, as shown in the following code:

```
var builder = WebApplication.CreateBuilder(args);
...
var app = builder.Build();
...
app.UseHsts();
app.UseHttpsRedirection();
```

A05:2025 – Injection

This category includes SQL Injection, Command Injection, and so on. For example, vulnerabilities due to concatenating user inputs in SQL queries.

Employ parameterized queries with Entity Framework or use stored procedures to prevent injection flaws. Use parameterized queries with ADO.NET or LINQ to Entities to avoid SQL injection vulnerabilities. Never construct SQL queries with string concatenation. Object-Relational Mapping (ORM) tools like EF Core naturally protect against SQL injection by using parameterized queries for data access.

Validate and sanitize all user input. Ensure that all input, whether from users, files, databases, or external services, is validated against a strict specification. This means checking data for type, length, format, and range. Use .NET's built-in methods for HTML encoding and URL encoding to sanitize inputs that will be displayed on pages or included in URLs to prevent **Cross-Site Scripting** (**XSS**) attacks.

A06:2025 – Insecure Design

This is a new category focusing on risks related to design flaws. For example, designing an application without considering security from the start, leading to fundamental vulnerabilities.

Adopt a **Secure by Design** approach. Utilize threat modeling and embrace security design principles and patterns from the outset of your project.

A07:2025 – Authentication Failures

When an attacker is able to trick a system into recognizing an invalid or incorrect user as legitimate, this vulnerability is present. For example, weak password policies allowing brute force attacks or session hijacking due to insecure handling of session tokens.

Implement strong authentication mechanisms using ASP.NET Core Identity and enforce strong password policies and secure session management practices.

A08:2025 – Software and Data Integrity Failures

A new category that focuses on making unauthorized modifications to software or data, and the lack of integrity verification. For example, not verifying the integrity of third-party code or data before its execution or use within the application.

Use digital signatures or similar mechanisms to verify the integrity of third-party software, components, and data.

A09:2025 – Logging and Alerting Failures

This emphasizes the lack of or insufficient logging and monitoring. For example, failing to log security events or not monitoring logs for suspicious activity.

Implement robust logging using ASP.NET Core's logging features. Ensure that logs include security-relevant information and are monitored for anomalies.

Customize error messages to avoid revealing sensitive information about your application's internal workings, which could be exploited by attackers. Log security-relevant events without recording sensitive data. Ensure log files are stored securely and monitored for suspicious activity.

A10:2025 – Mishandling of Exceptional Conditions

This is a new category for 2025. Mishandling exceptional conditions in software happens when programs fail to prevent, detect, and respond to unusual and unpredictable situations, which leads to crashes, unexpected behavior, and sometimes vulnerabilities. This can involve one or more of the following 3 failings; the application doesn't prevent an unusual situation from happening, it doesn't identify the situation as it is happening, and/or it responds poorly or not at all to the situation afterwards.

Exceptional conditions can be caused by missing, poor, or incomplete input validation, or late, high level error handling instead at the functions where they occur, or unexpected environmental states such as memory, privilege, or network issues, inconsistent exception handling, or exceptions that are not handled at all, allowing the system to fall into an unknown and unpredictable state. Any time an application is unsure of its next instruction, an exceptional condition has been mishandled. Hard-to-find errors and exceptions can threaten the security of the whole application for a long time.

Many different security vulnerabilities can happen when we mishandle exceptional conditions, such as logic bugs, overflows, race conditions, fraudulent transactions, or issues with memory, state, resource, timing, authentication, and authorization. These types of vulnerabilities can negatively affect the confidentiality, availability, and/or integrity of a system or its data. Attackers manipulate an application's flawed error handling to strike this vulnerability.

OWASP Top 10 summary

For .NET developers, understanding and addressing these Top 10 risks is crucial for building secure web applications. Leveraging the security features provided by .NET and following best practices can help mitigate these risks and protect your applications from potential attacks.

Adopting these secure coding practices will help .NET developers build more secure applications, protect user data, and comply with regulatory requirements. It's also important to stay informed about the latest security trends and threats, as cybersecurity is an ever-evolving field.

> The latest OWASP Top 10 can be found at the following link: `https://owasp.org/Top10/`.

Threat modeling

Threat modeling is a critical process in securing applications, aimed at identifying potential threats and vulnerabilities early in the design phase so that they can be mitigated before deployment. For .NET developers, engaging in threat modeling means systematically analyzing the architecture of .NET applications to identify security risks. Microsoft offers guidance and tools specifically designed for this purpose, which can be highly beneficial in the .NET context. Here's an overview.

Microsoft Threat Modeling Tool

The Microsoft Threat Modeling Tool is perhaps the most directly relevant and powerful resource for .NET developers. It's a free tool designed to help in identifying and mitigating security threats early in the software development lifecycle.

The Microsoft Threat Modeling Tool comes with templates that are tailored for different types of applications, including web, cloud, and general software applications. These templates help in identifying common threats by focusing on relevant areas based on the application type.

The Microsoft Threat Modeling Tool allows for the creation of **Data Flow Diagrams (DFDs)** that represent the components of your application and the data flow between them. DFDs look like flow charts because that's basically what they are. This visual representation makes it easier to understand how data moves through your application and where potential vulnerabilities might exist. Based on the DFDs, the tool applies a predefined set of rules to automatically identify potential security threats, making it easier for developers to focus on mitigating identified risks.

While not specific to .NET applications, its integration capabilities with other Microsoft products and services can make it particularly useful in environments heavily reliant on Microsoft technologies.

Security Development Lifecycle (SDL)

Microsoft's **Security Development Lifecycle (SDL)** provides a software development process that helps developers build more secure software and address security compliance requirements while reducing development costs. The SDL offers guidance, practices, and tools for all phases of software development, including threat modeling.

OWASP resources

While not specifically designed for .NET, OWASP offers two resources that are highly relevant to .NET developers engaged in threat modeling.

The first is OWASP Threat Dragon. This is an open-source threat modeling tool that can be used for web and mobile applications. It provides an interactive modeling environment where you can draw data flow diagrams and automatically determine potential threats.

The other is the OWASP Cheat Sheets, which offer concise, actionable advice on a wide range of security topics, including threat modeling. These can be a great resource for understanding specific threats and mitigations.

Azure Security and Compliance Blueprints

For .NET applications hosted on Azure, Microsoft provides Azure Security and Compliance Blueprints. These blueprints offer a set of guidelines and automated deployment tools for configuring Azure resources in a way that aligns with specific compliance standards and best practices, effectively incorporating threat modeling considerations into the design of cloud-hosted applications.

.NET security best practices

Finally, Microsoft's own documentation on .NET security best practices is an invaluable resource for developers. It covers a range of topics from securing ASP.NET applications to working with cryptographic APIs in .NET. While not a tool per se, this guidance is crucial for understanding the security features available in .NET and how to effectively use them in your applications.

By leveraging these tools and resources, .NET developers can systematically identify and mitigate potential security threats, ensuring the development of secure applications. It's important to incorporate threat modeling as an integral part of the software development lifecycle, ideally revisiting and updating threat models as the application evolves and as new threats emerge.

Practicing and exploring

Test your knowledge and understanding by answering some questions, getting some hands-on practice, and exploring the topics covered in this chapter with deeper research.

Exercise 12.1 – Online-only material

The OWASP Top 10 is primarily an awareness document. If you want to use the OWASP Top 10 as a coding or testing standard, you must accept that it is just a starting point.

One of the difficulties of using the OWASP Top 10 as a standard is that its goal is to document ranked security risks, not to identify security issues that are easily testable. You cannot comprehensively detect, test, or protect against the full OWASP Top 10 due to the nature of several of the risks. For example, A04:2021 – Insecure Design is impossible to test automatically with a tool.

OWASP encourages anyone wanting to adopt an application security standard to use the OWASP **Application Security Verification Standard** (**ASVS**), as it's designed to be verifiable and tested, and can be used in all parts of a secure development lifecycle. You can read about it at the following link: `https://github.com/OWASP/ASVS/blob/master/README.md`.

> **Good practice**: Enforce the following rules for passwords: `https://pages.nist.gov/800-63-4/sp800-63b.html#passwordver`.

Exercise 12.2 – Practice exercises

Review the dev tunnels command-line reference at the following link: `https://learn.microsoft.com/en-us/azure/developer/dev-tunnels/cli-commands`.

Exercise 12.3 – Test your knowledge

Answer the following questions. If you get stuck, try googling the answers, if necessary, while remembering that if you get totally stuck, the answers are in *Appendix A*:

1. What is the relationship between test doubles, mocks, spies, stubs, fakes, and dummies?
2. For integration testing, what types of external systems should you test, and which should you mock?
3. What are dev tunnels and how are they useful to .NET developers?
4. Where should a .NET developer start with security testing?
5. What is the Microsoft Security Development Lifecycle?

> *Appendix A, Answers to the Test Your Knowledge Questions,* is available to download from the following link: `https://github.com/markjprice/tools-skills-net10/blob/main/docs/B31468_Appendix%20A.pdf`.

Exercise 12.4 – Explore topics

Use the links on the following page to learn more details about the topics covered in this chapter: `https://github.com/markjprice/tools-skills-net10/blob/main/docs/book-links.md#chapter-12---integration-and-security-testing`.

Summary

In this chapter, you learned:

- The basics of integration testing
- How to perform integration testing with data stores
- How to test services using dev tunnels
- About some concepts of security testing including OWASP Top 10

In the next chapter, you will learn about benchmarking performance using tools like BenchmarkDotNet and load and stress testing using tools like Bombardier and NBomber.

13

Benchmarking Performance, Load, and Stress Testing

Benchmarking is the process of measuring the performance of your code, applications, or systems under controlled conditions to understand how efficiently they run. In software development, this involves running carefully designed tests to determine how long specific operations take, how much memory they consume, and how well they scale under different workloads. Benchmarking is essential for .NET developers because writing functional code isn't enough. The code must also be fast, efficient, and reliable.

Optimizing performance early can prevent scalability problems, reduce infrastructure costs, and improve user experience. Without benchmarking, you're essentially guessing where performance bottlenecks exist, which can lead to wasted effort or even degraded application behavior. Accurate measurements help you make informed decisions about optimizations and trade-offs rather than relying on assumptions.

In the .NET ecosystem, **BenchmarkDotNet** is the most widely used library for benchmarking code performance. It simplifies the process of writing, running, and analyzing benchmarks by handling warmups, statistical analysis, and reporting automatically. Using BenchmarkDotNet, you can measure execution times with high precision and compare different implementations side by side.

Beyond benchmarking individual pieces of code, developers often need to understand how entire applications behave under real-world usage. This is where load testing and stress testing come in. Load testing evaluates how your application performs under expected levels of traffic, while stress testing pushes it beyond normal capacity to identify breaking points and ensure graceful degradation under extreme conditions.

Benchmarking is important for .NET developers for many reasons, and they boil down to ensuring that the code they write is efficient as well as functional.

This chapter covers the following topics:

- Benchmarking performance
- BenchmarkDotNet for benchmarking performance
- Load and stress testing
- Bombardier – a fast cross-platform HTTP benchmarking tool
- NBomber – a load testing framework

Benchmarking performance

Benchmarking is about identifying bottlenecks and inefficient code paths that could slow down your code. By comparing different algorithms or strategies under the same conditions, you can pinpoint which one offers the best performance, whether it's faster execution, lower memory usage, or better CPU efficiency.

Regular benchmarking can also expose issues that might not surface under normal development testing, like memory leaks, concurrency problems with multiple threads, or scalability issues when handling large volumes of data or high traffic.

When you have concrete data on how various implementations compare to each other, you can make informed decisions. Whether it's choosing between different libraries, frameworks, or architectural patterns, benchmarking provides the evidence needed to make a confident decision. This will help you avoid premature optimizations or going down the path of using a trendy new tool or technique that might not actually be the best fit for your project. For example, do you really need to use an efficiently optimized gRPC microservice or would a simple web service suffice?

For applications where speed and efficiency are critical, like high-frequency trading platforms, real-time analytics, and gaming, being able to process data faster or handle more users simultaneously can make or break your .NET projects.

The performance of your software also affects the user experience. Users have little patience for slow-loading websites, laggy applications, or crashes due to resource exhaustion. Regular benchmarking and optimization based on those results can lead to higher user satisfaction.

In cloud computing environments, where resources are billed based on usage, efficient code can significantly reduce operational costs. Benchmarking helps identify areas where resources are being wasted or where a more cost-effective approach could be adopted without compromising performance.

By embracing benchmarking, you can not only enhance your skills and be more valuable to your employer but also significantly contribute to the success of your projects and the satisfaction of your users. It's another one of those areas where your investment in time and resources pays off many times over.

One of the most important concepts in benchmarking is recording baseline measurements. Let's find out why.

Importance of a baseline

Recording a baseline is crucial because it sets the context for everything that comes after. Without a baseline, it is impossible to know if any changes you make are a benefit or a detriment.

Technology environments are dynamic, with frequent changes to code, infrastructure, and usage patterns. A baseline recorded at the beginning of a project or during a stable period serves as a reference point to monitor performance over time. This ongoing comparison can alert you to performance regressions, scalability issues, or the need for further optimization.

A baseline provides a concrete, initial set of data against which all future changes, optimizations, and modifications can be compared. Without this reference point, you cannot objectively assess whether a particular change has improved performance, degraded it, or had no significant impact.

Recording a baseline gives you a detailed snapshot of how your system or application performs under specific conditions. This snapshot can include metrics like:

- Response times
- Throughput
- Resource utilization, for example, CPU, memory, and disk I/O

Which you choose depends on what aspects of performance are most important to your goals. By understanding the current performance levels, organizations can set realistic, achievable goals for improvement. Without a baseline, you might aim too high and set unachievable targets.

In many cases, optimizations require investment, whether it's in developer time, new hardware, or software tools. A baseline provides the evidence needed to justify these investments by demonstrating evidence of improvements. It's much easier to secure resources when you can show concrete data on current performance and articulate how proposed changes could lead to measurable gains.

Some projects are subject to regulatory requirements or must meet specific **Service Level Agreements (SLAs)**, so establishing a baseline not only demonstrates current compliance but also helps ensure that future changes don't inadvertently cause violations of these obligations.

Imagine that you're trying to lose weight. You spend six months exercising and eating better, and then weigh yourself on a scale and measure your waistline. How do you know that you've achieved your goal? You must weigh yourself and measure your waistline *before* you spend six months performing actions to lose weight as well as *after*!

By understanding where you're starting from, you can make informed decisions, track progress over time, and ultimately drive improvements that matter. A baseline is your anchor, ensuring that your efforts lead to tangible, positive outcomes.

When discussing performance and comparing options to improve it, it is useful to have standard ways of describing the time and space complexity of a problem that takes time and resources to execute. Let's see some common ways to do this.

Big O notation

Big O notation and related performance concepts are fundamental in understanding the efficiency of algorithms, especially in terms of time and space (memory) complexity. These concepts help programmers and computer scientists predict how an algorithm will perform, both in the worst-case scenario and as the size of the input data grows.

Big O notation is a mathematical notation that describes the upper bound of an algorithm's running time or space requirement in the worst-case scenario. It provides a high-level understanding of the algorithm's efficiency by describing how its performance scales with the size of the input data, which is denoted as "n."

The main purpose of Big O notation is to provide a way to compare the efficiency of algorithms by abstracting away constants and lower-order terms, and focusing on the main factors that contribute to the growth rate of the runtime or memory usage.

Big O notation time complexity descriptions with algorithm examples are shown in *Table 13.1*:

Notation	Time	Description	Example
`O(1)`	Constant	The execution time of an algorithm is fixed and does not change with the size of the input data set.	Accessing any element in an array by index.
`O(n)`	Linear	The execution time grows linearly with the input size.	Searching for an element in an unsorted array.
`O(log n)`	Logarithmic	The execution time grows logarithmically as the input size increases.	Binary search in a sorted array.
`O(n log n)`	Linearithmic	The execution time grows faster than linear but not exponentially.	Sorting algorithms like mergesort and heapsort.
`O(n^2)`	Quadratic	The execution time grows quadratically with the input size.	Bubble sort algorithm for sorting.
`O(2^n)`	Exponential	The execution time doubles with each additional element in the input data. Algorithms with this complexity are often seen in brute-force solutions for combinatorial problems.	Recursive solution to the Fibonacci sequence problem.

Table 13.1: Big O notation time complexity descriptions and example algorithms

To better grasp the differences between the notations, some Big O notation example values are shown in *Table 13.2*:

n	log n	n log n	n^2	2^n
1	-	-	1	2
2	0.3	0.60	4	4
5	0.7	3.49	25	32
20	1.3	26.02	400	1,048,576
50	1.7	84.95	2,500	1,125,899,906,842,620

Table 13.2: Big O notation time complexity example values

Space complexity refers to the amount of memory an algorithm needs to complete its execution as a function of the size of the input data. Like time complexity, it can also be expressed using Big O notation. Taking space complexity into account allows the development of algorithms that do not exceed the memory limitations of a system, especially for large datasets or constrained environments like embedded systems.

Supplementary notations for Big O include:

- **Theta (Θ) notation** describes the exact upper and lower bounds of an algorithm's runtime. It's a tighter bound than Big O, providing a more precise measure of an algorithm's efficiency.
- **Omega (Ω) notation** represents the lower bound of an algorithm's running time, indicating the minimum time required by the algorithm for any input.

By describing algorithms with these notations, developers can predict their performance, and make informed choices about which algorithms to use based on the context and requirements of their projects.

Statistical metrics

P95 and P99 are statistical metrics used to describe the performance characteristics of web services, applications, and systems, especially in terms of latency or response times. These metrics are percentiles, which provide a way to understand the distribution of a dataset. What they specifically represent is described in the following bullets:

- **P95 (95th percentile):** This value indicates that 95% of the response times are below this value, and 5% are above. For example, if the P95 latency of a web service is 200 milliseconds, it means that 95% of all requests are processed in 200 milliseconds or less, and only 5% of requests take longer than that. It's a strong indicator of the general user experience under normal operating conditions, as it excludes the slowest 5% of requests, which might be outliers due to exceptional conditions.

- **P99 (99th percentile)**: This value shows that 99% of the response times are below this value, and 1% are above. If the P99 latency is 500 milliseconds, it means that 99% of all requests are processed in 500 milliseconds or less, with only 1% taking longer. This metric helps you understand the performance outliers and ensures that even the slowest responses are within acceptable limits. It's particularly important for services with high reliability and performance requirements, as it addresses the experience of the "worst-off" users.

P95 and P99 help in understanding the overall experience for most users, including those who might experience longer-than-average wait times. These percentiles are valuable for identifying and troubleshooting performance bottlenecks. By focusing on the higher percentiles, developers can pinpoint issues that only arise under heavy load or due to unusual conditions.

Understanding the distribution of response times, including the extremes, aids in effective capacity planning. It ensures that systems can handle not just the average case but also the edge cases with grace. Many SLAs include percentile metrics to define acceptable performance thresholds, making P95 and P99 vital for compliance.

P95 and P99 percentiles provide a more nuanced view of system behavior than average response times, highlighting the experiences of those who encounter the slowest responses. Optimizing for these percentiles can significantly improve user satisfaction and system robustness, especially in applications where performance is key.

Now, let's look at one of the most popular practical tools for benchmarking.

Using BenchmarkDotNet for benchmarking performance

There is a popular benchmarking NuGet package for .NET that Microsoft uses in its blog posts about performance improvements, and newsletter and LinkedIn posters frequently use it to provide evidence for a faster approach to solving a .NET problem. It is therefore important for .NET developers to know how BenchmarkDotNet works and how to use it for their own performance testing.

Writing benchmarks is a bit like writing unit tests. You need to create a class with methods that represent different benchmark tests. With BenchmarkDotNet, you decorate the methods with the `[Benchmark]` attribute. One of those methods must be set as the baseline using the `[Benchmark(Baseline = true)]` attribute to which the other benchmark methods will be compared.

Comparing string concatenation and string builder

Let's see how we could use it to compare performance between the `string` concatenation (which will be our baseline) and `StringBuilder` (which we expect will be an improvement):

1. Use your preferred code editor to add a new console app to the `Chapter13` solution named `BenchmarkApp`.

2. In the BenchmarkApp project, treat warnings as errors, statically and globally import Console, and add a package reference to BenchmarkDotNet, as shown in the following markup:

```
<ItemGroup>
  <Using Include="System.Console" static="true" />
</ItemGroup>

<ItemGroup>
  <PackageReference Include="BenchmarkDotNet" />
</ItemGroup>
```

3. Build the BenchmarkApp project to restore packages.
4. Add a new class file named StringBenchmarks.cs.
5. In StringBenchmarks.cs, add statements to define a class with methods for each benchmark you want to run, in this case, two methods that both combine 100 comma-separated numbers using either the string concatenation or StringBuilder, as shown in the following code:

```
using BenchmarkDotNet.Attributes; // To use [Benchmark].

// Same null namespace as in Program.cs.

public class StringBenchmarks
{
  int[] numbers;

  public StringBenchmarks()
  {
    numbers = Enumerable.Range(
      start: 1, count: 100).ToArray();
  }

  [Benchmark(Baseline = true)]
  public string StringConcatenationTest()
  {
    string s = string.Empty; // e.g. ""

    for (int i = 0; i < numbers.Length; i++)
    {
      s += numbers[i] + ", ";
    }

    return s;
  }
```

```
  [Benchmark]
  public string StringBuilderTest()
  {
    System.Text.StringBuilder builder = new();

    for (int i = 0; i < numbers.Length; i++)
    {
      builder.Append(numbers[i]);
      builder.Append(", ");
    }

    return builder.ToString();
  }
}
```

6. In `Program.cs`, delete the existing statements, import the namespace for running benchmarks, and add a statement to run the benchmarks class, as shown in the following code:

```
using BenchmarkDotNet.Running; // To use BenchmarkRunner.

BenchmarkRunner.Run<StringBenchmarks>();
```

7. Use your preferred code editor to run the console app with its release configuration:
   - In Visual Studio, in the toolbar, set **Solution Configurations** to **Release**, and then navigate to **Debug** | **Start Without Debugging**.
   - In VS Code, in a terminal, use the `dotnet run --configuration Release` command.

> **Good practice:** When running benchmark projects, you must always compile and run a release configuration to get accurate measurements.

8. Note the results, including some artifacts like exported report files and, most importantly, a summary table that shows that the `string` concatenation took a mean of 2,484.6 ns and `StringBuilder` took a mean of 780.6 ns, which is less than one third of the time, as shown in the following partial output:

```
// Validating benchmarks:
// ***** BenchmarkRunner: Start   *****
// ***** Found 2 benchmark(s) in total *****
// ***** Building 1 exe(s) in Parallel: Start   *****
```

```
// start dotnet  restore /p:UseSharedCompilation=false
/p:BuildInParallel=false /m:1 /p:Deterministic=true /p:Optimize=true
in C:\tools-skills-net10\Chapter13\BenchmarkApp\bin\Release\
net10.0\36a5f5cd-d053-416c-92e9-a04028e30b91
...
// ***** Done, took 00:00:18 (18.09 sec)   *****
// Found 2 benchmarks:
//   StringBenchmarks.StringConcatenationTest: DefaultJob
//   StringBenchmarks.StringBuilderTest: DefaultJob
...
// ***** BenchmarkRunner: Finish  *****
// * Export *
  BenchmarkDotNet.Artifacts\results\StringBenchmarks-report.csv
  BenchmarkDotNet.Artifacts\results\StringBenchmarks-report-github.md
  BenchmarkDotNet.Artifacts\results\StringBenchmarks-report.html
// * Detailed results *
StringBenchmarks.StringConcatenationTest: DefaultJob
Runtime = .NET 10.0.2 (10.0.224.6711), X64 RyuJIT AVX-
512F+CD+BW+DQ+VL+VBMI; GC = Concurrent Workstation
Mean = 2.485 us, StdErr = 0.012 us (0.50%), N = 18, StdDev = 0.053 us
Min = 2.418 us, Q1 = 2.438 us, Median = 2.481 us, Q3 = 2.520 us, Max =
2.588 us
IQR = 0.082 us, LowerFence = 2.315 us, UpperFence = 2.644 us
ConfidenceInterval = [2.435 us; 2.534 us] (CI 99.9%), Margin = 0.049 us
(1.98% of Mean)
Skewness = 0.29, Kurtosis = 1.7, MValue = 2
-------------------- Histogram --------------------
[2.416 us ; 2.469 us) | @@@@@@@@@
[2.469 us ; 2.544 us) | @@@@@@@
[2.544 us ; 2.601 us) | @@
---------------------------------------------------
StringBenchmarks.StringBuilderTest: DefaultJob
Runtime = .NET 10.0.2 (10.0.224.6711), X64 RyuJIT AVX-
512F+CD+BW+DQ+VL+VBMI; GC = Concurrent Workstation
Mean = 780.606 ns, StdErr = 3.884 ns (0.50%), N = 63, StdDev = 30.832 ns
Min = 734.198 ns, Q1 = 768.066 ns, Median = 774.160 ns, Q3 = 783.365 ns,
Max = 944.730 ns
IQR = 15.299 ns, LowerFence = 745.118 ns, UpperFence = 806.313 ns
ConfidenceInterval = [767.187 ns; 794.025 ns] (CI 99.9%), Margin = 13.419
ns (1.72% of Mean)
Skewness = 2.96, Kurtosis = 14.79, MValue = 2
-------------------- Histogram --------------------
```

```
[724.028 ns ; 744.242 ns) | @
[744.242 ns ; 764.820 ns) | @@@@@@@@@@@@
[764.820 ns ; 785.160 ns) | @@@@@@@@@@@@@@@@@@@@@@@@@@@@@@@@@@@@@@
[785.160 ns ; 817.544 ns) | @@@@@@@@@
[817.544 ns ; 837.885 ns) |
[837.885 ns ; 874.367 ns) | @@
[874.367 ns ; 894.707 ns) |
[894.707 ns ; 915.047 ns) |
[915.047 ns ; 934.560 ns) |
[934.560 ns ; 954.900 ns) | @
---------------------------------------------------
// * Summary *
BenchmarkDotNet v0.13.12, Windows 11 (10.0.22631.3235/23H2/2023Update/
SunValley3)
11th Gen Intel Core i7-1165G7 2.80GHz, 1 CPU, 8 logical and 4 physical
cores
.NET SDK 10.0.100
  [Host]     : .NET 10.0.2 (10.0.224.6711), X64 RyuJIT AVX-
512F+CD+BW+DQ+VL+VBMI
  DefaultJob : .NET 10.0.2 (10.0.224.6711), X64 RyuJIT AVX-
512F+CD+BW+DQ+VL+VBMI
| Method                    | Mean       | Error     | StdDev    | Ratio |
RatioSD |
|------------------------- |-----------:|----------:|----------:|------:|--
------:|
| StringConcatenationTest | 2,484.6 ns | 49.14 ns | 52.58 ns |  1.00 |
0.00 |
| StringBuilderTest       |   780.6 ns | 13.42 ns | 30.83 ns |  0.32 |
0.02 |
// * Hints *
Outliers
  StringBenchmarks.StringBuilderTest: Default -> 18 outliers were removed
(1.00 us..1.47 us)
// * Legends *
  Mean    : Arithmetic mean of all measurements
  Error   : Half of 99.9% confidence interval
  StdDev  : Standard deviation of all measurements
  Ratio   : Mean of the ratio distribution ([Current]/[Baseline])
  RatioSD : Standard deviation of the ratio distribution ([Current]/
[Baseline])
  1 ns    : 1 Nanosecond (0.000000001 sec)
// ***** BenchmarkRunner: End *****
```

```
Run time: 00:01:44 (104.27 sec), executed benchmarks: 2
Global total time: 00:02:02 (122.6 sec), executed benchmarks: 2
// * Artifacts cleanup *
Artifacts cleanup is finished
```

Your results will vary, of course. Note that there might not be a `Hints` and an `Outliers` section if there are no outliers when you run your benchmarks!

Comparing Fibonacci implementations

Now, let's compare ways to implement an algorithm for Fibonacci:

1. In the `BenchmarkApp` project, add a new class file named `FibonacciBenchmarks.cs`.
2. In `FibonacciBenchmarks.cs`, add statements to define a class with methods for each benchmark you want to run, as shown in the following code:

```
using BenchmarkDotNet.Attributes; // To use [Benchmark].

public class FibonacciBenchmarks
{
  private const long n = 10;

  public long RecursiveFibonacci(long n)
  {
    if (n <= 0) return 0;
    if (n == 1) return 1;
    return RecursiveFibonacci(n - 1) + RecursiveFibonacci(n - 2);
  }

  [Benchmark(Baseline = true)]
  public long RecursiveTest()
  {
    return RecursiveFibonacci(n);
  }

  public static long BinetsFibonacci(long n)
  {
    double sqrt5 = Math.Sqrt(5);
    double phi = (1 + sqrt5) / 2;
    double psi = (1 - sqrt5) / 2;

    return (long)((Math.Pow(phi, n) - Math.Pow(psi, n)) / sqrt5);
  }
```

```
    [Benchmark]
    public long BinetsTest()
    {
      return BinetsFibonacci(n);
    }
}
```

Binet's formula provides a direct way to calculate the nth Fibonacci number without recursion, significantly improving the performance. This formula uses the golden ratio, denoted by phi (φ), and its conjugate, psi (ψ). You can learn more at the following link: `https://artofproblemsolving.com/wiki/index.php/Binet%27s_Formula`.

3. In `Program.cs`, comment out the existing statement that runs the string benchmarks, and then add a statement to run the Fibonacci benchmarks class, as shown in the following code:

```
// BenchmarkRunner.Run<StringBenchmarks>();
BenchmarkRunner.Run<FibonacciBenchmarks>();
```

4. Use your preferred code editor to run the console app with its release configuration:
    - In Visual Studio, in the toolbar, set **Solution Configurations** to **Release**, and then navigate to **Debug** | **Start Without Debugging**.
    - In VS Code, in a terminal, use the `dotnet run --configuration Release` command.
5. Note the results that show that when `n=10` the recursive method took a mean of 155.22 ns and Binet's method took a mean of 40.34 ns, which is almost only one quarter of the time, as shown in the following partial output:

```
| Method        | Mean      | Error     | StdDev    | Ratio |
|-------------- |----------:|----------:|----------:|------:|
| RecursiveTest | 155.22 ns | 2.940 ns  | 2.750 ns  |  1.00 |
| BinetsTest    |  40.34 ns | 0.385 ns  | 0.360 ns  |  0.26 |
```

Avoiding benchmarking mistakes

As with any tool, BenchmarkDotNet's effectiveness depends on how it's used.

Isolating benchmarking code from setup or teardown

One common mistake is not isolating the code you're benchmarking from the setup or teardown logic. BenchmarkDotNet provides the `[GlobalSetup]` and `[GlobalCleanup]` attributes to separate the setup and cleanup code from the actual benchmarking code. Not using these properly can lead to including setup time in the benchmark results, skewing the performance metrics.

Let's walk through an example of how to properly use BenchmarkDotNet's `[GlobalSetup]` and `[GlobalCleanup]` attributes to isolate your benchmarking code from the setup and teardown logic:

1. In the `BenchmarkApp` project, add a class file named `SortingBenchmarks.cs`.
2. In `SortingBenchmarks.cs`, define a class that measures the performance of a method that sorts an array. We'll compare two different sorting methods, `Array.Sort` and a custom implementation of bubble sort, as shown in the following code:

```
using BenchmarkDotNet.Attributes; // To use [GlobalSetup] and so on.

public class SortingBenchmarks
{
  private int[] data = null!; // Disable null warnings for data.
  private int[] dataArraySort = null!;
  private int[] dataBubbleSort = null!;

  [GlobalSetup]
  public void Setup()
  {
    // Initialize the data array with random values.
    data = new int[1000];

    for (int i = 0; i < data.Length; i++)
    {
      data[i] = Random.Shared.Next(0, 10000);
    }

    // Create copies of the data array to ensure each run uses the same
unsorted data.
    dataArraySort = (int[])data.Clone();
    dataBubbleSort = (int[])data.Clone();
  }

  [Benchmark]
  public void ArraySort()
  {
    Array.Sort(dataArraySort);
  }

  [Benchmark]
  public void BubbleSort()
  {
```

```
        BubbleSort(dataBubbleSort);
    }

    private void BubbleSort(int[] array)
    {
        int n = array.Length;

        for (int i = 0; i < n - 1; i++)
        {
            for (int j = 0; j < n - i - 1; j++)
            {
                if (array[j] > array[j + 1])
                {
                    // Swap array[j] and array[j + 1].
                    int temp = array[j];
                    array[j] = array[j + 1];
                    array[j + 1] = temp;
                }
            }
        }
    }

    [GlobalCleanup]
    public void Cleanup()
    {
        // Clean up resources if necessary.
        data = [];
        dataArraySort = [];
        dataBubbleSort = [];
    }
}
```

Note the following about the preceding code:

- The `Setup` method is decorated with `[GlobalSetup]`. This method initializes the data array with random values. This setup ensures that every benchmark run starts with the same initial conditions.

> **Good practice:** Although you can use a constructor for initial setup, do so only when you need the absolute minimum bootstrapping to create an instance, and keep that constructor trivial. Prefer `[GlobalSetup]` in almost all cases because it pairs nicely with `[GlobalCleanup]` and it runs once per benchmarked method after BenchmarkDotNet has initialized your `[Params]` fields or properties. That means your setup code can depend on the parameter values that will be used in the run. A constructor runs earlier, before params are applied, so it can't reliably read them.

- The `ArraySort` method benchmarks `Array.Sort`. It clones the data array to ensure that each run works with the same unsorted data.
- The `BubbleSort` method benchmarks a custom bubble sort implementation. Like `ArraySort`, it clones the data array for consistency.
- The `Cleanup` method is decorated with `[GlobalCleanup]`. This method resets the data array to null. While this cleanup is trivial in this example, it demonstrates where you would release resources if necessary.

3. In `Program.cs`, run the benchmark, as shown in the following code:

```
BenchmarkRunner.Run<SortingBenchmarks>();
```

4. Run the project and note the results which show that `ArraySort` is approximately 122 times faster than `BubbleSort`, as shown in the following output:

```
| Method     | Mean       | Error     | StdDev    |
|----------- |-----------:|----------:|----------:|
| ArraySort  |   2.962 us | 0.0569 us | 0.0533 us |
| BubbleSort | 363.691 us | 7.1306 us | 7.6523 us |
```

This approach ensures your benchmarks are accurate and reflect the true performance of the methods being tested, without being skewed by setup or teardown logic.

Trust the tool

The **Just-In-Time** (**JIT**) compiler optimizes code during runtime, which can affect benchmarking results if not accounted for. BenchmarkDotNet automatically handles JIT warming up, but misunderstanding or trying to manually manage this process can lead to incorrect assumptions about code performance. Always trust the tool to manage JIT effects properly.

By default, BenchmarkDotNet tries to run a sufficient number of iterations to achieve statistically significant results. However, altering the default settings without a thorough understanding, for example, reducing the iteration count to save time, can result in unreliable data due to insufficient sample size or variability in execution times.

Compare like to like

Comparing results from different machines, environments, or configurations can lead to misleading conclusions. BenchmarkDotNet provides the ability to export and compare results, but it's important to ensure that comparisons are made under similar conditions and that the differences in hardware or environment settings are accounted for.

Failing to version control benchmark results makes it difficult to track performance changes over time. BenchmarkDotNet can export results in various formats like Markdown and CSV, which should be version controlled alongside code to document performance improvements or regressions.

Running benchmarks against debug builds instead of release builds can provide misleading results due to the lack of optimizations in debug builds. Always ensure that benchmarks are run in an environment as close to production as possible, typically using release builds.

Beware of environmental variations

Benchmark results can be affected by statistical noise caused by background processes, operating system (OS) scheduling, hardware variability, and so on. It's important to understand and recognize the variability in benchmark results and not make performance decisions based on small differences that fall within the margin of error.

Identifying poor blog posts about performance

These days, it is common to see people try to earn clout on social networking sites like LinkedIn by posting about performance. Let's see how to identify posts that might be misusing BenchmarkDotNet or similar benchmarking tools in a way that leads to incorrect conclusions about method performance.

When browsing LinkedIn or technical blogs for performance comparisons, there are some red flags that might suggest a misuse of BenchmarkDotNet or a misinterpretation of its results, as shown in the following list:

- **Lack of context**: If the post does not provide context about the environment in which the benchmarks were run, for example, hardware specifications, runtime version, and OS, then the results might not be reliable or applicable to other environments.
- **Not mentioning the BenchmarkDotNet version**: BenchmarkDotNet is actively developed, and performance metrics can change between versions due to improvements in the tool itself. Posts should specify the version used for transparency and reproducibility.
- **Ignoring statistical significance**: BenchmarkDotNet provides statistical analysis of the run, including error margins. Posts that claim one method is better than another without discussing the statistical significance of the difference might be misleading.
- **Comparing different workloads**: Ensure the methods being compared are doing equivalent work. A common mistake is comparing two methods that seem similar but actually perform different amounts of work or handle edge cases differently.
- **Overlooking the cold start impact**: The first execution of a method can be slower due to JIT compilation and other initialization overheads. Posts that do not account for this by allowing a warm-up period might not accurately represent the typical performance of a method.

- **Focusing solely on speed:** Optimizations often come with trade-offs in memory usage, maintainability, or readability. Posts that focus exclusively on execution speed without discussing these trade-offs provide an incomplete picture.
- **Small sample sizes:** BenchmarkDotNet allows the configuration of the number of iterations and warm-up iterations. Results based on too few iterations can be noisy and less reliable.
- **Cherry picking results:** Be wary of posts that only show selected results favoring one method without providing the full context of the tests, including cases where the other method might perform better.
- **Rarely executed workloads:** Even when everything else is good, if the workload being optimized is something that your project will almost never run, what's even the point? An example of this that seems to have become common recently is converting an `enum` value into its text, with the comparison being between calling `ToString()` and calling `nameof()`. Using `nameof()` is dramatically faster because the conversion happens once at compile time instead of runtime.

When evaluating performance comparisons, look for posts that provide a comprehensive view of the tests conducted, including setup, configuration, and an in-depth analysis of the results. Critical thinking and a healthy skepticism can help you discern whether a performance comparison is genuinely useful or potentially misleading.

A genuine performance expert is Feng Yuan, an ex-performance architect at Microsoft, ex-host of FrugalTips, and a published author. He recently retired to raise goats on his farm (yes, really), but he is still often seen on LinkedIn pointing out all the poor performance tip posts and explaining why they are half-baked. If you are on LinkedIn, I recommend following his account at the following link: `https://www.linkedin.com/in/dryuan/`. He was the main author of tips on Frugal Cafe, found at the following link: `https://frugalcafe.beehiiv.com/`.

Good practice: If you'd like to write your own benchmarking blog posts, then I strongly recommend that you use Stephen Toub's posts as good examples to follow. You can find the most recent post at the following link: `https://github.com/markjprice/tools-skills-net10/blob/main/docs/book-links.md#net-performance-improvements`.

Now, let's move on to load and stress testing, which are types of performance testing.

Load and stress testing

Load testing is a type of performance testing used to determine a system's behavior under both normal and anticipated peak load conditions. It helps to identify any bottlenecks and how the system handles up to the maximum expected volume of requests. Load testing ensures that your application can handle peak traffic moments smoothly, which helps maintain a positive user experience.

One of the primary purposes of load testing is to verify that an application can scale up to support the maximum expected volume of users. This involves scaling resources efficiently to maintain performance standards without degradation as the load increases.

You would typically measure performance at various loads, as described in *Table 13.3*:

Load	Description
Typical load	Average expected load on a typical day.
Peak load	Maximum expected user load. For example, if you expect a maximum of 1,000 user requests to the home page per second or 100 shopping cart checkouts per second.
Peak + 20%	The maximum expected user load plus a margin to represent those times when unexpected load may occur. It is useful to know how the system reacts when the load is more than expected, what throughput can still be achieved, or what experience some or all of those users will have when this occurs. For example, if only some users experience timeouts, but the system can still process the expected load, that's good. But if every user is negatively impacted, you might want to make changes to your architecture.
Overload	The load that causes the system to fail to deliver the required throughput. You keep increasing from the peak until you hit that limit and then record the load. This can be stored with the documentation so you know in advance what load will cause your system to overload. This is also known as stress testing.

Table 13.3: Various types of load

By simulating real-world usage, load testing helps ensure that your application remains stable and reliable under various conditions. It can uncover issues that might not arise during development or standard testing, such as race conditions, memory leaks, or database lockups, which could lead to downtime or poor user experience.

Another aspect of load testing is identifying bottlenecks within the system. These could be in the application's code, database, network, or infrastructure setup. Understanding where these bottlenecks occur allows developers to make targeted improvements to increase overall performance and efficiency.

For businesses that experience seasonal traffic spikes or those launching marketing campaigns expected to drive significant traffic, load testing helps with planning. It reduces the risk of system failures during these critical periods by ensuring the application can handle the expected load.

Stress testing, on the other hand, aims to determine the application's robustness and error-handling capabilities under extreme conditions. It's designed to push the application to its limits and beyond, to see how it behaves under stress and how it recovers when returning to normal conditions.

The focus of stress testing is on stability and recovery. It involves testing the application with load and input beyond normal operational capacity, often to the point of breaking it, to identify how the system fails and what its breaking points are.

The insights gained from stress testing help you understand the boundaries of an application. It highlights how the system reacts to failure, how gracefully it degrades, and how it recovers (or fails to recover) once the load returns to normal levels. This is particularly important for applications where failure can have significant repercussions.

Load testing is used to validate that the system can handle expected traffic, supporting performance tuning and scalability efforts. Stress testing is used to identify conditions under which the system will fail, how it fails, and what indicators can be monitored to predict and prevent future failures.

Both load testing and stress testing are integral to a comprehensive performance testing strategy. They provide different, yet complementary, insights into an application's performance, stability, and resilience. While load testing ensures that the application can meet day-to-day demands, stress testing prepares it for the unexpected, ensuring that any potential failure does so with minimal impact and with known recovery paths. Together, they help in building robust, efficient, and user-friendly applications that can withstand both the expected and the unforeseen.

Let's briefly talk about a tool, Apache JMeter, that can automate load and stress testing, and then look at another tool, Bombardier, in more detail.

> **Warning!** Before being deprecated, **Visual Studio's Load Test** was a popular choice among .NET developers for conducting web performance and load testing directly within Visual Studio. It allowed the testing of web applications, services, and Azure resources. Despite its deprecation, you will still find resources referring to it. Microsoft recommends using alternatives like Apache JMeter for new projects.

Apache JMeter

Apache JMeter runs on the Java platform, so it is inherently cross-platform like .NET. JMeter tests can be integrated into **continuous integration/continuous deployment** (**CI/CD**) pipelines. For .NET projects, this means you can automate performance testing as part of your build and deployment process, using tools like Jenkins, TeamCity, or Azure DevOps.

This integration helps catch performance issues early in the development cycle, making it easier to address them before they affect production environments.

.NET developers working on web applications using ASP.NET Core can use JMeter to simulate a heavy load on their applications to test performance under stress. JMeter can mimic multiple users accessing the website or service simultaneously, allowing you to understand how your project behaves under high demand. JMeter has capabilities to test web services by sending various HTTP requests to these services, validating their responses, and ensuring they meet performance benchmarks.

JMeter can be used to test the performance of SQL queries or stored procedures. By simulating concurrent database operations, developers can identify slow-running queries or transactions that might become performance issues in production environments.

JMeter is open source and free so you can add performance testing without investing in expensive tools. It has community support and extensive documentation to make it easy to get started. Most of my readers do not want to install Java on their computer so we will not look at Apache JMeter examples in this book. Instead, we will use some alternatives, including Bombardier.

You can learn more about Apache JMeter at the following link: `https://jmeter.apache.org/`.

Bombardier – a fast cross-platform HTTP benchmarking tool

Bombardier is a high-performance, cross-platform HTTP benchmarking tool written in Go. It's designed to generate a significant load to test the performance of web servers and services with minimal impact on the system itself. Bombardier can produce many requests per second, making it suitable for stress testing and load testing web applications to understand how they behave under heavy traffic conditions.

Features of Bombardier include the following:

- **Concurrency support**: Bombardier can simulate numerous concurrent connections to a web service, enabling developers to understand how their applications handle simultaneous requests.
- **Fast HTTP engine**: Bombardier can quickly send a vast number of requests, making it an excellent tool for high-load testing.
- **Cross platform**: Being written in Go, Bombardier can be compiled and run on various OS', including Windows, Linux, and macOS, making it accessible to .NET developers regardless of their development environment.
- **Customizable requests:** It allows for the customization of headers, payloads, and HTTP methods, enabling more detailed and targeted testing scenarios.
- **Detailed statistics**: After running tests, Bombardier provides detailed statistics, including request counts, success rates, latencies, and throughput, offering valuable insights into the performance characteristics of the web service.

Let's start by reviewing the usual steps to use Bombardier, and then you can follow a practical example step by step.

Using Bombardier

Bombardier can be downloaded as a precompiled binary or as source code from its GitHub repository or using package managers on some platforms.

Before benchmarking, ensure your web service is deployed in an environment that closely mimics the production setup. If you cannot closely mimic the production setup, then this could be on a local development machine, in a staging environment, or even in a scaled-down version of the production environment.

You can execute Bombardier tests against your web service by specifying the target URL and various command-line options to adjust the load and behavior of the tests.

For example, to send 10,000 requests with 100 concurrent connections, you might use:

```
bombardier -c 100 -n 10000 http://yourwebservice.com/api/resource
```

After the test completes, analyze the output provided by Bombardier. Key metrics to pay attention to include the number of requests per second, average latency, and the percentage of successful requests. These metrics can help identify bottlenecks, understand capacity limits, and plan for scaling.

Use Bombardier iteratively to test different aspects of your web service by altering request payloads, headers, or the HTTP method. This approach helps identify specific areas for optimization.

For advanced use cases, consider integrating Bombardier into your CI/CD pipelines to automatically run performance tests against your web service with each deployment or update. This can help catch performance regressions early in the development cycle.

Downloading Bombardier

Let's get Bombardier:

1. Navigate to `https://github.com/codesenberg/bombardier/releases`. The latest release at the time of writing in November 2025 is version 2.0.2 from March 2025.
2. Download the appropriate executable to a suitable directory. For example, for Windows x64, download the file named `bombardier-windows-amd64.exe`.
3. Rename the downloaded executable as `bombardier.exe`.
4. Optionally, set the system path to include the directory containing `bombardier.exe`.
5. At the command prompt or terminal, confirm that Bombardier is responding by asking for help, as shown in the following command:

   ```
   bombardier --help
   ```

More help is available using `--help-long` and `--help-man`.

Note some of the most important Bombardier command line switches, as shown in *Table 13.4*:

Switch	Description
`-c, --connections <integer>`	Maximum number of concurrent connections.
`-d, --duration <duration>`	Duration of test. For example, `10s` for ten seconds.
`-n, --requests <integer>`	Number of requests.
`-r, --rate <integer>`	Rate limit in requests per second.
`-t, --timeout <duration>`	Socket/request timeout. For example, `2s`.
`--http1`	Use `net/http` client with *forced* HTTP/1.x.

`--http2`	Use `net/http` client with *enabled* HTTP/2.0.
`-m, --method <string>`	Request method. For example, `GET`, `POST`.
`-H, --headers <string>`	HTTP headers to use (can be repeated).
`-b, --body <string>`	Request body.
`-f, --body-file <path>`	File to use as request body.
`-l, --latencies`	Print latency statistics.
`-p, --print <string>`	Specifies what to output. Comma-separated list of values `'intro'` (short: `'i'`), `'progress'` (short: `'p'`), and `'result'` (short: `'r'`).
`-o, --format <string>`	Specifies which format to use to output the result. Formats understood by Bombardier are `plain-text` (short: `pt`) or `json` (short: `j`). You can also specify a path to a user-defined template that uses Go's text/template syntax.

Table 13.4: Common Bombardier command line switches

Next, we need projects to test and compare using Bombardier. Recently, the .NET team added a great new performance feature for web service development: native **Ahead-Of-Time** (**AOT**) compilation. Let's use Bombardier to see how much better an AOT service is than a traditional service.

Comparing an AOT and a non-AOT web service

Native AOT produces apps and services that are AOT compiled into native code, meaning a faster start-up time and a potentially smaller memory footprint. This can have a positive impact when you have lots of instances (for example, when deploying massively scalable microservices) that are frequently stopped and restarted.

Native AOT compiles **intermediate code** (**IL**) to native code at the time of publishing, rather than at runtime using the JIT compiler. But how much faster and more efficient are they?

Let's create a pair of weather web services, one using the normal compiler and one using the AOT compiler. Both will be configured to support HTTP only and without `OpenAPI` support to minimize complexity:

1. Use your preferred code editor to add a web API project, as defined in the following list:
    - Project template: **ASP.NET Core Web API** / `webapi --no-https --no-openapi`
    - Solution file and folder: `Chapter13`
    - Project file and folder: `Northwind.WebApi`
    - **Authentication type: None**
    - **Configure for HTTPS**: Cleared
    - **Enable container support**: Cleared
    - **Enable OpenAPI support**: Cleared
    - **Do not use top-level statements**: Cleared
    - **Use controllers**: Cleared
    - **Enlist in Aspire orchestration**: Cleared

If using the command prompt or terminal, in the `Chapter13` directory, enter the following command:

```
dotnet new webapi --no-https --no-openapi -o Northwind.WebApi
```

2. Create a second web service project with all the same options but named `Northwind.WebApiAot`. We will then manually convert it to use AOT so that you can be sure that there is no "magic" involved from using a different project template.

   If using the command prompt or terminal, in the `Chapter13` directory, enter the following command:

```
dotnet new webapi --no-https --no-openapi -o Northwind.WebApiAot
```

3. In the `Northwind.WebApiAot.csproj` project file, enable AOT publishing, as shown highlighted in the following markup:

```
<Project Sdk="Microsoft.NET.Sdk.Web">

  <PropertyGroup>
    <TargetFramework>net10.0</TargetFramework>
    <Nullable>enable</Nullable>
    <ImplicitUsings>enable</ImplicitUsings>
    <PublishAot>true</PublishAot>
  </PropertyGroup>

</Project>
```

4. In the `Northwind.WebApiAot` project, in `Program.cs`, make the changes shown in the following bullets and as highlighted in the following code:

   - Import the namespace for working with JSON serialization
   - Change the call from `CreateBuilder` to `CreateSlimBuilder`
   - Register a JSON serializer context
   - Comment out the statement to use HTTPS redirection
   - At the bottom of the file, define a JSON serializer context class

```
using System.Text.Json.Serialization; // To use JsonSerializerContext.

var builder = WebApplication.CreateSlimBuilder(args);

// Add services to the container.
builder.Services.ConfigureHttpJsonOptions(options =>
{
  options.SerializerOptions.TypeInfoResolverChain
    .Insert(0, AppJsonSerializerContext.Default);
```

```
});

var app = builder.Build();

// Configure the HTTP request pipeline.

var summaries = new[]
{
  "Freezing", "Bracing", "Chilly", "Cool", "Mild", "Warm",
  "Balmy", "Hot", "Sweltering", "Scorching"
};

app.MapGet("/weatherforecast", () =>
{
  var forecast = Enumerable.Range(1, 5).Select(index =>
      new WeatherForecast
      (
        DateOnly.FromDateTime(DateTime.Now.AddDays(index)),
        Random.Shared.Next(-20, 55),
        summaries[Random.Shared.Next(summaries.Length)]
      ))
      .ToArray();
  return forecast;
});

app.Run();

internal record WeatherForecast(DateOnly Date, int TemperatureC, string?
Summary)
{
  public int TemperatureF => 32 + (int)(TemperatureC / 0.5556);
}

[JsonSerializable(typeof(WeatherForecast[]))]
internal partial class AppJsonSerializerContext : JsonSerializerContext
{
}
```

The `CreateSlimBuilder` method does not include support for HTTPS or HTTP/3, although you can add those back in yourself if you need them. It does support JSON file configuration for `appsettings.json` and logging.

5. In the `Northwind.WebApi` project folder, at the command prompt or terminal, publish the web service, as shown in the following command:

```
dotnet publish
```

6. Start **File Explorer**, open the `bin\Release\net10.0\publish` folder, and you can see that the EXE file is about 140 KB. This and the DLL are the only files that need to be deployed onto another computer for the web service to work. The `appsettings.json` files are only needed to override configuration if needed. The PDB file is only needed if debugging.

> The compiled assembly is not OS specific so you could copy it to a Windows, Mac, or Linux computer and it can execute there.

7. In the `Northwind.WebApiAot` project folder, at the command prompt or terminal, publish the web service using native AOT, as shown in the following command:

```
dotnet publish
```

> The compiled assembly is specific to the OS which you compile it on. If you compile it on Windows, the assembly can only execute on Windows. You should also note that it will take much longer to compile the AOT version of the project.

> **Warning for Rider!** You must have installed **Build Tools for Visual Studio** to enable AOT compilation or you will get: `error : Platform linker not found`. You can install them from the following link: `https://visualstudio.microsoft.com/downloads/#build-tools-for-visual-studio-2026`.

Testing the two web services with Bombardier

Now, let's test the two web services that you've just built:

1. Start **File Explorer** and open the `bin\Release\net10.0\win-x64\publish` folder and note the EXE file is about 9,272 KB. This is the only file that needs to be deployed onto another Windows computer for the web service to work. The `appsettings.json` files are only needed to override configuration if needed. The PDB file is only needed if debugging. The compiled assembly is OS specific. It is compiled to native Windows x64.
2. At the command prompt or terminal, in the `bin\Release\net10.0\publish` folder, start the web service using port `5131`, as shown in the following command:

```
.\Northwind.WebApi --urls="http://localhost:5131"
```

Warning! To start an executable if your terminal uses PowerShell, you need to prefix with `.\`. Other shells might not require it but they won't be hurt by adding it.

3. At the command prompt or terminal, in the `bin\Release\net10.0\win-x64\publish` folder, start the web service using port `5132`, as shown in the following command:

```
.\Northwind.WebApiAot --urls="http://localhost:5132"
```

4. Start your preferred browser and confirm that you can get a weather forecast from both web services using the following links:

```
http://localhost:5131/weatherforecast
http://localhost:5132/weatherforecast
```

5. At the command prompt or terminal, use Bombardier to make one million requests using 125 connections (simulated users) to the normal web service, which is listening on port `5131`, as shown in the following command:

```
bombardier -c 125 -n 1000000 http://localhost:5131/weatherforecast
```

6. Note the results, as shown in the following output:

```
Bombarding http://localhost:5131/weatherforecast with 1000000 request(s)
using 125 connection(s)
 1000000 / 1000000 [=========================================================
=========================] 100.00% 85310/s 11s
Done!
Statistics        Avg      Stdev        Max
  Reqs/sec     86113.31   14277.37  142372.22
  Latency        1.44ms   171.32us    27.01ms
  HTTP codes:
    1xx - 0, 2xx - 1000000, 3xx - 0, 4xx - 0, 5xx - 0
    others - 0
  Throughput:    51.39MB/s
```

In my results, the web service handled an average of 86,113 HTTP GET requests per second and a maximum of 142,372. The average latency of each request was 1.44 ms and the maximum was 27.01 ms. Remember these are local requests on the same computer.

7. At the command prompt or terminal, use Bombardier to make one million requests using 125 connections (simulated users) to the AOT web service, which is listening on port `5132`, as shown in the following command:

```
bombardier -c 125 -n 1000000 http://localhost:5132/weatherforecast
```

8. Note the results, as shown in the following output:

```
Bombarding http://localhost:5132/weatherforecast with 1000000 request(s)
using 125 connection(s)
 1000000 / 1000000 [=====================================================
=========================] 100.00% 94956/s 10s
Done!
Statistics        Avg      Stdev        Max
  Reqs/sec     95165.74   11185.27  142047.69
  Latency        1.30ms   600.72us     50.20ms
  HTTP codes:
    1xx - 0, 2xx - 1000000, 3xx - 0, 4xx - 0, 5xx - 0
    others - 0
  Throughput:    56.78MB/s
```

> In my results, the web service handled an average of 95,165 HTTP GET requests per second and a maximum of 142,047. The average latency of each request was 1.30 ms and the maximum was 50.20 ms. Requests per Second (RPS) and latency are about 10% better with the AOT web service.

9. At the command prompt or terminal, use Bombardier to make as many requests as possible for 10 seconds using 200 connections to the normal web service and output the latency distribution, as shown in the following command:

```
bombardier -c 200 -d 10s -l http://localhost:5131/weatherforecast
```

10. Note the results, as shown in the following output:

```
Bombarding http://localhost:5131/weatherforecast for 10s using 200
connection(s)
[========================================================================
=========================================] 10s
Done!
Statistics        Avg      Stdev        Max
  Reqs/sec     87073.67    9378.44  103406.56
  Latency        2.28ms   356.54us     68.68ms
  Latency Distribution
     50%     2.07ms
     75%     2.81ms
```

```
      90%     3.21ms
      95%     3.56ms
      99%     4.31ms
  HTTP codes:
    1xx - 0, 2xx - 877089, 3xx - 0, 4xx - 0, 5xx - 0
    others - 0
  Throughput:     52.16MB/s
```

The latency distribution shows us that 95% of requests are returned within 3.56 ms. 5% of requests take longer than 3.56 ms. 99% of requests are returned within 4.31 ms. The worst 1% of requests take longer than 4.31 ms. During the ten seconds, a total of 877,089 requests were successfully returned.

11. Repeat for the AOT web service and note the result, as shown in the following output:

```
Bombarding http://localhost:5132/weatherforecast for 10s using 200
connection(s)
[=========================================================================
========================================] 10s
Done!
Statistics        Avg      Stdev        Max
  Reqs/sec     96390.06   25083.96  242524.25
  Latency        2.06ms   807.55us     65.86ms
  Latency Distribution
     50%     2.00ms
     75%     2.47ms
     90%     3.16ms
     95%     4.00ms
     99%     6.51ms
  HTTP codes:
    1xx - 0, 2xx - 968744, 3xx - 0, 4xx - 0, 5xx - 0
    others - 0
  Throughput:     57.61MB/s
```

The latency distribution shows us that 95% of requests are returned within 4.00 ms. 5% of requests take longer than 4.00 ms. 99% of requests are returned within 6.51 ms. The worst 1% of requests take longer than 6.51 ms. For the worst 5% or 1% of requests, the latency is *worse* for the AOT web service than the non-AOT web service. During the ten seconds, a total of 968,744 requests were successfully returned. This is about 10% better for the AOT web service than the non-AOT web service.

Interpreting Bombardier results

It's important to understand how to interpret Bombardier results, as described in *Table 13.5*:

Metric	Meaning and how to interpret
RPS	Measures how many requests your web service can handle per second. It's an indicator of the service's ability to handle load. Higher RPS indicates better performance and greater capacity to handle concurrent users or requests. Compare RPS against expected traffic volumes to determine whether your service can handle peak loads.
Latency	Represents the time taken for a request to travel from the client to the server and back. It includes the time taken to process the request on the server. Lower latency means a faster response time for users. Pay attention to average latency, but also consider percentiles like P95 and P99 to understand the experience of the slowest users.
Throughput	Represents the amount of data transferred over a given period. It's usually measured in kilobytes per second (KBps). Throughput gives you an idea of the bandwidth usage of your web service. Higher throughput might indicate more data being transferred per request, which could affect costs and scalability.
Success rate	Shows the percentage of requests that were successfully handled by the web service without errors. A success rate lower than 100% may indicate issues under load, such as timeouts, server errors (5xx responses), or other failures. Investigate any errors to improve reliability.
Errors	Bombardier reports any failed requests, including timeouts and HTTP error codes. Review error types and frequencies to identify and troubleshoot specific issues in your web service. Frequent timeouts might suggest performance bottlenecks, while HTTP errors could point to faulty logic or resource limits.
Connection times	This includes metrics like the fastest, slowest, and average connection times, providing insight into the variability and reliability of connections. Look for significant variations in connection times, which might suggest network or server instability. Consistently slow connections could indicate a need for server optimization or increased capacity.

Table 13.5: Bombardier metrics explained

While Bombardier itself doesn't report CPU and memory usage, you should monitor these metrics separately in your environment during testing. High CPU or memory usage during testing might indicate inefficient code or a need for more powerful hardware. Monitoring these metrics can help identify resource bottlenecks.

Understand that results can vary based on the testing environment (development, staging, production) and the specific conditions under which the test was run (network speed, server load, and so on). Performance testing is not a one-time task. Regularly benchmarking your web service as you make changes can help you understand the impact of those changes on performance.

When interpreting Bombardier results, focus on understanding how your web service performs under various loads, identify bottlenecks or errors under stress, and use this information to guide optimizations. Combining Bombardier's metrics with monitoring tools like Prometheus and Grafana or ELK Stack (Elasticsearch, Logstash, and Kibana), which can track resource usage and application insights, will give you a comprehensive view of your web service's performance and stability.

> You can learn more about Bombardier from its GitHub repository at the following link: `https://github.com/codesenberg/bombardier`.

NBomber – a load testing framework

NBomber is a .NET-friendly load testing framework for building performance testing scenarios. It supports writing test scenarios in C#, so it is a comfortable choice for .NET developers. NBomber can be used for testing web services, SQL databases, and even custom protocols. It provides rich reporting and can scale out tests across multiple nodes.

NBomber scenarios

Scenarios in NBomber are essentially test plans that define what actions or operations will be performed during the test, how many users or concurrent tasks will simulate those actions, and how long the test will run.

A scenario in NBomber is composed of several key components:

- **Steps**: These are the individual operations or actions that will be executed. For example, in the context of a web application, a step could be a specific HTTP request to an endpoint.
- **Load simulations**: This defines how the load will be generated, specifying the number of concurrent users or requests and the duration of the test. NBomber supports various load simulation strategies, such as simulating a steady load over time or gradually ramping up or down the load.
- **Scenario settings**: Additional settings for the scenario, such as global headers for HTTP requests or setup and cleanup actions, that should be executed before and after the scenario runs.

> You can read more about scenarios at the following link: `https://nbomber.com/docs/nbomber/scenario`.

Load simulations

If you expect your service to get a maximum of up to 120 RPS, then you can simulate that scenario. First, you might want to slowly ramp up from 0 to 120 RPS. Then, you'd want to sustain that maximum for a while before finally ramping back down.

Let's review some examples of load simulations:

- To ramp up to 120 invocations every second over one minute; since the interval is 1 second, the rate will increase by 2 invocations per second:

```
Simulation.RampingInject(rate: 120,
  interval: TimeSpan.FromSeconds(1),
  during: TimeSpan.FromMinutes(1))
```

- To maintain a steady rate of injecting 120 invocations every second for two minutes:

```
Simulation.Inject(rate: 120,
  interval: TimeSpan.FromSeconds(1),
  during: TimeSpan.FromMinutes(2))
```

- To ramp down to 0 invocations every second over 30 seconds; since the interval is 1 second, the rate will decrease by 4 invocations per second:

```
Simulation.RampingInject(rate: 0,
  interval: TimeSpan.FromSeconds(1),
  during: TimeSpan.FromSeconds(30))
```

NBomber types and methods

Important NBomber types are shown in *Table 13.6*:

Type	Description
`Scenario`	A scenario defined with a name and a delegate to run.
`LoadSimulation`	A load simulation defined with a target rate, an interval between injections, and a duration. A ramped injection means you can ramp the number of requests up and down during the test.
`Simulation`	A class factory that creates `LoadSimulation` instances using methods like `Inject` and `RampingInject`.
`Response`	A class and class factory that creates `Response` instances using methods like `Ok()` and `Fail()`.
`NBomberRunner`	The class that defines one or more scenarios using the `RegisterScenarios` method and then runs them using the `Run` method.
`IScenarioContext`	Represents the execution context of the currently running `Scenario`. It provides functionality to log events, gets information about the test, and enables you to stop all or a specific scenario manually by calling the `StopCurrentTest` and `StopScenario` methods.

Table 13.6: NBomber types

Important NBomber methods are shown in *Table 13.7*:

Method	Description
`WithInit`	Used to initialize Scenario and all its dependencies. You can use it to prepare your target system, populate the database, or read and apply the JSON configuration for your scenario.
`WithClean`	Used to clean the scenario's resources after the test finishes.
`WithWarmUpDuration`	Sets the duration of the warm-up phase. By default, the warm up duration is 30 seconds.
`WithoutWarmUp`	Disables warm up.
`WithLoadSimulations`	Configures the load simulations for the current `Scenario`. Load simulation allows the configuration of parallelism and workload profiles. Learn more at the following link: `https://nbomber.com/docs/nbomber/load-simulation/`.
`WithMaxFailCount`	`FailCount` is incremented on every failure or failed `Response`. When a scenario reaches `MaxFailCount`, NBomber will stop the whole load test. By default, the `MaxFailCount` is 5,000.

Table 13.7: NBomber methods

NBomber project example

Let's explore an example:

1. Use your preferred code editor to add a new console app to the `Chapter13` solution named `NBomberApp`.
2. In the `NBomberApp` project, treat warnings as errors, statically and globally import `Console`, and add a package reference to `NBomber` for defining HTTP scenarios, as shown in the following markup:

```
<ItemGroup>
  <Using Include="System.Console" static="true" />
</ItemGroup>

<ItemGroup>
  <PackageReference Include="NBomber" />
  <PackageReference Include="NBomber.Http" />
</ItemGroup>
```

3. Build the `NBomberApp` project to restore packages.

4. In `Program.cs`, delete any existing statements, then write statements to define a load simulation, create an NBomber scenario, and run it, as shown in the following code:

```
using NBomber.Contracts; // To use ScenarioProps.
using NBomber.CSharp; // To use Scenario, Simulation, NBomberRunner.
using NBomber.Http; // To use HttpMetricsPlugin.
using NBomber.Http.CSharp; // To use Http.
using NBomber.Plugins.Network.Ping; // To use PingPlugin.

// Use System.Net.Http.HttpClient to make HTTP requests.
using HttpClient client = new();

LoadSimulation[] loads = [

  // Ramp up to 50 RPS during one minute.
  Simulation.RampingInject(rate: 50,
    interval: TimeSpan.FromSeconds(1),
    during: TimeSpan.FromMinutes(1)),

  // Maintain 50 RPS for another minute.
  Simulation.Inject(rate: 50,
    interval: TimeSpan.FromSeconds(1),
    during: TimeSpan.FromMinutes(1)),

  // Ramp down to 0 RPS during one minute.
  Simulation.RampingInject(rate: 0,
    interval: TimeSpan.FromSeconds(1),
    during: TimeSpan.FromMinutes(1))
];

ScenarioProps scenario = Scenario.Create(
  name: "http_scenario",
  run: async context =>
{
  HttpRequestMessage request = Http.CreateRequest(
    "GET", "http://localhost:5131/weatherforecast")
    .WithHeader("Accept", "application/json");

  // Use WithHeader and WithBody to send a JSON payload.
  // .WithHeader("Content-Type", "application/json")
  // .WithBody(new StringContent("{ some JSON }", Encoding.UTF8,
"application/json"));
```

```
  Response<HttpResponseMessage> response = await Http.Send(client,
request);
  return response;
})
  .WithoutWarmUp()
  .WithLoadSimulations(loads);

NBomberRunner
  .RegisterScenarios(scenario)
  .WithWorkerPlugins(
    new PingPlugin(PingPluginConfig.CreateDefault("nbomber.com")),
    new HttpMetricsPlugin([ HttpVersion.Version1 ])
  )
  .Run();
```

5. Start the `NBomberApp` project without debugging.
6. Wait for three minutes to pass and then review the results, as shown in the following partial output:

```
13:20:39 [INF] NBomber "5.5.0" started a new session: "2024-03-
12_13.20.19_session_ef615dae"
...
13:20:39 [INF] Starting bombing...
...
scenario: http_scenario
  - ok count: 6030
  - fail count: 0
  - all data: 2.5 MB
  - duration: 00:03:00
load simulations:
  - ramping_inject, rate: 50, interval: 00:00:01, during: 00:01:00
  - inject, rate: 50, interval: 00:00:01, during: 00:01:00
  - ramping_inject, rate: 0, interval: 00:00:01, during: 00:01:00
┌────────────────────┬────────────────────────────────────────────
────────────┐
│               step │ ok stats
│
├────────────────────┼────────────────────────────────────────────
────────────┤
│               name │ global information
│
│      request count │ all = 6030, ok = 6030, RPS = 33.5
│
```

```
|            latency | min = 0.16 ms, mean = 0.87 ms, max = 55.25 ms,
StdDev = 0.82   |
| latency percentile | p50 = 0.9 ms, p75 = 0.97 ms, p95 = 1.08 ms, p99 =
1.28 ms      |
|      data transfer | min = 0.406 KB, mear = 0.419 KB, max = 0.438 KB,
all = 2.5 MB |
└────────────────────┴────────────────────────────────────────────────────
────────────┘

status codes for scenario: http_scenario
┌─────────────┬───────┬─────────┐
| status code | count | message |
├─────────────┼───────┼─────────┤
|          OK | 6030  |         |
└─────────────┴───────┴─────────┘
...
13:23:44 [INF] Reports saved in folder: "C:\tools-skills-net10\Chapter13\
NBomberApp\bin\Release\net10.0\reports\2024-03-12_13.20.19_session_
ef615dae"
13:23:44 [WRN] THIS VERSION IS FREE ONLY FOR PERSONAL USE. You can't use
it for an organization.
```

7. Shut down the web services and console apps.

You can learn more about NBomber at the following link: https://nbomber.com/.

Practicing and exploring

Test your knowledge and understanding by answering some questions, getting some hands-on practice, and exploring the topics covered in this chapter with deeper research.

Exercise 13.1 – Online-only material

You can read the official documentation for BenchmarkDotNet at the following link: https://benchmarkdotnet.org/articles/overview.html.

In particular, you should review the good practice section at the following link: https://benchmarkdotnet.org/articles/guides/good-practices.html.

This fascinating website allows developers to submit their benchmarks and comment on others: https://dotnetbenchmarks.com.

Deep dive into .NET performance and native AOT | BRK205H

A deep dive into .NET performance and native AOT compilation, covering various tools and techniques involved in optimizing .NET apps, including reducing allocations, minimizing startup time, and exploring minimal container constraints, at the following link:

`https://www.youtube.com/watch?v=1eHjemGKfRw`.

Benchmarking mistakes

One of my favorite .NET influencers is Nick Cosentino aka Dev Leader. Nick has a weekly newsletter (sign up at `https://subscribe.devleader.ca`), courses (`https://devleader.ca/courses`), and GitHub repositories (`https://github.com/ncosentino/`).

Recently, he discovered that he had made a mistake in one of his .NET performance videos. Instead of trying to hide his mistake, he actively wrote about it. As Nick says:

1. "It's okay to make mistakes. We're all human."
2. "Mistakes are a great way to take ownership and show others that we can grow from messing up!"
3. "Failing is one of the best ways to learn. I had absolutely no idea MatchCollection was lazy after probably 10+ years of using Regex in C#."

Nick's transparency and willingness to help others learn is one of the reasons I trust his advice.

You can read about his regular expression benchmarks and how lazy evaluation messed up his results at the following link: `https://dev.to/devleader/c-regular-expression-benchmarks-how-to-avoid-my-mistakes-2cef`.

Exercise 13.2 – Practice exercises

You can explore more about Big O notation using Polyglot Notebooks by reading an article by Matt Eland, author of the Packt book, **Refactoring with C#**. The article is found at the following link: `https://newdevsguide.com/2023/05/16/polyglot-notebooks-big-o/`.

You can try BenchmarkDotNet templates at the following link: `https://benchmarkdotnet.org/articles/guides/dotnet-new-templates.html`.

Exercise 13.3 – Test your knowledge

Answer the following questions. If you get stuck, try googling the answers, if necessary, while remembering that if you get totally stuck, the answers are in *Appendix A*:

1. What is Big O notation?
2. What are some common mistakes when benchmarking, and what does BenchmarkDotNet provide to help avoid them?
3. What is the difference between stress and load testing?
4. What is Bombardier, and why is it useful for developers?
5. When using NBomber, what does a scenario consist of?

Exercise 13.4 – Explore topics

Use the links on the following page to learn more details about the topics covered in this chapter: `https://github.com/markjprice/tools-skills-net10/blob/main/docs/book-links.md#chapter-13---benchmarking-performance-load-and-stress-testing`.

Summary

In this chapter, you learned:

- About benchmarking performance concepts like baselines and Big O notation
- How to use BenchmarkDotNet to benchmark the performance of your code
- How to use Bombardier to benchmark the performance of services
- How to use NBomber to load test services

In the next chapter, you will learn about functional and end-to-end testing to ensure that your .NET solutions work as expected from the user's perspective and fulfill the specified requirements.

14

Functional and End-to-End Testing of Websites and Services

This chapter is about **functional** and **End-to-End (E2E)** testing, which ensure that your .NET solutions work as expected from the user's perspective and fulfill specified requirements. In this chapter, you will see specific examples that illustrate how these testing approaches can be applied in .NET environments and the common tools that you will use. Then you will learn, in more detail, how to use Microsoft Playwright to test web user interfaces and xUnit to test web services.

This chapter covers the following topics:

- Understanding functional and end-to-end testing
- Testing web user interfaces using Playwright
- Interacting with a web user interface
- Generating tests with the Playwright Inspector
- Testing web services using xUnit

Understanding functional and end-to-end testing

Functional testing verifies that individual components or features of an application work as intended by comparing actual outcomes against specified requirements. It is granular, often automated, and tests inputs and expected outputs without delving into the system's internals.

End-to-end testing simulates real user scenarios by testing the entire application flow from start to finish, encompassing multiple integrated components to ensure that they work properly together. This type of testing validates the complete system, identifying issues that may arise from interactions between different parts of the application, thus providing a more holistic assurance of software functionality and reliability.

We will start with some examples that span various common functionalities in modern .NET applications, from web services to user interfaces. As you will see, E2E tests are more complex and involve multiple features, whereas functional tests focus more on testing a single feature.

Example 1: Testing a Web API service

Imagine you have an ASP.NET Core Web API that serves as the backend for a task management application. The API includes endpoints to create, retrieve, update, and delete tasks.

End-to-end test scenario: A user creates a new task, updates it, marks it as completed, and then retrieves it to confirm the changes. The test steps would be:

1. Call the `POST` endpoint to create a new task with specific details.
2. Call the `PUT` endpoint to update the task's title and description.
3. Call another `PUT` endpoint to mark the task as completed.
4. Call the `GET` endpoint to retrieve the task and verify that all changes have been applied correctly.

You could use Postman for manual testing, create these tests with their AI assistant named Postbot, or write automated tests using RestSharp or your own client library along with xUnit.

Functional test scenario: Ensuring that the task creation endpoint correctly handles input validation. The test steps would be:

1. Call the `POST` endpoint with invalid input, for example, missing required fields.
2. Verify that the API returns a `400 Bad Request` status code with a descriptive error message, usually generated using the `ProblemDetails` class in the .NET service.

You could use xUnit to write the test, FluentAssertions for more expressive assertions, and NSubstitute for mocking, as you learned about in *Chapter 11, Unit Testing and Mocking*.

Example 2: Testing an ASP.NET Core website

Consider an ASP.NET Core MVC or a Blazor app project for an e-commerce website that includes functionality to browse products, add them to a cart, and proceed through a checkout process.

End-to-end test scenario: A visitor navigates the product catalog until they find what they are looking for, adds a product to their cart, and completes the checkout process. The test steps would be:

1. Navigate to the product listing page and select a product.
2. Add the selected product to the shopping cart.
3. Navigate to the cart page, confirm that the product is listed, and proceed to checkout.
4. Complete the checkout form and submit the order.
5. Verify that a confirmation page is displayed with the order details.

You could use Playwright for automating browser interactions, integrated with xUnit for the testing framework.

Functional test scenario: Verifying that adding a product to the cart updates the cart's item count and total price correctly. The test steps would be:

1. Add a specific product to the cart.
2. Retrieve the cart's details and verify that the item count and total price reflect the addition of the new product.

You could use xUnit for the test framework, and NSubstitute for mocking any database calls or other external services and systems.

Example 3: Testing a SignalR real-time application

If you're developing a real-time chat application using SignalR, testing the real-time communication features is critical.

End-to-end test scenario: Two users send messages to each other in a chat room and verify that they receive the messages in real time. The test steps would be:

1. User A sends a message in the chat room.
2. Verify that User B receives the message in real time.
3. User B responds to the message.
4. Verify that User A receives the response in real time.

You could use Playwright with custom logic to interact with the real-time aspects of the application. For automated testing, a mock SignalR server or client might be used to simulate the real-time communication.

Functional test scenario: Testing the message broadcasting functionality to ensure messages are correctly sent to all connected clients. The test steps would be:

1. Simulate multiple clients connecting to a chat room.
2. Send a message from one client.
3. Verify that all connected clients receive the message.

You could use xUnit for structuring the test, with a mocked SignalR environment using NSubstitute to simulate multiple clients.

Now that you have seen some examples that illustrate how E2E and functional tests target different aspects of .NET applications, ensuring comprehensive coverage across all functionalities, let's look at a great framework for testing web user interfaces.

Testing web user interfaces using Playwright

Playwright is an open-source framework for the automated testing of websites and web apps across various browsers. Developed by Microsoft, Playwright enables developers and testers to write scripts that simulate user interactions with web pages. These interactions can include anything from navigating pages, filling out forms, and clicking buttons to more complex scenarios like handling single-page applications, web components, and even file downloads and uploads.

The most popular browsers to test with are WebKit, Firefox, Google Chrome, Microsoft Edge, and other Chromium-based browsers. Playwright uses open-source Chromium builds. The Chromium project is ahead of the branded browsers, so when the latest branded release is Google Chrome N, Playwright already supports Chromium N+1, which will be released in branded browsers a few weeks later.

Chromium is an open-source web browser project started by Google. It serves as the foundation for Google Chrome and many other modern browsers. The project provides the core browser engine, networking stack, JavaScript engine, and user interface components, but lacks some proprietary features included in Chrome, such as automatic updates, licensed codecs, and integrated Google services.

Playwright's Firefox version uses the most recent Firefox Stable build. Playwright's WebKit version uses the most recent WebKit trunk build before it is used in Apple Safari and other WebKit-based browsers. Playwright doesn't work with the branded version of Firefox or Safari since they rely on patches.

Playwright can operate against branded browsers available on your computer. In particular, the current Playwright version will support the Stable and Beta channels of these browsers – for example, to configure Microsoft Edge, as shown in the following markup:

```
<?xml version="1.0" encoding="utf-8"?>
<RunSettings>
  <Playwright>
    <BrowserName>chromium</BrowserName>
    <LaunchOptions>
      <Channel>msedge</Channel>
    </LaunchOptions>
  </Playwright>
</RunSettings>
```

When running a test project, you can then specify the browser and channel, as shown in the following command:

```
dotnet test -- Playwright.BrowserName=chromium Playwright.LaunchOptions.
Channel=msedge
```

Different browsers can render web pages differently due to variations in their underlying engines. By specifying the browser, developers can ensure that their applications work correctly across multiple browsers. This helps in catching browser-specific issues early in the development process. Specifying the channel is particularly useful for ensuring compatibility with the latest browser features or with certain versions that users might still be using.

Some bugs may only appear in certain browsers or channels. By explicitly specifying these in tests, developers can catch and address browser-specific bugs, enhancing the overall reliability and user experience of the web application.

You can run Playwright tests against multiple browsers at once. You can specify multiple browsers using command-line arguments, although this approach is less common than using a configuration file. By default, Playwright runs tests in parallel. When configured to run against multiple browsers, it will parallelize the tests across those browsers as well. This can significantly speed up the testing process and provide comprehensive coverage quickly.

Playwright has specific packages that integrate with NUnit and MSTest. For other testing systems, like xUnit, or if you just want to write tests in a console app, then you can just reference the main Playwright package, as we will in this chapter.

Benefits for .NET developers

For .NET developers, Playwright offers a comprehensive set of benefits that can streamline the development and testing processes, including those shown in the following list:

- **Cross-browser support**: Playwright supports testing across all modern browsers, including Chrome, Firefox, Safari, and Edge. This is particularly beneficial for ensuring application compatibility and performance across different user environments without having to manually test each browser.
- **Rich set of APIs**: Playwright provides a rich API for automating web interactions, including support for modern web features like web components, shadow DOM, and asynchronous operations. This allows for more sophisticated and accurate tests that closely mimic real user behavior.
- **Speed and reliability**: Playwright tests are designed to be fast and reliable. Its architecture minimizes flakiness and improves test stability, which is crucial for agile development and fast iteration cycles.
- **Headless mode**: Playwright can run browsers in headless mode, meaning the browser is invisible, which is faster and uses less memory than a full browser UI, making it ideal for automated test pipelines and **continuous integration** (CI) systems. While Selenium supports headless mode, Playwright's implementation is more optimized, resulting in faster execution times.
- **Parallel test execution**: Playwright supports running tests in parallel, significantly reducing the time required to execute extensive test suites. This feature is incredibly beneficial in a CI/CD environment, where speed and efficiency are paramount.

Alternatives to Playwright

There are several alternatives to Playwright that .NET developers might consider, including the two main competitors shown in the following list:

- **Selenium**: One of the most well-known and widely used tools for web application testing, Selenium offers a mature ecosystem and extensive browser support. However, it may be slower and less efficient than Playwright in some scenarios, especially with modern web applications. For example, Playwright automatically waits for elements to be ready before performing actions on them. This reduces flakiness and the need for explicit waits or sleep commands, which are more common in Selenium scripts and can slow down test execution. Parallelization is more sophisticated in Playwright compared to Selenium, which tends to be slower due to its architecture and the overhead of the WebDriver protocol. Single-page applications rely heavily on JavaScript for rendering content dynamically; Playwright can interact with these apps more seamlessly because it was designed to work with modern JavaScript frameworks and handle the complexity of client-side navigation better than Selenium. Selenium requires different WebDriver implementations for each browser, adding complexity and potential inconsistency.

- **Puppeteer**: Developed by the Chrome DevTools team, Puppeteer is another popular choice for browser automation, primarily focused on Chrome and Chromium-based browsers. While it offers a similar feature set to Playwright, it lacks native support for other browsers like Firefox and Safari.

Both of these tools have their strengths and weaknesses, and the best choice depends on the specific needs of your project, including the browsers you need to support, the complexity of your web application, and your development environment.

The biggest benefit of Selenium over Playwright is its mature ecosystem and extensive community support. Selenium has been around since 2004, making it one of the oldest and most widely adopted web automation tools. This long history means it has a well-established ecosystem, with extensive documentation, numerous tutorials, and a vast array of third-party tools and integrations.

Playwright, with its comprehensive browser support and .NET integration, represents a compelling option for .NET developers looking for a modern and efficient way to automate their web application testing.

Common Playwright testing types

Playwright provides some useful types to test the user interface of a website, as described in *Table 14.1*:

Type	Description
`IPlaywright`	Represents the Playwright system. Has properties like `Chromium`, `Firefox`, and `Webkit` that represent browsers, and properties like `Selectors` that configure how you can select elements on a web page to automate testing.
`IBrowser`	Represents a web browser. Has properties like `Contexts`, `IsConnected`, `BrowserType`, and `Version`. Has methods like `NewContextAsync` and `NewPageAsync`.
`IBrowserContext`	Represents a browser session. Has properties like `APIRequest` and `Pages`. Has methods like `NewPageAsync`, `AddCookiesAsync`, `CookiesAsync`, and `StorageStateAsync`. The methods `SetGeolocationAsync` and `SetOfflineAsync` can be used to simulate those features. A good practice is to create a browser context and then create a page within that context. Cookies and cached objects are not shared between contexts.
`IResponse`	Represents an HTTP response from the web server. Has properties like `Headers`, `Ok`, `Status`, and `StatusText`. Has methods like `BodyAsync`, `JsonAsync`, and `TextAsync` to get the body of the response.
`IPage`	Represents a web page. Each page belongs to a browser context, aka session, and shares its cookies and cache.
`ILocator`	Represents one or more HTML elements within a web page.

Table 14.1: Common Playwright testing types

Common Playwright testing methods

Playwright provides some useful methods to automate and test a web page represented by an IPage instance, as described in *Table 14.2*:

IPage method	Description
GotoAsync, GoBackAsync, GotForwardAsync	Navigates to the specified resource or navigates back and forward. Returns an IResponse instance.
ContentAsync	Gets the full HTML content of the page.
TitleAsync	Gets the page title.

Table 14.2: Common Playwright page automation methods

Common Playwright locator methods

Playwright provides some useful methods to get one or more elements on a web page, and they all return an ILocator instance, as described in *Table 14.3*:

Method	Description
GetByRole	Match elements based on accessibility role. Specify the role and additional values, as shown in the following code: GetByRole(AriaRole.Heading, new() { Name = "Sign up" })). These roles and values select the following element: <h3>Sign up</h3>, or GetByRole(AriaRole.Button, new() { Name = "Sign in" }). This element will in turn select the following element: <button>Sign in</button>.
GetByLabel	Use to fill input fields in a form. For example, GetByLabel("Password").FillAsync("secret") would fill the following element: <label>Password <input type="password" /></label>.
GetByPlaceholder	Also useful to fill input fields in a form. For example, GetByPlaceholder("name@example.com").FillAsync("playwright@microsoft.com") would fill the following element: <input type="email" placeholder="name@example.com" />.
GetByTestId	Test IDs are specified by adding the data-testid attribute to an element.
GetByText	Find an element by the text it contains, like <div>, <span>, <p>, and so on.
GetByTitle	Locate an element with a matching title attribute. For example, use GetByTitle("Unread messages") to locate <span title='Unread messages'>3</span>.
GetByAltText	You can locate an image based on the text alternative. For example, GetByAltText("playwright logo") would find the following image: <img alt="playwright logo" src="/img/playwright-logo.svg" width="100" />.
Locator	Return an ILocator instance that matches the specified CSS or XPath selector specified using css= or xpath= although these prefixes are optional. This should be avoided in favor of one of the GetBy... methods. CSS and XPath selectors are less resilient to changes.

`And`, `Or`	Combine multiple locators into a Boolean matching expression.
`First`, `Last`, `Nth`	Return the first, last, or nth element when there are multiple matches. But avoid these methods because, when your page changes in the future, Playwright may click on an element you did not intend.

Table 14.3: Common Playwright locator methods

> **Good practice:** Use role locators to locate elements as much as possible because it is the closest way to how users and assistive technology perceive the page.

Common Playwright locator automation methods

Playwright provides some useful methods for testing part of a page using an `ILocator` instance, and most will throw an exception if more than one element is matched by the locator, as described in *Table 14.4*:

ILocator method	Description
`CheckAsync`, `UncheckAsync`	Selects or clears a check box or a radio button.
`SelectOptionAsync`	Selects an option in a list box.
`ClickAsync`	Clicks a button or other element.
`DblClickAsync`	Double-clicks a button or other element.
`FillAsync`	Fills an input element like a text box.
`FocusAsync`	Sets the focus to an element.
`HoverAsync`	Hovers the mouse pointer over an element.
`PressAsync`	Presses a key in the element.
`PressSequentiallyAsync`	Presses a sequence of keys in the element.
`ScreenshotAsync`	Takes a screenshot of the element.
`ScrollIntoViewIfNeededAsync`	Scrolls the view port to show the element.
`SelectTextAsync`	Selects text within an element.
`TapAsync`	Taps on an element.

Table 14.4: Common Playwright locator automation methods

> **Warning!** All operations on locators that imply a single DOM element will throw an exception if more than one element matches. For example, if you have a locator that matches all buttons and call `ClickAsync`, then an exception is thrown.

> You can learn more about locators at the following link: `https://playwright.dev/dotnet/docs/locators`.

Downloading and reviewing eShopOnWeb

Playwright enables a wide range of automated testing scenarios, from basic navigations to complex user interactions and validations.

We need a website to test, so let's use the Microsoft **eShopOnWeb** ASP.NET Core reference application, which demonstrates a single-process (monolithic) application architecture and deployment model.

> The `eShopOnWeb` repository was archived on January 13, 2025. It is now read-only. But it is still suitable for our needs because it demonstrates a single-process (monolithic) application architecture for an ecommerce website suitable for testing its user interface.

In this first step-by-step task, you will download the eShopOnWeb repository and run the website. We will walk through some key pages and functionality that we will then test later. Let's get started:

1. Navigate to the eShopOnWeb repository at the following link: `https://github.com/dotnet-architecture/eShopOnWeb`.
2. Download or clone the eShopOnWeb repository.
3. Open the `eShopOnWeb.sln` solution file in your preferred code editor.
4. Build the solution.
5. Start the `Web` project without debugging. (We do not need the web service project or the admin Blazor projects and the `Web` project can run independently of them.)
6. At the command prompt or terminal, note that the database is created and seeded with sample data during the first start, as shown in the following output:

```
info: Web[0]
      App created...
info: Web[0]
      Seeding Database...
info: Microsoft.EntityFrameworkCore.Database.Command[20101]
      Executed DbCommand (194ms) [Parameters=[], CommandType='Text',
CommandTimeout='60']
      CREATE DATABASE [Microsoft.eShopOnWeb.CatalogDb];
...
info: Microsoft.EntityFrameworkCore.Database.Command[20101]
      Executed DbCommand (1ms) [Parameters=[], CommandType='Text',
CommandTimeout='30']
      CREATE TABLE [Baskets] (
          [Id] int NOT NULL IDENTITY,
```

```
            [BuyerId] nvarchar(40) NOT NULL,
            CONSTRAINT [PK_Baskets] PRIMARY KEY ([Id])
        );
...
info: Web[0]
      Adding Development middleware...
info: Web[0]
      LAUNCHING
info: Microsoft.Hosting.Lifetime[14]
      Now listening on: https://localhost:5001
info: Microsoft.Hosting.Lifetime[14]
      Now listening on: http://localhost:5000
info: Microsoft.Hosting.Lifetime[0]
      Application started. Press Ctrl+C to shut down.
info: Microsoft.Hosting.Lifetime[0]
      Hosting environment: Development
info: Microsoft.Hosting.Lifetime[0]
      Content root path: C:\GitHub\eShopOnWeb\src\Web
```

7. If a browser is not started automatically, then start your preferred browser, navigate to `https://localhost:5001/`, and note the home page, as shown in *Figure 14.1*:

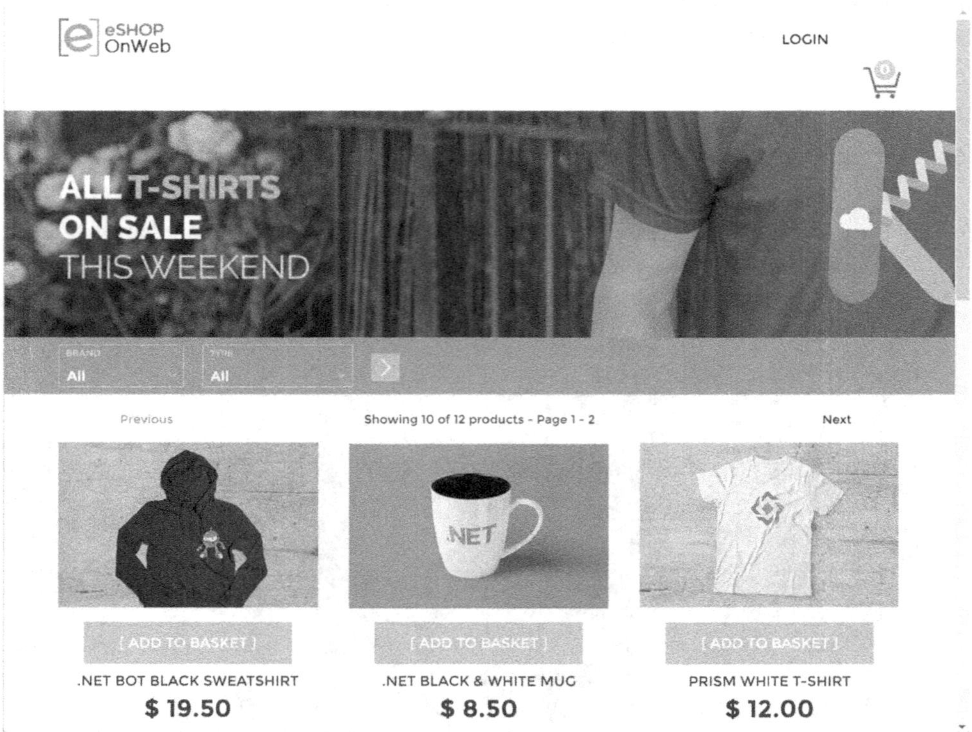

Figure 14.1: eShopOnWeb home page

8. Right-click in the middle of the white page header, select **View page source**, and note the `<title>` element in the `<head>` and the `<div>` for showing the number of items in the shopping cart, as shown highlighted in the following markup:

```
<!DOCTYPE html>
<html>
<head>
    <meta charset="utf-8" />
    <meta name="viewport" content="width=device-width, initial-scale=1.0"
/>
    <title>Catalog - Microsoft.eShopOnWeb</title>
...
      <a class="esh-basketstatus" href="/Basket">
        <div class="esh-basketstatus-image">
            <img src="/images/cart.png" />
        </div>
        <div class="esh-basketstatus-badge">
          0
        </div>
      </a>
...
```

9. Right-click the **BRAND** dropdown list, select **Inspect**, and note the two `<select>` elements in `<label>` elements and the `<input>` element in the `<form>` element, as shown in the following markup:

```
<form method="GET">
  <label class="esh-catalog-label" data-title="brand">
    <select class="esh-catalog-filter"
            id="CatalogModel_BrandFilterApplied"
            name="CatalogModel.BrandFilterApplied">
      <option>All</option>
      <option value="2">.NET</option>
      <option value="1">Azure</option>
      <option value="5">Other</option>
      <option value="4">SQL Server</option>
      <option value="3">Visual Studio</option>
    </select>
  </label>
  <label class="esh-catalog-label" data-title="type">
    <select class="esh-catalog-filter"
            id="CatalogModel_TypesFilterApplied"
            name="CatalogModel.TypesFilterApplied"><option>All</option>
```

```
      <option value="1">Mug</option>
      <option value="3">Sheet</option>
      <option value="2">T-Shirt</option>
      <option value="4">USB Memory Stick</option>
    </select>
  </label>
  <input class="esh-catalog-send" type="image" src="/images/arrow-right.
svg">
</form>
```

Good practice: This HTML is provided by the eShopOnWeb solution. If we wrote this markup in our own project, we should make two changes. First, labels should contain the text shown in the user interface like **BRAND** and **TYPE,** but these labels use `data-title` attributes instead. Second, elements that we might want to automate, like the `<select>` dropdown lists, should have a `data-testid` attribute set to a unique value. Later, we will have to use less optimal techniques to find and automate these page elements.

10. Close the browser's inspection pane.
11. On the home page, in the **BRAND** dropdown list, select **.NET**.
12. In the **TYPE** dropdown list, select **Mug**.
13. To the right of the **TYPE** dropdown list, click the right-pointing arrow image, and note that the products on the home page are filtered to only show the mug branded with .NET named **.NET BLACK & WHITE MUG**.
14. At the top of the home page, click **LOGIN**.
15. Right-click the white background of the page, select **View page source**, and note the two labels, two inputs, and button to log in, as shown in the following markup:

```
<label for="Input_Email">Email</label>
<input class="form-control" type="email" data-val="true" data-val-
email="The Email field is not a valid e-mail address." data-val-
required="The Email field is required." id="Input_Email" name="Input.
Email" value="" />
...
<label for="Input_Password">Password</label>
<input class="form-control" type="password" data-val="true" data-
val-required="The Password field is required." id="Input_Password"
name="Input.Password" />
...
<button type="submit" class="btn btn-default">Log in</button>
```

16. Close the page source tab.

17. Fill in the **Log in** form with an **Email** of `admin@microsoft.com` and a **Password** of `Pass@word1`, click the **Log in** button, and note that the email is now shown at the top of the home page.
18. Close the browser and shut down the web server. You can do this at the command prompt or terminal by pressing *Ctrl* + *C*.

Let's review some common examples of tests that developers often automate using Playwright, starting with basic website navigation.

Page navigation and title verification

A fundamental test case is to navigate to a webpage and verify its title to ensure the correct page is loaded. This test can be used as a **smoke test** for website availability and correct routing.

Let's go:

1. Leave the eShopOnWeb solution and its projects open in its code editor and start a new instance of your code editor.
2. Use your preferred code editor to add a new **xUnit Test Project [C#]** / `xunit` project named `WebUITests` to a `Chapter14` solution. For example, at the command prompt or terminal in the `Chapter14` folder, enter the following commands:

```
dotnet new sln
dotnet new xunit -o WebUITests
dotnet sln add WebUITests
```

3. In the `WebUITests.csproj` project file, reference the Playwright package, as shown in the following markup:

```
<PackageReference Include="Microsoft.Playwright" />
```

4. Build the `WebUITests` project to restore packages.
5. Navigate to `WebUITests\bin\Debug\net10.0` and, at the command prompt or terminal, install browsers for Playwright to automate, as shown in the following command:

```
pwsh playwright.ps1 install
```

> **Warning!** Some readers might get an error, `The command "pwsh" is not recognized`. The most likely problem is that PowerShell is not installed properly on their computer (i.e. not installed at all, or installed but not set up so it is found from the command prompt). To install PowerShell on Windows, Linux, and macOS, please read the following link: `https://learn.microsoft.com/en-us/powershell/scripting/install/installing-powershell`.
>
> However, for some readers, the following command might fix the issue:
>
> `dotnet tool update --global PowerShell`
>
> Some of the answers here might also help: **getting started instructions dont work** #1865: `https://github.com/microsoft/playwright-dotnet/issues/1865`.

> Playwright needs special versions of browser binaries to operate. You must use the Playwright PowerShell script to install these browsers. If you have issues, you can learn more at the following link: `https://playwright.dev/dotnet/docs/browsers`.

6. Note that Playwright downloads its own copies of Chrome, Firefox, and WebKit, as shown in the following output:

```
Downloading Chromium 123.0.6312.4 (playwright build v1105) from https://playwright.azureedge.net/builds/chromium/1105/chromium-win64.zip
122.2 MiB [====================] 100% 0.0s
Chromium 123.0.6312.4 (playwright build v1105) downloaded to C:\Users\markj\AppData\Local\ms-playwright\chromium-1105
Downloading Firefox 123.0 (playwright build v1440) from https://playwright.azureedge.net/builds/firefox/1440/firefox-win64.zip
83.4 MiB [====================] 100% 0.0s
Firefox 123.0 (playwright build v1440) downloaded to C:\Users\markj\AppData\Local\ms-playwright\firefox-1440
Downloading Webkit 17.4 (playwright build v1983) from https://playwright.azureedge.net/builds/webkit/1983/webkit-win64.zip
47.2 MiB [====================] 100% 0.0s
Webkit 17.4 (playwright build v1983) downloaded to C:\Users\markj\AppData\Local\ms-playwright\webkit-1983
```

> If you do not run this script, then when you try to run Playwright tests, they will fail, and you will see the following message in the test output: **Looks like Playwright was just installed or updated. Please run the following command to download new browsers:** `pwsh bin/Debug/netX/playwright.ps1 install`.

7. In the `WebUITests` project, rename `UnitTest1.cs` to `eShopWebUITests.cs`.
8. In `eShopWebUITests.cs`, define a class with a method to set up Playwright to use Chromium, and a test method that will confirm that the home page is returned successfully (the page is not null and the request for it returned a 200 OK status code). Then check that the title of the home page is the text that we expect, and finally, ask Playwright to take a screenshot and save it to the desktop so that we can see the home page as it appeared during the test, as shown in the following code:

```
using Microsoft.Playwright; // To use Playwright, IBrowser, and so on.

namespace WebUITests;

public class eShopWebUITests
{
  private IBrowser? _browser;
```

```
    private IBrowserContext? _session;
    private IPage? _page;
    private IResponse? _response;

    private async Task GotoHomePage(IPlaywright playwright)
    {
      _browser = await playwright.Chromium.LaunchAsync(
        new BrowserTypeLaunchOptions { Headless = false });

      _session = await _browser.NewContextAsync();
      _page = await _session.NewPageAsync();
      _response = await _page.GotoAsync("https://localhost:5001/");
    }

    [Fact]
    public async Task HomePage_Title()
    {
      // Arrange: Launch Chrome browser and navigate to home page.
      // using to make sure Dispose is called at the end of the test.
      using IPlaywright? playwright = await Playwright.CreateAsync();
      await GotoHomePage(playwright);
      string actualTitle = await _page.TitleAsync();

      // Assert: Navigating to home page worked and its title is as
  expected.
      string expectedTitle = "Catalog - Microsoft.eShopOnWeb";
      Assert.NotNull(_response);
      Assert.True(_response.Ok);
      Assert.Equal(expectedTitle, actualTitle);

      // Universal sortable ("u") format: 2009-06-15 13:45:30Z
      // : and spaces will cause problems in a filename
      // so replace them with dashes.
      string timestamp = DateTime.Now.ToString("u")
        .Replace(":", "-").Replace(" ", "-");

      await _page.ScreenshotAsync(new PageScreenshotOptions
      {
        Path = Path.Combine(Environment.GetFolderPath(
          Environment.SpecialFolder.Desktop),
          $"homepage-{timestamp}.png")
      });
    }
  }
```

9. In the eShopOnWeb solution, start the Web project without debugging.
10. Run the test and note the result is that it passes. You will note that the Chrome browser briefly appears on your screen.
11. On your desktop, open the image and confirm that it is a screenshot of the home page.
12. In eShopWebUITests.cs, in the GotoHomePage method, change the browser to Headless, as shown highlighted in the following code:

```
browser = await playwright.Chromium.LaunchAsync(
  new BrowserTypeLaunchOptions { Headless = true });
```

> You could also just call the LaunchAsync method without passing a BrowserTypeLaunchOptions object because Headless defaults to true.

13. Run the test again and note the result is that it passes. This time, the browser does not appear and the test executes faster.

Now let's try some more complex examples.

Interacting with a web user interface

Common web user interface interactions include selecting items from dropdown lists, clicking elements like buttons and icons, filling in and submitting forms, and validating that elements contain specific text or are visible to the visitor.

Selecting dropdown items and clicking elements

The eShopOnWeb home page shows a shopping cart with a numeric badge showing the number of items in the cart, and it allows the visitor to filter the products by selecting from two dropdown lists and clicking an image. Let's automate this:

1. In eShopWebUITests.cs, statically import the Assertions class so that we can use its Expect method, as shown in the following code:

```
using static Microsoft.Playwright.Assertions; // To use Expect.
```

2. In eShopWebUITests.cs, add a test to check that the shopping cart is empty and is visible to the visitor, as shown in the following code:

```
[Fact]
public async Task HomePage_CartEmptyAndVisible()
{
  // Arrange: Launch Chrome browser and navigate to home page.
  using IPlaywright? playwright = await Playwright.CreateAsync();
  await GotoHomePage(playwright);
```

```
    // The only way to select the cart badge is to use a CSS selector.
    ILocator element = _page.Locator("css=div.esh-basketstatus-badge");

    // The text content will contain whitespace like \n so we
    // must trim that away.
    string? actualCount = (await element.TextContentAsync())?.Trim();

    // Assert: Shopping cart badge is as expected.
    string expectedCount = "0";
    Assert.Equal(expectedCount, actualCount);
    await Expect(element).ToBeVisibleAsync();
  }
```

3. In `eShopWebUITests.cs`, add a test to check that the filtering products feature works correctly, as shown in the following code:

```
[Fact]
public async Task HomePage_FilterCategories()
{
  // Arrange: Launch Chrome browser and navigate to home page.
  using IPlaywright? playwright = await Playwright.CreateAsync();
  await GotoHomePage(playwright);

  // By default, GetByTestId looks for the data-testid attribute
  // which is not used by eShopOnWeb so we must tell Playwright
  // to use the id attribute instead.
  playwright.Selectors.SetTestIdAttribute("id");

  // Set the BRAND list box to .NET.
  ILocator brand = _page.GetByTestId("CatalogModel_BrandFilterApplied");
  await brand.SelectOptionAsync(".NET");

  // Set the TYPE list box to Mug.
  ILocator type = _page.GetByTestId("CatalogModel_TypesFilterApplied");
  await type.SelectOptionAsync("Mug");

  // Click the image to apply the filter.
  ILocator apply = _page.Locator("css=input.esh-catalog-send");
  await apply.ClickAsync();

  // Assert: One product is shown.
  ILocator topPager = _page.Locator("css=span.esh-pager-item").First;
  string? actualPager = (await topPager.TextContentAsync())?.Trim();
  string expectedPager = "Showing 1 of 1 products - Page 1 - 1";
```

```
    Assert.Equal(expectedPager, actualPager);

    string timestamp = DateTime.Now.ToString("u")
      .Replace(":", "-").Replace(" ", "-");

    await _page.ScreenshotAsync(new PageScreenshotOptions
    {
      Path = Path.Combine(Environment.GetFolderPath(
        Environment.SpecialFolder.Desktop),
        $"dotnet-mug-{timestamp}.png")
    });
  }
```

Good practice: There are two pagers on the home page, one at the top and one at the bottom of the table of products (if you cannot find them, search for `pager-item`). Due to strict mode, you will get an error if you do not use `First` or `Nth` to select which of those two elements you want to interact with.

4. If necessary, in the `eShopOnWeb` solution, start the `Web` project without debugging.
5. Run all the tests, and note that they all succeed and the screenshot taken by Playwright shows the one matching product correctly.

Form submission, authentication, and validation

Automating form submissions and validating the responses or resulting actions is a common scenario for testing web applications. Playwright can fill out forms, click submit buttons, and verify whether the submission leads to the expected outcome, such as a thank you page, a validation error, or the creation of a new database record.

Testing user authentication flows, including login and logout functionality, is another common use case. Playwright can simulate a user logging in to an application, perform actions as an authenticated user, and then log out, as shown in the following code:

```
// Navigate to log in page.
await page.GotoAsync("https://example.com/login");
await page.FillAsync("input#username", "dummyuser");
await page.FillAsync("input#password", "123456");
await page.ClickAsync("button#login");

// Verify login was successful by checking for a logout button
// and a welcome message.
bool isLoggedIn = await page.IsVisibleAsync("button#logout");
Assert.True(isLoggedIn);

string successMessage = await page.InnerTextAsync("div.success");
```

```
Assert.Equal("Welcome, Dummy!", successMessage);

// Perform actions as logged-in user and then logout
...
await page.ClickAsync("button#logout");
```

Responsive design testing

Testing your web user interfaces for how well they implement responsive design is important in modern web development. Let's review some common scenarios.

Emulating screen sizes

With Playwright, you can test how your application behaves on different screen sizes, which is essential for ensuring a good user experience across devices, like making sure that an important section is visible to mobile visitors, as shown in the following code:

```
await page.SetViewportSizeAsync(640, 480); // Set to a mobile view.
await page.GotoAsync("https://example.com");
bool isLoggedIn = await page.IsVisibleAsync("div#importantSection");
Assert.True(isLoggedIn);
```

You can set the view port back to desktop size, as shown in the following code:

```
await page.SetViewportSizeAsync(1920, 1080); // Set to a desktop view
```

Emulating devices

You can emulate specific devices when you create a browser context, as shown in the following code:

```
browser = await playwright.Chromium.LaunchAsync(
  new BrowserTypeLaunchOptions { Headless = false });

BrowserNewContextOptions iphone13 = playwright.Devices["iPhone 13"];
IBrowserContext context = await browser.NewContextAsync(iphone13);
```

Emulating locale, time zone, and geolocation

You can emulate the device locale and time zone, as shown in the following code:

```
BrowserNewContextOptions options = new()
{
  Locale = "de-DE", // Accept-Language header.
  TimezoneId = "Europe/Berlin"
};
IBrowserContext context = await browser.NewContextAsync(options);
```

Valid time zones for Chromium are documented at the following link: `https://source.chromium.org/chromium/chromium/deps/icu.git/+/faee8bc70570192d82d2978a71e2a615788597d1:source/data/misc/metaZones.txt`.

You can grant geolocation permissions and set geolocation to a specific area like the Colosseum in Rome, as shown in the following code:

```
BrowserNewContextOptions options = new()
{
  Permissions = [ "geolocation" ],
  Geolocation = new() { Longitude = 41.890221F, Latitude = 12.492348F }
};
IBrowserContext context = await browser.NewContextAsync(options);
```

If you need to dynamically change the geolocation for example, to the Eiffel Tower in Paris, then you can call a method, as shown in the following code:

```
await context.SetGeolocationAsync(new()
  { Longitude = 48.858455F, Latitude = 2.294474F });
```

Emulating dark mode and color schemes

You can emulate dark mode, as shown in the following code:

```
BrowserNewContextOptions options = new()
  { ColorScheme = ColorScheme.Dark };

IBrowserContext context = await browser.NewContextAsync(options);
```

If you need to dynamically change the color mode, then you can call a method on a page, as shown in the following code:

```
await page.EmulateMediaAsync(new()
  { ColorScheme = ColorScheme.Dark });
```

Emulating the user agent, disabling JavaScript, and going offline

Other configuration options include customizing the user agent, disabling JavaScript, and going offline, as shown in the following code:

```
BrowserNewContextOptions options = new()
{
  UserAgent = "My User Agent",
  JavaScriptEnabled = false,
  Offline = true
};

IBrowserContext context = await browser.NewContextAsync(options);
```

You can learn more about emulation at the following link: `https://playwright.dev/dotnet/docs/emulation`.

Single-Page Applications (SPAs) and dynamic content

Playwright excels in handling complex web applications that use JavaScript heavily for dynamic content loading, SPAs, and AJAX calls. You can wait for elements to become visible or load, or for network requests to complete before proceeding with tests, as shown in the following code:

```
await page.GotoAsync("https://example.com/spa");
await page.ClickAsync("button#loadData");

// Wait for data to load.
await page.WaitForSelectorAsync("div.dataLoaded");
string loadedData = await page.InnerTextAsync("div.dataLoaded");
```

Now let's see how you can get Playwright to generate the testing code for you.

Generating tests with the Playwright Inspector

Code generation with Playwright for .NET is a super cool feature that can significantly speed up your test automation workflow. Code generation is like having a personal assistant who watches over your shoulder as you browse through your web application and automatically writes the test scripts for you. In essence, it's a way to automate the automation, which is meta in a good way.

The Playwright Inspector tool allows you to create comprehensive test scripts in a fraction of the time it would take to write them manually. It captures user interactions with high precision, reducing the chance of errors that can occur when writing tests by hand. Even if you're new to test automation, you can get started quickly. It's also a great way to learn how Playwright structures its tests by examining the generated code.

As you navigate through your application, Playwright records your actions like clicks, text inputs, and navigations, and then generates the corresponding C# test code in real time. Once you're done, you can stop the code generation tool, and it will output the generated script. You can then review this code, make any necessary adjustments, and integrate it into your test suite.

After integrating the generated code into your project, you can run your tests using the Playwright test runner, ensuring that your application behaves as expected across different browsers and devices. The generated code is a great starting point, but don't be afraid to refine and customize it to suit your testing needs better.

Playwright Inspector walkthrough

Let's see it in action:

1. If necessary, start the `Web` project without debugging.
2. In the `WebUITests` project folder, at the command prompt or terminal, enter the command to start the code generator:

```
pwsh bin/Debug/net10.0/playwright.ps1 codegen https://localhost:5001/
```

3. Note that two application windows will open, one for the special version of the Chromium browser, which has a "Chrome" icon in shades of blue, and one for **Playwright Inspector**, which has a pair of colorful actor masks, as shown in *Figure 14.2*:

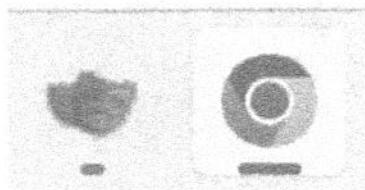

Figure 14.2: Playwright Inspector and Chromium icons in the Windows Taskbar

1. In the **Chromium** window, note that it has a floating toolbar with buttons for **Record**, **Pick locator**, **Assert visibility**, **Assert text**, and **Assert value**, and **Assert snapshot**, and when you move your mouse cursor over an element on the page, like the right-arrow button that applies a filter to products, it suggests a locator to select that element, as shown in *Figure 14.3*:

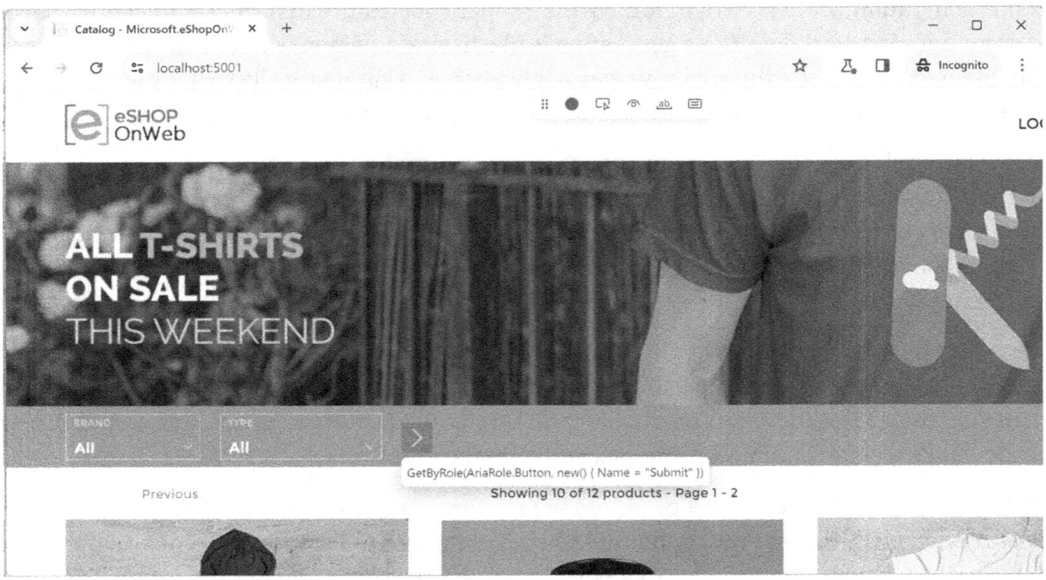

Figure 14.3: Chromium with the Playwright Inspector toolbar

2. In the **Playwright Inspector** window, note the initial C# code to automate the browser test; in the top-right corner is a dropdown list of targets that can be set to any of multiple languages and testing frameworks like **.NET C# - Library** or **NUnit**, or **Node.js - Test Runner**, as shown in *Figure 14.4*:

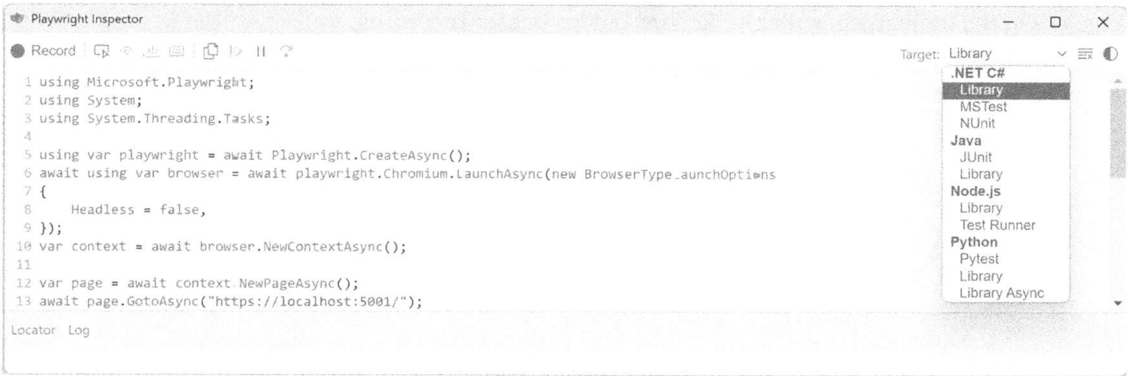

Figure 14.4: Playwright Inspector showing initial C# code to automate the browser test

Warning! When the **Record** button is red, you are recording. When the **Record** button is black, you are *not* recording. Playwright Inspector starts recording automatically.

Record actions in the web browser

Now we can perform actions as if we were a user:

1. Switch to the Chromium browser window.
2. Optionally, arrange the two application windows to be side by side and both visible so that you can see the code written for you as you perform actions in the Chromium browser window.
3. On the website home page, in the top navigation, click **LOGIN** and note that a new statement is written for you to select, and then click that element, as shown in the following code:

```
await page.GetByRole(AriaRole.Link, new() { Name = "Login"
}).ClickAsync();
```

4. In the **Email** box, enter `admin@microsoft.com`.
5. In the **Password** box, enter `Pass@word1`.
6. Click the **Log in** button.
7. On the home page, in the toolbar, click **Assert text.**
8. Click **admin@microsoft.com.**
9. In the **Assert that element contains text** popup window, note the value `admin@microsoft.com`, and in the top-right corner, click the **Accept** tick icon to accept that text.
10. In the table of products, for the **Cup<T> White Mug** product, click the **Add To Basket** button.
11. In the **Quantity** box, enter `3`, click the **Update** button, and then click the **Checkout** button.
12. On the **Review** page, click the **Pay Now** button.
13. On the website home page, in the top navigation, hover over or click **admin@microsoft.com** and then click **LOG OUT**.

14. On the toolbar, click the red **Record** button to stop recording.

Review the recorded code

Now we can review what code was written based on our actions in the web browser:

1. In the **Playwright Inspector** window, note the code:

```
using Microsoft.Playwright;
using System;
using System.Threading.Tasks;

using var playwright = await Playwright.CreateAsync();

await using var browser = await playwright.Chromium.LaunchAsync(
  new BrowserTypeLaunchOptions
{
    Headless = false,
});

var context = await browser.NewContextAsync();
var page = await context.NewPageAsync();

await page.GotoAsync("https://localhost:5001/");
await page.GetByRole(AriaRole.Link, new() { Name = "Login"
}).ClickAsync();
await page.GetByLabel("Email").ClickAsync();
await page.GetByLabel("Email").FillAsync("admin@microsoft.com");
await page.GetByLabel("Email").PressAsync("Tab");
await page.GetByLabel("Password").FillAsync("Pass@word1");
await page.GetByLabel("Password").PressAsync("Tab");
await page.GetByRole(AriaRole.Button, new() { Name = "Log in"
}).ClickAsync();

await Expect(page.Locator("#logoutForm"))
  .ToContainTextAsync("admin@microsoft.com");

await page.Locator("form").Filter(
  new() { HasText = "[ ADD TO BASKET ] Cup<T>" })
  .GetByRole(AriaRole.Button).ClickAsync();

await page.GetByRole(AriaRole.Spinbutton).ClickAsync();
await page.GetByRole(AriaRole.Spinbutton).FillAsync("3");
await page.GetByRole(AriaRole.Button,
```

```
  new() { Name = "[ Update ]" }).ClickAsync();
await page.GetByRole(AriaRole.Link,
  new() { Name = "[ Checkout ]" }).ClickAsync();
await page.GetByRole(AriaRole.Button,
  new() { Name = "[ Pay Now ]" }).ClickAsync();
await page.GetByText("admin@microsoft.com").ClickAsync();
await page.GetByRole(AriaRole.Link,
  new() { Name = "Log Out" }).ClickAsync();
```

Note the assertion using the `Expect` method, as shown in the following code:

```
await  Expect(page.Locator("#logoutForm")).ToContainTextAsync
("admin@microsoft.com");.
```

2. You would now copy and paste this code into your test project and edit it to remove unnecessary statements like clicking on text boxes or pressing the *Tab* key, as shown in the following code:

```
// This statement is not needed.
await page.GetByLabel("Email").ClickAsync();

// This statement is not needed.
await page.GetByLabel("Email").PressAsync("Tab");
```

You can start the Playwright Inspector with emulation options like setting a view port size, as shown in the following command:

```
pwsh bin/Debug/net10.0/playwright.ps1 codegen --viewport-size=800,600 https://
localhost:5001/
```

You could emulate a device, as shown in the following command:

```
pwsh bin/Debug/net10.0/playwright.ps1 codegen --device="iPhone 13" https://
localhost:5001/
```

Learn more about code generation with Playwright Inspector at the following link: `https://playwright.dev/dotnet/docs/codegen`.

Testing web services using xUnit

There are multiple ways to test web services:

- Automated testing frameworks like xUnit, NUnit, and MSTest
- HTTP request editors like REST Client for VS Code or HTTP Editor in Visual Studio
- GUI tools like Postman, NSwag, or Swagger UI

One of the trickier aspects of testing web services is how to host the web service during testing and how to simulate an HTTP context. Integration tests for ASP.NET Core projects require the following:

- A test project to contain and execute the tests. The test project has a reference to the website or web service project aka the **system under test** (SUT).
- The test project creates a test web host for the SUT and uses a test server client to handle requests and responses with the SUT.

The `Microsoft.AspNetCore.Mvc.Testing` package handles the following tasks:

- Sets the content root to the SUT's project root so that static files and pages/views are found when the tests are executed
- Provides the `WebApplicationFactory` class to streamline bootstrapping the SUT with the `TestServer` class

We will create an example weather service using the built-in project template. Then we will write integration tests for it.

`WebApplicationFactory<Program>` is used to create an instance of the application under test, where `Program` is the class that contains your minimal API's `Main` method. The `CreateClient` method of `WebApplicationFactory<T>` creates an `HttpClient` configured to send requests to this instance.

The first test will send a `GET` request to the `/weatherforecast` endpoint and assert that the response is successful by checking for a status code in the range 200–299. The second test will make the same request and check that there are five weather forecasts in the deserialized JSON response.

By using `WebApplicationFactory<T>`, the tests will automatically handle the setup and teardown of the test server for you. This means you get to test your application in an environment very close to production, without the overhead of deploying and hosting the web service.

Creating a web service ready for testing

Let's create a web service ready for testing:

1. Use your preferred code editor to add a new project to the `Chapter14` solution:
    - Project template: **ASP.NET Core Web API** / `webapi`
    - Solution file and folder: `Chapter14`
    - Project file and folder: `WeatherService`
    - **Authentication type: None**
    - **Configure for HTTPS**: Selected
    - **Enable container support**: Cleared
    - **Enable OpenAPI support**: Selected
    - **Do not use top-level statements**: Cleared

Good practice: For web services that need to be easily tested, if you are targeting .NET 9 or earlier then avoid using the top-level program feature, and instead have the `Program` class explicitly defined so that you can make it `public` and, therefore, accessible outside the project. With .NET 10 and later, a new feature automatically makes your top-level program generated `Program` class public so it can be hosted for testing.

- **Use controllers**: Cleared
- **Enlist in Aspire orchestration**: Cleared

2. Build the `WeatherService` project.
3. Optionally, start the `WeatherService` project and confirm that it returns random weather forecasts. When you are done, close the browser and shut down the web server.

Creating the test project

Now we can create a test project that references the web service project:

1. Use your preferred code editor to add a new **xUnit Test Project** / `xunit` project named `WebServiceTests` to the `Chapter14` solution.
2. In the `WebServiceTests.csproj` project file, add a package reference for ASP.NET Core testing, as shown in the following markup:

```
<PackageReference Include="Microsoft.AspNetCore.Mvc.Testing" />
```

3. In the `WebServiceTests.csproj` project file, add a project reference to the web service, as shown in the following markup:

```
<ItemGroup>
  <ProjectReference Include="..\WeatherService\WeatherService.csproj" />
</ItemGroup>
```

4. In the `WebServiceTests` project, rename `UnitTest1.cs` to `WeatherForecastTests.cs`.
5. In `WeatherForecastTests.cs`, define a class with test methods, as shown in the following code:

```
using Microsoft.AspNetCore.Mvc.Testing; // To use
WebApplicationFactory<T>.
using System.Net.Http.Json; // To use ReadFromJsonAsync.
using WeatherService; // To use Program.

namespace WebServiceTests;

public class WeatherForecastTests :
  IClassFixture<WebApplicationFactory<Program>>
{
  private readonly WebApplicationFactory<Program> _factory;
```

```
  private const string relativePath = "/weatherforecast";

  public WeatherForecastTests(WebApplicationFactory<Program> factory)
  {
    _factory = factory;
  }

  [Fact]
  public async Task Get_WeatherForecasts_ReturnsSuccessStatusCode()
  {
    // Arrange
    HttpClient client = _factory.CreateClient();

    // Act
    HttpResponseMessage response =
      await client.GetAsync(relativePath);

    // Assert
    Assert.True(response.IsSuccessStatusCode); // Status Code 200-299.
  }

  [Fact]
  public async Task Get_WeatherForecasts_ReturnsFiveForecasts()
  {
    // Arrange
    HttpClient client = _factory.CreateClient();

    // Act
    HttpResponseMessage response = await client.GetAsync(relativePath);
    WeatherForecast[]? forecasts = await response.Content
      .ReadFromJsonAsync<WeatherForecast[]>();

    // Assert
    Assert.NotNull(forecasts);
    Assert.True(forecasts.Length == 5);
  }
}
```

6. Run the tests in the `WebServiceTests` project and note that they succeed without needing to start the web service project because the web service is hosted in a `TestServer` instance in the test project.

Practicing and exploring

Test your knowledge and understanding by answering some questions, getting some hands-on practice, and exploring the topics covered in this chapter with deeper research.

Exercise 14.1 – Online-only material

You can read the official documentation for Playwright for .NET at the following link: `https://playwright.dev/dotnet/docs/intro`.

Exercise 14.2 – Practice exercises

If you are done with Playwright and you want to remove the special browsers (`chromium`, `firefox`, and `webkit`) of the current Playwright installation, then run the Playwright PowerShell script with the `uninstall` option, as shown in the following command:

```
pwsh bin/Debug/ret10.0/playwright.ps1 uninstall
```

To remove browsers of other Playwright installations as well, add the `--all` switch, as shown in the following command:

```
pwsh bin/Debug/ret10.0/playwright.ps1 uninstall --all
```

Exercise 14.3 – Test your knowledge

Answer the following questions. If you get stuck, try googling the answers, while remembering that if you get totally stuck, the answers are in *Appendix A*:

1. What browsers does Playwright use when running its tests?
2. What are the main interfaces that represent important objects when writing tests for Playwright?
3. Using Playwright, what are some methods to get one or more elements on a web page?
4. What happens if more than one element matches and you call a method that implies a single DOM element like `ClickAsync`?
5. What does the Playwright Inspector do?

> *Appendix A, Answers to the Test Your Knowledge Questions*, is available to download from the following link: `https://github.com/markjprice/tools-skills-net10/blob/main/docs/B31468_Appendix%20A.pdf`.

Exercise 14.4 – Explore topics

Use the links on the following page to learn more details about the topics covered in this chapter: `https://github.com/markjprice/tools-skills-net10/blob/main/docs/book-links.md#chapter-14---functional-testing-of-websites-and-services`.

Summary

In this chapter, you learned:

- About the difference between functional and end-to-end testing
- How to test a web user interface using Playwright
- How to generate tests with Playwright Inspector
- How to test web services using xUnit

In the next chapter, you will learn about containerization using Docker.

Learn more on Discord

To join the Discord community for this book – where you can share feedback, ask questions to the author, and learn about new releases – follow this QR code:

`https://packt.link/TS2e`

Join .NETPro — It's Free

Staying sharp in .NET takes more than reading release notes. It requires real-world tips, proven patterns, and scalable solutions. That's what .NETPro, Packt's new newsletter, is all about.

Scan the QR code or visit the link to subscribe:

`https://landing.packtpub.com/dotnetpronewsletter/`

15

Containerization Using Docker

This chapter delves into the concept of containerization, a transformative technology that encapsulates applications along with their dependencies into isolated units, ensuring consistent performance across diverse computing environments.

In particular, you will see practical containerization through the use of Docker, a leading platform that simplifies the creation, deployment, and management of containerized applications. We'll explore Docker's core components, its ecosystem, and real-world applications, providing you with the tools and skills to harness the full potential of containerization in your development workflow.

Unlike traditional **virtual machines** (**VMs**), which emulate entire operating systems (OSs), containers share the host OS kernel, making them more lightweight and efficient.

This chapter covers the following topics:

- Introducing containerization
- Understanding Docker concepts
- Managing containers with Docker
- Working with Testcontainers

Introducing containerization

Containerization is a technology that is about making software development, deployment, and execution more efficient, consistent, and scalable.

A containerization analogy

To use a simple analogy, imagine that you are planning to set up several different themed parties (software applications) inside a large event hall (a physical server). Each party needs its own space, decorations, DJ (operating system), and music playlist (application dependencies) to create the right atmosphere.

Using VMs is like renting multiple smaller rooms within the event hall. Each room is separate from the others, with its own walls (hypervisor), locks (isolated OS), and all the specific decorations and music it needs, as shown in *Figure 15.1*:

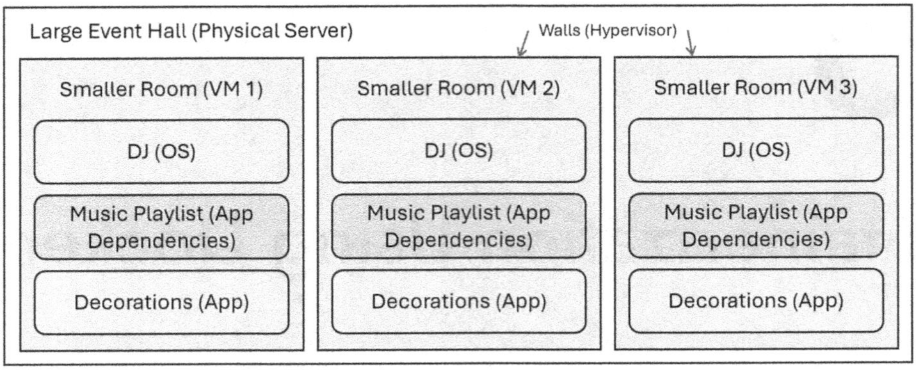

Figure 15.1: Using VMs is like renting multiple smaller rooms

This setup ensures that each party can happen without interference from the others, and each has everything it needs to operate independently. However, renting all these rooms and setting them up individually takes a lot of space, time, and money because each one needs a complete setup from scratch, including its own DJ and sound system.

Containerization is like deciding to host all the different parties in the same big room but using movable partitions to divide the space (the equivalent of the container runtime). Instead of each party having its own DJ and sound system, there's one big sound system (the host OS's kernel) that everyone shares. Each partitioned area is set up with its unique decorations and music playlist (the application and its dependencies), but the underlying infrastructure is shared, as shown in *Figure 15.2*:

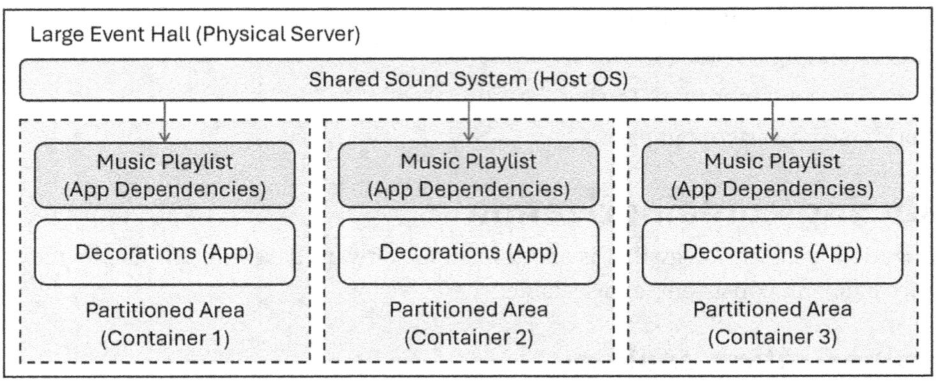

Figure 15.2: The same big room with movable partitions to divide the space

For this analogy to work, we must assume that humanity has invented a "cone of silence" technology that completely isolates the partitions with their own music.

This approach is more space and cost efficient because you're not duplicating the expensive components (like DJs and sound systems). It's easier and quicker to move the partitions around or change the themes of the parties than it would be to tear down and rebuild entire rooms. Plus, you can host more parties in the same space because each one requires less room to set up.

So, as we can see, VMs are like renting multiple rooms, providing complete isolation but with higher costs and more overhead. Containerization is about smartly sharing the space to host multiple parties more efficiently and flexibly. Both approaches have their place depending on the needs of the event (or application), but containerization offers a way to maximize resources and streamline setups in many scenarios.

Containerization wraps up software in a complete file system that contains everything the software needs to run including code, runtime, system tools, and system libraries. This guarantees that the software will always run the same, no matter where it is deployed. Think of it as a "code container" that plays nice within any environment, be it your personal laptop, a private data center, or the cloud.

This uniformity solves a big headache in software development and deployment known as the "it works on my machine" syndrome. With containers, developers can focus on their code without worrying about the environment where it will ultimately run.

Benefits and downsides of containers

Containers run on a single machine's OS kernel and share that kernel with other containers. They're lightweight because they don't need the extra load of a hypervisor that manages VMs. Containers run directly within the host machine's kernel. This makes them more efficient, faster, and less resource intensive than traditional VMs that require a full-blown OS for each VM.

The primary benefits of containerization are shown in the following list:

- **Portability**: Once a container image is created, it can be run anywhere, making it easy to move applications across different environments with confidence.
- **Consistency**: Containers provide a consistent environment for applications from development through to production, reducing bugs and inconsistencies.
- **Isolation**: Each container is isolated, so it doesn't interfere with others or the host system.
- **Efficiency**: Containers use system resources more efficiently than VMs, allowing you to get more out of your hardware.
- **Scalability**: Containers can be easily scaled up or down, making it simple to adjust resources to meet demand.
- **Speedy deployments**: Containers can be created and destroyed in seconds, making it easier to dynamically adjust to workload demands.

No technology solution is perfect, so let's review some of the potential downsides to containerization:

- **Security concerns:** Since containers share the host OS kernel, a vulnerability in the kernel could potentially compromise all containers running on that host. Containers provide process isolation, but it is not as robust as the hardware-level isolation provided by VMs. This can increase the risk of container escape attacks, where a malicious container could access the host system.

- **Management complexity:** In production, managing a large number of containers requires orchestration tools like Kubernetes, which add complexity and require significant expertise to configure and maintain. During development, managing containers can be significantly improved using Aspire, as you will see in the next chapter. Container networking can become complex, especially when dealing with multi-host networking, service discovery, and network policies.
- **Persistent storage management:** Containers are designed to be ephemeral, which can make managing persistent storage challenging. Solutions like volume mounts and network-attached storage must be carefully implemented to ensure data persistence and consistency.
- **Compatibility issues:** Not all applications are easily containerized, particularly legacy applications that may depend on specific hardware or OS features.
- **Debugging challenges:** The layered nature of container images and the complexity of container orchestration can make debugging more challenging compared to traditional applications.

While containerization offers significant advantages in terms of efficiency, scalability, and consistency, you should consider the potential downsides.

Now, let's get you introduced to some specific technologies that enable containerization.

Docker, Kubernetes, and Aspire

Docker is a platform that popularized containerization and made it accessible to developers by providing an open standard for packaging and distributing containerized applications. Building, shipping, and running applications are streamlined with Docker, making development workflows more predictable and scalable. It packages applications and their dependencies into a container, which can then be run on any Linux server or Windows that supports Docker. These containers are lightweight, ensuring that you can pack a lot of applications into a single host.

Beyond Docker, there's a whole ecosystem to support containerization, including orchestration tools like **Kubernetes**, which automates the deployment, scaling, and management of containerized applications in production. **Aspire** performs a similar role on a developer's computer during local development.

Docker and Kubernetes serve different but complementary roles in the world of containerization. If we consider containerization as organizing and shipping goods, Docker would be the packaging system that wraps up the goods (applications and their dependencies) into neat, transportable containers, while Kubernetes would be the shipping hub that manages where and how these containers are shipped, stored, and scaled.

Docker provides the tools for managing the life cycle of containers: building images, running containers, moving them around, managing versions, and so on. It simplifies the process of creating containers, making it accessible even to those new to the technology.

Docker containers can be integrated into CI/CD pipelines to automate the deployment process, making it faster and reducing the chances of errors.

> Podman is an alternative that is Docker compatible and is supported by Aspire. You can learn more at the following link: `https://podman.io/`.

Kubernetes

Kubernetes aka k8s is a container orchestration system for Docker and other container tools. Once you have containers, Kubernetes helps you manage them at scale. It handles how and where those containers run, how they communicate, and how they are scaled up or down based on demand.

Kubernetes offers features like automatic deployment, scaling, and operation of application containers across clusters of hosts. It also deals with networking between containers, load balancing, security, and storage orchestration. Kubernetes provides the infrastructure to build a container-based cloud, so it is used when you need to manage multiple containers across a cluster of machines. It's ideal for production environments where you need high availability, scalability, and distributed systems.

While Docker also offers its own tools for container orchestration (like **Docker Swarm**), Kubernetes has better scalability, flexibility, and strong community support. Essentially, Docker simplifies creating and managing your containers' life cycles, and Kubernetes takes those containers and deploys them in a way that optimizes resource usage, automates scaling and healing, and ensures your applications are always running efficiently.

This book focuses on tools and skills for .NET developers to use on their own local computers. Production deployments are beyond the scope of this book, so it does not cover Kubernetes in any detail. Many organizations find that Kubernetes is too complicated for their needs and choose to use a less complex deployment process like cron-job scripts that deploy based on reading Docker container labels.

Aspire (formerly .NET Aspire)

Aspire started its life as part of the broader .NET ecosystem, focusing on modernizing .NET with the latest technologies and practices. This includes embracing cloud-native practices, microservices architectures, and, notably, containerization technologies like Docker. Containerizing .NET applications with Docker enables developers to take full advantage of the portability, efficiency, and isolation that containers offer.

With Aspire 13, released alongside .NET 10, Aspire dropped the prefix .NET and skipped ahead a few versions to differentiate itself from .NET. Aspire is now polyglot, meaning it is not just for .NET developers. It can be used to orchestrate multiple projects created in many languages, with especially strong support for Python and JavaScript (Node.js).

> Aspire is very useful for local .NET development, and automates some of the process of working with containers, so it is covered in *Chapter 16, Cloud-Native Development Using Aspire*.

Container registries

A container registry is a storage and distribution system for container images. Think of it as a library or repository where you can store various versions of container images and then pull them when you need to deploy or run containers based on those images. This enables developers to easily share, store, and manage container images across development teams and production environments. Container registries often provide features such as version control, access control, and security scanning to ensure the images are safe from vulnerabilities.

The most common container registries used by .NET developers are shown in *Table 15.1*:

Registry	Description
Docker Hub	The default registry for Docker images and the largest public container image registry. It hosts official images from various software vendors, open-source projects, and community contributors. It also allows users to push their private images to Docker Hub. You will find official .NET and ASP.NET Core images, as well as other community or third-party images that .NET developers might use in their projects. Here's the link: `https://hub.docker.com/`.
Microsoft Container Registry (MCR), now known as Microsoft Artifact Registry	Microsoft's own container registry, hosting container images and other artifacts for Microsoft products and services, including .NET. When .NET Core transitioned to .NET 5 and beyond, Microsoft began to recommend using MCR as the primary source for .NET container images. While MCR hosts the images, Docker Hub provides the discovery and user interface experience. This means you can find Microsoft images on Docker Hub, but when you pull these images, they are served directly from MCR. This setup allows Microsoft to control and distribute their images efficiently while leveraging Docker Hub's vast user base for discoverability. MCR serves as the official source for Microsoft container images, including Windows Server with .NET, SQL Server, and many others. This guarantees that developers are getting authenticated and up-to-date images for their development and production needs. Here's the link: `https://mcr.microsoft.com/`.
GitHub Container Registry (GHCR)	Integrated with GitHub, GHCR lets developers easily publish and consume container images within the GitHub ecosystem. It supports Docker image storage and can be used in conjunction with GitHub Actions for CI/CD workflows. It's suitable for .NET developers who manage their code repositories on GitHub and want to streamline their CI/CD pipelines with containerized .NET applications. Here's the link: `https://github.com/container-registry/`.

Azure Container Registry (ACR)	A paid, private container registry service provided by Microsoft, designed to store and manage container images for Azure deployments. It offers close integration with Azure services, making it a convenient choice for .NET developers deploying applications to Azure. It's perfect for .NET developers looking for a secure, private registry with advanced features like geo-replication, vulnerability scanning, and tight integration with Azure Kubernetes Service (AKS) and Azure DevOps. Here's the link: `https://azure.microsoft.com/en-us/products/container-registry/`.
Amazon Elastic Container Registry (ECR)	A paid, private container registry that makes it easy for developers to store, manage, and deploy Docker container images. It's integrated with Amazon Web Services (AWS), providing a workflow for deploying containerized applications on AWS. Ideal for .NET developers deploying applications on AWS, especially those using Amazon Elastic Container Service (ECS) or Amazon Elastic Kubernetes Service (EKS). Here's the link: `https://aws.amazon.com/ecr/`.

Table 15.1: Common container registries

> The container registries shown in *Table 15.1* are the most common but there are many others, including ones hosted by GitLab and Harbor: `https://goharbor.io/`.

When choosing a container registry, .NET developers should consider factors such as integration with their current development and deployment workflows, security features, ease of use, and cost. Public registries like Docker Hub are great for accessing and sharing public images, while private registries like ACR and ECR offer more control and security for enterprise applications. Integration with CI/CD pipelines and cloud services is also an important consideration, making services like GHCR, ACR, and ECR popular choices for .NET developers working within those ecosystems.

Containerization is a fundamental shift in how we build and deploy applications. It offers a standardized way to package your solution and its dependencies into one or more units that run consistently across any environment. This technology has massive implications for improving development workflows, infrastructure efficiency, and application scalability.

The most popular core containerization technology that a .NET developer uses on their local computer is Docker, so that's what the remaining sections of this chapter will cover in more detail.

Understanding Docker concepts

When working with Docker, understanding its core concepts and terminology is important for the effective development, deployment, and management of containerized applications. Here are about a dozen essential terms and concepts for Docker that every .NET developer should know, as shown in *Table 15.2*:

Term	Description
Docker Engine	The core software that manages containers, allowing users to build and containerize applications. It's the engine, aka runtime, that executes containers based on Docker images.
Docker Image	A lightweight, standalone, executable package that includes everything needed to run a piece of software, including the code, runtime, libraries, environment variables, and configuration files. Images are immutable and act as a template for creating containers.
Docker Registry	A storage and content delivery system, holding named Docker images, available in different tagged versions. Users interact with a registry by using Docker push and pull commands. Examples include Docker Hub and MCR.
Docker Container	An instance of a Docker image. Containers run the actual applications, encapsulating them in a package that can be run anywhere the Docker daemon is installed. Containers are isolated from each other and the host system but can communicate via a network if needed.
Dockerfile	A text file that contains all the commands a user could call on the command line to assemble an image. Dockerfiles automate the process of creating Docker images.
Docker Compose	A tool for defining and running multi-container Docker applications. With Compose, you use a YAML file to configure your application's services, networks, and volumes, and then create and start all the services with a single command.
Docker Daemon	The background service running on the host that manages building, running, and distributing Docker containers. The daemon is the process that runs in the OS that clients talk to.
Docker Client	The command line tool that allows the user to interact with the Docker daemon. Through commands such as `docker run`, the client sends these commands to Docker Daemon, which carries them out.
Docker Volume	A mechanism for persisting data generated by and used by Docker containers. Volumes are managed by Docker and are isolated from the core functioning of the host machine, providing a way to persist or share data across containers.
Docker Network	Docker's networking feature allows containers to communicate with each other and with the outside world via the host machine. Docker provides various networking models, including bridge, host, and overlay networks.
Docker Swarm	A Docker-native clustering system that turns a group of Docker hosts into a single virtual Docker host. It uses the standard Docker API, so any tool that works with Docker can use Swarm to scale to multiple hosts.

Table 15.2: Essential Docker terms and concepts

As you become more familiar with Docker, you'll find these concepts integral to various operations and workflows within the Docker ecosystem. Now, let's see some important tools and technologies for Docker.

Docker tools and technologies

Here's a curated list of tools and technologies for .NET developers related to Docker, as shown in *Table 15.3*:

Tool	Description
Docker Desktop	Provides an easy-to-use interface for managing the life cycle of containers and images, including building, running, and stopping containers. There are versions for Windows, MacOS, and Linux. You will install Docker Desktop in a hands-on task in the next section.
Docker Compose	Defines and runs multi-container Docker applications. With a single command, developers can spin up an entire application stack, including services, networks, and volumes, as defined in a `docker-compose.yml` file. Aspire provides similar capabilities using C# code in an Aspire project that you add to your solution. Docker Desktop includes the Docker CLI, which includes Docker Compose.
Docker Scout	Analyzes image contents and generates a detailed report of packages and vulnerabilities that it detects. It can provide you with suggestions for how to remediate issues discovered by image analysis. This is a paid service accessed via Docker Desktop.
Code editor extensions	These extensions provide features like adding Docker support to projects, generating Dockerfiles, and managing containers and images. Install them via your code editor.

Table 15.3: Docker tools and technologies

Docker command-line interface (CLI) commands

Docker provides a suite of CLI commands that allow developers to manage containers, images, volumes, and networks. Here are some of the most common Docker commands along with examples to illustrate their use. These commands form the foundation for interacting with Docker, managing the container life cycle, and manipulating images and other resources.

Now, let's review some common commands, as shown in *Table 15.4*:

Command Example	Description
`docker --help`	Shows help for the CLI.
`docker <command> --help`	Shows help for the named command. For example, `docker pull --help`.
`docker images`	Lists all local images.
`docker pull <image-name>:<tag>`	Downloads an image with a tag from a container registry. For example, `docker pull mcr.microsoft.com/dotnet/sdk:10.0`.
`docker rmi mcr.microsoft.com/dotnet/sdk:10.0`	Removes one or more images.

`docker build -t my-dotnet-app .`	Builds Docker images from a Dockerfile.
`docker run -d -p 8080:80 --name webapp mcr.microsoft.com/dotnet/samples:aspnetapp:10.0`	Creates and starts a container from an image.
`docker ps`	Lists running containers.
`docker ps -a`	Lists running and stopped containers.
`docker stop webapp`	Stops one or more running containers.
`docker start webapp`	Starts one or more stopped containers.
`docker restart webapp`	Restarts a container.
`docker rm webapp`	Removes one or more containers.
`docker logs webapp`	Fetches the logs of a container.
`docker exec -it webapp bash`	Runs a command interactively (`-it`) in a running container.
`docker network create my-network`	Creates a new network.
`docker network ls`	Lists all networks.
`docker network rm my-network`	Removes one or more networks.
`docker network connect my-network webapp`	Connects a container to a network.
`docker network disconnect my-network webapp`	Disconnects a container from a network.
`docker volume create my-volume`	Creates a volume for persistent data storage.
`docker volume ls`	Lists all volumes.
`docker volume rm my-volume`	Removes one or more volumes.

Table 15.4: Docker commands

These commands are useful for daily Docker use, from developing applications to deploying them in a production environment. Mastering these commands will significantly improve your ability to work effectively with Docker.

> The official documentation for the Docker CLI can be found at the following link: `https://docs.docker.com/reference/cli/docker/`.

Building images using Dockerfiles

A **Dockerfile** is a text document that contains all the commands a user could call on the command line to assemble an image. The format of a Dockerfile is designed to be simple and readable, consisting of various instructions, each serving a specific purpose in the image creation process.

The basic format looks something like this:

```
# Comment
INSTRUCTION arguments
```

Note that comments start with # and continue to the end of the line.

Let's review some common instructions in *Table 15.5*:

Instruction	Description
FROM	Specifies the base image from which you are building. This is always the first instruction in a Dockerfile (except for parser directives, comments, and ARG instructions that may precede it). For example: FROM ubuntu:20.04.
LABEL	Adds metadata to an image, such as the maintainer, version, or description of the image. For example, LABEL maintainer=sam.smith@example.com.
RUN	Executes any commands on top of the current image layer and commits the results. Used to install software into containers. For example, RUN apt-get update && apt-get install -y python3.
CMD	Provides defaults for executing a container. There can only be one CMD instruction in a Dockerfile. If you list more than one CMD, then the last CMD will take effect. For example, CMD ["echo", "Hello world"].
EXPOSE	Informs Docker that the container listens on specific network ports at runtime. It does not actually publish the port. For example, EXPOSE 80.
ENV	Sets environment variables. For example, ENV MY_NAME="Sam Smith".
ADD, COPY	Instructions to copy new files, directories, or remote file URLs from <src> and add them to the file system of the image at the path <dest>. For example, COPY ./app /app.
ENTRYPOINT	Configures a container that will run as an executable. Command line arguments passed to docker run <image> get appended to the ENTRYPOINT. For example, ENTRYPOINT ["python3", "-m", "http.server"].
WORKDIR	Sets the working directory for any RUN, CMD, ENTRYPOINT, COPY, and ADD instructions that follow it. For example, WORKDIR /app.
USER	Sets the user name or UID to use when running the image and for any RUN, CMD, or ENTRYPOINT instructions that follow it. For example, USER myuser.
VOLUME	Creates a mount point with the specified name and marks it as holding externally mounted volumes from native hosts or other containers. For example, VOLUME /myvol.

Table 15.5: Common instructions in a Dockerfile

Configuring ports and running a container

A Docker container that cannot communicate with the outside world is not very useful. It is common to need to open ports in the container. The `docker run` command allows you to specify ports using the `-p` or `--publish` switch, which maps a port on the host to a port in the container. The syntax is `-p <hostPort>:<containerPort>`.

For an ASP.NET Core web application that listens on port 8080 within the container, you might want to map it to port 8000 on the host, making the application accessible at `http://localhost:8000`, as shown in the following command:

```
docker run -p 8000:8080 -d --name myaspnetapp mcr.microsoft.com/dotnet/
samples:aspnetapp:latest
```

This command starts a container named `myaspnetapp` from the `mcr.microsoft.com/dotnet/samples:aspnetapp:latest` image, detaches it (`-d`), and maps port 8000 on the host to port 8080 in the container.

> **Warning!** ASP.NET Core container images changed in .NET 8 to listen on port 8080, by default. .NET 6 and 7 were configured to listen on port 80.

.NET applications can also be configured to use HTTPS. If your application inside the container listens on port 443 (the default HTTPS port), and you want to map this to port 8443 on the host, you would use the following command:

```
docker run -p 8443:443 -d --name mysecureapp mcr.microsoft.com/dotnet/
samples:aspnetapp:latest
```

This allows you to access the application over HTTPS at `https://localhost:8443`. Note that additional configuration and certificates might be required for HTTPS to work correctly.

Sometimes, applications might need multiple ports open, like when an application communicates over HTTP but also has a management or metrics endpoint on a different port. For example, if your .NET application uses port 80 for the web interface and exposes a metrics endpoint on port 8081, you can map both:

```
docker run -p 8080:80 -p 5001:8081 -d --name mydotnetapp mcr.microsoft.com/
dotnet/samples:aspnetapp:latest
```

In this command, `-p 8080:80` maps the HTTP port, and `-p 5001:8081` maps the metrics endpoint port from the host to the container.

Good practice: When specifying ports for Docker containers, especially for development or testing purposes, it's common to choose host ports that avoid conflicts with any services already running on the host machine. Always ensure the chosen host ports are not already in use to prevent binding errors.

In complex scenarios, you might need to perform a container task in separate steps:

1. Download an image to use as a base.
2. Build a custom image.
3. Run a container based on the custom image.

The most common action is to download and run an image immediately. The `docker run` command can be used to both download an image and immediately start a container using it, as shown in the following command:

```
docker run --rm -it -p 8000:8080 mcr.microsoft.com/dotnet/samples:aspnetapp
```

The `--rm` switch automatically removes the container when it exits.

Interactive mode

The `-it` switch in the `docker run` command is a combination of two separate flags, `-i` and `-t`, which together facilitate interactive processes by allocating a pseudo-TTY (teletypewriter):

- `-i` or `--interactive` keeps the **standard input** (**STDIN**) open for the container even if not attached. This flag allows the container to receive input from the terminal.
- `-t` or `--tty` allocates a pseudo-TTY, which simulates a terminal, like what you might find when you connect via SSH. It makes the container start in an interactive shell mode. The TTY is important for interactive applications because it formats the output in a user-friendly way and allows for user input via the keyboard.

When you use `-it` together, it enables you to interact with the CLI or application within the container. For example, if you're running a Linux container and want to interact with its shell, you would use:

```
docker run -it ubuntu /bin/bash
```

This command would start an Ubuntu container, open a bash shell, and allow you to interact with it directly from your terminal. You'll be able to type commands within the container's shell, see the output, and interact with the file system or applications running inside the container.

Using `-it` is essential for debugging, configuration, or when the primary purpose is to interact with applications within the container directly. Without `-it`, the Docker container would run in the background, and you wouldn't have a way to interact with it directly from the command line.

Other common configurations are performed by setting environment variables.

Setting environment variables

Some images will require environment variables to be set when you run a container based on that image. For example, SQL Server images require two environment variables to be set, and one that should be set but has a default value, as shown in *Table 15.6*:

Environment variable	Description
`ACCEPT_EULA`	Confirms your acceptance of the End-User Licensing Agreement.
`MSSQL_SA_PASSWORD`	Database system administrator (`sa`) password used to connect to SQL Server once the container is running. This password must include at least 8 characters of at least three of these four categories: uppercase letters, lowercase letters, numbers, and non-alphanumeric symbols.
`MSSQL_PID`	**Product ID** (**PID**) or Edition that the container will run with. Acceptable values include `Developer`, `Express`, or the product ID for your license. If you do not explicitly set this, then `Developer` is used by default.

Table 15.6: Environment variables for SQL Server image

The complete list of environment variables that can be set for SQL Server can be found at the following link: `https://learn.microsoft.com/en-us/sql/linux/sql-server-linux-configure-environment-variables`.

Environment variables are set using the `-e` switch, as shown in the following command:

```
docker run
  -e "ACCEPT_EULA=Y"
  -e "MSSQL_SA_PASSWORD=yourStrong(!)Password"
  -e "MSSQL_PID=Developer"
  -p 1433:1433  --name sqlserver1 --hostname sqlserver1
  -d mcr.microsoft.com/mssql/server:2022-CU10-ubuntu-22.04
```

Warning! The preceding command is formatted to make it easier to read in a printed book. At a terminal or command prompt it must be entered all on one line as a single command.

Common Docker container images

There are thousands of prebuilt container images that you can spin up and use, including some common ones shown in *Table 15.7*:

Name	Link
SQL Server	https://hub.docker.com/_/microsoft-mssql-server
SQL Server Edge	https://hub.docker.com/_/microsoft-azure-sql-edge
PostgreSQL	https://hub.docker.com/_/postgres
RabbitMQ	https://hub.docker.com/_/rabbitmq
Redis	https://hub.docker.com/_/redis
MongoDB	https://hub.docker.com/_/mongo
Elasticsearch	https://hub.docker.com/_/elasticsearch
nginx (Reverse Proxy)	https://hub.docker.com/_/nginx
Grafana	https://hub.docker.com/r/grafana/grafana
.NET SDK	https://hub.docker.com/_/microsoft-dotnet-sdk/
.NET Runtime	https://hub.docker.com/_/microsoft-dotnet-runtime/
ASP.NET Core Runtime	https://hub.docker.com/_/microsoft-dotnet-aspnet/
.NET Samples	https://hub.docker.com/_/microsoft-dotnet-samples/

Table 15.7: Common Docker container images

.NET container images

.NET provides various container images for different scenarios. The following characteristics are used to differentiate images:

- The **target framework moniker** (**TFM**) of the app
- The OS, version, and architecture
- The image type (for example, `runtime`, `aspnet`, `sdk`)
- The image variant (for example, `*-distroless`, `*-chiseled`)
- The image feature (for example, `*-aot`, `*-extra`)

> You can learn more about tagging patterns and policies that are used for the official .NET container images at the following link: `https://github.com/dotnet/dotnet-docker/blob/main/documentation/supported-tags.md`.

Some .NET container images are smaller because they don't include globalization dependencies like time zone data. These images only work with apps that are configured for globalization invariant mode. To configure an app for invariant globalization, add the following property to the project file:

```
<PropertyGroup>
  <InvariantGlobalization>true</InvariantGlobalization>
</PropertyGroup>
```

The four most common official images for .NET and ASP.NET Core are included at the bottom of *Table 15.7,* but if you want to review the most recent full list, then please use the following link: `https://hub.docker.com/_/microsoft-dotnet`.

CVEs and Chiseled Ubuntu

Common Vulnerabilities and Exposures (CVE) is a standardized identifier for a specific cybersecurity vulnerability or exposure. The CVE system is designed to provide a common reference point for identifying and discussing vulnerabilities across different tools, databases, and services.

Each CVE entry consists of an ID in the format CVE-YYYY-NNNN, where "YYYY" represents the year that the CVE was assigned or made public, and "NNNN" is a sequential number that starts at 0001 at midnight on January 1 of the current year and increases as new CVEs are recorded within that year. For example, CVE-2023-1234 would be the 1,234th CVE entry of the year 2023. Each CVE entry includes a brief description of the vulnerability or exposure. This typically covers the nature of the issue, the affected software or hardware, and the potential impact of the vulnerability.

CVE Numbering Authorities (CNAs) are organizations authorized to assign CVE IDs to vulnerabilities affecting their own products or in their scope of responsibility. These can include software vendors, research organizations, and security service providers.

By using CVE IDs, security professionals, researchers, and vendors can communicate more effectively about specific vulnerabilities, streamlining the processes of vulnerability management, reporting, and remediation. CVE IDs are used by many security tools and databases, including vulnerability scanners, intrusion detection systems, and patch management systems. This integration facilitates automated vulnerability management and improves the overall security posture.

Chiseled container images are Ubuntu container images with a minimal set of components required by the .NET runtime. These images are ~100 MB smaller than the regular Ubuntu images and have fewer CVEs since they have fewer components. They don't contain a shell or package manager, which significantly improves their security profile. They also include a non-root user and are configured with that user enabled.

You can learn more at the following link: `https://devblogs.microsoft.com/dotnet/announcing-dotnet-chiseled-containers/`.

Managing containers with Docker

Enough theory; let's get practical. In this section, we'll explore how to manage containers with Docker.

Installing Docker and using prebuilt images

Let's install Docker and explore how to use it to manage containers:

1. If you do not already have **Docker Desktop** installed on your computer, please install it now from the following link: `https://www.docker.com/products/docker-desktop/`.

2. Start **Docker Desktop** and note the user interface, including the **Containers** view, which will probably be empty if you have not run any containers yet, as shown in *Figure 15.3*:

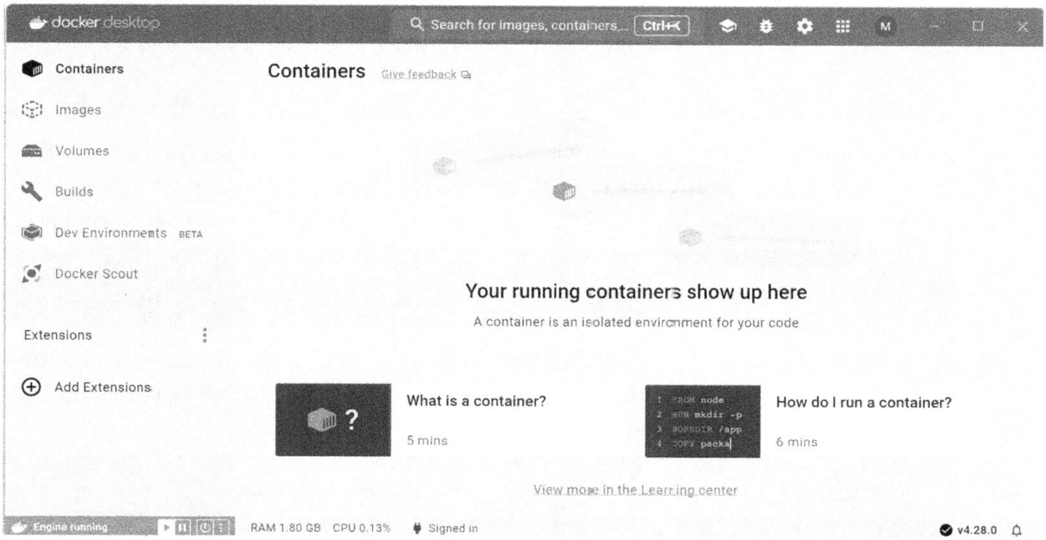

Figure 15.3: The Containers view in Docker Desktop

3. In the left navigation bar, click **Images**, and note that on my machine I already have a few Docker images downloaded, as shown in *Figure 15.4*:

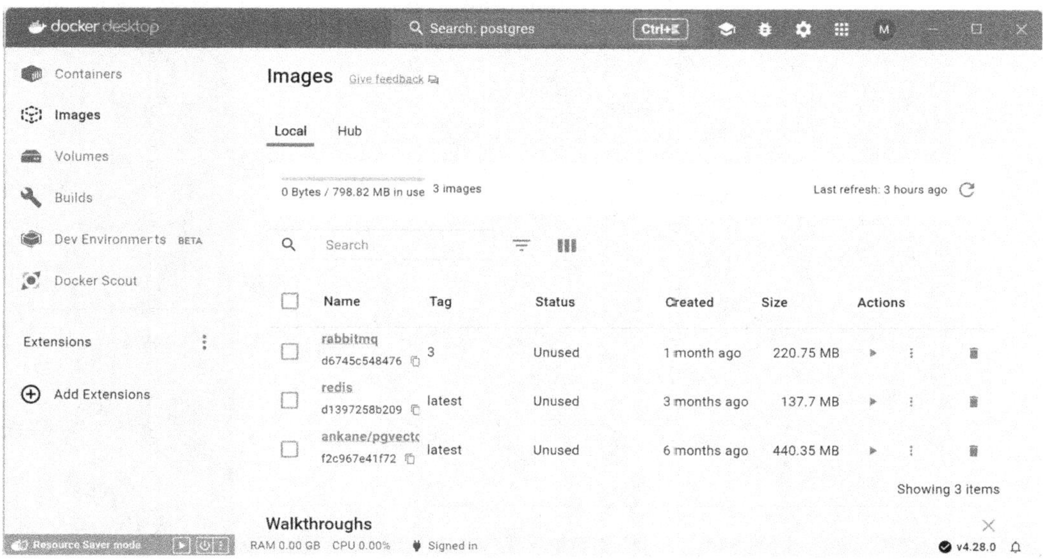

Figure 15.4: The Images view in Docker Desktop

4. At a command prompt or terminal, list the Docker images, as shown in the following command:

```
docker images
```

5. Note the results on my computer, as shown in the following output that matches *Figure 15.4*:

```
REPOSITORY          TAG         IMAGE ID        CREATED          SIZE
rabbitmq            3           d6745c548476    4 weeks ago      221MB
redis               latest      d1397258b209    2 months ago     138MB
ankane/pgvector     latest      f2c967e41f72    5 months ago     440MB
```

6. At the command prompt or terminal, download the Docker image for the sample ASP.NET Core project image and run it with external port 8000 mapped to internal port 8080, interactive TTY mode (`-it`), and remove it when the container stops (`--rm`), as shown in the following command:

```
docker run --rm -it -p 8000:8080 mcr.microsoft.com/dotnet/
samples:aspnetapp
```

7. Note the results, including downloading the image, starting the container, and outputting the console output from inside the container that is hosting the ASP.NET Core sample project, as shown in the following output:

```
Unable to find image 'mcr.microsoft.com/dotnet/samples:aspnetapp' locally
aspnetapp: Pulling from dotnet/samples
4abcf2066143: Pull complete
4e1692478f05: Pull complete
73df137ef55b: Pull complete
0ab1344a44f8: Pull complete
c9a33571af57: Pull complete
458c6e372327: Pull complete
d57ff6e481d4: Pull complete
Digest:
sha256:0bca5ff4b566b29c7d323efc0142ee506681efb31a7839cec91a9acbf760dfa8
Status: Downloaded newer image for mcr.microsoft.com/dotnet/
samples:aspnetapp
warn: Microsoft.AspNetCore.DataProtection.Repositories.
FileSystemXmlRepository[60]
      Storing keys in a directory '/root/.aspnet/DataProtection-Keys'
that may not be persisted outside of the container. Protected data will
be unavailable when container is destroyed. For more information go to
https://aka.ms/aspnet/dataprotectionwarning
warn: Microsoft.AspNetCore.DataProtection.KeyManagement.XmlKeyManager[35]
      No XML encryptor configured. Key {419c59e8-3d0b-43fa-bf2c-
4574734788c4} may be persisted to storage in unencrypted form.
info: Microsoft.Hosting.Lifetime[14]
      Now listening on: http://[::]:8080
info: Microsoft.Hosting.Lifetime[0]
      Application started. Press Ctrl+C to shut down.
info: Microsoft.Hosting.Lifetime[0]
```

```
      Hosting environment: Production
info: Microsoft.Hosting.Lifetime[0]
      Content root path: /app
warn: Microsoft.AspNetCore.HttpsPolicy.HttpsRedirectionMiddleware[3]
      Failed to determine the https port for redirect.
```

8. Start your preferred web browser, navigate to `http://localhost:8000/`, and you can see that the home page shows information about the container, as shown in *Figure 15.5*:

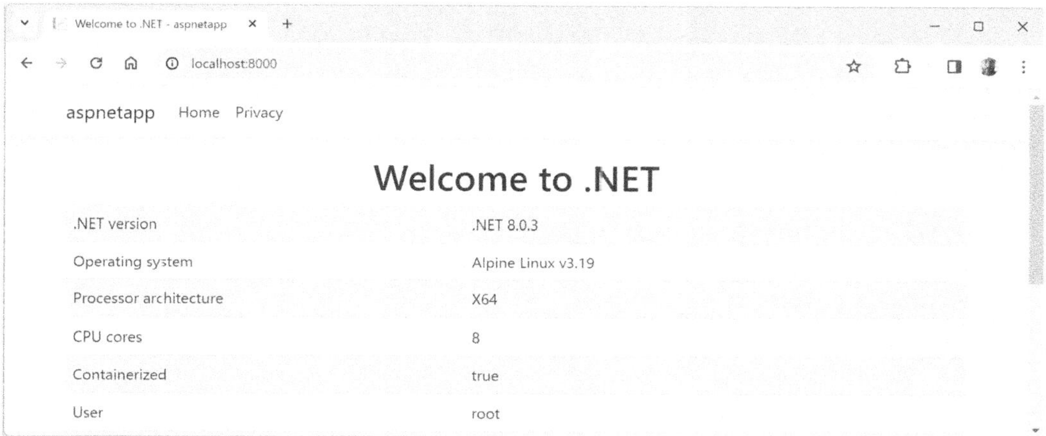

Figure 15.5: An ASP.NET Core website hosted in a Docker container

9. In **Docker Desktop**, you can see that the container is running with a random name, as shown in *Figure 15.6*:

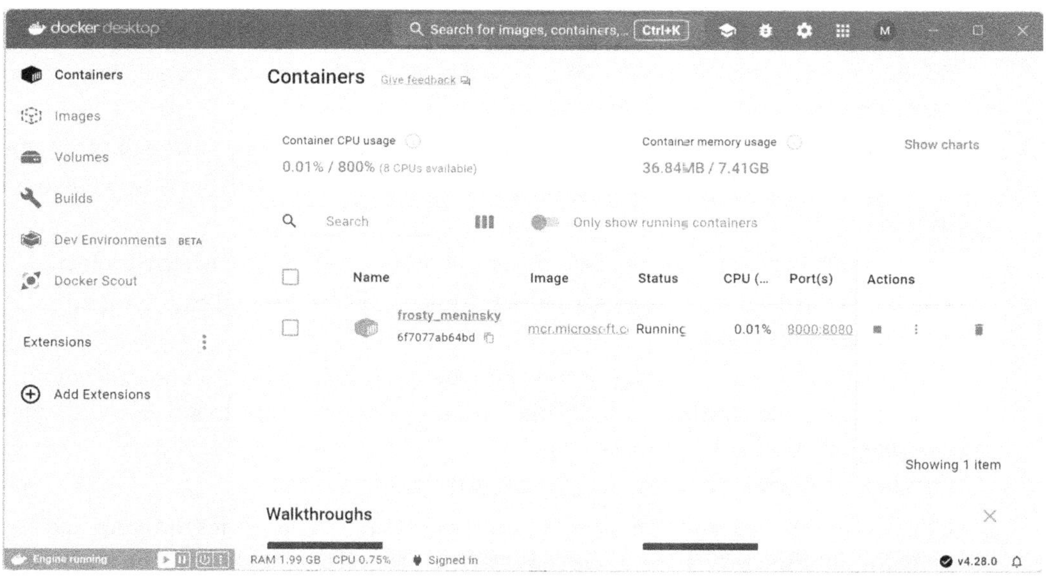

Figure 15.6: Randomly named running container

10. Close the browser and at the command prompt or terminal, shut down the web server.
11. In **Docker Desktop**, note the container automatically removes itself due to the `--rm` switch but the image remains on the local disk.

Example Dockerfile for a .NET application

Here's a simple example of a Dockerfile for a .NET application. This Dockerfile demonstrates how to build and run a basic .NET console app project inside a Docker container, as shown in the following code and visualized later in *Figure 15.7*:

```
# Use the .NET 10 SDK image to build the application.
FROM mcr.microsoft.com/dotnet/sdk:10.0 AS build-env
WORKDIR /Chapter15ConsoleApp
# Copy everything in current directory to /Chapter15ConsoleApp.
COPY . ./
# Restore any dependencies (via NuGet).
RUN dotnet restore
# Build and publish a release.
RUN dotnet publish -c Release -o out
# Use the ASP.NET Core 10 runtime image to host the application.
FROM mcr.microsoft.com/dotnet/runtime:10.0
WORKDIR /Chapter15ConsoleApp
COPY --from=build-env /Chapter15ConsoleApp/out .
ENTRYPOINT ["dotnet", "AboutMyEnvironment.dll"]
```

Note the following about the preceding instructions:

- `FROM mcr.microsoft.com/dotnet/sdk:10.0 AS build-env`: This line starts the first stage of the build, using the .NET 10.0 SDK image. The `AS build-env` part names this stage for later reference.
- `WORKDIR /Chapter15ConsoleApp`: This sets the working directory inside the container.
- `COPY . ./`: This copies all the project files from your host to the container's current working directory.
- `RUN dotnet restore`: This restores the NuGet packages required for the project.
- `RUN dotnet publish -c Release -o out`: This publishes the application to the out directory in a release configuration.
- `FROM mcr.microsoft.com/dotnet/aspnet:10.0`: This starts the second stage of the build by using the .NET 10 runtime image. This is a lighter-weight image that doesn't include the SDK, suitable for running the project.
- `WORKDIR /Chapter15ConsoleApp`: This sets the working directory.
- `COPY --from=build-env /Chapter15ConsoleApp/out .`: This copies the compiled application from the out directory in the `build-env` stage to the current directory in the runtime container.

- `ENTRYPOINT ["dotnet", "AboutMyEnvironmentMyApp.dll"]`: This specifies the command to run the application. It assumes the project has a `Main` entry point defined in `Program.cs`. Replace `AboutMyEnvironmentMyApp.dll` with the name of your application's DLL.

This Dockerfile is structured to use **multi-stage builds**. The first stage uses the SDK image to build the application, and the second stage uses the runtime image to run it. This approach keeps the final image size smaller, as the final image doesn't include the SDK and build artifacts, only the runtime and the application's published output. By using `docker build`, users can create an automated build that executes several command-line instructions in succession.

The official Dockerfile documentation can be found at the following link: `https://docs.docker.com/reference/dockerfile/`. Multi-stage builds documentation can be found at the following link: `https://docs.docker.com/build/building/multi-stage/`.

Docker image hierarchy and layers

Docker images are built using a layered architecture. When you create a Docker image, each instruction in the Dockerfile creates a new layer in the image. These layers represent a hierarchy of images, where each layer depends on the layer below it, as shown in *Figure 15.7*:

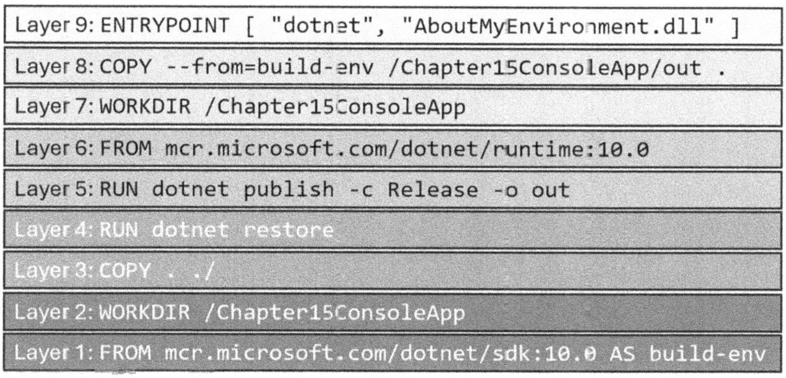

Figure 15.7: Docker's instructions and their layers

Each layer in a Docker image is simply a set of differences from the layer below it. The layers are stacked on top of each other. When you change a file, Docker only updates the layer containing that file, rather than creating a new image from scratch. This makes building and sharing images much faster and more storage efficient.

Each layer is immutable, meaning it cannot be changed once it's created. Only new layers can be added on top. If a layer changes, Docker creates a new layer to represent that change, rather than altering the existing layer.

The foundation of an image hierarchy is the base image, which is the first layer of an image that other layers build upon. It typically contains the minimum necessary environment, like an OS, for example, Ubuntu or Alpine.

Built on top of the base image, child images add additional layers that include application code, libraries, dependencies, and environment variables. These are the custom layers that differentiate one image from another and tailor it to a specific application or service.

Each instruction adds a layer on top of the base image, forming a hierarchy that culminates in the final image. When you run a container from this image, Docker combines these layers into a single cohesive file system.

This architecture allows Docker to be highly efficient in storing and transporting images, as only the layers that have changed need to be pushed or pulled, reducing the amount of data that needs to be transferred.

Reviewing image layers

Now that we have a Docker image to work with, let's dig deeper into how they are made:

1. In **Docker Desktop**, select **Images**, and then click the ASP.NET Core samples image.
2. In the **Image hierarchy** section, make sure the first image, **alpine-3**, is selected. You can see that it is an official Docker image, it has 19 packages, and it is made by the first 2 of 13 layers numbered 0 and 1, as shown in *Figure 15.8*:

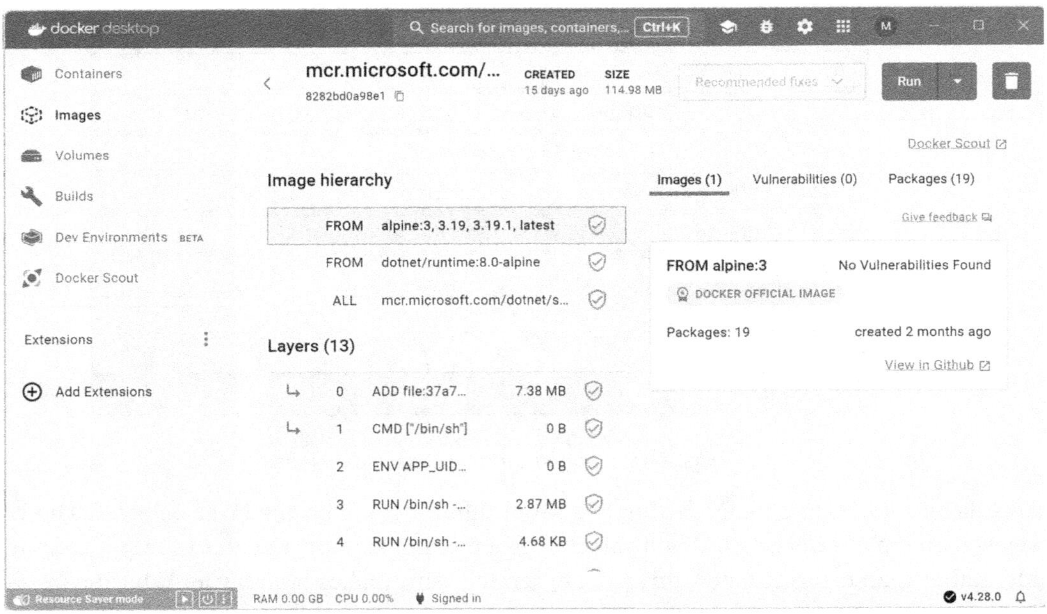

Figure 15.8: Image hierarchy and layers for dotnet/samples:aspnetapp

3. In the **Image hierarchy** section, select the second image, **dotnet/runtime:10.0-alpine**; you can see that it has 190 packages, and it is made by layers 2 to 6, as shown in *Figure 15.9*:

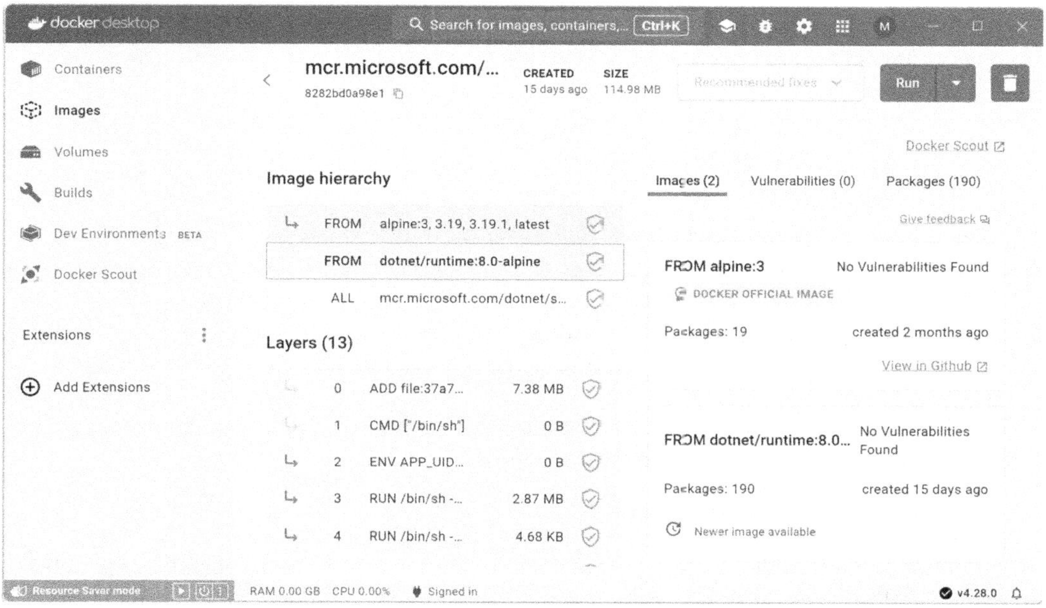

Figure 15.9: Second image and its layers for dotnet/samples:aspnetapp

4. Select layer **2**, click the **Command** tab, and you can see that it sets some environment variables, as shown in the following `ENV` instruction:

```
ENV APP_UID=1654 ASPNETCORE_HTTP_PORTS=8080 DOTNET_RUNNING_IN_
CONTAINER=true DOTNET_SYSTEM_GLOBALIZATION_INVARIANT=true
```

5. Select layer **6**, and you can see that it downloads the .NET runtime for Linux, as shown in the following **RUN** instruction:

```
RUN /bin/sh -c wget -O dotnet.tar.gz https://dotnetcli.
azureedge.net/dotnet/Runtime/$DOTNET_VERSION/dotnet-
runtime-$DOTNET_VERSION-linux-musl-x64.tar.gz && dotnet_
sha512='bbed0cf924d103e15d07e069522fc89d921e8d91adccbd4e161345b52fc8bdb2683
7a18c83d06ccd092d14d3df0e6acbe3b8d348e0825822807a1cbc1c8f549f' && echo
"$dotnet_sha512 dotnet.tar.gz" | sha512sum -c - && mkdir -p /usr/share/
dotnet && tar -oxzf dotnet.tar.gz -C /usr/share/dotnet && rm dotnet.tar.
gz && ln -s /usr/share/dotnet/dotnet /usr/bin/dotnet # buildkit
```

6. In the **Image hierarchy** section, select the third and last image, **mcr.microsoft.com/dotnet/samples:aspnteapp**, and you can see that it has 331 packages and is made by layers 7 to 12.
7. Select layer **7**, and you can see that it sets an environment variable for the ASP.NET Core version, as shown in the following `ENV` instruction:

```
ENV ASPNET_VERSION=10.0.0
```

8. Select layer **8**, and you can see that it downloads the ASP.NET Core runtime for Linux, as shown in the following `RUN` instruction:

```
RUN /bin/sh -c wget -O aspnetcore.tar.gz https://dotnetcli.azureedge.net/
dotnet/aspnetcore/Runtime/$ASPNET_VERSION/aspnetcore-runtime-$ASPNET_
VERSION
-linux-musl-x64.tar.gz && aspnetcore_
sha512='438ed9f5fef9cc63bae18f52af4209
a80d8265ef6f9c7b92661e5276538b76163a7
9e6c59f5fe3d40133e8cdbed7ba50135ce365194358f4abe9df9231a124a5'
&& echo "$aspnetcore_sha512 aspnetcore.tar.gz" | sha512sum -c - && tar
-oxzf
aspnetcore.tar.gz -C /usr/share/dotnet ./shared/Microsoft.AspNetCore.App
&& rm aspnetcore.tar.gz # buildkit
```

9. Select layer **9**, and you can see that it tells the container that it exposes internal port 8080, as shown in the following `EXPOSE` instruction:

```
EXPOSE map[8080/tcp:{}]
```

By adopting Docker, .NET developers can make their applications more portable, scalable, and easier to deploy and manage, which modernizes the development, deployment, and maintenance of .NET applications.

Now, let's see how to create a new .NET project from scratch and then containerize it.

Containerizing a Console App project

So far in this chapter, we have learned about containerization concepts and the Docker tools. Now, let's see how to use these new tools and skills with .NET development.

In this section, we will look at two types of .NET projects: a console app and an ASP.NET Core website.

Let's start with a class library and console app:

1. Use your preferred code editor to add a new **Class Library** / `classlib` project named `EnvironmentLib` to a `Chapter15` solution.
2. Rename `Class1.cs` to `EnvironmentInfo.cs`.
3. In `EnvironmentInfo.cs`, replace the existing statements with statements to store information about the current environment, as shown in the following code:

```
using System.Net; // To use Dns.
using System.Runtime.InteropServices; // To use RuntimeInformation.

namespace EnvironmentLib;

public class EnvironmentInfo
{
```

```
  public string UserName { get; } = Environment.UserName;
  public string HostName { get; } = Dns.GetHostName();
  public string DotNet { get; } = RuntimeInformation.
FrameworkDescription;
  public string OS { get; } = RuntimeInformation.OSDescription;
  public string Architecture { get; } =
    RuntimeInformation.OSArchitecture.ToString();
  public int Processors { get; } = Environment.ProcessorCount;
  public bool InContainer { get; } = Environment
    .GetEnvironmentVariable("DOTNET_RUNNING_IN_CONTAINER") is not null;
}
```

4. Build the `EnvironmentLib` project.
5. Use your preferred code editor to add a new **Console App** / `console` project named `AboutMyEnvironment` to the `Chapter15` solution.
6. Optionally, make the `AboutMyEnvironment` project the startup project for the solution.
7. In the `AboutMyEnvironment.csproj` project file, statically and globally import the `Console` class, add a reference to the Spectre Console package, and add a reference to the `EnvironmentLib` project, as shown in the following markup:

```
<ItemGroup>
  <Using Include="System.Console" Static="true" />
</ItemGroup>

<ItemGroup>
  <PackageReference Include="Spectre.Console" />
</ItemGroup>

<ItemGroup>
  <ProjectReference Include="..\EnvironmentLib\EnvironmentLib.csproj" />
</ItemGroup>
```

8. In `Program.cs`, delete any existing statements, and then write statements to output the properties of an instance of the `EnvironmentInfo` class in a Spectre table, as shown in the following code:

```
using Spectre.Console; // To use Table.

EnvironmentLib.EnvironmentInfo info = new();

Table t = new();
t.AddColumn("Property");
t.AddColumn("Value");
```

```
t.AddRow("User", info.UserName);
t.AddRow("Host", info.HostName);
t.AddRow("OS", info.OS);
t.AddRow("Architecture", info.Architecture);
t.AddRow("Platform", info.DotNet);
t.AddRow("Processors", info.Processors.ToString());
t.AddRow("In a container", info.InContainer.ToString());

AnsiConsole.Write(t);

WriteLine("I will output the time every five seconds.");
WriteLine("Press Ctrl + C to stop.");
while (true)
{
  await Task.Delay(TimeSpan.FromSeconds(5));
  WriteLine(DateTime.Now.ToLongTimeString());
}
```

9. Run the `AboutMyEnvironment` project and note the result, as shown in the following output:

```
┌────────────────┬──────────────────────────────┐
│ Property       │ Value                        │
├────────────────┼──────────────────────────────┤
│ User           │ markj                        │
│ Host           │ DESKTOP-J1PQHR7              │
│ OS             │ Microsoft Windows 10.0.22631 │
│ Architecture   │ X64                          │
│ Platform       │ .NET 10.0.0                  │
│ Processors     │ 8                            │
│ In a container │ False                        │
└────────────────┴──────────────────────────────┘
I will output the time every five seconds.
Press Ctrl + C to stop.
16:04:59
16:05:04
16:05:09
```

10. Press *Ctrl* + *C* to stop the console app.

Publishing to a Docker container

Now, let's deploy this project to a container:

1. At the command project or terminal, in the `Chapter15` folder, publish the two projects using their release configurations, as shown in the following command:

```
dotnet publish -c Release
```

2. Note the results, as shown in the following output:

```
MSBuild version 18.0.0-01+07fd5d51f for .NET
Restore complete (1.0s)
  EnvironmentLib succeeded (0.2s) → EnvironmentLib\bin\Release\net10.0\
publish\
  AboutMyEnvironment succeeded (2.5s) → AboutMyEnvironment\bin\Release\
net10.0\publish\
```

3. In the `Chapter15` folder, create a file named `Dockerfile`.
4. In `Dockerfile`, add instructions to create an image to build the projects using the .NET SDK, and then create an image to run the `AboutMyEnvironment` console app, as shown in the following commands:

```
# Use the .NET 10 SDK image to build the application.
FROM mcr.microsoft.com/dotnet/sdk:10.0 AS build-env
WORKDIR /Chapter15ConsoleApp
# Copy everything in current directory to /Chapter15ConsoleApp.
COPY . ./
# Restore any dependencies (via NuGet).
RUN dotnet restore
# Build and publish a release.
RUN dotnet publish -c Release -o out
# Use the .NET 10 runtime image to host the application.
FROM mcr.microsoft.com/dotnet/runtime:10.0
WORKDIR /Chapter15ConsoleApp
COPY --from=build-env /Chapter15ConsoleApp/out .
ENTRYPOINT ["dotnet", "AboutMyEnvironment.dll"]
```

The `ENTRYPOINT` instruction sets `dotnet` as the host for the assembly. It's possible to instead use the app executable itself, `ENTRYPOINT ["./AboutMyEnvironment"]`, which causes the app to be executed directly and relies on the app host and the underlying OS.

5. At the command project or terminal, in the `Chapter15` folder, build the container, as shown in the following command:

```
docker build -t aboutmyenvironment-image -f Dockerfile .
```

> **Warning!** Repository image names must be all lowercase.

6. Note the results, as partially shown in the following output:

```
[+] Building 9.0s (14/14) FINISHED
docker:default
 => [internal] load build definition from Dockerfile        0.0s
 => => transferring dockerfile: 442B                        0.0s
 => [internal] load metadata for mcr.../runtime:10.0        0.4s
...
=> [build-env 2/5] WORKDIR /Chapter15                       0.1s
=> [build-env 3/5] COPY . ./                                0.1s
 => [build-env 4/5] RUN dotnet restore                      3.1s
 => [build-env 5/5] RUN dotnet publish -c Release -o out    5.0s
 => [stage-1 3/3] COPY --from=build-env /Chapter15/out .    0.0s
 => exporting to image                                      0.0s
...
View build details: docker-desktop://dashboard/build/default/default/
lms97oh3e670otwuv89jexa2l
List the Docker images, as shown in the following command:
docker images
Note the results, as shown in the following output:
REPOSITORY                         TAG         IMAGE ID       SIZE
aboutmyenvironment-image           latest      8e046d9d8358   194MB
mcr.microsoft.com/dotnet/samples   aspnetapp   8282bd0a98e1   115MB
```

> You will also be able to see the image in Docker Desktop.

7. Create a Docker container named `ame` from the image named `aboutmyenvironment-image`, as shown in the following command:

```
docker create --name ame aboutmyenvironment-image
```

8. Note a GUID value like `1124bbf17c58` will be returned.
9. List all the containers, as shown in the following command:

```
docker ps -a
```

10. Note the results that show a container named `ame` has been created, as shown in the following output:

```
CONTAINER ID   IMAGE                        COMMAND
CREATED           STATUS     PORTS      NAMES
1124bbf17c58   aboutmyenvironment-image   "dotnet AboutMyEnvir…"   25
seconds ago   Created                ame
```

You will also be able to see the container in Docker Desktop.

11. Start the `ame` container and attach its standard input and output to the current command prompt or terminal, as shown in the following command:

```
docker start ame -ai
```

The `-ai` switches are short for `--attach --interactive`, which means attach `STDOUT/STDERR` and forward signals and attach the container's `STDIN`. This allows us to see output from the console app in the container and send the input using the keyboard.

12. Note the results, as shown in the following output:

```
┌─────────────────┬──────────────────────────────────┐
│ Property        │ Value                            │
├─────────────────┼──────────────────────────────────┤
│ User            │ root                             │
│ Host            │ 1124bbf17c58                     │
│ OS              │ Debian GNU/Linux 12 (bookworm)   │
│ Architecture    │ X64                              │
│ Platform        │ .NET 10.0.0                      │
│ Processors      │ 8                                │
│ In a container  │ True                             │
└─────────────────┴──────────────────────────────────┘
I will output the time every five seconds.
Press Ctrl + C to stop.
16:51:15
16:51:20
```

13. At the command project or terminal, press *Ctrl* + *C* to stop the console app (which will also stop its container).
14. Instead of manually creating, starting, and stopping a container, run it with a randomly generated container name like `agitated-mahavira`, as shown in the following command and *Figure 15.10*:

```
docker run -it --rm aboutmyenvironment-image
```

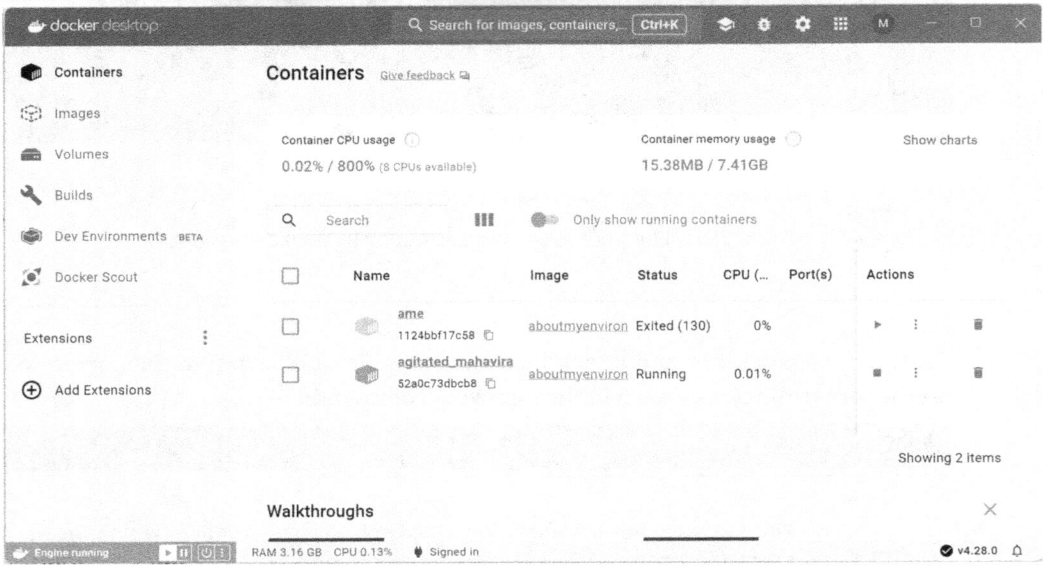

Figure 15.10: Container with a randomly generated name

15. At the command project or terminal, press *Ctrl* + *C* to stop the console app (which will also stop *and remove* its container due to the `--rm` switch).
16. At the command prompt or terminal, run and connect to the container without running the console app immediately by overriding the entry point, as shown in the following command:

```
docker run -it --rm --entrypoint "bash" aboutmyenvironment-image
```

17. Note the command prompt that shows the user and current directory, as shown in the following output:

```
root@f01f9d2cda94:/Chapter15#
```

18. List the directory contents using `ls` or `dir`, and note the results, as shown in the following output:

```
AboutMyEnvironment                AboutMyEnvironment.pdb
EnvironmentLib.dll
AboutMyEnvironment.deps.json  AboutMyEnvironment.runtimeconfig.json
EnvironmentLib.pdb
AboutMyEnvironment.dll            EnvironmentLib.deps.json
Spectre.Console.dll
```

19. Run the console app using `dotnet`, as shown in the following command:

```
dotnet AboutMyEnvironment.dll
```

20. After at least ten seconds, press *Ctrl* + *C* to stop the console app.
21. Run the console app using its executable, as shown in the following command:

```
./AboutMyEnvironment
```

22. After at least ten seconds, press *Ctrl* + *C* to stop the console app.
23. Change to the parent directory using `cd ..`, list the directory contents using `ls` or `dir`, and note the results, as shown in the following output:

```
Chapter15  bin  boot  dev  etc  home  lib  lib64  media  mnt  opt  proc
root  run  sbin  srv  sys  tmp  usr  var
```

24. Exit `bash`, and you can see that the container automatically gets removed, as shown in the following command:

```
exit
```

Now, let's look at a more complex example.

Containerizing an ASP.NET Core project

Publishing a simple console app to Docker is a useful first step to learning how to use Docker with .NET. In the real world, you are more likely to containerize ASP.NET Core projects, so that's what we will look at next. Let's go:

1. Use your preferred code editor to open the `Chapter15` solution.
2. Add an MVC website project with authentication accounts stored in a database, as defined in the following list:
    - Project template: **ASP.NET Core Web App (Model-View-Controller) [C#]** / `mvc`
    - Project file and folder: `Northwind.Mvc`
    - Solution file and folder: `Chapter15`
    - **Authentication type: Individual Accounts** / `--auth Individual`
    - **Configure for HTTPS:** Selected
    - **Enable container support:** Selected
    - **Container OS:** Linux
    - **Container build type:** Dockerfile
    - **Do not use top-level statements:** Cleared

For VS Code, in the `Chapter15` solution folder, use `dotnet new mvc --auth Individual -o Northwind.Mvc` and `dotnet sln add Northwind.Mvc`.

For Rider, right-click the `Chapter15` solution, navigate to **Add** | **New Project...**, in the **New Project** dialog box, select **ASP.NET Core Web Application**, for **Type**, select **Web App (Model-View-Controller)**, and for **Auth**, select **Individual authentication**, and then click **Create**.

3. Navigate to **View** | **Output**.
4. In the **Output** window, for **Show output from:**, select **Container Tools**, and note that Visual Studio verifies that Docker Desktop is installed, and that appropriate images are downloaded, and creates a Docker image named `northwindmvc` for the `Northwind.Mvc` project with a tag of `dev`.

I have not shown the output in the book because it would take multiple pages and the details are not especially interesting. I recommend scanning through the output on your own computer just to become familiar with what it shows, which is it piecing together the image from the Dockerfile, and you can review the contents of that file in the previous section.

5. In the `Northwind.Mvc.csproj` project file, add a reference to the `EnvironmentLib` class library project, as shown in the following markup:

```
<ItemGroup>
  <ProjectReference Include="..\EnvironmentLib\EnvironmentLib.csproj" />
</ItemGroup>
```

6. Build the `Northwind.Mvc` project.
7. In the `Northwind.Mvc` project, in the `Controllers` folder, in `HomeController.cs`, in the `Index` method, add statements to get information about the environment and pass it to the view as its model, as shown highlighted in the following code:

```
public IActionResult Index()
{
  EnvironmentLib.EnvironmentInfo model = new();
  return View(model);
}
```

8. In the `Views\Home` folder, in `Index.cshtml`, replace the paragraph with the link to documentation with markup to render information about the environment, as shown highlighted in the following markup:

```
@model EnvironmentLib.EnvironmentInfo
@{
  ViewData["Title"] = "Home Page";
}
<div class="text-center">
  <h1 class="display-4">Welcome</h1>
  <table class="table table-bordered table-sm">
    <tr><th>Property</th><th>Value</th></tr>
    <tr><td>User</td><td>@Model.UserName</td></tr>
    <tr><td>Host</td><td>@Model.HostName</td></tr>
    <tr><td>OS</td><td>@Model.OS</td></tr>
    <tr><td>Architecture</td><td>@Model.Architecture</td></tr>
    <tr><td>Platform</td><td>@Model.DotNet</td></tr>
    <tr><td>Processors</td><td>@Model.Processors</td></tr>
    <tr><td>In a container</td><td>@Model.InContainer</td></tr>
  </table>
</div>
```

9. If you are using Visual Studio, navigate to **Debug** | **Start Debugging**, press *F5*, or click **Container (Dockerfile)** in the toolbar, and a browser starts and navigates to the home page of the `Northwind.Mvc` website, as shown in *Figure 15.11*:

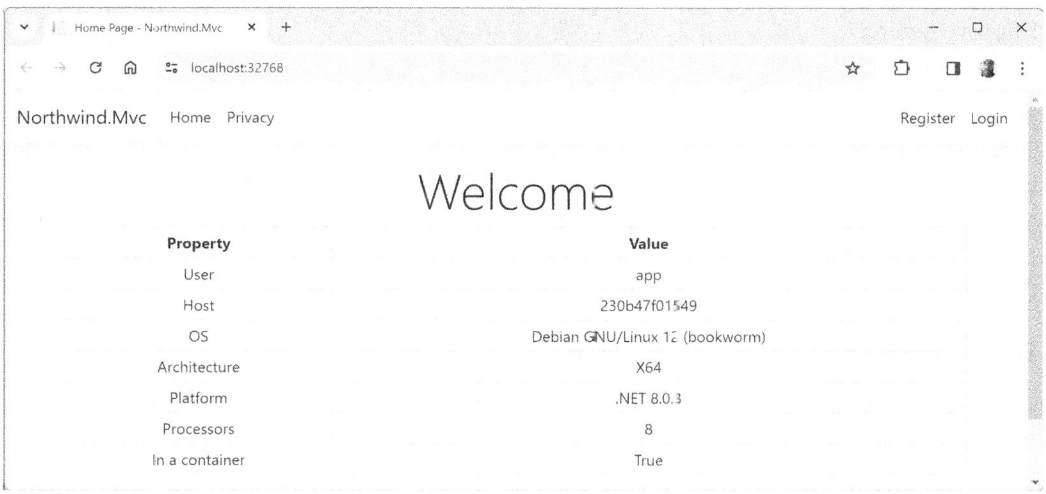

Figure 15.11: The Northwind.Mvc website hosted in Docker

10. If you are using Visual Studio, you can see the **Containers** window showing the `northwindmvc:dev` image running with its output in the **Logs** tab, as shown in *Figure 15.12*:

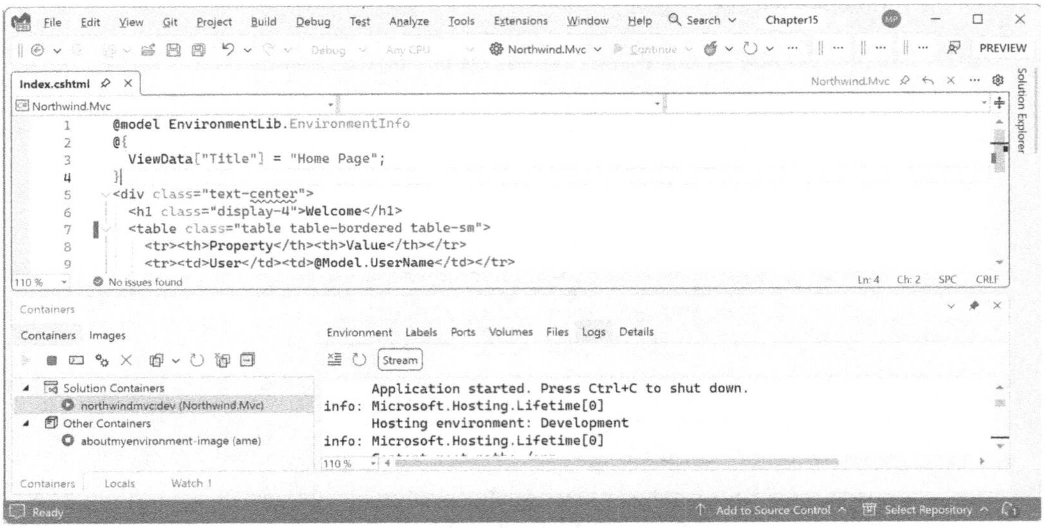

Figure 15.12: Containers window in Visual Studio

You can also publish without a Dockerfile, as shown in the following command:

```
dotnet publish $PROJECT_PATH --os linux --arch arm64 /t:PublishContainer
/p:ContainerImageTags=$CI_JOB_DATE -c Release
```

You've now seen a couple of practical examples of a console app project and an ASP.NET Core project being published to Docker containers and executed. Next, we will look at Testcontainers that help improve testing.

Working with Testcontainers

Testcontainers is a library that supports integration tests, using Docker containers to simulate external services and systems. Originally developed for Java, Testcontainers has seen adaptations in several programming languages, including .NET, thanks to its powerful concept and flexibility. Testcontainers for .NET is a managed implementation that leverages Docker to create lightweight, disposable instances of databases, browsers, or anything else that can run in a Docker container, directly from .NET test code.

How Testcontainers for .NET works

The core idea behind Testcontainers is to use Docker containers to provide external dependencies required by integration tests, such as:

- Databases, for example, SQL Server, PostgreSQL, MongoDB
- Caches, for example, Redis
- Messaging systems, for example, RabbitMQ

- Web browsers for Playwright and other web automation tests
- Any other service that can be containerized

This approach ensures that the integration tests run in an environment closely mirroring the production setup, leading to more reliable test outcomes.

Each test can run against a fresh instance of the required services, ensuring test isolation and avoiding side effects between tests. Developers can define containerized dependencies directly in their test code, making it easier to understand the test context and requirements.

Since the dependencies are containerized, the tests can be run in any environment where Docker is available, enhancing the portability of the test suite. Testcontainers supports a wide range of containerized services, making it versatile for various testing scenarios.

Usage example

Here's a simplified example of how you might use Testcontainers in a .NET test project to test against a SQL Server database.

First, you would add references to appropriate Testcontainers packages, as shown in the following markup:

```
<PackageReference Include="Testcontainers" />
<PackageReference Include="Testcontainers.MsSql" />
```

Second, you would write integration tests, as shown in the following code:

```
using Testcontainers.MsSql; // To use MsSqlContainer.

namespace NorthwindTests;

public class DatabaseIntegrationTests
{
  private MsSqlContainer _sqlContainer;

  private async Task SetUp()
  {
    _sqlContainer = new(new(
      database: "Northwind",
      username: "sa",
      password: "s3cret-n1nj@"
    ));

    await _sqlContainer.StartAsync();
  }
```

```
    [Fact]
    public async Task TestDatabaseConnection()
    {
      await SetUp();

      // Use _sqlContainer.ConnectionString to connect and interact with the SQL
Server
      await TearDown();
    }

    private async Task TearDown()
    {
      await _sqlContainer.StopAsync();
    }
  }
```

In this example, `MsSqlContainer` is a class from the Testcontainers library that manages an SQL Server container. Before each test, it starts a new SQL Server instance with a specified configuration. The tests can then use this database, ensuring they run against a known, isolated environment. After the tests, the container is stopped and removed, ensuring no state persists between test runs.

Testcontainers for .NET is an invaluable tool for developers looking to enhance their integration testing strategies with real-world dependencies without the overhead of managing those dependencies manually.

> You can learn more about Testcontainers at the following link: `https://dotnet.testcontainers.org/`.

Practicing and exploring

Test your knowledge and understanding by answering some questions, getting some hands-on practice, and exploring the topics covered in this chapter with deeper research.

Exercise 15.1 – Online-only material

You can read an e-book about containerization with .NET at the following link: `https://learn.microsoft.com/en-us/dotnet/architecture/microservices`.

Exercise 15.2 – Practice exercises

Explore the Docker Desktop user interface at the following link: `https://docs.docker.com/desktop/use-desktop/`.

Exercise 15.3 – Test your knowledge

Answer the following questions. If you get stuck, try googling the answers, if necessary, while remembering that if you get totally stuck, the answers are in *Appendix A*:

1. What makes containers lightweight compared to virtual machines?
2. How are Docker and Kubernetes related?
3. What is the relationship between a Docker registry, a Docker image, and a Docker container?
4. What is the difference between the `docker start` and `docker run` commands?
5. In a `Dockerfile`, how do you specify the base image?

> *Appendix A, Answers to the Test Your Knowledge Questions,* is available to download from the following link: `https://github.com/markjprice/tools-skills-net10/blob/main/docs/B31468_Appendix%20A.pdf`.

Exercise 15.4 – Explore topics

Use the links on the following page to learn more details about the topics covered in this chapter: `https://github.com/markjprice/tools-skills-net10/blob/main/docs/book-links.md#chapter-15---containerization-using-docker`.

Summary

In this chapter, you learned:

- About the concepts around containerization
- About the concepts, tools, and technologies for Docker
- How to manage containers with Docker
- How to containerize console apps and ASP.NET Core projects
- How to work with Testcontainers

In the next chapter, you will learn about Aspire, which uses similar techniques as Testcontainers but takes the concept much further.

16

Cloud-Native Development Using Aspire

This chapter is about cloud-native development using Aspire, a feature introduced with .NET 8 that improves the local development experience when building distributed cloud-native solutions.

The general availability of Aspire was announced at Microsoft Build on May 21, 2024. Overall, developers are still excited about Aspire's capabilities and its potential impact on cloud-native development. For example, Pramesh KC, an ordinary .NET developer like you, described Aspire as a game-changer in the .NET 8 lineup. He emphasized that it has quickly become his favorite feature. You can read more in his article at the following link: `https://dev.to/prameshkc/discovering-the-gem-in-net-8-introducing-net-aspire-1mlo`.

Another developer, Creyke, posted to the Aspire channel on Microsoft's DotNetEvolution Discord server, as shown in the following quote:

> *"late to the party, but i've been using aspire for two nights and i just wanted to say it's really, really impressive. the abstractions are tight, writing custom extensions has been a delight, and everything has worked first time so far. great defaults too! if this is marketed right, has the right tooling, and community buy in, it's going to be huge compliments to all chefs."*

> Aspire 13 is polyglot (meaning it supports multiple languages) so Aspire orchestrates apps in C#, Java, Python, JavaScript, TypeScript, Go, and more. It is more than just a .NET feature now so the branding drops ".NET" from the old name, ".NET Aspire". During the transition you are likely to see the old name, .NET Aspire. The new official website for Aspire can be found at the following link: `https://aspire.dev/`.
>
> If you used previous versions of Aspire, you should note that Aspire components have been renamed to Aspire integrations. You can learn more about this change at the following link: `https://devblogs.microsoft.com/dotnet/announcing-dotnet-aspire-8-2/`.

This chapter covers the following topics:

- Introducing Aspire
- Exploring the Aspire starter template
- Diving deeper into Aspire
- Aspire for new and existing solutions

Introducing Aspire

What is Aspire? From the announcement blog post at: `https://devblogs.microsoft.com/dotnet/introducing-dotnet-aspire-simplifying-cloud-native-development-with-dotnet-8/`, "*.NET Aspire is an opinionated stack for building resilient, observable, and configurable cloud-native applications with .NET.*"

It is worth noting each carefully chosen phrase in that description:

- **Opinionated stack:** One of the trickier aspects of building modern distributed solutions is there is too much choice. For each feature of your solution, there are multiple integrations that you could pick from. For each of those integrations, there are multiple ways to configure them based on your needs. Aspire has an opinion about which integrations you should use and how you should configure them, which is explained in the *Aspire integrations* section later in the chapter. If you concur with those opinions, then Aspire is especially great, and if not, you can always override the default configuration.
- **Resilient:** Aspire is designed to be resilient by implementing best practices for cloud solutions, like implementing caching, queuing, and implementing fault tolerance using Polly.

> Using Polly to add fault tolerance to your apps and services is covered in my book, *Apps and Services with .NET 10*, and you can read Polly's documentation at the following link: `https://www.pollydocs.org/`. But if you use Aspire, Polly is one of Aspire's integrations that is included and configured for you by default.

- **Observable:** Aspire enables tracing, logging, and metrics using the most popular telemetry framework for .NET and other platforms, OpenTelemetry. Aspire also includes a dashboard to monitor all activity across the many complex tiers of your solution.
- **Configurable:** Aspire has sensible defaults for configuring all its integrations but is open to be configured however you want. Of course, you can override the defaults, but if your needs are genuinely different, then you won't get as much out of Aspire as other developers who are happy to go along with the recommended integrations with the most popular configuration that works best for most distributed solutions.
- **Cloud-native:** Aspire projects assume they will be eventually deployed to the cloud in containers. For local testing, Aspire projects have a dependency on Docker Desktop or Podman. You learned about Docker in *Chapter 15, Containerization Using Docker*. You can learn about Podman at the following link: `https://podman.io/`.

Aspire includes service discovery, telemetry, resilience, and health checks by default. Aspire simplifies the local developer experience and makes it easy to discover, acquire, and configure essential dependencies.

Aspire previews were first made available with the launch of .NET 8 in November 2023. Aspire version "1.0" was released at the Microsoft Build conference on May 21, 2024, but it was versioned as 8.0 because Aspire was part of .NET 8.

Aspire 13 shipped alongside .NET 10 in November 2025, but it is no longer part of .NET. This is why the branding drops the ".NET" prefix and the version number jumped to 13, making a more obvious break with .NET 10. With Aspire 13, the orchestration projects must still be written using C# and target .NET, while the functional projects can be non-.NET languages like Python and JavaScript (Node.js). In future versions of Aspire, even the orchestration projects will be able to be written in non-.NET languages.

Some of the new features of Aspire 13 include the following:

- First-class support for Python and JavaScript as well as .NET. The new `AddJavaScriptApp` method replaces the older `AddNpmApp`.
- The Aspire CLI `aspire do` command introduces a customizable pipeline for build, publish, and deploy tasks.
- Aspire's **Model Context Protocol (MCP)** server enables AI chat integration to the Dashboard, allowing you to use natural language to analyze logs and telemetry to determine and solve problems.
- Aspire's Dashboard continues to be refined.
- .NET 10's file-based apps feature can be used to simplify your AppHost projects.

What does the Aspire team say?

To better understand the purpose of Aspire, it's useful to hear some quotes directly from the Aspire team that were made during a recorded standup, available to watch at the following link: `https://www.youtube.com/watch?v=0sf7_ZxRlvw`.

> *"Aspire projects allow you to model and simulate infrastructure for your application or a subset of your application for local development. The orchestrator runs executables and containers and makes networking seamless between them." David Fowler*
>
> *"When do we think Aspire starts adding value? As soon as you have more than one node in the logical map that is your application. So, if you have a web app that talks to a database. Or a web app that talks to an API service. Or a web app that talks to anything else. As soon as you have more than one project that you deploy... then Aspire is useful." Damien Edwards*
>
> *"As a developer observing and using Aspire, I'm finding that just for the very simplest case of an app talking to an API or even just having a database... having that dashboard and immediately having the launch URLs for everything, and instead of popping around different terminal windows and seeing what didn't start, it's transformed the dev experience for me." Jon Galloway*

What stands out for me personally is that all .NET developers will benefit from using Aspire as soon as they work on a solution with more than one project, database, or service like Redis. Microsoft has historically performed well in the enterprise market because it understands the needs of corporate developers and produces tools that genuinely support that workflow.

Now let's review support for Aspire in your developer toolset.

Code editor and CLI support for Aspire

Support for Aspire is built into Visual Studio version 17.10 and later. Everything else, including VS Code, can use the CLI tools, and over time I expect support to be improved.

> You can learn more about Aspire support in VS Code at the following links: `https://marketplace.visualstudio.com/items?itemName=microsoft-aspire.aspire-vscode` and `https://devblogs.microsoft.com/dotnet/may-release-of-csharp-dev-kit/`.

To use Aspire 13, you must have the following prerequisites:

1. .NET SDK 10 or later.
2. An OCI compliant container runtime, like Docker Desktop or Podman.

> Although you must have .NET 10 SDK installed to use Aspire 13, the functional projects in an Aspire solution like your web services and websites can target earlier versions like .NET 8 and .NET 9 as well as .NET 10 or later.

To install the Aspire for .NET project templates for use with the `dotnet` CLI and common code editors like Visual Studio, enter the following command:

```
dotnet new install Aspire.ProjectTemplates
```

To install the Aspire CLI that streamlines your development workflow with an interactive-first experience, enter the following PowerShell command:

```
irm https://aspire.dev/install.ps1 | iex
```

> **Warning!** You must use PowerShell, not the normal Windows command prompt or Terminal.

Alternatively, for other operating systems, you can use the following Bash command:

```
curl -sSL https://aspire.dev/install.sh | bash
```

You can read more details about how to install the Aspire CLI at the following link: `https://aspire.dev/get-started/install-cli/`.

Warning! The Aspire CLI requires the .NET 10 SDK to be installed on your machine. However, Aspire can orchestrate applications targeting .NET 8 or later.

You can learn about the Rider plugin for Aspire at the following link:

`https://blog.jetbrains.com/dotnet/2024/02/19/jetbrains-rider-and-the-net-aspire-plugin/`.

Using the Aspire CLI to create a starter project

The Aspire CLI is interactive by default. It will become more important as Aspire becomes more polyglot. Let's try creating a complete starter project:

1. Create a new folder named `AspireTemp`, for example, `C:\AspireTemp`.
2. At the command prompt or terminal, in the `AspireTemp` folder, use the Aspire CLI to interactively create a new project, as shown in the following command:

```
aspire new
```

3. Select **Blazor & Minimal API starter**, as shown in the following output:

```
Select a template:

> Blazor & Minimal API starter
  React (Vite) & FastAPI starter
  Empty AppHost
```

4. For the project name, enter `Aspire4Net`.
5. For the output path, press *Enter* to accept the default.
6. For the template version, press *Enter* to accept the default.
7. For **Use *.dev.localhost URLs**, select **No**.
8. For **Use Redis Cache**, select **Yes**.
9. For a test project, select **Yes**, and then select **xUnit.net v2**.

10. Wait for the projects to be created, as shown in the following output:

```
Enter the project name (aspiretemp): Aspire4Net
Enter the output path: (./Aspire4Net): ./Aspire4Net
✓  Using Redis Cache for caching.
✓  Using xUnit.net for testing.
📦  Using project templates version: 13.0.0
✓  Project created successfully in C:\aspiretemp\Aspire4Net.
```

11. If Docker is not running, start Docker Desktop, which will start the Docker service.
12. Run the Aspire solution, as shown in the following command:

```
aspire run
```

13. Wait for the projects to start, as shown in the following output:

```
🔍  Finding apphosts...
Aspire4Net\Aspire4Net.AppHost\Aspire4Net.AppHost.csproj

📄  Created settings file at '.aspire/settings.json'.

      AppHost:  Aspire4Net\Aspire4Net.AppHost\Aspire4Net.AppHost.csproj

    Dashboard:  https://localhost:17089/
login?t=4091a9b841b209f29e5b5abc639d4083

         Logs:  C:\Users\markj\.aspire\cli\logs\
apphost-17948-2025-11-25-10-00-16.log

Press CTRL+C to stop the apphost and exit.
```

14. Use your browser to navigate to the Dashboard link and note the Aspire dashboard with a Minimal API web service named `apiservice`, a Blazor website named `webfrontend`, and a Redis cache named `cache`.
15. In the **webfrontend** row of the resources table, click its URL, and note that the Blazor web app opens and you can click the **Weather** menu to call the web service.
16. Close the browser.
17. At the command prompt or terminal, press *Ctrl* + *C* to stop the apphost.

Now let's review in more detail how to work with Aspire solutions.

Starting an Aspire solution

To start an Aspire solution, you have three experiences to choose from, depending on your code editor:

- Press *F5* in Visual Studio or VS Code or Rider, which attaches the debugger to all projects. If you want to make a code change while running, you can use Hot Reload.

- Press *Ctrl* + *F5* in Visual Studio or VS Code or Rider, which runs the solution without debugging. You can make changes to individual projects and Visual Studio will automatically restart them.
- At the command prompt or terminal, enter `dotnet watch`. This has basic support for watching projects and restarting them when code files change. The Aspire team is working on improved Hot Reload support.

Aspire project types

To work, Aspire solutions need two special projects:

- **AppHost:** This is a console app that starts all the other projects and ensures the correct configuration for all resources and endpoints.
- **ServiceDefaults:** This is a class library that centralizes the configuration of all the Aspire resources, including integrations like databases and .NET projects.

The `AppHost` project will run any .NET projects, containers, or executables needed as part of your cloud-native distributed application. If you are using Visual Studio, then debugging will attach to all the running projects, allowing you to step into and across each service.

The `ServiceDefaults` project contains common service and integration logic that applies to each of the projects in the app. This is where integrations like service discovery, telemetry, and health checks are configured. It is a centralized convention where you would go to customize the configuration to be developer-friendly.

All Aspire solutions will have these two special projects, as well as any other projects that make up your complete distributed solution, as shown in *Figure 16.1*:

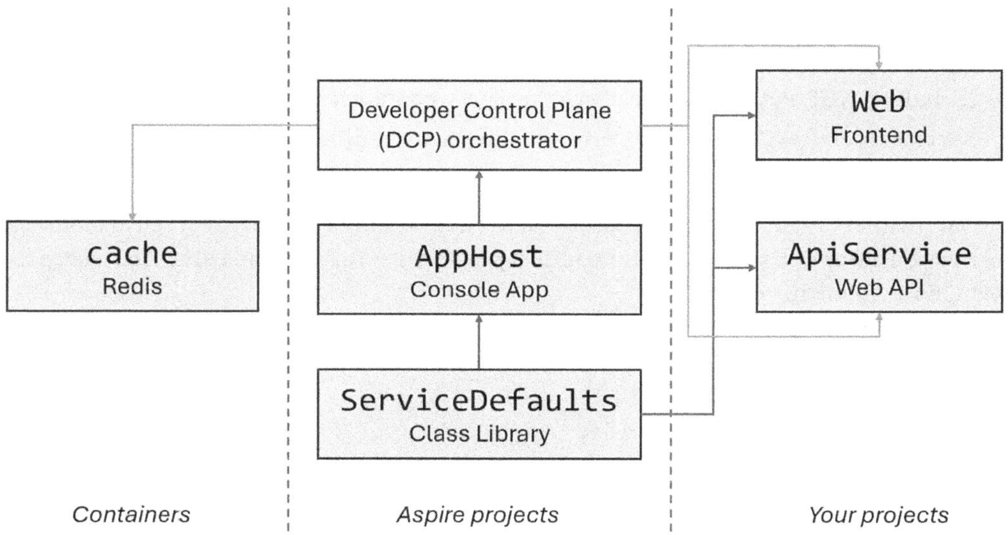

Figure 16.1: DCP, Aspire projects, your projects, and containers in an Aspire application model

The **Developer Control Plane** (**DCP**) is a closed source orchestrator used by Aspire. The team doesn't like to talk about it much because it is closed source and therefore not open to developers to customize. Everything else about Aspire is designed to be open and extendable.

The `AppHost` project reads configuration from the `ServiceDefaults` project and uses the DCP to orchestrate the startup of any containers and your projects. Your projects should read the configuration from the `ServiceDefaults` project too.

Aspire resource types

In Aspire, the built-in resource types are:

- **Project**: A project. For example, an ASP.NET Core web service, or Python or JavaScript (Node.js) website
- **Container**: A container image. For example, a Docker image of Redis or RabbitMQ
- **Executable**: An executable file

For container resources, you can either have Aspire launch a container during development or connect to an existing resource via connection strings.

Aspire application model and orchestration

Aspire orchestration is designed to simplify and control the connections and configurations between all the integrations of a cloud-native solution.

Aspire orchestration assists with the following tasks:

- **Solution composition**: The `AppHost` project defines resources that make up the application, including .NET, Python, and JavaScript projects, containers, executables, and cloud resources
- **Service discovery**: The `AppHost` project maps how the different resources communicate with each other

In a similar manner to ASP.NET Core projects that use a class named `WebApplication` to build configuration for the website or web service, Aspire AppHost projects use a class named `DistributedApplication`, as shown in the following code:

```
var builder = DistributedApplication.CreateBuilder(args);
```

This builder object can then call methods to map the resources in a distributed Aspire application model, as shown in *Table 16.1*:

Method	Description
`AddContainer`	Adds a container resource to the Aspire application model. If you add a package reference to an Aspire package like `Aspire.Hosting.Redis`, then you can use extension methods like `AddRedis` that will add a container specifically for Redis.
`AddExecutable`	Adds an executable resource to the Aspire application model.
`AddProject`	Adds a project resource to the Aspire application model. This dynamically scans the referenced project for configuration in `launchSettings.json` like URLs.
`AddResource`	Adds a generic resource to the Aspire application model.

Table 16.1: Methods to map the resources in a distributed Aspire application model

For example, to add a Redis container, you call the `AddRedis` method, as shown in the following code:

```
var cache = builder.AddRedis("cache");
```

To add an ASP.NET Core Web API service project, you would call the `AddProject` method, as shown in the following code:

```
var apiService = builder.AddProject
  <Projects.AspireStarter_ApiService>("apiservice");
```

Good practice: When you add an Aspire resource, you give it a short name like `cache` or `apiservice`. These are then used throughout your other projects to dynamically refer to that resource's endpoints and so on. For example, `http://apiservice`. Note that this is not a true URL. The actual URL and port numbers will be replaced dynamically during Aspire service discovery.

As well as methods for building the Aspire application model, there are methods to add settings, as shown in *Table 16.2*:

Method	Description
`AddConnectionString`	If you've already provisioned resources outside of the app host and want to use them.
`AddParameter`	Parameter values are read from the `Parameters` section of the app host's configuration and are used to provide values to the app while running locally. When deploying the app, the value will be asked for the parameter value. You can learn more about external parameters at the following link: `https://learn.microsoft.com/en-us/dotnet/aspire/fundamentals/external-parameters`.

Table 16.2: Methods to add settings for Aspire integrations

To connect the resources in an Aspire application model using service discovery, you call one of the `With` methods, as shown in *Table 16.3*:

Method	Description
`WithReference`	Links resources so they can use the correct configuration to communicate with each other by passing service discovery information for the referenced projects.
`WithExternalHttpEndpoints`	Configures a web project to have external HTTP endpoints that can be automatically configured for any related Aspire integrations and projects.
`WithHttpEndpoint`, `WithHttpsEndpoint`	Uses code to configure named endpoints.
`WithArgs`	Adds a callback to be executed with a list of command-line arguments when a container resource is started.
`WithEnvironment`	Adds an environment variable to the resource.

Table 16.3: Methods to connect and configure Aspire integrations

For example, to add a web frontend project that will call the web service and Redis container, you call the `AddProject` method and then connect to its dependencies by calling the `WithReference` method, as shown in the following code:

```
builder.AddProject<Projects.AspireStarter_Web>("webfrontend")
    .WithExternalHttpEndpoints()
    .WithReference(cache)
    .WithReference(apiService);
```

Any distributed solution needs the ability to call remote services. While building Aspire, the team created a new service discovery library named `Microsoft.Extensions.ServiceDiscovery`. This provides the core abstraction and several implementations of client-side service discovery and load balancing. It enables integration with `HttpClientFactory` and **Yet Another Reverse Proxy (YARP)** (`https://microsoft.github.io/reverse-proxy/`) for local development, as well as Kubernetes in deployed environments.

> You can learn more about service discovery at the following link:
>
> `https://learn.microsoft.com/en-us/dotnet/aspire/service-discovery/overview`

Aspire project templates

Aspire for .NET CLI has ten project templates to choose from:

- **Aspire Starter Application** / `aspire-starter`: A solution with four or five projects and an optional Redis container, depending on the options selected. This is used to learn about Aspire.

- **Aspire Python Starter Application** / `aspire-py-starter`: A solution with four or five projects and an optional Redis container, depending on the options selected. This is used to learn about Aspire.
- **Aspire Empty App** / `aspire`: A solution with the two required projects, `AppHost` and `ServiceDefaults`. This is used for new greenfield projects that will use Aspire.
- **Aspire App Host** / `aspire-apphost`: A project with minimum setup for an app host. This is used to add Aspire to an existing solution when you do not use Visual Studio's tooling.
- **Aspire Single-File App Host** / `aspire-apphost-singlefile`: A project with minimum setup for an app host including using the .NET 10 file-based app without a project file.
- **Aspire Service Defaults** / `aspire-servicedefaults`: A project with minimum setup for service defaults. This is used to add Aspire to an existing solution when you do not use Visual Studio's tooling.
- **.NET MAUI for Aspire Service Defaults** / `maui-aspire-servicedefaults`: A project with minimum setup for service defaults. This is used to add Aspire to an existing .NET MAUI solution.
- **Aspire Test Project (xUnit)** / `aspire-xunit`: A project to add integration tests using xUnit to an Aspire solution.
- **Aspire Test Project (NUnit)** / `aspire-nunit`: A project to add integration tests using NUnit to an Aspire solution.
- **Aspire Test Project (MSTest)** / `aspire-mstest`: A project to add integration tests using MS Test to an Aspire solution.

You can list the project templates at the command prompt or terminal, as shown in the following command:

```
dotnet new list aspire
```

As well as the project templates, Visual Studio has tooling support to add Aspire orchestration and the two required projects to an existing solution. You will see this later in this chapter.

Now let's use the starter project template to review some key concepts and implementation details of Aspire.

Exploring the Aspire starter template

The **Aspire Starter Application** project template is designed to get you started with a working Aspire solution that you can try out. It's a great way to initially understand how all the Aspire parts fit together.

The project template solution is made up of four or five projects and an optional Redis cache, as described in the following list:

- A **Blazor Web Application** project named `<Solution_Name>.Web` as the frontend user interface
- An **ASP.NET Core Web API** (using Minimal APIs) project named `<Solution_Name>.ApiService` as a backend weather information service
- A **Aspire App Host** project named `<Solution_Name>.AppHost`
- A **Aspire Service Defaults** project named `<Solution_Name>.ServiceDefaults`

- An optional **xUnit Test** project named <Solution_Name>.Tests
- An optional container for Redis hosted in Docker (by default) or hosted in Podman

Now that you understand the basics of what to expect from the Aspire starter project template, let's see it in action.

Creating the Aspire starter application

Let's create an Aspire starter application using the project template:

1. Use your preferred code editor to add a new **Aspire Starter Application** / `aspire-starter` project with a solution named `AspireStarter` in a new folder in a `Chapter16` folder, as shown in *Figure 16.2*:

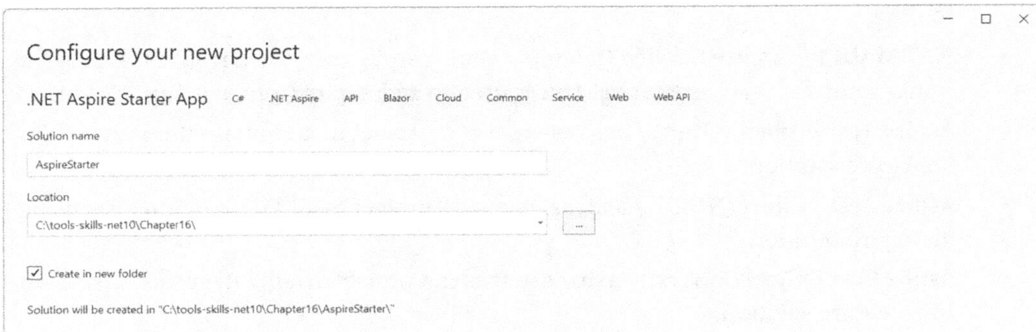

Figure 16.2: Configure your new project for the Aspire starter template

> **Warning!** This project template does not allow you to specify a project name because it creates multiple projects for you. Instead, you specify a solution name that is then used as a prefix for the names of all its projects. In this chapter, you will use the folder named `Chapter16` to contain multiple solutions, each of which contains multiple projects.

2. Click **Next**.
3. On the **Additional information** step, choose the following options:
   - **Framework: .NET 10 (Long Term Support)**
   - **Configure for HTTPS**: Selected
   - **Aspire version: 13.0**
   - **Use Redis for caching**: Selected (this will create the optional container for Redis)
   - **Create a test project**: xUnit.net (this will create the optional project for integration tests)
   - **xUnit.net version: v2**
   - **Use the .dev.localhost TLD in the application URL**: Cleared
4. In **Solution Explorer**, note the five projects and that the `AspireStarter.AppHost` project is set as the startup project (it's in bold), and note that you will see errors because we are using CPM, as shown in *Figure 16.3*:

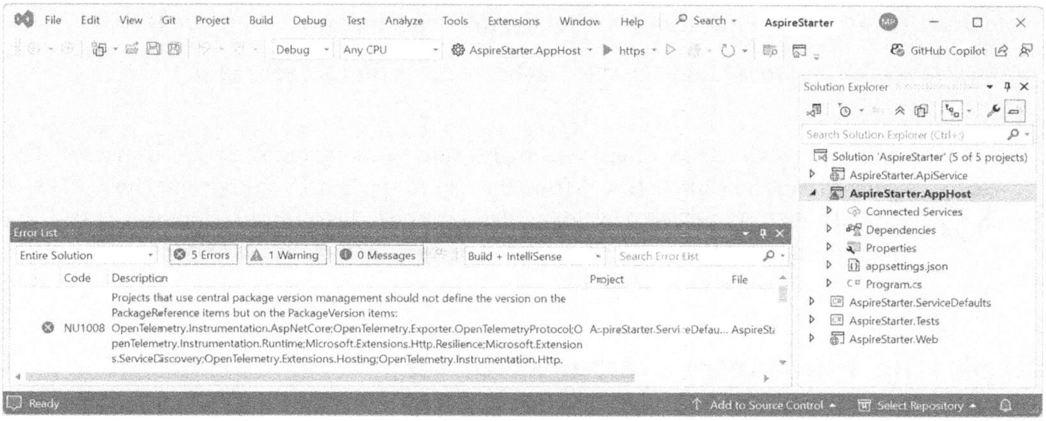

Figure 16.3: Aspire starter application solution with five projects

5. In each project file, for each package reference, remove the version attribute. For example, in `AspireStarter.AppHost.csproj`, remove the `Version="13.0.0"` from the Redis package reference, as shown in the following markup:

```
<ItemGroup>
  <PackageReference Include="Aspire.Hosting.Redis" />
</ItemGroup>
```

6. Start **Docker Desktop**. This will also start the Docker daemon.
7. Start the `AspireStarter.AppHost` project with the debugger attached by navigating to **Debug** | **Start Debugging**, or clicking the **https** button, or pressing *F5*.
8. Note the successful launch of the app host console app and the Aspire dashboard on a random port, in my case `17143`, as shown in the following output:

```
info: Aspire.Hosting.DistributedApplication[0]
      Aspire version: 13.0.0+7512c2944094a58904b6c803aa824c4a4ce42e11
info: Aspire.Hosting.DistributedApplication[0]
      Distributed application starting.
info: Aspire.Hosting.DistributedApplication[0]
      Application host directory is: C:\tools-skills-net10\Chapter16\
AspireStarter\AspireStarter.AppHost
info: Aspire.Hosting.DistributedApplication[0]
      Now listening on: https://localhost:17143
info: Aspire.Hosting.DistributedApplication[0]
      Login to the dashboard at https://localhost:17143/
login?t=88c817f3679614a06778de42009aa624
info: Aspire.Hosting.DistributedApplication[0]
      Distributed application started. Press Ctrl+C to shut down.
```

Note the URL to "Login to the dashboard" at the following link (with a unique GUID):

`https://localhost:17056/login?t=486c304bd3c61961cfdef9d58eb8d8e7.`

> There are scenarios where you might want to allow an unsecured transport. The dashboard can run without `HTTPS` from the Aspire app host by configuring the `ASPIRE_ALLOW_UNSECURED_TRANSPORT` setting to `true`. You can learn more about this at the following link: `https://learn.microsoft.com/en-us/dotnet/aspire/troubleshooting/allow-unsecure-transport`.

Exploring the Aspire starter solution

Now that we've seen how to successfully create and start the Aspire starter solution, let's explore it:

1. Note that the dashboard in the browser shows that a Redis container named `cache` is running, as well as two projects, the Web API service named `apiservice` and the Blazor client named `webfrontend`, as shown in *Figure 16.4*:

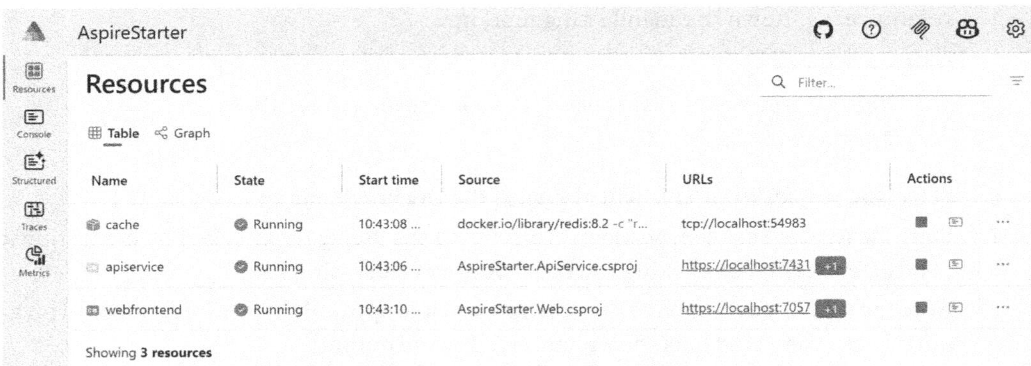

Figure 16.4: The Aspire dashboard shows one container and two projects

2. In the **apiservice** row, in the **URLs** column, click the **+1** button to show the second endpoint with its port number, then click the `https` link to call the web service, and note the message saying the API service is running.
3. Append `weatherforecast` to the end of the address bar, and note the weather forecast that results, as shown in *Figure 16.5*:

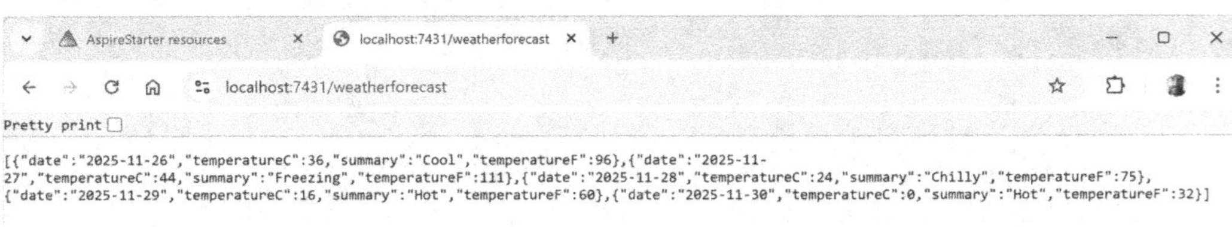

Figure 16.5: Fake weather forecast from the web service

4. In the Aspire dashboard, in the **webfrontend** row, in the **URLs** column, click the `https` link to open the Blazor client, then navigate to the **Weather** page, and note the table of weather forecasts, as shown in *Figure 16.6*:

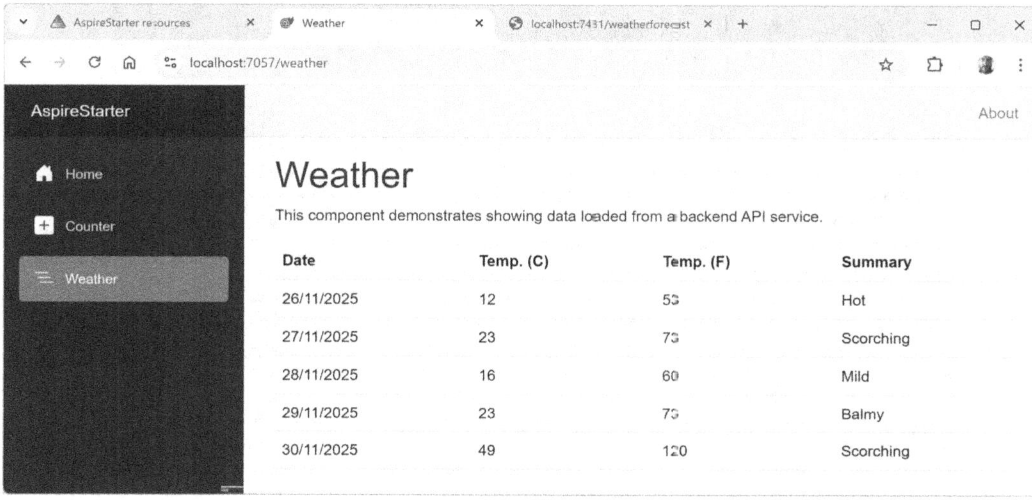

Figure 16.6: Blazor web frontend

5. In the Aspire dashboard, navigate to **Console**, and select each of the three resources in turn to view their console output, as shown in *Figure 16.7*:

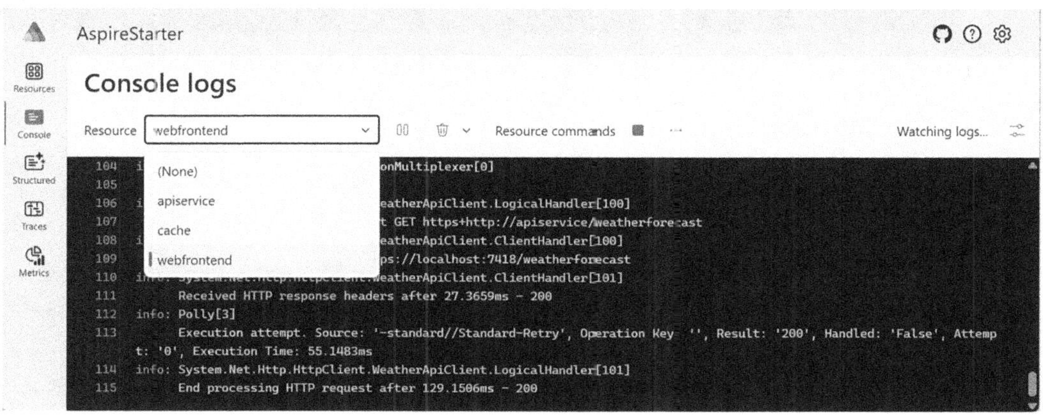

Figure 16.7: Console logs in the Aspire dashboard

You can also click on the **View** links in the **Logs** column for each resource row to directly view its logs.

6. Note that the console logs for `webfrontend` show that it successfully connected to the Redis container and made a successful request to the web service using Polly for retries, as shown in the following partial output:

```
info: StackExchange.Redis.ConnectionMultiplexer[0]
      Connecting (sync) on .NET 10.0.0 (StackExchange.Redis:
v2.8.31.52602)
...
info: StackExchange.Redis.ConnectionMultiplexer[0]
      localhost:58709/Interactive: Connected
...
2024-04-info: System.Net.Http.HttpClient.WeatherApiClient.
ClientHandler[100]
      Sending HTTP request GET https://localhost:7403/weatherforecast
2024-04-info: System.Net.Http.HttpClient.WeatherApiClient.
ClientHandler[101]
      Received HTTP response headers after 18.2274ms - 200
info: Polly[3]
      Execution attempt. Source: '-standard//Standard-Retry', Operation
Key: '', Result: '200', Handled: 'False', Attempt: '0', Execution Time:
'68.7295'
info: System.Net.Http.HttpClient.WeatherApiClient.LogicalHandler[101]
      End processing HTTP request after 178.3335ms - 200
```

7. Navigate to **Structured** to show the structured logs, as shown in *Figure 16.8*:

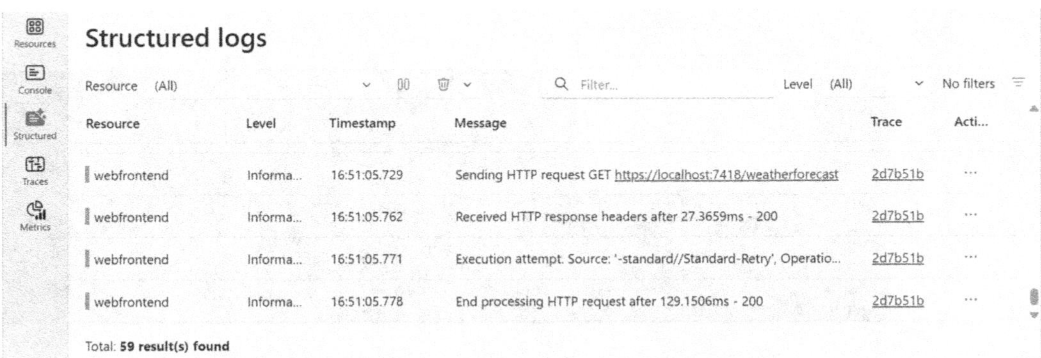

Figure 16.8: Structured logs in the Aspire dashboard

8. In the **Trace** column, click the GUID value, and note that the `/weather` route in the Blazor app triggered a request to the Redis cache, then to the web service because it hadn't been cached yet, and again to the Redis cache to store the data for the next request, as shown in *Figure 16.9*:

Figure 16.9: Details of a trace including calls between Aspire project resources

9. Navigate to **Metrics** and note you can select and see graphs and tables for data like `process.runtime.dotnet.thread_pool.threads.count` and `http.server.request.duration`.
10. Close the browser, and at the command prompt or terminal for the Aspire app host, press *Ctrl* + *C* to shut down the distributed application.

Now let's review in more detail what you've just seen.

Diving deeper into Aspire

There are a lot of parts to Aspire. Let's dive in and see what role all the parts of Aspire play.

Developer dashboard for monitoring

As you have seen, starting an Aspire project brings you to the developer dashboard. This is an essential tool for debugging distributed applications because it gives you a unified view of your services alongside their logs, metrics, and traces.

You can use it to see logs and traces across all projects, for example, a distributed trace showing a request to the weather page. Traces are very helpful in diagnosing problems in distributed applications.

The developer dashboard uses all the same open standards you would use in production when you configure your production telemetry systems like Grafana and Prometheus.

The Aspire developer dashboard is visible while the `AppHost` project is running and will launch automatically when you start the project. The left navigation provides links to the different parts of the dashboard, as described in the following list:

- **Resources**: This is the home page of the dashboard, and it lists all the projects, containers, executables, and other resources in your Aspire solution. It shows the state of each resource and gives you links directly to parts of the solution like web services and web user interfaces. It also highlights errors when they are logged so that you can easily jump to more details to zero in on problems.

- **Console:** This provides access to the logs of all the parts of your Aspire solution that write to the console or standard output using plain text.
- **Structured:** This provides a filterable view of your logs. The structured logs maintain the properties of your log messages so that they can be filtered and searched on, compared to the console log, which merges all properties into a single string message.
- **Traces:** This shows the path of a single action through all the layers of your solution as a distributed trace. This helps you to find the root cause of errors and performance bottlenecks, and diagnose other behaviors.
- **Metrics:** This shows all the metrics for your application.

> You can learn more about the Aspire dashboard at the following link: `https://learn.microsoft.com/en-us/dotnet/aspire/fundamentals/dashboard/overview`.
>
> Information about how you can run the dashboard standalone without an Aspire solution is found at the following link: `https://learn.microsoft.com/en-us/dotnet/aspire/fundamentals/dashboard/standalone`.

AppHost project for orchestrating resources

The `AppHost` project lets you express the needs of your solution, and it orchestrates the running of your app on your local developer computer.

Aspire provides abstractions that allow you to orchestrate service discovery, environment variables, and container configurations without having to manage the details manually (unless you want to).

Let's see how it works in the starter template:

1. In the `AspireStarter.AppHost.csproj` project file, note that the project is a console app (`Exe`) that targets the Aspire AppHost SDK, references the two functional projects, and references the `Aspire.Hosting.Redis` package, as shown highlighted in the following markup:

```
<Project Sdk="Aspire.AppHost.Sdk/13.0.0">

  <PropertyGroup>
    <OutputType>Exe</OutputType>
    <TargetFramework>net10.0</TargetFramework>
    <ImplicitUsings>enable</ImplicitUsings>
    <Nullable>enable</Nullable>
    <UserSecretsId>1d713f01-3bf2-4a15-9910-799f70fe499f</UserSecretsId>
  </PropertyGroup>

  <ItemGroup>
    <ProjectReference Include=
      "..\AspireStarter.ApiService\AspireStarter.ApiService.csproj" />
    <ProjectReference Include=
```

```
      "..\AspireStarter.Web\AspireStarter.Web.csproj" />
  </ItemGroup>

  <ItemGroup>
    <PackageReference Include="Aspire.Hosting.Redis" />
  </ItemGroup>

</Project>
```

A `<ProjectReference>` in an Aspire host project is not like a traditional project reference to a class library. Instead of building the referenced project and copying the `.dll` to the local project `bin` folder where it will be found at runtime, a `<ProjectReference>` in an Aspire host project tells the tooling to manage connections via endpoints including ports and paths by processing any `launchSettings.json` files. We will explore this in more detail later in the chapter.

2. In the `Properties` folder, in the `launchSettings.json` file, note that it includes URLs to access the dashboard named `applicationUrl`, as well as the URL for the endpoint that hosts an **Open Telemetry Protocol (OTLP)** service and receives telemetry, the URL for an MCP endpoint for AI integrations, and the URL for the gRPC endpoint to which the dashboard connects for its data, as shown highlighted in the following markup:

```
{
  "$schema": "https://json.schemastore.org/launchsettings.json",
  "profiles": {
    "https": {
      "commandName": "Project",
      "dotnetRunMessages": true,
      "launchBrowser": true,
      "applicationUrl": "https://localhost:17020;http://localhost:15099",
      "environmentVariables": {
        "ASPNETCORE_ENVIRONMENT": "Development",
        "DOTNET_ENVIRONMENT": "Development",
        "DOTNET_DASHBOARD_OTLP_ENDPOINT_URL": "https://localhost:21184",
        "DOTNET_DASHBOARD_MCP_ENDPOINT_URL": "https://localhost:23143",
        "DOTNET_RESOURCE_SERVICE_ENDPOINT_URL": "https://localhost:22057"
      }
    },
```

3. In `AppHost.cs` (equivalent to `Program.cs` in a normal console app), note that we orchestrate the container for Redis and the two web projects, including calling the `WaitFor` method introduced in Aspire 9 to make sure the Redis cache and the web service are running before showing them as ready in the Aspire dashboard, as shown in the following code:

```
var builder = DistributedApplication.CreateBuilder(args);

var cache = builder.AddRedis("cache");

var apiService = builder.AddProject<Projects
  .AspireStarter_ApiService>("apiservice")
  .WithHttpHealthCheck("/health");

builder.AddProject<Projects.AspireStarter_Web>("webfrontend")
  .WithExternalHttpEndpoints()
  .WithHttpHealthCheck("/health")
  .WithReference(cache)
  .WaitFor(cache)
  .WithReference(apiService)
  .WaitFor(apiService);

builder.Build().Run();
```

4. Click in the `AspireStarter_ApiService` type and press *F12* or right-click and select **Go To Definition**, and note the `ProjectPath` property, as shown in the following code:

```
// <auto-generated/>

namespace Projects;

[global::System.CodeDom.Compiler.GeneratedCode("Aspire.Hosting", null)]
[global::System.Diagnostics.CodeAnalysis.ExcludeFromCodeCoverage(
  Justification = "Generated code.")]
[global::System.Diagnostics.DebuggerDisplay(
  "Type = {GetType().Name,nq}, ProjectPath = {ProjectPath}")]
public class AspireStarter_ApiService : global::Aspire.Hosting.
IProjectMetadata
{
  public string ProjectPath => """C:\tools-skills-net10\Chapter16\
AspireStarter\AspireStarter.ApiService\AspireStarter.ApiService.
csproj""";
```

This autogenerated code is created when you add a project reference to an Aspire host project. In effect, all it does is store the path to the other project so that the tooling can read information about the project and find related files like its `launchSettings.json` file to know how to connect endpoints using service discovery.

When you add a project to an `AppHost` project, it is *not* the same as adding a usual .NET-to-.NET project reference! The SDK works magic to fake it and autogenerate code. You can add a reference to a .NET Framework project, and that project will get added to the dashboard, but it won't get any special integrations, and so on.

> Aspire resources are not .NET specific. They could be any executable or type of project.

When you call `AddProject`, Aspire dynamically reads the `launchSettings.json` file to discover the URL and port numbers, and so on. An `AppHost` project has its own `launchSettings.json` file so it can have multiple URLs for all the projects it references.

You can pass an extra parameter to `AddProject` to specify an alternative profile, `launchProfileName: "https"`. Setting it to `null` means disable, or for a port, it means generate a random port, as shown in the following code:

```
.WithEndpoint("https", e => e.Port = null) // Generate random port number.
```

ServiceDefaults project for centralized configuration

The `ServiceDefaults` project provides a central place to configure all the Aspire services and integrations. Let's review how it works:

1. In the `AspireStarter.ServiceDefaults.csproj` project file, note that it is a class library that is configured as an Aspire shared project, it has a framework reference to `Microsoft.AspNetCore.App`, and it references multiple packages for implementing features like resilience, service discovery, and instrumentation for OpenTelemetry, as shown highlighted in the following markup:

```
<Project Sdk="Microsoft.NET.Sdk">

  <PropertyGroup>
    <TargetFramework>net10.0</TargetFramework>
    <ImplicitUsings>enable</ImplicitUsings>
    <Nullable>enable</Nullable>
    <IsAspireSharedProject>true</IsAspireSharedProject>
  </PropertyGroup>

  <ItemGroup>
    <FrameworkReference Include="Microsoft.AspNetCore.App" />
```

```
    <PackageReference Include=
     "Microsoft.Extensions.Http.Resilience" />
    <PackageReference Include=
     "Microsoft.Extensions.ServiceDiscovery" />
    <PackageReference Include=
     "OpenTelemetry.Exporter.OpenTelemetryProtocol" />
    <PackageReference Include=
     "OpenTelemetry.Extensions.Hosting" />
    <PackageReference Include=
     "OpenTelemetry.Instrumentation.AspNetCore" />
    <PackageReference Include=
     "OpenTelemetry.Instrumentation.Http" />
    <PackageReference Include=
     "OpenTelemetry.Instrumentation.Runtime" />
  </ItemGroup>

</Project>
```

2. In `Extensions.cs`, note the `Extensions` class is defined in the `Microsoft.Extensions.Hosting` namespace and defines extension methods for `IHostApplicationBuilder`, as shown in the following list:

   - `AddServiceDefaults`: This method should be called within any project that wants to participate in the distributed application, like the web service and Blazor website. Then it calls the next method.
   - `ConfigureOpenTelemetry`: This method sets up OpenTelemetry with sensible defaults for logging, adds metrics for ASP.NET Core, HTTP clients, and .NET runtime counters, and adds tracing for ASP.NET Core and HTTP clients. Then it calls the next method.
   - `AddOpenTelemetryExporters`: This method reads configuration like the appropriate environment variable to know whether it should enable OTLP exporters.
   - `AddDefaultHealthChecks`: This method adds a basic health check to ensure a service is responding to requests.
   - `MapDefaultEndpoints`: This method maps the health checks endpoint to `/health` and the liveness endpoint to `/alive`.

Good practice: If you have other shared functionality, put it in a separate class library. The Aspire service defaults class library project should only be used to configure Aspire services and integrations.

Participating functional projects

Now let's see what is different about your functional projects, the web service and web user interface, that allows them to participate in this Aspire distributed solution:

1. In the `ApiService` project, in its project file, note that it has a reference to the service defaults project. This is so the project can call the `AddServiceDefaults` method.
2. In the `ApiService` project, in `Program.cs`, note that it adds a call to `AddServiceDefaults`, as shown in the following code:

```
// Add service defaults & Aspire client integrations.
builder.AddServiceDefaults();
```

3. In the `Web` project, in its project file, note that it also has a reference to the service defaults project. This is so the project can call the `AddServiceDefaults` method.
4. In the `Web` project, in its project file, note that it has a package reference to `Aspire.StackExchange.Redis.OutputCaching`.

> This is an example of an **Aspire integration**. Aspire integrations are wrapper class libraries that configure a feature like Redis to operate well in a cloud-native environment. We will learn more about them later in this chapter.

5. In the `Web` project, in `Program.cs`, note that it adds a call to `AddServiceDefaults` and to add Redis for output caching, as shown in the following code:

```
// Add service defaults & Aspire integrations.
builder.AddServiceDefaults();
builder.AddRedisOutputCache("cache");
```

> The name `cache` comes from when Redis was registered as an Aspire resource in the app host project, as shown in the following code: `builder.AddRedis("cache")`.

6. In the `Web` project, in `Program.cs`, note the statement to configure the web frontend to be able to call the weather web service API, as shown in the following code:

```
builder.Services.AddHttpClient<WeatherApiClient>(client =>
  {
    // This URL uses "https+http://" to indicate HTTPS is preferred over
HTTP.
    // Learn more about service discovery scheme resolution at https://
aka.ms/dotnet/sdschemes.
    client.BaseAddress = new("https+http://apiservice");
  });
```

The name `apiservice` comes from when the web service was registered as an Aspire resource in the app host project, as shown in the following code:

```
builder.AddProject<Projects.AspireStarter_ApiService>("apiservice").
```

Aspire runs your projects and their dependencies and configures them appropriately, allowing them to communicate. Aspire removes the need to know the ports and connection strings from the developer experience. This is achieved by a service discovery mechanism that allows you to use logical names like `apiservice` instead of IP addresses and ports when making HTTP calls.

In the preceding URL, you can use the name `apiservice` when making HTTP calls via `IHttpClientFactory`. The calls made using this method will also automatically retry and handle transient failures because Aspire preconfigures integration with Polly for resilience features.

Now let's see how a developer could integrate Redis into their projects, first manually, and then automatically using Aspire.

Configuring Redis traditionally

Let's look at what a developer traditionally needs to do to configure Redis:

1. Add a reference to the Redis package.
2. Add a reference to a health checks library so your app can respond to Redis being unavailable.

> **Good practice:** Adding health checks to confirm that a required resource like Redis is available makes your solutions more resilient but it is frequently missed. Luckily, this is a key step that Aspire does for you. You will see this in action later in this chapter for RabbitMQ in the section titled *Reviewing the eShop with the Aspire reference application*, in steps 9 to 11, and the principle is the same for Redis.

3. Configure the Redis connection string.
4. Configure the Redis client library to send log output to your telemetry system.
5. Configure logs and metrics for Redis.
6. Decide on resiliency using a retry policy and wrap Redis calls with a library like Polly that can implement your policies.

> **Good practice:** Deciding on and implementing suitable resiliency with a retry policy is something that most developers do not have detailed knowledge about. So, they release a solution without any policy at all, and something breaks that could've been avoided with a good retry policy. You can learn about retry policies in my book, *Apps and Services with .NET 10*, or at the following link: `https://github.com/App-vNext/Polly/blob/main/docs/strategies/retry.md`.

Configuring Redis with Aspire

Contrast that with using Aspire:

1. Add a reference to the Aspire Redis package.
2. Call `AddRedis`.

There is no step 3!

The Aspire Redis integration configures the Redis client to use the connection string provided automatically. This avoids many common errors in your setup for local development.

Of course, you could override the default configuration if necessary, but the Aspire Redis integration is designed to provide you with an optimal production-ready configuration without hiding the underlying Redis SDK. And performance is never a factor since your code uses the same underlying Redis client library.

> **Warning!** Redis recently changed its license, as you can read about at the following link: `https://redis.com/blog/redis-adopts-dual-source-available-licensing/`. Consider switching to compatible alternatives in production, like Dragonfly: `https://www.dragonflydb.io/redis-alternative` or KeyDB `https://docs.keydb.dev/`. There is no need to change anything in your code since both alternatives support the Redis protocol.

Now that you've seen a specific example of how the Aspire Redis integration improves the local development experience, let's learn more details about Aspire integrations.

Aspire integrations

Aspire integrations are designed to solve the biggest roadblock to getting started with cloud-native development. The roadblock is that there is too much configuration that you must get right, and it often is not obvious what path to start with.

Aspire helps this by being opinionated about what an integration needs to provide, mandating that all integrations, at a minimum, provide resiliency defaults, health checks, set up telemetry, and integrate with DI.

Every Aspire integration must comply with the following requirements:

- An Aspire integration must provide a JSON schema so that statement completion works when editing `appsettings.json`.
- An Aspire integration must have default but configurable resilience patterns such as retries, timeouts, and circuit breakers to maximize availability.
- An Aspire integration must have health checks that enable Aspire solutions to track and respond to its health.
- An Aspire integration must provide integrated logging, metrics, and tracing using modern .NET abstractions like `ILogger`, `Meter`, and `Activity`.
- An Aspire integration must provide `AddXxx` extension methods that connect the services from the SDK to the DI container with the right lifetime for the types being registered.

Currently, Aspire provides the integrations shown in *Table 16.4*:

Integration	Description
SQL Server EF Core	For accessing SQL Server databases using EF Core. This is for application-side integrations. Your EF Core context is wrapped in healthy Aspire infrastructure: OpenTelemetry metrics, logs, and health probes all come alive by default. The code is in the client app and does not set up the containers and resources.
SQL Server	For accessing SQL Server databases. This is for infrastructure-side integrations i.e. running or managing the actual SQL Server instance, typically in a container orchestrated by Aspire itself. The code is in AppHost and sets up the containers and resources.
PostgreSQL EF Core	For accessing PostgreSQL databases using Entity Framework Core.
PostgreSQL	For accessing PostgreSQL databases.
RabbitMQ	For accessing RabbitMQ.
Redis Distributed Caching	For accessing Redis caches for distributed caching.
Redis Output Caching	For accessing Redis caches for output caching.
Redis	For accessing Redis caches.
Apache Kafka	For producing and consuming messages from an Apache Kafka broker.
MongoDB Driver	For accessing MongoDB databases.
Oracle EF Core	For accessing Oracle databases with Entity Framework Core.
MySqlConnector	For accessing MySQL databases.

Table 16.4: Aspire integrations

Currently, Aspire also provides the Azure-specific integrations shown in *Table 16.5*:

Integration	Description
Azure AI OpenAI	For accessing Azure AI OpenAI or OpenAI functionality.
Azure Blob Storage	For accessing Azure Blob Storage.
Azure Cosmos DB EF Core	For accessing Azure Cosmos DB databases with Entity Framework Core.
Azure Cosmos DB	For accessing Azure Cosmos DB databases.
Azure Key Vault	For accessing Azure Key Vault.
Azure Service Bus	For accessing Azure Service Bus.
Azure Storage Queues	For accessing Azure Storage Queues.

Table 16.5: Aspire Azure-specific integrations

> You can see the current list of Aspire integrations at the following link: `https://learn.microsoft.com/en-us/dotnet/aspire/fundamentals/integrations-overview#official-integrations`.

Logging, tracing, and metrics for observability

For a solution to be observable:

- All integrations in the distributed solution need to provide data in a way you can consume. This includes .NET itself, any libraries that you use, and your own project code.
- The data needs to be sent somewhere that you can access.
- The tools to view, query, and analyze the data need to be set up.

Aspire solutions are observable by default. This means that you can see what is going on in your solution from all the data being collected from the running resources and their logs, metrics, and traces.

.NET teams have invested in OpenTelemetry by adopting OpenTelemetry's naming and structure and for getting data into tools by using OTLP. You learned about OpenTelemetry in *Chapter 5, Logging, Tracing, and Metrics for Observability*.

Aspire provides the code to enable OpenTelemetry by default in the `ServiceDefaults` project. By using a shared code project instead of hardcoding this implementation, the conventions Aspire uses, like the name of health endpoints, can be customized if you need to. The alternative would have been to put them in a library with configuration settings for customization, which would ultimately be more complex.

Aspire presents all the logs, metrics, and traces from your solution in its developer dashboard. The **Traces** view makes finding things like user actions that cause inefficient paths through the solution easy.

You can see issues like multiple potentially unnecessary database calls or individual services that are slowing down other parts of the system. These types of issues can be difficult to discover without this type of data and a view of the data.

Docker versus Podman for containers

With the initial version of Aspire, you have two choices for hosting containers: Docker (the default) and Podman.

Docker pros:

- More established ecosystem
- Larger community
- More third-party integrations
- Features like Docker Compose to manage multi-container solutions

Podman pros:

- Lower cost of licenses

Unless you have a good reason to use Podman, like your team has already standardized on using it, I recommend that you use Docker because the Aspire team chose it as the default for the good reasons listed above.

Waiting for containers to be ready

If you're familiar with Docker Compose, then you might know that a common issue is that, during startup, the Docker Compose `depends_on` instruction does not wait until a container is "ready"; it only waits until it's "running." This can cause issues because if you have a relational database system that needs to start its own services before being able to handle incoming connections, then another service may call the database before it is truly ready.

Aspire had a similar issue because calling `WithReference` does something like the Docker Compose `depends_on` instruction. However, the Aspire team knows that the capability to truly make a resource depend on another resource is one of the top asks from the .NET community.

Aspire 9 introduced a `WaitFor` method that uses health checks to provide a better experience.

Alternatively, you can implement retries for automatic resiliency while the dependent resources get ready.

What about Dapr, Orleans, and Project Tye?

Microsoft has other related products that are like Aspire or can work with Aspire, but the situation can be confusing to understand. Here's a brief description of each of these technologies so that you can understand how they are related and could fit together.

Dapr

Short for **Distributed Application Runtime**, Dapr is an open-source project designed to make it easier for developers to build resilient, microservice-oriented applications that are platform-agnostic. It abstracts some of the most common challenges associated with building microservices, like state management, service-to-service communication, and observability, into a set of APIs that are simple to use and implement.

Dapr utilizes a **sidecar architecture pattern**, meaning that each microservice is paired with a Dapr runtime instance. This sidecar acts as a proxy, handling tasks such as inter-service communication, integration with external systems, and more, all without requiring changes to the microservice code.

Dapr supports multiple programming languages and frameworks, making it accessible to a broad developer community. You can interact with Dapr through HTTP or gRPC APIs, which allows for easy integration into existing applications.

Dapr benefits from contributions from a large community and is backed by significant industry players, not just Microsoft. This ensures that it stays relevant and evolves in response to real-world use cases and feedback. You can use both Dapr and Aspire together. Check out `https://github.com/dotnet/aspire-samples/tree/main/samples/AspireWithDapr` for a sample.

> You can learn more about Dapr at the following link: `https://dapr.io/`. Do not confuse Dapr with Dapper, which you can learn about at the following link: `https://github.com/DapperLib/Dapper`.

Orleans

This is a framework for building distributed, high-scale computing applications. Orleans was created by Microsoft Research and has been used extensively within the company, powering services for games like *Halo*, as well as in other large-scale applications.

Orleans is based on the actor model, but it introduces the concept of **virtual actors**, called "**grains**" in the framework. These grains are the fundamental units of computation and state storage. Orleans abstracts away the complexities of creating, destroying, and managing the lifecycle of these actors.

Orleans provides built-in mechanisms to handle failures, including activating backup grains if a server fails. Developers using Orleans write code as if all grains are on the same server, without needing to worry about the underlying details of data location and communication between grains. Orleans supports grain state persistence in a straightforward manner.

The framework supports event streams, enabling grains to subscribe to and publish events, which facilitates building event-driven architectures. Orleans has built-in support for timers and reminders that can trigger events or actions within grains at specified times.

Orleans is particularly well-suited for applications that require high throughput and low latency, such as real-time gaming, IoT, and real-time analytics. Orleans is a good solution for implementing large-scale distributed apps and is a more flexible and scalable architecture than traditional microservices.

The Aspire team has created a sample of Aspire and Orleans integration working, available in the Aspire sample repository at the following link: `https://github.com/dotnet/aspire-samples/tree/main/samples/OrleansVoting`.

> You can learn more about Orleans at the following link: `https://learn.microsoft.com/en-us/dotnet/orleans/`.

Project Tye

Project Tye was an experimental developer tool that aimed to simplify the process of developing, testing, and deploying microservices and distributed applications. It addressed common challenges faced when dealing with multiple services, such as orchestrating these services during development and simplifying the deployment of services to production environments.

Aspire evolved from Tye. You can think of Tye as the initial experiment and Aspire as the production implementation of a similar idea. For example, the developer dashboard was originally created as part of Tye, and now it's part of Aspire.

> You can read about the *The end of the Tye experiment* issue at the following link: `https://github.com/dotnet/tye/issues/1622`.

Choosing between Dapr, Orleans, and Aspire

During a public Aspire standup meeting, the team gave their opinion about choosing between these various technologies:

> *"There's the answer. And then there's what people want to hear. These questions lead me down the path that people want to hear, which one to use? Right? You're never going to get that answer from me. There are many options, and you have to know what you get out of the tech. Orleans is really great for virtual actors. Dapr is really great when you have multiple languages. Aspire orchestration specifically works with both of those concepts. Aspire does not attempt to abstract the cloud. Aspire works with whatever client libraries you have, whatever existing systems you have." David Fowler*

A developer gave their opinion in the chat:

> *"aspire is pure joy with dapr" Laurent Kempe*

> You can view more comments at the following link: `https://devblogs.microsoft.com/dotnet/introducing-dotnet-aspire-simplifying-cloud-native-development-with-dotnet-8/`.

Aspire for new and existing solutions

Now that you've reviewed the starter template to get a basic idea of the various parts of Aspire and how they all work together to provide a great local development experience when building distributed cloud-native solutions with .NET, let's get more realistic and see how you can create new Aspire solutions and how you can add Aspire to existing solutions.

Creating a new Aspire solution

At this point, we have reviewed a complete Aspire solution with common projects and components like a web service and web user interface, alongside a container for Redis. If you have a brand new solution to create, you can use the **Aspire Empty App** project template.

Imagine that you need to create a greenfield solution that uses a PostgreSQL database, a SQL Server database, and an ASP.NET Core Web API.

Let's create an initial Aspire solution for that now:

1. Use your preferred code editor to create a new **Aspire Empty App** / `aspire` project with a solution named `AspireNew` in a new folder in the `Chapter16` folder.

   Warning! Make sure that you create a new solution rather than add to the existing starter solution. The solution should be created in `C:\tools-skills-net10\Chapter16\AspireNew\`.

2. Note that your solution should have two projects, named `AspireNew.AppHost` and `AspireNew.ServiceDefaults`.
3. In the `AspireNew.ServiceDefaults` project file, remove the version attributes from all package references because we are using CPM.
4. In the `AspireNew.ServiceDefaults` project, in `Extensions.cs`, note the `AddServiceDefaults` method implementation that configures OpenTelemetry, health checks, service discovery, and adds resilience (via Polly) and service discovery to HTTP clients, as shown in the following code:

```
public static TBuilder AddServiceDefaults<TBuilder>(
  this TBuilder builder) where TBuilder : IHostApplicationBuilder
{
  builder.ConfigureOpenTelemetry();

  builder.AddDefaultHealthChecks();

  builder.Services.AddServiceDiscovery();

  builder.Services.ConfigureHttpClientDefaults(http =>
  {
    // Turn on resilience by default
    http.AddStandardResilienceHandler();

    // Turn on service discovery by default
    http.AddServiceDiscovery();
  });

  // Uncomment the following to restrict the allowed schemes for service
discovery.
  // builder.Services.Configure<ServiceDiscoveryOptions>(options =>
  // {
```

```
  //     options.AllowedSchemes = ["https"];
  // });

  return builder;
}
```

5. In `Extensions.cs`, note the two `string` constants for paths, as shown in the following code:

```
private const string HealthEndpointPath = "/health";
private const string AlivenessEndpointPath = "/alive";
```

6. In `Extensions.cs`, note the `MapDefaultEndpoints` method implementation that maps health check endpoints when running in development, as shown highlighted in the following code:

```
public static WebApplication MapDefaultEndpoints(
  this WebApplication app)
{
  // Adding health check endpoints to applications in non-development environments has security implications.
  // See https://aka.ms/dotnet/aspire/healthchecks for details before enabling these endpoints in non-development environments.
  if (app.Environment.IsDevelopment())
  {
    // All health checks must pass for app to be considered ready to accept traffic after starting
    app.MapHealthChecks(HealthEndpointPath);

    // Only health checks tagged with the "live" tag must pass for app to be considered alive
    app.MapHealthChecks(AlivenessEndpointPath, new HealthCheckOptions
    {
      Predicate = r => r.Tags.Contains("live")
    });
  }

  return app;
}
```

7. In the `AspireNew.AppHost` project, in `AppHost.cs`, note that, currently, a distributed application builder is created and run without any resources defined, as shown in the following code:

```
var builder = DistributedApplication.CreateBuilder(args);

builder.Build().Run();
```

8. Add a Web API project to the `AspireNew` solution, as defined in the following list:
   - Project template: **ASP.NET Core Web API** / `webapi`
   - Solution file and folder: `AspireNew`
   - Project file and folder: `Northwind.WebApi`
   - **Authentication type: None**
   - **Configure for HTTPS:** Selected
   - **Enable container support:** Cleared
   - **Enable OpenAPI support:** Selected
   - **Do not use top-level statements:** Cleared
   - **Use controllers:** Cleared
   - **Enlist in Aspire orchestration:** Selected
9. In the `Northwind.WebApi.csproj` project file, remove the `Microsoft.AspNetCore.OpenApi` package version number because we are using CPM.
10. In the `Northwind.WebApi` project, in `Program.cs`, note the call to the `AddServiceDefaults` and `MapDefaultEndpoints` methods, as shown highlighted in the following code:

```
var builder = WebApplication.CreateBuilder(args);

builder.AddServiceDefaults();

// Add services to the container.
// Learn more about configuring OpenAPI at https://aka.ms/aspnet/openapi
builder.Services.AddOpenApi();

var app = builder.Build();

app.MapDefaultEndpoints();
```

11. In the `AspireNew.AppHost` project, in `AppHost.cs`, note that the distributed application builder now has a project resource defined for the Web API project, as shown highlighted in the following code:

```
var builder = DistributedApplication.CreateBuilder(args);

builder.AddProject<Projects.Northwind_WebApi>("northwind-webapi");

builder.Build().Run();
```

12. In **Solution Explorer**, right-click the `AspireNew.AppHost` project, select **Add | Aspire package...**, and note that the **NuGet Package Manager** uses a filter (`owner:Aspire tags:integration+hosting`) to limit packages to only those suitable for adding to an Aspire `AppHost` project.
13. In the filter box, after the existing text, type `postgresql`, and then select the `Aspire.Hosting.PostpreSQL` package, select the latest stable version, and then click the **Install** button. If necessary, accept any license agreement.
14. In the filter box, after the existing text, replace `postgresql` with `sqlserver`, and then select the `Aspire.Hosting.SqlServer` package, select the latest stable version, and then click the **Install** button. If necessary, accept any license agreement.
15. In the `AspireNew.AppHost.csproj` project file, note the packages for hosting PostgreSQL and SQL Server with Aspire, as shown in the following markup:

```
<ItemGroup>
  <PackageReference Include="Aspire.Hosting.PostgreSQL" />
  <PackageReference Include="Aspire.Hosting.SqlServer" />
</ItemGroup>
```

16. Save all changes.
17. Build the `AspireNew.AppHost` project to restore packages.
18. In `AppHost.cs`, after creating the `builder`, add statements to configure the two databases, as shown highlighted in the following code:

```
var builder = DistributedApplication.CreateBuilder(args);

builder.AddPostgres("postgres")
  .WithPgAdmin()
  .AddDatabase("cms");

builder.AddSqlServer("sqlserver")
  .AddDatabase("northwind");

builder.AddProject<Projects.Northwind_WebApi>("northwind-webapi");

builder.Build().Run();
```

19. Start **Docker Desktop.**
20. Start the `AspireNew.AppHost` project.

21. When the browser opens the Aspire developer dashboard, note that it is likely to take a bit longer for the two database servers to start, especially if the appropriate images need to be downloaded, as shown in *Figure 16.10*:

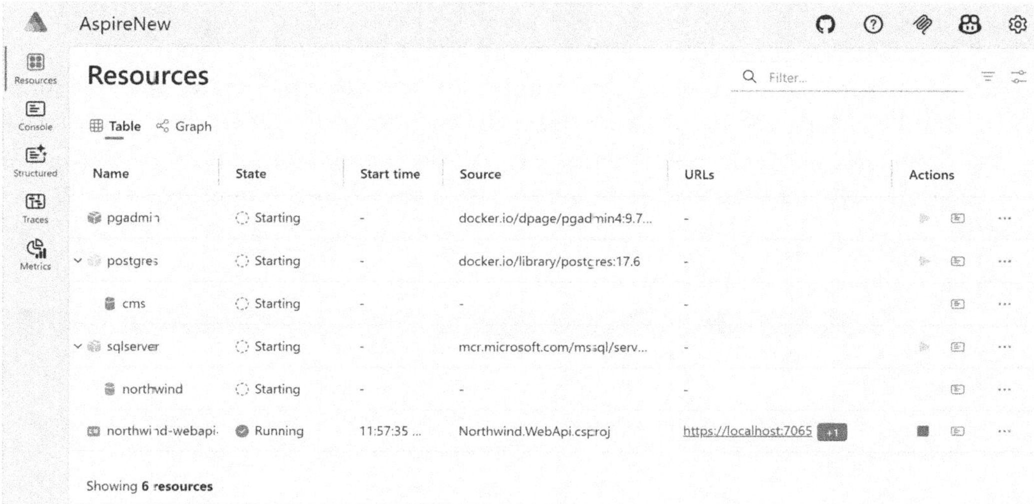

Figure 16.10: The two database servers are still starting

22. Eventually, the two database servers will be running, their endpoints will be active, and the two databases will be available, as shown in *Figure 16.11*:

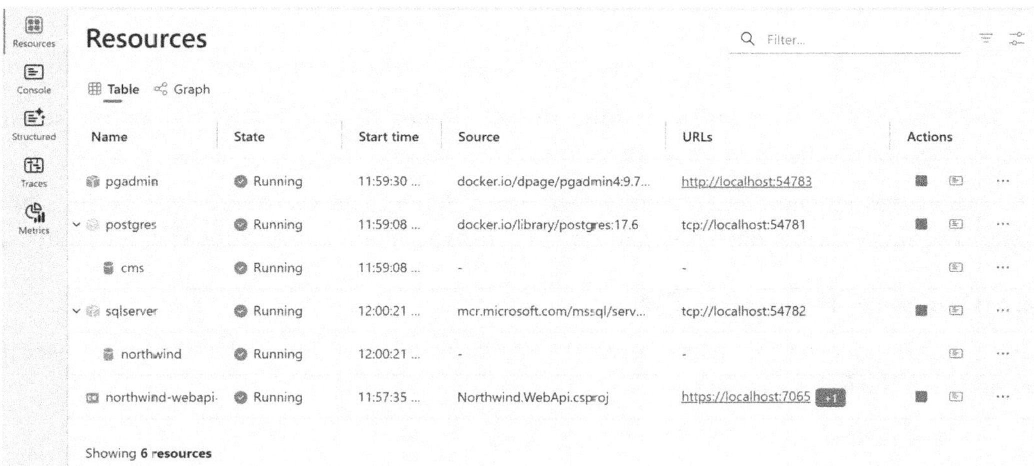

Figure 16.11: Running database servers and their databases

> **Warning!** When you call `AddSqlServer`, it uses a random port by default, as you can see in *Figure 16.11*, so you must fix it to **1433** if you want to use the default settings that SQL clients will expect.

23. In Docker Desktop, note the three containers that were spun up for you: one for `postgres` for the CMS database, one for `pgadmin`, and one for SQL Server for the Northwind database.
24. From the dashboard, click the endpoint for **postgres-pgadmin**, and note the web user interface for managing the PostgreSQL server and its databases, as shown in *Figure 16.12*:

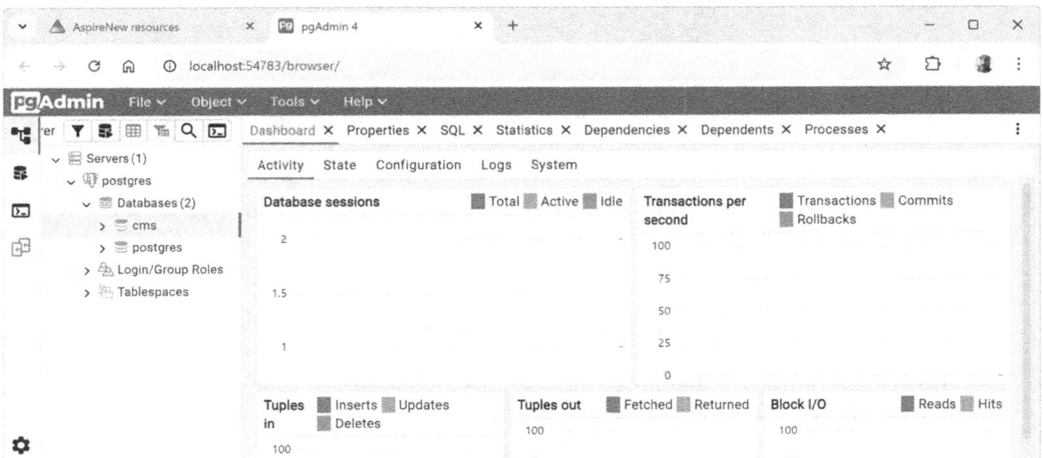

Figure 16.12: The pgadmin web user interface

25. Close the browser and shut down the distributed Aspire app. Note the three containers in Docker automatically shut down too.

You've now created a new Aspire solution and run it. Now let's review some of what you've seen in more detail, keeping in mind that it is equally applicable to both new and existing solutions that use Aspire.

Aspire and PostgreSQL

In the `AppHost` project, you might register PostgreSQL as a service with its admin web user interface, as shown in the following code:

```
var postgress = builder.AddPostgres("my-pgsql")
  .WithPgAdmin()
  .AddDatabase("mydb");
```

Note that the name of the PostgreSQL server is `my-pgsql` and the name of the database is `mydb`. Aspire identifies resources by these names so they must be unique. By convention, the connection string name to connect to the `mydb` database will be assumed to be `mydb`, as shown in the following configuration:

```
{
  "ConnectionStrings": {
    "mydb": "Host=localhost;Port=5432;Database=myDataBase;User
ID=root;Password=myPassword; "
  },
}
```

In a service that needs to connect to the database, you might register that you need the EF Core data context for the PostgreSQL database, as shown in the following code:

```
// Will look for connection string with the name my-pgsql.
builder.AddNpgsqlDbContext<NorthwindContext>("my-pgsql");
```

You should match the connection string name `mydb`, as shown in the following code:

```
// Will look for connection string with the name mydb.
builder.AddNpgsqlDbContext<NorthwindContext>("mydb");
```

Or, you could override the name of the connection string, as shown in the following code:

```
// Override the connection string convention.
builder.AddNpgsqlDbContext<NorthwindContext>("my-pgsql", o =>
  o.ConnectionString = builder.Configuration.GetConnectionString("mydb")
);
```

It can be useful to understand what types are returned by Aspire methods, as described in *Table 16.6*:

Method	Returns	Description
`AddPostgres`	`PostgresServerResource`	Adds a PostgreSQL resource to the application model. A container is used for local development.
`AddDatabase`	`PostgresDatabaseResource`	If you call `AddDatabase` without specifying a database name, then it uses the server name.

Table 16.6: Aspire builder for PostgreSQL

The `WithReference` method has an optional `connectionName` parameter, which becomes the connection string name.

Using data volumes and configuring a stable password

When you use a data volume, the randomly generated password is saved there. Then Aspire generates a new password when you next run the Aspire solution, and so if you do not account for this, it fails. This issue is described at the following link: `https://github.com/dotnet/aspire/issues/3669`.

Using the `WithDataVolume` method requires setting a stable password rather than relying on the default of a new one being generated each time you run the project. The easiest way to fix this is to put a password in user secrets for your `AppHost` project using the key `Parameters:my-pgsql-password`.

> You can learn more about this issue and how the Aspire team plans to make this smoother at the following link: `https://github.com/dotnet/aspire/issues/1151`.

Adding Aspire to an existing solution

Aspire can also be used with existing applications so you can incrementally adopt the parts of the stack. Aspire is only available with .NET 8 or later. If you have existing projects that target earlier versions, then you will need to upgrade to at least .NET 8 before you use any of the parts of the Aspire stack. You will also need Visual Studio version 17.10 or later if you want to use the Visual Studio tooling.

Let's try adding Aspire to an existing solution:

1. Use your preferred code editor to create a new **ASP.NET Core Web API** / `webapi` project named `Northwind.WebApi` in a solution named `AspireExisting` in a new folder in the `Chapter16` folder:
    - Project template: **ASP.NET Core Web API** / `webapi`
    - Solution file and folder: `AspireExisting`
    - Project file and folder: `Northwind.WebApi`
    - **Authentication type: None**
    - **Configure for HTTPS**: Selected
    - **Enable container support**: Cleared
    - **Enable OpenAPI support**: Selected
    - **Do not use top-level statements:** Cleared
    - **Use controllers**: Cleared
    - **Enlist in Aspire orchestration**: Cleared

    > **Warning!** Do *not* select the **Enlist in Aspire orchestration** check box! The entire point of this section is to start with a project that does *not* have Aspire already in it so that we can then see how to add it to an existing solution. And make sure that you create a new solution rather than add to the existing solution. The project should be created in `C:\tools-skills-net10\Chapter16\AspireExisting\Northwind.WebApi`.

2. In the `Northwind.WebApi.csproj` project file, remove the `Microsoft.AspNetCore.OpenApi` package version number because we are using CPM.
3. Start the project without debugging.
4. Confirm that the web service returns some randomly generated weather forecasts in JSON.
5. Close the browser and shut down the web service.
6. In **Solution Explorer**, right-click the project and select **Add | Aspire Orchestrator Support...**.
7. In the **Add Aspire Orchestrator Support** dialog box, review the options and then click **OK**, as shown in *Figure 16.13*:

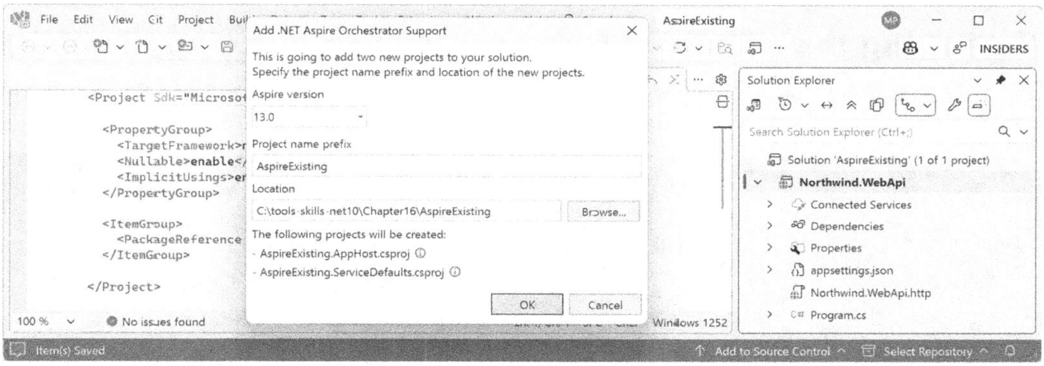

Figure 16.13: Adding Aspire Orchestrator Support

8. In the `Northwind.WebApi.csproj` project file, note the project reference to the Aspire service defaults project.
9. In the `Northwind.WebApi` project, in `Program.cs`, note the statements that call `AddServiceDefaults` and `MapDefaultEndpoints`.
10. In the `AspireExisting.AppHost` project, in `AppHost.cs`, note the statement that calls `AddProject` to connect to the web service, as shown in the following code:

```
var builder = DistributedApplication.CreateBuilder(args);

builder.AddProject<Projects.Northwind_WebApi>("northwind-webapi");

builder.Build().Run();
```

11. Optionally, in the `AspireExisting.ServiceDefaults.csproj` project file, remove the `version` attributes from all the package references.
12. Close the solution.

If you are not using Visual Studio, you can manually create new instances of the `AppHost` and `ServiceDefaults` projects using `dotnet new` and then add them to an existing solution, but they will not already reference an existing project.

Switching to Aspire integrations

If your existing projects used any NuGet packages that have Aspire equivalents (like Redis, MySQL, PostgreSQL, and so on), then you can now switch over to the Aspire integrations. This will hopefully allow you to remove some explicit configuration.

Aspire integrations do not need to be used only in Aspire-orchestrated solutions. You can also use Aspire integrations in any .NET 8 or later project. This will provide you with the resiliency and other easy configuration provided by that integration. What you won't get is the rest of Aspire, like the dashboard, service discovery, automatic ports and URLs, or connection strings.

Reviewing the eShop with the Aspire reference application

The eShop reference application is a fictional website named **Northern Mountains**. It is a .NET e-commerce website using a services-based architecture, as shown in *Figure 16.14*:

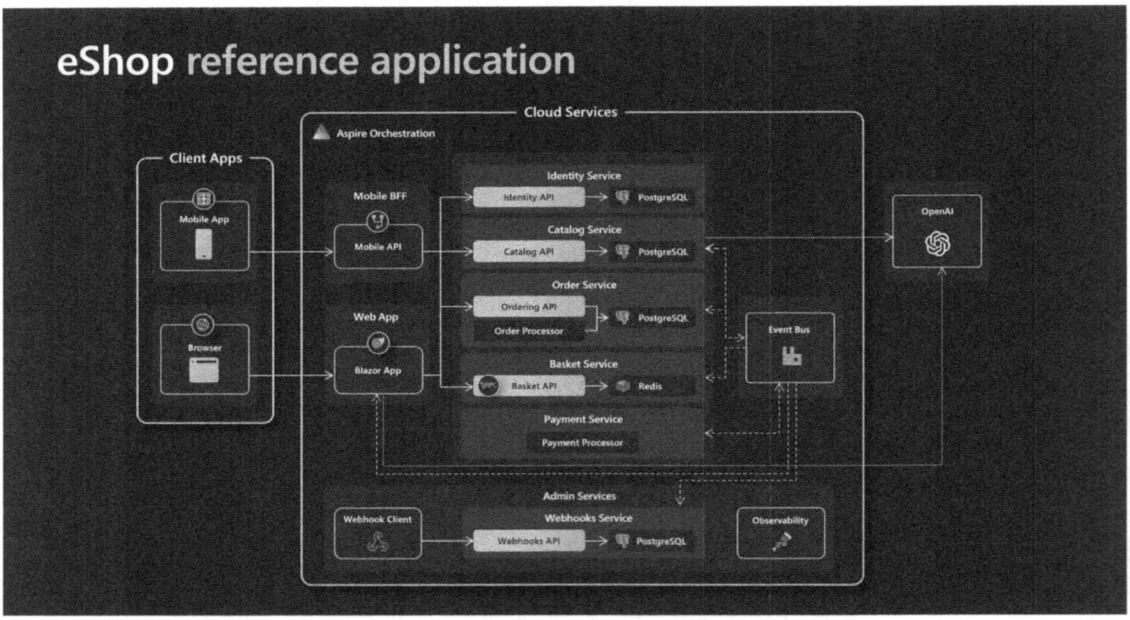

Figure 16.14: eShop reference application architecture diagram from Microsoft's repository

> You can see a larger image at the following link: `https://raw.githubusercontent.com/dotnet/eShop/main/img/eshop_architecture.png`.

The sample catalog data is defined in `catalog.json`. The product names, descriptions, and brand names are fictional and were generated using GPT-35-Turbo. The corresponding product images were generated using DALL·E 3.

Let's see eShop with Aspire in action:

1. Navigate to the eShop repository at the following link: `https://github.com/dotnet/eShop`.
2. Download or clone the eShop project:
    - To download, click the green **Code** button and then select **Download ZIP**. In your `Downloads` folder, extract the ZIP to `C:\eShop\` or something similar.
    - To clone, click the green **Code** button and then select **Open with GitHub Desktop**.
3. Open the `eShop.slnx` solution file in your preferred code editor. Be patient while it loads, as it has 24 projects (19 projects in the `src` folder and 5 in the `tests` folder).
4. In the `eShop.AppHost.csproj` project file, note that it references Aspire integration packages for RabbitMQ, Redis, PostgreSQL, and Azure Cognitive Services, as well as 10 .NET projects, as shown in the following markup:

```
<Project Sdk="Aspire.AppHost.Sdk/13.0.0">

  <PropertyGroup>
    <OutputType>Exe</OutputType>
    <TargetFramework>net10.0</TargetFramework>
    <Nullable>enable</Nullable>
    <IsPackable>false</IsPackable>
    <UserSecretsId>b99dbce4-17d4-41d2-858a-2b0529d60bb8</UserSecretsId>
  </PropertyGroup>

  <ItemGroup>
    <PackageReference Include="Aspire.Hosting.AppHost" />
    <PackageReference Include="Aspire.Hosting.RabbitMQ" />
    <PackageReference Include="Aspire.Hosting.Redis" />
    <PackageReference Include="Aspire.Hosting.PostgreSQL" />
    <PackageReference Include="Aspire.Hosting.Azure.CognitiveServices" />
    <PackageReference Include="Aspire.Hosting.Yarp" />
    <PackageReference Include="CommunityToolkit.Aspire.Hosting.Ollama" />
  </ItemGroup>

  <ItemGroup>
    <ProjectReference Include="..\Basket.API\Basket.API.csproj" />
    <ProjectReference Include="..\Catalog.API\Catalog.API.csproj" />
    <ProjectReference Include="..\Identity.API\Identity.API.csproj" />
    <ProjectReference Include="..\Ordering.API\Ordering.API.csproj" />
    <ProjectReference Include="..\OrderProcessor\OrderProcessor.csproj"
/>
```

```
    <ProjectReference Include="..\PaymentProcessor\PaymentProcessor.
csproj" />
    <ProjectReference Include="..\Webhooks.API\Webhooks.API.csproj" />
    <ProjectReference Include="..\WebApp\WebApp.csproj" />
    <ProjectReference Include="..\WebhookClient\WebhookClient.csproj" />
  </ItemGroup>
</Project>
```

5. Build the solution. This can take about five minutes so be patient.

> **Warning!** If you get errors, it is probably due to missing workloads. At the command prompt or terminal, enter the following command: `dotnet workload restore`

6. Start **Docker Desktop**.
7. Start the `AppHost` project without debugging.
8. At the command prompt or terminal, note that the distributed application starts and shows the URL for the dashboard for the cases when the browser does not start and navigate to it automatically, as shown in the following output:

```
info: Aspire.Hosting.DistributedApplication[0]
      Aspire version: 13.0.0+6596fdc41a8d419876a6bf4abc17b7c66b9ef63a
info: Aspire.Hosting.DistributedApplication[0]
      Distributed application starting.
info: Aspire.Hosting.DistributedApplication[0]
      Application host directory is: C:\GitHub\eshop\src\eShop.AppHost
info: Aspire.Hosting.DistributedApplication[0]
      Now listening on: https://localhost:19888
info: Aspire.Hosting.DistributedApplication[0]
      Login to the dashboard at https://localhost:19888/
login?t=42930028c8398321487a942b8aeb6cd0
info: Aspire.Hosting.DistributedApplication[0]
      Distributed application started. Press Ctrl+C to shut down.
```

9. In the Aspire developer dashboard, wait for all the Aspire resources to successfully start and have a **State** value of **Running**, as shown in the following list and in *Figure 16.15*:
   - Four containers (3D box icons): **eventbus** (RabbitMQ), **mobile-bff**, **postgres**, and **redis**
   - Four PostgreSQL databases: **catalogdb**, **identitydb**, **orderingdb**, and **webhooksdb**Nine projects (</> icons): **basket-api**, **catalog-api**, **identity-api**, **order-processor**, **ordering-api**, **payment-processor**, **webapp**, **webhooks-api**, and **webhooksclient**

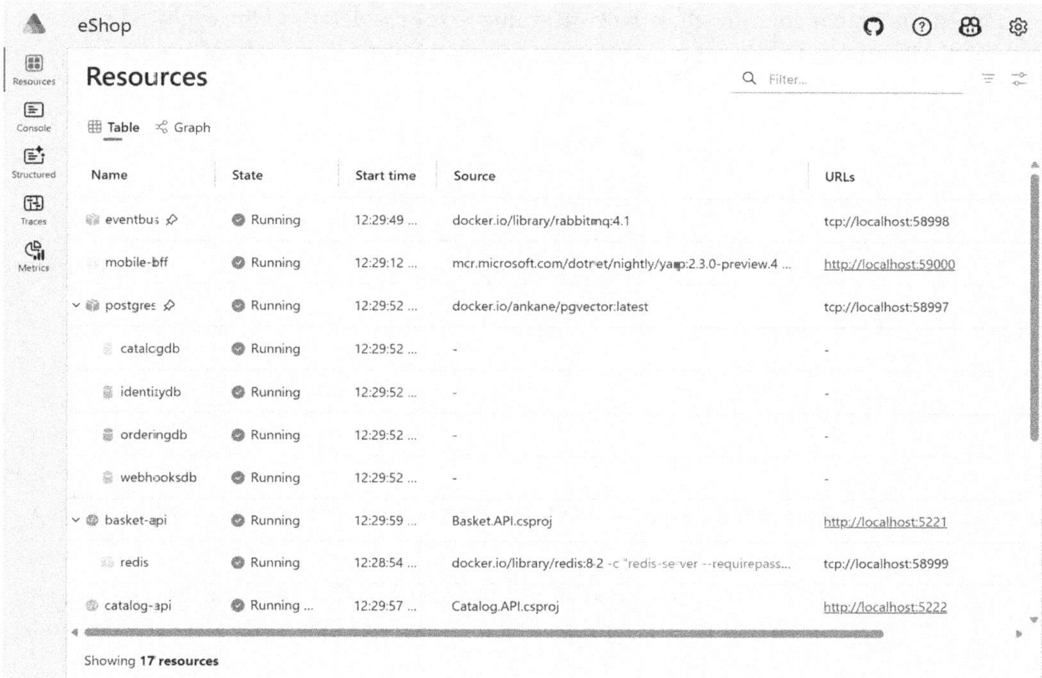

Figure 16.15: Seventeen resources running in the dashboard for the eShop solution

10. Note that, initially, on the **Structured logs** page with a **Level** filter of **Error**, you are likely to see errors logged due to resources like RabbitMQ taking time to fully start and be ready to respond to requests, as shown in *Figure 16.16*:

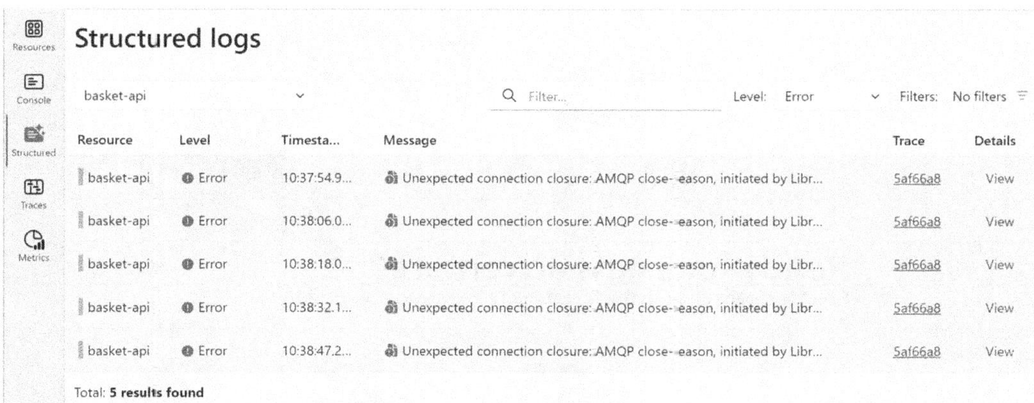

Figure 16.16: Five AMQP (RabbitMQ) errors from the basket-api web service

11. In the **Traces** column, click the GUID value to see the details of the repeated calls to RabbitMQ that failed until after about a minute, when RabbitMQ was ready and successfully responded, as shown in *Figure 16.17*:

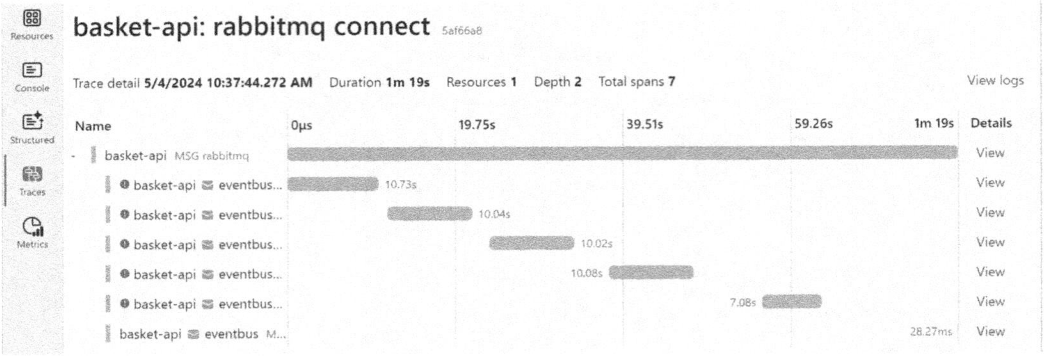

Figure 16.17: Five failed calls to RabbitMQ over about one minute until it was ready

> This behavior is one of the major benefits of Aspire. You don't have to write your own code to handle waiting for resources like RabbitMQ and Redis to be ready for your projects to call.

12. Navigate back to **Resources.** In the **webapp** row, click the `https` link, and note the website home page, as shown in *Figure 16.18*:

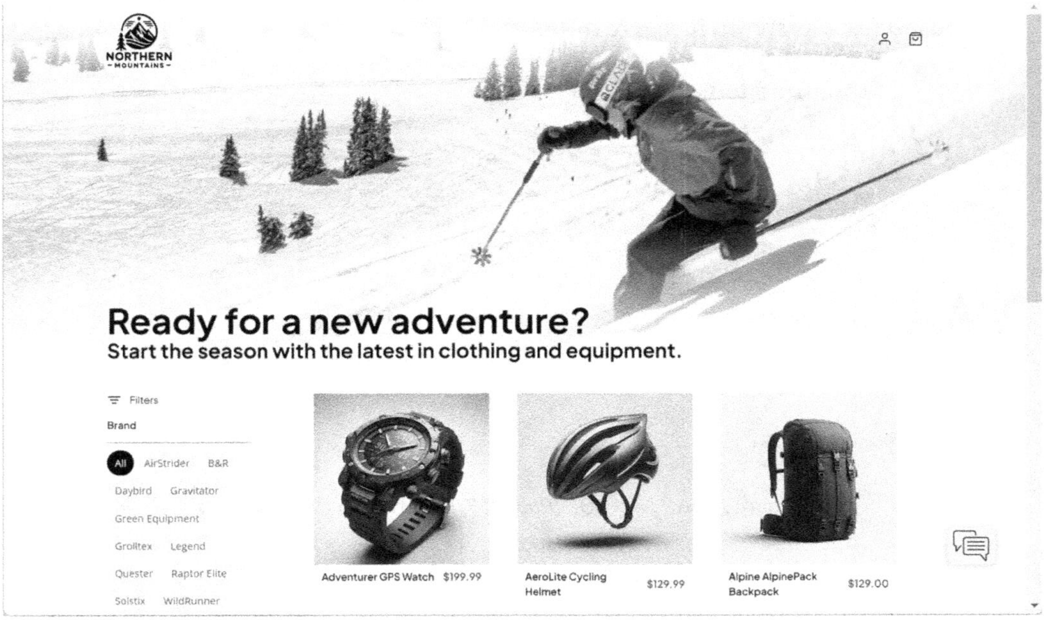

Figure 16.18: Northern Mountains website home page

13. Click on any item, log in as `alice` or `bob` with a password of `Pass123$`, add the item to your cart, and then return to the Aspire dashboard and view the most recent traces for the **webapp** resource, and note the resource usage, as shown in *Figure 16.19*:

Figure 16.19: Aspire dashboard traces for Northern Mountains

14. In the row that calls the **basket-api** resource, click **View**, and note the sequence diagram for how the website calls the services to add an item to the basket, as shown in *Figure 16.20*:

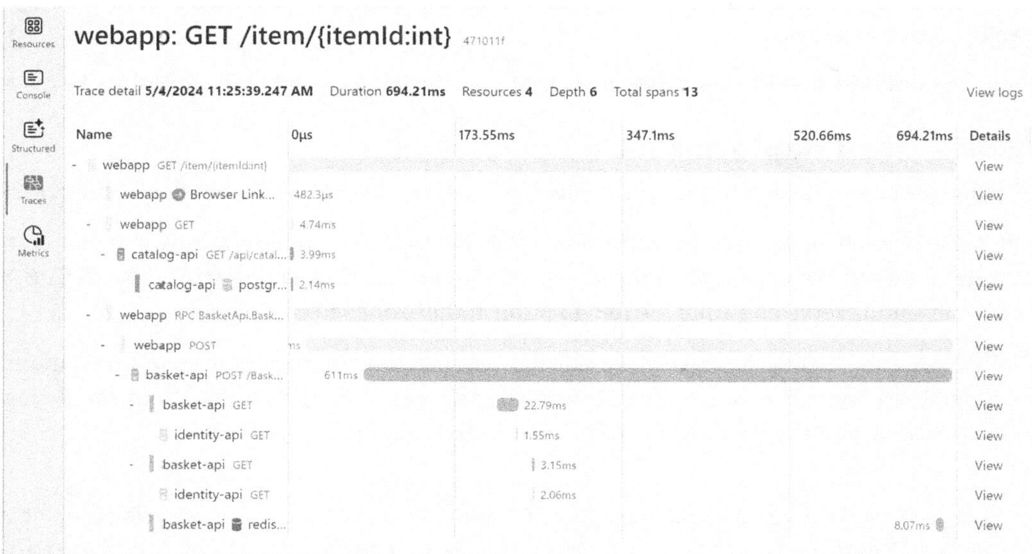

Figure 16.20: Aspire resources working together to add an item to the basket

15. Close the browser and shut down the distributed application.

Now let's see how you could deploy an Aspire solution into production.

Deployment with Aspire

The `AppHost` project has two execution modes, run and publish:

- Run mode is used during the developer inner loop on your local computer
- Publish mode produces a manifest file that statically describes the application model that can be used in deployment scenarios

> **Warning!** The `AppHost` project itself is not deployed and does not run outside of local development and test scenarios.

Understanding Aspire manifests

The application model can produce a manifest definition that describes the solution's relationships and dependencies that tools can consume, augment, and build upon for deployment.

With this manifest, you can get your Aspire solution into Azure using Azure Container Apps in the simplest and fastest way possible. The Azure Developer CLI and Aspire work together to enable you to quickly provision and deploy the Azure resources in one step. The Azure Developer CLI can also create Bicep from the manifest to allow developers and platform engineers to audit or augment the deployment processes.

Bicep is a **domain-specific language** (DSL) that uses declarative syntax to deploy Azure resources.

Aspire cloud deployments

Although Aspire today works best for deploying to Azure, it is open to other deployment systems.

The final artifacts of an Aspire application are .NET apps and configurations that can be deployed to your cloud environments. With the strong container-first mindset of Aspire, the .NET SDK native container builds serve as a valuable tool to publish these apps to containers.

While Aspire itself doesn't natively provide a direct mechanism to deploy your applications to their final destinations, the Aspire application model that you build knows all about the dependencies, configurations, and connections to all the distributed solution's resources.

> You can learn about deploying to Azure Container Apps at the following link: `https://devblogs.microsoft.com/dotnet/how-to-deploy-dotnet-aspire-apps-to-azure-container-apps/`.

Aspir8 deployment YAML files

Another deployment tool is **Aspir8**, which can generate a deployment YAML file for a Aspire AppHost project.

You can learn more about Aspir8 at the following link: https://prom3theu5.github.io/aspirational-manifests/getting-started.html.

Aspir8's GitHub repository can be found at the following link: https://github.com/prom3theu5/aspirational-manifests.

Practicing and exploring

Test your knowledge and understanding by answering some questions, getting some hands-on practice, and exploring the topics covered in this chapter with deeper research.

Exercise 16.1 – Online-only material

You can read official materials from Microsoft at the following links:

- Announcement: https://devblogs.microsoft.com/dotnet/introducing-dotnet-aspire-simplifying-cloud-native-development-with-dotnet-8/
- GA release: https://devblogs.microsoft.com/dotnet/dotnet-aspire-general-availability/
- Documentation: https://learn.microsoft.com/en-us/dotnet/aspire/get-started/aspire-overview
- Sample code: https://github.com/dotnet/aspire-samples
- Aspire Community Toolkit Repository: https://github.com/CommunityToolkit/Aspire
- Introducing the Aspire Community Toolkit: https://devblogs.microsoft.com/dotnet/introducing-the-dotnet-aspire-community-toolkit/

You can read more about Aspire from third-party sites at the following links:

- Dashboard: https://anthonysimmon.com/dotnet-aspire-dashboard-best-tool-visualize-opentelemetry-local-dev/
- Frequently asked questions: https://learn.microsoft.com/en-us/dotnet/aspire/reference/aspire-faq

In this book, we do not want any dependencies on Azure or AWS resources because they cost money. But you should know that there are Azure-specific methods for configuring Aspire, as shown in *Table 16.7*:

Package	Link
Azure hosting	https://www.nuget.org/packages/Aspire.Hosting.Azure/
AWS hosting	https://www.nuget.org/packages/Aspire.Hosting.AWS/

Table 16.7: Azure and AWS cloud hosting packages

You can learn more about Dapr with the book found at the following link: https://www.amazon.com/Practical-Microservices-Dapr-NET-cloud-native/dp/1803248122/.

Exercise 16.2 – Practice exercises

Build and test resilient apps in .NET with Dev Proxy

"When building apps that connect to APIs, we typically focus on getting the app to work. But what happens when the API is slow, returns errors, or becomes unavailable? But it's hard to simulate how your app will handle these scenarios when you don't control the APIs you integrate with. Unless you use Dev Proxy."

Learn how Dev Proxy can help you test how your app handles any behavior, of any API that you connect to, without you having to change a line of code in your app at the following link:

`https://devblogs.microsoft.com/dotnet/build-test-resilient-apps-dotnet-dev-proxy/`.

Using Podman

Instead of using Docker, try using Podman for the coding tasks in this chapter.

You can tell Aspire to use Podman by setting the `DOTNET_ASPIRE_CONTAINER_RUNTIME` environment variable to `podman`, as shown in the following PowerShell command:

```
$env:DOTNET_ASPIRE_CONTAINER_RUNTIME = "podman"
```

Aspireify

You can find lots of articles and tutorials to practice with Aspire at **aspireify.net** by Jeff Fritz, `@csharpfritz`, found at the following link: `https://aspireify.net/`.

Exercise 16.3 – Test your knowledge

Answer the following questions. If you get stuck, try googling the answers if necessary, while remembering that if you get totally stuck, the answers are in *Appendix A*:

1. What are the three main Aspire resource types?
2. What role does the `AppHost` project play in an Aspire solution?
3. What role does the `ServiceDefaults` project play in an Aspire solution?
4. What does the `AddProject` method do?
5. What does the `WithReference` method do?
6. What can you see in the Aspire developer dashboard?
7. What are the benefits of referencing an Aspire integration package instead of the usual package for an integration like Redis?
8. How does Aspire compare to Dapr and Orleans?
9. What container technologies are supported by Aspire?
10. How can you make sure a stable password is used for databases like PostgreSQL?

Appendix A, Answers to the Test Your Knowledge Questions, is available to download from the following link: `https://github.com/markjprice/tools-skills-net10/blob/main/docs/B31468_Appendix%20A.pdf`.

Exercise 16.4 – Explore topics

Use the links on the following page to learn more details about the topics covered in this chapter: `https://github.com/markjprice/tools-skills-net10/blob/main/docs/book-links.md#chapter-16---cloud-native-development-using-aspire`.

Summary

In this chapter, you learned about:

- The key concepts around Aspire
- How to create new Aspire solutions
- How to add Aspire to existing solutions
- How Aspire solutions can be deployed

In the next chapter, you will learn about design patterns and principles.

17

Design Patterns and Principles

This chapter is about design patterns and principles that provide tried-and-tested solutions to common problems. By using this guidance, developers avoid reinventing the wheel, which saves time and effort and leads to more reusable and maintainable code. This benefit applies to all the advice in this chapter.

As you read this chapter, especially about guidelines that developers should follow, you might find yourself rolling your eyes. Many of these ideas could be categorized as "common sense." Sadly, "common sense" is less common than one might hope!

In any case, it is useful to have a checklist of good practices. And knowing all the acronyms and concepts covered in this chapter could save you from an embarrassing, "Sorry, I haven't heard of that" in an interview. Design patterns and principles create a common vocabulary among developers. When a team member refers to a pattern or principle, other developers instantly understand the approach and structure being discussed. This shared language enhances collaboration and reduces misunderstandings.

Using design patterns and principles ensures consistency across different projects. This consistency makes it easier for developers to move between projects and maintain a high standard of code quality.

> As with all things, the key is balance. Use the good practices, design patterns, and principles in this chapter to guide you, but do not fall into the trap of following them dogmatically. The reason why is rooted in the need for flexibility, contextual adaptation, and pragmatic decision-making. While the design patterns and principles in this chapter can guide your decisions and improve the quality of your solutions, software development requires balancing the unique demands of each project.

This chapter covers the following topics:

- SOLID principles
- Design patterns
- Design principles
- Algorithms and data structures

SOLID principles

One of the most common acronyms you will come across as a .NET developer is SOLID, which stands for the following principles (each of which is its own acronym):

- Single Responsibility Principle (SRP)
- Open/Closed Principle (OCP)
- Liskov Substitution Principle (LSP)
- Interface Segregation Principle (ISP)
- Dependency Inversion Principle (DIP)

The SOLID principles are primarily designed for **Object-Oriented Programming** (**OOP**), but their core concepts can be adapted and applied to other programming paradigms like functional programming or procedural programming as well.

Principles are harder to follow than rules. Rules are explicit and specific. Principles are broad and abstract. To follow a principle, you need to interpret how it applies to your situation and judge the extent to which you follow it.

Let's review each of these five principles in turn.

Single Responsibility Principle (SRP)

The **Single Responsibility Principle** (**SRP**) says that a class should have only one reason to change. This means a class should have only one job or responsibility. By adhering to the SRP, you can create more maintainable, flexible, and understandable code.

Adding multiple responsibilities to a single class leads to tight coupling between those responsibilities. This makes it hard to modify one part of the class without affecting the others, increases the risk of bugs, and makes unit testing more challenging. Unless a developer makes the effort to actively adhere to the SRP, they might overlook these costs until they become significant issues.

SRP example

Let's start with a simple example that follows the SRP, involving a user profile and its manager, as shown in the following code:

```
public class UserProfile
{
  public string UserName { get; set; }
  public string Email { get; set; }
}

public class UserProfileManager
{
  public void SaveUserProfile(UserProfile user)
  {
```

```
    // Save user profile to a database.
  }
}
```

In this example, `UserProfile` is a simple class that holds user data. The `UserProfileManager` class has a single responsibility: managing the persistence of `UserProfile` objects to a database. This design adheres to the SRP because each class is focused on a single aspect of the system.

SRP violation example

Now, let's look at an example that violates the SRP. Here is a class with multiple responsibilities, as shown in the following code:

```
public class UserOperations
{
  public void SaveUser(string userName, string email)
  {
    // Save user to a database.
  }

  public void SendEmail(string email, string message)
  {
    // Send an email to the user.
  }
}
```

In this example, the `UserOperations` class is handling both user persistence and email notifications. This design violates the SRP because the class has more than one reason to change: changes to how users are saved and changes to how emails are sent.

SRP-adhering refactoring

To make this class adhere to the SRP, we should split it into two separate classes, each with its own responsibility, as shown in the following code:

```
public class UserSaver
{
  public void SaveUser(string userName, string email)
  {
    // Save user to a database.
  }
}

public class EmailSender
{
  public void SendEmail(string email, string message)
```

```
    {
      // Send an email to the user.
    }
}
```

This separation of concerns makes the system easier to maintain and extend (and test).

SRP common mistakes

The most common mistake developers make related to the SRP is overloading a class with too many responsibilities. This typically stems from a misunderstanding or underestimation of what constitutes a "single responsibility." Developers often misinterpret "responsibility" as a broad, generic task category, such as "handling user data," which can lead them to combine different functionalities into the same class.

Violations of SRP can happen long after a class is initially written. Due to a quick fix or tight deadlines, it's tempting to add a method to an existing class because it's convenient or because the class already has similar methods. This "just add it here" mentality gradually leads to bloated classes that are difficult to maintain.

When designing a class, developers might not anticipate how requirements could change in the future. They would see their current design as satisfying the SRP because, at that moment, it does. However, as new requirements emerge, the class might change for more than one reason, thus violating SRP.

To avoid these pitfalls, it's helpful to regularly review and refactor code with SRP in mind. Asking questions like "Is this functionality integral to the class's primary responsibility?" can guide you to adhere more closely to SRP.

Additionally, embracing practices like code reviews and pair programming can help catch SRP violations early on because you're more likely to spot violations in someone else's code rather than your own. Shocking, I know!

SRP takeaways

Here are the key takeaways for the SRP:

- **Adhering to the SRP**: Ensure each class has a single responsibility, making your code more modular, understandable, and flexible. But don't go overboard. If all your classes end up with only a single method each, that's a red flag too!
- **Refactoring to the SRP**: When you identify a class that's doing too much, consider splitting it into multiple classes, each with a focused responsibility.
- **Designing for the SRP**: Start with the SRP in mind to avoid the complexities of tightly coupled systems and to make future modifications easier.

Open/Closed Principle (OCP)

The **Open/Closed Principle** (OCP) states that software entities like classes and functions should be open for extension but closed for modification. This means that you should be able to add new functionality to an entity without changing its existing code. This principle encourages a more modular and flexible design, which is easier to maintain and extend over time.

OCP example

The following code shows a basic report generation system that adheres to the OCP:

```
public abstract class ReportGenerator
{
  public abstract void GenerateReport();
}

public class PDFReportGenerator : ReportGenerator
{
  public override void GenerateReport()
  {
    // Generate a PDF report.
  }
}

public class ExcelReportGenerator : ReportGenerator
{
  public override void GenerateReport()
  {
    // Generate an Excel report.
  }
}
```

In this example, `ReportGenerator` is an abstract class that defines a contract for generating reports. `PDFReportGenerator` and `ExcelReportGenerator` are concrete implementations that extend `ReportGenerator` without modifying it, adhering to the OCP. If we want to introduce a new report format for Word, we would create another class that extends `ReportGenerator`.

OCP violation example

The following code shows a design that violates the OCP:

```
public class ReportGenerator
{
  public void GenerateReport(string reportType)
  {
    if (reportType == "PDF")
    {
      // Generate a PDF report.
    }
    else if (reportType == "Excel")
    {
      // Generate an Excel report.
    }
  }
}
```

In this example, `ReportGenerator` is a single class with a method that decides how to generate the report based on a `reportType` parameter. To add new report types, you'd have to modify the `GenerateReport` method directly, violating the OCP.

To refactor this to comply with the OCP, we should use an approach like our initial example.

OCP common mistakes

The most common mistake developers make related to the OCP is not designing their software with extension points in mind. Without abstract classes or interfaces, adding new functionality typically means modifying existing code, which violates the OCP. The lack of abstraction forces changes to the core logic of the system for every new feature or variation, increasing the risk of bugs and making the code harder to maintain.

Another mistake is not leveraging OOP features like inheritance or composition effectively. By failing to use these mechanisms, developers miss out on creating a flexible system architecture where new functionalities can be added as new classes that extend or compose existing ones. This results in a rigid design that necessitates direct modifications to existing components to introduce new behaviors.

Sometimes, to make their code as efficient as possible from the outset, developers might tightly couple components and logic. While optimization is important, premature optimization can lead to a design that doesn't leave room for easy extension without modification, violating the OCP.

Developers sometimes misunderstand the OCP as a principle that applies universally to all parts of the software, leading them to over-engineer solutions by making everything extensible. This can add unnecessary complexity to the system. The OCP should be applied mostly to the parts of the application that are most likely to change over time.

To avoid these pitfalls, you should:

- **Use abstractions:** Design with interfaces and abstract classes that define clear contracts for behavior. This allows for the implementation details to vary without needing to change the code that depends on these abstractions.
- **Plan for extension:** Identify areas of the code that are likely to change or expand in the future and design these areas to be easily extensible.
- **Embrace composition:** Consider using composition over inheritance in situations where it provides greater flexibility for extending behavior.
- **Balance flexibility and simplicity:** Apply the OCP where it makes sense, focusing on the system's parts that are most likely to change. Avoid over-engineering by not making every part of the system extensible.

By anticipating changes and designing software components to be extendable from the outset, developers can create systems that better adhere to the OCP. This approach leads to more maintainable, robust, and flexible software.

OCP takeaways

Here are the key takeaways for the OCP:

- **Adhering to the OCP:** Design your system so that new functionality can be added with new code, rather than changing existing code.
- **Strategy for the OCP:** Use abstraction and polymorphic C# language features like abstract classes or interfaces in .NET to create flexible systems that can grow and change over time.

By carefully designing classes and interfaces with the OCP in mind, developers can build .NET applications that are more resilient to change and easier to extend with new features or behaviors.

Liskov Substitution Principle (LSP)

The **Liskov Substitution Principle (LSP)** was introduced by Barbara Liskov in a 1987 conference keynote. The LSP states that objects of a superclass should be replaceable with objects of a subclass without altering the correctness of the program aka the implementation of your code. This principle encourages the design of more modular systems, where subclasses can be used in place of superclass objects seamlessly.

LSP example

Let's start with a simple example that adheres to the LSP, as shown in the following code:

```
public abstract class Shape
{
  public abstract double CalculateArea();
}

public class Rectangle : Shape
```

```
{
  public double Width { get; set; }
  public double Height { get; set; }

  public override double CalculateArea()
  {
    return Width * Height;
  }
}

public class Circle : Shape
{
  public double Radius { get; set; }

  public override double CalculateArea()
  {
    return Math.PI * Radius * Radius;
  }
}
```

In this example, `Rectangle` and `Circle` are both subclasses of `Shape`. Each implements the `CalculateArea` method according to its geometric formula. You can use objects of `Rectangle` or `Circle` interchangeably without altering the correctness of the program that utilizes these objects through a `Shape` reference. This adheres to the LSP by ensuring that subclasses are fully substitutable for their base class.

LSP violation example

The following code shows an example that violates the LSP:

```
public class Rectangle
{
  public virtual double Width { get; set; }
  public virtual double Height { get; set; }

  public double CalculateArea()
  {
    return Width * Height;
  }
}

public class Square : Rectangle
{
```

```
    public override double Width
    {
      get => base.Width;
      set => base.Width = base.Height = value;
    }

    public override double Height
    {
      get => base.Height;
      set => base.Height = base.Width = value;
    }
  }
```

At first glance, it might seem logical that a `Square` is a type of `Rectangle`. However, enforcing a `Square`'s `Width` and `Height` to always be equal violates the LSP because it changes the behavior when substituting a `Rectangle` with a `Square`. For example, setting the `Width` of a `Square` also changes its `Height`, which is not expected behavior for a `Rectangle`.

LSP-adhering refactoring

To comply with the LSP, we should avoid inheritance between `Rectangle` and `Square` where their behaviors diverge in such a fundamental way, as shown in the following code:

```
  public abstract class Shape
  {
    public abstract double CalculateArea();
  }

  public class Rectangle : Shape
  {
    public double Width { get; set; }
    public double Height { get; set; }

    public override double CalculateArea()
    {
      return Width * Height;
    }
  }

  public class Square : Shape
  {
    public double SideLength { get; set; }
```

```
    public override double CalculateArea()
    {
      return SideLength * SideLength;
    }
  }
```

In this refactored version, both `Rectangle` and `Square` inherit from a common `Shape` abstract class but are implemented separately, ensuring that objects of `Shape` can be replaced with either `Rectangle` or `Square` without affecting the program's correctness, thus adhering to the LSP.

LSP common mistakes

The most common mistake developers make related to the LSP involves creating subclasses that don't fully adhere to the behavior expected by the base class's contract. This can lead to a variety of issues where substituting a base class with a derived class alters the functioning of the program, violating the LSP.

Developers sometimes override methods in a subclass in ways that fundamentally change the expected behavior defined by the base class. This could include throwing new exceptions not declared by the base class, significantly altering the semantics of operations, or producing side effects unexpected by clients of the base class. Using deep inheritance hierarchies can also lead to violations of LSP.

Another common mistake is strengthening preconditions in a subclass. For instance, if the base class method accepts any non-null string as an input, a subclass method that imposes additional restrictions, such as that the string must also be of a certain length, violates the LSP because it's not substitutable in all contexts where the base class is expected.

To avoid these common mistakes:

- **Understand the base class contract**: Before extending a class, thoroughly understand the contract it establishes, including method behaviors, preconditions, postconditions, and invariants. One way to do this is to create the documentation for it. By forcing yourself to document the method thoroughly, you understand it better.
- **Design with substitution in mind**: When designing subclasses, always consider whether they can be used as drop-in replacements for their base classes in any context without altering the program's correctness.
- **Use composition when inheritance doesn't fit**: Sometimes, composition can be a more flexible alternative to inheritance, especially if achieving substitutability through inheritance leads to awkward or brittle designs.
- **Test substitutability**: Automated testing strategies that verify a subclass can be substituted for its base class without changing the correctness of the program can help catch violations of the LSP.

By avoiding these common mistakes and designing with LSP in mind, developers can create more robust and flexible object-oriented systems that are easier to maintain and extend.

LSP in .NET

The .NET BCL provides a variety of stream classes for reading and writing to different kinds of data sources, such as memory, files, network, and so on. Streams are a great example of the LSP in action because you can substitute one stream for another without altering the correctness of the program, provided you're using them through their common base class or interface.

To contrast, consider a hypothetical situation where a developer decides to create a specialized stream that behaves differently from the standard .NET streams. If `CustomStream's Read` method doesn't adhere to the expected behavior of a `Stream`, for example, it ignores parameters like `count` or alters the data in unexpected ways, it could break functionality that expects a standard `Stream` behavior. This would violate the LSP because `CustomStream` cannot be substituted for `Stream` without altering the correctness of the program.

LSP takeaways

Here are some key takeaways for the LSP:

- **The LSP encourages robust design**: By designing classes that can be substituted for one another without affecting the application, you create a more flexible and maintainable system.
- **Watch for inheritance misuse**: Not all "is-a" relationships are suitable for inheritance, especially if substituting a subclass alters the expected behavior.
- **Use the LSP as a guide**: The LSP can serve as a guideline for detecting problematic inheritance hierarchies that could lead to brittle and error-prone code.

Interface Segregation Principle (ISP)

The **Interface Segregation Principle (ISP)** advises that no client should be forced to depend on methods it does not use. The ISP promotes the segregation of large interfaces into smaller and more specific ones so that clients only need to know about the methods that are of interest to them. This approach leads to a more decoupled and maintainable system.

ISP example

Let's consider a document printing system where different kinds of documents can be printed, scanned, and faxed. If we apply the ISP, we would create separate interfaces for each of these functionalities, as shown in the following code:

```
public interface IPrinter
{
  void Print(Document d);
}

public interface IScanner
{
  void Scan(Document d);
}
```

```
public interface IFax
{
  void Fax(Document d);
}

public class Document
{
}

public class MultiFunctionPrinter : IPrinter, IScanner, IFax
{
  public void Print(Document d)
  {
    // Implementation
  }

  public void Scan(Document d)
  {
    // Implementation
  }

  public void Fax(Document d)
  {
    // Implementation
  }
}
```

In this example, by segregating the functionalities into separate interfaces (`IPrinter`, `IScanner`, `IFax`), we ensure that clients that only need printing capabilities are not forced to depend on the scanning or faxing methods.

ISP violation example

The following code shows an approach that violates the ISP:

```
public interface IMultiFunctionDevice
{
  void Print(Document d);
  void Scan(Document d);
  void Fax(Document d);
}
```

```
public class Document
{
}

public class MultiFunctionPrinter : IMultiFunctionDevice
{
  public void Print(Document d)
  {
    // Implementation
  }

  public void Scan(Document d)
  {
    // Implementation
  }

  public void Fax(Document d)
  {
    // Implementation
  }
}
```

In this example, there is a single interface (`IMultiFunctionDevice`) for all device functionalities. This design forces clients who might only need a subset of the functionalities, like only printing, to depend on the entire interface, including unused methods for scanning and faxing. This violates the ISP and leads to a less flexible system design.

ISP-adhering refactoring

To correct this and adhere to the ISP, we would break down the `IMultiFunctionDevice` interface into smaller interfaces, as shown in the preceding code example.

ISP common mistakes

The most common mistake developers make related to the ISP is creating large, "fat" interfaces. A "fat" interface is one that includes more methods than a client needs to perform its function.

When an interface is not segregated, client classes implementing the interface are forced to implement methods they don't need. This can clutter the class with irrelevant method implementations, making the code harder to understand and maintain.

Large interfaces increase coupling in the system. Classes may depend on parts of an interface they don't use, making the system more rigid and less flexible. Any changes to the interface, even if unrelated to a class's functionality, can force changes in that class.

The goal of interfaces is to promote reusability by defining contracts that can be implemented in various ways. However, when interfaces are not segregated, they become less reusable. Clients might need only a small part of the interface, but the presence of additional, unnecessary methods can make the interface less appealing or even unusable in some contexts.

To avoid making this common mistake, developers should:

- **Segregate interfaces based on client use cases:** Instead of a single, monolithic interface, provide several smaller interfaces that clients can implement as needed. This approach follows the ISP by ensuring that clients only depend on the methods that are necessary for them.
- **Analyze and understand client needs:** Regularly review and analyze how clients use interfaces. If different clients use different sets of methods, it's a sign that the interface should be broken down into smaller, more specific interfaces.
- **Prefer composition over inheritance:** If a class needs functionality from multiple unrelated interfaces, use composition to bring these capabilities together instead of forcing the class to implement a large interface that combines all these methods.
- **Iterate and refactor as needed:** As software evolves, so do the needs of its clients. Be prepared to refactor interfaces and their implementations to better adhere to the ISP. This may involve splitting interfaces, modifying client classes, or introducing new patterns like Adapter (covered later in this chapter) or Facade to better organize functionality.

ISP in .NET

One could argue that certain interfaces or classes in the .NET BCL might feel too broad or not perfectly segregated for specific use cases, but these are not clear-cut violations of the ISP. Instead, they reflect the challenges of designing a highly general and versatile framework intended to cover a wide array of programming needs.

For example, the `Stream` class is an abstract base class for representing streams, which includes methods for reading, writing, seeking, and more. In some cases, not all operations are supported. For example, a `FileStream` supports seeking, but a `NetworkStream` does not. While `Stream` provides a mechanism to check capabilities, like `CanRead`, `CanWrite`, and `CanSeek`, one could argue that having separate interfaces for readable, writable, and seekable streams might more strictly adhere to the ISP for cases where a type of stream only needs to be consumed in a specific manner. However, this design is a trade-off chosen for flexibility and usability across a wide range of stream types and operations.

In large, general-purpose libraries like the .NET BCL, certain design choices are made to balance usability, performance, and versatility across a vast number of use cases. Additionally, backward compatibility concerns can limit how much existing designs can be changed, even when newer principles like the ISP become more widely recognized and adopted.

While it's beneficial to think about and learn from these design choices, it's also important to recognize the context and constraints under which they were made. In practice, the .NET BCL does an excellent job of providing a broad and usable set of functionalities, and any deviations from design principles often reflect necessary compromises rather than oversights. Just because the .NET team violates a SOLID principle, it does not make that principle useless, nor does it make their decision to violate it wrong.

ISP takeaways

Here are some key takeaways:

- **Decoupling:** The ISP helps in decoupling the system by ensuring that classes do not depend on interfaces they do not use.
- **Flexibility and maintainability:** By applying the ISP, systems become more flexible and maintainable, as changes to one part of the system are less likely to require changes to unrelated parts.
- **Use of interfaces:** Proper use of interfaces is crucial in .NET and other object-oriented systems to achieve the benefits of the ISP. It promotes cleaner, more modular code and a more robust system architecture.

Dependency Inversion Principle (DIP)

The **Dependency Inversion Principle (DIP)** aims to reduce dependencies among high-level modules and low-level modules by introducing an abstraction layer. Specifically, the DIP states two key things:

- High-level modules should not depend on low-level modules. Both should depend on abstractions.
- Abstractions should not depend upon details. Details should depend upon abstractions.

This principle encourages decoupling in software architecture, which leads to more maintainable and flexible code.

DIP example

Let's suppose that you have a high-level module, `CustomerService`, that performs operations on customer data using a lot of abstractions and little implementation and a low-level module, `CustomerRepository`, that deals with database access, as shown in the following code:

```
public interface ICustomerRepository
{
  void Add(Customer customer);
  // Other data access methods.
}

public class CustomerRepository : ICustomerRepository
{
  public void Add(Customer customer)
  {
    // Implementation details for adding customer
  }
}

public class CustomerService
{
```

```
    private readonly ICustomerRepository _customerRepository;

    public CustomerService(ICustomerRepository customerRepository)
    {
      _customerRepository = customerRepository;
    }

    public void RegisterCustomer(Customer customer)
    {
      _customerRepository.Add(customer);
      // Additional high-level operations
    }
}
```

In this example, both `CustomerService` (a high-level module) and `CustomerRepository` (a low-level module) depend on the `ICustomerRepository` abstraction. This setup follows the DIP by decoupling the service from the specifics of data access.

DIP violation example

Here's how you might structure the code without adhering to the DIP:

```
public class CustomerRepository
{
  public void Add(Customer customer)
  {
    // Implementation details for adding customer
  }
}

public class CustomerService
{
  private readonly CustomerRepository _customerRepository
    = new CustomerRepository();

  public void RegisterCustomer(Customer customer)
  {
    _customerRepository.Add(customer);
    // Additional high-level operations
  }
}
```

In this example, `CustomerService` directly depends on the concrete `CustomerRepository`. This violates the DIP because the high-level module (`CustomerService`) is directly dependent on a low-level module (`CustomerRepository`) rather than an abstraction. Changing the data access logic or substituting a different data access mechanism would require changes to the `CustomerService` class, making the code less flexible and more tightly coupled.

DIP common mistakes

The most common mistake developers make related to the DIP is to directly instantiate dependencies within a class instead of injecting them through constructors or properties. This hardcodes specific implementations into the class, violating the DIP. It makes the code less flexible and more difficult to modify or test because the class is tightly coupled to its dependencies.

Dependency Injection (**DI**) is a technique for complying with the DIP by passing dependencies from outside rather than creating them inside the class. You learned about DI in *Chapter 10, Dependency Injection, Containers, and Service Lifetime*. However, simply using a DI framework doesn't guarantee compliance with the DIP if the dependencies injected are still concrete classes rather than abstractions. The essence of the DIP is in the use of abstractions, not just in the mechanism of injection.

The DIP is often applied within specific layers of an application but ignored when it comes to the interaction between different layers, for example, UI, business logic, and data access. Each layer should depend on abstractions and not on the concrete implementations of another layer to promote true decoupling.

A tricky balance must be struck when applying the DIP. Under-abstracting, or not creating sufficient abstractions, leaves the code tightly coupled. Conversely, over-abstracting, or creating too many unnecessary interfaces and abstract classes, can lead to a bloated and overly complex codebase where the benefit of decoupling is lost to the overhead of managing numerous abstractions.

Follow these guidelines to avoid these mistakes:

- **Consistently use abstractions**: Always depend on interfaces or abstract classes rather than concrete implementations. This includes the design of class libraries, APIs, and even the internal components of an application.
- **Apply the DIP thoughtfully across the application**: Ensure that DIP is applied not just within layers but also across different layers of the application architecture.
- **Use dependency injection wisely**: Utilize DI frameworks to manage dependencies, but always inject abstractions rather than concrete instances.
- **Find the right level of abstraction**: Strive for a balance where each abstraction brings genuine flexibility and decoupling to the design without unnecessary complexity.

DIP takeaways

Here are some key takeaways:

- **Decoupling through abstraction**: The DIP emphasizes using interfaces or abstract classes to decouple high-level business logic from low-level implementation details.

- **Flexibility and maintainability**: By adhering to the DIP, software systems become more flexible and easier to maintain. Changes in low-level modules (like switching from a relational database to a NoSQL database for data access) require minimal to no changes in high-level modules.
- **Testability**: Following the DIP also enhances testability, as high-level modules can be easily tested by mocking the abstract interfaces they depend on, rather than dealing with concrete implementations of lower-level modules.

Implementing the DIP and the other SOLID principles effectively in .NET applications leads to cleaner, more modular code that is easier to extend, maintain, and test.

Design patterns

Design patterns are like templates for solving common problems in software design. They're not finished designs you can transform directly into code, but guidelines you can follow to solve problems in a variety of contexts. They're solutions to problems that software developers have found themselves facing repeatedly.

There are three major kinds of design patterns: creational, structural, and behavioral:

- **Creational patterns** are about object creation mechanisms, in a manner suitable to the situation. The basic form of object creation could result in design problems or added complexity to the design because the developer must manually create every instance using the `new` keyword and then compose complex objects themselves in ways that might not be expected. Creational design patterns solve this problem by controlling this object creation. Examples include the Singleton, Factory Method, Abstract Factory, Builder, and Prototype patterns.
- **Structural patterns** are about class and object composition. They help ensure that if one part of a system changes, the entire system doesn't need to do the same. They help to create a structure that promotes flexibility. Examples include the Adapter, Bridge, Composite, Decorator, Facade, Flyweight, and Proxy patterns.
- **Behavioral patterns** are about identifying common communication patterns between objects and providing implementations of them. These patterns increase flexibility in carrying out communication. Examples include the Observer, Mediator, Iterator, Strategy, Command, Memento, State, Visitor, Chain of Responsibility, and Template Method patterns.

You should use design patterns because they can speed up the development process by providing tested, proven development solutions. Effective software design requires considering issues that may not become visible until later in the implementation. Reusing design patterns helps to prevent subtle issues that can cause major problems later and improves code readability for coders and architects familiar with the patterns.

> **Good practice:** Do not force patterns onto your problems. Patterns are solutions to problems, not solutions looking for a problem. They should be applied wisely. Overusing them can lead to code that's harder to understand and maintain.

Before we look at design patterns in more detail, let's review a summary of common design patterns, including a brief description, and examples of their implementation in the .NET Base Class Library, ASP.NET Core, or common third-party libraries.

First, creational design patterns, as shown in *Table 17.1*:

Design Pattern	Brief Description	.NET BCL / ASP.NET Core / Third-Party Types Examples
Singleton	Ensures a class has only one instance and provides a global point of access to it.	`SqlConnection` (BCL, for connection pooling), `ILogger` in ASP.NET Core (when configured as singleton)
Factory Method	Defines an interface for creating an object but allows subclasses to decide which class to instantiate.	`WebClient` (BCL), `HttpClientFactory` (ASP.NET Core)
Abstract Factory	Provides an interface for creating families of related or dependent objects without specifying their concrete classes.	`DbProviderFactory` (BCL), `ILoggerFactory` (ASP.NET Core)
Builder	Separates the construction of a complex object from its representation, allowing the same construction process to create various representations.	`StringBuilder` (BCL), `WebHostBuilder` (ASP.NET Core)
Prototype	Creates new objects by copying an existing object, known as the prototype.	`ICloneable` (BCL)

Table 17.1: Creational design patterns, concepts, and usage in .NET

Next, structural design patterns, as shown in *Table 17.2*:

Design Pattern	Brief Description	.NET BCL / ASP.NET Core / Third-Party Types Examples
Adapter	Allows incompatible interfaces to work together. Uses a wrapper to translate calls to an interface into a different interface.	`StreamAdapter` (BCL), various ORM adapters like Dapper
Bridge	Decouples an abstraction from its implementation, allowing the two to vary independently.	`DbConnection` (BCL), `ILogger` (ASP.NET Core)
Composite	Composes objects into tree structures to represent part-whole hierarchies, allowing clients to treat individual objects and compositions uniformly.	`DirectoryInfo` (BCL), `IApplicationBuilder` (ASP.NET Core)

Decorator	Allows behavior to be added to an individual object, either statically or dynamically, without affecting the behavior of other objects from the same class.	Stream (BCL, e.g., FileStream, MemoryStream), Middleware in ASP.NET Core
Façade	Provides a simplified interface to a complex subsystem.	HttpClient (BCL), WebClient (BCL)
Flyweight	Minimizes memory usage or computational expenses by sharing as much as possible with similar objects.	String.Intern (BCL)
Proxy	Provides a surrogate or placeholder for another object to control access to it.	WCF Proxy (BCL), IActionResult in ASP.NET Core for action result proxies

Table 17.2: Structural design patterns, concepts, and usage in .NET

Finally, behavioral design patterns, as shown in *Table 17.3*:

Design Pattern	**Brief Description**	**.NET BCL / ASP.NET Core / Third-Party Types Examples**
Observer	Defines a dependency between objects so that when one object changes state, all its dependents are notified and updated automatically.	IObservable<T> / IObserver<T> (BCL), INotifyPropertyChanged (BCL)
Mediator	Reduces coupling between classes communicating with each other by having them communicate indirectly through a mediator object.	IMediator in MediatR (Third-party)
Iterator	Provides a way to access the elements of an aggregate object sequentially without exposing its underlying representation.	IEnumerable / IEnumerator (BCL)
Strategy	Defines a family of algorithms, encapsulates each one, and makes them interchangeable. Strategy lets the algorithm vary independently from clients that use it.	IComparer / IComparable (BCL)
Command	Encapsulates a request as an object, thereby allowing the parameterization of clients with queues, requests, and operations.	ICommand in WPF (BCL), CommandHandler in MediatR
Memento	Without violating encapsulation, it captures and externalizes an object's internal state so that the object can be returned to this state later.	DataContractSerializer (BCL) for state snapshot

State	Allows an object to alter its behavior when its internal state changes. The object will appear to change its class.	`StateServerMode` in ASP.NET (BCL)
Visitor	Represents an operation to be performed on elements of an object structure. Visitor lets a new operation be defined without changing the classes of the elements on which it operates.	`ExpressionVisitor` (BCL)
Chain of Responsibility	Passes the request along a chain of handlers. Upon receiving the request, each handler decides either to process the request or to pass it to the next handler in the chain.	`DelegatingHandler` in `HttpClient` (ASP.NET Core), Middleware in ASP.NET Core
Template Method	Defines the skeleton of an algorithm in the superclass but lets subclasses override specific steps of the algorithm without changing its structure.	`Stream` (BCL, with methods like `Read` and `Write` that subclasses implement), `ControllerBase` in ASP.NET Core (with action methods overridden in derived controllers)

Table 17.3: Behavioral design patterns, concepts, and usage in .NET

I have written detailed explanations of all the design patterns. They are available online in the GitHub repository for this book at the following link: `https://github.com/markjprice/tools-skills-net10/blob/main/docs/design-patterns/readme.md`. One design pattern from each category has been included in the print book so that you can get used to the standard structure I have used to describe each pattern.

Creational patterns

The first set of design patterns that programmers learn are usually creational patterns because you can't do anything without first creating one or more objects. Instead of your program directly instantiating objects, creational patterns provide a way to encapsulate this task within the program, making it more modular, flexible, and maintainable. They abstract the instantiation process, making the system independent of how its objects are created, composed, and represented.

The full set of creational patterns are available online in the GitHub repository at the following link: `https://github.com/markjprice/tools-skills-net10/blob/main/docs/design-patterns/creational.md`.

As an example of a creational design pattern to include in the print book, I chose Builder because it is used to configure ASP.NET Core projects, which are the most common type of .NET project that you will work with.

Builder pattern

The core idea of the **Builder** pattern is to separate the construction of a complex object from its representation, allowing the same construction process to create different representations. This is especially useful in .NET when dealing with objects that have numerous properties, some of which may be optional.

The Builder pattern is beneficial when:

- You want to avoid a constructor with too many parameters
- You have an object that requires intricate initialization
- You want to provide a clear API for constructing complex objects

Typically, the Builder pattern involves the following components:

- **Builder**: An abstract interface for creating parts of an object.
- **Concrete Builder**: Implements the Builder interface, constructs and assembles parts of the product by implementing the Builder interface. Defines and keeps track of the representation it creates.
- **Director**: Constructs an object using the Builder interface.
- **Product**: The object being built.

Builder pattern example

Let's walk through an example of the Builder pattern in .NET, where we construct a complex `UserProfile` object, as shown in the following code:

```
public class UserProfile
{
  public string FirstName { get; set; }
  public string LastName { get; set; }
  public int Age { get; set; }
  public string Email { get; set; }
  public string Address { get; set; }
}
```

First, you create the Builder Interface, with methods to set each of the Product's properties, and a `Build` method to return the constructed Product, as shown in the following code:

```
public interface IUserProfileBuilder
{
  IUserProfileBuilder SetFirstName(string firstName);
  IUserProfileBuilder SetLastName(string lastName);
  IUserProfileBuilder SetAge(int age);
  IUserProfileBuilder SetEmail(string email);
  IUserProfileBuilder SetAddress(string address);
  UserProfile Build();
}
```

Next, you implement the Concrete Builder, as shown in the following partial code:

```
public class UserProfileBuilder : IUserProfileBuilder
{
  private UserProfile _userProfile = new UserProfile();

  public IUserProfileBuilder SetFirstName(string firstName)
  {
    _userProfile.FirstName = firstName;
    return this;
  }

  public IUserProfileBuilder SetLastName(string lastName)
  {
    _userProfile.LastName = lastName;
    return this;
  }

  public IUserProfileBuilder SetAge(int age)
  {
    _userProfile.Age = age;
    return this;
  }

  ...

  public UserProfile Build()
  {
    return _userProfile;
  }
}
```

Then, you could utilize the Builder, as shown in the following code:

```
UserProfile userProfile = new UserProfileBuilder()
  .SetFirstName("John")
  .SetLastName("Doe")
  .SetAge(30)
  .SetEmail("john.doe@example.com")
  .SetAddress("123 Main St")
  .Build();
```

In this example, `UserProfileBuilder` serves as the Concrete Builder that implements the `IUserProfileBuilder` interface. It provides a fluent API for setting properties of `UserProfile`, allowing for clear and flexible object creation. The `Build` method finalizes the construction process and returns the resulting `UserProfile` object.

This pattern is common in .NET, allowing for clean, maintainable code when constructing complex objects. It avoids the need for overloaded constructors or objects with partially initialized states, making your code more intuitive and less prone to errors.

Builder pattern in ASP.NET Core and other examples

The Builder pattern is frequently seen in ASP.NET Core and many third-party libraries utilized by .NET developers. It's commonly used to set up and configure services, middleware, and applications through fluent APIs.

In ASP.NET Core, the `WebHostBuilder` and `HostBuilder` are used to configure and launch an ASP.NET Core application. These builders allow for the fluent configuration of various aspects, such as server settings, logging, dependency injection services, and more.

ASP.NET Core also uses the Builder pattern for configuring services within the application's dependency injection container. `IServiceCollection` uses builder pattern-like methods like `AddControllersWithViews` and `AddRazorPages` to register services for the application.

Entity Framework Core utilizes the Builder pattern extensively for model configuration in the `OnModelCreating` method of the `DbContext`. This approach allows for fluent configuration of entities, relationships, and database mappings.

Serilog, a widely used logging library, also uses the Builder pattern to configure logging options through a fluent API.

Structural design patterns

Structural design patterns are about organizing different classes and objects to form larger structures and provide new functionality. The focus is on simplifying the design by identifying a simple way to realize relationships among entities. They help ensure that if one part of a system changes, the entire system doesn't need to do the same, thus promoting reusability and modularity.

> The full set of structural patterns are available online in the GitHub repository at the following link: `https://github.com/markjprice/tools-skills-net8/blob/main/docs/design-patterns/structural.md`.

As an example of a structural design pattern, I chose Adapter because it is used to configure ASP.NET Core middleware.

Adapter a.k.a. the Wrapper pattern

The **Adapter pattern** allows objects with incompatible interfaces to collaborate. It's like having two different electronic devices with different power plugs but using an adapter to make one fit into the other's socket, allowing them to work together seamlessly.

The Adapter pattern is used when you want an existing class to work with another class that has an incompatible interface. This situation often arises in software development when you need to integrate new features or components that weren't initially designed to work with your existing codebase.

The Adapter pattern involves three key components:

- **Target**: The interface that the client expects or uses
- **Adaptee**: The class that needs to be adapted to fit the target interface
- **Adapter**: The class that implements the target interface and translates calls to the adaptee

Adapter pattern example

Let's imagine that you're working on a system that processes text data. You have an existing system component that expects data in a structured format defined by an `ITextProcessor` interface, but you're now integrating a new component that has a valuable text analytics capability, only it presents a completely different interface, `IAdvancedTextAnalytics`.

You might define these interfaces and classes, as shown in the following code:

```
public interface ITextProcessor
{
  void ProcessText(string text);
}

public class TextProcessor : ITextProcessor
{
  public void ProcessText(string text)
  {
    // Implementation for processing text in a basic way.
    WriteLine($"Processing text: {text}");
  }
}

public interface IAdvancedTextAnalytics
{
  void AnalyzeTextComplexity(string text);
  void FindKeyPhrases(string text);
}

public class AdvancedTextAnalytics : IAdvancedTextAnalytics
```

```
{
  public void AnalyzeTextComplexity(string text)
  {
    // Imagine some complex text analysis here.
    WriteLine($"Analyzing text complexity: {text}");
  }

  public void FindKeyPhrases(string text)
  {
    // And some advanced key phrase detection here.
    WriteLine($"Finding key phrases in: {text}");
  }
}
```

To use the Adapter design pattern, we must define an Adapter that makes `AdvancedTextAnalytics` compatible with `ITextProcessor`, as shown in the following code:

```
public class TextAnalyticsAdapter : ITextProcessor
{
  private readonly IAdvancedTextAnalytics _advancedTextAnalytics;

  public TextAnalyticsAdapter(IAdvancedTextAnalytics advancedTextAnalytics)
  {
    _advancedTextAnalytics = advancedTextAnalytics;
  }

  public void ProcessText(string text)
  {
    // Adapter translates the method call to the new system.
    _advancedTextAnalytics.AnalyzeTextComplexity(text);
    _advancedTextAnalytics.FindKeyPhrases(text);
  }
}
```

And finally, you can use this adapter in your application, as shown in the following code:

```
ITextProcessor processor = new TextProcessor();
processor.ProcessText("Hello, world!");

// Now let's use the advanced analytics via the adapter.
IAdvancedTextAnalytics analytics = new AdvancedTextAnalytics();
ITextProcessor advancedProcessor = new TextAnalyticsAdapter(analytics);
advancedProcessor.ProcessText("Exploring the Adapter pattern in .NET");
```

In this example, `TextAnalyticsAdapter` allows you to use `AdvancedTextAnalytics` in places where `ITextProcessor` is expected, without altering the original classes. This approach keeps your code flexible and open for extension, adhering to SOLID design principles while accommodating new requirements or third-party components.

Adapter pattern ASP.NET Core example

The Adapter pattern is used in ASP.NET Core middleware to allow them to interact with each other seamlessly despite having different interfaces. In modern middleware, the `Invoke` or `InvokeAsync` methods are called with the `HttpContext` and perform the middleware's logic.

To integrate legacy middleware that does not conform to the standard middleware signature, you could implement the Adapter pattern. This pattern is especially useful for maintaining compatibility and reusability without modifying existing codebases.

Behavioral design patterns

Behavioral design patterns manage complex interactions and communication between objects and classes in a system. They are all about efficient communication and the assignment of responsibilities between objects. They help in defining not just how objects are structured or created, but how they behave and operate together.

> The full set of behavioral patterns are available online in the GitHub repository at the following link: `https://github.com/markjprice/tools-skills-net8/blob/main/docs/design-patterns/behavioral.md`.

As an example of a behavioral design pattern, I chose Template Method because it is used in many .NET BCL types like `Stream` and `ControllerBase`.

Template Method pattern

The Template Method pattern defines the skeleton of an algorithm in the superclass but allows its subclasses to override specific steps of the algorithm without changing its structure. This pattern is particularly useful when multiple classes share a common method but have different implementations of some steps in that method. By using the Template Method pattern, you can encapsulate the invariant parts of the algorithm in a base class and let subclasses implement the variant parts.

Components of the Template Method pattern:

- **Template:** Defines abstract methods for the steps that need to be customized and implements the template method defining the skeleton of an algorithm. The Template Method calls the abstract methods, as well as other methods.
- **Concrete classes:** Implements the abstract methods to complete the algorithm's specific steps.

Template Method pattern example

Let's illustrate the Template Method pattern with an example of cooking recipes. Suppose we have a general process for cooking a meal, but the details vary depending on the specific meal being prepared.

First, define the abstract class with the template method, as shown in the following code:

```
public abstract class CookingRecipe
{
  // Template method.
  public void CookMeal()
  {
    PrepareIngredients();
    Cook();
    Serve();
  }

  protected abstract void PrepareIngredients();
  protected abstract void Cook();

  // Common method used by all subclasses.
  protected void Serve()
  {
    WriteLine("Serving the meal.");
  }
}
```

Next, implement concrete classes for specific meals, as shown in the following code:

```
public class PastaRecipe : CookingRecipe
{
  protected override void PrepareIngredients()
  {
    WriteLine("Preparing pasta and sauce.");
  }

  protected override void Cook()
  {
    WriteLine("Cooking pasta in boiling water.");
  }
}

public class SaladRecipe : CookingRecipe
{
  protected override void PrepareIngredients()
  {
    WriteLine("Chopping vegetables.");
  }
```

```
    protected override void Cook()
    {
      WriteLine("Mixing vegetables with dressing.");
    }
  }
```

Finally, demonstrate the Template Method in action, as shown in the following code:

```
CookingRecipe pasta = new PastaRecipe();
pasta.CookMeal();

CookingRecipe salad = new SaladRecipe();
salad.CookMeal();
```

In this example, `CookingRecipe` defines the template method `CookMeal()` that outlines the steps for cooking a meal. The steps `PrepareIngredients()` and `Cook()` are declared as abstract methods, forcing subclasses (`PastaRecipe` and `SaladRecipe`) to provide their own implementations for these steps. The `Serve()` method is a concrete implementation within the abstract class because it's common across all subclasses.

This setup allows the subclasses to alter parts of the algorithm by overriding certain steps without changing the algorithm's structure defined by the template method. The Template Method pattern is beneficial for enforcing a certain structure while allowing flexibility in the details of the execution.

Template Method pattern examples in .NET

In the .NET ecosystem, the Template Method pattern is frequently used. For example, the `Task` and `Task<TResult>` classes use the Template Method to define the basic structure for asynchronous operations, while derived classes or instances override specific methods to provide the actual implementation of the task.

The `Stream` class defines the template methods for reading, writing, and seeking operations. Derived classes like `FileStream`, `MemoryStream`, and `NetworkStream` provide specific implementations for these operations.

The `Controller` and `ControllerBase` classes in ASP.NET Core provide template methods for handling HTTP requests. Methods can be overridden to customize the behavior of controllers.

The `TagHelper` class uses the Template Method pattern to allow developers to define custom tag helpers in Razor views. Methods like `Process` can be overridden to implement custom behavior for HTML elements.

Design principles

Like all the design patterns and principles in this chapter, the design principles we will review next are guidelines to help you write better, more maintainable, and more efficient code.

The common principles we will review in this section are shown in the following list:

- Don't Repeat Yourself (DRY)
- Keep It Simple, Stupid (KISS)
- You Ain't Gonna Need It (YAGNI)
- Law of Demeter (LoD) or the principle of least knowledge
- Composition over Inheritance
- Principle of least astonishment

DRY

The **Don't Repeat Yourself (DRY)** principle is a fundamental concept in software development that emphasizes the importance of avoiding duplication in code. This principle encourages reducing the repetition of software patterns by abstracting out common functionality into a single place, thus enhancing the maintainability, readability, and scalability of code.

Here are some key takeaways about DRY:

- **Avoid repetition:** Always look for patterns or logic that are repeated and abstract them into their methods or classes.
- **Improve maintainability:** By adhering to DRY, you make your code more maintainable since changes in the future will likely only need to be made in a single place.
- **Enhance readability:** DRY code is generally more readable and understandable, as it avoids the clutter of repeated logic, making the unique parts of each method or class stand out more.

Following the DRY principle is a key part of writing clean, efficient, and easy-to-maintain code in .NET and any other programming environment.

KISS

The **Keep It Simple, Stupid (KISS)** principle is a design guideline emphasizing the value of simplicity in design and implementation. In software development, adhering to KISS means creating solutions that are straightforward, easy to understand, and devoid of unnecessary complexity. This principle encourages developers to strive for simplicity in their code, making it more readable, maintainable, and less prone to errors.

Here are some key takeaways about KISS:

- **Strive for simplicity:** Aim to solve problems with the simplest solutions rather than overcomplicating things with premature optimizations or unnecessary features.
- **Improve code quality:** Simpler code is usually more reliable and easier to test, reducing the likelihood of bugs.
- **Enhance maintainability:** Simple, straightforward code is easier to understand and maintain, saving time and effort in the long run.

Keeping code simple, as advocated by the KISS principle, is not about choosing the most basic or naive implementation but about finding the most straightforward and effective solution for the problem at hand.

YAGNI

The **You Ain't Gonna Need It (YAGNI)** principle is a reminder to developers not to add functionality until it is necessary. This **Agile** development principle emphasizes avoiding spending time on features or code that are not required for the current needs of the project, based on the assumption that future requirements may not materialize as expected. Following YAGNI can lead to faster development times and reduce the complexity of a project by keeping the codebase as simple and streamlined as possible.

Here are some key takeaways about YAGNI:

- **Focus on the present:** Implement features only when they are immediately needed, not because they might be needed in the future.
- **Reduce waste:** By not spending time on unneeded functionality, you can focus resources on features that provide actual value.
- **Simplify development:** Adhering to YAGNI keeps the project simpler and more manageable, making it easier to understand, maintain, and extend.

Following YAGNI helps to avoid over-engineering and keeps the development process lean and focused on delivering value efficiently. In .NET and other programming environments, this principle encourages more sustainable and pragmatic software development practices.

Law of Demeter

The **Law of Demeter (LoD)**, also known as the **principle of least knowledge**, is a guideline for designing object-oriented systems. It suggests that a module should only have knowledge of and talk directly to closely related modules. In practice, this means an object should avoid calling methods on a returned object (the result of another call), which leads to tightly coupled code. The LoD can be summarized as "only talk to your immediate friends."

LoD example

Suppose you have a `BankAccount` class and a `Customer` class. Instead of having the customer access the bank account's balance directly, you provide a method within the `Customer` class to get the balance, adhering to the LoD, as shown in the following code:

```
public class BankAccount
{
  public decimal Balance { get; private set; }

  public BankAccount(decimal initialBalance)
  {
    Balance = initialBalance;
  }

  public decimal GetBalance()
  {
    return Balance;
```

```
    }
}

public class Customer
{
    private BankAccount account;

    public Customer(BankAccount account)
    {
        this.account = account;
    }

    public decimal CheckAccountBalance()
    {
        return account.GetBalance();
    }
}
```

In this example, the `Customer` class talks directly to its immediate friend, the `BankAccount`, and does not navigate its properties or call methods further than one level deep.

Now, consider an example where a `Customer` directly accesses the account's balance property, potentially through multiple levels of object navigation, as shown in the following code:

```
public class Wallet
{
    public BankAccount Account { get; set; }
}

public class Customer
{
    public Wallet Wallet { get; set; }

    public decimal GetAccountBalance()
    {
        // Directly accessing the BankAccount's Balance property violates LoD
        return Wallet.Account.Balance;
    }
}
```

In this example, the `Customer` class violates the LoD by accessing the `BankAccount` through the `Wallet` using `Wallet.Account.Balance`. This creates a dependency not just on the `Wallet` but also on the `BankAccount` and its internal `Balance` property, leading to tighter coupling and less maintainable code.

LoD takeaways

Here are some key takeaways about the LoD:

- **Promote loose coupling**: Adhering to the LoD can lead to a design that promotes loose coupling and enhances module independence.
- **Enhance maintainability**: By limiting an object's knowledge and interaction to its close associates, you make the overall system easier to maintain, since changes in distant modules are less likely to require changes in unrelated modules.
- **Improve modularity**: The LoD encourages a more modular design by discouraging wide-reaching interactions between components, leading to a system that's easier to understand, debug, and extend.

Composition over Inheritance

Composition over Inheritance is a design principle guiding software developers to achieve code reuse by composing objects rather than inheriting from a base or parent class. This approach leads to more flexible, maintainable, and scalable systems, as it favors a loosely coupled architecture where components can be mixed and matched as needed without being bound by a rigid inheritance hierarchy.

Composition over Inheritance example

Suppose you have various services in your application, and each needs logging capability. Instead of inheriting from a base class that provides logging, you can compose each service with a logging component, as shown in the following code:

```
public interface ILogger
{
  void Log(string message);
}

public class ConsoleLogger : ILogger
{
  public void Log(string message)
  {
    Console.WriteLine(message);
  }
}

public class FileLogger : ILogger
{
  public void Log(string message)
  {
    // Write message to a file
  }
```

```
}

public class OrderService
{
  private readonly ILogger _logger;

  public OrderService(ILogger logger)
  {
    _logger = logger;
  }

  public void ProcessOrder()
  {
    _logger.Log("Processing order");
    // Order processing logic
  }
}
```

In this example, `OrderService` is composed with an `ILogger` instance, allowing flexible logging. You can easily switch between `ConsoleLogger`, `FileLogger`, or any other `ILogger` implementation without changing the `OrderService`'s code.

Composition over Inheritance violating example

Compare the preceding example to one using inheritance, as shown in the following code:

```
public abstract class BaseService
{
  protected void Log(string message)
  {
    Console.WriteLine(message);
  }
}

public class OrderService : BaseService
{
  public void ProcessOrder()
  {
    Log("Processing order");
    // Order processing logic.
  }
}
```

`OrderService` inherits from `BaseService` to gain logging functionality. This design tightly couples `OrderService` to `BaseService`, making it less flexible. For example, changing the logging mechanism would affect all subclasses of `BaseService`.

Composition over Inheritance takeaways

Here are some key takeaways for the principle of Composition over Inheritance:

- **Flexibility**: Composition allows for more flexible designs where behavior can be easily changed or extended by composing objects with different implementations of their components.
- **Maintainability**: Systems designed with composition are often easier to maintain, as changes to a component's behavior do not ripple through an inheritance chain.
- **Reusability**: Components in a composition-based design can be reused across different parts of an application without the need for a shared inheritance hierarchy.

Adopting composition over inheritance encourages a design that is more aligned with the principles of modularity and separation of concerns, leading to software that is easier to understand, extend, and maintain.

Principle of Least Astonishment

The **Principle of Least Astonishment (PoLA)**, also known as the **Principle of Least Surprise**, advises that software should behave in a way that is least surprising to its users or developers. This principle impacts user interface design, software functionality, and API design, aiming to ensure that code and features behave in expected ways to minimize confusion and errors.

PoLA example

Here's an example of applying the PoLA to make intuitive method names, as shown in the following code:

```
public class EmailService
{
  public void SendEmail(string toAddress, string subject, string body)
  {
    // Logic to send an email.
  }
}
```

In this example, the `SendEmail` method clearly communicates its purpose through its name and parameters. Developers using this class would have a clear understanding of what the method does and what is expected without needing to delve into its implementation.

The following code shows an example of confusing or misleading method names:

```
public class DataProcessor
{
  public void ProcessData(int mode)
  {
    if (mode == 1)
    {
      // Load data.
    }
    else if (mode == 2)
    {
      // Save data.
    }
  }
}
```

The `ProcessData` method and its use of a magic number (`mode`) to dictate behavior can be confusing. It's not clear from the method signature what mode refers to or what `ProcessData` does specifically. This can lead to errors or misunderstandings for developers unfamiliar with the method's implementation, violating the PoLA.

To enhance compliance with the PoLA and make the `DataProcessor` class less surprising, we could define an `enum` for the mode, or split the `ProcessData` method into two better-named methods, as shown in the following code:

```
public enum DataMode
{
  Load,
  Save
}

public class DataProcessor
{
  public void LoadData()
  {
    // Load data.
  }

  public void SaveData()
  {
    // Save data.
  }
}
```

In the improved example, `LoadData` and `SaveData` methods are explicitly named for their function, eliminating ambiguity and adhering to the PoLA. The use of an enumeration (`DataMode`) could further clarify intentions if modes are necessary, making the API's behavior more predictable and understandable.

PoLA takeaways

Here are some key takeaways for the PoLA:

- **Use clear naming conventions**: Use intuitive and descriptive names for methods, classes, and variables to clearly convey their purpose and behavior.
- **Avoid magic numbers**: Replace magic numbers with named constants or enums to make code intentions explicit.
- **Documentation**: When the given behavior might not be immediately obvious, provide clear documentation to minimize surprises.

Following the PoLA helps create .NET applications and libraries that are more intuitive and less error-prone, enhancing the developer experience and software quality.

Now let's wrap up this chapter with a brief section about common algorithms and data structures.

Algorithms and data structures

.NET is a versatile framework with rich libraries that abstract away the need to implement common algorithms and data structures from scratch. However, understanding them and knowing when to apply them is what separates good developers from great ones.

The common algorithms and data structures can be grouped into the following categories:

- Sorting algorithms
- Searching algorithms
- Data structure algorithms
- Hashing algorithms
- Recursive algorithms

Algorithms and data structures are often used as brain-trainers for coding interviews and can be useful for real-world problem solving. For a .NET developer, knowing these algorithms is about showing you've got a solid foundation in computer science concepts, not just language-specific skills. You show that although you use the built-on ones, that you could build your own if needed.

When preparing for interviews, don't just memorize algorithms; understand their mechanics and where they can be applied. Practice coding them in C# to get comfortable with the syntax and .NET library methods that can simplify your implementations.

Let's break down the most common algorithms.

Sorting algorithms

Sorting algorithms are the code and caffeine (a programmer's bread and butter) of interview questions. The most important to learn are:

- **QuickSort**, which is like that efficient friend who divides and conquers tasks. Average Time Complexity: O(n log n). Worst Time Complexity: $O(n^2)$ (when the pivot choice is poor, e.g. already sorted input without randomization). QuickSort works by selecting a pivot and partitioning the array into elements less than and greater than the pivot, then recursively sorting the subarrays. In the average case, the pivot divides the array evenly → about log n levels of recursion, each handling n elements → O(n log n). In the worst case (e.g., sorted data + bad pivot), the recursion degenerates into n levels with n work each → $O(n^2)$.
- **MergeSort**, which is about breaking things down into manageable chunks and then combining them. Time Complexity: O(n log n). Space Complexity: O(n). MergeSort recursively splits the array in half until you have single elements, then merges them back in sorted order. Splitting takes O(log n) levels (because we halve each time). Merging at each level takes O(n) work. So total = O(n log n). Needs O(n) extra space for the temporary arrays used in merging.
- **BubbleSort**, which is the straightforward one, but not the most time-efficient for large datasets. It works by repeatedly stepping through the list, comparing adjacent pairs and swapping them if they are in the wrong order, continuing this process until the list is sorted. Average and Worst Time Complexity: $O(n^2)$. Best Time Complexity: O(n) (when already sorted, using an optimized version with a swapped-flag). Space Complexity: O(1). BubbleSort repeatedly compares adjacent elements and swaps them if they're out of order. It does roughly n passes, and in each pass compares up to n elements → $O(n^2)$. If you optimize it to stop early when no swaps occur, the best case (already sorted) is O(n).

Searching algorithms

Like reading, searching is fundamental. The most important search algorithms to learn are:

- **Binary search** for sorted arrays (it's like playing a smart guessing game halving the search area each time). Time Complexity: O(log n). Space Complexity: O(1) for iterative, O(log n) for recursive. Binary search works on a sorted array. It repeatedly halves the search interval: Each step cuts the problem size in half → takes about $\log_2(n)$ steps. That's why its time complexity is O(log n).
- **Linear search** for unsorted data (the go-to method when things aren't organized). Time Complexity: Best case: O(1) (if target is the first element), Average/Worst case: O(n). Space Complexity: O(1). Linear search simply checks every element until the target is found or the list ends. Worst case, you examine all n elements → O(n).

Data structure algorithms

Knowing how to manipulate data structures like trees and graphs can solve complex problems elegantly. The most important data-structure algorithms to learn are:

- **Tree Traversal** (Inorder, Preorder, Postorder) for navigating hierarchical data.
- **Graph Algorithms** like **Dijkstra's Algorithm** for shortest-path problems (think Google Maps finding the quickest route) and **Depth-First Search (DFS)** and **Breadth-First Search (BFS)** for exploring nodes.

Hashing algorithms

Used for everything from data retrieval to security, hashing is a way to encode data into a fixed-size string of bytes. Understanding how hash tables work under the hood is crucial, including dealing with collisions and designing a good hash function.

As you learned in *Chapter 8*, *Protecting Data and Apps Using Cryptography*, you should never implement your own cryptographic algorithms, so you should never need to learn how to implement hashing algorithms, unless you want to show off in an interview. You only need to know the concept and which ones to select for your scenario.

Recursive algorithms

It's a concept rather than an algorithm, but understanding recursion is key to solving complex problems by breaking them down into simpler versions of themselves. Recursion is a common solution for problems like Tower of Hanoi or generating permutations of a set.

In an interview, it's important to demonstrate an understanding of both the power and the pitfalls of recursion. Recursion relies on the call stack, and each recursive call consumes stack space, so you can often run out of memory. Recursive solutions can sometimes be less efficient than iterative ones, especially in terms of time complexity. Recursive code can look more elegant, but it is also harder for the average developer to understand and debug. Unless you are willing to commit to maintaining your code beyond your passing, consider a simpler solution!

Where to learn more about algorithms and data structures

If you feel like you need to learn algorithms and data structures in more detail, then I recommend reading the following book, as shown in *Figure 17.1*:

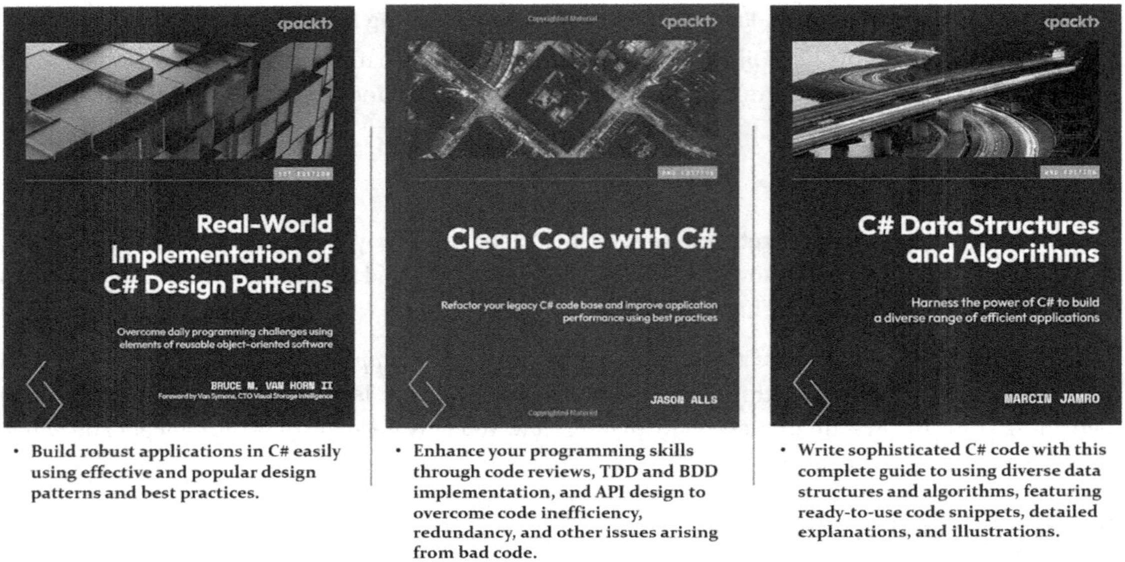

Figure 17.1: C# design patterns, clean code, data structures, and algorithms books from Packt

Practicing and exploring

Test your knowledge and understanding by answering some questions, getting some hands-on practice, and exploring the topics covered in this chapter with deeper research.

Exercise 17.1 – Online-only material

An oldie but a goodie article about design patterns, *Discover the Design Patterns You're Already Using in the .NET Framework* by Rob Pierry, can be found at the following link: `https://learn.microsoft.com/en-us/archive/msdn-magazine/2005/july/discovering-the-design-patterns-you-re-already-using-in-net`.

Exercise 17.2 – Practice exercises

Websites like LeetCode, HackerRank, and CodeSignal are gold mines for honing your skills:

- LeetCode: `https://leetcode.com/`
- HackerRank: `https://www.hackerrank.com/`
- CodeSignal: `https://codesignal.com/`

Exercise 17.3 – Test your knowledge

To get the best answer to some of these questions, you will need to do your own research. I want you to "think outside the book," so I have deliberately not provided all the answers in the book. I want to encourage you to get into the good habit of looking for help elsewhere, following the principle of "teach a person to fish."

1. What does the SOLID acronym represent?
2. What are the three major kinds of design patterns?
3. What is the Strategy design pattern? Give an example in the .NET base class library.
4. The Singleton design pattern is often implemented in .NET using a `static` class with an `Instance` property and a private constructor. What is a better way?
5. What is the Law of Demeter design principle?

Exercise 17.4 – Explore topics

Use the links on the following page to learn more details about the topics covered in this chapter: `https://github.com/markjprice/tools-skills-net10/blob/main/docs/book-links.md#chapter-17---design-patterns-and-principles`.

Summary

In this chapter, you learned about:

- SOLID principles
- Design patterns
- Design principles

You were also introduced to the importance of understanding algorithms and data structures.

Mastering design patterns and principles is a hallmark of a seasoned developer. It demonstrates a deep understanding of software development and problem-solving, making you more marketable and effective. This knowledge also provides a foundation for learning more advanced concepts and architectural styles.

In the next chapter, you will learn about the foundations of solution and software architecture.

18

Software and Solution Architecture Foundations

This chapter introduces you to the foundations of software and solution architecture. You will learn about the concepts and choices involved in architecting successful software solutions.

The goal of this chapter is not to teach you all the details of every architecture. Instead, the goal of this chapter is to introduce you to the key concepts of the most common architectures, styles, and methodologies, ensuring that you can participate in team discussions and understand why a team leader or manager decided to use a particular architecture for the project you are working on.

By learning about multiple architectures, you will see commonalities between them and the subtle pros and cons of each.

This chapter covers the following topics:

- Introducing software and solution architecture
- Uncle Bob's Clean Architecture
- Diagramming design using Mermaid

Introducing software and solution architecture

The terms "software architecture" and "solution architecture" often stir up some confusion, partly because their scopes overlap in the realms of software development and IT project planning, as shown in *Figure 18.1*:

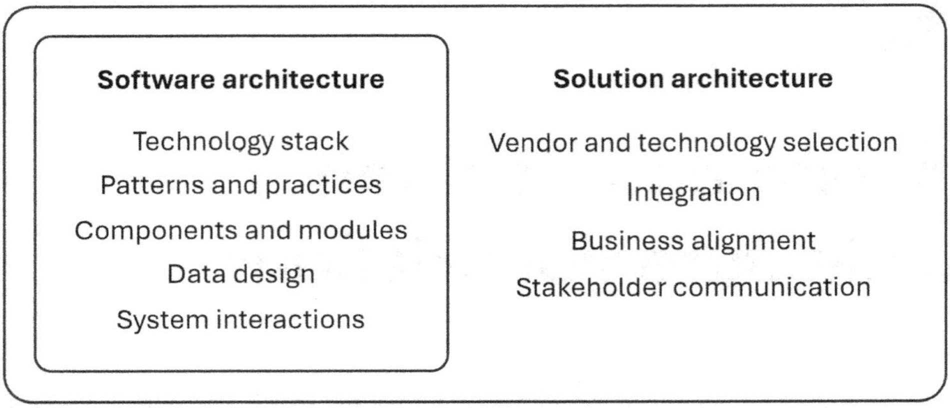

Figure 18.1: Software and solution architecture

Both software architecture and solution architecture are necessary for the success of a .NET project, but they focus on different aspects of the planning and design process. Let's look at each one in turn, before going into more detail on both.

Software architecture

Software architecture is primarily concerned with the structure and design of software systems. It involves defining a solution to meet all the technical and operational requirements while optimizing common quality attributes, such as performance, security, and manageability.

With software architecture, the focus is on the technology used within the software itself, including:

- **The technology stack**: Choosing the appropriate technologies, languages, and frameworks. If you are reading this book, then .NET is likely to be a major technology in your chosen stack.
- **Patterns and practices**: Applying design patterns, coding standards, and best practices to ensure a system is scalable, maintainable, and secure. You learned about many of these in *Chapter 17, Design Patterns and Principles*.
- **Components and modules**: Identifying the software's various parts and how they interact. A major decision here is between Monolith, Modular Monolith, and Microservices architectures.
- **Data design**: Structuring databases and data communication methods.
- **System interactions**: Defining how the system interacts with other software systems, APIs, and external services.

Software architecture is deeply technical, often requiring detailed knowledge of coding, system design, and technology trends. A good software architecture enables flexibility in the development process and provides a blueprint for developers to follow.

Solution architecture

Solution architecture is more holistic and business-oriented. It encompasses not just the software but also the hardware, human resources, and processes needed to solve a business problem or meet a specific business requirement.

Solution architects must understand and integrate various technological solutions and align them with business goals and constraints. This role involves:

- **Integration**: Ensuring that software and hardware components work together across different systems and platforms.
- **Business alignment**: Aligning the solution with business goals, strategies, and processes.
- **Project scope**: Defining the boundaries and requirements of the project, including cost and timeline estimates.
- **Stakeholder communication**: Bridging the gap between technical and non-technical stakeholders, ensuring that the technical solutions meet business needs.
- **Vendor and technology selection**: Choosing appropriate technologies and vendors based on requirements, cost, compatibility, and future-proofing.

Solution architecture is broader than software architecture, with a focus that extends beyond the software to include the entire ecosystem of a solution. It requires a blend of technical knowledge and business acumen, focusing on delivering value to a business while ensuring the solution is technically sound and sustainable.

Solution architects usually need at least a decade of experience, so if you're just starting out with software development, you can set becoming a solution architect as a goal, but be realistic about how long it will take to get there. It's great to have it as a long-term goal or guiding star in your career. Meanwhile, you could actively ask your manager if you can attend architecture meetings that are outside the scope of the part of the system that you work on, as this is how you grow.

Software architecture concepts

Software architecture concepts help in breaking down the complexity of software systems into more manageable components, each addressing different facets of software design and implementation.

Some concepts of software architecture are shown in *Table 18.1*:

Concept	**Description**
Design patterns	Design patterns are standard solutions to common problems in software design. They represent best practices used by experienced object-oriented software developers. Patterns are about reusable designs and interactions of objects. You learned about many of these in *Chapter 17, Design Patterns and Principles.*
Architectural styles	An architectural style, or architectural pattern, is a specific method of construction, characterized by the features that make it notable. Examples include Microservices, Monolithic, Layered (n-tier), Event-Driven, and **Service-Oriented Architecture** (**SOA**). Each style has its own set of principles and best practices that address different technical and business concerns. You will learn more about architectural styles later in this section.
Quality attributes	Quality attributes are the non-functional requirements of a software system that make the software desirable. These include scalability, reliability, availability, security, and performance. Quality attributes directly affect how well the system serves its users and adheres to its requirements.
Scalability and Performance Engineering	These concepts focus on designing systems that can scale effectively to meet increased demand and ensure that systems perform well under such conditions. This includes understanding load balancing, distributed systems design, caching strategies, and database optimization.
DevOps	DevOps is a set of practices that combines software development (Dev) and IT operations (Ops), aimed at shortening the system development lifecycle and providing continuous delivery with high software quality. DevOps practices, such as CI/CD, are crucial for automating the software release process and improving deployment frequency.
Security architecture	This involves designing software architecture with security policies and procedures in mind. Security architecture focuses on protecting against threats and vulnerabilities through authentication, authorization, encryption, and other security mechanisms. You learned some of this in *Chapter 12, Integration and Security Testing.*
Cloud-native and serverless architectures	Cloud-native is an approach to building and running applications that exploit the advantages of the cloud computing delivery model. Serverless architecture is a further evolution where the cloud provider dynamically manages the allocation of machine resources. Both concepts emphasize scalability, resilience, and agility.

Table 18.1: Summary of software architecture concepts

Understanding and applying these concepts allows architects and developers to build systems that meet their intended purposes effectively and efficiently.

Domain-Driven Design (DDD)

DDD is an approach to software development that emphasizes collaboration between technical and domain experts to create software models that solve complex business problems. It focuses on building a domain model that reflects a deep understanding of the business domain. This approach influences architecture by advocating for models based on the real-world business domain.

DDD is not strictly an architecture; instead, it is a methodology that influences architecture. DDD focuses on complex needs by connecting the implementation to an evolving model of the core business concepts. It emphasizes close collaboration between technical experts and domain experts to iteratively refine a conceptual model that addresses complex business challenges. DDD often results in architectures like microservices, where each service encapsulates a specific domain of business expertise.

Software Development Lifecycle (SDLC) methodologies

SDLC methodologies describe phases of the software cycle and the order in which those phases are executed. Each methodology follows a particular lifecycle to ensure success in the process of software development. The choice of SDLC model affects architectural decisions significantly.

Each SDLC methodology comes with its own set of principles, practices, advantages, and challenges, aiming to address different aspects of software development. Other methodologies for software development are shown in *Table 18.2*:

Methodology	Description
Agile	Agile is more of a philosophy than a strict methodology, underpinned by the Agile Manifesto's values and principles. It emphasizes flexibility, customer collaboration, and the ability to adapt to change. Agile promotes iterative development, where requirements and solutions evolve through collaborative efforts. Scrum and Kanban are among the most popular frameworks that implement Agile principles.
Scrum	Scrum is a subset of Agile that adds specific processes and roles, such as the Scrum Master, Product Owner, and Development Team. It structures development in cycles called Sprints, typically lasting two to four weeks, within which goals are set and completed. Scrum is characterized by regular stand-up meetings, reviews, and retrospectives to ensure continuous improvement.
Kanban	Kanban is another Agile framework that focuses on visualizing the entire development process, often with a Kanban board. It aims to manage work by balancing demands with available capacity and improving the handling of system-level bottlenecks. Work items are visually displayed on the board, allowing team members to see the state of every piece of work at any time.
Lean	Originating from lean manufacturing principles, Lean Software Development adapts those principles to software development. It focuses on minimizing waste (anything that doesn't add value to the customer), amplifying learning, delaying decision-making until the last responsible moment, and delivering as fast as possible. It's all about efficiency and sustainability.

Waterfall	The Waterfall model is one of the oldest methodologies, characterized by a linear and sequential approach where each phase must be completed before the next phase can begin. It's straightforward and easy to understand, making it suitable for projects with well-defined requirements that are unlikely to change. However, its rigidity can be a drawback in dynamic environments.
Extreme Programming (XP)	XP is a software development methodology designed to improve software quality and responsiveness to changing customer requirements. It promotes frequent "releases" in short development cycles, which improves productivity and introduces checkpoints where new customer requirements can be adopted.
Rapid Application Development (RAD)	RAD focuses on the quick development and delivery of high-quality systems with minimal planning. It emphasizes the use of software and user feedback over strict planning and requirements recording. RAD encourages rapid prototyping instead of long drawn-out development and testing cycles.

Table 18.2: Summary of software development methodologies

Each of these methodologies addresses different aspects of the software development process, from management and collaboration to design and deployment. The choice of methodology often depends on a project's specific needs, team size, deadlines, and the complexity of the project. The best approach might even be a hybrid, combining elements from multiple methodologies to suit a team's unique workflow and project requirements.

Software architecture styles

There are several software architecture styles that have become something of an industry standard, due to their reliability, scalability, and efficiency in handling specific project requirements.

It is important to note that architectural styles are not an exclusive choice. Just as a physical building can mix architectural styles like Gothic and Art Nouveau (like Sagrada Familia in Barcelona, Spain), developers can mix architectural styles. For example, Modular Monolith is a mixture of styles to get the best of all of them.

When I lived in Vancouver while studying screenwriting in 2005, I loved visiting the Vancouver Public Library because it blends postmodern and Roman architectural styles. Its coliseum-like form and contemporary materials create a dynamic and functional public space that bridges historical and modern design. It was perfect as a backdrop to scenes in the remake of Battlestar Galactica because it needed to be futuristic and Roman-based polytheistic.

A summary of the most common styles is shown in *Table 18.3*:

Architecture	Description
Monolithic	This is a single-tiered software application where the user interface and data access code are combined into a single project from a single platform. Simple to develop, deploy, and manage, it's a good fit for small, straightforward applications. However, large monolithic applications can be difficult to understand and modify. Scaling specific functionalities of the application can require scaling the entire application. As the application grows, the build and deployment processes can become slower, affecting productivity and the ability to respond to market changes rapidly.
Modular Monolithic	An evolution of the classic Monolithic architecture, this is designed to mitigate some of its drawbacks while preserving its benefits. It seeks to address these challenges by organizing a monolithic application into modules or components. Each module focuses on a specific business domain or functionality and is highly decoupled from other modules. Although the application is still deployed as a single unit, individual modules can be designed to scale more independently within the application, using techniques like multi-threading. The deployment process remains as straightforward as that of the classic monolith but with improved build times and the potential for more targeted optimizations, thanks to the modularity.
Microservices	Imagine a complex machine made up of independent components, each responsible for a specific function and capable of running on its own. That's the microservices architecture. It structures an application as a collection of services that are highly maintainable and testable, loosely coupled, independently deployable, and organized around business capabilities. This architecture is great for large, complex applications that require high scalability and flexibility. Netflix famously leveraged microservices to scale their massive, global services.
Service-Oriented Architecture (SOA)	SOA is like a city plan, where different services (like electricity, water, and waste management) are provided as separate but interoperable services. It focuses on service reuse across an entire organization, aiming for agility in integrating disparate systems and promoting interoperability. 25 years ago, Jeff Bezos infamously issued an edict to all the departments within Amazon that they must implement strict SOA for their services. That caused heaps of pain for the company initially, but eventually, it led to Amazon, an eCommerce company, being at the forefront of offering cloud services to other companies, with Amazon Web Services (AWS), and they were well positioned to adopt newer architectures like Microservices.

Architecture	Description
Layered aka N-Tier	This architecture is like a multi-story building, where each floor has a specific function, such as presentation, business logic, and data access layers. It's one of the most common architectures because of its simplicity in separating concerns, which makes it easier to manage and scale. Applications can be divided into layers that communicate with each other through clearly defined interfaces. It's a rather 1990s architecture, designed pre-internet. This architecture is well-suited for enterprise applications, web applications, and mobile backends.
Event-Driven (EDA)	Imagine a network of sensors and actuators in a smart home. Each sensor (like a motion sensor or a door sensor) triggers events that actuators (like lights or alarms) respond to. EDA is designed around the production, detection, and reaction to events. This architecture excels in environments where scalability and responsiveness to events in real time are crucial. It's particularly well-suited for asynchronous systems with sporadic or unpredictable traffic.
Serverless	In a serverless architecture, you're essentially outsourcing the responsibilities of managing servers, databases, and some logic to third-party services (like AWS Lambda). It allows developers to focus on writing code specific to their business logic without worrying about the underlying infrastructure. It's cost-efficient for certain workloads, highly scalable, and can significantly reduce operational complexity.
Clean	Clean Architecture aims to create systems that are easy to maintain, test, and adapt over time, focusing on the separation of concerns. It requires diligence in keeping the software's layers separate, especially the core business logic from external concerns. While it may seem complex or overkill for small projects, the benefits of Clean Architecture become more apparent as projects grow in size and complexity. It's highly regarded in the software development community.
Hexagonal	Similar in goals to Clean Architecture, Hexagonal Architecture (aka **Ports and Adapters**) aims at creating loosely coupled components that can be connected to their surroundings through ports and adapters. This allows an application to be equally driven by users, programs, or automated tests, and to be developed and tested in isolation from its eventual runtime devices and databases. It emphasizes the interchangeability of the input and output channels without changing the core logic.
Onion	Onion Architecture is like Clean Architecture and Hexagonal Architecture in that it focuses on the core domain logic of an application but structures the application into several layers. The innermost layers are the domain models and domain services. As you move outward, the layers become more specific to the mechanism of interaction with external agents. The main difference lies in how dependencies are structured; they flow inward, and the outer layers implement interfaces defined in the inner layers.

Architecture	Description
Vertical Slice	This is an approach to software development that emphasizes creating functional slices through an application's layers from the user interface down to the data storage, focusing on delivering complete features one at a time. This approach contrasts with more traditional, layer-oriented development, where individual layers of the application (such as the UI, business logic, and data access layers) are developed separately and in sequence. This architecture allows greater flexibility in using different technologies and approaches within each slice, as long as they can integrate with the overall system. By breaking down the application into smaller, manageable pieces that encompass all layers, developers can focus on delivering business value feature by feature, simplifying the development and testing processes.

Table 18.3: Summary of software architecture styles

Each of these architectures has its own set of advantages and trade-offs. Which one you choose depends on the specific needs of the project, including scalability, flexibility, maintainability, and the development team's expertise. One of the most popular, and therefore the one you should learn more details about, even if you don't use it immediately yourself, is Clean Architecture (and others that are very similar, like Hexagonal and Onion). You will learn about Clean Architecture later in this chapter, in the section titled *Uncle Bob's Clean Architecture*.

From the outside world, many of these architectural styles are so similar that it is difficult to see why they exist. Proponents can get fanatical about the smallest difference.

Command Query Responsibility Segregation (CQRS)

CQRS is a design pattern and architectural style that separates models to read and update data. This approach stems from a fundamental principle in computer science known as **Command-Query Separation (CQS)**, which states that every method should either be a command that performs an action or a query that returns data to the caller, but not both. Building on this, CQRS takes it a step further by applying this separation at the architectural level.

CQRS has many advantages, including:

- **Simplified Design**: By separating commands and queries, models become more simplified and focused. It's easier to optimize the read model for query performance and the write model for update performance.
- **Scalability**: CQRS allows for the read and write sides of the system to be scaled independently. If your application experiences a heavy read load, you can scale up the read model without affecting the write model, and vice versa.
- **Flexibility**: This pattern supports multiple views of your data for different purposes. For example, you can have a denormalized view for fast reads while maintaining a normalized form for updates.
- **Improved Security**: Separating the read and write models can lead to better security. Commands might require different authorization levels compared to queries.

While CQRS can offer significant benefits, it's not a silver bullet for all systems. Implementing CQRS can introduce complexity, especially in systems where the distinction between commands and queries is blurred or where the overhead of maintaining separate models is not justified by the benefits.

In systems where the write and read models are separated, ensuring that the read model is up to date with the write model can introduce challenges related to data consistency.

CQRS is particularly useful in complex domains where the tasks of updating information differ significantly from the tasks of reading information. It's also beneficial in scenarios requiring high performance and scalability, and where clear separation of concerns can lead to cleaner, more maintainable codebases.

CQRS is a powerful pattern when applied correctly, particularly in large, complex applications requiring scalable, flexible, and maintainable architectures. However, it's essential to assess the complexity and overhead it introduces against the specific benefits it offers to your project. Like any architectural pattern, the decision to use CQRS should be based on the specific requirements and constraints of your application.

Solution architecture concepts

Here are some key concepts integral to solution architecture, shown in *Table 18.4*:

Concept	Description
Requirements analysis	This involves gathering and interpreting the functional and non-functional requirements of the project. Understanding what the stakeholders need from the system is crucial for defining the scope of the solution and ensuring that the final product meets business objectives.
Technology selection	One of the primary roles of a solution architect is to select the technologies that will be used in a solution. This includes programming languages, frameworks, databases, cloud platforms, and other tools. The selection is based on various factors like performance, scalability, cost, and the current technological ecosystem of the organization.
Integration design	Most solutions don't exist in a vacuum but need to integrate with existing systems within an organization. Integration design covers how different systems will communicate with each other, data exchange formats, and protocols to ensure seamless interoperability.
Security design	Security is paramount in solution architecture. This subconcept encompasses the strategies and technologies used to ensure data confidentiality, integrity, and availability. Security design covers aspects like authentication, authorization, encryption, and compliance with relevant security standards and regulations.

Infrastructure architecture	While solution architecture often focuses on software, the underlying infrastructure – whether on-premises or in the cloud – plays a critical role. Infrastructure architecture involves designing the hardware, networks, and services required to support the deployment, operation, and scaling of the solution.
Data architecture	This pertains to how data is stored, organized, and accessed in a system. It includes database design, data modeling, data flow design, and considerations for data scalability, persistence, and data integrity. It's crucial for ensuring that data is used effectively and efficiently across an organization.
Scalability and performance planning	Solutions must be designed not just for current requirements but also with an eye toward future growth. This involves planning for horizontal and vertical scaling, optimizing performance, and ensuring that a system can handle increased loads without degradation.
Disaster recovery and high availability design	Designing solutions to be resilient in the face of failures and to ensure continuous operation is key. This involves strategies for data backup, system redundancy, failover processes, and recovery procedures.
User experience (UX) design	Although traditionally associated with product design, UX considerations are also important in solution architecture, especially for systems with direct user interaction. Ensuring that a system is intuitive and efficient to use can significantly impact user satisfaction and productivity.
Compliance and governance	Solutions must adhere to relevant laws, regulations, and internal policies. This includes data protection regulations (like GDPR in Europe), industry standards, and internal IT governance policies. Compliance and governance considerations influence various aspects of the solution design, from data handling to user management.
Cost management	Cost is a critical factor in solution architecture, particularly with the prevalence of cloud-based resources. Architects need to consider the financial impact of their technology choices and design solutions that are cost-effective without compromising on performance or scalability.
DevOps and CI/CD integration	Integrating DevOps practices and CI/CD pipelines into solution architecture facilitates automation, improves deployment frequency, and enhances the quality of the software. It involves planning for automation tools, testing environments, and deployment strategies that support continuous integration and continuous delivery.

Table 18.4: Summary of solution architecture concepts

Solution architecture is a multifaceted discipline that requires a holistic understanding of both business and technical domains. By considering these concepts, solution architects can design systems that are not only technologically sound but also align closely with business goals and objectives. Solution architects must take into account not just technical concerns but also monetary and legal. Technology problems are the least of it.

Conclusion

In many projects, especially in smaller organizations, the roles of software architecture and solution architecture may overlap or be fulfilled by the same person. However, understanding their differences is important, so let's highlight them:

- Software architecture is about making key decisions on the structure and design of a software system.
- Solution architecture takes a step back, focusing on integrating that software within a broader business and technology ecosystem to solve a particular problem or meet a specific business requirement.

While software architects lay the foundation for a system's design and how it operates internally, solution architects ensure that the solution fits within the broader business context, addressing not just the technical but also the operational and strategic needs of an organization. Both roles are vital for creating effective, efficient, and sustainable technology solutions.

You could write an entire book just about each of the software architectures in detail. For our purposes of introducing you to the most important concepts, and preparing you for interviews, we will focus on the most popular ones. Like learning human languages, once you've learned one formally (beyond your native language), it becomes easier to learn more because there is common grammar (i.e., problems) that they all try to solve, just with different priorities. As mentioned earlier in this chapter, a common architecture that other architectures are based on is Clean Architecture, so let's look at that one in more detail next.

Uncle Bob's Clean Architecture

Clean Architecture is a software design philosophy that emphasizes the separation of concerns among the different elements of a software application. This approach aims to create systems that are independent of frameworks, UI, database, and any external agency.

The main goal is to produce a system that is easy to manage, test, and scale over time, with a particular focus on enabling the development of business policies that are independent of external influences.

The concept of Clean Architecture was introduced by Robert C. Martin (aka Uncle Bob), who provided a structured way to think about software architecture that promotes the use of practices that lead to more maintainable code.

> You can learn more about Uncle Bob and his contributions to computing at `https://en.wikipedia.org/wiki/Robert_C._Martin`, or if you don't trust Wikipedia, you can go to his own personal website at `http://cleancoder.com/`, but keep in mind that Bob's own site is unlikely to be as unbiased as the Wikipedia editors'.

Clean architecture concepts

The core concepts of Clean Architecture include the following:

- **Independence of Frameworks:** The architecture does not depend on the existence of some library or framework. This allows you to use such frameworks as tools, rather than having to fit your system into their limited constraints.
- **Testability:** Business rules can be tested without the UI, database, web server, or any other external element.
- **UI Independence:** The UI can change easily, without changing the rest of the system. A web UI could be replaced with a console UI, for example, without changing the business rules.
- **Database Independence:** You can swap out Oracle or SQL Server for a filesystem, or something else. Your business rules are not bound to the database.
- **External Agency Independence:** The business rules don't know anything about the outside world (such as the UI, database, web, etc.).

Clean Architecture proposes a circular architecture divided into multiple layers, each representing a different area of software design, as shown in *Figure 18.2*:

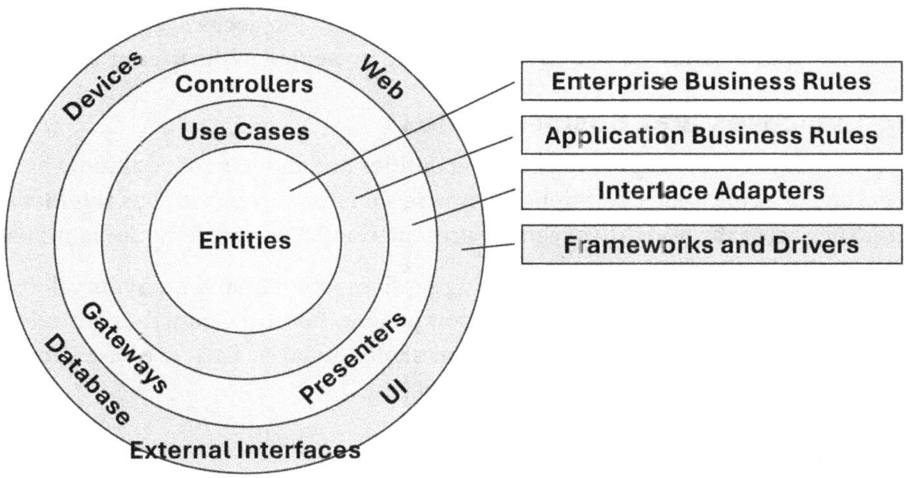

Figure 18.2: Clean Architecture circular layers

From the innermost layers to the outermost ones, these layers are:

1. **Enterprise Business Rules/Entities:** The innermost layer containing the enterprise-wide business rules. Entities encapsulate the most general and high-level rules. They are the least likely to change when something external changes.
2. **Application Business Rules/Use Cases:** The application-specific business rules layer. It encapsulates and implements all the use cases of the system. In .NET, you'd define these using C# types in class libraries with clearly defined interfaces to improve modularity for use in any architecture, from modular monolith to microservices.

3. **Interface Adapters:** This layer contains adapters that convert data from the format most convenient for the external agencies and frameworks to the format most convenient for the use cases and entities. This includes controllers, gateways, and presenters. For .NET projects, this is often an object-relational mapper like EF Core, or lower-level APIs like ADO.NET SqlClient.
4. **Frameworks and Drivers:** The outermost layer where frameworks and tools such as databases like SQL Server and web frameworks like ASP.NET Core reside.

Implementing Clean Architecture involves adherence to its principles throughout the software development process.

Defining entities

Entities in clean architecture are the business objects of your application. They encapsulate the most general and high-level rules. They are the least likely to change when something external changes. For example, if your application will not change its operation or business rules, entities will remain largely unaffected by changes in the database, UI, or external integrations.

In .NET, entities should be **plain old C# objects (POCOs)** with no dependencies on external frameworks or libraries. They should focus purely on business rules and properties that are critical to the domain.

For example, a `User` entity might contain methods to validate the user's age or email format, but it shouldn't know anything about the way these details are presented to the user or stored.

Defining use cases and business rules

Use cases control the flow of data to and from the entities and implement additional business rules specific to particular application operations. These are sometimes referred to as **Interactors** in Clean Architecture. They act as the bridge between the presentation/UI layer and the domain/business logic.

In .NET, implementing use cases involves creating services or command/query handlers that encapsulate application-specific business rules. These components take data from the controllers, perform operations using entities, and return data to the presentation layer. Each use case should be highly focused, managing a specific business rule or transaction.

Implementing interfaces

Interfaces in Clean Architecture define the boundaries and interactions between different components, for example, between use cases and entities, or use cases and infrastructure services. They maintain the decoupling necessary for clean architecture.

In .NET, you can define interfaces for repository access, external services like APIs or third-party services, and data flow between use cases and entities.

For example, an `IUserRepository` interface might declare methods for user data retrieval and storage, which can then be implemented by any data-access mechanism you choose, for example, Entity Framework Core or Dapper with ADO.NET SqlClient.

Implementing presenters

Presenters are part of the output boundary in Clean Architecture. They take data from use cases and format it for the frameworks and drivers layer. This allows the frameworks and drivers layer to remain isolated from the use cases and entities.

In .NET, implement presenters that transform model data from the use cases into view models or **Data Transfer Objects (DTOs)**, using `record` types that are then sent to the frontend. This separation ensures that changes to the presentation logic do not impact the core business logic.

Implementing controllers

In a web-based .NET application using frameworks like ASP.NET Core, controllers act as the input boundary of the clean architecture. They are responsible for handling incoming requests, delegating business processing to the appropriate use cases, and returning the appropriate response to the client.

In .NET, controllers should be lean, focusing on routing and validation. They should avoid business logic, which should instead reside in the use cases or entities. Dependency injection should be used to supply the controllers with instances of the necessary use cases or services.

Good practices in .NET Clean Architecture

Good practices to implement Clean Architecture with .NET include the following:

- **Dependency Inversion:** Central to Clean Architecture is the principle of dependency inversion, which is that high-level modules should not depend on low-level modules. Both should depend on abstractions (e.g., interfaces).
- **Persistence Ignorance:** The domain entities and business logic should be ignorant of the persistence mechanisms. This means designing entities and business rules without regard to how they will be stored or retrieved.
- **Testing:** It is good practice to test your code. There is less excuse not to follow this with Clean Architecture because by isolating business logic from other concerns, it becomes much easier to write unit tests for the business rules without worrying about external dependencies like databases or web frameworks.

Adopting Clean Architecture in a .NET environment involves a disciplined approach to software design, focusing on the separation of concerns and encapsulation. It requires a shift from thinking about software as a set of operations that execute in a sequence to a collection of independent models and operations that communicate through well-defined interfaces. This shift not only helps to build robust systems but also ensures that the system is easier to test, maintain, and scale.

Diagramming design using Mermaid

As you now know from *Chapter 6, Documenting Code, APIs, and Services*, Mermaid is a tool for generating diagrams through text in a Markdown-like syntax, making it a favorite among developers for documentation and design purposes, especially because it integrates seamlessly into many documentation tools and platforms.

> You can read the **Mermaid User Guide** at the following link: `https://mermaid.js.org/intro/getting-started.html`.

Mermaid for software and solution architecture

Mermaid is particularly useful for software and solution architecture because Mermaid diagrams are written in plain text, so they can be version-controlled along with code and documentation. This makes it easier to track changes, collaborate, and manage updates. Mermaid supports various types of diagrams that are commonly used in software architecture, such as flowcharts, sequence diagrams, class diagrams, state diagrams, and entity-relationship diagrams. This variety allows architects to represent different aspects of a system's architecture and workflows effectively.

Mermaid diagrams can be generated or updated programmatically, which is useful for creating dynamic diagrams that reflect the current state of the system or data. Diagrams can even be generated or updated automatically as part of continuous integration and deployment pipelines, ensuring that documentation stays up to date with code changes.

Use cases include:

- System architecture diagrams that represent the overall structure of software systems, including components, services, and their interactions.
- Workflow and process diagrams that visualize business processes, workflows, and user interactions with a system.
- Data models and **entity-relationship** (**ER**) diagrams that illustrate database schemas, entity relationships, and data flow within a system.
- Sequence diagrams that detail the interactions between system components over time, which is useful for understanding specific use cases and processes.
- Deployment diagrams that show how software components are deployed across different environments and infrastructures.

Mermaid diagram types

Here are several types of diagrams you can create with Mermaid that are particularly useful in software design and architecture:

- **Flowchart**: Perhaps the most common and versatile diagram, flowcharts with Mermaid can illustrate the flow of logic, data, or processes within a system. They're great for outlining algorithms, process flows, and system designs, making complex logic visually understandable.
- **Sequence Diagram**: Sequence diagrams are crucial for detailing the interactions between parts of a system in a time-sequential order. They're perfect for visualizing how objects in a system interact through method calls, which is particularly useful in object-oriented programming.
- **Class Diagram**: Mermaid can generate class diagrams to represent the structure of a system by showing the system's classes, their attributes, methods, and the relationships among objects. This is particularly useful for visualizing the architecture of a software application.
- **State Diagram**: Also known as statechart diagrams, these depict the states an entity can be in as well as the transitions between these states. This is useful for modeling the behavior of applications, especially those with complex conditional or looping control flows.
- **Entity Relationship Diagram (ERD)**: ERDs are essential for database modeling, showing the relationships between different data entities or structures. With Mermaid, you can easily outline the database schema, making it invaluable for designing database applications.
- **Gantt Chart**: Although not traditionally associated with software architecture, Gantt charts in Mermaid can be used to plan and visualize project timelines, including the development phases, milestones, and dependencies of software projects. This helps in project management and scheduling.
- **Component Diagram**: Component diagrams are used to visualize the organization and relationships of various components within a system. They help in understanding the high-level structure of software systems, making them critical for architectural documentation.
- **User Journey**: This is a more narrative approach to diagrams, illustrating how a user interacts with a system to achieve a goal. This can be invaluable for user-centered design, ensuring the software architecture aligns with user needs and experiences.

Mermaid's syntax is straightforward, allowing you to create these diagrams directly in your documentation without the need for external drawing tools. This not only saves time but also ensures that diagrams stay updated with the text they're describing, providing a single source of truth that's easy to maintain.

The most flexible Mermaid diagram type is the flowchart, so let's start with that.

Mermaid flowcharts

Flowcharts can represent a variety of processes and workflows, making them applicable to numerous scenarios in software development and architecture, including documenting the steps in a process or workflow, visualizing the flow of logic in algorithms, showing decision points and the outcomes of each decision, and illustrating the flow of data or control within a system.

Flowcharts are intuitive and easy to understand, even for non-technical stakeholders. Flowcharts can encapsulate both high-level overviews and detailed step-by-step processes, making them suitable for different levels of abstraction.

Flowchart syntax

The basic syntax for defining a flowchart is shown in *Table 18.5*:

<table>
<tr><th>Syntax</th><th>Example(s)</th><th>Description</th></tr>
<tr><td><code>flowchart <direction></code></td><td><code>TD, TB, LR, RL, BT</code></td><td>Top-down, top-bottom, left-right, right-left, and bottom-top. The default is <code>TD</code>.</td></tr>
<tr><td><code>node</code></td><td><code>A, B, C</code></td><td>Defines identifiers for nodes.</td></tr>
<tr><td><code>node[label]</code></td><td><code>A[Start], C[Access Dashboard]</code></td><td>Labels a node in a rectangle. Represents the steps or actions in the process.</td></tr>
<tr><td><code>node{label}</code></td><td><code>B{Is User Logged In?}, D{Is Username and Password Correct}</code></td><td>Labels a node in a diamond. Represents the decision points, where the flow can diverge based on the condition's outcome.</td></tr>
<tr><td><code>--></code></td><td><code>A --> B</code></td><td>The arrow between nodes. Represents the direction of the workflow from one step or decision to another.</td></tr>
<tr><td><code>-->|label|</code></td><td><code>B -->|Yes| D</code></td><td>Adds a labeled arrow between nodes.</td></tr>
<tr><td><code>classDef style_name style_settings</code></td><td><code>classDef startend fill:#f9f,stroke:#333,stroke-width:4px;</code></td><td>Defines a named style aka class. Valid settings include <code>fill</code>, <code>stroke</code>, and <code>stroke-width</code>.</td></tr>
<tr><td><code>class node_list style_name;</code></td><td><code>class A,L startend;</code></td><td>Applies a named style to a comma-separated list of nodes.</td></tr>
</table>

Table 18.5: Flowchart syntax

Other shapes include the following:

- Use (...) for a rounded rectangle
- Use ((...)) for a circle
- Use (((...))) for a double circle
- Use ([..]) for a pill
- Use [[...]] for a subroutine
- Use [(...)] for a cylinder, commonly used to represent a database
- Use {{...}} for a hexagon
- Use [/.../] or [\...\] for a parallelogram
- Use [/...\] or [\.../] for a trapezoid
- Use >...] for a rectangle with a triangle cut out on the left side

Let's explore examples using Mermaid syntax that will demonstrate different scenarios and how you might represent them in a flowchart. To view these diagrams, you would typically paste the Mermaid code into a Markdown file in an environment that supports Mermaid, such as GitHub or a Markdown editor with the Mermaid plugin.

Example flowchart – a user login process

This flowchart outlines a basic user login process, including decision points for successful authentication and handling forgotten passwords, as shown in *Figure 18.3* and the following markup:

```
flowchart LR
 A[Start] --> B{Is User Logged In?}
 B -->|Yes| C[Access Dashboard]
 B -->|No| D{Is Username and Password Correct?}
 D -->|Yes| C
 D -->|No| E[Display Error Message]
 E --> F{Did User Forget Password?}
 F -->|Yes| G[Redirect to Password Reset]
 F -->|No| D
 G --> D
```

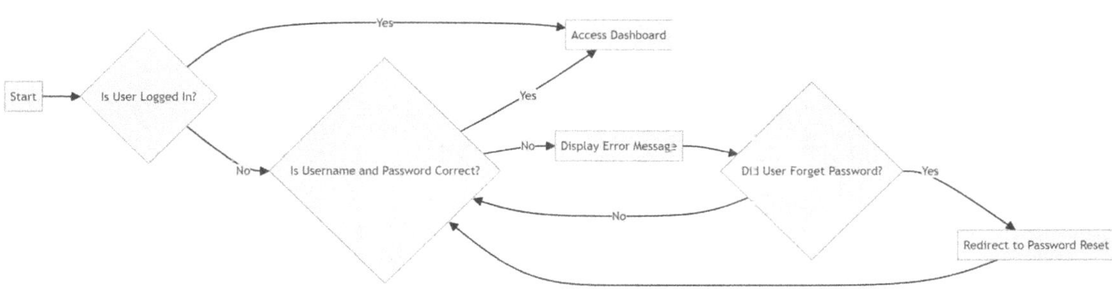

Figure 18.3: Flowchart of a basic user login process

Example flowchart – a software development process

This flowchart represents a simplified software development process, from initial requirement gathering to deployment.

Class definitions at the end are used to style different types of nodes, making the diagram more visually distinct and easier to follow. For instance, `startend` is applied to the `A[Start]` and `L[End]` nodes to make them stand out, while `process` and `decision` styles differentiate between actions and decision points, as shown in *Figure 18.4* and the following markup:

```
flowchart
 A[Start: Bug Identified] --> B[Log Bug in Tracker]
 B --> C{Bug Reproducible?}
 C -->|Yes| D[Fix Bug]
 C -->|No| E[Request More Info]
 E --> F[More Info Provided?]
 F -->|Yes| C
 F -->|No| G[Close as Cannot Reproduce]
 D --> H[Test Fix]
 H --> I{Is Bug Fixed?}
 I -->|Yes| J[Deploy Fix to Production]
 I -->|No| D
 J --> K[Close Bug in Tracker]
 K --> L[End: Bug Resolved]
 classDef startend fill:#f9f,stroke:#333,stroke-width:4px;
 classDef process fill:#bbf,stroke:#333,stroke-width:2px;
 classDef decision fill:#fbf,stroke:#333,stroke-width:2px;
 class A,L startend;
 class B,D,E,F,G,H,J,K process;
 class C,I decision;
```

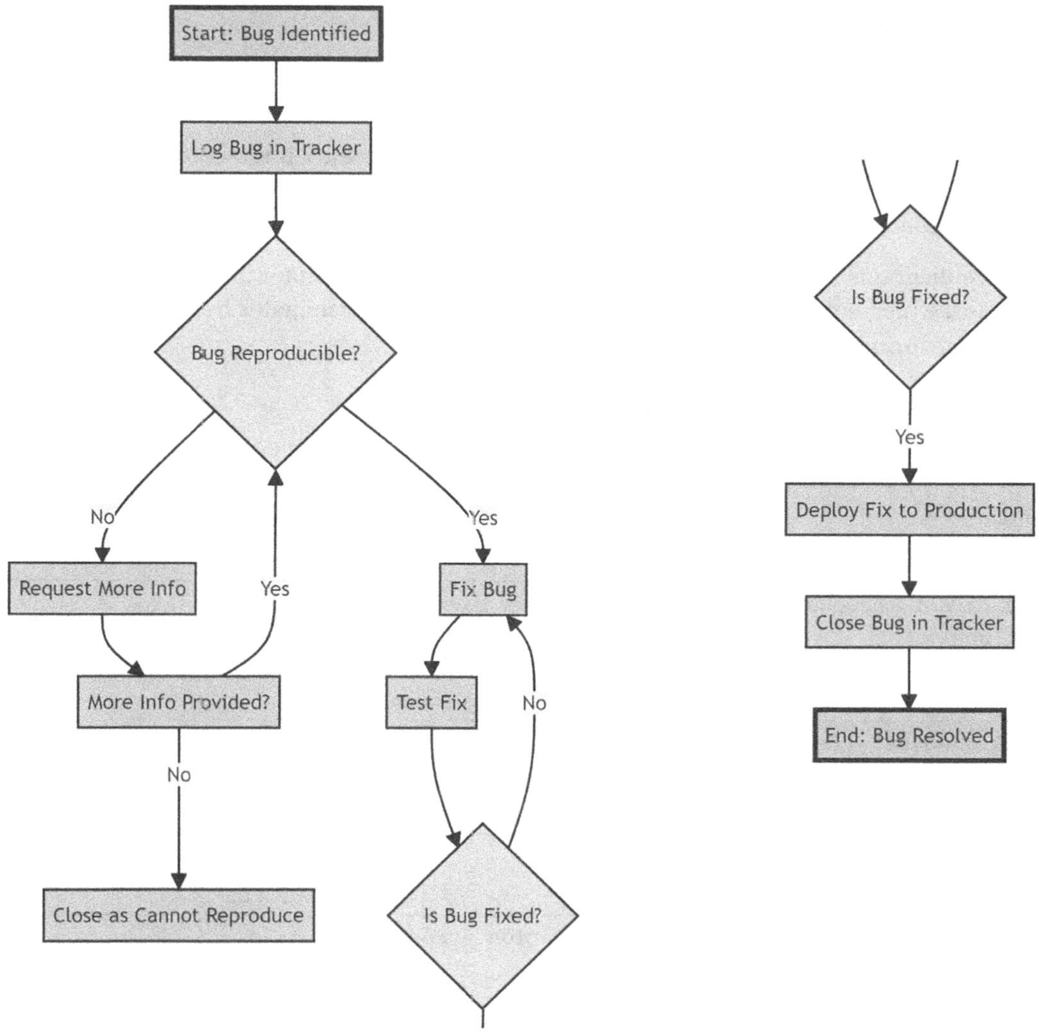

Figure 18.4: Flowchart of a bug track and fix process

While flowcharts are highly flexible and commonly used, there are other diagram types in Mermaid that are also popular and useful in different contexts. Sequence diagrams are used to show interactions between different parts of a system over time, which is useful for illustrating use cases and scenarios. Let's look at sequence diagrams in more detail.

Mermaid sequence diagrams

Sequence diagrams help in understanding the dynamic behavior of a system, illustrating how processes operate sequentially, and showing the flow of messages and events.

This aids in identifying potential issues, ensuring that all necessary interactions are accounted for, and improving communication among team members by providing a common, easily understandable visual representation.

Sequence diagrams are particularly useful in specifying and documenting the exact sequence of operations, which enhances the accuracy of system design and facilitates better planning and troubleshooting during development.

Sequence diagram syntax

The basic syntax for defining a sequence diagram is shown in *Table 18.6*:

Syntax	Example(s)	Description
`sequenceDiagram`	`sequenceDiagram`	Defines a sequence diagram.

`participant <nodename> as <label>`	`participant U as User`
	`participant F as Front-End`
	`participant B as Back-End`
		Defines participants that will appear at the top and bottom of the sequence diagram.

`node1->>node2: <label>`	`U->>F: Clicks Register` `F->>B: POST /register`	Defines a message or action directed from one participant to another.
`alt <label>`	`alt successful registration`	Defines the start of an alternative branch block.
`else <label>`	`else registration error`	Defines a subsequent alternative branch.
`end`	`end`	Defines the end of a block.
`loop <label>`	`loop Data Validation`	Defines the start of a loop block.

Table 18.6: Sequence diagram syntax

Example sequence diagram – a user registration process

Here is a sequence diagram that illustrates the process of a user registering on a website, including interactions between the user and the frontend and backend systems, as shown in the following markup and *Figure 18.5*:

```
sequenceDiagram
  participant U as User
  participant F as Front-End
  participant B as Back-End
```

```
 U->>F: Clicks Register
 F->>B: POST /register
 alt successful registration
B->>F: Return Success
F->>U: Display Success Message
else registration error
B->>F: Return Error
F->>U: Display Error Message
end
```

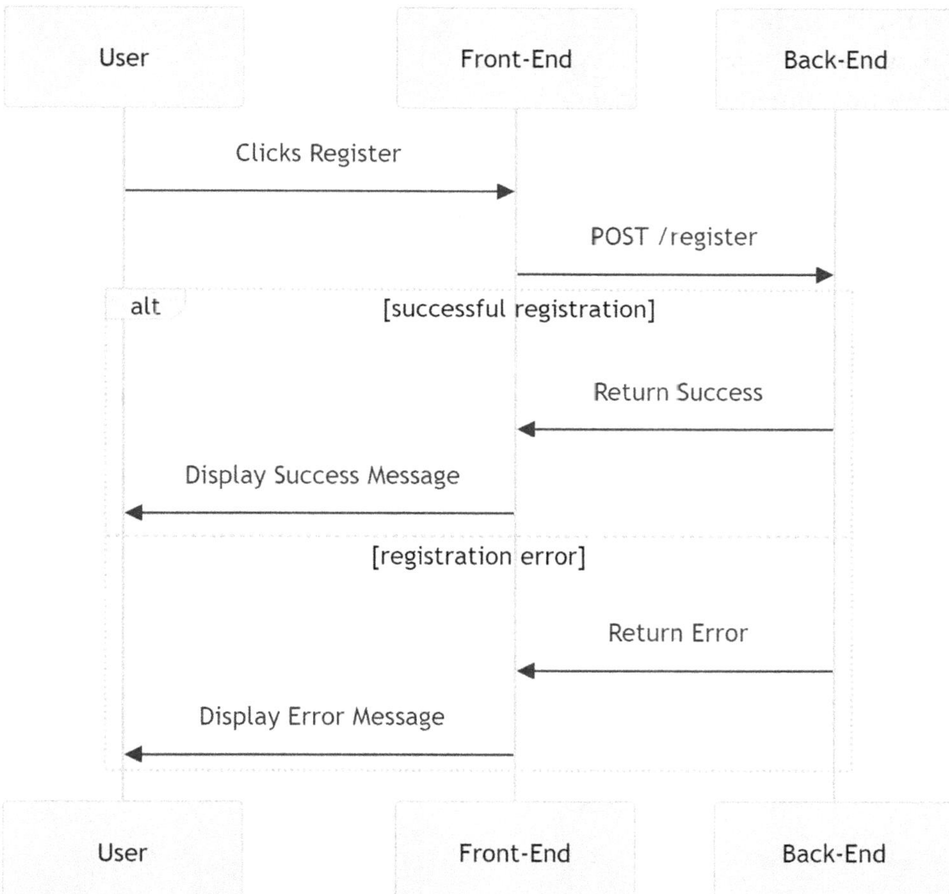

Figure 18.5: A sequence diagram showing a user registration process

In the preceding diagram:

- Participants are labeled and represent different entities in the process like User, Front-End, and Back-End.
- The `->>` symbol denotes messages or actions directed from one participant to another.
- The `alt` block is used to show alternative paths based on the outcome of the registration process (success or error). Indicate the end of the `alt` block with `end`.

There are several arrow styles for messages or actions directed from one participant to another:

- Solid line arrow: `->>`
- Dotted line arrow: `-->>`
- Arrow to an active participant: `->>+`
- Arrow from an active participant: `->>-`

> The preceding example diagram does not show all these types of arrows.

Arrows can go from a participant to itself.

Example sequence diagram – website querying a database

The next example demonstrates a simple scenario where a website queries a database for user information and processes the response, as shown in the following markup and *Figure 18.6*:

```
sequenceDiagram
  participant W as Website
  participant D as Database
  W->>+D: Query User Data
  D-->>-W: Return User Data
  W->>W: Process User Data
  loop Data Validation
 W->>W: Validate Data Fields
 end
 W->>W: Display User Profile
```

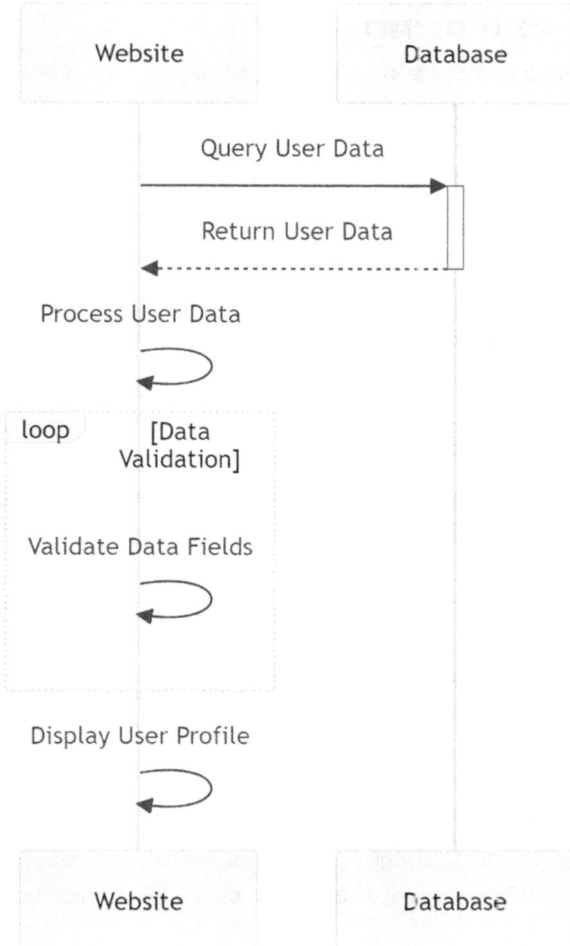

Figure 18.6: A sequence diagram showing a website querying a database

Key features illustrated here include:

- The `->>+` and `-->>-` symbols, which denote a message to a database that initiates a process and the return message, respectively, highlighting the start and end of an interaction.
- The `loop` block, which shows a repetitive action, in this case, validating data fields, which is an internal process within the website.

These diagrams serve as a clear visual aid in understanding the sequence of interactions and operations in various processes, showcasing the power of Mermaid to document and design software systems. Sequence diagrams, with their straightforward syntax, can significantly enhance the comprehensibility of complex interactions in software development projects.

Practicing and exploring

Test your knowledge and understanding by answering some questions, getting some hands-on practice, and exploring the topics covered in this chapter with deeper research.

Exercise 18.1 – Online-only material

In the first edition of this chapter, I have only covered flowcharts and sequence diagrams using Mermaid. If you would like me to cover other types in future editions, please let me know which ones would be most useful to include in the print book.

Meanwhile, you can see examples of other types at the following links:

- Class diagrams represent the structure of a system by showing its classes, attributes, operations, and relationships. They are commonly used in object-oriented design: `https://mermaid.js.org/syntax/classDiagram.html`.
- State diagrams describe the states of an object and the transitions between those states. They are useful for modeling the lifecycle of objects in a system: `https://mermaid.js.org/syntax/stateDiagram.html`.
- ERDs show the relationships between entities in a database. They are useful for database design and data modeling: `https://mermaid.js.org/syntax/entityRelationshipDiagram.html`.
- Gantt chart diagrams are used for project management to represent tasks, durations, and dependencies. They are helpful to plan and track project progress: `https://mermaid.js.org/syntax/gantt.html`.

Exercise 18.2 – Practice exercises

Have a chat with your favorite LLM about software and solution architecture. Below is a suggested question to get you started. When you get a response, pick a few topics that the LLM mentions to dig deeper into:

"Please act as an expert on software and solution architecture with .NET and related technologies. I work for a company that is implementing a project for an eCommerce platform. What design decisions should we consider? What questions should we ask ourselves about the architecture we should pick? Please give code examples and diagrams using Mermaid when relevant. Do not assume prior knowledge of third-party libraries, so explicitly call them out and their benefits when mentioning them, even if only in a separate section at the end."

Exercise 18.3 – Test your knowledge

Answer the following questions. If you get stuck, try googling the answers; if you get totally stuck, the answers are in *Appendix A*:

1. What is the difference between "software architecture" and "solution architecture"?
2. Briefly describe three software architecture styles.
3. What is Domain-Driven Design (DDD)?
4. What is Command Query Responsibility Segregation (CQRS)?
5. Who is Uncle Bob and why is he important to .NET developers?

Exercise 18.4 – Explore topics

Use the links on the following page to learn more details about the topics covered in this chapter: `https://github.com/markjprice/tools-skills-net10/blob/main/docs/book-links.md#chapter-18---software-and-solution-architecture-foundations`.

There are also a few Packt books that cover software and solution architecture in much more detail, as shown in *Figure 18.7*:

- A book for the aspiring .NET software architect - design scalable and high-performance enterprise solutions using the latest features of C# 12 and .NET 8.
- Backend design like you've never seen it before - a guide to building SOLID ASP.NET Core web apps that stand the test of time. Featuring more Minimal APIs, more testing, more building blocks, and the modular monolith!
- Embark on a transformative journey to becoming a cloud solution architect with a roadmap, expert insights, and practical knowledge to excel in your career.

Figure 18.7: Packt books for software and solution architecture

Summary

In this chapter, you learned:

- The key concepts of software and solution architecture
- The key concepts of Uncle Bob's Clean Architecture
- How to create diagrams for software and solution architecture using flowcharts and sequence diagrams with Mermaid

In the next chapter, you will learn about what to do to improve your career prospects and, especially, how to do your best in job interviews.

19

Your Career, Teamwork, and Interviews

This chapter is about working in a team as a career professional, applying for jobs, and passing interviews for .NET software engineer and related job positions.

The title of this book is *Tools and Skills for .NET 10*, so I assume that you want to learn about those tools and skills because you want to get a job working with .NET, which mostly means getting a software engineer position or another related job position. This whole book helps you learn those topics with the end goal of getting you that job.

This chapter covers the following topics:

- Working on a development team
- Applying for a job
- Sample interview questions

> Answers to the sample interview questions are found online at the following link: `https://github.com/markjprice/tools-skills-net10/blob/main/docs/interview-qa/readme.md`.

Working on a development team

Some of the readers of my .NET books are amateurs rather than professionals, meaning they program for fun rather than being paid to do so. They want to learn .NET for a personal challenge or to create software only for their own use.

But most of my readers are either professional .NET developers or aspire to be eventually. Although some professional .NET developers work on their own, most work on a development team with other developers and related roles.

Being a software engineer

As a .NET software engineer, your daily life can be quite varied, depending on the type of projects you're working on and the organization that you work for. But there are common tasks that you will need to be good at, as shown in the following list:

- **Coding and development:** Of course, the primary task is writing, debugging, and maintaining code using C# and .NET. This involves developing websites, apps, services, and APIs, fixing bugs, updating software to improve performance, and adding new features as needed. All my books cover these core topics.
- **Collaboration:** You will work closely with other developers, designers, product managers, and stakeholders to ensure your software meets organizational requirements.
- **Testing:** You will write unit tests, integration tests, and sometimes automated UI tests to ensure code quality and reliability.
- **Code reviews:** You are likely to participate in code reviews to improve code quality and share knowledge.
- **Documentation:** You will need to write documentation for other developers and end users, ensuring that your code is understandable and maintainable.
- **Learning and development:** You must keep up with the latest trends and updates in the .NET ecosystem, as well as general software development best practices.
- **Meetings:** Unfortunately, you cannot avoid meetings. These could be stand-ups, sprint planning, retrospectives, and other agile ceremonies.

The key technical skills of a .NET software engineer include:

- **C# and .NET:** The primary language for .NET development
- **ASP.NET Core:** For developing web applications
- **Entity Framework Core:** For database interactions
- **Web front-end technologies:** Basic understanding of HTML, CSS, and JavaScript
- **Databases:** Knowledge of SQL Server or other relational databases
- **Version control:** Proficiency with Git and platforms like GitHub or Azure DevOps
- **Cloud services:** Familiarity with Azure or other cloud providers

The key soft skills of a .NET software engineer include:

- **Problem-solving:** The ability to think critically and solve complex issues
- **Communication:** Clear and effective communication with team members and stakeholders
- **Teamwork:** Collaboration with other developers, designers, and business analysts
- **Adaptability:** The ability to quickly learn and adapt to new technologies and methodologies
- **Attention to detail:** Ensuring code quality and reducing bugs

Software engineers can be known by various titles depending on the specific role or company:

- **Software Developer**: Writes and maintains code for various applications and systems to meet specific user needs.
- **Back-end Developer**: Specializes in server-side development, focusing on databases, server logic, and **application programming interfaces** (**APIs**).
- **Full-Stack Developer**: Works on both the front-end and back-end of applications, handling the entire development process from server to user interface.
- **Application Developer**: Creates, tests, and maintains software applications for specific devices or operating systems like Windows and macOS, or iPhone and Android.
- **Systems Developer**: Designs and implements systems software, which includes operating systems, network control systems, and database management systems.
- **Web Developer**: Develops and maintains websites, focusing on front-end design, user experience, and sometimes back-end server functionality.
- **DevOps Engineer**: Bridges the gap between development and operations by automating deployment processes, ensuring system reliability, and improving software development cycles.

Software engineer career path

The typical career path for a software engineer is:

1. **Entry-Level, Junior Developer**: You will focus on learning and writing code under supervision. Internships are valuable for gaining hands-on experience.
2. **Mid-Level, Software Developer**: You will have more responsibility, contributing to design and architecture, and mentoring juniors. You might choose to specialize in areas like DevOps, database management, or front-end development.
3. **Senior-Level, Senior Developer**: You will be involved in high-level design decisions, leading projects, and mentoring. As a Technical Lead, you might lead a team of developers, ensuring technical standards are met.

One of the reasons I chose software engineering as a career path was that success as a .NET software engineer requires a blend of technical and creative problem-solving. The role requires a strong foundation in coding and development practices, as well as a surprising amount of soft skills like communication and managing upwards.

The career path is flexible, with opportunities to specialize, lead, or move into related fields. Whether you're just starting or looking to advance, being a software engineer offers a dynamic and evolving career with plenty of opportunities for growth.

As a .NET software engineer or an aspiring software engineer, it's important for you to know the types of role that you will work with and how you can collaborate with them.

Roles on a development team that you will collaborate with

In the life of a .NET software engineer, daily interactions can span a broad range of roles, each contributing in different ways to the project's goals.

Understanding the roles and responsibilities of these collaborators not only helps with effective communication but also enhances the efficiency and quality of the project outcomes. The more a .NET engineer is attuned to the inputs and needs of these varied roles, the smoother the project execution will likely be.

Let's review some key roles that a .NET engineer might regularly interact with, their core responsibilities, and the typical collaborative tasks involved.

Project manager aka project owner

The responsibilities of a **Project Manager (PM)** include overseeing the project timeline and deliverables, managing resources and budget, and ensuring that the project meets its objectives and stakeholders' expectations.

A .NET software engineer like yourself might work with the PM to clarify requirements, provide updates on development progress, and discuss any roadblocks that could affect deadlines or project scope.

To work well with a PM, make sure your predicted work timelines are as accurate as possible, and think outside the box with suggestions on how to remove roadblocks.

Business analyst

The responsibilities of a **Business Analyst (BA)** include gathering and defining business requirements from stakeholders, translating business needs into technical specifications, and validating the implemented features against business requirements.

A .NET software engineer will often need to understand the business logic detailed by the BA, ensuring that the technical solutions accurately reflect the business needs. They might also assist the BA in understanding the feasibility of proposed solutions.

If you can explain a complex technology in an easy-to-grasp manner to the BA, they will appreciate it since they will be explaining the same to higher-ups with even less technical prowess.

Quality assurance analyst or tester

The responsibilities of a **Quality Assurance (QA) analyst** or **tester** include designing test plans and scripts based on project requirements, conducting tests to ensure the software meets quality standards, and identifying bugs and issues for the development team to address.

A .NET software engineer will work closely with QA to understand the defects found during testing, prioritize bug fixes, and sometimes help in automating tests or providing specific unit tests.

The more tests that you write yourself, the better you will understand the needs of a QA analyst or tester. As you work with testers, you will start to write better code yourself that avoids the common mistakes that cause tests to fail, and if you build a good rapport with a tester, then the cycle of implementing a feature, testing it, and fixing it, gets smaller and faster, and the PMs will love you both.

User experience designer

The responsibilities of a **User Experience (UX) designer** include designing user interfaces, crafting user experiences that meet the needs of the end users, and creating and maintaining design wireframes, mockups, and specifications.

Collaborating with UX designers is important for a .NET software engineer to ensure that the application's front-end integrates seamlessly with back-end services. Feedback loops between the engineer and the designer help refine UI/UX elements.

Most software engineers I know are terrible at UI/UX design. If you can spend time with a UX designer, then you can improve these skills and build a better sense of UI taste. When Bill Gates and Steve Jobs were interviewed together at the D5 Conference on May 30, 2007, they were asked about their individual strengths and the impact they had on the technology industry. Gates said that Jobs had good taste, as shown in the following quote:

> *I'd give a lot to have Steve's taste. [...] He has natural—it's not a joke at all. I think in terms of intuitive taste, both for people and products, you know, the way he does things is just different and I think it's magical. [...] And in that case, wow.*
>
> -- *Bill Gates*

Good taste is often lacking in software engineering. I believe that improving that area in your own work will be noticed and appreciated.

Database administrator

The responsibilities of a **Database Administrator (DBA)** include designing, optimizing, and maintaining the database schema and performance, and ensuring data integrity and security.

A .NET software engineer needs to work with DBAs to ensure that their queries are optimized, data models are aligned with the application requirements, and any database changes do not adversely affect the application's performance. Recognize the DBA's specialized knowledge and seek their input on database design, performance optimization, and data integrity.

Engage the DBA early in the project lifecycle, especially during the database schema design phase, to ensure scalability and performance. Collaborate on indexing strategies to optimize query performance, and be open to their suggestions for improvements. Work together to anticipate future data growth and plan for database scalability and maintenance.

DevOps engineer aka Site Reliability Engineer (SRE)

The responsibilities of a **DevOps engineer** or Site Reliability Engineer (SRE) include managing CI/CD pipelines, ensuring system reliability and scalability, and implementing automation tools for deployment and testing.

A .NET software engineer collaborates with DevOps to streamline development workflows, deploy code efficiently, and troubleshoot deployment issues. They may also help in setting up environment-specific configurations.

Learning about and using tools like Docker and .NET Aspire for local development and containerizing your apps and services will make working with DevOps easier.

Front-end (FE) developer

The responsibilities of a **FE developer** include implementing the visual and interactive elements of a website or web application and ensuring cross-browser compatibility and responsiveness.

Although a .NET software engineer might also handle front-end tasks, in larger teams, the FE developers would specifically need to integrate APIs and back-end services developed in .NET with the front-end, ensuring seamless data exchange and functionality.

Most .NET developers avoid FE work for the same reason they are less comfortable with UX design. But it is important for a .NET developer to understand what helps and what hinders an FE developer when they need to integrate with your back-end projects.

Technical lead or architect

The responsibilities of a **technical lead** or **technical architect** include defining the project's technical architecture, ensuring best practices are followed, guiding the development team, and providing technical leadership.

Regular interaction with the technical lead or architect is essential for a .NET software engineer to align their development efforts with the project's architecture and to seek guidance on complex technical challenges.

Onboarding process

The onboarding process for a .NET software engineer can vary from one organization to another, but generally includes several key phases aimed at helping new hires integrate smoothly into their roles and the company culture. A typical onboarding process is laid out in stages in *Table 19.1*:

Stage	Description
Pre-Onboarding	Before the new engineer even starts, companies often prepare by setting up their IT systems, including email accounts, necessary software, and access permissions. HR might send out paperwork in advance for benefits and payroll setup. This phase ensures the engineer can hit the ground running on their first day.
First Day Introductions	The very first day usually focuses on HR orientation, which covers company policies, workplace rules, benefits, and administrative procedures. This is followed by an introduction to the team and key colleagues, including managers, peers, and other relevant staff they'll be working with. This may include a tour of the office and facilities.

Initial Training and Setup	In the first week, the engineer typically undergoes technical onboarding, which involves setting up their development environment with all necessary tools and accesses, such as Visual Studio, database access, cloud services, or other specific tools used by the team. Next will be an introduction to company technology stacks, including code repositories, current projects, and internal tools. This often involves cloning and running the existing projects to understand the codebase. Finally, there will be compliance and security training, particularly important in regulated industries or companies handling sensitive data.
Project Ramp-Up	Once the initial setups are complete, the focus shifts to integrating the engineer into the actual work including project assignments, starting with smaller, manageable tasks to familiarize them with the project workflows and codebase. Later, there will likely be mentorship, where a more experienced colleague might be assigned to guide the new hire through their first months, answering questions and providing support as needed.
Ongoing Development and Training	There will be regular check-ins with managers and mentors to assess progress, set goals, and discuss any challenges. Training sessions can be scheduled throughout the first few months to cover advanced topics, proprietary technologies, or soft skills like project management and communication. Feedback and evaluations are often formalized through a review at the end of the probation period to discuss performance, fit, and future goals.
Integration into the Company Culture	Social events and team-building activities help new hires establish relationships within and outside their immediate teams. Participation in company-wide meetings and town halls allows them to better understand the broader company objectives and developments.

Table 19.1: Stages of the onboarding process

Good practice: Onboarding good practices include clear documentation and resources. If your organization has not provided this, don't be afraid to ask for it. If it doesn't exist, make sure your manager knows that the lack of documentation and resources will impede your progress.

How to ask for training and development

When you want to ask your manager for training and development, I recommend that you present a clear, well-justified request. Take a strategic approach to effectively communicate and justify your training needs.

Identify specific training needs

Before approaching your manager, you should clearly define what training you need and why. This involves:

- **Identifying skill gaps:** Determine which skills need improvement or updating to meet current or upcoming project demands or to keep up with industry advancements like new .NET versions, cloud technologies, or best practices.
- **Researching training options:** Look for specific books, courses, certifications, workshops, or conferences that address these gaps. Consider factors like cost, duration, format (online or in-person), and the reputation of the training provider. Sometimes the organization will have an annual budget for training, and your manager might spend it all at once on a single training event for you. You don't have to just accept this. Ask your manager what the budget is per employee and suggest alternatives with similar or lower costs.

For your style of learning, buying a set of .NET books, combined with a subscription to an LLM like Gemini Pro, ChatGPT, or Claude, a .NET weekly newsletter, or access to a suite of video learning courses might be money better spent than a couple of days of classroom training.

Align training with business goals

You should link your training needs to the business's objectives and goals:

- **Enhance project performance:** Explain how the training will directly improve your work on specific projects. For example, a course on the latest version of ASP.NET Core could help you to build more efficient and secure codebases.
- **Increase team capabilities:** Show how your enhanced skills will benefit the team or department, such as bringing new capabilities in-house, reducing dependency on external consultants, or speeding up project delivery.
- **Support long-term business growth:** Illustrate how the skills gained will help in scaling operations, entering new markets, or innovating products and services. Paying attention during monthly all-company meetings is especially useful. What does the CEO spend time talking about? What are their priorities this quarter? How can you align your needs with the business's needs? Remember, often it's not your direct manager who needs persuading; they will need to persuade their manager, and up and up. So give your manager the ammunition they need to get you what you want.

Prepare a cost-benefit analysis

To make a compelling case, prepare a cost-benefit analysis that includes:

- **Direct costs:** Training fees, travel expenses (if applicable), and any required materials
- **Indirect costs:** Time away from work and the potential temporary reduction in productivity
- **Benefits:** Quantify the potential returns such as cost savings from faster project completion, better quality output, reduction in errors, or customer satisfaction improvements

Propose a flexible plan

Offer flexible solutions to minimize the impact of your absence during the training period. This might include:

- **Scheduling:** Propose doing the training during a slower period for the team or suggest splitting it into parts to reduce the impact on daily operations.
- **Workload management:** Outline how you plan to manage or redistribute your current workload. Offer to train colleagues on essential tasks to ensure continuity.
- **Post-training sharing:** Commit to sharing the knowledge gained with your team through a presentation or workshop, which adds value to the entire team. This also gives you practice in public speaking and clear communication, which are vital skills to accelerate your career.

Request a meeting and present your case

Arrange a formal or informal meeting to discuss your proposal. During the meeting:

- **Be concise and focused:** Clearly outline your training request, the reasons behind it, and the benefits to the team and company.
- **Be prepared for questions:** Your manager may ask about the specifics of the training, its relevance, or how you plan to manage your duties during the training period.
- **Show enthusiasm and commitment:** Demonstrate your dedication to personal growth and to contributing to the company. But be sure to stress the company benefits more than your personal growth!

After the meeting, follow up with an email summarizing your request and the key points discussed. Thank your manager for considering your proposal and express your willingness to adjust aspects of your plan to better fit team needs or constraints.

By carefully preparing and aligning your training request with the business's needs, you not only increase your chances of approval but also demonstrate your proactive stance on personal and organizational development. This approach helps ensure that your interests are aligned with the company's strategic goals, making it a win-win proposition for both you and your employer.

Pair programming

Pair programming is a software development technique that involves two programmers working together at one workstation. One programmer, the "driver," writes the code while the other, the "observer" or "navigator," reviews each line of code as it is typed in. The roles are frequently switched between the two, promoting collaborative work and more creative problem-solving. This method is a core practice in Agile development methodologies and Extreme Programming (XP).

The typical workflow in pair programming includes:

- **Role switching:** Regularly switching roles ensures that both the driver and the navigator engage actively in the coding process, contributing to both the strategic direction of the code and the detail-oriented task of coding itself.

- **Continuous review**: Having two sets of eyes on the code at all times helps catch errors early, improves code quality, and reduces debugging time later.
- **Brainstorming solutions**: The collaborative environment allows for immediate discussion and problem-solving, fostering innovative solutions and faster decision-making.
- **Knowledge sharing**: Pair programming is an effective way to share knowledge about the codebase and programming techniques between the more experienced developers and newcomers or between specialists in different areas.

> Your code editor might allow you to do pair programming remotely, and this can work especially well when integrated with Microsoft Teams or Discord. Both programmers can edit and debug a project simultaneously and see each other's edits. You can read about this at the following link: `https://visualstudio.microsoft.com/services/live-share/`.

Could an LLM replace a human paired programmer?

While an LLM like ChatGPT can assist in many tasks associated with programming, it cannot yet fully replace a human in the role of a paired programmer. However, it can be used as a supplementary tool in the programming process.

The pros of an LLM paired programmer include:

- **Instant lookup**: LLMs can quickly provide information about programming concepts, syntax, and best practices, speeding up the coding process
- **Code suggestions**: LLMs can generate code snippets or suggest improvements to existing code, acting as a pseudo-navigator by reviewing and suggesting changes
- **Debugging help**: LLMs can help in debugging by interpreting error messages and suggesting fixes

The cons of an LLM paired programmer include:

- **Hallucinations**: These occur because the model predicts based on patterns in its training data rather than factual accuracy, leading to outputs that seem plausible but are wrong. For example, the LLM might generate a function call to an API that doesn't exist, or the LLM might provide a flawed implementation of an algorithm. It might suggest an optimization that doesn't actually improve performance or is impractical, or it might suggest code that introduces security vulnerabilities.
- **Lack of understanding context**: The LLM might not fully grasp the broader context or the specific project goals, which can lead to less relevant suggestions. Sadly, in my experience, this is common for humans too. Make sure that you understand the wider context of your development decisions and suggestions; otherwise, you're no better than an LLM.
- **Inability to make judgments**: LLMs lack the ability to make nuanced judgments about design decisions, which often depend on understanding project-specific constraints and objectives. This is also a key difference between a junior and senior .NET software engineer.

- **No emotional intelligence**: Emotional intelligence and personal interaction are key in pair programming for motivation and maintaining a positive working relationship. LLMs cannot replicate these human aspects. In the IT field, many humans also lack emotional intelligence. I recommend that you put extra effort into learning to be as empathetic as possible.
- **Limited adaptability**: While LLMs can learn from a vast amount of data, they do not yet adapt in real time to the evolving needs of a project or learn from the project's specific past experiences in the same way a human does. But give them a few years.

While ChatGPT and similar LLMs offer valuable assistance in the coding process by automating information retrieval and generating code snippets, they cannot (yet) replace the interactive, dynamic, and context-sensitive nature of human collaboration in pair programming. The real value of pair programming lies not just in writing code but in the shared understanding, creative problem-solving, and continuous learning between the pair—aspects that are currently beyond the capabilities of AI models.

While AI can augment the capabilities of a programming team, human insight, oversight, and interaction remain indispensable, especially in complex and collaborative tasks like software development.

My recommendation is to "skate to where the puck is going," because, although today, even in 2025-26, you still need to know how to write C#, in five years, you might not. Sooner than you think, your pair programmer will be an AI. If you know the pros and cons of AI pair programmers, then you can put more effort into enhancing your skills that are more human, like a better understanding of the context of coding decisions, making judgments, and so on.

Applying for a job

Applying for a job as a .NET software engineer involves several key steps that can help you effectively showcase your skills and stand out as a candidate. By following these steps, you'll be well prepared to apply for .NET software engineering positions and make a strong impression throughout the hiring process.

Before you apply

Before you contact a potential employer, there is some work you should do to prepare.

Refine your skills and knowledge

Before you start applying, ensure you have a strong foundation in .NET technologies and related skills, as shown in the following list:

- **Core technologies**: Be proficient in C#, ASP.NET, .NET Core, and Entity Framework, and be familiar with front-end technologies like JavaScript, HTML, and CSS if the job involves full-stack development.
- **Databases**: Have a good understanding of SQL Server or other databases like MySQL, Oracle, or NoSQL databases such as MongoDB.
- **Version control**: Be adept at using tools like Git.
- **Development tools**: Familiarize yourself with Visual Studio and VS Code.

- **Cloud services:** Knowledge of Microsoft Azure, AWS, or Google Cloud can be a big plus. But note that there is a backlash building against cloud services. If you can gain experience with migrating from cloud to self-hosting, this is a very current desired skill.

A good set of books like my .NET quartet can help you with most of the above .NET technologies and related skills.

Obtain certifications

While not always necessary, certifications can enhance your resume, especially if you're starting your career and do not yet have experience to lean on. Certifications demonstrate your commitment and proficiency in .NET and related Microsoft technologies.

For example, Microsoft has a new foundational certification for C# alongside a free 35-hour online course. You can read more about how to qualify for the certification at the following link: `https://www.freecodecamp.org/learn/foundational-c-sharp-with-microsoft/`.

Search for job openings

Job openings are listed in many places:

- **Job boards:** Use websites like LinkedIn, Indeed, Glassdoor, and Stack Overflow Jobs to find .NET software engineer positions.
- **Company websites:** Target specific companies you're interested in and apply through their career pages.
- **Networking:** Leverage your network as many jobs are filled via referrals. Attend .NET meetups, conferences, or seminars to connect with potential employers.

According to ChatGPT 5, as of mid-2025, there are more than 10,000 open .NET developer positions worldwide, as listed on the WeAreDevelopers website: `https://www.wearedevelopers.com/en/jobs/s/.net`. Before you exclaim, "That could be a hallucination!", consider that even if it were 100% accurate, it's an utterly useless factoid. It's not like you, dear reader, can apply for all those open positions. It's only a handful that are close to your geographic location that are relevant.

If there were 10,000 open positions for .NET/C# and 20,000 open positions for Java, would you really switch to Java? No! You only need one open position that suits your skills and interests and that pays decently.

The number of open positions highlights a strong global demand for .NET developers. The roles vary from junior developers to senior positions and full-stack developers, indicating opportunities at multiple career stages. Positions are available in major technology hubs as well as remote opportunities, offering flexibility for developers in different geographic locations and work preferences.

Salaries for .NET developers can vary widely based on location, experience, and specific job requirements. For example, mid-level to senior .NET developers in the U.S. can expect to earn between $75,000 and $150,000 annually, with hourly rates for contract positions ranging from $50 to $85.

You can search for yourself at the following common job sites:

- Indeed: `https://www.indeed.com/`
- LinkedIn Jobs: `https://www.linkedin.com/jobs`
- Remote OK: `https://remoteok.com/`
- Stack Overflow Jobs: `https://stackoverflow.com/jobs`
- ZipRecruiter: `https://www.ziprecruiter.com/`
- Asia – JobStreet: `https://www.jobstreet.com/`
- India – Naukri: `https://www.naukri.com/`

Craft your job application, resume, and online profiles

Unless you've literally only just started with your current job and you're already wanting to jump to another position, then your documents for applying for jobs will likely be out of date, so update your resume and online profiles:

- **Resume**: Tailor your resume to highlight your .NET development experience, projects, and specific technologies you're proficient in. Include measurable achievements and use action verbs. This chapter covers more details about resumes in the next section.
- **LinkedIn**: Make sure your LinkedIn profile is up to date and reflects your resume. Engage with .NET-related content and follow companies you're interested in.
- **GitHub/portfolio**: Maintain a GitHub repository with samples of your code or contribute to open-source projects. If possible, create a portfolio website showcasing your projects and technical skills.
- **Cover letter**: Write a concise cover letter that explains why you are a good fit for the position, highlighting your .NET skills and any specific projects that are relevant to the job.
- **Custom applications**: Tailor each application to the job description, emphasizing the skills and experience that match the employer's requirements.

Your job application, resume, and online profiles paint a picture of you, your skills, and your experience. We'll focus on resumes next.

Your resume or curriculum vitae

When crafting a resume as a .NET developer, it's important to highlight your technical skills, project experiences, and your ability to adapt and solve problems using the .NET framework.

Here's a structured template to help you organize your resume effectively: `https://github.com/markjprice/tools-skills-net10/blob/main/docs/resume.md`.

If you have no professional (paid) experience, here's a template that you'll find more helpful: `https://github.com/markjprice/tools-skills-net10/blob/main/docs/resume-no-experience.md`.

These templates aim to showcase not just your technical capabilities but also your impact on projects and your role within teams. Tailor each section to reflect your experiences and strengths, ensuring that your resume stands out to potential employers in the .NET development field.

The terms "resume" and "curriculum vitae (CV)" are often used interchangeably, but they refer to different types of documents, particularly in an international context. A resume is a concise document tailored for a specific job application. It highlights an individual's skills, experiences, and accomplishments relevant to the position they are applying for. Its typical length is 1 to 2 pages.

A CV provides a comprehensive and detailed overview of an individual's academic and professional history. It can grow to 10 or more pages for someone with extensive experience. CVs are commonly used in Europe, Asia, Africa, and the Middle East. They are also used in the U.S. and Canada for academic, research, medical, and scientific positions. A CV is often a static document that is not tailored to specific jobs but, rather, updated regularly as one's career progresses.

My recommendation for applying for .NET software developer jobs is to maintain a CV for those countries that prefer them but send a resume with initial job applications. You can always include a note in your cover letter that you can provide a full CV if needed.

Ask an LLM to improve your resume

To help you enhance your resume effectively for a specific job opening, you can follow these steps:

1. **Provide the job description**: Share details or key excerpts from the job description. Understanding the requirements and preferred qualifications will allow the LLM to help tailor your resume to highlight the most relevant skills and experiences.
2. **Share your current resume**: Provide the content of your resume. You don't need to upload the actual document, but providing the text, especially sections like your objective or summary, professional experience, skills, and education, will be crucial.
3. **Specify any particular concerns**: If there are any specific areas on your resume that you feel need improvement—whether it's clarity, impact, or relevance—mention them so that the LLM can focus more on those aspects.

Based on this information, an LLM can suggest modifications such as:

- **Revising the objective or summary**: Tailoring this section to align closely with the job you're applying for.
- **Highlighting relevant experience**: Adjusting bullet points under your professional experience to emphasize the skills and responsibilities that directly align with the job description.
- **Enhancing the Skills section**: Ensuring the keywords and skills that match the job requirements are prominently featured.
- **Formatting adjustments**: Making sure the layout is professional and easy to read, and that the formatting is consistent throughout the document.

Good practice: As always, when working with LLMs, use their output with caution!

Interview preparation

Like a good scout, you should always be prepared:

- **Technical preparation**: Be ready to discuss your past projects and demonstrate your expertise in .NET technologies. You might be asked to solve programming problems or explain the design decisions in your previous work.
- **Behavioral preparation**: Prepare to answer questions about your teamwork, problem-solving abilities, and how you handle deadlines and pressure.
- **Mock interviews**: Consider conducting mock interviews with peers or mentors to build confidence and improve your interview skills.

When preparing for an interview for a .NET software engineer position, it's important to be well-rounded in your preparation, covering technical skills, problem-solving abilities, and cultural fit. The interview process can vary between companies but typically involves several key components:

1. **Initial screening**: This might be a phone or video call, often with HR or a recruiter, to assess your general fit for the position, communication skills, and background. Expect questions about your resume, your interest in the company, and your career goals.
2. **Technical screen**: This often follows the initial screening and can be a coding test or technical questions administered over the phone or through a platform like HackerRank or Codility. For .NET positions, this might involve solving problems using C# and could cover:
    - **Basic and advanced programming concepts**: OOP principles, data structures, algorithms, and system design.
    - **.NET-specific knowledge**: Understanding of the .NET framework, CLR, and nuances of languages like C#. You might be asked about ASP.NET Core for web development, Entity Framework Core for data access, and LINQ for data manipulation. Make sure to review everything covered in my book, *C# 14 and .NET 10 – Modern Cross-Platform Development Fundamentals*.
    - **Debugging, testing, and optimization**: Ability to diagnose and improve poorly performing code or systems. This book is critical for these topics.
3. **On-site interview**: This usually involves a series of interviews with team members and managers. These can be technical deep dives, system design interviews, and sometimes pair programming sessions. For a .NET engineer, expect:
    - **In-depth technical questions**: Focused on .NET, C#, and possibly related technologies like SQL Server or front-end technologies if the role is full stack.
    - **System design**: Especially for senior roles, showing your ability to design scalable systems using .NET technologies.
    - **Soft skills assessment**: Problem-solving approach, communication skills, and ability to work collaboratively.

- **Experience:** Interviewers will often start with a general question about your experience and leave it up to you to decide what the most important experience you have had to talk about. From there, they can come up with more questions and gain a good understanding of your contribution to past projects.

4. **Cultural fit and behavioral interview:** You might encounter questions intended to gauge how well you'll fit into the company's culture. These often revolve around past experiences, how you handle conflict, and your adaptability to change.

Do not use an LLM during an interview

While it is acceptable to use LLMs before an interview to help you polish your resume, learn technologies, and so on, you should never use an LLM live while participating in an interview.

Remote interviews happen more frequently these days, and this has opened the door to cheating using LLMs. Sadly, it is becoming more and more common for interviewees to have ChatGPT open in one window while using Zoom to do an interview in another window. When the interviewer asks a question, they say, "Let me think about that," while typing the question into ChatGPT, and then a few seconds later, they read out the response. No one is fooled by this. Do NOT do it!

I used to be a trainer for a company that offered accelerated courses to prepare developers for Microsoft developer certification exams. Once, I had 20 developers in a classroom, and in the back row, in the corner, where I couldn't easily walk past and see what he was up to, was a gentleman who would ask oddly specific, off-topic questions throughout the day. During a break, the student sitting next to him came to me and told me this guy was asking questions from a "brain dump."

This is when an actual set of real exam questions and answers are stolen from Microsoft and dumped in a dark corner of the Internet. I had to ban this gentleman from my classroom and prevent him from taking the exam at the end of the course. Cheaters always get caught because they are never the sharpest tool in the shed.

> **Warning!** LLMs are useful but only when combined with human judgment. If you are just the "typist" between the interviewer and the LLM, then, seriously, what's the point? If that's all you can do, you'll be the first to be replaced by the machines. Work with AI to augment and develop your own skills; don't just use it to replace your brain completely.

Interviewing at the big companies

Interviewing with top tech companies like Microsoft, Amazon, Google, Apple, and Meta (Facebook), as well as major game companies, is a unique challenge. Each company has its own culture, values, and specific things they look for in candidates. Here are some targeted tips and anecdotes for each of these giants, which could help you make a strong impression during your interview process:

Company	Tips
Microsoft	Microsoft values collaboration and how effectively you can work within a team. Be prepared to discuss past projects and how you contributed to team success. Having a good grasp of Microsoft's product suite and the underlying technologies can be a big plus. Mentioning your experiences or insights about products like Azure, Office 365, or Windows can show your enthusiasm and knowledge. Many candidates mention that storytelling is crucial in Microsoft interviews. One candidate described how framing their project experiences as stories, highlighting challenges and solutions, helped engage the interviewers more effectively.
Amazon	Amazon is famous for its 16 Leadership Principles. Be ready to discuss examples from your past experiences that align with these principles. Many questions are likely to revolve around Amazon's principle of customer obsession. Think of instances where you went above and beyond to meet a customer's needs. Amazon has a unique role in its interview process known as the Bar Raiser, who ensures that hiring standards are consistently high. Impress this person with your problem-solving skills and readiness to take on complex challenges.
Google	Google places a strong emphasis on your coding ability and problem-solving skills through algorithms and data structures. Practicing coding challenges on platforms like LeetCode can be highly beneficial. Be prepared to show deep technical knowledge relevant to the position you're applying for, whether it's in systems design, AI, or web development. Highlight your ability to own and lead projects, as Google values entrepreneurial spirit even in technical roles.
Apple	Apple values innovation, so highlighting any creative solutions or products you've developed can be a plus. Also, attention to detail is crucial; Apple prides itself on the polish and intuitiveness of its products. Given Apple's strong stance on privacy, showing knowledge in these areas, especially if you're applying for a role related to cloud services or user data, can be advantageous. Showing passion for Apple's products and an understanding of what makes them unique and favored in the market can help you connect with the interviewers.
Meta (Facebook)	Facebook looks for candidates who can demonstrate the impact of their work. Prepare to discuss your achievements in terms of real-world impact, user engagement, or growth metrics. Emphasizing your ability to work efficiently and adapt quickly can resonate well with Facebook's fast-paced work environment. Zuckerberg infamously said he liked to "move fast and break things," but you can stress that attitude among software engineers has changed for the better. Expect rigorous coding interviews, with an emphasis on writing clean, efficient code.
Video game companies (like Blizzard, EA, and Riot Games)	Demonstrating a genuine passion for gaming, knowledge about the company's games, and ideas on how they can be improved is crucial. For developers, strong programming skills are a must, often in C++ or Unity (depending on the studio). Be prepared to discuss game-specific algorithms, such as pathfinding and collision detection. Game companies often look for a good cultural fit, so expressing your alignment with the company's values and showing how you can contribute to the team spirit is important.

Table 19.2: What the big companies look for when interviewing

General tips that apply to all organizations include the following:

- **Practice whiteboard coding:** Many of these companies still use whiteboard coding during their interviews, so practicing this can be crucial.
- **Mock interviews:** Engage in mock interviews with peers or mentors who have experience with these companies to get used to the style and rigor of the questions.
- **Stay calm and positive:** These interviews can be grueling. Maintaining a positive attitude and staying calm under pressure can help you think clearly and perform better.

Each interview is an opportunity to learn, so take each experience as a chance to improve your skills and understand what these leading companies are looking for in top-tier talent.

Applying for more experienced positions

When experienced developers or candidates apply for senior positions at top tech companies, the interview process can involve additional complexities and expectations. The focus shifts more toward leadership, architectural understanding, strategic thinking, and a proven track record of impact on previous projects.

Here are some key aspects that are often emphasized in interviews for senior roles:

- **Leadership and influence:**
  - **Team leadership:** Expect questions about leading teams, mentoring junior developers, and managing cross-functional projects. You'll need to demonstrate your ability to inspire, lead, and deliver through others.
  - **Conflict resolution:** Interviewers often ask about situations where you had to handle conflicts or make tough decisions. They are looking to see how you balance technical correctness, project timelines, and interpersonal relationships.
  - **Driving change:** Companies look for leaders who can drive technological and procedural changes to improve efficiency or outcomes. Be prepared to discuss how you have initiated and managed change.
- **Architectural depth:**
  - **System design:** For senior roles, a deep understanding of system design is crucial. You might be asked to design complex systems on the spot or critique the architecture of existing systems.
  - **Scalability and performance:** Demonstrating knowledge of scalability, performance optimization, and system security is often a requirement. These elements are crucial as systems grow and evolve.
  - **Technology evaluation:** Senior developers are often tasked with evaluating and choosing technologies that best fit project needs. You may be asked how you evaluate new tools or technologies and your process for integrating them.

- **Strategic thinking:**
  - **Vision and strategy:** You might be asked about your long-term vision for a project you've led or your strategic approach to technology. This can include product lifecycle management, foreseeing market or tech trends, and aligning technology strategies with business goals.
  - **Resource management:** Questions may also focus on how you allocate resources, manage budgets, or prioritize work to meet strategic goals.
- **Technical mentorship:**
  - **Knowledge sharing:** Senior developers are expected to be repositories of knowledge and experience that they can share with their team. You might be asked about times you've mentored others or contributed to the professional growth of your colleagues.
  - **Advocating best practices:** Demonstrating your commitment to best practices in coding, testing, security, and maintenance is important, as well as your ability to advocate and implement these practices within your teams.
- **Impact and results:**
  - **Measurable outcomes:** Be ready to discuss specific examples where your contributions led to measurable improvements in productivity, performance, or revenue.
  - **Project management:** Experience in managing projects, particularly in an Agile environment, can be crucial. You may need to illustrate your methodological approach and how it led to successful project completions.
- **Cultural contribution:**
  - **Cultural fit:** Especially at senior levels, being a cultural fit for the organization becomes as important as a technical fit. You may be assessed on how well your values and work style align with the company's culture.
  - **Innovative mindset:** Companies often seek senior developers who not only adapt to change but also drive innovation within the company. Be prepared to discuss how you've fostered innovation in your previous roles.

Preparation tips for senior roles include the following:

- **Prepare impact stories:** Have a few key stories ready that highlight your contributions, leadership, problem-solving, and outcomes. Ensure these stories articulate the context, your actions, the challenges faced, and the results.
- **Brush up on new technologies:** Even if you are an experienced developer, staying up to date with the latest technologies and trends is vital, as it shows your commitment to continual learning.
- **Mock interviews:** Engaging in mock interviews focused on leadership and strategic questions can be particularly helpful.

Interviewing for a senior position means demonstrating not just your technical skills but also your ability to lead and think strategically. It's about showing that you can drive the company forward, not just keep up with it.

Applying for tester positions

Applying for a tester or QA position involves a distinct set of preparation steps and focuses compared to developer roles. While technical skills are still important, the emphasis shifts more toward precision, problem-solving, and understanding of testing methodologies. Here's what an applicant for a tester position should consider doing differently:

- **Understand different testing methodologies:**
    - **Study up:** Familiarize yourself with various testing methodologies like Agile testing, Waterfall, and more contemporary approaches such as **Behavior-Driven Development** (**BDD**) and **Test-Driven Development** (**TDD**).
    - **Certifications:** Consider obtaining certifications like **ISTQB** (**International Software Testing Qualifications Board**) or **CSTE** (**Certified Software Tester**), which can demonstrate your knowledge and commitment to the testing field.
- **Focus on detail-oriented skills:**
    - **Error detection:** Testers need a keen eye for detail to spot inconsistencies and errors that others might miss. Practice by reviewing code, apps, or even websites to identify bugs or UI issues.
    - **Documentation:** Strong documentation skills are crucial. You should be able to write clear and concise bug reports, test cases, and testing plans that are understandable and actionable.
- **Technical proficiency:**
    - **Tool familiarity:** Gain proficiency in tools commonly used in testing such as Playwright, Jira, or Postman. Knowing how to automate tests using scripting languages like Python or JavaScript can be particularly advantageous.
    - **Understand the stack:** Have a basic understanding of the software stack that you will be testing. For instance, if you're testing web applications, you should know HTML, CSS, and JavaScript basics.
- **Soft skills:**
    - **Communication:** Effective communication is vital as you will often need to explain bugs to developers and ensure there is a clear understanding of the issue and how it can be replicated.
    - **Problem-solving:** Highlight your problem-solving skills during interviews. You might be given scenarios where you need to figure out how to test certain functionalities or identify potential problems in a hypothetical situation.
- **Prepare for testing-specific interview questions:**
    - **Practical demonstrations:** Be prepared to participate in practical tests during the interview, such as finding bugs in a block of code, writing test cases for a given scenario, or critiquing a piece of software.

    - **Scenario questions**: You may be asked to outline how you would test a particular application or feature. Be ready to discuss your approach methodically and logically.
- **Showcase past testing experience:**
    - **Portfolio of bugs**: If possible, keep a record of significant bugs you've identified in past projects and how your findings contributed to improving the product.
    - **Impact of your work**: Discuss the impact your testing had on previous projects. This could include how it improved user satisfaction, reduced bug counts, or helped streamline the development process.
- **Demonstrate a quality-first mindset:**
    - **Advocate for quality**: Show that you are an advocate for product quality and user satisfaction. Discuss how you have contributed beyond just bug finding to improve the overall quality of a project.
    - **Proactive approach**: Illustrate your ability to think ahead about potential areas of failure in applications and how proactive testing can mitigate these risks.
- **Understand the product and user:**
    - **User-centric testing**: Demonstrate your understanding of the end user's needs and how you tailor your testing practices to ensure the final product meets these needs effectively.
    - **Product knowledge**: If possible, research the company's products thoroughly before the interview to suggest thoughtful, targeted testing strategies.

Testers play a critical role in software development, ensuring the reliability and performance of the final product. By focusing on these specialized areas, you can effectively prepare for a tester position and demonstrate your unique value in the interview process.

Selection of questions

The selection of interview questions is typically designed to measure both the breadth and depth of a candidate's technical capabilities, as well as their cultural fit with the company. Here's how questions are often selected:

- **Relevance to the job**: Questions are chosen based on the specific skills and knowledge that are necessary for the job. For .NET positions, this means a heavy focus on the .NET ecosystem, C# programming, and commonly used tools and libraries in the .NET community.
- **Testing problem-solving skills**: Employers often select questions that assess a candidate's ability to solve problems under pressure. These questions also help interviewers gauge a candidate's thinking process and ability to articulate their thoughts.
- **Assessing the potential for growth**: Questions might also be aimed at understanding a candidate's capacity for learning and growth, especially important in the fast-evolving tech landscape.
- **Cultural fit**: Companies also choose questions that help determine if a candidate aligns with the company's values, work ethic, and team dynamics. The two biggest qualities interviewers look for are passion that they can "see in the eyes," and someone they can relate to. One of my favorite questions to ask is "Tell me about something you're proud of."

Here are some preparation tips:

- **Review the basics:** Make sure your fundamental knowledge of C#, .NET, and common frameworks is solid.
- **Practice coding:** Utilize platforms like LeetCode or CodeSignal to practice coding challenges.
- **Understand the company's tech stack:** Research the specific technologies and tools the company uses.
- **Mock interviews:** Consider mock interviews or speaking with mentors who can provide feedback.

By understanding these facets of the interview process, you can better prepare and present yourself as a well-rounded candidate for any .NET software engineer position.

Behavioral questions

Behavioral interview questions are a common part of the interview process, especially for roles that require significant interpersonal interaction or decision-making. These questions help employers predict your future behavior based on your past experiences.

When answering behavioral interview questions, the quality of your response can significantly influence the interviewer's perception of your suitability for the role.

Here's how to frame responses to three commonly asked questions, highlighting one bad response and two good responses for each.

1. Tell me about a time when you faced a significant challenge at work. How did you handle it?

This question aims to assess your problem-solving and critical-thinking skills. Interviewers are interested in understanding how you approach complex situations and overcome obstacles. They want to see evidence of persistence, creativity, and resourcefulness.

Bad response: "I really can't think of any significant challenges. I guess I just do my work and things generally go smoothly."

Why it's bad: This response fails to answer the question, suggests a lack of challenging experiences, and may imply you're not used to handling difficult situations.

Good response 1: "At my previous job, we were facing a tight deadline on a critical project where we were short-staffed. I recognized the urgency, so I took the initiative to redistribute the workload, including taking on additional responsibilities myself. I also organized brief daily check-ins to keep everyone motivated and on track. We managed to complete the project two days ahead of schedule, which really helped maintain our team's reputation for reliability."

Why it's good: It demonstrates initiative, leadership, and the ability to handle stress effectively.

Good response 2: "Once, I encountered a significant software bug during the final testing phase, which threatened to delay our release deadline. I stayed late for several evenings, researching and ultimately resolving the issue by revising our codebase. I also documented the process to prevent similar issues in the future. This experience taught me valuable lessons in persistence and detailed documentation."

Why it's good: Shows problem-solving skills, commitment, and a proactive approach to learning from challenges.

2. Describe a situation where you had to work closely with someone whose personality was very different from yours.

Here, the focus is on teamwork and your ability to collaborate effectively with diverse personalities. The interviewer wants to gauge your interpersonal skills, flexibility and how you handle conflict or differences in the workplace. This question also tests your empathy and your ability to understand and work with different perspectives.

Bad response: "I had a coworker who was really difficult to work with because of his attitude. I just tried to avoid him as much as possible and did my work independently."

Why it's bad: It shows an inability to collaborate effectively or adapt to interpersonal challenges.

Good response 1: "In a previous role, I worked with a colleague who was very extroverted and spontaneous, while I am more introverted and like to plan my work meticulously. Initially, it was challenging, but I saw it as an opportunity to develop my adaptability. We found a middle ground by scheduling regular planning sessions, which helped him organize his thoughts and allowed me to be more spontaneous in my interactions. This approach led to a successful project outcome and a surprisingly innovative workflow."

Why it's good: Demonstrates adaptability, willingness to meet halfway, and ability to leverage diverse working styles for better outcomes.

Good response 2: "I once worked with someone who preferred email communication, whereas I thrive on face-to-face interactions. To address our differences, I proposed a blend of weekly in-person meetings supplemented by emails. This not only improved our project coordination but also enhanced our mutual understanding and respect for each other's preferences."

Why it's good: Shows communication skills, flexibility, and initiative in finding effective solutions to teamwork challenges.

3. Can you give an example of a goal you didn't meet and how you handled it?

The intent behind this question is to understand your resilience and accountability. It reveals how you deal with failure and whether you can learn from your mistakes. Employers are looking for candidates who are honest about their shortcomings but are proactive about making improvements and can bounce back from setbacks.

Bad response: "Once, I missed a sales target by a wide margin. I guess I just accepted it because sometimes you win, sometimes you lose."

Why it's bad: Indicates a lack of responsibility and does not demonstrate any learning or corrective actions.

Good response 1: "Last year, I set a personal goal to increase my quarterly sales by 20%, but I fell short by 5%. I analyzed my sales strategies and realized I hadn't fully adapted to new consumer trends. I took this as a learning opportunity, enrolled in a digital marketing course, and worked with my manager to refine my approach. The next quarter, I exceeded my original goal by 10%."

Why it's good: Shows honesty, the ability to self-reflect, and a commitment to personal development.

Good response 2: "In a previous role, I aimed to lead a project rollout that unfortunately was postponed due to external factors beyond my control. I used this setback as a chance to gather more user feedback and refine our deployment strategy. The project was eventually a success and received positive feedback for its user-centric approach."

Why it's good: Illustrates resilience, strategic thinking, and the ability to turn setbacks into opportunities.

Applying for jobs is tough and can feel demoralizing. Try to remember that organizations are often desperate to find a good applicant. They want you to succeed and be the one that fills the position so they can go back to their real job. It's as frustrating for them as it is for you.

STAR method

These examples highlight the importance of illustrating your thought process, the actions you took, and the outcomes or lessons learned in a positive light.

When answering behavioral interview questions, it's beneficial to use the **STAR** method (**Situation, Task, Action, Result**). This structured approach helps you deliver clear and concise responses that highlight your skills and experiences in a relevant manner. Each answer should briefly outline the situation, describe the tasks involved, detail the actions you took, and explain the results of those actions.

With the STAR method, you respond to behavioral interview questions by organizing your answer into four distinct parts: Situation, Task, Action, and Result. This method helps you present a clear, concise, and compelling narrative of your past experiences, making it easier for the interviewer to understand how you approach and solve problems. Here's a breakdown of each component.

1. Situation

Begin your answer by setting the context for your story. Describe the background of the situation you were in, ensuring that it's relevant to the question. This part should give the interviewer a clear understanding of the environment and the circumstances leading up to the task or challenge you faced. It's crucial to be specific enough to paint a vivid picture but concise enough to keep the listener engaged.

Example: "In my previous role as a project manager, we were tasked with launching a new product on a tight deadline due to unexpected market demand."

2. Task

After setting the scene, explain the task you were assigned or the challenge you needed to overcome. This section clarifies your specific responsibilities in the scenario. It should convey what was expected of you, who was involved, and any particular objectives that had to be met. This is your opportunity to highlight the direct role you played.

Example: "I was responsible for coordinating between software development, marketing, and sales teams to ensure that all aspects of the product launch were synchronized and met the two-month timeline."

3. Action

This is the core of your answer, where you detail the steps you took to address the task or challenge. Focus on what you specifically did, rather than what the team or group accomplished. Use this section to showcase your skills, problem-solving abilities, and initiative. Describe your actions clearly and precisely, and don't shy away from mentioning any innovative or creative solutions you employed.

Example: "I organized weekly cross-departmental meetings to facilitate communication and address any bottlenecks. I also introduced a real-time dashboard for stakeholders to track progress and set up a quick-response team to handle last-minute issues."

4. Result

Conclude your story by sharing the outcome of your actions. Highlight the results achieved through your efforts and make sure these are quantifiable if possible. Discuss what you learned from the experience and, if applicable, mention any recognition you received for your performance. This part demonstrates the impact of your actions and reinforces the value you brought to the organization.

Example: "The product was successfully launched on schedule and exceeded initial sales projections by 15%. The project's success led to my recommendation for a leadership role in the company. Additionally, the dashboard I implemented became a standard tool used in future projects."

Using the STAR method effectively

When using the STAR method, it's important to:

- **Be specific**: Provide enough detail to ensure that the interviewer understands the complexity and significance of your story.
- **Be concise**: Although details are important, your answer should be succinct and to the point to maintain the interviewer's interest. You can even check in occasionally, asking the interviewer if they want more details, or move on to the next part.
- **Focus on yourself**: Even if you worked as part of a team, highlight your contributions and the actions you personally took.
- **Tailor your stories**: Choose stories that best match the job role and the company's values or highlight the skills that are most relevant to the position.

By structuring your responses using the STAR method, you can effectively communicate your past achievements and make a compelling case for your candidacy in behavioral interviews.

Tips during interviews

Remember that both you and the interviewer have limited time during the interview. The idea is that the interviewer just needs to hear enough to be convinced that you know a topic area. Unfortunately, when the interviewer asks you about a topic that you love and know a lot about, it is tempting to drone on and on because you're comfortable. But be sure to "read the room."

Give opportunities for an "off ramp" to allow the interviewer to switch to a different topic. For example, after speaking for a couple of minutes, say something like, "I could go into more detail if you like?"

Then they can either prompt you to continue, steer you to a more specific area within the same topic that you would be equally familiar with, or change to another topic entirely. You're showing that you are respectful of their needs and understand the process.

Some common general questions that you might get asked are shown in *Table 19.3*:

Question	Reasoning
Can you tell me about a project you're particularly proud of, and what your contribution was?	This question helps the interviewer understand what you consider important and your role in successful outcomes.
What motivated you to apply for this position?	This reveals your desires and expectations about the role and whether they align with what the company offers.
How do you handle stress and pressure, especially with tight deadlines or challenging projects?	Insights into your coping mechanisms can indicate how you'll manage day-to-day stress in the role.
What are your biggest strengths and weaknesses?	This classic question can still yield useful information about how self-aware you are and whether you're proactive about personal development.
Where do you see yourself in five years?	Your response can help gauge your long-term career aspirations and your potential longevity with the organization.
Can you describe a time when you had to work with someone who was difficult to get along with? How did you handle it?	This tells the interviewer about your interpersonal skills and adaptability.
How do you prioritize your work when you have multiple projects to handle at the same time?	Effective time management is crucial in any role, and this question assesses your ability to organize and prioritize.
What do you like to do outside of work?	This can give a glimpse into whether you might share interests with other team members, enhancing team cohesion.
What type of work environment do you thrive in?	This can help the interviewer decide if you'll fit into the work culture and physical environment of the organization.
Do you have any questions for us?	Your questions can be as telling as your answers to the interviewer's questions. It shows your level of interest and engagement with the organization.

Table 19.3: Common general questions

These questions are designed to prompt detailed responses and give the interviewer a comprehensive view of your abilities and potential fit within the organization.

Good practice: Be sure to prepare some questions for the interviewer, and not just about the salary and benefits!

When you're the interviewee, asking thoughtful questions at the end of an interview is crucial. It shows your interest in the role and company and helps you determine if the position is a good fit for your skills and career goals. Some insightful questions you might consider asking are shown in *Table 19.4*:

Question	Reasoning
Can you describe a typical day in this position?	This question helps clarify the day-to-day responsibilities and the workload you can expect.
What are the immediate projects that need to be addressed?	This gives you insight into what your first few weeks or months will look like and what the company prioritizes.
What are the most important qualities for someone to excel in this role?	Understanding what the employer values most can help you determine if your skills and qualities align with the position.
What opportunities for professional development does the company offer?	This shows your interest in growth and learning, which is important for long-term career progression.
How does the company measure success in this role?	Knowing how a company measures success can help you understand what it will take to excel and what expectations they have.
What are the typical career paths for someone in this role?	This question helps you understand the potential for advancement and future opportunities within the organization.
Can you tell me about the team I'll be working with?	This can reveal more about the team's size, structure, and the dynamics you can expect to encounter.
What is the company's approach to teamwork and collaboration?	This question helps assess whether the company's collaboration style aligns with your preferred working style.
What are the company's core values and how are they reflected in daily operations?	Understanding the company's values can help you see if there's a good cultural fit.
How is feedback given here?	Regular feedback is vital for professional growth; knowing how it's delivered can help you understand if the environment will support your development.

What are the biggest challenges facing the company right now?	This question can provide insights into what obstacles you might face and how the company anticipates handling them.
Where do you see the company in the next five years?	This shows your interest in the company's future and your potential role in its growth.
How does this company differentiate itself from its competitors?	Understanding the company's market position can give you a better sense of stability and innovation within the company.
Is there anything else you need from me, like references or work samples?	This shows your eagerness to move forward and ensures you've provided all they need to make their decision.
What are the next steps in the interview process?	This helps you understand the timeline and what to expect next, allowing you to plan accordingly.

Table 19.4: Common general questions you can ask

Be ready with answers to these questions yourself! After asking a question like, "What are the most important qualities for someone to excel in this role?", the interviewer might turn the question around to you. For example, they might ask, "What do *you* think the most important qualities for someone to excel in this role are?"

These questions not only demonstrate your enthusiasm for the role and the company but also provide you with crucial information that can help you make an informed decision if you are offered the position.

How to handle difficult coding questions

Facing coding questions in an interview that you find challenging or can't complete is a common issue, particularly under the pressure of an interview setting. Here's how you can handle such situations effectively:

1. **Keep calm**: First and foremost, try to stay composed. It's important to manage your stress in the moment, as panic can hinder your ability to think clearly. Take a deep breath and focus on the problem at hand.
2. **Communicate your thought process:** Even if you're unsure about the solution, start by explaining your initial thoughts and how you would approach the problem. Interviewers are often more interested in seeing your problem-solving process rather than just the correct answer.
3. **Break the problem into smaller parts:** If the problem seems overwhelming, try to break it down into manageable parts. This can help you tackle one aspect at a time and potentially uncover a solution piece by piece.
4. **Ask clarifying questions:** If anything about the problem is unclear, don't hesitate to ask questions. This can help demonstrate your attention to detail and your commitment to understanding the problem fully before diving into a solution.
5. **Discuss similar problems:** If you've solved similar problems before, discuss them and how you might adapt those solutions to the current problem. This can show your ability to leverage past knowledge effectively.

6. **Mention resources**: It's okay to mention that, in a real work scenario, you would consult documentation or resources like Stack Overflow to refine your solution. This honesty about your process can be refreshing and realistic.
7. **Make an attempt**: Even if you're not sure, make an attempt to solve the problem. It's better to try and work through your logic than to give up entirely. You can even write pseudocode or outline what you would do next if you had more time or resources.
8. **Ask for feedback**: If you reach a point where you can't proceed, you might ask the interviewer for a hint or their thoughts on your approach so far. This can turn the experience into a learning opportunity and show that you're open to feedback and learning.
9. **Reflect on your performance**: After the interview, reflect on what was challenging and why. Practicing coding problems under timed conditions or doing mock interviews can help you get more comfortable over time.
10. **Follow up in your thank you note**: In your follow-up thank you email, you might briefly mention your thoughts on the coding problem if you have come up with a better solution post-interview, or express your eagerness to learn and adapt based on the interview experience.

Facing challenging coding problems in interviews is a common hurdle, and how you handle these situations can demonstrate your problem-solving skills, resilience, and ability to learn from tough situations. Remember, demonstrating a thoughtful approach and a willingness to tackle difficult problems can be just as valuable as providing the correct answer.

When I was in college, many decades ago, I applied for a part-time job with Talking Pages, a phone service where customers could ask for details of plumbers and other companies in their local area. Part of the interview process was a test on British placenames. Audio was played and I had to write the correct spelling. Britain is infamous for placenames with very different spellings to how they are pronounced, like Loughborough ("LUFF-bur-uh" with the emphasis on the first syllable).

I failed the test.

I left feeling embarrassed and wandered around the town center for a while. Then I decided I would ask to try again. I phoned the work agency and asked if I could come back the next day and test again. I bought a road atlas and learned the placenames, went back, passed the test, and got the job.

How to handle unprepared interviewers

You will be super prepared for the interview, but the interviewer may not. This is extremely unprofessional but happens more than you might think. Many organizations do not help their employees learn how to job candidates well.

Dealing with an unprepared or unprofessional interviewer can be a challenging and uncomfortable situation. However, how you handle it can still leave a positive impression and potentially salvage the interview. Here are some strategies to consider:

- **Maintain your composure**: No matter the interviewer's behavior, keep your responses and demeanor professional. This demonstrates your ability to handle difficult situations gracefully.

- **Try to steer the conversation:** If the interviewer seems off-track or disorganized, gently guide the conversation back to relevant topics. For example, you might say, "I read about your recent project in X; I believe my experience with Y could be beneficial in this context."
- **Offer subtle assistance:** If the interviewer seems to have lost track of their questions or the interview's purpose, you might help by suggesting, "Would it help if I shared more about my experience in [specific area]?" This can provide a nudge in the right direction without appearing confrontational.
- **Clarify confusing questions:** If questions are unclear or poorly formulated, it's okay to ask for clarification to ensure you understand what's being asked. You might respond with, "I want to make sure I address your question correctly; could you clarify what you mean by...?"
- **Assess the company culture:** Consider whether the interviewer's behavior might reflect the company's broader culture. An unprepared interviewer could be a red flag about organizational issues or a lack of respect for employees.
- **Use the closing to get clarity:** At the end of the interview, you can ask questions that help you understand future interactions, such as, "Can you describe the next steps in the interview process?" or "Who will be my point of contact moving forward?"
- **Follow up professionally:** Send a thank-you email to express your gratitude for the opportunity to interview. This keeps the communication lines open and positive, regardless of the initial impression.
- **Decide if the job is right for you:** Reflect on the experience and decide if the behavior was a one-off or indicative of deeper issues within the company. If the role still interests you, consider proceeding with caution, but if the negatives outweigh the positives, it might be best to look elsewhere.

Navigating an interview with an unprepared or unprofessional interviewer requires tact and patience. How you handle it can provide valuable insights into your ability to manage difficult situations, which is a valuable skill in any job.

What to never do

When applying for jobs, there are several key behaviors and practices you should definitely avoid to maintain your professionalism and integrity. These missteps can jeopardize your chances of securing a position and harm your reputation in the industry.

By avoiding these pitfalls, you'll present yourself as a responsible and desirable candidate, increasing your chances of successfully landing a job that fits your skills and career aspirations.

Here are some important "never dos":

- **Never lie on your resume or in an interview:** Embellishing your skills, experience, or education can lead to disastrous consequences if discovered. Always be truthful about your qualifications.
- **Never apply to multiple positions in the same company simultaneously:** This can give the impression that you are not focused or genuinely interested in a specific role. Instead, apply for the job that best matches your skills and career goals.

- **Never skip customizing your application:** Avoid sending a generic resume and cover letter. Tailor your materials to each job, emphasizing how your skills and experiences align with the specific role and company.
- **Never ignore the instructions in the job posting:** If the posting asks for certain documents, a particular format, or to include specific information, make sure you follow these instructions carefully. Failing to do so can get your application discarded before it's even reviewed.
- **Never speak negatively about past employers or colleagues:** This can be seen as unprofessional and raise concerns about your teamwork and conflict management skills. Focus on positive experiences and what you've learned from past roles.
- **Never use an unprofessional email address:** Always use a professional email address, ideally one based on your name. Addresses that are casual or inappropriate can make a poor first impression.
- **Never send your application without proofreading:** Typos, grammatical errors, and formatting issues can make you seem careless. Always proofread your documents, or have someone else review them before submission.
- **Never forget to prepare for the interview:** Failing to prepare can lead to poor performance during the interview. Research the company, rehearse your answers to common interview questions, and prepare some questions to ask the interviewer.
- **Never arrive late for an interview:** Punctuality is critical. Arriving late can start the interview off on the wrong foot and suggest poor time management skills. Aim to arrive a few minutes early.
- **Never ghost an employer after an interview:** Always follow up with a thank-you note, and if you decide to decline a job offer or withdraw your application, communicate this decision politely and professionally.
- **Never burn bridges:** Even if you're not selected for a role, respond graciously and maintain a professional demeanor. Networking and industry reputation are important, and you never know when another opportunity might arise at the company.

Sample interview questions

Now let's review 60 commonly asked questions in .NET software engineer position interviews.

The first three items include a question, a good answer, and a poor answer with an explanation of why it is poor. In my opinion, you will learn as much from reviewing poor answers as good ones! The other 57 items only have the question.

> Answers for all 60 questions can be found online at the following link: `https://github.com/markjprice/tools-skills-net10/blob/main/docs/interview-qa/readme.md`.

I encourage you to get access to a whiteboard and ask a friend to read the questions to you. Answer them verbally and record your responses on video to review later. This will force you to practice writing code on a whiteboard in a stressful environment.

As you review these sample interview questions, you will note commonalities, especially in the poor answers:

- **Oversimplification:** A poor response will oversimplify the concept, technology, or process. This is a sign that the interviewee may only have learned a few key phrases related to the question, without any deeper understanding. At a minimum, you should have written code and seen it run for any technology you get asked about. It's fine to be honest and explain that you have not implemented a technology they ask you about in a real project, or only in learning exercises.
- **Unaware of best practices:** A poor response will often neglect the best practices in a technology area.
- **Misunderstanding:** A poor response will miss the point of the question or show that the interviewee does not understand the topic area. It is better to acknowledge areas where you have a vaguer understanding. Most employers would rather an employee ask questions when they are unsure rather than pretend that they know what they are doing!

Creating a comprehensive list of topics for a .NET software engineer interview can help candidates prepare effectively and ensure that interviewers cover all necessary aspects of .NET development. The following is a detailed set of topics that could be asked about during such an interview.

1. .NET CLI tools

"Can you explain the role of .NET CLI tools in the development process? Please provide examples of how you would use these tools to manage a .NET project throughout its lifecycle."

Good answer

".NET CLI tools play a crucial role in managing the lifecycle of a .NET application. They offer a comprehensive, cross-platform toolkit for developing, building, running, and publishing .NET applications. Here's how .NET CLI tools can be utilized throughout different stages of a project:

- **Project creation:** You can create various types of .NET projects using templates available via the CLI. For example, to create a new ASP.NET Core web application, you would use:

```
dotnet new webapp -n MyWebApp
```

- **Building the project:** To compile the project and check for compilation errors without running the application, you can use:

```
dotnet build
```

- **Running the project:** To run your application locally during development, you can simply execute:

```
dotnet run
```

- **Adding dependencies:** The CLI allows you to manage NuGet package dependencies directly. For instance, to add Entity Framework Core to your project, you can use:

```
dotnet add package Microsoft.EntityFrameworkCore
```

- **Migrations and database updates:** For projects using Entity Framework, managing database migrations is straightforward with the CLI:

```
dotnet ef migrations add InitialCreate
dotnet ef database update
```

- **Testing:** The CLI supports running unit tests using the `dotnet test` command, which identifies test projects in your solution and runs the tests:

```
dotnet test
```

- **Publishing:** Finally, to deploy your application, the CLI provides the `dotnet publish` command, which compiles the application, reads through its dependencies specified in the project file, and publishes the resulting set to a directory:

```
dotnet publish -c Release -o ./publish
```

These tools enhance productivity by allowing developers to perform all necessary tasks from the command line, making it easier to integrate with various IDEs and continuous integration pipelines."

Commonly given poor answer

"To manage a .NET project, you only need to use the Visual Studio IDE; the .NET CLI tools are just for those who prefer not to use an IDE."

Explanation of why this is wrong:

- **Underestimation of CLI capabilities:** This answer significantly underestimates the importance and capabilities of .NET CLI tools, suggesting that they are secondary to an IDE like Visual Studio. In reality, .NET CLI tools provide essential functions that are often faster and more flexible than using an IDE, especially in environments where an IDE may not be available, such as continuous integration servers or when developers prefer using lightweight editors like VS Code.
- **Misunderstanding of tooling ecosystem:** It overlooks the CLI's role in automation and scripting, which are critical for modern development practices like DevOps. The CLI allows for scripting of commands in a way that IDEs do not, facilitating automated builds and deployments.
- **Lack of recognition for cross-platform development:** The statement fails to acknowledge that .NET CLI tools are cross-platform, enabling development on Windows, Linux, and macOS, whereas Visual Studio is primarily Windows-based.

The mistake typically stems from a lack of exposure to the full spectrum of development environments and scenarios where .NET CLI tools are not only useful but essential

2. Git fundamentals

"Can you explain the fundamental concepts and commands of Git that every .NET developer should know? How would these Git operations be used in a typical development workflow?"

Good answer

"Git is a distributed version control system crucial for managing changes to software projects, allowing multiple developers to work on the same codebase concurrently. Key concepts and commands include:

- **Repositories:** A Git repository hosts the content of your project including all the files and the entire revision history. You can have local repositories on your machine and remote repositories to share with others.
- **Basic commands:**
  - `git init`: Initializes a new Git repository.
  - `git clone [url]`: Creates a copy of a remote repository on your local machine.
  - `git add [file]`: Stages changes in specific files preparing them for a commit.
  - `git commit -m "[message]"`: Saves the staged changes locally along with a descriptive message.
  - `git push [remote] [branch]`: Sends committed changes to a remote repository.
  - `git pull [remote] [branch]`: Fetches updates from the remote repository and merges them into the current branch.
- **Branching and merging:**
  - `git branch [branch-name]`: Creates a new branch.
  - `git checkout [branch-name]`: Switches to another branch.
  - `git merge [branch]`: Merges the specified branch into the current branch.
- **Workflow:** In a typical .NET development workflow, developers clone a repository, create a new branch for each feature or bug fix, commit changes locally, and push the branch to the remote repository. After peer review, changes from the feature branch are merged into the main branch. Regular `git pull` operations ensure the local repository is up to date with the main branch, minimizing merge conflicts.

Here is an example of creating a new feature branch and pushing it to the remote repository:

```
git checkout -b feature/new-feature
# Development work happens here, files are edited
git add .
git commit -m "Add new feature"
git push origin feature/new-feature
```

Using these Git commands and practices allows teams to manage changes efficiently, track the history of changes, and revert to previous states if necessary, all while collaborating effectively."

Commonly given poor answer

"Just use `git commit` and `git push` for everything you do. It doesn't matter much what branch you're on as long as your code gets into the `main` branch eventually."

Explanation of why this is wrong:

- **Lack of branching strategy**: This answer shows a misunderstanding of the importance of branches in Git. Branching is fundamental for managing features, fixes, and releases separately. Neglecting branches can lead to conflicts and instability in the main codebase.
- **Oversimplification of commands**: Suggesting to use only `git commit` and `git push` ignores other essential Git operations like `git pull`, `git branch`, and `git checkout` that are crucial for a collaborative and effective workflow.
- **Poor collaboration and version control practices:** The response disregards good practices like code reviews and merging strategies, which are critical in a team environment to maintain code quality and trackability.

The mistake usually stems from a lack of formal training in version control systems or from working in solo environments where rigorous source control protocols might not have been necessary. This oversight can lead to significant issues in larger, more complex projects where code maintainability and collaboration are essential.

3. Entity Framework Core

"Can you explain how Entity Framework Core can be used to handle database operations in .NET applications? Provide an example of configuring EF Core with a SQL Server database in a .NET application and explain how you would perform basic CRUD operations using this setup. Why would you use EF Core in a .NET project?"

Good answer

"Entity Framework Core is an advanced **ORM** (**Object-Relational Mapping**) framework that allows developers to work with a database using .NET objects, eliminating the need for most data-access code. EF Core supports a wide range of database providers such as SQL Server, SQLite, and PostgreSQL.

To use EF Core in a .NET application, you first need to set up the database context and register it with the dependency injection system. To configure it with a SQL Server database, create a class that derives from `DbContext` and includes `DbSet<T>` properties for the tables in the database, as shown in the following code:

```
using Microsoft.EntityFrameworkCore;

public class ApplicationDbContext : DbContext
{
  public ApplicationDbContext(
    DbContextOptions<ApplicationDbContext> options) : base(options)
  {
  }

  public DbSet<Product> Products { get; set; }
}
```

```
public class Product
{
  public int Id { get; set; }
  public string Name { get; set; }
  public decimal Price { get; set; }
}
```

Next, register the context with the SQL Server provider in the `Program.cs`, as shown in the following code:

```
var builder = WebApplication.CreateBuilder(args);

builder.Services.AddDbContext<ApplicationDbContext>(options =>
  options.UseSqlServer(builder.Configuration
  .GetConnectionString("DefaultConnection")));
```

You can now perform CRUD operations, as shown in the following code:

```
using var scope = app.Services.CreateScope();

var context = scope.ServiceProvider.GetRequiredService<ApplicationDbContext>();

// Create a new product.
Product newProduct = new() { Name = "New Product", Price = 9.99M };
context.Products.Add(newProduct);
context.SaveChanges();

// Read all the products.
List<Product> products = context.Products.ToList();
```

The key benefits of using EF Core in a .NET project include the following:

- **Productivity**: Automates database schema creation and data manipulation, reducing development time
- **Maintainability**: Changes to the data model can be propagated to the database through migrations, facilitating easy database schema updates
- **Abstraction**: Provides a high-level abstraction over database interactions, making code cleaner and more readable

EF Core's integration into .NET with its built-in dependency injection and configuration systems makes it an ideal choice for developing robust, maintainable database applications."

Commonly given poor answer

"Just install Entity Framework Core, create your database tables as classes, and it automatically handles everything for you without needing any configuration."

Explanation of why this is wrong:

- **Oversimplification of configuration and setup:** This answer incorrectly suggests that EF Core requires no explicit configuration or initialization. In reality, EF Core needs proper setup in the application's startup configuration, including specifying the database provider and connection string.
- **Misunderstanding of automatic operations:** It assumes that EF Core automatically syncs classes with database tables without any additional setup like migrations or database context configuration. This neglects the necessary steps to ensure the database schema matches the data models defined in the code.
- **Neglect of best practices:** The response fails to mention best practices such as managing database connections through dependency injection, which are crucial for developing scalable and maintainable applications.

This type of mistake often stems from a lack of detailed knowledge about EF Core's capabilities and requirements, perhaps based on superficial experiences or misunderstandings about how modern ORM tools function within larger application frameworks.

4. Interfaces and abstract classes

"In .NET, when should you use an interface and when should you use an abstract class? Please provide scenarios where one would be more appropriate than the other."

> In the print book, only the questions are included for items 4 to 60. View the full questions and answers online in the GitHub repository for the book at the following link: `https://github.com/markjprice/tools-skills-net10/blob/main/docs/interview-qa/readme.md`.

5. Properties and indexers

"Can you explain the difference between properties and indexers in C# and provide examples of scenarios where each would be appropriately used?"

6. Generics

"Can you explain the benefits of using generics in .NET applications, and provide an example of a scenario where using generics can significantly improve code quality and performance?"

7. Delegates and events

"Can you explain the difference between delegates and events in C# and how they are used to implement the Observer pattern? Please provide an example of a scenario where you would use them."

8. Language Integrated Query (LINQ)

"Can you describe what LINQ is and how it can be used in .NET applications? Provide examples of different types of LINQ providers and explain a scenario where using LINQ enhances code readability and efficiency."

9. Asynchronous programming with async and await

"Can you explain how the `async` and `await` keywords enhance .NET applications? Include in your answer a brief explanation of how these keywords work and provide an example of a scenario where asynchronous programming is particularly beneficial."

10. Memory management and garbage collection

"Can you explain the role of garbage collection in .NET and describe how it helps manage memory? Also, discuss any potential issues developers might face with garbage collection and how they can mitigate these issues."

11. Differences between modern .NET and .NET Framework

"Can you explain the key differences between modern .NET and .NET Framework? Also, discuss scenarios where one might be more appropriate than the other."

12. Cross-platform capabilities

"Can you discuss the cross-platform capabilities of modern .NET? Explain how these capabilities benefit software development and provide an example of a scenario where cross-platform support is crucial."

13. .NET Standard

"Can you explain the purpose of .NET Standard and discuss its relevance with the advent of modern .NET versions like .NET 5 and later? How does .NET Standard impact cross-platform code sharing?"

14. Dependency injection in .NET

"How do you implement dependency injection in a .NET application, and what are the key advantages of using DI? Please provide code examples demonstrating how to configure and use DI for managing services and dependencies."

15. Middleware in ASP.NET Core

"Can you explain the role of middleware in ASP.NET Core applications? Please provide an example of how you might implement custom middleware in a .NET application and describe a scenario where this middleware could be particularly useful."

16. Configuration and Options pattern

"Can you describe how to implement the Options pattern in .NET for managing application settings? Please provide an example of configuring and accessing settings from a configuration file."

17. Hosting and Kestrel server

"Can you explain what Kestrel is in the context of ASP.NET Core? How would you configure an ASP.NET Core application to use Kestrel and IIS together in a production environment, and why might this configuration be beneficial?"

18. Data types

"Can you explain the differences between value types and reference types in .NET, and provide examples of when you would use each?"

19. Globalization and localization

"Can you explain how you would implement globalization and localization in an ASP.NET Core MVC website project to support multiple languages and cultures?"

20. Control structures

"In C#, can you describe the various control structures available for handling decision-making and iteration, and provide a scenario where each might be used effectively?"

21. Exception handling

"Can you explain the importance of exception handling in .NET and describe how you would implement it in a real-world application? Please include different types of exceptions you might encounter and how you would manage them."

22. Git branching strategies

"Can you describe a Git branching strategy that you have used in your projects, and explain how it helps manage development and release cycles effectively?"

23. Code reviews and pair programming

"Can you describe the benefits of code reviews and pair programming in a .NET development team? Also, provide examples of how you have successfully implemented these practices in past projects."

24. Agile and Scrum methodologies

"Can you explain how Agile and Scrum methodologies can be beneficial in .NET software development projects? Additionally, describe how you have applied Scrum practices in your past projects."

25. Documentation standards

"Can you discuss the importance of documentation standards in .NET development and explain how tools like DocFX and Mermaid markup can be utilized to enhance project documentation?"

26. Problem-solving skills

"Can you describe a challenging technical problem you encountered in a .NET project and explain how you approached solving it? What tools and strategies did you use, and what was the outcome?"

27. Project management tools

"Can you describe your experience with project management tools in the context of managing .NET projects? Highlight how you have used these tools to improve project efficiency and team collaboration."

28. Estimation techniques

"Can you describe different estimation techniques you have used in your .NET projects and explain how these techniques have helped you ensure project delivery within timelines?"

29. Team collaboration

"Can you describe how you foster team collaboration in .NET software development projects? What strategies and tools do you use to ensure effective communication and integration among team members?"

30. Leadership and mentorship

"Can you discuss your approach to leadership and mentorship within a .NET software development team? How do you ensure that your leadership positively impacts both project outcomes and team member development?"

31. MVC pattern

"Can you explain the MVC pattern and how you have implemented it in your .NET projects? Please provide a specific example of how you have utilized MVC to improve application architecture in a .NET project."

32. Razor syntax

"Can you explain the Razor syntax used in ASP.NET Core applications? Provide an example to demonstrate how Razor can be used to dynamically generate HTML based on model data in a .NET 8 project."

33. Web API development

"Can you explain how you would design and implement a Web API using the Minimal API features introduced in .NET 6 and extended in .NET 8? Please describe the steps involved in creating a Minimal API and how it simplifies API development compared to earlier versions."

34. RESTful services best practices

"Can you discuss the best practices for designing and implementing RESTful services in .NET applications? Please include examples of how these practices ensure efficient and maintainable API services."

35. SignalR for real-time web functionality

"Can you explain how you would implement a real-time notification system using SignalR in a .NET 8 application? Describe the key components involved and how you ensure the system is scalable and performant."

36. State management

"Can you discuss different state management strategies available in .NET applications? Please provide examples of scenarios where you would use each strategy and include how you implement state management in a .NET 8 application."

37. Authentication and authorization

"How would you implement authentication and authorization in a .NET 8 ASP.NET Core application using Minimal APIs? Provide specific examples of configuring these security measures and applying them to ensure secure data access."

38. Blazor WebAssembly

"Can you describe how you would build a client-side web application using Blazor WebAssembly in .NET 8? Include details on how you would set up the project, manage dependencies, and handle API calls."

39. Benefits of microservices

"Can you explain the benefits of using a microservices architecture in .NET applications?"

40. Challenges in microservices architecture

"What are some of the challenges associated with implementing a microservices architecture in .NET applications, and how would you address these challenges?"

41. Docker containers and .NET

"Can you explain how Docker can be used to enhance the development, testing, and deployment of .NET applications? Provide specific examples of how you would configure and deploy a .NET 8 application using Docker."

42. Microservices communication patterns

"Can you explain different communication patterns used in microservices architectures and how you would implement these in a .NET 8 application using Minimal APIs? Provide specific examples, including the handling of asynchronous communication."

43. Resilience and transient fault handling

"Can you describe how you would implement resilience and transient fault handling? Please provide examples of techniques and tools you would use to ensure your application can gracefully handle and recover from failures."

44. Distributed tracing

"How would you implement distributed tracing to monitor and debug microservices interactions? Please provide examples of tools and methodologies you would use."

45. Health checks and monitoring

"How would you implement health checks and monitoring in a .NET 8 service? Please describe the tools and methodologies you would use to ensure robust application health management."

46. AutoMapper vs. extension method vs. implicit operator

"Can you compare the use of AutoMapper, extension methods, and implicit operators for object mapping in .NET applications? Discuss the advantages and scenarios best suited for each approach. Provide examples for each method using .NET 8 and Minimal APIs."

47. ADO.NET fundamentals

"How would you utilize ADO.NET to manage database operations in a .NET 8 application using Minimal APIs? Please describe how you handle connection management, execute queries, and manage transactions."

48. Entity Framework Core performance tuning

"How would you optimize the performance of Entity Framework Core? Please provide specific examples of techniques and configurations you would use to enhance the efficiency of database interactions."

49. Unit testing frameworks like xUnit

"How would you use xUnit to implement unit tests in a .NET application? Please describe the process of setting up xUnit, writing a basic test case, and how you would run these tests. Include any best practices you follow when writing unit tests."

50. Mocking frameworks like NSubstitute

"Can you explain how you would use NSubstitute in a .NET application to facilitate unit testing? Provide examples of how to create mocks for dependencies and verify that they behave as expected."

51. Integration testing strategies

"Can you describe your approach to integration testing in .NET applications? Please explain how you would plan, implement, and automate these tests, including any specific tools or frameworks you would use."

52. Performance testing

"Can you describe your approach to performance testing in .NET applications? Please explain the steps you take from planning and tool selection to execution and analysis of results."

53. Security testing

"What is your approach to security testing in .NET applications? Please explain the steps you take to identify and mitigate security vulnerabilities."

54. Automated UI testing

"How do you approach UI testing for .NET applications? Please explain the tools and techniques you use to ensure comprehensive UI test coverage."

55. SOLID principles

"What are the SOLID principles, and how do they apply to .NET software development?"

56. Singleton pattern

"What is the Singleton pattern, and how would you implement it in a .NET application? Can you discuss its advantages and potential drawbacks?"

57. Factory pattern

"Explain the Factory pattern and how it can be implemented in .NET applications. Provide an example of when you would use the Factory pattern."

58. Memory leak identification

"How would you identify and troubleshoot memory leaks in a .NET application?"

59. Development methodologies

"What development methodologies are you familiar with, and how do you choose the most appropriate one for a .NET project?"

60. Big O

"In a .NET application, you have an array of integers where each number represents the ID of a user. You need to implement a function that identifies and returns any duplicate user IDs in the array. Describe how you would implement this function and discuss the time complexity of your approach using Big O notation."

When you're failing, you're learning

When I was a trainer helping prepare students for their exams, some students would be upset if they got questions that I had asked them wrong. In my opinion, this attitude misunderstands the point of answering practice questions before an exam (or interview).

Imagine that I asked you ten questions, and you got them all correct. Have you made any progress? No!

Now imagine that I asked you ten questions, you got them all wrong, but you then learned why you were wrong and what the correct answer would be. Have you made progress? Yes! Lots!

Celebrate every time you "fail" because now you have identified where you can do the work to improve for next time. That's how you know you're getting closer to your goal.

Practicing and exploring

Test your knowledge and understanding by answering some questions, getting some hands-on practice, and exploring the topics covered in this chapter with deeper research.

Exercise 19.1 – Online-only material

The best .NET developer roadmap for 2025: `https://www.educative.io/blog/net-developer-roadmap`.

C# coding challenges to master your .NET technical job interview:

`https://www.youtube.com/watch?v=f31n3TeX19s`.

Exercise 19.2 – Practice exercises

Mock interviews with LLMs like ChatGPT can help you prepare for an interview, especially if you reference the online job description and your own online resume when asking the chat to give you questions. Here's a prompt you can try:

"Please help me prepare for an interview for a job position. Here is the job advertisement URL: [JOB_URL]. Additionally, here is the URL to my resume: [RESUME_URL]. Please summarize the key responsibilities and qualifications listed in the job advertisement. Please identify the areas of my resume that are most relevant to the job requirements and suggest ways to highlight these experiences during the interview. Provide a list of common interview questions that are likely to be asked for this type of position and suggest strategies for answering them effectively. Give examples of behavioral interview questions related to the job and tips on structuring my answers using the STAR method. Suggest thoughtful questions I can ask the interviewer to demonstrate my interest in the role and company. Provide a brief overview of the company, including its mission, values, recent news, and any other relevant information that can help me tailor my responses. Thank you!"

Exercise 19.3 – Test your knowledge

To get the best answer to some of these questions, you will need to do your own research. I want you to "think outside the book," so I have deliberately not provided all the answers in the book. I want to encourage you to get into the good habit of looking for help elsewhere, following the principle of "teach a person to fish."

1. What are the responsibilities of a Business Analyst (BA), and how might you, as a .NET software engineer, collaborate with them?
2. What is pair programming?
3. Could an LLM like ChatGPT or Llama3 replace a .NET software engineer?
4. What types of questions can you expect during an interview?
5. When learning a topic, why is it useful to see wrong answers as well as correct answers?

> *Appendix A*, *Answers to the Test Your Knowledge Questions*, is available to download from the following link: `https://github.com/markjprice/tools-skills-net10/blob/main/docs/B31468_Appendix%20A.pdf`.

Exercise 19.4 – Explore topics

Use the links on the following page to learn more details about the topics covered in this chapter: `https://github.com/markjprice/tools-skills-net10/blob/main/docs/book-links.md#chapter-19---your-career-teamwork-and-interviews`.

Summary

In this chapter, you learned how to:

- Work on a development team
- Apply for a job
- Answer some sample interview questions

In the Epilogue, you will learn what your next steps could be.

Epilogue

I wanted this book to be different from the others on the market. I hope that you found it to be a brisk, fun read, packed with practical hands-on walk-throughs of each subject.

This epilogue contains the following short sections:

- Next steps on your .NET learning journey
- Companion books to continue your learning journey
- Other Packt .NET books to take your learning further
- Good luck!

Next steps on your .NET learning journey

There is never enough space in a book written for print to include everything one might want. For subjects that you wanted to learn more about, I hope that the notes, good practice tips, and links in the GitHub repository pointed you in the right direction: `https://github.com/markjprice/tools-skills-net10/blob/main/docs/book-links.md`.

Companion books to continue your learning journey

This is one of four books in a quartet that provides a learning journey through .NET 10:

1. The first book, *C# 14 and .NET 10 - Modern Cross-Platform Development Fundamentals*, covers the fundamentals of the C# language, the .NET libraries, and modern ASP.NET Core technologies for web development. It is designed to be read linearly because skills and knowledge from earlier chapters build up and are needed to understand later chapters.
2. The second book, *Real-World Web Development with .NET 10*, covers mature and proven web development technologies like ASP.NET Core MVC and controller-based Web API web services, as well as OData, FastEndpoints, and Umbraco CMS for building real-world web projects on .NET 10. You will learn how to test your web services using xUnit and test the user interfaces of your websites using Playwright, and then how to containerize your projects ready for deployment.
3. The third book, *Apps and Services with .NET 10*, covers how to build graphical user interfaces for websites, desktop, and mobile apps with Blazor, Avalonia, and .NET MAUI respectively. Then you will learn more specialized library topics like internationalization and popular third-party packages including Serilog and NodaTime. You will learn how to build native AOT-compiled web services with ASP.NET Core Minimal API and how to improve performance, scalability, and reliability using caching, queues, and background services. You will implement more services using GraphQL, gRPC, and SignalR, as well as learn how to integrate LLMs to add intelligence to your solutions.

4. The fourth book, *Tools and Skills for .NET 10* (the one you're reading now), covers important tools and skills for a professional .NET developer. These include design patterns and solution architecture, debugging, memory analysis, all the important types of testing, whether unit, performance, or web and mobile, and then containerization for deployment topics like Docker and Aspire. Finally, the book looks at how to prepare for an interview to get the .NET developer career that you want.

A summary of the .NET 10 quartet and their most important topics is shown in *Figure E.1*:

Figure E.1: Quartet of books for learning C# .NET 10

To see a list of all the books that I have published with Packt, you can use the following link: `https://subscription.packtpub.com/search?query=mark+j.+price`.

To see my author page on Amazon, you can use the following link: `https://www.amazon.com/Mark-J-Price/e/B071DW3QGN/`.

Other Packt .NET books to take your learning further

If you are looking for other books from my publisher that cover .NET-related subjects, there are many to choose from that follow on from topics in this book, as shown in *Figure E.2*:

Figure E.2: Packt books to take your tools and skills with .NET learning further

Good luck!

I hope to see you on the book's Discord channel. Join me and other readers at the following link: `https://packt.link/TS2e`.

I wish you the best of luck with all your .NET projects!

Join .NETPro – It's Free

Staying sharp in .NET takes more than reading release notes. It requires real-world tips, proven patterns, and scalable solutions. That's what .NETPro, Packt's new newsletter, is all about.

Scan the QR code or visit the link to subscribe:

`https://landing.packtpub.com/dotnetpronewsletter/`

Share your thoughts

Now you've finished *Tools and Skills for .NET 10, Second Edition,* we'd love to hear your thoughts! Scan the QR code below to go straight to the Amazon review page for this book and share your feedback or leave a review on the site that you purchased it from.

`https://packt.link/r/183588251X`

Your review is important to us and the tech community and will help us make sure we're delivering excellent quality content.

Unlock Your Exclusive Benefits

Your copy of this book includes the following exclusive benefits:

- Next-gen Packt Reader
- DRM-free PDF/ePub downloads

Follow the guide below to unlock them. The process takes only a few minutes and needs to be completed once.

Unlock this Book's Free Benefits in 3 Easy Steps

Step 1

Keep your purchase invoice ready for *Step 3*. If you have a physical copy, scan it using your phone and save it as a PDF, JPG, or PNG.

For more help on finding your invoice, visit `https://www.packtpub.com/unlock-benefits/help`.

> **Note:** If you bought this book directly from Packt, no invoice is required. After *Step 2*, you can access your exclusive content right away.

Step 2

Scan the QR code or go to `packtpub.com/unlock`.

On the page that opens (similar to *Figure X.1* on desktop), search for this book by name and select the correct edition.

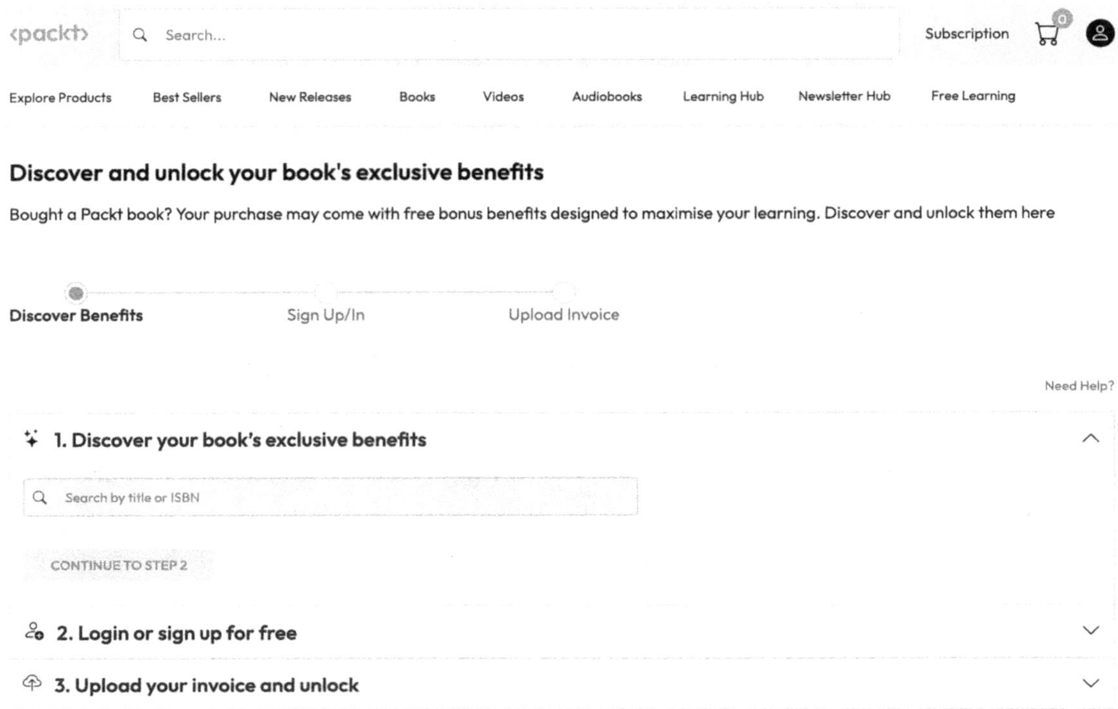

Figure X.1: Packt unlock landing page on desktop

Step 3

After selecting your book, sign in to your Packt account or create one for free. Then upload your invoice (PDF, PNG, or JPG, up to 10 MB). Follow the on-screen instructions to finish the process.

Need help?

If you get stuck and need help, visit `https://www.packtpub.com/unlock-benefits/help` for a detailed FAQ on how to find your invoices and more. This QR code will take you to the help page.

Note: If you are still facing issues, reach out to `customercare@packt.com`.

Index

Symbols

A

D

G

H

I

J

K

L

M

N

O

P

U

V

W

X

Y

www.ingramcontent.com/pod-product-compliance
Lightning Source LLC
LaVergne TN
LVHW081612120126
829565LV00072B/1369
9781835882504